Handbook of
Girls' and Women's Psychological Health

Handbook of
Girls' and Women's Psychological Health

Judith Worell

Carol D. Goodheart

EDITORS

UNIVERSITY PRESS

2006

OXFORD
UNIVERSITY PRESS

Oxford University Press, Inc., publishes works that further
Oxford University's objective of excellence
in research, scholarship, and education.

Oxford   New York
Auckland   Cape Town   Dar es Salaam   Hong Kong   Karachi
Kuala Lumpur   Madrid   Melbourne   Mexico City   Nairobi
New Delhi   Shanghai   Taipei   Toronto

With offices in
Argentina   Austria   Brazil   Chile   Czech Republic   France   Greece
Guatemala   Hungary   Italy   Japan   Poland   Portugal   Singapore
South Korea   Switzerland   Thailand   Turkey   Ukraine   Vietnam

Published by Oxford University Press, Inc.
198 Madison Avenue, New York, New York, 10016

www.oup.com

Oxford is a registered trademark of Oxford University Press

Library of Congress Cataloging-in-Publication Data

Handbook of girls' and women's psychological health / edited by Judith Worell
and Carol D. Goodheart.
p.   cm. — (Oxford series in clinical psychology)
Includes bibliographical references and index.
ISBN-13 978-0-19-516203-5
ISBN 0-19-516203-X
1.   Women—Psychology.   2.   Women—Health and hygiene.   3.   Women—Mental health.
4.   Girls—Psychology.   5.   Girls—Health and hygiene.   6.   Girls—Mental health.
I.   Worell, Judith, 1928–   II.   Goodheart, Carol D.   III.   Series.
HQ1206.H23855 2005
155.3'33—dc22   2004027119

9 8 7 6 5 4 3 2 1

Printed in the United States of America
on acid-free paper

To all the women who have given us so much:
Our mothers, daughters, grandmothers, granddaughters,
teachers, students, colleagues, clients, patients, and friends

And to our husbands Bud Smith and Hugh Goodheart, who
genuinely like women and support our efforts to make a
better world for them.

Foreword

NORINE G. JOHNSON

The importance of psychology and health, multicultural-ism, and a focus on strengths and positive psychology are the dynamic issues of psychology in this new millennium. These central issues in psychological research and practice today form the backbone of the *Handbook of Girls' and Women's Psychological Health.* To encounter all three inte-grated into a handbook on women and girls is like fantasiz-ing a feast and having it appear on your table.

In 2001, during my year as President of the American Psy-chological Association (APA), the organization affirmed the primacy of psychology in health, amending its mission statement to read: "The objects of the American Psycholog-ical Association shall be to advance psychology as a science and profession and as a means of promoting health, educa-tion and human welfare . . ." (APA, 2001).

My APA presidential initiative, "Psychology Builds a Healthy World," cochaired by Carol Goodheart, Rodney Hammond, and Ronald Rozensky, undertook to inform psychologists of cutting-edge research and practice in health; to inform the public of psychology's contributions to health; and to expand health-based partnerships with the public, policy makers, and other professionals (Johnson, 2003a). The initiative's immersion in the research and practice of psychology and health resulted in a recommendation to consider a new approach to health policy, to include culture as a primary component in models of health, and to expand the biopsychosocial model to a biopsychosocial *cultural* model of health (Johnson, 2003b).

Using the lens of the biopsychosocial cultural model of health, editors Judith Worell and Carol Goodheart have produced a resource of such depth and breadth that users of the *Handbook* will be at the apex of a new way of conceptualizing girls' and women's health. The contributors to the *Handbook* were challenged to discuss health cohesively through the lens of gender, culture, life span development, and well-being and positive aspects. The valuing of multiculturalism alone would make this comprehensive volume of girls/women and health an important addition; the fusion of all these elements makes the *Handbook* one of a kind.

The social construction of gender influences health policy and the availability and delivery of services. Today it is documented that women have received inappropriate health interventions because the research underpinning the medical decisions used only men as subjects, that women's descriptions of their health needs have been discounted too often in the medical and mental health systems, and that poor women and women of color have had difficulty accessing health services.

Editors Worell and Goodheart move the discussion to another level by having the *Handbook* contributors include vulnerabilities and risks for girls and women and then go beyond these problems to give the reader information regarding protective or supportive factors that facilitate effective coping, positive growth, strength, and resilience. In addition, by focusing on health and well-being, effective coping, strength, and resilience, this comprehensive *Handbook* links into the practice and research network of strengths-based psychological models.

The research is clear—women and girls are not always well served by our nation's healthcare system. Poor women, aging women, and women of color have the poorest health outcomes, the most difficulty accessing services, and the difficult position of continuing to be caretakers when they are the ones needing care. Recommended policies to address these disparities are included in the *Handbook*. Also, women in these positions have strengths and sources of resilience that are identified in the *Handbook* and can be built upon by health professionals and community advocates.

The scope of this *Handbook* is bold. The coeditors and contributors bring the best psychological knowledge to the gender, health, and life span perspective presented in this volume. Both editors are visionaries. They know what is crucial out of the myriad of materials, and have been able to organize this plethora of information into a compelling whole that allows the reader a reference for today's top thinking and a direction for tomorrow's research and practice. Overlooking the field of psychology from my perspective as a past APA president and a psychologist who has spent a lifetime learning, teaching, practicing, and advocating for the psychological health of girls and women, I am pleased that the *Handbook* anticipates the future directions in girls'/women's health and delivers a volume that empowers its readers to build a healthier world for them.

REFERENCES

American Psychological Association. (2001, February). *Council of Representatives, February 23–25, 2001. Draft minutes.* Washington, DC: Author.

Johnson, N. G. (2003a). Introduction: Psychology and health—Taking the initiative to bring it together. In R. H. Rozensky, N. G. Johnson, C. D. Goodheart, & W. R. Hammond (Eds.), *Psychology builds a healthy world* (pp. 3–31). Washington, DC: American Psychological Association.

Johnson, N. G. (2003b). Psychology and health: Research, practice, and policy. *American Psychologist, 58,* 670–677.

Acknowledgments

We extend our thanks and gratitude first to the many people who made a difference, either small or profound, in how we have come to view and understand the lives of girls and women in contemporary society. We want to thank especially the host of family, friends, colleagues, mentors, students, clients, and patients from whom we learned so much about the multitude of factors that both challenge and support the development of strong and healthy women. We are especially grateful to Gerald Koocher, Ph.D., and the entire Clinical Advisory Board of Oxford University Press for inviting us to develop this volume.

The quality and content of the volume reflect the outstanding contributions of the wonderful authors who agreed to work with us in producing an original and exciting approach to girls' and women's psychological health. We are enriched by all of them. We also appreciate the efforts and guidance of the staff at Oxford who assisted in both the development and production stages: Joan Bossert, Maura Roessner, Jessica Sonnenschein, Norman Hirschy, and Heather Hartman. And finally, we owe a debt of love and gratitude to our spouses, who supported and encouraged us during the long process of bringing this book to fruition. To all, we say thank you. We hope you will read and enjoy these insightful chapters.

Contents

**Part I
Gender and
Psychological Health**

**Part II
Risks and Strengths
Across the Life Span**

**Part III
Phases of
Development Within
the Life Span**

**Part IV
Special Problems
and Resources**

**Part V
Conclusion**

Contributors

Jennifer Bailey, Ph.D.
Research Analyst, Social Development Research Group
University of Washington
Seattle, WA

Susan A. Basow, Ph.D.
Charles A. Dana Professor of Psychology
Lafayette College
Easton, PA

Lula A. Beatty, Ph.D.
Chief, Special Populations Office, Office of the Director
National Institute on Drug Abuse/NIH
Bethesda, MD

Linda J. Beckman, Ph.D.
Professor, California School of Professional Psychology
Alliant International University
Los Angeles, CA

Deborah Belle, Ed.D.
Professor, Department of Psychology
Boston University
Boston, MA

Patricia A. Bennett, Ph.D.
Senior Instructor, Department of Psychiatry (Psychology),
    University of Rochester Medical Center
Faculty, Department of Obstetrics/Gynecology,
    Rochester General Hospital
Rochester, NY

Nancy E. Betz, Ph.D.
Professor, Department of Psychology
Ohio State University
Columbus, OH

Jeshmin Bhaju
Doctoral Student, Department of Psychology
Auburn University
Auburn, AL

Kalina M. Brabeck, M.A.
Doctoral Candidate, Counseling Psychology
University of Texas at Austin
Austin, TX

Mary M. Brabeck, Ph.D.
Professor of Applied Psychology
Steinhardt School of Education
New York University
New York, NY

Judith S. Bridges, Ph.D.
Professor Emerita of Psychology
University of Connecticut at Hartford
Hartford, Connecticut

Phyllis Bronstein, Ph.D.
Professor, Department of Psychology
University of Vermont
Burlington, VT

Veronica Cardenas, M.A.
Research Assistant, Older Adult and Family Center
Stanford University School of Medicine
VA Palo Alto Health Care System
Menlo Park, CA

Deborah Carr, Ph.D.
Assistant Professor, Department of Sociology and Institute
    for Health, Health Care Policy and Aging Research
Rutgers, The State University of New Jersey
New Brunswick, NJ

Rona Carter
Doctoral Student, Developmental Psychology Program,
    Department of Psychology
Child and Family Psychosocial Research Center
Florida International University
Miami, FL

Faye J. Crosby, Ph.D.
Professor of Psychology
University of California, Santa Cruz
Santa Cruz, CA

Cynthia de las Fuentes, Ph.D.
Associate Professor, Department of Psychology
Our Lady of the Lake University
San Antonio, TX

Natasha Demidenko, M.A.
School of Psychology
University of Ottawa
Ottawa, ON, Canada

Rene Dickerhoof, M.A.
Graduate Student
University of California, Riverside
Riverside, CA

Jennifer Dillinger, B.A.
Research Assistant, Older Adult and Family Center
Stanford University School of Medicine
VA Palo Alto Health Care System
Menlo Park, CA

Lisa Dodson, Ph.D.
Research Professor, Department of Sociology
Boston College
Chestnut Hill, MA

Debra Lina Dunivin, Ph.D.
Deputy Chief and Director of Training,
    Department of Psychology
Walter Reed Army Medical Center
Washington, DC

Jacquelynne S. Eccles, Ph.D.
Professor, Department of Psychology
The University of Michigan
Ann Arbor, MI

Nicole Else-Quest, M.S.
Doctoral Candidate, Department of Psychology
University of Wisconsin
Madison, WI

Claire A. Etaugh, Ph.D.
Professor, Department of Psychology
Bradley University
Peoria, IL

James M. Frabutt, Ph.D.
Associate Director, Center for Youth, Family,
    and Community Partnerships
University of North Carolina at Greensboro
Greensboro, NC

Dolores Gallagher-Thompson, Ph.D.
Director, Older Adult and Family Center,
    VA Palo Alto Health Care System
Professor, Research, Department of Psychiatry
    and Behavioral Medicine,
    Stanford University School of Medicine
Menlo Park, CA

Kimberly Gamble, M.A.
Graduate Student, Virginia Consortium Program
    in Clinical Psychology
Psychology Department
Old Dominion University
Norfolk, VA

Kenneth J. Gergen, Ph.D.
Mustin Professor of Psychology
Swarthmore College
Swarthmore, PA

Mary M. Gergen, Ph.D.
Professor of Psychology and Women's Studies
Penn State University Delaware County
Media, PA

Lucia Albino Gilbert, Ph.D.
Vice Provost
Professor of Educational Psychology
Frank C. Irwin, Jr. Centennial Honors Professor
University of Texas at Austin
Austin, TX

Sherry Glied, Ph.D.
Professor and Chair, Department of Health Policy
    and Management
Mailman School of Public Health
Columbia University
New York, NY

Carol D. Goodheart, Ed.D.
Psychologist in Independent Practice
Princeton, NJ

Heather L. Gray, B.A.
Programs Coordinator, Older Adult and Family Center
Stanford University School of Medicine
VA Palo Alto Health Care System
Menlo Park, CA

Jung-Hwa Ha, M.A., M.S.W.
Doctoral Candidate, Departments of Sociology
    and Social Work
University of Michigan
Ann Arbor, MI

Diane F. Halpern, Ph.D.
Director, Berger Institute for Work, Family, and Children
Professor of Psychology
Claremont McKenna College
Claremont, CA

Ay Ling Han, Ph.D.
Psychologist, Student Counseling Services and Adjunct
    Instructor
Smith College
Northampton, MA

Michele Harway, Ph.D.
Core Faculty in Psychology
Antioch University
Santa Barbara, CA

Susan S. Hendrick, Ph.D.
Professor, Department of Psychology
Texas Tech University
Lubbock, TX

Veronica M. Herrera, Ph.D.
Assistant Professor, Department of Criminal Justice
Indiana University
Bloomington, IN

Shannon Hsu, B.S.
Research Assistant, Department of Psychiatry
    and Behavioral Sciences
Stanford University School of Medicine
Menlo Park, CA

Dionne J. Jones, Ph.D.
Health Sciences Administrator, Services Research Branch
Division of Epidemiology, Services,
    and Prevention Research
National Institute on Drug Abuse/NIH
Bethesda, MD

Lisa K. Kearney, Ph.D.
Postdoctoral Psychology Resident
South Texas Veterans Health Care System
San Antonio, TX

Cathy Kessel, Ph.D.
Mathematics Education Consultant
Berkeley, CA

Sharon Kofman, Ph.D., M.P.H.
Faculty and Supervising Psychoanalyst
William Alanson White Institute of Psychoanalysis,
    Psychiatry, and Psychology
New York, NY

Mary P. Koss, Ph.D.
Professor, College of Public Health
University of Arizona
Tucson, AZ

Annette M. La Greca, Ph.D.
Professor of Psychology and Pediatrics
Director of Clinical Training
University of Miami
Coral Gables, FL

Erika L. Lichter
Postdoctoral Research Fellow
Department of Maternal and Child Health
Harvard School of Public Health
Boston, MA

Marcia C. Linn, Ph.D.
Professor, Graduate School of Education
University of California, Berkeley
Berkeley, CA

Sonja Lyubomirsky, Ph.D.
Associate Professor, Department of Psychology
University of California, Riverside
Riverside, CA

Eleanor Race Mackey, M.S.
Graduate Student, Department of Pediatric
    Health Psychology
University of Miami
Coral Gables, FL

S. Deborah Majerovitz, Ph.D.
Associate Professor, Department of Psychology
York College, City University of New York
Jamaica, NY

Oksana Malanchuk, Ph.D.
Senior Research Associate, Institute for Research
    on Women and Gender
The University of Michigan
Ann Arbor, MI

Bonnie Markham, Ph.D., Psy.D.
Psychologist in Independent Practice, Metuchen, NJ
Adjunct Faculty, Department of Psychiatry, UMDNJ-
    Robert Wood Johnson Medical School, Piscataway, NJ

Diane T. Marsh, Ph.D.
Professor, Department of Psychology
University of Pittsburgh at Greensburg
Greensburg, PA

M. C. McCrudden, M.Ed.
Doctoral Student, Department of Psychology
Duke University
Durham, NC

Susan H. McDaniel, Ph.D.
Professor of Psychiatry and Family Medicine
Director, Division of Family Programs, Psychiatry
Director, Wynne Center for Family Research
Associate Chair, Family Medicine
University of Rochester School of Medicine and Dentistry
Rochester, NY

Vanessa L. McGann, Ph.D.
Derner Institute of Advanced Psychological Studies
Adelphi University
Garden City, NY

Judith L. Meece, Ph.D.
Professor, Department of Education
University of North Carolina at Chapel Hill
Chapel Hill, NC

Karen Bearman Miller, Ph.D.
Postdoctoral Trainee, Child Development Center
St. Mary's Hospital
West Palm Beach, FL

Roberta L. Nutt, Ph.D.
Professor, Department of Psychology and Philosophy
Texas Woman's University
Denton, TX

Virginia E. O'Leary, Ph.D.
Professor, Department of Psychology
Auburn University
Auburn, AL

Rhoda Olkin, Ph.D.
Professor, California School of Professional Psychology
Alliant International University
Walnut Creek, CA

Lucia F. O'Sullivan, Ph.D.
Assistant Professor of Clinical Psychology,
    Department of Psychiatry
Columbia University
New York, NY

Niva Piran, Ph.D.
Professor, Department of Adult Education
    and Counseling Psychology
Ontario Institute for Studies in Education
University of Toronto
Toronto, ON, Canada

Lillian M. Range, Ph.D.
Professor, Department of Psychology
The University of Southern Mississippi
Hattiesburg, MS

Rena L. Repetti, Ph.D.
Professor, Department of Psychology
University of California, Los Angeles
Los Angeles, CA

Bridget M. Reynolds, M.A.
Graduate Student, Department of Psychology
University of California, Los Angeles
Los Angeles, CA

Joy K. Rice, Ph.D.
Clinical Professor, Department of Psychiatry
University of Wisconsin Medical School
Madison, WI

Adele B. Roman, M.S.
Deputy Women and Gender Research Coordinator
National Institute on Drug Abuse
Bethesda, MD

Erin Ross, M.A.
Graduate Student, Department of Adult Education
    and Counseling Psychology
Ontario Institute for Studies in Education
University of Toronto
Toronto, ON, Canada

Laura Sabattini
Doctoral Candidate, Department of Psychology
University of California, Santa Cruz
Santa Cruz, CA

Janis Sanchez-Hucles, Ph.D.
Professor, Department of Psychology
Old Dominion University
Norfolk, VA

Kathryn Scantlebury, Ph.D.
Associate Professor, Department of Science Education
University of Delaware
Newark, DE

Wendy K. Silverman, Ph.D.
Professor, Department of Psychology
Child and Family Psychosocial Research Center,
    Florida International University
University Park
Miami, FL

Lani Singer, M.A.
Project Coordinator, Older Adult and Family Center
Stanford University School of Medicine
VA Palo Alto Health Care System
Menlo Park, CA

Karyn M. Skultety, Ph.D.
Geropsychology Postdoctoral Fellow
Palo Alto Veterans Administration Health Care System
Palo Alto, CA

Linda Smolak, Ph.D.
Samuel B. Cummings Jr. Professor of Psychology
Kenyon College
Gambier, OH

Janice M. Steil, Ph.D.
Professor, Derner Institute of Advanced
    Psychological Studies
Adelphi University
Garden City, NY

Deborah L. Tolman, Ed.D.
Professor, Department of Human Sexuality Studies
San Francisco State University
San Francisco, CA

Cheryl Brown Travis, Ph.D.
Professor, Department of Psychology
University of Tennessee
Knoxville, TN

Melba J. T. Vasquez, Ph.D.
Psychologist in Independent Practice
Austin, TX

Lenore E. A. Walker, Ed.D.
Professor of Psychology and Coordinator of Clinical
    Forensic Psychology Concentration
Nova Southeastern University
Ft. Lauderdale, FL

Cora Lee Wetherington, Ph.D.
Women and Gender Research Coordinator
National Institute on Drug Abuse
Bethesda, MD

Valerie E. Whiffen, Ph.D.
Professor, School of Psychology
University of Ottawa
Ottawa, ON, Canada

Susan Krauss Whitbourne, Ph.D.
Professor, Department of Psychology
University of Massachusetts, Amherst
Amherst, MA

Jacquelyn W. White, Ph.D.
Professor, Department of Psychology
University of North Carolina at Greensboro
Greensboro, NC

Carol Williams-Nickelson, Psy.D.
Associate Executive Director
American Psychological Association of Graduate
    Students (APAGS)
American Psychological Association
Washington, DC

Judith Worell, Ph.D.
Professor Emerita, Department of Educational
    and Counseling Psychology
University of Kentucky
Lexington, KY

Karen Fraser Wyche, Ph.D.
Associate Professor, Department of Psychology
University of Miami
Coral Gables, FL

Nicole P. Yuan, Ph.D.
Research Associate, Department of Family
    and Community Medicine
Arizona Health Sciences Center, College of Medicine
Tucson, AZ

Gender and Psychological Health

CAROL D. GOODHEART

An Integrated View of Girls' and Women's Health: Psychology, Physiology, and Society

Girls and women in developed nations have more opportunities than at any previous time in history, yet they continue to be pressed by internal and external forces that affect their well-being. Their sex is biologically determined, but their gender and status are socially and culturally defined. And there is the rub. It is surprising how many inequities remain for them in this new century and how many of their compelling strengths and capacities for resilience are overlooked. The consequences of persistent gender disparities lead to a profound and differential impact on health and well-being. This book celebrates and illuminates women's health, and it underlines the disparities that prevent their strengths from being fully actualized.

Health appears different in different contexts. Looking at psychological health for girls and women is akin to looking through a kaleidoscope. Just when a pattern seems stable and clear a small movement occurs, the pieces of colored glass are displaced, and they tumble into a new pattern. The individual pieces of glass remain the same, but their arrangement differs as the perspective changes. In this *Handbook*, we turn the kaleidoscope and offer many views of females' lives, risks, challenges, strengths, and resources. It is our goal to offer a comprehensive and nuanced understanding of women's psychological health and well-being.

OVERVIEW OF THE HANDBOOK

The *Handbook* is based upon a biopsychosocial perspective of psychological health. In a landmark proposal for a new conceptualization of health, Engel (1977) introduced the biopsychosocial model. His model built upon the physiological systems foundation of sickness and health to incorporate dimensions outside of the person: family, community, culture, society, and the environment. Unfortunately, many of the healthcare delivery systems in developed countries today continue to bifurcate mental and physical health services, the classic mind/body split. However, there are important specialty areas in which the biopsychosocial model is gaining in influence: primary care, internal medicine, pediatrics, family medicine, and psychology (McDaniel, Bennett Johnson, & Sears, 2004).

Within the biopsychosocial framework of this volume, we integrate mind and body, risks and resilience, research and interventions, cultural diversity, and public policy into a comprehensive view of psychological health. We have chosen the term psychological health because it is broader than the traditional term mental health and is in keeping with the modern perspective of health presented throughout the *Handbook*. Many of the contributors are in the forefront of advancing such an integrative and multifaceted model for understanding and improving the psychological and physical health of girls and women. Insofar as possible, each chapter integrates available information about ethnic minority and lesbian woman, rather than segregating the concerns of these groups of women in separate chapters.

There is an intentional focus on both risks and strengths as vital components in a cogent view of health. Contributors present gender aspects of girls' and women's development in terms of internal and external vulnerabilities and risks and in terms of the protective or supportive factors that facilitate effective coping, positive growth, strength, and resilience. The interactions among physical, psychological, and sociocultural factors are considered in overview (part I), across the life span (part II), within each period of development (part III), and for special problems and resources (part IV). Within all cultural groups, gender socialization for female development and behavior has an impact on self-evaluation and identity processes as well as on the social roles that girls and women adopt. Externally induced risks such as poverty and violence present further challenges to healthy development. The effects of these factors appear in many of the concerns and disorders for which girls and women seek or are referred for psychological help.

In many areas of psychological function there are greater differences among women than between women and men, and these differences need attention. Broad categorizations may mask considerable differences. It is not possible to understand the functioning of any girl or woman in a singular context, although gender is salient for each of them. Psychological health status is directly affected by age, socioeconomic status, ethnocultural identity, and sexual orientation variables, each of which interacts with gender to contribute to the health continuum.

CONTEXTS FOR HEALTH

Women are the major consumers of medical and psychological health services in the United States and many other countries. Women are also the primary caretakers of others and are likely to make decisions about seeking or advocating services for their children, spouses, and aging parents. However, only recently have scholars directed concerted attention to the variables that influence the particular concerns that women bring to the health service system.

Caretaking

Caretaking is a familiar role that is assumed by a large majority of women, a role with two faces. One face is love, connection, and the fostering of growth, healing, and comfort. The other face is caregiver burden.

In one study, more than two thirds of mothers who brought their children to a mental health center for services suffered from their own untreated depression and anxiety disorders; more than half of the problems were undiagnosed previously (National Institute of Mental Health [NIMH], 2001). In another large study, grandmothers who cared for healthy grandchildren more than nine hours a week faced a significantly higher risk of coronary heart disease than those not taking care of grandchildren (Lee, Colditz, Berkman, & Kawachi, 2003).

When women need caretaking due to physical illness, it may not be readily available to them. Women comprise three out of four caregivers for dying cancer patients, but when they are terminally ill themselves, they are less likely than men to receive family care and must rely on paid assistance (Emanuel et al., 1999). However, paid home health care is being reduced across the country in the national effort to lower health-care costs. Home health-care workers in New York City went on strike in 2004 to secure a wage increase from $7 to $10 per hour (Greenhouse, 2004). Neither figure is a living wage for working women caretakers in a major metropolitan area. They are squeezed by health system cost-containment measures and, in addition, are largely without the health insurance, vacation days, or overtime pay necessary to meet their own needs. At the same time in New York City, day-care workers in centers serving more than 30,000 low-income children also went on strike for better wages (Kaufman, 2004).

Ethnic minority women caregivers bear a disproportionate burden. An AARP survey (2001) revealed group differences among the percentage of individuals caring for aging parents: 19% Whites, 28% African Americans, 34% Hispanic/Latinas, and 42% Asian Americans.

Caretaking for children, the elderly, the disabled, and the ill is a fact of life for most women. Young girls and boys see them in these roles every day, which creates expectations for their own futures. Caring for others can be meaningful and fulfill important family and cultural values, but it is also a source of strain. There are some studies that show a growing more equitable distribution of caregiving between the sexes, but overall, women caregivers spend 50% more time than do men caregivers (U.S. Department of Health and Human Services, June, 1998). Caregiver burden can be reduced substantially by respite services, community training and education, and public policy changes in how those tasks are valued by society and funded (e.g., Goodheart, in press).

Social Changes: Two Steps Forward, One Step Back

There have been many changes for women in society over the past generation and they may affect psychological health either directly or indirectly. Women have increased freedom from sex-role stereotypes and a greater awareness of options for work, motherhood, and the division of labor in families. They have greater entitlement to sexual knowledge, relationships, pleasure, and ownership over their own bodies. There is more public awareness of the staggering personal, social, and health costs of violence, coercion, and abuse. On the other hand, more women struggle with traditional men's issues, such as spending time with their children, being downsized out of a job, and developing new health risks such as the rising lung cancer rates for women.

There are mixed social messages that contribute to frustration. Many girls are encouraged in modern families to realize their potential and aspirations. They believe they can achieve equally with the boys who are their peers. As adults, however, they face discrimination such as the "glass ceiling" that holds back career advancement, the double binding criticism for both mothers who work outside the home and those who do not, and the legal risk for lesbian mothers losing custody of their children based on sexual orientation. Women still earn substantially less than men do. For every dollar that a man in the United States earns, a woman earns only 79 cents, and some groups of women earn even less: African American women earn only 70 cents and Hispanic/Latinas 58 cents (U.S. Department of Labor, 2004).

There may be better news on the horizon. At least some portion of the gender wage gap may be bridged as women recognize opportunities and learn to ask for more money with the same expectations as men, rather than accept initial offers by employers or prospective employers without negotiating (Babcock, Gelfand, Small, & Stayn, 2004). Also, women are striding out on their own with success in the work world. There are large increases in women business ownership and the number of people they employ. Within a ten-year period the number of women-owned businesses grew by 78%; one out of three firms in the United States is now owned and operated by a woman and these companies provide 18.5 million jobs (Small Business Administration, 1997).

Heroism has been recognized and associated traditionally with men and masculine roles such as the military and firefighting, but recent research by Becker and Eagly (2004) fills in a missing part of the picture. They report that women's acts of heroism are as risky and courageous as men's but have been less visible in society, such as rescuing holocaust victims, donating a kidney, and volunteering for duty overseas with Doctors of the World.

Sociocultural status may increase the risk of being in harm's way for members of some groups, but cultural heritage can provide well-developed protective and coping resources to counterbalance some of that risk. A high degree of ethnic identity has been shown to be a buffer against HIV for African American women at high risk, as women with higher ethnic identity scores reported fewer instances of sexual risk-taking behavior (Beadnell et al., 2003). Also, African

American caregivers show more resilience than Whites on measures of depression and life satisfaction, although they remain vulnerable to increases in physical symptoms over time (Haley, West, Wadley, & Ford, 1995; Roth, Haley, Owen, Clay, & Goode, 2001).

The good stories and the ugly ones continue to unfold, although the pace of change is quickening, and the reasons behind some of the changes are not fully understood. Pregnancy rates for adolescent girls dropped almost 30% over ten years to a historic low, with African Americans showing the greatest decline of 40% since 1991 (CDC, 2004). In the same decade, crime rates were falling, too. However, as arrests for men declined almost 6%, arrests for women increased 14.1% (Federal Bureau of Investigation, 2003).

Professionals, educators, and researchers have progressed beyond the isolation of mental and physical factors for health and well-being, knowing that biology is only part of the story. They have come to understand psychological, social, and cultural contributions to health as dominant forces in the lives of girls and women. Clear links have been established between social circumstances and mortality, between psychosocial processes and health (Berkman & Kawachi, 2000).

Behavior, genetics, and the environment interact to produce or prevent disease, as well as psychological distress. Therefore, it is important to understand these basic processes in order to prevent and treat chronic conditions. Once disease or dysfunction is present, symptoms may be affected by behavior, cognition, emotion, and interpersonal dynamics. Overall, the application of psychological interventions for chronic diseases and conditions results in improvements in psychological functioning and more appropriate use of medical services (Goodheart, 2004).

COMPONENTS OF PSYCHOLOGICAL HEALTH

There are physiological differences between women and men, such as reproductive function. There are advances in the scientific understanding of how mind and body influence each other, such as the growing body of research in psychoneuroimmunology discussed below. There are

changes in society, such as roles, work, awareness of violence, and demographic shifts. These factors have contributed both to advances and to setbacks for women. As a result, the picture of their psychological health contains both positive and negative aspects.

Definitions of Health

What does it mean to be psychologically healthy? Health needs a more articulate and dynamic definition than "the absence of illness and pathology." The concept of health applies to everyone, including those who are well, those who live with a disability or chronic disease, and those who are ill with physical or psychological conditions. It is possible to be psychologically healthy in the presence of chronic diseases, mental or physical limitations, or hardships in life, if the burdens are not too cumulative or pervasive.

In *Health and Health Care 2010*, health is defined as a state of physical, mental, social, and spiritual well-being; it is a composite of interdependent components and implies functioning as fully as possible under current circumstances (Institute for the Future, 2000). Conversely, the neglect of a component may result in an unhealthy state or may place individuals at risk for disease or dysfunction. This broad definition of health signals a shift away from a limited biomedical framework and away from the splitting of physical and mental health into two distinct spheres of health care. The mounting evidence for the expanded view of health presented in the Institute's report is expected to create pressure for changes in the U.S. health-care system: from a biomedical model to multifactorial model, from acute episodic illness to management of chronic illness, from a focus on individuals to a focus on communities and other defined populations; from cure as the goal to best adjustment and adaptation when there is no cure, and from focus on disease to focus on the person and the disease. Apart from disease, the expanded view of health also recognizes the influence of "social, cultural, mental, behavioral, environmental, occupational, economic, and circumstantial elements" (p. 196) on injuries, which are a result of traffic and alcohol/drug accidents, abuse, criminal acts, and work site accidents. In the not too distant future, emerging models of health may be able to better explain factors that allow some people to grow beyond adaptation to transcendence and thriving.

The specific subcategory of mental health (which would be better characterized as psychological health) is defined as "successful mental functioning, resulting in productive activities, fulfilling relationships, and the ability to adapt to change and cope with adversity" (U.S. Department of Health and Human Services, 2000, p. 37). Additional factors that underlie psychological function include cognitive abilities, emotional regulation, dispositional traits, beliefs, and expectations.

Determinants of Health

Critical variables that determine health for individuals, families, and communities may be seen in figure 1.1. The schematic drawing shows the reciprocal relationships between and among a person's biology, behavior, social and physical environments, and it shows the influence of access to care, interventions, and social policy.

The interaction of physical and psychological factors is apparent in the fact that the underlying causes for eight of the top ten determinants of death in the United States are related to behavioral problems: tobacco, diet, lack of exercise, alcohol, motor vehicles, firearms, sexual behavior, and illicit drug use (Mokdad, Marks, Stroup, & Gerberding, 2004). Proportional contributions to

health status are: access to care 10%, genetics 20%, environment 20%, and lifestyle behaviors 50% (CDC, cited in Institute for the Future, 2000, p. 23).

Psychological factors have a significant impact on immune function and health, and an understanding of the psychoneuroendocrine pathways by which this occurs is well under way in the literature on psychoneuroimmunology. Acute and chronic stress, negative emotions, social support availability, marital conflict, coping style, and hostility have all been shown to affect the body's immune activity and health (see Kiecolt-Glaser, McGuire, Robles, & Glaser, 2002b, for a 10-year research review). Further, stress induced negative emotions stimulate the production of pro-inflammatory cytokines, and inflammation poses a threat for multiple problems as people age: cardiovascular disease, diabetes, arthritis, osteoporosis, some cancers, Alzheimer's disease, periodontal disease, frailty, and functional decline. This distress-related immune dysregulation is a likely core mechanism underlying a large number of health risks (Kiecolt-Glaser, McGuire, Robles, & Glaser, 2002a).

In a discussion of the psychobiology of stress, Kemeny (2003) challenges the assumption of one general physiological response to all stressors. Instead, she presents an integrated specificity model, in which specific stressful circumstances and the specific way a person appraises them can trigger qualitatively distinct emotional and bodily responses. The examples given include appraisals of threat (vs. challenge), uncontrollability, and negative social evaluation, all of which have been shown to provoke specific psychobiological responses. It seems likely these kinds of appraisals would be influenced by gender-related circumstances.

Health Trends

Quite a few promising trends for girls and women in health research, services, and policy are converging on a biopsychosocial approach.

Multiple Levels of Intervention and Approach

Stanton has examined the intersection of gender, stress, and health by locating women's health in

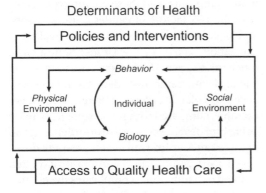

FIGURE 1.1 Determinants of health. Source: U.S. Department of Health and Human Services (2000).

three contexts: the environmental, interpersonal, and personal spheres (Stanton & Courtenay, 2004). Her review of empirical developments and emerging perspectives on health determinants for women considers sociodemographic factors (e.g., poverty, social roles, and traditions of medical care for and research about women), interactional factors (e.g., violence and the relationship between marriage and health), and personal attributes (e.g., gendered coping styles). She concludes that multiple levels of intervention (for individuals, couples, and systems) are necessary to improve women's health and decrease the harmful effects of barriers to care, ethnic disparities, caregiver burden, and violence.

The Institute of Medicine (IOM) report *Promoting Health: Intervention Strategies From Social and Behavioral Research* (Smedley & Syme, 2000) also recommends multiple-level interventions for individuals, families, and communities. In addition, multiple approaches are recommended, including behavioral change programs, social support, education, and public policy. The National Institutes of Health report *New Horizons in Health: An Integrative Approach* (Singer & Ryff, 2001), recommends research priorities for the Office of Behavioral and Social Sciences Research; these include the identification of biopsychosocial factors and pathways that contribute both to disease and to positive health and resilience, the social and environmental variables that shape gene expression, the mechanisms that contribute to health disparities, and the characteristics of communities and environments that have an impact on health.

Women's Health Initiative

For decades women have been underrepresented in health research; finally, the Women's Health Initiative (WHI) is well under way. This is a large 15-year national health study under the auspices of the National Institutes of Health (see Matthews et al., 1997, for a discussion of the psychosocial aspects of the study). The WHI mission is to better understand the determinants of health for postmenopausal women and to evaluate the efficacy of preventive interventions aimed at the major causes of mortality and morbidity. The overlapping studies involve almost 165,000 women aged 50–79 and include three components: randomized controlled clinical trials, an observational study, and a community prevention study. Results should yield a greatly enhanced understanding of the relationships between behaviors and health in women. The design is noteworthy in several respects. It focuses on women, assesses biopsychosocial factors related to multiple health outcomes, and incorporates an ethnically diverse population of women. In fact, some of the research sites have focused directly on enrolling Hispanic/Latina, African American, Asian American, and Native American women.

It has been widely publicized that the WHI experimental trial of estrogen plus progestin versus a placebo for the prevention of coronary artery diseases was halted because the health risks for women outweighed any benefits (Rossouw et al., 2002). Less well known are other promising psychosocial aspects of WHI—for example, the research related to women and social support. It has long been understood that social support is correlated with better health. In the current research, newer measures for different types of support are being used to gain a clearer picture of the paths by which this occurs. For example, social strain may emerge as even more predictive of mental health declines than poor social support (Matthews et al., 1997).

Comorbidity

The co-occurrence of different conditions is a common and challenging theme in the converging approaches to health. There are high rates of comorbidity for depression, anxiety, and somatic symptoms, and these are interconnected with the risk factors of gender roles, stressors, and negative life experiences (World Health Organization, 2004). In the United States, as in much of the world, women and men suffer equally from mental disorders, but they experience particular disorders at differential rates. For example, compared with men, women are twice as likely to develop depressive disorders and two to three times as likely to develop anxiety disorders (NIMH, 2001). Depression and anxiety often go hand in hand, which complicates the picture. Depression co-occurs with medical problems (e.g., chronic diseases), with social problems (e.g., poverty and abuse), with marital problems, and with many psychological problems (e.g., eating disorders, anxiety disorders, especially post-traumatic stress disorder (NIMH, 2001; Nolen-Hoeksema & Keita, 2003).

In children and adolescents, depression co-occurs frequently with anxiety, disruptive behavior, substance abuse, and physical illnesses such as diabetes (Angold & Costello, 1993). Because depression risk for girls and boys is similar in childhood, but the risk for girls becomes twice that for boys in adolescence (Birmaher et al., 1996), the likelihood of co-occurring problems for girls increases also. Only integrated models of health research, policy, and care will be able to address this complex comorbidity picture for girls and women. The section of the *Handbook* on problems and risks, and its sister section on strengths and resources, shed light on the state of knowledge, needs, protective factors, and interventions that can help.

Genetic Testing

Another health trend is related to the genetics revolution, which is based on the new field of genomics. Individuals are believed to have many mutated genes, perhaps dozens, which carry risk for common problems such as cancer, heart disease, and depression (Collins, 1999), although some may be found to contribute only a very small fraction of risk. Genetic testing that allows for the identification of risk in people who are currently healthy and without symptoms creates opportunities for treatment and even prevention in the future. It also creates biopsychosocial challenges to be faced as the public's hopes and fears rise. For example, genetic mutations called BRCA 1 and BRCA 2 have been identified; the risk for women with these mutations ranges from 56% to 85% for breast cancer and 20% to 60% for ovarian cancer (see Patenaude, Guttmacher, & Collins, 2002, for a research review, a discussion of the psychological implications of genetic testing, and the presentation of core competencies for health professionals from all disciplines; see Patenaude, 2005, for psychological approaches to help individuals and families with the implications of genetic testing). Only a small percentage of women who develop breast cancer have the gene mutation, but extensive media coverage has led to worrisome concerns about heritability among many more breast cancer families.

Women with breast cancer (as well as other cancers and other diseases) and their relatives have many questions: Should I have the genetic test? What will it mean if I test positive for the presence of the gene? Can I live with knowing the results? Who will I tell and not tell? Should I tell my teenage daughter? Can the information help me to plan for the future? How can I protect myself from job and insurance discrimination? What if testing for my family members is planned, but one of my relatives does not want to participate?

The increased availability of genetic testing will affect everyone. It will affect those who choose testing and those who refuse, those who can afford it and those who cannot, and those who understand and those who do not. Researchers and clinicians need to understand better the overlapping dimensions relevant to genetic testing that have an impact on well-being. These include coping skills, communication abilities, family relationships, access to care, cultural meanings of genetic information, the complexity of prediction for risks that involve the interaction of genes and environment and behavior, the willingness to make use of preventive interventions (such as prophylactic surgery), and the factors that may lead a teen or woman to decide to adopt new health behaviors.

Divorce

More than 1 million new children are affected by divorce each year (U.S. Bureau of the Census, 1998). Some children of divorced families live in single parent homes; some divide their time between the homes of the two parents; some live in blended families with stepparents and stepsiblings. The challenging circumstances of ruptured marital relationships have long been known to place children at risk. Newer models of research and intervention are focused increasingly on the identification of protective factors for children of divorce, the development of competence, and the enhancement of resilience. These newer resilience approaches are useful for children in other difficult circumstances too, such as poor urban environments. For an overview of the trend related to divorce research, practice, and policy see Pedro-Carroll (2001).

The trends showcased above can give only the briefest glimpse of the utility of biopsychosocial approaches to health. Overall, however, it seems unwise to continue with fragmented and segmented models of care in the face of the knowledge reflected in these trends. There are lively and ongoing discussions among professionals about evidence-based practice in medicine, psychology, education, and public policy. Biopsychosocial models of care draw upon broad and deep streams of evidence, expertise, and respect for the values of the girls, women, and families who seek health services. This comprehensive base is underscored throughout the *Handbook*.

Chesney (1993) built upon the lessons learned from the epidemic of HIV and summarized five trends in health psychology and medicine with important implications for the future. They are still highly relevant today and consistent with our biopsychosocial perspective for psychological health:

1. Early identification of people at risk
2. Rising expectations for behavior change programs
3. Growing numbers of people who live with chronic diseases of all kinds
4. Inclusion of community and public health perspectives
5. An increasing urgency to address health problems on a global scale

ADVANCES IN UNDERSTANDING AND TREATING WOMEN

Society's changes over the past 30 years or so have produced researchers, educators, and practitioners who focus on girls' and women's psychological health. More women are in these positions now. More diverse questions are asked. More research is done with women participants, and the evolving theories are more suitable for women, thus enlarging the universe of good interventions. Training and service institutions pay more attention to gender and culture and conceptualize both women and men in more di-

verse ways. Women's psychological health is less often judged by male standards and norms in research and practice.

Research

In breaking new ground, researchers and theoreticians stimulate advances for women with heuristic questions and processes that create a ripple effect of influence. For example, Taylor and her research group proposed the first new stress response model for coping in more than 70 years (Taylor et al., 2000). Previously, the human stress response was described as fight-or-flight for both females and males, although most of the research was based on men and male rats. The new model suggests that although the core physiological responses may be similar for both sexes, females' behavioral responses show a different pattern called "tend-and-befriend." Despite the concerns in some quarters that this biological model would be constraining for women, it is not. Instead, the proposal has stimulated consideration of the ways in which biological tendencies to nurture and maintain social networks may interact with life experiences and coalesce into individual expressions. Several contributors in the *Handbook* refer to the tend-and-befriend model as it applies to their topics.

The *Handbook* contains multiple citations of influential theories and findings that have furthered our knowledge; for example: Tolman on women's diverse sexuality, Barnett and Hyde on work and family role juggling, Bakan on the balance of communion and agency, Kiecolt-Glaser on mind/body, Walker on the battered woman, Koss on sexual assault, Steil on egalitarian relationships, Stanton on stress, Eagly on transformational leadership, Herman on trauma, and Worell on feminism in psychology.

Practice

The atmosphere for putting theory and research into practice has changed markedly in recent years. There is a proportionally larger pool of women health professionals from which the public may choose, especially among psychologists and physicians. Feminist principles for treatment and therapeutic relationships have become more widely known and have influenced traditional methods of treatment. The integrative perspective of Worell and Remer (2003) identifies four principles of best practices for the treatment of women: attention to the diversity of women's personal and social identities, the influence of gender and role strictures in personal/family/work problems, the need for egalitarian relationships between client and health professional, and the creation of a therapeutic process that is genuinely valuing of women. Their empowerment model is adaptable to diverse circumstances and may be combined and integrated with many psychological treatment orientations—for example, cognitive-behavioral, family, humanistic, psychodynamic, systems, and psychoeducational approaches. It also applies to the field of medicine.

Treatments for psychological problems have been embedded for a long time in a traditional medical model of psychopathology. The *Diagnostic and Statistical Manual of Mental Disorders*, Fourth Edition (*DSM-IV*; American Psychiatric Association, 1994), is the standard medically based diagnostic classification system in the United States. It has been criticized as sexist and not sensitive to culture, ethnicity, or situational context (for analyses see Becker, 2001; Lopez & Guaranaccia, 2000; Worell & Remer, 2003). However, there are signs of expansion into new directions that are more consonant with a biopsychosocial perspective.

One sign of progress in thinking about assessments and treatments for a broad array of health problems is the development of the *International Classification of Functioning, Disability, and Health* (*ICF*; World Health Organization, 2001). The *ICF* is a companion classification for the *ICD-10* (*International Statistical Classification of Diseases and Related Health Problems*; World Health Organization, 1992). The *ICD-10* classifies diseases, disorders, and injuries and is the standard system used internationally for mental health diagnoses, except in the United States where the *DSM* system predominates. The *ICF* is based on a biopsychosocial orientation and classifies function, not disease. It describes how people live with a health condition; classifies health, health related domains, and some health related components of well-being both in terms of person-level activities and social participation; includes a classification of environmental factors that support or impede function; and provides a framework on which assessment and measurement tools may be based. According to Geoffrey Reed (G. Reed, personal communication), the American Psychological Association representative working on the *ICF Procedural Manual* (American Psychological Association, 2003), the system is designed to work in real-world clinical settings with varying assessment techniques, such as psychometric measures, clinical interviews, direct observations, and self-report. Because of the limitations of the current medical framework in the United States that does not capture a broad picture of health, we are pleased to see a promising new model with the potential to help clinicians improve assessment, description, and ultimately the treatments provided. The *ICF* system is likely to be particularly beneficial for girls and women, who have not always been served well by disease models of psychological function.

For the first time in 2002, new health assessment and behavior procedures for people with physical health problems who need psychological interventions were recognized in the Current Procedure Terminology (CPT) coding system of the American Medical Association (American Psychological Association, 2002). The CPT coding system is used to bill all insurers for procedures performed by physicians, psychologists, and other health professionals. In these new codes, the focus is on biopsychosocial factors rather than mental disorders. Psychologists may now offer psychosocial prevention, treatment, and management of physical health conditions without inappropriately labeling individuals as having mental disorder diagnoses. This is a welcome and necessary expansion of the types of assessment and intervention that can be offered to girls and women with acute and chronic illnesses.

With the vision and leadership of American Psychological Association 2001 President Norine Johnson, the organization amended its mission statement to include the term health in its aims: "to advance as a science and a profession, and as a means of promoting *health* and human welfare" (American Psychological Association, n.d.). Psychology is changing from a mental health profession to a health profession. As it does, there is a growing spectrum of current and potential biopsychosocial health services that require a range of professional skills.

Some psychologists who treat girls and women will continue to practice solely within the mental health system. Specialty-trained clinical health psychologists will continue to offer specialized services to those with diseases. But as more integration of psychological and medical services occurs, increasing numbers of clinical and counseling psychologists will want to generalize the skills from their training and develop new ones that are helpful in bridging the mind/body divide. For practitioners who want to provide services to people with physical problems as well as psychological ones, Belar and colleagues (2001) offer a way to evaluate readiness, "Self-Assessment in Clinical Health Psychology: A Model for Ethical Expansion of Practice."

Finally, there is continuing movement toward strengths-based treatment approaches for girls and women with psychological risks. Resilience is common in both children and adults. Child development specialists (Masten, 2001; Wyman, Sandler, Wolchik, & Nelson, 2000) recommend that practice be directed toward cumulative competence promotion and stress protection rather than toward deficits, especially for interventions with children facing adversity and disadvantage. Similarly, strengths-based approaches are being extended not only to high-functioning middle-class women with abundant resources but also to women in trying circumstances, such as those who are elderly, on welfare, in the criminal justice system, or facing domestic violence.

Changes in research, professional practice, society, and policy are reflected in the chapters to follow. For expert readers, some of the topics may be an organized review; for readers new to women's psychological health issues. the material will chart new territory.

In the end, aggregate information can only carry us so far. Then we must make a conceptual leap to envision the lives of girls and women, what they are and what they can become. The *Handbook* offers the foundation of knowledge and understanding from which to make the leap.

REFERENCES

AARP. (2001, June). *In the middle: A report on multicultural boomers coping with family and aging issues.* Washington, DC: Author.

American Psychiatric Association. (1994). *Diagnostic and statistical manual of mental disorders* (4th ed.). Washington, DC: Author.

American Psychological Association. (2002). APA Practice Directorate announces new health and behavior CPT codes. *APA Online.* Retrieved June 2004 from http://www.apa.org/practice/cpt_2002.html

American Psychological Association. (2003). *Procedural manual and guide for a standardized application of the International Classification of Functioning Disability and Health (ICF): A manual for health professionals.* Sample and prototype. Washington, DC: Author.

American Psychological Association. (n.d.). About APA. mission statement: Bylaws I.1. Retrieved June 2004 from http://www.apa.org/about/

Angold, A., & Costello, E. J. (1993) Depressive comorbidity in children and adolescents: Empirical, theoretical, and methodological issues. *American Journal of Psychiatry, 150*(12), 1779–1791.

Babcock, L., Gelfand, M. J., Small, D., & Stayn, H. (2004). *Propensity to initiate negotiations: A new look at gender variations in negotiation behavior.* IACM 15th Annual Conference, Working Paper Series. Retrieved June 2004 from http://papers.ssrn.com/sol3/papers.cfm?abstract_id=305160

Beadnell, B., Stielstra, S., Baker, S., Morrison, D. M., Knox, K., Gutierrez, L., et al. (2003). Ethnic identity and sexual risk-taking among African American women enrolled in an HIV/STD prevention intervention. *Psychology, Health, & Medicine, 8,* 187–198.

Becker, D. (2001). Diagnosis of psychological disorders: *DSM* and gender. In J. Worell (Ed.), *Encyclopedia of women and gender: Sex similarities and differences and the impact of society on gender* (Vol. 1, pp. 333–343). San Diego, CA: Academic Press.

Becker, S. W., & Eagly, A. H. (2004). The heroism of women and men. *American Psychologist, 59*(3), 163–178.

Belar, C. D., Brown, R. A., Hersch, L. E., Hornyak, L. M., Rozensky, R. H., Sheridan, E. P., et al. (2001). Self-assessment in clinical health psychology: A model for ethical expansion of practice. *Professional Psychology: Research and Practice, 32,* 135–141.

Berkman, L., & Kawachi, I. (2000). A historical framework for social epidemiology. In L. Berkman, & I. Kawachi (Eds.), *Social epidemiology* (pp. 3–12). New York: Oxford University Press.

Birmaher, B., Ryan, N. D., Williamson, D. E., Brent, D. A., Kaufman, J., Dahl, R. E., et al. (1996). Childhood and adolescent depression: A review of the past 10 years. Part I. *Journal of the American Academy of Child and Adolescent Psychiatry, 35*(11), 1427–1439.

CDC National Center for Health Statistics. (2004). NCHS data on teen age pregnancy. Retrieved June 2004 from http://www.cdc.gov/nchs/data/factsheets/teenpreg.pdf

Chesney, M. A. (1993). Health psychology in the 21st century: Acquired immunodeficiency syndrome as a harbinger of things to come. *Health Psychology, 12*(4), 259–268.

Collins, F. S. (1999). Shattuck lecture: Medical and societal consequences of the Human Genome Project. *New England Journal of Medicine, 341,* 28–37.

Emanuel, E. J., Fairclough, D. L., Slutsman, J., Alpert, H., Baldwin, D., & Emanuel, L. L. (1999). Assistance from family members, friends, paid care givers, and volunteers in the care of terminally ill patients. *New England Journal of Medicine, 341*(13), 956–963.

Engel, G. (1977). The need for a new medical model: A challenge for biomedicine. *Science, 196,* 129–136.

Federal Bureau of Investigation. (2003, December 29). Uniform Crime Report, Bureau of Justice Statistics. Cited in *New York Times* (page not available).

Goodheart, C. D. (1998/2004). Psychological interventions in adult disease management. In G. Koocher, J. Norcross, & S. Hill (Eds.), *Psychologists' desk reference* (2nd ed., pp. 274–278). New York: Oxford University Press.

Goodheart, C. D. (in press). The impact of health disparities on cancer caregivers. In R. C. Talley, R. McCorkle, & W. Baile (Eds.), *Caregiving for individuals with cancer.* New York: Oxford University Press.

Greenhouse, S. (2004, June 8). Thousands of home aides begin a strike. *New York Times,* p. B1.

Haley, W. E., West, C. A. C., Wadley, V. G., & Ford, G. R. (1995). Psychological, social, and health impact of caregiving: A comparison of Black and White demential family caregivers and noncaregivers. *Psychology and Aging, 10*(4), 540–552.

Institute for the Future. (2000). *Health and Health Care 2010.* San Francisco: Jossey-Bass.

Kaufman, L. (2004, June 9). Strike today to complicate day care for the poor. *New York Times,* p. B4.

Kemeny, M. (2003). The psychobiology of stress. *Current Directions in Psychological Science, 12*(4), 124–129.

Kiecolt-Glaser, J. K., McGuire, L., Robles, T. F., & Glaser, R. (2002a). Emotions, morbidity, and mortality: New perspectives from psychoneuroimmunology. *Annual Review of Psychology, 53*(1), 83–107.

Kiecolt-Glaser, J. K., McGuire, L., Robles, T. F., & Glaser, R. (2002b). Psychoneuroimmunology: Psychological influences on immune function and health. *Journal of Consulting and Clinical Psychology, 70*(3), 537–547.

Lee, S., Colditz, G., Berkman, L., & Kawachi, I. (2003). Caregiving to children and grandchildren and risk of coronary heart disease in women. *American Journal of Public Health, 93,* 1939–1944.

Lopez, S. R., & Guaranaccia, P. J. J. (2000). Cultural psychopathology: Uncovering the social world of mental illness. *Annual Review of Psychology, 51,* 571–598.

Masten, A. S. (2001). Ordinary magic: Resilience processes in development. *American Psychologist, 56*(3), 227–238.

Matthews, K., Shumaker, S., Bowen, D., Langer, R., Hunt, J., Kaplan, R., et al. (1997). Women's health initiative: Why now? What is it? What's new? *American Psychologist, 52*(2), 101–116.

McDaniel, S. H., Bennett Johnson, S., & Sears, S. F. (2004). Psychologists promote biopsychosocial health for families. In R. H. Rozensky, N. G. Johnson, C. D. Goodheart, & W. R. Hammond (Eds.), *Psychology builds a healthy world: Opportunities for research and practice* (pp. 49–75). Washington, DC: American Psychological Association.

Mokdad, A. H., Marks, J. S., Stroup, D. F., & Gerberding, J. L. (2004). Actual causes of death in the United States, 2000. *Journal of the American Medical Association, 291*(10), 1238–1246. Retrieved June 2004 from http://www.cdc.gov/nccdphp/factsheets/death_causes2000_access.htm

National Institute of Mental Health. (2001). NIMH research on women's mental health: Highlights FY 1999–FY 2000. Retrieved January 2004 from http://www.nimh.nih.gov/wmhc/highlights.cfm

Nolen-Hoeksema, S., & Keita, G. (2003). Women and depression: An introduction. *Psychology of Women Quarterly, 27,* 89–90.

Patenaude, A. F. (2005). *Genetic testing for cancer: Psychological approaches for helping patients and families.* Washington, DC: American Psychological Association.

Patenaude, A. F., Guttmacher, A. F., & Collins, F. S. (2002). Genetic testing: New roles, new responsibilities. *American Psychologist, 57*(4), 271–282.

Pedro-Carroll, J. (2001). The promotion of wellness in children and families: Challenges and opportunities. *American Psychologist, 56*(11), 993–1004.

Rossouw, J. E., Anderson, G. L., Prentice, R. L., LaCroix, A. Z., Kooperberg, C., Stefanick, M. L., et al. (2002). Risks and benefits of estrogen plus progestin in healthy postmenopausal women: Principal results from the Women's Health Initiative randomized controlled trial. *Journal of the American Medical Association, 288,* 312–333.

Roth, D. L., Haley, W. E., Owen, J. E., Clay, O. J., & Goode, K. T. (2001). Appraisal, coping, and social support as mediators of well-being in Black and White family caregivers of patients with Alzheimer's disease. *Psychology and Aging, 16*(3), 427–436.

Singer, B. H., & Ryff, C. D. (Eds.). (2001). *New horizons in health: An integrative approach.* Washington, DC: National Academies Press.

Small Business Administration & National Foundation for Women Business Owners. (1997). Startling new statistics. *SBA Online Women's Business Center.* Retrieved July 2004 from http://www.onlinewbc.gov/docs/starting/new_stats.html

Smedley, B. D., & Syme, S. L. (Eds.). (2000). *Promoting health: Intervention strategies from social and behavioral research.* Washington, DC: National Academies Press.

Stanton, A., & Courtenay, W. (2004). Gender, stress and health. In R. H. Rozensky, N. Johnson, C. D. Goodheart, & W. R. Hammond (Eds.), *Psychology builds a healthy world: Opportunities for research and practice* (pp. 105–135). Washington, DC: American Psychological Association.

Taylor, S. E., Klein, L. C., Lewis, B. P., Gruenewald, T. L., Gurung, R. A. R., & Updegraff, J. A. (2000). Biobehavioral responses to stress in females: Tend-and-befriend, not fight-or-flight. *Psychological Review, 107*(3), 411–429.

U.S. Bureau of the Census. (1998). *Statistical abstract of the United States* (118th ed.). Washington, DC: U.S. Government Printing Office.

U.S. Department of Health and Human Services. (1998, June). *Informal caregiving: Compassion in action.* Washington, DC: U.S. Department of Health and Human Services, Office of the Assistant Secretary for Planning, Evaluation, and Administration on Aging.

U.S. Department of Health and Human Services. (2000, November). *Healthy people 2010: Understanding and improving health* (2nd ed.). Washing-ton, DC: U.S. Government Printing Office. Available at http://www.healthypeople.gov/Document/Word/uih/uih.doc

U.S. Department of Labor, Bureau of Labor Statistics. (2004, July). *Table 2. Median usual weekly earnings of full-time wage and salary workers by age, race, Hispanic or Latino ethnicity, and sex, fourth quarter 2004 averages, not seasonally adjusted.* Retrieved July 2004 from http://stats.bls.gov/news.release/wkyeng.t02.htm

Worell, J., & Remer, P. (2003). *Feminist perspectives in therapy* (2nd ed.). New York: John Wiley & Sons.

World Health Organization. (1992). *International statistical classification of diseases and related health problems* (1989 revision). Geneva, Switzerland: Author.

World Health Organization. (2001). *International classification of functioning, disability, and health (ICF).* Geneva, Switzerland: Author.

World Health Organization. (2004). Gender and women's mental health. Retrieved June 2004 from http://www.who.int/mental_health/prevention/genderwomen/en/print.html

Wyman, P. A., Sandler, I., Wolchik, S., & Nelson, K. (2000). Resilience as cumulative competence promotion and stress protection: Theories and intervention. In D. Cicchetti, J. Rappaport, I. Sandler, & R. P. Weissberg (Eds.), *The promotion of wellness in children and adolescents* (pp. 133–184). Washington, DC: Child Welfare League of America Press.

Gender is ubiquitous and at the same time nebulous—everywhere but nowhere. Often it is so embedded in everyday details as to be invisible. Yet in the aggregate, that which seems prosaic and ordinary is often compelling in ways not easily recognized. Birth announcements and clothing for newborns proclaim gender. Toys, games, and even such unlikely artifacts as lunch pails and umbrellas are codes for gender. Nonverbal gestures, postures, and mannerisms are similarly displays of gender. Gender stereotypes include prescriptions for emotional expression, temperament, competitiveness, relational style, and cognitive ability. Certain roles within the family and in society are firmly associated with gender, and exceptions usually receive a special label or designation. For example, common parlance has included the term "working mom" but not "working dad." The universal presence of gender in so many aspects of identity and experience make it a worthwhile starting point from which to consider the disruptive and somber planes of life.

As a pivotal variable, gender provides a useful, and seldom irrelevant, basis for theorizing about risks to psychological health and development across the life span. Unfortunately *female* gender encompasses a number of perils to healthy development. By intention, this chapter examines the negative and the harmful aspects of health and development; however, this is not the complete picture, and in the following chapter strengths are addressed.

GENDER DIFFERENCE AND DYNAMICS OF ENTITLEMENT

The social context of gender is fundamental to an analysis of threats to healthy development. Scholars in the psychology of women generally agree that American society differentially values male over female. In this sense, gender is a marker variable that reflects the combined effects of differential entitlement, status, and power. It is not so much the qualities unique to a particular gender, but rather the ways in which each is allowed identity, expression, opportunity, resources, and ease of access to alternatives. The differential valuing and status of male over female can be seen in concrete outcomes such as

CHERYL BROWN TRAVIS

Risks to Healthy Development: The Somber Planes of Life

lower pay for women engaged in identical professions and lower pay for women engaged in different, but comparable, work roles (U.S. Department of Labor, 2001). It can also been seen in more subtle ways in evaluative judgments of the same behavior performed by people of different genders. For example, assertiveness by a woman may be off-putting, while coworkers or other role partners may welcome the same behavior in a man as a mark of leadership (Carli, 1990).

Gender is enacted and re-enacted within the dynamics of differential value and status. This social construction shapes day-to-day interactions and personal experience. It influences expectations and implicit understandings about reality and meaning. I propose here, along with others (West & Zimmerman, 1991), that gender is not so much a set of fixed qualities but rather something one does. Gender has an emergent, negotiated component that is jointly constructed with specific role partners in a societal context. It is shaped by the fact that participants carry with them varying degrees of entitlement, expectations, resources, scripts, and vested interests. A significant and often unrecognized feature of context is the extent to which it fosters and supports certain understandings, assumptions, and realities about self-identity and social relationships, while making other realities and relationships seem strange or problematic.

Additionally, gender reflects most of the elements of a status variable. Therefore, a framework of analysis that emphasizes gender must also examine the varying resources, alternatives, and entitlement associated with gender. *Resources* might be as concrete as the money by which one may have, without thinking too hard about it, housing, telephone service, food, entertainment, health care, and so on. Resources also may be intangible—for example, social skill, work experience, beauty. These can be gauged in terms of their portability or universal value. Money is highly portable whereas work experience within a particular company is somewhat less portable, and physical beauty is relatively transient.

Alternatives by which one might reach desirable outcomes is yet another dimension of gender and status. Certainly some of the stresses experienced by many women are the limited viable alternatives to their present relationships or to their current economic situation. Alternatives usually reflect the compound effects of choices made over time, although it is not entirely a matter of choice. When girls have been led to understand that their happiness is easily won by being agreeable, attentive, and appealing (i.e., harmless), it won't occur to them that they might someday need the authority of alternative resources beyond charm. However, the point in life when this becomes blazingly clear to them is often after an accumulation of many small steps of action and of inaction so that other options are not readily available. Finally, it is not simply the presence of alternatives, but how costly it might be to reach for them.

Entitlement encompasses a range of phenomena; defining one's own reality and being taken seriously is one of them. The differential valuing and status associated with gender also has a component of entitlement. This speaks to the legitimacy of one's experience and the right to act on the basis of it. However, what women experience and want is often judged by society as irrational, unpredictable, confusing, opaque, or even dangerous. They are frequently in the position of needing to explain themselves. These dynamics operate across all dimensions that are the typical bases for classifying people, certainly gender, but also age, class, color, ethnicity, physical ability, religion, and sexual orientation. Lips (1991) identifies these dynamics as reflections of power and notes that most stereotypic male-female differences result from this imbalance.

Marginal status and the differential valuing of girls and women contribute to a wide range of risks and poor outcomes. Subsequent chapters that discuss specific risks and life experiences all address issues that may be examined in terms of gender and the elements of status and of entitlement confounded within gender. Although female gender constitutes one crosscutting framework of risk, there are certainly other bases by which inequity is enacted. Central themes in the analysis for this chapter are that gender covaries with status (resources, alternatives, and entitlement); that gender is emergent in a social and cultural context; and that the meaning of life events are often socially constructed in ways that preserve the status quo. Gendered features of risk are considered here in three clusters: violence across the life span, selfhood and identity, and social roles and relationships.

VIOLENCE ACROSS THE LIFE SPAN

Violence unfortunately is common throughout the lives of girls and women. Child abuse is strongly gendered, and retrospective self-report studies indicate that women are two to three times more likely than men to report childhood sexual abuse (de Paul, Milner, & Mugica, 1995). Data from the Department of Health and Human Services (DHHS) Children's Bureau indicated that 903,000 children were confirmed victims of abuse or neglect in 2001, a rate of approximately 12 per 1,000 children (DHHS, 2003). Individual perpetrators may engage the very young child in a play or make-believe script that enforces the idea of "our special secret." In these ways, victims are silenced and denied their own reality. As girls develop, patterns of violence continue in the alarming incidence of sexual assault and date rape. Here, too, differential power invested in gender affects dynamics of rape and interpersonal violence. Many boys and young men learn that attention-getting behaviors, bravado, and pugnacity can lead to agreeable outcomes and may be viewed with a tacit social tolerance that "boys will be boys." It's a short step to identify aggression as a legitimate and natural tool of instrumental behavior. Alternatively, many girls and young women learn that aggression is a sign of failure.

Media messages contribute by offering the depersonalized female body as fundamentally a sexual object. To some extent, almost all women internalize aspects of this objectification message (Fredrickson & Roberts, 1997) and accordingly modify their expectations of the treatment to which they are entitled (Holland & Eisenhart, 1990). Instances of sexual harassment are especially prone to social constructions concerning what actually happened and what it means. For example, men frequently perceive the friendly behavior of women as indicating sexual interest the women themselves did not intend (Abbey, McAuslan, Zawacki, Clinton, & Buck, 2001). At the same time, men may perceive their own sex-

ualizing of a situation as being merely affable. Indeed commonly understood scripts for dating held by female as well as male adolescents normalize a scenario of gaming and competition. In some instances this may include forcefulness, where sexual predation may be seen as natural among boys (Tolman, Spencer, Rosen-Reynoso, & Porche, 2003). Individual teens will have varying experiences that do not include all features of this script. However, the general script does exist as one part of cultural norms.

Implications for Treatment

Though abuse and sexual violence are not the only risks to healthy development, a multitude of sequelae may follow, including anxiety disorders and depression, as well as drug dependence, poor scholastic achievement, later sexual risk taking, and problems for close relationships. Victims of childhood abuse often exhibit symptoms that reflect an internalizing of problems—for example, depression—and also an externalizing of problems—for example, fighting. In addition, early abuse and sexual victimization increases the risk of later re-victimization. For example, children who experienced abuse involving intercourse were eight times as likely to have attempted suicide and more than nine times as likely to be at risk later for rape (Nelson et al., 2002).

The relevance of power and influence in recognizing and dealing with sexual abuse and violence is highlighted by the fact that aspects of the events may not be disclosed to others for years or even decades. Factors that normalize violence and that objectify women tend to silence women's active protest. It is not rare that this differential access to voice leads women to feelings of guilt for these events and, on occasion in cases of rape, may lead them even to wish for more signs of physical damage so as to validate the violation and anguish they have experienced.

SELFHOOD AND IDENTITY

A range of developmental tasks emerges in adolescence involving a sense of identity and worth, the capacity for friendship, and psychological intimacy, as well as a more conscious integration of a gender identity. While historic traditions in psychology have emphasized the mental health benefits of traditional gender role socialization, more recent thinking has included the idea that socialization into restricted feminine roles may be harmful to the self-esteem and the overall well-being and development of girls (Pipher, 1994). Risk factors for low self-esteem for girls in general include the reality of being part of a social group that is less valued and that occupies relatively lower status (Katz, Joiner, & Kwon, 2002).

To the extent that girls begin to assume the scripted role of caretaker for the feelings and welfare of others, they may find it increasingly difficult to express their own preferences or thoughts. Factors of particular relevance to girls may include gender intensification and growing role strain between instrumental achievement and interpersonal relationships (Basow & Rubin, 1999). Ubiquitous effects may involve chronic low self-esteem and body image disorders, especially among adolescent girls. Lifetime risks for anxiety disturbance or clinical depression are similarly high. Although less frequent, substance abuse and suicide are critical risks with gendered variations in development and process.

Self-Esteem

There is some debate about the exact size and extent of self-esteem problems. A meta-analysis[1] of 216 studies involving 16,000 people found that on average there is a small gender difference that favors boys, $d = .21$, or about one fifth of one standard deviation; this difference is somewhat larger when only adolescents are included ($d = .33$) (Kling, Hyde, Showers, & Buswell, 1999). Both girls and boys appear to experience a general decline in their sense of competence, but the size and direction of gender differences varies with the domain being assessed (Jacobs, Lanza, Osgood, Eccles, & Wigfield, 2002).

It also is worthwhile to consider variations and diversities among girls and women themselves. A recent longitudinal survey conducted by the National Heart Lung and Blood Institute of the National Institutes of Health (NIH) looked at components of self-esteem for White and African American adolescent girls aged 9–14. The self-esteem of White, but not African American, girls declined notably over the five-year period of the study (Brown et al., 1998). (The primary measurement scale was the Self-Perception Profile for Children [SPPC]). One might ask how the vigor and self-esteem of African American women is shaped by the negotiations of gender within ethnic communities. Since ethnic minority women face a double jeopardy of sexism and racism, dynamics of self-esteem in the lives of these women may inform more broadly the understanding of self-esteem in general.

Hispanic/Latina ethnicity offers additional perspectives on gender and self-esteem, although the constructions of gender in traditional Hispanic/Latina cultures include many of the same biased social constructions found in White culture. Nurturance, self-sacrifice, sexual virtue, deference, and diffidence are extolled as laudable for Hispanic/Latina girls and women. In Hispanic/Latina culture, this role is sometimes referred to as *marianismo*, and is somewhat complementary to the male *machismo* (Breuner, 1992; Comas-Diaz, 1984). Despite variations across ethnicities, a variety of sequelae may follow when self-esteem is undermined.

Sequelae

Self-esteem issues are related to body image disturbance and a variety of eating disorders. Beauty has become a defining element in sexuality, of worth, and of status (Travis, Meginnis, & Siebrecht, 2000). While both adolescent males and females are concerned about physical appearance, the standards for women are relatively strict and, for girls, violations may entail more sanctions. This is likely to be most problematic when the cultural ideal of a perfect body becomes internalized in the feelings and experiences of individual women. Lower status for girls and women is regularly conveyed in the sexualized, idealized depictions of the female body (Malkin, Wornian, & Chrisler, 1999). Research has documented that exposure to these images is associated with poor body image and symptoms of disordered eating (Thompson & Smolak, 2001; Vaughan & Fouts, 2003). These factors also have been associated with more general depressive symptoms (Stice & Bearman, 2001; Stice, Spangler, & Agras, 2001).

A corollary of low self-esteem may shape the classroom behaviors of college women who report that in many instances they don't participate in class discussions because they are afraid of looking dumb or because their ideas are not well formulated (Crawford & MacLeod, 1990). The combination of factors may influence a variety of educational and career choices. It is possible that the cumulative impact on education and occupational aspirations is to increase the likelihood of conservative choices in the classes students select and later in career choices. Eccles (1994) has described these academic and life choices in terms of the interaction of expectations of success and the extent to which success, if achieved, promotes access to other valued outcomes. It seems that even when girls have achieved high levels of academic success, they gradually come to doubt that their achievements are due to superior ability, whereas high achieving boys continue to credit themselves with exceptional talent (Arnold, 1993). Even when women college students achieve a high grade point average in a field such as engineering or computer science, they are more likely than men to change majors (Selingo, 1998).

Anxiety and Depression

It has been long acknowledged that women are more likely to suffer from anxiety and depressive disorders. This difference appears in adolescence and has been related to gender role orientation. Specifically, a more masculine gender identity seems to offer some protection (Ginsburg & Silverman, 2000). The two conditions, anxiety and depression, are thought to be interrelated, and research has found that women are indeed more likely to be diagnosed with these dual comorbid conditions than are men (Simonds & Whiffen, 2003).

Throughout their lives women are at a higher risk for depression. This is true despite a wide range in the ways it is defined—for example, hospital admission, diagnosis of major clinical depressive disorder, checklists acknowledging a certain number of depressive symptoms, and

self-reports of feeling blue. Gender stereotypes clearly influence perceptions of mental health and foster a link between female gender and reports of depression. Much of the medical literature on women and depression follows a reductionist approach that considers psychology an offshoot of physiology, especially the physiology of women's reproductive hormones. Psychological theory has often accounted for links between gender and depression in factors internal to the individual. One approach suggests that girls and women have more permeable boundaries and relationship-oriented definitions of selfhood that make them more vulnerable to internalization of symptoms and associated depression, while boys and men have more firm boundaries of selfhood that lead to more externalization of symptoms (Rosenfield, Vertefuille, & McAlpine, 2000).

Social conditions of status and entitlement again may provide the contextual background for understanding some of the increased risk for women. Gove, a sociologist, was one of the first scholars to link women's depression to their lower status roles in marriage (Gove, 1972). Other analyses have subsequently included consideration of women's status as well as the intersection of ethnic minority status and gender (Landrine, 1995; McGrath, Keita, Strickland, & Russo, 1990). Relevant factors include the early socialization of girls that places relatively more emphasis on pleasing others, praise for decorum and dutiful behavior and relatively less emphasis on instrumental achievement. Additionally there is a risk of being ostracized for being too assertive, and general cultural messages that give greater emphasis to girls' appearance over, for example, career achievement. Often these factors are played out in subtle everyday events that individually seem unremarkable. Not all girls will experience all these factors at all times, but these factors do contribute to an ambience in which girls develop.

SOCIAL ROLES AND RELATIONSHIPS

There is often a cultural expectation that women will find their most satisfying fulfillment in intimate (heterosexual) relationships. Mothers especially are lauded for emotional investment, nurturing, and strengthening of the family. In fact, girls and women are likely to have a good deal of achievement motivation in association with their close relationships. While this relational focus has been recognized as reflecting strengths, it is not without risks.

Emotional Investments

Investment in close relationships frequently offers a sense of well-being, purpose, and accomplishment for both women and men, but it also can produce a degree of vulnerability and dependency, particularly if resources and alternatives available to the partners are unequal or difficult to access. Personal flexibility and agreeableness are key to maintaining these relationships, and in order to secure and maintain these all-important relationships, girls and women may suppress important aspects of their identity and emotional experiences. To the extent that women have invested relatively more of their resources and of their future opportunities in a relationship, they may be more vulnerable to exploitation and inequity.

Defining equity in these close relationships may depend in part on economic resources each partner provides, and these are likely to be higher for men than women. Equity in the costs and benefits of (heterosexual) couple relationships often seem lopsided, with men partners receiving relatively more emotional care as well as more personal services. For example, studies of the relative contribution of husbands and wives to household tasks regularly show much greater contributions from women, yet the women themselves may define the situation as equitable (Baxter, 1997) and indeed may not feel entitled to better treatment.

In order to sustain compatibility in their relationships, women may be hesitant to directly express their wishes, reluctant to convey disagreement, or unable to express anger. Since women are almost universally socialized to contain or suppress anger, this seems an especially fertile area for therapeutic work. Van-Velsor and Cox (2001) suggest that anger may energize recovery and may serve as a vehicle for wellness instead of being a symptom of illness. The expression of anger seems particularly key to women's depression involving relationships. They may engage in a muffling or silencing of themselves, with depression being the result (Jack, 1991, 2003). Women may also learn to express or redirect anger in positive ways (Jack, 2001). Stoppard (1999) maintains that approaches that offer a central role to the experiences of women are a critical element of therapy, as opposed to—for example, cognitive behavior—therapies that tend to challenge clients' negative beliefs (Hurst & Genest, 1995).

Married women experiencing depression come with regular frequency to therapy having complaints of not "being heard," and they often feel that their complaints are dismissed or otherwise invalidated (Papp, 2003). Methods of negotiating one's reality and of being heard vary systematically by gender and power in relationships (Falbo & Peplau, 1980). Women and those with less power in a relationship tend to use indirect and unilateral tactics—for example, hinting, hoping, or withdrawing. Unfortunately, such efforts to preserve relationship by continually protecting and favoring the needs and comfort levels of a partner may ultimately undermine the very intimacy the woman (or man) hopes to guard. Worell (Worell, 2000; Worell & Remer, 2003) suggests that an empowerment approach may be particularly valuable for women, as well as those who have been marginalized or silenced by virtue of socioeconomic class, ethnicity, sexual orientation or other conditions of social status.

Work

Having it all was at one time an inspirational goal for women emerging into a new gender consciousness of the sixties. However, since women often do much of the emotional work for the family, as well as logistical household management, having it all often means working a double shift (Hochschild, 1989) and simultaneously feeling inadequate and guilty for not meeting all the demands associated with ideal homemaking. The common expectation of young women as they contemplate whether or not they even want careers often centers on the image of too many tasks to complete at home and at work and the picture of the mother who struggles to juggle roles (Crosby & Jaskar, 1993).

Theoretical models based on fixed resources suggest that investments in one realm automatically detract from another. However, psychological research suggests there may be a protective function associated with multiple roles. Research by Barnett and Hyde (2001) discloses a somewhat more positive and hopeful picture. Multiple roles offer increased opportunities for achievement, self-esteem, and social support for many women. A further, nontrivial, consideration is that although women as a whole earn less than men, women's wages constitute a significant contribution to total family income and stability.

In addition, women may bring strengths to the economic and work environment. The economy, educational institutions, health care, and research laboratories may all benefit from an increased and enthusiastic workforce. Studies of managerial style indicate that women are more likely to engage in transformational styles and in more contingent reward behaviors than men (Eagly, Johannesen-Schmidt, & van Engen, 2003). Presenting to young women the possibility that they may have unique and really important contributions to make in the workplace might be particularly affirming and might allow them to imagine more options for self-actualization in work outside the home. However, simply increasing aspirations among individual young women is not a complete solution.

Career development can be a source of frustration and stress for women. Professional women often work as minorities in their place of employment and may find the atmosphere more reflective of male preferences and male-centered norms regarding work. In particular, promotions and advancement may favor men while ignoring the contributions and competence of women. This is such an omnipresent phenomenon that it has been labeled the "glass ceiling." Cultural beliefs about traditional femininity suggest an assumed incongruity between being feminine and being a leader, thus women leaders who are assertive and direct may receive poor evaluations (Eagly & Karau, 2002). The result may be a subtle discounting of women's accomplishments or the manner in which these are achieved. Although subtle, the cu-

mulative effects may be quite large. For example, roughly 40% of employees in Fortune 500 corporations are women, while less than 1% are CEOs (Wellington & Giscombe, 2001).

Poverty

Developmental tasks of adulthood encompass large issues such as generativity and the existential need, finally, "to get it right." But more often than not, daily tasks deal with the ordinary elements of making a living and sustaining committed relationships. Here, too, differential status, influence, and power continue to be evident, specifically poverty, divorce, and single mothering. The majority of women work full time in the labor force; this includes the majority of women with children. On average, women who work full time earn 74% of what men earn (U.S. Department of Labor, 2001, table 37). Effectively, women must work approximately 15 months to make what men earn in 12 months. Another way to think of it is that for wages to be equal, women on average would need to have a 35% salary increase. The lifetime impact per woman, including compounded interest on wages *and* retirement benefits, has been estimated to be over a half million dollars. Psychologically, some women may accept gender differences in salary because they compare their salaries to the norm for other women rather than men (Major, 1989). That is, their sense of entitlement is restricted by implicit gender-based norms.

Despite employment outside the home, many women and their children remain in poverty. The official poverty level for a family of four in 2001 was $18,104; 33 million people fell below this level (Proctor & Dalakar, 2002). The incidence of poverty varies significantly by gender and family type. Poverty also varies dramatically by ethnic minority designation, with the poverty level ranging from 21% to 23% for ethnic minorities in contrast to poverty among Whites (non-Hispanic) at 7.8% (Proctor & Dalakar, 2002). When women are the sole financial heads of their own households, it becomes increasingly likely that they will fall below the poverty level; this is especially true for Hispanic women who are single heads of households (U.S. Department of Labor, 2001). Poverty in itself limits the alternatives and choices of women. Given that poverty increases uncertainty in general and the possibility of catastrophic events, it is likely to undermine confidence and problem solving.

GOING FORWARD

As following chapters indicate, girls and women face a plethora of risks to healthy development. There also are a range of strengths and resources that may be developed, and many later chapters discuss opportunities for empowerment and growth. Analyses of problems and of possible solutions may benefit from systematically attending to the gendered aspects of both. In particular, the differential valuing of girls and women can be seen to have a pervasive influence on development and health across the life span. Empowering women to hold and exercise authority in their personal lives and in public political realms is a fundamental component in the resolution of these problems. This includes building authenticity and the confidence to define one's reality and have it taken seriously. Becoming an agent of action and acquiring the conviction to effect change is another aspect of this process.

NOTE

1. Meta-analysis is a statistical technique whereby mean differences are re-formulated in terms of a common standard unit that makes the results comparable across studies. The average mean difference can then be calculated for all the studies in combination.

REFERENCES

Abbey, A., McAuslan, P., Zawacki, T., Clinton, A. M., & Buck, P. O. (2001). Attitudinal, experimental, and situational predators of sexual assault perpetration. *Journal of Interpersonal Violence, 16,* 784–807.

Arnold, K. D. (1993). Academically talented women in the 1970s: The Illinois Valedictorian Project. In K. D. Hulbert & D. Tickton (Eds.), *Women's lives through time* (pp. 393–414). San Francisco: Jossey-Bass.

Barnett, R. C., & Hyde, J. S. (2001). Women, men, work, and family: An expansionist theory. *American Psychologist, 56,* 781–796.

Basow, S. A., & Rubin, L. R. (1999). Gender influences on adolescent development. In N. G. Johnson, N. G., Roberts, M. C., & Worell, J. (Eds.), *Beyond appearance: A new look at adolescent girls* (pp. 25–52). Washington, DC.: American Psychological Association.

Baxter, J. (1997). Gender equality and participation in housework: A cross-national perspective. *Journal of Comparative Family Studies, 28*(3), 220–247.

Breuner, N. F. (1992). The cult of the Virgin Mary in southern Italy and Spain. *Ethos, 20*(1), 66–95.

Brown, K. M., McMahon, R. P., Biro, F. M., Crawford, P., Schreiber, G. B., Shari, L., et al. (1998). Changes in self-esteem in Black and White girls between the ages of 9 and 14 years. *Journal of Adolescent Health, 23,* 7–19.

Carli, L. (1990). Gender, language, and influence. *Journal of Personality and Social Psychology, 59,* 941–951.

Comas-Diaz, L. (1984). Content themes in group treatment with Puerto Rican women. *Social Work With Groups, 7*(3), 75–84.

Crawford, M., & MacLeod, M. (1990). Gender in the college classroom: An assessment of the "chilly climate" for women. *Sex Roles, 23*(34), 101–122.

Crosby, F. J., & Jaskar, K. L. (1993). Women and men at home and at work: Realities and illusions. In. S. Oskamp & M. Costanzo (Eds.), *Gender issues in contemporary society. Claremont Symposium on Applied Social Psychology* (Vol. 6, pp. 143–171).

Department of Health and Human Services Administration on Children, Youth and Families. (2003). *Child Maltreatment 2001.* Washington, DC: U.S. Government Printing Office.

de Paul, J., Milner, J. S., & Mugica, P. (1995). Childhood maltreatment, childhood social support, and child abuse potential in a Basque sample. *Child Abuse Neglect, 19,* 907–920.

Eagly, A. H., Johannesen-Schmidt, M. C., & van Engen, M. L. (2003). Transformational, transactional, and laissez-faire leadership styles: A meta-analysis comparing women and men. *Psychological Bulletin, 129*(4), 569–591.

Eagly, A. H., & Karau, S. J. (2002). Role congruity theory of prejudice toward female leaders. *Psychological Review, 109,* 573–598.

Eccles, J. S. (1994). Understanding women's educational and occupational choices: Applying the Eccles et al. model of achievement-related choices. *Psychology of Women Quarterly, 18,* 585–610.

Falbo, T., & Peplau, L. A. (1980). Power strategies in intimate relationships. *Journal of Personality and Social Psychology, 38,* 618–628.

Fredrickson, B. L., & Roberts, T. A. (1997). Objectification theory: Towards understanding women's lived experience and mental health risks. In T. A. Roberts (Ed.), *The Lanahan readings in the psychology of women* (pp. 376–400). Baltimore: Lanahan.

Ginsburg, G. S., & Silverman, W. K. (2000). Gender role orientation and fearfulness in children with anxiety disorders. *Journal of Anxiety Disorders,* *14*(1), 57–67.

Gove, W. R. (1972). The relationship between sex roles, marital status, and mental illness. *Social Forces, 51*(1), 34–44.

Hochschild, A. (1989). *The second shift: Working parents and the revolution at home.* New York: Viking.

Holland, D. C., & Eisenhart, M. A. (1990). *Educated in romance: Women, achievement, and college culture.* Chicago: University of Chicago Press.

Hurst, S. A., & Genest, M. (1995). Cognitive behavioural therapy with a feminist orientation: A perspective for therapy with depressed women. *Canadian Psychology, 36*(3), 236–257.

Jack, D. C. (1991). *Silencing the self: Women and depression.* Cambridge, MA: Harvard University Press.

Jack, D. C. (2001). Understanding women's anger: A description of relational patterns. *Health Care for Women International, 22*(4), 385–400.

Jack, D. C. (2003). The anger of hope and the anger of despair: How anger relates to women's depression. In J. M. Stoppard, & L. M. McMullen (Eds.), *Situating sadness: Women and depression in social context* (pp. 62–87). New York: New York University Press.

Jacobs, J. E., Lanza, S., Osgood, D. W., Eccles, J. S., & Wigfield, A. (2002). Changes in children's self-competence and values: Gender and domain differences across grades one though twelve. *Child Development, 73*(2), 509–527.

Katz, J., Joiner, T. E., Jr., & Kwon, P. (2002). Membership in a devalued social group and emotional well-being: Developing a model of personal self-esteem, collective self-esteem, and group socialization. *Sex-Roles, 47*(9–10), 419–431.

Kling, K. C., Hyde, J. S., Showers, C. J., & Buswell, B. N. (1999). Gender differences in self-esteem: A meta-analysis. *Psychological Bulletin, 125*(4), 470–500.

Landrine, H. (Ed.). (1995). *Bringing cultural diversity to feminist psychology.* Washington, DC: American Psychological Association.

Lips, H. (1991). *Women, men, and power.* Mountain View, CA: Mayfield.

Major, B. (1989). Gender differences in comparisons and entitlement: Implications for comparable worth. *Journal of Social Issues, 45*(4), 99–115.

Malkin, A. R., Wornian, K., & Chrisler, J. C. (1999). Women and weight: Gendered messages on magazine covers. *Sex Roles, 40,* 647–655.

McGrath, E., Keita, G. P., Strickland, B. R., & Russo, N. F. (Eds.). (1990). *Women and depression: Risk factors and treatment issues: Final report of the American Psychological Association's National Task Force on Women and Depression.* Washington, DC: American Psychological Association.

Nelson, E. C., Health, A. C., Madden, P. A. F., Cooper, L., Dinwiddie, S. H., Bucholz, K. K., et al. (2002). Association between self-reported childhood sexual abuse and adverse psychosocial outcomes. *Archives of General Psychiatry, 59,* 139–145.

Papp, P. (2003). Gender, marriage, and depression. In L. Silverstein and T. J. Goodrich (Eds.), *Feminist family therapy* (pp. 211–223). Washington, DC: American Psychological Association.

Pipher, M. (1994). *Reviving Ophelia: Saving the selves of adolescent girls.* New York: G. P. Putnam's Sons.

Proctor, B., & Dalakar, J. B., U.S. Census Bureau. (2002). Poverty in the United States: 2001. *Current Population Reports* (pp. 60–219). Washington, DC: U.S. Government Printing Office.

Rosenfield, S., Vertefuille, J., & McAlpine, D. D. (2000). Gender stratification and mental health: An exploration of dimensions of the self. *Social Psychology Quarterly, 63*(3), 208–223.

Selingo, J. (1998, February 20). Science-oriented campuses strive to attract more women. *Chronicle of Higher Education,* pp. A53–A54.

Simonds, V. M., & Whiffen, V. E. (2003). Are gender differences in depression explained by gender differences in co-morbid anxiety? *Journal of Affective Disorders, 77*(3), 197–202.

Stice, E., & Bearman, S. K. (2001). Body-image and eating disturbances prospectively predict increases in depressive symptoms in adolescent girls: A growth curve analysis. *Developmental Psychology, 37,* 597–607.

Stice, E., Spangler, D., & Agras, W. S. (2001). Exposure to media-portrayed thin-ideal images adversely affects vulnerable girls: A longitudinal experiment. *Journal of Social and Clinical Psychology, 20,* 270–288.

Stoppard, J. M. (1999). Why new perspectives are needed for understanding depression in women. *Canadian Psychology, 40*(2), 79–90.

Thompson, J. K., & Smolak, L. (2001). *Body image, eating disorders, and obesity in youth: Assessment, prevention, and treatment.* Washington, DC: American Psychological Association.

Tolman, D. L., Spencer, R., Rosen-Reynoso, M., & Porche, M. V. (2003). Sowing the seeds of violence in heterosexual relationships: Early adolescents narrate compulsory heterosexuality. *Journal of Social Issues, 59*(1), 159–178.

Travis, C. B., Meginnis, K., & Siebrecht, K. (2000). Beauty, sexuality, and identity: The social control of women. In C. B. Travis & J. W. White (Eds.), *Sexuality, society, and feminism: Psychological perspectives on women* (pp. 237–272). Washington, DC: American Psychological Association.

U.S. Department of Labor, Bureau of Labor Statistics. (2001). *Employment and earnings.* Table 37. Washington, DC: Government Printing Office.

Van-Velsor, P., & Cox, D. L. (2001). Anger as a vehicle in the treatment of women who are sexual abuse survivors: Reattributing responsibility and accessing personal power. *Professional Psychology: Research and Practice, 32*(6), 618–625.

Vaughan, K. K., & Fouts, G. T. (2003). Changes in television and magazine exposure and eating disorder symptomatology. *Sex Roles, 49,* 313–320.

Wellington, S., & Giscombe, K. (2001). Women and leadership in corporate American. In C. Costello & A. Stone (Eds.), *The American women, 2001–2002* (pp. 87–106). New York: Norton.

West, C., & Zimmerman, D. (1991). Doing gender. In J. Lorber & S. A. Farrell (Eds.), *The social construction of gender* (pp. 13–37). Thousand Oaks, CA: Sage.

Worell, J. (2000, August). *Searching for the power in empowerment.* Invited address to annual meeting of the American Psychological Association, Chicago.

Worell, J., & Remer, P. (2003). *Feminist perspectives in therapy: Empowering diverse women* (2nd ed.). New York: John Wiley & Sons.

Do not follow where the path may lead.
Go instead where there is no path and leave
a trail.

—Ralph Waldo Emerson

JUDITH WORELL

Pathways to Healthy Development: Sources of Strength and Empowerment

Women today are stronger, more hopeful, energetic, optimistic, and healthy than ever before in our history. But we know that major challenges to a safe and healthy existence still face many women globally, and in the United States, women continue to be the major consumers of health services. Across the life span, significant developmental changes occur for each person that present challenges in adaptation and effective coping; some people appear to accommodate to these changes more successfully than others. Additionally, most people will experience one or more stressful events or trauma, such as serious injury or illness, loss of a loved one, prolonged poverty, unemployment, or unpredictable violence. Many chapters in this *Handbook* document the gender-related conditions that persist for girls and women from diverse cultures in terms of threats to health, economic and social inequities, and physical or sexual assault.

The questions that challenge psychology and other health disciplines are to understand why, in the face of normal or expected life changes, societal discrimination, and traumatic events, some individuals succumb to despair and decline in health and well-being, yet others accommodate to changing circumstances and adapt comfortably over time. Still, some girls and women, whether through natural circumstances, their own efforts, or with therapeutic help, appear to benefit from adversity; they are able to grow productively and thrive despite their challenging experiences. For example, prior to the 1964 Federal Civil Rights Act, a young African American woman won a prize for her thesis on democracy, but was later denied entrance to the hotel where the prizes were being handed out. This experience, as well as other similar ones, motivated her to "buck the system" by becoming the first African American woman to enter and graduate from a local university and nursing school in her state. She went on to greater achievements as the first woman of her ethnicity in many other professional domains (*Herald Leader*, 2004).

In the psychological and health-related literature, there are abundant resources on theory, research, and intervention related to developmental disorders, disability, illness, and psychopathology; there has been relatively little related to the variables that influence women's psychological health, resilience, and well-being. In the past few decades, however, a growing literature has been exploring the health-promoting sources of personal and community strength and well-being. This trend holds out promise that a major paradigm shift, with a change in focus from illness to health, is taking hold and flourishing in both research and practice communities (Icovics & Park, 1999; O'Leary & Icovics, 1995).

This chapter moves from pain to gain, offering a strength and resilience perspective on women's psychological health. I review some of the factors that contribute to girls' and women's strength, resilience, productive growth, and psychological well-being. What are the ingredients that contribute to the development of effective coping strategies, increased resilience to stress, a secure and confident sense of self, a satisfying and productive life style, and robust enthusiasm and zest for living?

ACTIVISM: OPENING LEGAL, EDUCATIONAL, AND SOCIAL OPPORTUNITIES

The personal and social benefits of gaining voice and control over one's life circumstances have been recognized throughout history. For women in United States, a giant step in this direction was achieved in 1920 with legislation that entitled them to vote in state and national elections. It was not until the 1960s that women's continued awareness of their unequal position in society activated new efforts to implement changes in the educational, social, and political environment. In tandem to these awakenings, community-supported crisis centers for battered and sexually assaulted women opened their welcoming doors, responding to the growing awareness that women did not have to live with violence. These community resources have become established institutions in most areas of the United States, and still provide essential services to protect and heal women from interpersonal assault and its aftermath (Gondolf, 1998).

The outcomes of these activities were gradual transformations in sociocultural gender-role expectations, an aroused public consciousness that promoted legislation to advance opportunity for girls and women, and new directions in research and psychological practice with women (Worell & Johnson, 1997). Almost four decades of research on women's psychological health have brought women of diverse social and economic groups out of the background and into the forefront of psychological focus. Growing awareness of widespread gender and ethnic discrimination brought demands for institutional reform, and triggered research on epidemiology, assessment, prevention, and intervention for interpersonal violence. This literature also revealed the extent to which some normative coping responses to such stressors have been medically and socially defined as pathology.

Rekindled attention to women's health also brought many positive correlates, including an emphasis on strength over pathology and well-being over illness. Conceptions of normative behavior and "adjustment" for girls and women have changed, moving beyond the traditional goals of returning clients to their status quo. Revised goals for healthy lifestyles required new approaches to assessment and evaluation of the effectiveness of psychological interventions. It becomes imperative to develop and include assessment of positive, constructive, and affirmative outcomes as well as remission of symptoms (Worell, 2001). More is currently known about evaluating and ameliorating pain and distress than about the range of personal and environmental ingredients that contribute to a satisfying life well-lived for a broad range of girls and women.

Education Promotes Well-Being

During the same period, a committed coalition of activist women, enlightened men, and sympathetic legislators advocated successfully for passage by the U.S. Congress of Title IX of the Elementary and Secondary Education Act. This landmark legislation advanced the status and opportunities for all women by prohibiting discrimination on the basis of gender at all levels of educational institutions. It opened doors for girls and women to enter institutions previously denied them. Now more women than men in the United States graduate from high school, and roughly equal numbers of women and men receive college degrees.

Prior to Title IX, funding and facilities for women's sports were often limited or absent, thus denying equal access to training, space, equipment, travel, and so on. This legislation enabled girls and women to participate in a variety of activities that facilitate the development of physical, emotional, and behavioral skills. In turn, new opportunities for healthy collaboration and competition, positive self-esteem, and psychological well-being were established. Title IX also opened opportunities for girls and women to develop a variety of new career paths that have contributed substantially to their financial and emotional health. A current trend toward reverting to same-sex education, which divides girls and boys into separate classes in the elementary schools, has received mixed reviews. It is too early to make firm judgments about whether it is advantageous for girls to be given separate learning environments where they are free to learn undisturbed by the greater attention paid to boys in classrooms or competition with boys. If strength develops in response to challenge, then perhaps the mixture of the sexes and ethnicities in classrooms presents some distinct advantages.

Satisfying Employment Promotes Well-Being

The promotion and support of women's education as a national goal provided a new perspective for most women on the meaning of work. Although many rural and urban women have always worked outside the home, especially those of color and/or low income, they tended to regard themselves, and were seen by others, as merely holding a job or bringing in necessary economic support. Once they became empowered to enter the portals of higher education and achieve advanced degrees, the prospect of a career became possible and attainable. In contrast to work as jobs, which tend to provide low levels of satisfaction and opportunity for advancement, careers are characterized by self-development toward personal goals. Careers also offer women opportunities for achievement, higher levels of functioning and increased income, and life-long commitment to developing and improving one's competency in a skill or discipline (Betz, 2002; Kahn & Juster, 2002).

Now, most young girls and women anticipate having both a family and career. Programs for women in rural or isolated communities offer training in employment skills, instilling hope for more advanced employment and better life circumstances (Frances, 1999). Women have become established in a range of career tracks that were formerly occupied by men, such as business, academic teaching and scientific research, computer science, law, medicine, and the military (Fassinger, 2001). Although White majority and ethnic minority women still earn less than their male counterparts and are more scarce than men at the top echelons of organizations, they bring particular contributions and strengths. Relatively recent organizational policies such as facilitative mentoring relationships, affirmative action policies, flexible scheduling, and day care for children have had an important impact on women's career entry, advancement, and satisfaction. Workplace environments are becoming more diverse and inclusive, and women in professional roles can serve as role models for youth and incoming employees (Murrell, 2001).

Most contemporary married women are in "dual earner" families, in which partners value equally both home and job or career. A burgeoning literature of research supports the health-promoting value of multiple roles for both women and men, with appropriate supports by partner, family, and the workplace (Barnett & Hyde, 2001). Multiple roles provide women with opportunities for increased income and thus reduced financial stress, greater self-efficacy, and a broader view of life that leads to a more complex and satisfying sense of self. Although most heterosexual married women still carry the burden of family and child care (Gilbert & Rader, 2001), studies find that egalitarian relationships, with equitable division of home and child-related tasks and shared decision making provide both partners with increased satisfaction and emotional intimacy (Steil, 1997).

GENDER TRANSFORMATIONS IMPACT WOMEN'S PSYCHOLOGICAL HEALTH

The changing meanings and expectations associated with sex and gender have been one of the major social upheavals of 20th-century social structures. The revolution of what it means to be a woman or man in society is still in flux, as individuals struggle with how to process their personal identities in a fluid and multicultural environment, and how to negotiate their relationships with family, friends, and work environments. The traditional "opposite sex" view of gender posits that women and men differ biologically in their traits and abilities; such perspectives tend to invite gender stereotyping, encourage separate social roles and activities, and limit women's opportunities. These attitudes are still in vogue for both laypersons and professionals, as exemplified by popular books and media. In contrast, we approach gender from a sociocultural identity composed of personal experiences and social expectations associated with being a girl or boy, woman or man, in any group or culture (Deaux & Major, 1987). To the extent that these expectations vary or converge, so will the personal and social identities and opportunities available for an individual in a particular group or society.

Developing a Healthy Gender and Ethnocultural Identity

As girls and women develop and grow, life circumstances change and individuals move in many different contexts. They are continually negotiating and modifying their gender-related behaviors and identities across situations and social interactions. The sense of being a girl or woman probably remains stable for most, yet the meanings and consequent behaviors attached to this identity will change with age and life circumstances (Deaux & Stewart, 2001).

The construction and meanings of gender will also vary depending on the individual's ethnicity, culture, social class, economic status, national origin, sexual orientation, and so on. For example, the experience of being either a Latina or an African American woman may be qualitatively different, as will be the gender experiences of lesbians or bisexuals as compared with heterosexual girls and women. There is support for the strength-promoting contribution of encouraging a firm integration among ethnic, gender, and sexual identities as girls and women develop (Worell & Remer, 2003). For example, Harris (1995) reported that African American women who had a secure ethnic identity status and few anti-White feelings held more favorable attitudes toward their own physical appearance and engaged in more health-promoting behaviors than those who were less secure in their cultural and ethnic identity. Professionals who work with developing youth need to be particularly aware, sensitive, and open to the personal and ethnocultural variations in both gender and sexual identities as they emerge and are expressed in social situations.

INFLUENCE OF THE POSITIVE PSYCHOLOGY MOVEMENT

An overview of recent literature reveals an increasing emphasis on the positive face of psychology and the health-promoting aspects of physical and psychological well-being. Theory and research have illuminated many strength-building concepts such as hardiness (Kobassa, Maddi, & Kahn, 1982), optimism (Seligman, 1991), posttraumatic growth (Tedeschi & Calhoun, 1995), self-efficacy (Bandura, 1997), hope (Snyder, Rand, & Sigman, 2002), problem-solving appraisal (Heppner, Witty, & Dixon, 2004), empowerment (Worell, 2002), personal control (Thompson & Wierson, 2000), and thriving (O'Leary, 1998). The focus on personal strength and affirmative behaviors has pointed to the importance of going beyond considerations of remission and symptom reduction in our interventions for personal and social distress.

The "positive psychology" movement championed by Seligman (Seligman & Csikszentmihalyi, 2000) seemed to mirror many of the tenets and values of the women researchers, theoreticians, and practitioners who have worked hard to infuse these ideas into the mainstream of psychology. The positive psychology perspective also rejects the illness and disease model of human behavior in favor of a paradigm of psychological health, proposing "a science of strength and resilience" (p. 8). Among the contributions of the positive psychology movement have been its energetic focus on promoting wellness over illness, clear definitions of important concepts, attention to healthy environmental contexts, and insistence on objective assessment of concepts and outcomes that can apply across diverse populations. The subsequent publication of several volumes of theory, application, and classification has added useful dimensions to the dialogue (cf., Peterson & Seligman, 2004; Snyder & Lopez, 2002). The positive psychology approach reminds us to seek and support the strengths that reside in every individual, and to recognize that attention to context is essential: families, schools, communities, and public institutions. Where do girls and women fit into this picture?

A CALL FOR NEW MODELS OF WOMEN'S PSYCHOLOGICAL HEALTH

There is a continuing need for models that recognize factors contributing to risks and challenges to women's psychological health, as well as opportunities for promoting wellness, resilience in the face of challenge and adversity, strength, persistence, and empowerment. The concept of empowerment has been used in many ways, often by agencies that serve underprivileged communities or marginalized populations, such as women of color (Gutierrez & Lewis, 1999) and those with disabilities. It has also been used by feminist and other professional groups to promote the well-being of diverse populations of girls' and women's well-being (Worell & Remer, 2003; Wyche & Rice, 1997). Concepts of empowerment in the literature highlight the importance to each girl and women of gaining and owning a sense of personal entitlement, or what she believes she deserves.

Empowerment is a powerful concept. It includes: competency for self-valued domains, a sense of personal control or choice over life circumstances, skills in decision making and prob-

lem solution, confidence in one's ability to reach out and engage the love and support of others, self-efficacy or the expectancy that one has the ability to achieve desired outcomes, and the multiple skills required to effect changes in both the self and in the proximal environment (Worell, 2002). The assumption underlying all empowerment interventions is that with appropriate support, individuals and groups can acquire the knowledge, motivation, and skills to improve their health, well-being, and their equitable access to meaningful resources. For minority communities with limited resource access, a multicultural approach emphasizes the "inherent resilience . . . embedded within interdependence among people, including collective wisdom, shared resources, and commitment to community" (Lee & Ramirez, 2000). For communities that value a collective approach to their identity, variables other than assertiveness or achievement in Western individualistic cultures may be relevant for the development and maintenance of self-competency (Ruiz, Roosa, & Gonzales, 2002). The signal role of empowerment strategies for women's well-being is discussed further in the chapter.

ECOLOGICAL MODELS THAT PROMOTE STRENGTH AND WELL-BEING

A broad ecological model to promote women's strength and well-being considers both internal and external variables in an interactive relationship. Relevant factors may include genetic predispositions or personality traits, embedded and displayed differently within the cultures and communities in which people are born and develop. External factors include: a supportive and affirming family and extended caring networks; clean, safe, connected, and invigorating neighborhoods; stimulating, inclusive, and empowering schools; fair employment and career opportunities; loving and nourishing peer, partner, and community relationships; financial sufficiency and access to beneficial community and health institutions; and sufficient freedom or autonomy to consider options for satisfying life choices. No single model can capture the complex range of these factors, and each deserves a full understanding. Many of the chapters in this volume address these enabling factors. They point to some of the multicultural variables that intersect with them, and propose educational and professional interventions to promote the psychological health and well-being of girls and women.

THE ROLE OF SUPPORTIVE AND FLEXIBLE FAMILIES

Across the life span, a major component of subjective well-being and psychological health is the experience of having positive, warm, and affirming relationships with others. At varying times, this will include parents, a spouse or significant other, friends, children, teachers, mentors, and extended family or interpersonal networks (Markus, Ryff, Curhan, & Palmersheim, 2004).

Support for High Self-Esteem, Multiple Skills, and Competency

Significant components of positive feelings and cognitions about the self typically develop in early childhood, within the context of the family. Parents or caretakers who provide interesting, challenging, and stimulating environments for children will kindle the flames of curiosity and exploration of their worlds. Mothers' education is found to be a key component in the development of children's early competency and later resiliency (Serbin & Karp, 2004). Other supportive factors include maternal warmth and involvement, a high degree of monitoring activities, encouragement and high expectations for girls' academic achievement and interests, and involvement of teachers or other adult mentors. As girls move from childhood to adolescence, the strains of separation and connectedness become more apparent. Even as they move away from parents into the world of peers, however, a continuing warm and supportive relationship with parents is important. Such relationships serve to reinforce positive values, maintain girls' self-esteem, and help to avoid disordered eating or substance abuse (Piran, Carter, Thompson, & Pajouhandeh, 2002).

The development and importance of the factors that contribute to self-esteem appear to vary across ethnic groups and ability domains, and as well across time and situations Self-esteem, or positive self-valuing at both cognitive and affective levels, has been traditionally viewed as one cornerstone of healthy well-being in the United States.

During the heyday of the movement to boost self-esteem, many elementary schools promoted programs to develop in each child a sense of self-valuing through programs such as having children wear a sign on their backs stating "I am capable and lovable" (W. E. Worell, personal communication). However, this approach was insufficient to help most youngsters feel competent and accepted by others, and some early self-esteem enhancing programs fell into disuse.

Studies generally find that in early adolescence, the self-esteem of girls drops substantially more than it does for boys, and continues to decline through the college-age years. These data diverge, however, when culture and ethnicity are examined, indicating that the construction of self-esteem and the standards by which girls self-evaluate may not be similar for all groups. For example, African American girls are found to demonstrate higher self-esteem than either European American girls or African American boys (Eccles, Barber, Jozefowicz, Malanchuk, & Vida, 1997). Further, when sources of self-esteem were examined between the two groups of girls, African American girls were more satisfied with their appearance and had higher self-concepts in academic, athletic, and social abilities. Several chapters in this volume discuss the consequences for adolescent girls in the United States of overvaluing their appearance and concern with body shape and weight that often lead to chronic body dissatisfaction, dieting, and plastic surgery. Early concepts of self-esteem were constructed on limited samples that did not include cultural variations in the sources self-valuing. Although parents may be less influential than peers as mediators of adolescent girls' self-evaluation of attractiveness, they can certainly play a part by supporting their daughters' needs for peer support and acceptance. Parents can place an emphasis on strengthening skills and competencies in other areas, such as academics, athletics or the arts.

Other studies have shown that girls' involvement with athletics is related to high self-esteem and satisfaction with competent performance (Delaney & Lee, 1995). Exciting examples of women's athletic achievement across a variety of group and individual sports were displayed at the 2004 Olympic Games in Athens, Greece. Some pioneering women from countries that previously had not allowed their participation competed as individuals in track and field events. In three team sports—basketball, softball, and soccer—American women excelled against competing teams from other countries, and won gold medals in each as the highest honor of excellence. The jubilation and pride of all these women reflected the importance of setting high competency aspirations related to their specific skills and the contribution to their self-worth of athletic participation. Although many of these teams comprised girls from diverse social and ethnic backgrounds, there may be intercultural differences in the factors that reinforce feelings of competency and high self-esteem. Emphasis on individual achievement in Western cultures may contrast with a collective orientation that values group relatedness as a source of self-valuing (Lehman, Chiu, & Schaller, 2004). For many African American families, parental encouragement and support for girls' competency and self-worth are crucial factors in developing their strength and positive self-valuing in a society that often offers them limited safety, respect, or acceptance (Ward, 1996).

Support for Flexible Gender Roles

From a health-promoting perspective, it seems that a more fluid and flexible gender-role identity is both attainable and desirable (Basow & Rubin, 1997). Individuals who function effectively in situations calling for agentic, instrumental, and assertive behaviors, as well as those requiring communal, expressive, and emotionally nurturing ones, are more likely than those with more traditional gender-role behaviors to have relatively high self-esteem, self-confidence, and low depression. Thus, a gender-balanced and gender-integrated identity enables girls and women to draw on a full range of personal and

social resources to cope and thrive across diverse situations.

The wealth of research on the advantages to both girls and boys of flexible gender-role development and behaviors contains clear implications for parents, educators, and professionals in their work with children and youth. In a contemporary environment filled with messages from peers and the media about how to be a "real" girl or woman, parents and youth may find it difficult to resist the cultural flow. As girls develop in a world of images portrayed by television and teen magazines, they may incorporate into their body and self concepts those messages that tell them they have failed to meet the current Western standards of female beauty. The cultural myth that "beauty is the most vital aspect of a woman's being" (Travis & Meginnis-Payne, 2001, p. 190) leads many girls and women into relentless dissatisfaction with their bodies, with chronic attempts to diet and to change their bodies through cosmetics and surgery.

Several chapters in this *Handbook* review research on healthy gender development. The strong and healthy models portrayed by the supremely athletic girls and women at the Olympic trials or by the many women who compete in the international professional tennis circuit can be important factors in instilling a positive body pride that comes from competence and achievement as well as by appearance. Sports programs in many schools and communities offer models for average girls at different levels of realistic possibility for attainment. For early adolescent girls, both European American and African American, confidence in their athletic ability is one of the predictors of high self-esteem (Eccles et al., 1997).

SOCIAL SUPPORT BY PEERS, FRIENDS, AND COMMUNITIES

Social support in its various forms contributes in beneficial ways to women's strength and psychological health. The concept of support refers to "the process by which individuals manage the psychological and material resources through their social networks to enhance their coping with stressful events, meet their social needs, and achieve their goals" (Rodriguez & Cohen, 1998, p. 536). Social support thus encompasses emotional ties and needs for a socially integrated identity, a stress-buffering function, and instrumental contributions to enhance life satisfaction.

From childhood through adolescence and beyond, the peer group plays an essential role in the development of interpersonal competence and connection. Skills in initiating and maintaining friendships and close ties to peers will have an impact on the long-term psychological health of girls and women. For younger children, coaching and training in social skills can increase peer acceptance for both girls and boys (Ladd, 1999). During adolescence, acceptance and inclusion by peers becomes essential, shaping the ways in which young girls define themselves, their attractiveness to others, and their capabilities.

Much has been written about the angst of young girls, in *Reviving Ophelia* (Pipher, 1994), for example, so that we tend to regard this as a period of extreme dissatisfaction with self. Supportive friends, or even one close buddy and confidante to whom she can confide, can mediate the climate of uncertainty or alienation. Most girls, from early childhood and on into adolescence and womanhood, seek to maintain a "best friend." They increasingly value intimacy, the ability to self-disclose and share thoughts and feelings with another whom they can trust. Reynolds and Repetti (chapter 31, this volume) point out the many health-promoting benefits of close peers relationships for adolescent girls, including less depression and higher levels of self-esteem. Supportive friends may also buffer the relationships with other unsupportive peers or parents, providing a haven of comfort and understanding. Further, girls with friends who model healthy behaviors such as attention to healthy self-care and safety practices may themselves tend to adopt such practices. These findings support the need for close parental monitoring and supervision, not only of time and place but also of the peers with whom their daughters associate.

Throughout the life span, friends and romantic partners play a critical role in providing support and confirmation of self-valuing and self-competence. Intimacy is significant for most women's close friends and romantic relationships, including emotional expressiveness, self-disclosure, mutuality, caring, respect, and trust. Friends and romantic partners may also provide supportive social networks of others who expand their community of those with whom can socialize and turn to in need (Hendrick, 2004).

The value of close ties to a network of others becomes even more important for the psychological health of women as they mature. Gergen and Gergen (chapter 44, this volume) speak of the health-promoting powers of "relational resources" in aging women, which help to maintain a sense of balance by interpreting the meanings and pleasures in life in the context of socially relevant groups. Not to be ignored is the function of women's support groups, through which girls and women can explore new ways of self-definition and personal growth, or find solace and peace in sharing their illness and grief with similar others. In group as well as in other interpersonal contexts, however, the negative aspects of social support can become problematic. Extended provision of social or material support to others can add an unwelcome burden that adds, rather than reduces, personal and family stress (Todd & Worell, 2000). More often, the act of giving and sharing contributes to feelings of self-esteem, competence, and quiet pleasure.

COMMUNITY GROUPS PROVIDE SUPPORT AND HEALTH PROMOTION

Key systems for promoting empowerment and resilience in the lives of girls and women include: schools, community groups and resources, and volunteer and religious organizations. Singly or in concert, these groups can provide positive identity, information, support, resources, education, and prevention programs. Adolescent girls who participate in after-school programs can discover new sources of social interaction and support, and adult mentors or role models in the form of coaches, teachers, or religious leaders. Participation in religious or faith-based communities has also been correlated with higher levels of self-rated happiness. Such associations can provide girls and women with a source of social support, and bring a sense of purpose and meaning to life (Myers, 2000). The importance of community support points to the many possibilities for social action programs and policies (Shinn & Toohey, 2003).

For women in poverty, single mothers, and many middle-class families as well, affordable health care is a pressing need that is frequently unfulfilled. Community empowerment initiatives tend to concentrate on health and wellness promotion programs, targeting all community members rather than only those at risk. Such broad programs depend on citizen as well as professional involvement in identifying health needs and initiating change (Eisen, 1994). Likewise, the use of multiple settings to promote health-care information—schools, the workplace, religious groups—increases the opportunity to reach underserved and alienated populations (Repucci, Woolard, & Fried, 1999). Results from these programs suggest that strategies and programs designed for one target group, such as elderly African American women (LaVeist, Sellers, Elliot Brown, & Nickerson, 1997), may not be effective with another, such Native Americans (Lemaster & Connell, 1994). As with all other interpersonal, group, or community interventions, careful attention to diversity is an essential component.

PROFESSIONAL SUPPORTS OFFER HOPE AND GROWTH THROUGH EMPOWERING INTERVENTIONS

New approaches to psychotherapy that integrate the realities of women's lives address risks to their safety and health, and the strengths that reside in every girl and woman. With the support of a safe and collaborative environment, girls and women are encouraged to explore the intersects of their personal and social identities. Here, they can normalize their experience in the context of these identities, so that they no longer feel subordinate, abnormal, or crazy. A safe and woman-centered space allows them share their pain, their secrets, and their distress without fear of disapproval or humiliation. Dispelling myths about interpersonal violence and sexual assault also enables women to explore, heal, and take action to prevent further assault on themselves or others. Woman-centered individual or group psychotherapies encourage optimism (I can feel better, I can change), a sense of self-efficacy (I

have the ability to handle this, I can reach my goals), hope (I know I can find ways to solve my problem, there is sunshine out there), and resilience (I believe I have some control over what happens to me, I can recover from this experience), all of which can lead to personal and social empowerment.

CONCLUSIONS

This chapter explores the many pathways that lead to personal and social empowerment for girls and women. Empowerment interventions facilitate skills and flexibility in problem identification and solution, in developing a full range of interpersonal and constructive life skills, and in developing strategies for effective community and institutional change. These interventions may include prevention and education to promote healthy lifestyles; remediation of personal pain and distress; support structures in families and communities that are affirming and enabling; strength-building strategies to increase personal pride, self-efficacy, and resilience to current and future stress; and community change strategies to modify structural barriers and aversive or toxic environments.

There are still undiscovered pathways to girls' and women's psychological health and well-being. The challenge remains to seek them through woman-sensitive research that leads to increased understandings and insights, and to incorporate them through interventions that support girls' and women's strength and empowerment. The remaining chapters of this *Handbook* expand on these themes. The early chapters cover the multiple risks that face girls and women, followed by chapters that explore the strength and protective factors that contribute to women's psychological health and well-being through their life spans. Throughout these pages, respect for the importance of ethnocultural diversity, and of sensitive and woman-centered research, permeates this volume.

REFERENCES

Bandura, A. (1997). *Self-efficacy: The exercise of control.* New York: W. H. Freeman.

Barnett, G. W., & Hyde, J. S. (2001). Women, men, work, and family: An expansionist theory. *American Psychologist, 56,* 781–796.

Basow, S. A., & Rubin, L. R. (1997). Gender influence on adolescent development. In N. G. Johnson, M. C. Roberts, & J. Worell (Eds.), *Beyond appearance: A new look at adolescent girls.* Washington, DC: American Psychological Association.

Betz, N. E. (2002). Women's career development: Weaving personal themes and theoretical constructs. *The Counseling Psychologist, 30,* 467–481.

Deaux, K., & Major, B. (1987). Putting gender into context: An interactional model of gender-related behaviors. *Psychological Bulletin, 94,* 369–389.

Deaux, K., & Stewart, A. J. (2001). Framing gendered identities. In R. K. Unger (Ed.), *Handbook of the psychology of women and gender* (pp. 84–97). New York: John Wiley & Sons.

Delaney, W., & Lee, C. (1995). Self esteem and sex roles among male and female high school students: Their relationships to physical activity. *Australian Psychologist, 30,* 84–87.

Eccles, J., Barber, B., Jozefowicz, D., Malanchuk, O., & Vida, M. (1997). Self-evaluation of task competence, task values, and self-esteem. In N. G. Johnson, M. C. Roberts, & J. Worell (Eds.), *Beyond appearance: A new look at adolescent girls* (pp. 53–84). Washington, DC: American Psychological Association.

Eisen, A. (1994). Survey of neighborhood comprehensive community empowerment initiatives. *Health Education Quarterly, 21,* 235–252.

Fassinger, R. (2001). Women in non-traditional work fields. In J. Worell (Ed.), *Encyclopedia of women and gender: Sex similarities and differences and the impact of society on gender* (Vol. 2, pp. 1169–1180). San Diego, CA: Academic Press.

Frances, C. (1999). *New Opportunity School for Women.* Berea College, KY: Author.

Gilbert, L. A., & Rader, J. (2001). Current perspective on women's adult roles: Work, family, and life. In R. K. Unger (Ed.), *Handbook of the psychology of women and gender.* New York: John Wiley & Sons.

Gondolf, E. W. (1998). *Assessing woman battering in mental health services.* Thousand Oaks, CA: Sage.

Gutierrez, L., & Lewis, E. (1999). *Empowering women of color.* New York: Columbia University Press.

Harris, S. M. (1995). Family, self, and sociocultural contributors to body-image of African-American women. *Psychology of Women Quarterly, 19,* 139–145.

Hendrick, S. S. (2004). *Understanding close relationships.* Boston: Allyn & Bacon.

Heppner, P. P., Witty, T. E., & Dixon, W. A. (2004). Problem-solving appraisal and human adjustment. *The Counseling Psychologist, 32,* 344–429.

Herald Leader. (2004, September). Lexington, KY.

Icovics, J. R., & Park, C. L. (Eds.). (1999). Thriving: Broadening the paradigm beyond illness to health. *Journal of Social Issues, 54*(2), whole issue.

Kahn, R. L., & Juster, F. T. (2002). Well-being: Concepts and measures. *Journal of Social Issues, 58,* 627–644.

Kobassa, S. C., Maddi, S. R., & Kahn, S. (1982). Hardiness and health: A prospective study. *Journal of Personality and Social Psychology, 42,* 168–177.

Ladd, G. W. (1999). Peer relationships and social competence during early and middle childhood. In J. T. Spence, J. M. Darley, & D. J. Foss (Eds.), *Annual Review of Psychology* (Vol. 50, pp. 333–360). Palo Alto, CA: Annual Reviews.

LaVeist, P. L., Sellers, R. M., Elliot Brown, K. A., & Nickerson, K. J. (1997). Extreme social isolation, use of community-based senior support services, and mortality among African American elderly women. *American Journal of Community Psychology, 25,* 721–732.

Lee, R. M., & Ramirez III, M. (2000). The history, current status, and future of multicultural psychotherapy. In I. Cuéllar & F. A. Paniagua, *Handbook of multicultural mental health* (pp. 280–310). San Diego, CA: Academic Press.

Lehman, D. R., Chiu, C., & Schaller, M. (2004). Psychology and culture. In S. A. Fiske, D. L. Schachter, & C. Zahn-Waxler (Eds.), *Annual review of psychology* (pp. 689–714). Palo Alto, CA: Annual Reviews.

Lemaster, P. L., & Connell, C. M. (1994). Health education interventions among Native Americans: A review and analysis. *Health Education Quarterly, 21,* 521–428.

Markus, H. R., Ryff, C. D., Curhan, K., & Palmersheim, K. (2004). In their own words: Well-being at midlife among high school and college educated adults. In O. G. Brim, C. D. Ryff, & R. Kessler (Eds.), *How healthy are we: A national study of well-being at midlife* (pp. 273–319). Chicago: University of Chicago Press.

Murrell, A. (2001). Career achievement: Opportunities and barriers. In J. Worell (Ed.), *Encyclopedia of women and gender: Sex similarities and differences and the contributions of society to gender* (Vol. 1, pp. 211–218). San Diego, CA: Academic Press.

Myers, D. G. (2000). The funds, friends, and faith of happy people. *American Psychologist, 55,* 56–67.

O'Leary, V. E. (1998). Strength in the face of adversity: Individual and social thriving. *Journal of Social Issues, 54,* 425–446.

O'Leary, V. E., & Icovics, J. R. (1995). Resilience and thriving in response to challenge: An opportunity for a shift in women's health. *Women's health: Research on Gender, Behavior, and Policy, 1,* 121–142.

Peterson, C., & Seligman, M. E. P. (2004). *Character strengths and virtues: A handbook and classification.* New York: Oxford University Press.

Pipher, M. (1994). *Reviving Ophelia: Saving the selves of adolescent girls.* New York: Ballantine Books.

Piran, N., Carter, W., Thompson, S., & Pajouhandeh, P. (2002). Powerful girls: A contradiction in terms?

Young women speak out about the experience of growing up in a girl's body. In S. Abbey (Ed.), *Ways of knowing in and through the body: Diverse perspectives on embodiment* (pp. 202–210). Welland, Ontario, Canada: Soleil.

Repucci, N. D., Woolard, J. D., & Fried, C. S. (1999). Social, community, and preventative interventions. In J. T. Spence, J. M. Darley, & D. J. Foss (Eds.), *Annual review of psychology* (Vol. 50, pp. 387–418). Palo Alto, CA: Annual Reviews.

Rodriguez, M., & Cohen, S. (1998). Social support. In H. S. Friedman (Ed.), *Encyclopedia of mental health* (Vol. 3, pp. 535–548). San Diego, CA: Academic Press.

Ruiz, S., Roosa, M., & Gonzales, N. A. (2002). Predictors of self-esteem for Mexican American and European American youths: A reexamination of the influence of parenting. *Journal of Family Psychology, 16*, 70–80.

Seligman, M. E. P. (1991). *Learned optimism.* New York: Knopf.

Seligman, M. E. P., & Csikszentmihalyi, M. (2000). Positive psychology: An introduction. *American Psychologist, 55*, 5–14.

Serbin, L. A., & Karp, J. (2004). Transfer of social risk: Mediators of vulnerability and resilience. In S. A. Fiske, D. L. Schachter, & C. Zahn-Waxler (Eds.), *Annual review of psychology* (pp. 333–363). Palo Alto, CA: Annual Reviews.

Shinn, M., & Toohey, S. B. (2003). Community contexts of human welfare. In S. T. Fiske, D. L. Schacter, & C. Zahn-Waxler (Eds.), *Annual review of psychology* (Vol. 54, pp. 427–459). Palo Alto, CA: Annual Reviews.

Snyder, C. R., & Lopez, S. J. (2002). *Handbook of positive psychology.* New York: Oxford University Press.

Snyder, C. R., Rand, K. L., & Sigman, D. R. (2002). Hope theory. In C. R. Snyder & S. J. Lopez, *Handbook of positive psychology* (pp. 257–276). New York: Oxford University Press.

Steil, J. M. (1997). *Marital equality.* Thousand Oaks, CA: Sage.

Tedeschi, R. G., & Calhoun, L. G. (1995). *Trauma and reformation.* Thousand Oaks, CA: Sage.

Thompson, S. C., & Wierson, M. (2000). Enhancing perceived control in psychotherapy. In C. R. Snyder & R. E. Ingram (Eds.), *Handbook of psychological change* (pp. 177–187). New York: John Wiley & Sons.

Todd, J. L., & Worell, J. (2000). Resilience in low-income employed, African American women. *Psychology of Women Quarterly, 24*, 119–128.

Travis, C. B., & Meginnis-Payne, K. L. (2001). Beauty politics and patriarchy: The impact on women's lives. In J. Worell (Ed.), *Encyclopedia of women and gender: Sex similarities and differences and the contributions of society to gender* (Vol. 1, pp. 189–200). San Diego, CA: Academic Press.

Ward, J. V. (1996). Raising resisters: The role of truth-telling in the psychological development of African American girls. In B. J. Ross Leadbeater & N. Way (Eds.), *Urban girls: Raising resisters, creating identities* (pp. 85–99). New York: New York University Press.

Worell, J. (2001). Feminist interventions: Accountability beyond symptom reduction. *Psychology of Women Quarterly, 25*, 335–343.

Worell, J. (2002, August). *Seeking the power in empowerment.* Carolyn Wood Sherif Award address presented at the annual convention of the American Psychological Association, Chicago.

Worell, J., & Johnson, N. G. (1997). *Shaping the future of feminist psychology: Education, research, and practice.* Washington, DC: American Psychological Association.

Worell, J., & Remer, P. (2003). *Feminist perspective in therapy: Empowering diverse women.* New York: John Wiley & Sons.

Wyche, K., & Rice, J. K. (1997). Feminist therapy: From dialogue to tenets. In J. Worell & N. G. Johnson (Eds.), *Shaping the future of feminist psychology: Education, research, and practice* (pp. 57–71). Washington, DC: American Psychological Association.

Risks and Strengths Across the Life Span

Problems and Risks

MARCIA C. LINN
and CATHY KESSEL

Assessment and Gender

This chapter explores sources of gender bias in assessments of psychological health and makes recommendations for recognizing, isolating, neutralizing, and investigating these effects. Measures used in assessments serve as proxies for constructs and, as a result, are open to invalid, inaccurate, and biased interpretation. Differences in social roles, societal expectations, opportunity to learn, or biological characteristics may confound assessment responses and interpretations for females and males. Training programs for mental health professionals may predispose individuals to take a biomedical, cultural, or a psychological view of health rather than combining them in a biopsychosocial perspective. Lack of research or clear recommendations about certain populations, such as adolescents, further confounds efforts to assess females and males. Establishing valid assessments for complex constructs such as depression, mathematics anxiety, or eating disorders may require differential norms for females and males, multiple indicators, or a team of interpreters. Gender bias can occur in the design, selection, administration, and interpretation of assessments; and may range from blatant discrimination to implicit expectations (Bargh & Chartland, 1999; Lustina et al., 1999; Steele, 1997; Valian, 1998).

Differences in outcomes between a group of females and a group of males are often labeled sex differences when they are attributed to biological factors and gender differences when they are attributed to nonbiological factors such as society, culture, or individual psychology. Because it is not easy to disentangle the effects of biological and nonbiological factors, we assume that the latter may always play a role in differences found for females and males. Consequently, we use the terms *gender* and *gender differences* throughout this chapter to describe these differences.

Although much research focuses on the differences between gender groups and cultural groups, this research tells us as much about all members of society as it does about the groups. There is a danger of expecting every member of a group to have a characteristic that occurs more frequently in their group. Variability within gender or cultural groups generally exceeds variability between groups. Only a few biopsychosocial dimensions occur exclusively in one group. For example, prostate cancer occurs only in males. Bias toward women, children, culture, and other characteristics of groups varies among individuals. The tendency to expect every adolescent girl to experience mathematics anxiety or every male to display aggression has been called the tyranny of the mean because each member of the group is expected to represent the average for their group rather than to display individual characteristics (Linn, 1994).

In this chapter we consider an assessment to be the administration of an instrument and interpretation of a client's responses to that instrument. In clinical settings administrator and interpreter may often be the same person, but it is useful to separate these roles when considering sources of bias. We think of the administration of an assessment as taking place in a social context in which expectations and actions of both administrator and client may affect the client's responses to the assessment. Thinking of an assessment as comprising these components provides a structure that encompasses educational and medical assessments as well as psychological ones. Viewed from this perspective, research on assessment in one area may suggest assessment considerations in others.

For example, Steele (1997) developed the concept of stereotype threat to describe and explain responses in educational assessments. Members of cultural groups stereotyped as poor performers in particular fields may perform more poorly on difficult assessments when indirectly reminded of the stereotype. In particular, Steele's research shows that African Americans or women tend to perform more poorly on difficult mathematics assessments if first requested to give information about ethnicity or gender. (For other examples, see Brownlow, McPheron, & Acks, 2003; Lustina et al., 1999.) Such findings suggest that administrators of any assessment need to be attentive to situations that might trigger stereotype threat for the client. For instance, clinicians might want to be cautious about using language that could trigger stereotypes about aging and memory when administering cognitive tests to older people.

Any assessment now takes place against the backdrop of rapid changes in opportunities to learn, cultural expectations, social roles, and reward structures for females and males of all ages.

For example, over the past 10 years, a growing number of students have continued their education beyond high school, the proportion of women in college, and in science and engineering has increased, yet the number of female university professors in these fields has not increased and the salaries of women remain about 75% those of men (Lewin, 2004). In the area of health, the life span has increased, women continue to live longer than men, and men engage in more health-risky behaviors such as smoking and binge-drinking than women. In addition, women are more likely than men to seek treatment for ailments and have health insurance.

A number of undifferentiated or difficult-to-sort-out constructs permeate the area of psychological health. Depression, serious mental illness, and other behavioral and biological conditions are often difficult to distinguish from each other and to diagnose effectively (Maj, Gaebel, López-Ibor, & Sartorius, 2002). In these situations, the cultural expectations of the individual, as well as the situation under which the individual is examined, can result in shifts of the construct, differences in presentation of symptoms, and differences in expectations for treatment (Brown, Abe-Kim, & Barrio, 2003; Murthy & Wig, 2002).

Differences in construct and treatment expectations are illustrated by an immigrant Hmong family's experiences with health workers involved with the care of their epileptic daughter (Fadiman, 1997). Hmong culture does not distinguish between mental and physical illness as often done in the United States, and considers epilepsy to have a strong spiritual component. The child's illiterate parents were understandably bewildered by rapidly changing recommendations for medication, as filtered through interpreters, and by the fact that the many different pills prescribed for their daughter looked identical. The U.S. doctors viewed the Hmong parents as unwilling to comply with medical practice and, therefore, as abusive parents, recommending foster care for the child. In contrast, the parents viewed themselves as providing the best possible care for their child and as balancing the recommendations of their culture with those of the doctors. These differing views, complicated by a seizure due to sepsis rather than epilepsy, led to tragedy (pp. 254–256).

Culture also interacts with gender roles and expectations about causes and treatments for problems in psychological health. In 1998, the Food and Drug Administration relaxed regulations on pharmaceutical advertising. Ads for prescription drugs increased 150 percent. Studies suggest that advertising for antidepressants, which target women, have increased demands for prescription drugs. Many advertisements make connections to culturally laden issues such as potential feelings of inadequacy experienced by mothers. These advertisements imply that such feelings stem from depression and suggest the need for medication (Metzl, 2003). These advertisements may benefit readers who seek and receive appropriate professional care but may injure those who insist on medication or perceive themselves as inadequate and do not seek care.

In the following sections, we discuss how gender bias can affect the reliability and validity of an assessment, influence personal decision making, and affect outcomes for individuals. We identify mechanisms that can bias assessment results and call on professionals to keep them in mind when interpreting results reported across the spectrum of social and cognitive dimensions. In addition, we identify research questions that deserve further attention.

GENDER BIAS

Gender bias can arise when gender is neglected as well as when gender is considered but is not relevant to the decision. Gender plays a role, for example, in determining whether a child is growing abnormally because male norms for height differ from female norms. Gender also plays a role in establishing drug treatments since women tend to be smaller than men and may need smaller doses of drugs to achieve the same effect and because interactions between drugs and hormones may differ for the genders. In contrast, the historical practice of maintaining gender-based quotas for medical school admissions has proved to be ungrounded. The quotas reflected the view that women were less suited for the profession, yet dropping quotas has revealed that women and men are equally likely to succeed and make useful contributions to the field of medicine.

Bias arises when designers and administrators of assessments have implicit or explicit expectations about gender roles. Bias shows up when designers create an assessment for one construct (such as mechanical aptitude) but require knowledge (such as familiarity with the components of an automobile engine) that males often have more opportunity to learn, given current gender-role norms. Bias arises when the ethnicity, culture, style, gender, or beliefs of an examiner implicitly or explicitly skew the interaction with some groups of examinees. Bias arises when a measurement situation (such as a standardized test) elicits anxiety or other reactions irrelevant to the construct being measured in one group but not others (for instance, when stereotype threat is triggered for some test-takers). And, bias may arise when a standardized measure is normed on one group but extended to another.

Assessments may either explicitly or inadvertently favor one gender over the other. For example, we know from retrospective studies that diagnoses of heart disease were biased because far more men than women were identified with heart disease, yet in actuality more women than men die of heart disease (Wizemann & Pardue, 2001, p. 161). Factors contributing to biased measurement of heart disease include changing demographics of the disease, differences between men and women in age of onset and symptoms, and expectations among medical professionals that men are more prone to heart disease than women. Biased expectations may stem from the greater incidence of heart disease in young men than in young women, as well as from an increase in the incidence of heart disease in women over the past 30 years. Biased diagnoses may arise because women are less likely than men to experience chest pain and more likely to experience extreme fatigue as a symptom of heart disease.

The detection of breast cancer in men and women is similarly skewed, although the base rate for breast cancer in men is far lower than it is for women. This lower incidence of breast cancer in men means that men are less likely to be screened, and therefore, breast cancer in men is less likely to be detected than it is in women. Assessment of depression also interacts with gender. Including adolescents, more women than men are diagnosed with depression, yet symptoms of depression are often overlooked in women. Life events such as poverty, abuse, and single parenthood are more common among women than men and increase the frequency and severity of depression but may interfere with accurate diagnosis. Intake interviewers may miss more depression in women than in men because women's behavior may seem reasonable based on their life circumstances, rather than symptomatic of depression. They may also misdiagnose depression because of a tendency to trivialize the symptoms of women (Hoffman & Tarzian, 2001, pp. 17–18). In these situations, cultural expectations influence the weight placed on information from females and males.

Health professionals may interpret interview information and case material for women and men based on social roles rather than criteria for depression. Authority figures may inadvertently demand different behaviors from females and males. Females often report that male examiners appear to distrust assertive statements and respond better to self-effacing narratives (Bargh & Chartrand, 1999). Such narratives may in turn reinforce the belief among authority figures in health-care situations that the symptoms and complaints of women are less serious. This phenomenon also arises in educational situations where professors often assert that women are less confident of their knowledge and women often complain that their assertive statements are discounted. In addition, the etiology of depression in men and women differs.

Bias may be inherent in the items of a test or inventory. College and graduate school admissions tests include measures of mathematical and verbal ability. Intelligence tests such as the Wechsler Intelligence Scale include measures of verbal and spatial ability. Extensive research shows that standardized measures of verbal, mathematical, and spatial ability tend to favor males while other indicators such as grades or pre- and posttests measuring impact of innovative instruction tend to favor females (Caplan, Crawford, Hyde, & Richardson, 1997; Linn & Kessel, 2003). These biases may stem from differential opportunity to learn. For example, measures of verbal ability may favor those who have studied more science if they use science passages or favor social scientists if they use literature passages on cultural issues.

In the area of mathematical ability, speeded multiple-choice formats may favor males over females, and essays may favor females over males (Gipps & Murphy, 1994), possibly because females have more opportunity to learn to write and less experience with speeded examinations (Brownlow et al., 2003). In the area of spatial ability, small amounts of practice (such as 30 minutes spent practicing similar items) can have a large impact on performance. Short training often favors females more than males, perhaps because males have already had some opportunity to learn these skills (Brownlow et al., 2003).

Care needs to be taken in interpretation of scores and responses. Tests or inventories may be normed or validated on one population or intended for one purpose, but used for another. For example, psychological tests used for clinical screening may be inappropriate for forensic evaluation (Hynan, 2004) or hiring decisions. Lack of accuracy may not cause serious problems if a test score is treated as a working hypothesis and the individual tested later receives appropriate treatment. In contrast, a misleading score may have disastrous consequences if used in a child custody case. Similarly, the SAT was developed as a college admissions test to be used in conjunction with high school grades, not to determine "mathematical ability" or the allocation of fellowships. Inappropriate use of tests may be not only unethical but also cause for legal action.

Moreover, users of assessment instruments need to view score interpretation guidelines with caution and appropriate skepticism. For example, Hynan notes that the Millon Clinical Multiaxial Inventory–III manual advises that standard scores be transformed according to the gender of the examinee, without giving a rationale. Statistics for the gender distribution of scores obtained in this manner for histrionic, narcissistic, and compulsive personality disorders are not consistent with those obtained by other measures. A possible explanation of this inconsistency is poor test development practices. In the development of the Millon scale, clients were rated on the basis of only one meeting. The score transformation was developed when inventory scores were compared with these ratings (Hynan, 2004).

Design practices intended to create comparable outcomes with different versions (often called forms) of standardized tests can perpetuate bias with regard to gender. For example, if biased tests of verbal and mathematical ability are updated using careful equating practices, the bias could be maintained. If tests were normed against external criteria such as grades in mathematics, the process could reduce gender bias and improve test accuracy. New statistical techniques, such as item response theory modeling, provide information about individual items and enable test developers to identify items that display differences by gender and items that do not. These techniques could help reduce bias and also contribute to a more nuanced understanding of the sources of bias.

Studies of heroism illustrate challenges of instrument design. Recent research shows that men are more likely than women to attempt to rescue people from fires, water hazards, and other dangers that could result in loss of life, but that women are more likely than men to have risked their lives to shelter Jews during the Holocaust. These findings suggest that context needs to be taken into account in order to make sense of the construct "heroism" (Becker & Eagly, 2004).

Diagnosis of dyslexia in young children has suffered from an implicit belief in conduct disorder as an indicator of dyslexia. Recent research with systematically administered assessments and brain scans demonstrates that dyslexia is quite evenly distributed between females and males in childhood (Wizemann & Pardue, 2001, p. 103). However, schools typically identify dyslexia in more boys than girls, in part because boys tend to concurrently display conduct disorder and dyslexia (Hartung & Widiger, 1998, p. 264). Ironically, older boys are more likely to remain dyslexic than girls. Compensated dyslexics (adults who were dyslexic as children but who are able to read as adults) tend to be women (Wizemann & Pardue, 2001). This finding could result from interactions between expectations for treatment success and gender; it deserves serious research.

Diagnosis of anorexia nervosa, bulimia nervosa, and other eating disorders may reflect biased instruments as well as cultural expectations. At-risk populations include women, especially adolescents, as well as gymnasts, ballet dancers, coxswains, and jockeys. White middle-class women are diagnosed with anorexia ner-

vosa more often than women and men in other groups, although it does not appear to be the case that this condition occurs more frequently in the middle class (van Hoeken, Lucas, & Hoek, 1998). One problem in diagnosis of anorexia nervosa concerns the role of the ethnic group. Some procedures predicate a diagnosis using factors such as eating behavior and body image together with actual weight relative to expected weight for age and height (following the definition in the *Diagnostic and Statistical Manual of Mental Disorders*). Aspects that may be assessed for diagnostic purposes include body composition, energy expenditure, energy intake, core psychopathology, and general psychopathology (Nathan & Allison, 1998). The Caucasian features of figural stimuli used in some measures of body image may make these measures unsuitable for use. By taking into account the weight and height norms for ethnic groups, an examiner's accuracy in diagnosis may be improved (Becker, Franko, Speck, & Herzog, 2003). In addition, factors such as bone size contribute to accurate diagnosis of anorexia nervosa. The diagnosis of eating disorders is further complicated by changing norms for immigrant populations when their nutritional needs are met. Finally, eating disorders tend to emerge in adolescence, at a time when hormonal effects may mask or exaggerate symptoms.

Interpretation of complex data sources, such as clinical interviews, brain scans, or other imprecise sources of evidence, can, when combined with information about the gender of the individual, result in biased interpretations. Well-meaning individuals may filter imprecise measures through their cultural expectations. As a result, it is not uncommon for authority figures and decision-makers to recommend differential paths of action to individuals depending on their gender, when in fact such individual paths may be unjustified on other grounds. For example, this interpretation effect extends to the evaluation of clinical cases and essays, when attributed to males or females. Individuals place far more weight on the gender of the individual than is justified by the evidence available (Hoffman & Tarzian, 2001; Valian, 1998).

Implicit societal beliefs about the behavior of men and women may adversely affect performance. If individuals perceive that their examiners do not expect them to succeed (for example, if interviewers are conducting oral examinations and believe that women are less likely to succeed in engineering), this belief may raise anxiety and reduce performance without being explicitly stated.

Furthermore, if small gender differences are publicized without explanatory context and appropriate statistical background, the publicity can nurture stereotype threat rather than provide useful information for individuals. Some individuals make career decisions based on their perceived performance and the performance of their group from their vantage point (Seymour & Hewitt, 1997). For example, the consistent gender gap of about 50 points on the mathematics SAT receives yearly publicity, but the population statistics showing equal male and female performance, as in the Third International Mathematics and Science Study, are less well known. The gender gap in SAT scores represents only two or three additional wrong answers but is accorded far more prominence. In addition, the fact that female SAT takers now outnumber males has not received wide publicity. As a group, female test takers have less mathematics course experience than males. Very small differences detected in large populations are easily described but may not be consequential for individual or policy decisions. Women may opt out of science or mathematics because they are dissatisfied with their own performance, even though it is above average, and because they believe that they need to be even more successful in order to compete in "a man's world."

In summary, the effects of instruments, examiners, and interpreters on assessment depend on a variety of important factors. Co-occurrence of several conditions, such as verbal ability and science course taking, depression and poverty, or dyslexia and presence or absence of conduct disorder, may lead to misinterpretation and erroneous assessment. In other cases, expectations about gender roles, such as passivity for women, interact with interpretations. In complex situations, interpreters may implicitly invoke cultural stereotypes rather than place appropriate weight on performance of the individual.

RELIABILITY

Bias can impact the reliability and validity of instruments. By reliability we refer to the likelihood that an individual will be assessed similarly on subsequent occasions. When instruments have low reliability they lack power for decisions about individuals and may show group differences. Reliability may differentially affect the assessment of females and males. For example, hormonal changes of adolescence affect females and males at different ages. Sources of reliability or unreliability affected by gender can come from the instrument selected, the examiner, the interpreter, the situation, and measurement practices.

Inconsistent results from different instruments, or instruments with differential consistency for disparate groups, can result in questionable decisions. For example, diagnoses of depression or serious mental illness depend on indicators such as the display of persistent sadness and social withdrawal behaviors or the enactment of paranoid beliefs. Depending on gender and situation, fears of strangers, abuse, or retaliation may be legitimate learned responses based on experiences of maltreatment. As a result, the same indicator of depression or serious mental illness may work differently for the genders. Using a combination of indicators and taking a thorough history can improve the chances for an accurate diagnosis but also has potential for bias if interpreters give unequal weight to some information or ask only questions that are consistent with their biases.

Instrument reliability may also vary with situation due to the familiarity of the individuals with the format or content of the assessment. For example, unusual requirements for examiners or individuals, such as scenario-based assessments of anxiety or unusual task formats such as selecting all but one correct answer, typically rely on experience that may be more available to one gender than to the other. Recent research in school districts that have undertaken more consequential and extensive standardized testing, as part of the No Child Left Behind legislation, has revealed effects of practice on format. In many schools, a 10% or greater increase in performance can result from students having experience with the test format (Koretz, Linn, Dunbar, & Shepard, 1991). This is particularly important for standardized tests where students could be diagnosed as retarded when really they are inexperienced. Similarly, inventories intended to tap mental health or cognitive constructs may give less accurate information for members of groups unfamiliar with multiple-choice formats.

Format effects for psychiatric screening were reported by Jacobson, Koehler, and Jones-Brown (1987). Structured interviews and written questionnaires both probed for history of sexual abuse or assault, but responses indicated rates of 35% and 52%, respectively, suggesting an interaction between format and content in this case.

Lack of reliability can result from the interactions of examiners and examinees. Interviewers can elicit reactions based on their gender, ethnicity, culture, and level of authority (Caplan et al., 1997; Lustina et al., 1999). Females may be more likely to distrust strangers based on prior experience or to view bearded individuals as having special status. Males may display aggression while females display passivity under conditions of anxiety. This variability may be difficult to detect and control. Health-care workers may erroneously expect women to have low pain thresholds and therefore miss physical disorders in depressed women (Wizemann & Pardue, 2001).

More subtle variability based on the comfort of individuals with their examiner or the examination setting can further exacerbate the problem. For example, when interviewed about their health-related behavior, females and males from different cultures or different family practices may provide more or less detail, or promote or demote symptoms that could be important to their diagnosis depending on whether the examiner is from their culture, race, or gender (Murthy & Wig, 2002).

Concentration and attention of individuals also varies depending on situations, time of day, and other factors. These variables introduce unreliability into diagnostic and testing situations. Often, harried examiners and expensive procedures fail to take into consideration these variables and may result in misdiagnoses. Males and females vary with regard to their response to drugs, fatigue, and attention-diverting situations,

which exacerbate the difficulty of establishing reliable measures (Maj et al., 2002).

Reliability of measurement between and within genders calls for careful interpretation of information about individuals and conclusions about group effects. Unreliable measures reduce the power of comparisons between groups. However, unreliability also introduces fluctuations, especially when sample sizes are small, as is common in some mental health studies and many studies involving brain scans or other expensive procedures. In selection decisions, unreliable measures cause serious problems. For example, some inventories define mental retardation, learning disabilities, or even phobias based on a specific score. If the score has a low reliability, many errors near the cut-off will result.

In summary, sources of unreliability for the measurement of females and males are particularly likely for measures involving interactions between the individual and an interviewer, experimenter, or interpreter of behavior such as a clinician. However, any instrument used to assign individuals to treatments could have bias for one gender. Reliability studies need to assess the contribution of gender to the variance across time.

VALIDITY

By validity, we refer to the likelihood that an assessment measures the dimension of individual performance intended. Earlier examples illustrate the difficulties in sorting out the constructs in the area of psychological health. Depression, serious mental illness, eating disorders, and other distressing conditions frequently overlap, and may be difficult to distinguish from each other and to diagnose definitively (Maj et al., 2002).

Many conditions co-occur and have interacting effects. Thus, heart disease and mood disorders, diabetes and depression, dyslexia and conduct disorder, and phobias and eating disorders, often occur in the same individuals. These conditions may be mediated by the same mechanisms, as is sometimes the case for diabetes and depression, or might result from side effects of drug treatments, which is possible for heart disease and mood disorders. Moreover, a chronic medical condition may itself be cause for depression or anxiety. These conditions may be caused by the interaction of sociocultural influences, individual psychology, and biological factors as appears to be the case for many eating disorders (Gordon, 1998). Thus, establishing distinct constructs and finding valid measures for them is difficult. The chapters in this volume discuss these complex interactions as well as changing perspectives of the constructs in psychological health. Further evidence for the complexity of construct definition comes from the changing recommendations found in clinical standards (American Psychiatric Association, 2000). Here we highlight some of the issues and call for caution as cultural, psychological, medical, and treatment research continuously raises new concerns.

New technologies such as brain imaging technologies have called definitions of constructs such as dyslexia into question by showing that brain imaging consistent with dyslexia occurs equally in women and men yet diagnosis is skewed toward men (Wizemann & Pardue, 2001, pp. 101–104). The results for drug and cognitive therapies illustrate connections among cortical, limbic–paralimbic, and subcortical functions (Goldapple et al., 2004).

From the standpoint of validity, a common recommendation is to use multiple indicators. Use of multiple indicators can increase the validity of an assessment or diagnosis, but can also strengthen bias if the only common variance in the indicators is attributable to a biased factor. Comorbid conditions such as dyslexia and conduct disorder, depression and poverty, anxiety and depression, or depression and borderline personality disorder can confound and perplex those making diagnoses and may end up overemphasizing gender-related behaviors, thus skewing gender distributions. Format effects, such as combining oral and written examinations, which might tap different constructs for females and males, can create difficulties in assessment. Finally, assertiveness and self-deprecation can contribute to the difficulty of establishing valid assessments of females and males. When assessments create debilitating anxiety in the gender that is stereotyped as not likely to succeed under the target conditions, the validity of the process is in doubt.

Opportunity to learn, or opportunity to experience dimensions of a situation can modify the construct that is measured. Individuals need opportunities to learn self-respect, science, mathematics, spatial reasoning, and independence, as well as other factors that frequently display gender disparities. Developmental experiences, such as opportunities to explore or venture from the home, appear to have important implications for later way-finding ability as well as for risk taking. Furthermore, cultural differences in gender roles or work ethic may predispose some individuals to experiences that modify the construct being measured (Caplan et al., 1997).

In summary, changing explanations and mechanisms for psychological health have resulted in modification and refinement of constructs. New technologies including data from brain functioning and results of studies of medications shed light on the mechanisms that lead to psychological health. For example, recent studies of placebo effects reveal the powerful impact of expectations on the efficacy of drug treatments. New uses for cognitive therapies have clarified the distinctions between disorders. All of these factors underscore the complexity of diagnosis and treatment in the area of psychological health and call for community-wide attention to potential sources of bias.

CONCLUSIONS

Individuals involved in mental health face complex assessment challenges. They need to sort out the effect of bias on the lives of those they treat as well as on the decisions of others involved in mental health. Gender bias affects cultural practices, opportunities to learn, expectations concerning who develops disorders, and views about how psychological problems should be treated. Such effects also influence individuals who are threatened by these expectations or who act on their own versions of them. Cultural mechanisms for gender bias include the tyranny of the mean—overvaluing mean differences for females and males (Linn, 1994), implicit beliefs, stereotyping, and stereotype threat. Aspects of assessment that may invoke or allow bias are co-occurring conditions, selection of instruments, instrument design and format, and mismatch between an instrument and the condition it is intended to measure.

To respond to bias, we offer several recommendations.

First, whenever feasible, use multiple, diverse indicators of biopsychosocial well-being. Combine interviews, surveys, observations, histories, medical data, and peer reports. Draw on input from experts in varied fields such as psychology, education, psychiatry, medicine, and social work. To ensure validity, allow experts to interpret their assessments autonomously before asking them to reconcile their views with those of others. Experts from varied backgrounds bring valid insights to complex situations that can be missed if one perspective is viewed as dominant.

Second, view each individual first as a person and second as a member of multiple interacting communities, cultures, and categories. There is often more variability within groups such as gender, ethnicity, or social class than between these groups. Assuming an individual has characteristics that occur slightly more often in a group that they belong to is a common source of invalid assessment. For example, assuming that a female complaining of fatigue and malaise is suffering from depression may miss important symptoms of heart disease.

Third, look for consistencies and discrepancies across indicators and seek explanations for both. Make sure that consistencies do not detract attention from valid but low probability alternatives. When possible, add indicators in areas where there are discrepancies to resolve differences. Assume that discrepancies stem from lack of reliability in indicators. If increased reliability does not resolve the problem, then seek explanations based on cultural, social, or situational factors.

For example, grades and scores provide discrepant information about capabilities in mathematics for many high school students. Adding more scores or grades may not clarify the discrepancy. Realizing that the sample taking tests is not representative of the whole population helps to resolve this dilemma but leaves some variance unexplained. Consideration of factors such as stereotype threat helps to resolve this dilemma. All these factors may be essential to assess the potential of an individual who has high success anxiety, belongs to a group that is not expected to succeed, and performs inconsistently.

Fourth, allocate assessment funds so that difficult cases get more attention. For example, start with a short assessment and add indicators to resolve discrepancies or improve outcomes. To help teams make sensible decisions about when to seek more information and about how to interpret information, encourage research that develops databases and collections of findings from multiple cases.

Fifth, use a process of trial and refinement to develop an explanation for the assessment findings that fully accounts for the available information and leads to improvement in well-being. As the example from the treatment of the Hmong child illustrates, assessment is an ongoing process that must take into account not only all the indicators from the initial assessment but the sequence of assessments as the individual responds to treatment. Weighing factors in complex biopsychosocial situations and determining when to gather more information, when to try a new treatment, and how to learn from the experience requires attention to a broad range of dimensions.

Sixth, raise awareness of sources of bias so that individuals can advocate for themselves and their loved ones. Incorporate these issues into introductory courses. For example, curriculum materials for K–12 education can discuss gender bias and cultural stereotypes. To avoid falling prey to the tyranny of the mean and to neutralize stereotype threat, students could benefit from understanding that the differences between men and women are far smaller than the differences within either group. Helping individuals to evaluate themselves in the population as well as in their gender or cultural group can improve personal decision making. Students could also benefit from existing materials, such as the Web-Based Inquiry Science Environment (WISE) (Linn, Davis, & Bell, 2004), to improve individual awareness. WISE activities, for example, address diagnosis of sexually transmitted diseases and tradeoffs among behavioral, drug-related, and environmental solutions to the worldwide threat of malaria. Such programs should illustrate complex decisions that concern individuals or their families and highlight situations in which gender is a factor.

Seventh, integrate attention to bias in assessment into professional development programs for all health professionals. Fadiman (1997, chapter 18) reports considerable benefit from understanding of Hmong culture, and suggests that education programs alerting health workers to cultural issues could result in better outcomes for culturally diverse individuals. Educational programs could help practitioners integrate biomedical and sociocultural perspectives (Rutter, 1995).

Eighth, encourage research programs on gender bias and on ways to reduce bias. We need research that investigates sources of bias and ways to ameliorate bias. We need a better understanding of stereotype threat, of methods used for interpreting ambiguous data, and of sources of bias that arise in ongoing complex situations. We need to sort out the mechanisms behind valid differences so that appropriate treatments can be designed. We should study promising suggestions such as the role of cultural brokers (Fadiman, 1997) in decision making. Programs that help people deal with potential stereotype threats and anxiety could have long-term benefits. These programs could help individuals understand how decision-makers, experimenters, and health workers make sense of information and show how stereotyping can play a role.

In short, gender bias threatens equal access to psychological and medical treatment. Research on psychological health assessment will have much broader impact if attention to gender bias in particular, and cultural bias more generally, becomes an essential area of study.

NOTE

This material is based upon research supported by the National Science Foundation (NSF) under grants, 9873180, 9805420, 0087832, and 9720384. Any opinions, findings, conclusions or recommendations expressed in this material are those of the authors and do not necessarily reflect the views of the National Science Foundation. The authors appreciate the help and encouragement of the Web-Based Inquiry Science Environment (WISE) research group. Preparation of this manuscript was made possible with help from Jonathan Breitbart and David Crowell.

REFERENCES

American Psychiatric Association. (2000). *Diagnostic and statistical manual of mental disorders* (4th ed.). Washington, DC: Author.

Bargh, J. A., & Chartrand, T. L. (1999). The unbearable automaticity of being. *American Psychologist, 54,* 462–479.

Becker, A., Franko, D. L., Speck, A., & Herzog, D. B. (2003). Ethnicity and differential access to care for eating disorder symptoms. *International Journal of Eating Disorders, 33,* 205–212.

Becker, S. W., & Eagly, A. H. (2004). The heroism of women and men. *American Psychologist 59*(3), 163–178.

Brown, C., Abe-Kim, J. S., & Barrio, C. (2003). Depression in ethnically diverse women. *Professional Psychology: Research and Practice, 34*(1), 1–19.

Brownlow, S., McPheron, T. K., & Acks, C. N. (2003). Science background and spatial abilities in men and women. *Journal of Science Education and Technology, 12*(4), 371–380.

Caplan, P., Crawford, M., Hyde, J., & Richardson, J. T. (1997). *Gender differences in human cognition.* New York: Oxford University Press.

Fadiman, A. (1997). *The spirit catches you and you fall down: A Hmong child, her American doctors, and the collision of two cultures.* New York: Farrar, Straus & Giroux.

Gipps, C., & Murphy, P. (1994). *A fair test? Assessment, achievement, and equality.* Philadelphia: Open University Press.

Goldapple, K., Segal, Z., Garson, C., Lau, M., Bieling, P., Kennedy, S., et al. (2004). Modulation of cortical-limbic pathways in major depression: Treatment-specific effects of cognitive behavior therapy. *Archives of General Psychiatry, 61,* 34–41.

Gordon, R. A. (1998). Concepts of eating disorders. In H. W. Hoek, J. L. Treasure, & M. A. Katzman (Eds.), *Neurobiology in the treatment of eating disorders* (pp. 5–25). Chichester, UK: John Wiley.

Hartung, C. M., & Widiger, T. A. (1998). Gender differences in the diagnosis of mental disorders. *Psychological Bulletin, 123,* 260–278.

Hoffman, D. E., & Tarzian, A. J. (2001). The girl who cried pain: A bias against women in the treatment of pain. *Journal of Law, Medicine and Ethics, 29,* 13–27.

Hynan, D. (2004). Unsupported gender differences on some personality disorder scales of the Millon Clinical Multiaxial Inventory—III. *Professional Psychology: Research and Practice, 35,* 105–110.

Jacobson, A., Koehler, J. E., & Jones-Brown, C. (1987). The failure of routine assessment to detect histories of assault experienced by psychiatric patients. *Hospital and Community Psychiatry, 38,* 786–792. Cited in D. A. Robinson & J. Worell, Issues in clinical assessment with women. In J. M. Butcher (Ed.), *Clinical personality assessment: Practical approaches* (2nd ed., pp. 190–207). New York: Oxford University Press.

Koretz, D., Linn, R. L., Dunbar, S. B., & Shepard, L. A. (1991, April). *The effects of high-stakes testing on achievement: Preliminary findings about generalization across tests.* Paper presented at the annual meeting of the American Educational Research Association, Chicago.

Lewin, T. (2004, January 15). Despite gain in degrees, women lag in tenure in two main fields. *New York Times*, p. A23.

Linn, M. C. (1994). The tyranny of the mean: Gender and expectations. *Notices of the American Mathematical Society, 41*(7), 766–769.

Linn, M. C., Davis, E. A., & Bell, P. (2004). *Internet environments for science education.* Mahwah, NJ: Erlbaum.

Linn, M. C., & Kessel, C. (2003). Gender differences in cognition and educational performance. In L. Nadel (Ed.), *Encyclopedia of cognitive science* (pp. 261–267). New York: Macmillan.

Lustina, M., Aronson, J., Good, C., Keough, K., Brown, J. L., & Steele, C. M. (1999). When white men can't do math: Necessary and sufficient factors in stereotype threat. *Journal of Experimental Social Psychology, 35*(1), 29–46.

Maj, M., Gaebel, W., López-Ibor, J., & Sartorius, N. (Eds.). (2002). *Psychiatric diagnosis and classification.* Chichester, UK: John Wiley.

Metzl, J. (2003). Selling sanity through gender. *Ms., 8*(3), 40–45.

Murthy, R. S., & Wig, N. N. (2002). Psychiatric diagnosis and classification in developing countries. In M. Maj, W. Gaebel, J. López-Ibor, & N. Sartorius (Eds.), *Psychiatric diagnosis and classification* (pp. 249–279). Chichester, UK: John Wiley.

Nathan, J. S. & Allison, D. B. (1998). Psychological and physical assessment of persons with eating disorders. In H. W. Hoek, J. L. Treasure, & M. A. Katzman (Eds.), *Neurobiology in the treatment of eating disorders* (pp. 47–96). Chichester, UK: John Wiley.

Rutter, M. (Ed.). (1995). *Psychosocial disturbances in young people: Challenges for prevention.* New York: Cambridge University Press.

Seymour, E., & Hewitt, N. (1997). *Talking about leaving.* Boulder, CO: Westview Press.

Steele, C. (1997). A threat in the air: How stereotypes shape intellectual identity and performance. *American Psychologist, 52*(6), 613–629.

Valian, V. (1998). *Why so slow?: The advancement of women.* Cambridge, MA: MIT Press.

van Hoeken, D., Lucas, A. R., & Hoek, H. W. (1998). Epidemiology. In H. W. Hoek, J. L. Treasure, & M. A. Katzman (Eds.), *Neurobiology in the treatment of eating disorders* (pp. 97–126). Chichester, UK: John Wiley.

Wizemann, T. M., & Pardue, M.-L. (Eds.). (2001). *Exploring the biological contributions to human health: Does sex matter?* Report by the Committee on Understanding the Biology of Sex and Gender Differences. Washington, DC: National Academy Press.

VALERIE E. WHIFFEN
and NATASHA DEMIDENKO

Mood Disturbance Across the Life Span

5

As the most frequently reported form of mood disturbance, depression is said to be the "common cold" of emotional distress. Sadness is a common, human response to loss, failure, rejection, or disappointment. This sadness can be profound, as it may be after the death of a loved one. However, sadness is not depression unless it becomes complicated by negative feelings about our futures and our selves. Depressed people feel badly about themselves, they blame themselves for things going wrong in their lives, and they have trouble imagining a better future. Depression that is clinically meaningful involves physical symptoms as well, including changes in appetite, energy levels, and sleeping patterns. Depression is usually preceded by one or more highly stressful life events, which typically involve loss or devaluation, such as the break up of a relationship, or failure at school or work (Brown & Harris, 1978). Even positive life events can entail an element of loss and so risk depressed mood. For instance, when women first become mothers, they may be overjoyed by the baby's birth but at the same time feel that they have lost freedom and control over their lives.

An important contextual factor that is related to depressive symptoms is poverty. Children who live in poverty endure a number of other conditions that may account for the link with depressive symptoms. For instance, poor children are more likely to live in neighborhoods with social problems, less likely to participate in activities outside of school, and more likely to have a mother who is depressed and who uses physical punishment to discipline them; these intervening variables appear to account for the association between child poverty and depressive symptoms (Eamon, 2002). Among adults, poverty is associated with being unmarried and living in a run-down, unsafe environment, both of which appear to account for the association with depressive symptoms (Ross, 2000).

One of the most robust yet mystifying facts about depression is that girls and women are twice as likely as boys and men to experience it. The lifetime rate of clinical depression is 20–25% for females and 7–12% for males (Nolen-Hoeksema, 1987). The rates are equal only before the age of 10 and after the age of 80 (Jorm, 1987). Thus, girls and women are more vulnerable than boys and men across most of the life span. In this chapter, we attempt to understand what it is about the lives of girls and women that make them vulnerable to depressed mood.

BIOLOGICAL EXPLANATIONS: HORMONES AND GENES

The fact that the gender gap first emerges in early adolescence has suggested hormonal origins to many researchers. Recent research confirmed that the gender difference emerges at puberty, regardless of the age at which that occurs (Angold, Costello, & Worthman, 1998). Girls experience a sharp increase in depression at this time, while boys experience a sudden decrease. However, the fact that puberty increases girls' risk for depression does not mean that hormones cause depression. The hormonal changes associated with puberty coincide with significant social and emotional changes in children's lives. Thus, pubertal girls may be at risk for depression because of hormonal or social factors, or a combination of both. For instance, negative life events seem to be more depressing for pubertal than prepubertal girls (Silberg et al., 1999).

Although researchers have long speculated that women's depression is caused by such hormonal events as puberty, menstruation, childbirth, and menopause, no specific hormonal mechanisms have been identified. There is no evidence that menopausal women are at special risk for developing depression (Ballinger, 1990), which makes a hormonal explanation for those depressions that do occur unlikely. The picture for premenstrual syndrome (PMS) and postpartum depression (PPD) is more complex but not yet clear. For instance, consistent with a hormonal explanation, there is a subgroup of women who are at high risk for depression after childbirth (Cooper & Murray, 1995). However, only thyroid dysfunction has been consistently associated with some cases of PPD (Hendrick, Altshuler, & Suri, 1998). Additionally, women who suffer with PMS (Graze, Nee, & Endicott, 1990) and PPD (Whiffen, 1992) are at risk for depression at other times in their lives, which indicates that their periods of depression coincide both with times of hormonal change and with times of stability.

It is possible that reproductive hormones have an impact on the neurotransmitters implicated in depression. Neurotransmitters are chemicals in the brain and nervous system that influence moods. Female hormones have an impact on how neurotransmitters are made and used by the nervous system. However, there is no evidence directly linking depression to female hormones. In addition, the hormones that are most clearly linked to depression, such as cortisol, do not differ between the sexes in a way that explains the gender difference.

In contrast, depression clearly has a genetic basis. While the genetic contribution to adult depression is equal in men and women (Kendler & Prescott, 1999), studies of adolescents show that genetic factors appear to play no role at all in adolescent boys' depressive symptoms (Jacobson & Rowe, 1999; Silberg et al., 1999). The meaning of this finding is not clear. Some researchers argue that the genes responsible for depression are "turned on" in girls during puberty (Silberg et al., 1999), while others argue that depression genes simply are more strongly expressed in girls than in boys (Jacobson & Rowe, 1999).

Psychological and Social Factors

Depression is associated with a variety of psychological and social risk factors, including dysfunctional beliefs (Beck, Rush, Shaw, & Emery, 1979), ruminative coping (Nolen-Hoeksema, 1987), a tendency to feel hopeless (Abramson, Alloy, & Metalsky, 1989), and personality traits such as dependency and self-criticism (Coyne & Whiffen, 1995). All models of depression are "diathesis-stress" models—that is, they assume that the underlying risk, whether biological or psychosocial, must be triggered by life stress in order for depressed mood to develop. In this chapter, we focus on two classes of risk factors that have been implicated in female depression throughout the life span: gender role and problematic relationships.

GENDER ROLE

The term gender role is broad and can refer to the socialization of gender-typed personality traits, to social conditions that typically are associated with one gender more than the other, or to the enactment of gender-typed behaviors such as caregiving.

Personality Traits

The socialization of boys encourages the development of instrumental personality traits such as independence and decisiveness, while girls' socialization encourages the development of interpersonal and expressive traits such as empathy and caring for others. By early adolescence, girls possess fewer instrumental traits than boys do. Nolen-Hoeksema and Girgus (1994) argued that this relative lack of instrumental traits impedes girls' ability to cope with the biological and social challenges of adolescence. Consistent with this hypothesis, adolescents who self-report high levels of instrumental traits are more confident about their ability to solve problems, which protects them from feeling depressed (Marcotte, Alain, & Gosselin, 1999). In addition, some researchers argue that depression is linked to the socialization of negative feminine traits, such as passivity and overinvolvement with others to the exclusion of self (Helgeson & Fritz, 1998).

Body Dissatisfaction

The normal changes associated with puberty mean that girls gain fat, especially in their breasts and buttocks, while boys become taller and more muscular. Thus, girls move away from societal ideals about thinness, while boys move closer to the ideal for men. As a result, body dissatisfaction is normative among adolescent girls, but rare among boys. This is problematic for girls because physical attractiveness is a central component of adolescents' self-esteem. Attractiveness determines popularity with both sexes and in girls may overshadow other characteristics such as intelligence and ability. Not surprisingly, body dissatisfaction is associated with depressive symptoms in both sexes. Girls who feel dissatisfied about normal physical changes have lower self-esteem and are more likely to be depressed than girls whose attitude toward their bodies is more positive (Wichstrom, 1999).

Interpersonal Violence

Girls and women are more likely than boys and men to be victims of violence, especially in intimate relationships. All forms of interpersonal violence, including sexual assault and physical abuse, are associated with depression, especially in girls and women (Weaver & Clum, 1995). In particular, researchers have focused on a history of childhood sexual abuse (CSA), which is strongly associated with adult women's depression. When a history of CSA is controlled for statistically, the gender difference in adult depressive symptoms disappears (Whiffen & Clark, 1997), which suggests that CSA may explain why girls and women experience more depressed mood than do boys and men.

A history of CSA may make it difficult for girls to cope with some of the challenges of adolescence, such as changes in their bodies and dating. Girls who were sexually abused as children may be ambivalent about normal, physical changes that make them attractive because sexual activity was a source of shame in the past. In addition, CSA may lead to the development of specific cognitive biases that are associated with depression. For example, when children are sexually abused, the assailant typically blames them for the abuse. The tendency to blame oneself for uncontrollable, negative events may become a stable part of the abused child's personality, such that even life events that are clearly out of one's control are perceived to be one's fault (Wenninger & Ehlers, 1998). CSA also may cause permanent changes to the nervous system that increase reactivity to stress (Weiss, Longhurst, & Mazure, 1999), which may make CSA survivors biologically prone to experience depression in the face of life stress.

CSA also has an indirect impact on adult depression through its influence on relationships. Close relationships, particularly with romantic partners, protect women from becoming depressed when they experience life stress (Brown and Harris, 1978). However, women with a history of CSA have more interpersonal problems than do women without this history (Rumstein-McKean & Hunsley, 2001). They report difficulties getting close to and trusting other people, and many report that they avoid having close relationships altogether. In addition, the quality of their romantic relationships may be poor. For instance, CSA survivors are more likely to be physically victimized by their romantic partners or to be sexually assaulted. Re-victimization is directly associated with episodes of depression during adulthood.

Work Outside the Home

Bebbington (1996) reviewed the role of gender-role enactment in adult women's depression. He pointed out that married women with young children are at the greatest risk for depression, except in countries and cultures where home-making is highly valued. Conversely, being employed outside the home is protective for women, despite the fact that the vast majority of working mothers report high levels of stress as a result of work-family conflict. Compared to stay-at-home mothers, working mothers have higher self-esteem and they feel more competent, even about their parenting. It may be useful to think of employment specifically and of gender roles generally, as factors that have a positive impact on the development of instrumental traits and behaviors. For instance, women who work outside their homes may have the opportunity to develop traits such as independence and self-confidence, as well as problem-solving skills that help them to cope with life stress.

PROBLEMATIC RELATIONSHIPS

While boys are socialized to value independence and competition, girls are socialized to value interpersonal relationships, particularly with their families and spouses. As a result, girls and women derive much of their self-esteem from their ability to establish and maintain positive connections with significant others (Josephs, Markus, & Tafarodi, 1992). There is substantial evidence that difficult interpersonal relations are linked to the onset of depression; once depressed, girls and women stay depressed in part by generating interpersonal conflicts (Hammen, 2003). In this section, we summarize the evidence that depression is related to two sources of interpersonal

strain: family relationships for adolescent girls and relationships with romantic partners throughout the life span.

Family Relationships

Depression in adolescents is strongly linked to dysfunctional family relationships (Cummings & Davies, 1999). Compared to nondepressed youth, depressed youth report lower levels of family cohesion and closeness, fewer social resources, lower levels of support and approval from their parents, more family conflict and poorer communication with parents, more parental control, and a negative family climate (Sheeber, Hops, & Davis, 2001). As girls make the transition into adolescence, they begin to place more importance on interpersonal relationships than do boys. Thus, difficult family relationships can have a significant impact on adolescent girls' mood even when they are not directly involved (i.e., parents' marital problems). One longitudinal study showed that girls were more vulnerable than boys to family problems such as marital conflict and low levels of family intimacy, which accounted for their social and emotional adjustment (Davies & Windle, 1997). Although adolescents typically spend less time with their parents than do younger children, they continue to identify their parents as their most significant sources of support. For girls, family relations are a better predictor of adolescent depressive symptoms than are peer relations, particularly when they are highly stressed (McFarlane, Bellissimo, Norman, & Lange, 1994).

Secure attachment bonds with parents allow girls to create positive cognitive models of the self and the self-in-relation. These models are important sources of information about girls' intrinsic worth, and about the emotional responsiveness of significant others. When researchers studied adolescents in an inpatient psychiatric setting, strong gender differences were found in attachment (Rosenstein & Horowitz, 1996). Adolescent girls were more likely than boys to be depressed and to be intensely worried that they would be abandoned by attachment figures. In contrast, boys were more likely than girls to have a dismissing attachment style characterized by self-sufficiency. This research suggests that adolescent girls who suffer from depression place a high importance on interpersonal bonds, but also that they have little confidence that people will be consistently available and responsive to their emotional needs. An insecure attachment relationship with one's primary attachment figure, usually the mother, appears to decrease girls' self-esteem, and increase the likelihood of depressed mood (Roberts & Monroe, 1999).

Mothers also are an important source of support for adolescent girls. Adolescent girls tend to experience more stressful life events and to be more reactive than boys are in response to these events. However, a warm, supportive relationship with one's mother attenuates the impact of stress on girls' but not boys' depressive symptoms (Ge, Lorenz, Conger, Elder, & Simons, 1994). Maternal support also may be implicated in the normal developmental process of individuation. Girls tend to feel depressed when they perceive discrepancies between who they are and who their parents wish them to be, which may reflect the relational basis of their self-esteem. However, these discrepancies are only problematic for girls who also perceive their mothers as unsupportive of their autonomy. Girls who see themselves as discrepant from what their mothers want for them, but see their mothers as supportive of their autonomy have high levels of self-esteem and low levels of depression (Moretti & Wiebe, 1999).

A discussion of family functioning and depression would not be complete unless it included mention of the impact of parental depression on adolescents. In interactions with their children, depressed parents show more negative mood and make more negative attributions, they communicate with vague, inconsistent and often confusing messages, they express more rejection and hostility, and they show less warmth and positive mood than nondepressed parents do (Chiariello & Orvaschel, 1995). Thus, depression makes it difficult for parents to meet their children's emotional needs on a consistent and reliable basis. Not surprisingly, the children of depressed parents are six times more likely to suffer from depression than are the children of nondepressed parents. Given that adolescent girls are already more likely than boys to become depressed, this risk becomes

alarmingly high in adolescent girls with a depressed parent.

Parental depression may have a direct negative impact on adolescent girls through poor parenting (Hammen, 2003). In addition, the children of depressed parents may feel guilty and be overly focused on the depressed parent (Cole-Detke & Kobak, 1996). Depressed parents may turn to their children to meet their own emotional needs and to alleviate their distress, which may cause the adolescent to neglect her own needs and assume the role of caregiver (Rosenstein & Horowitz, 1996). Because of their interpersonal focus, girls may be more likely than boys to take on a caregiver role with a depressed parent. Statistically, a depressed parent also is more likely to be a mother than a father, with additional consequences for daughters in the form of reduced maternal support. Thus, parental depression, particularly in mothers, may be another source of adolescent girls' risk for depressed mood.

Dating Relationships

Nondepressed adolescent girls believe that depression occurs when girls feel disconnected in their important relationships, particularly with boyfriends, or when they do not have a romantic partner (Hetherington & Stoppard, 2002). Consistent with this perception, adolescent girls are at risk for depression when romantic relationships end (Silberg et al., 1999). In late adolescence, girls may increasingly turn to romantic partners for the emotional support that earlier in their lives was provided by their parents. Lack of this form of intimacy may increase their vulnerability to depression. The acceptance and validation that is provided by an intimate romantic relationship may enable adolescent girls to regulate their negative moods. For instance, one study showed that girls who lacked intimacy in a romantic relationship were more likely to endorse dysfunctional beliefs about themselves when induced to have a negative mood (Williams, Connolly, & Segal, 2001).

However, romantic relationships are a double-edged sword. The results from a large-scale longitudinal study indicate that becoming involved in a romantic relationship also increases adolescent girls' depressed mood, in part because having a boyfriend can have a negative impact on girls' relationships with their parents (Joyner & Udry, 2000). Young women who are prone to depression may unwittingly select romantic partners who increase their risk of depression. Another study, which followed young women for up to five years after graduation from high school, found that young women who initially were unhappy went on to become involved with young men who tended to be aloof, guarded, unemotional, and unempathetic, and hence emotionally unsupportive (Daley & Hammen, 2002). This constellation of traits also increases depression levels in married women (Whiffen, Kallos-Lilly, & MacDonald, 2001). Thus, women who are prone to depression appear to choose romantic partners who are likely to exacerbate and maintain their depressive tendencies.

Marital Relations

Depression is associated with attachment insecurity in romantic relationships (Whiffen et al., 2001), and with marital distress (Whisman, 2001). There also is evidence that marital distress increases the risk of an episode of depression and predicts relapse after recovery. For instance, Whisman and Bruce (1999) showed that spouses who were maritally distressed but not depressed at baseline were nearly three times more likely to become clinically depressed over the subsequent year than were individuals who were neither maritally distressed nor depressed. Marital distress and depression are even more strongly associated among individuals who have a history of poor interpersonal relations. For example, women who were sexually abused during childhood are both better protected by good marital relations and more vulnerable to depressive symptoms when their relationships are of poor quality than are women without this history (Whiffen, Judd, & Aube, 1999).

Marital distress has an impact both on the level of conflict that a couple experiences and on the level of support they provide to one another. Both aspects heighten vulnerability to depression. Women who experience life stress are protected from becoming depressed by having some-

one in whom they can confide (Brown & Harris, 1978). Similarly, once a woman becomes depressed, having a warm and supportive spouse facilitates her recovery (McLeod, Kessler, & Landis, 1992). Husbands who denigrate the importance of relationships or who are indifferent to their wives are especially likely to maintain and exacerbate their wives' depression (Whiffen et al., 2001).

Women may be more sensitive than men to conflict and lack of support. When one partner is depressed, the couple tends to have hostile and conflicted interactions, regardless of whether the depressed person is the husband or the wife. However, when the wife is depressed, their interactions are measurably more negative. In addition, depressed women feel even more depressed after a hostile interaction with their spouses than do depressed men (Gotlib & Whiffen, 1989). Marital distress lowers women's self-esteem, which increases their vulnerability to depression (Culp & Beach, 1998). Unlike depressed men, once women become depressed, they tend to interact with their spouses in ways that perpetuate depression, for instance, by expecting their partners to be critical and by behaving unsupportively in marital interactions (Davila, Bradbury, Cohan, & Tochluk, 1997). Thus, marital distress and depression may form a unique negative feedback loop in women. Women also may need more support than men do to maintain their well being. On average, men and women do not differ in the levels of support that they receive. However, if women require more support and if they are more adversely affected by conflict with their spouses, then together these findings may explain why marital distress is more likely to induce depression in women than in men (Bebbington, 1996).

Women may be at risk for depression when their beliefs about the importance of relationships are taken to an extreme—that is, when they feel that harmony in their relationships must be maintained at all costs. Women who hold this view may "silence" themselves to preserve the illusion of harmony (Jack, 1991). "Self-silencing" involves suppressing negative thoughts or feelings that might threaten the relationship. This self-censorship alienates the woman from her own thoughts and feelings, which ultimately results in her becoming depressed. Self-silencing may be an interpersonal coping strategy that is particularly likely to develop when the romantic partner or spouse is critical and intolerant (Thompson, Whiffen, & Aube, 2001).

Finally, there is evidence that depressed mood is contagious (Joiner & Katz, 1999). Contagion effects are likely to be pronounced among women, who appear to be especially sensitive to their spouses' marital distress and depressed mood (Whiffen & Gotlib, 1989). Thus, women's risk for depression may come not only from their own marital distress but also from their husbands' distress.

SUMMARY AND INTEGRATION OF THE RESEARCH

We identified two linked themes, gender role and problematic relationships, that appear to place girls and women at risk for depressed mood. Girls are socialized to value interpersonal relationships and to value themselves for their skill in maintaining close and harmonious relations. Relationships can have a protective effect if they are healthy and secure or a detrimental effect in the context of discord and insecurity. Because of the emphasis girls and women place on relationships, they may ruminate about negative family events, they may feel caught or trapped in family problems, and they may become enmeshed in the problems of family members (Davies & Windle, 1997). In taking on gender socialized responsibilities for maintaining relationships, girls and women may put their own emotional needs aside, which ultimately may result in mood disturbance. Thus, the comparatively high rate of depressed mood in girls and women appears to be closely associated with the importance that girls and women place on harmony in their relationships, particularly those with their families and spouses. Unfortunately, girls and women who experience depression often grow up in families where relationships are distressed and where they are rejected, only to enter romantic relationships and marriages where they feel unsupported and criticized. In addition, they may perpetuate their emotional distress through the generation of interpersonal conflict. Thus, for many women, disturbed relationships are both the cause and consequence of depression (Hammen, 2003).

TREATMENT IMPLICATIONS

Psychological treatments need to take into account the interpersonal and social context in which women's depression occurs. A variety of standardized psychological treatments have been shown to be effective. Three treatments involve individual sessions between the depressed woman and her therapist: cognitive-behavioral therapy (CBT; Beck et al., 1979), interpersonal therapy (IPT; Frank & Spanier, 1995), and process-experiential therapy (PET; Watson, Gordon, Stermac, Kalogerakos, & Steckley, 2003). CBT is aimed at reducing dysfunctional beliefs about the self, world, and future that accompany depression. This treatment may help women change dysfunctional beliefs about relationships. IPT is focused directly on changing the disturbed interpersonal relations that give rise to depression. PET assists clients to process painful emotions and past experiences. After treatment, clients who received PET report fewer interpersonal problems. Marital therapy also is an effective treatment for women's depression when it co-occurs with marital distress (Jacobson, Dobson, Fruzzetti, Schmaling, & Salusky, 1991). Finally, attachment-based family therapy appears to be an effective treatment for adolescent depression (Diamond, Reis, Diamond, Siqueland, & Isaacs, 2002). Depression tends to be comorbid with other problems, most commonly anxiety and personality disorders (Melartin & Isometsae, 2000); the existence of co-occurring disorders usually complicates treatment.

REFERENCES

Abramson, L. Y., Alloy, L. B., & Metalsky, G. I. (1989). Hopelessness depression: A theory-based subtype of depression. *Psychological Review, 96,* 358–372.

Angold, A., Costello, E. J., & Worthman, C. M. (1998). Puberty and depression: The roles of age, pubertal status and pubertal timing. *Psychological Medicine, 28,* 51–61.

Ballinger, C. B. (1990). Psychiatric aspects of the menopause. *British Journal of Psychiatry, 156,* 773–787.

Bebbington, P. (1996). The origins of sex differences in depressive disorder: Bridging the gap. *International Review of Psychiatry, 8,* 295–332.

Beck, A. T., Rush, A. J., Shaw, B. F., & Emery, G. (1979). *Cognitive therapy of depression.* New York: Guilford Press.

Brown, G. W., & Harris, T. O. (1978). *Social origins of depression*. London: Free Press.

Chiariello, M. A., & Orvaschel, H. (1995). Patterns of parent-child communication: Relationship to depression. *Clinical Psychology Review, 15*, 395–407.

Cole-Detke, H. E., & Kobak, R. (1996). Attachment processes in eating disorder and depression. *Journal of Consulting and Clinical Psychology, 64*, 282–290.

Cooper, P. J., & Murray, L. (1995). Course and recurrence of postnatal depression: Evidence for the specificity of the diagnostic concept. *British Journal of Psychiatry, 166*, 191–195.

Coyne, J. C., & Whiffen, V. E. (1995). Issues in personality as diathesis for depression: The case of sociotropy/dependency and autonomy/self-criticism. *Psychological Bulletin, 118*, 358–378.

Culp, L. N., & Beach, S. R. H. (1998). Marriage and depressive symptoms: The role and bases of self-esteem differ by gender. *Psychology of Women Quarterly, 22*, 647–663.

Cummings, E. M., & Davies, P. T. (1999). Depressed parents and family functioning: Interpersonal effects and children's functioning and development. In T. Joiner & J. C. Coyne (Eds.), *The interactional nature of depression* (pp. 299–327). Washington, DC: American Psychological Association.

Daley, S. E., & Hammen, C. (2002). Depressive symptoms and close relationships during the transition to adulthood: Perspectives from dysphoric women, their best friends, and their romantic partners. *Journal of Consulting and Clinical Psychology, 70*, 129–141.

Davies, P. T., & Windle, M. (1997). Gender-specific pathways between maternal depressive symptoms, family discord, and adolescent adjustment. *Developmental Psychology, 33*, 657–668.

Davila, J., Bradbury, T. N., Cohan, C. L., & Tochluk, S. (1997). Marital functioning and depressive symptoms: Evidence for a stress generation model. *Journal of Personality & Social Psychology, 73*, 849–861.

Diamond, G. S., Reis, B. F., Diamond, G. M., Siqueland, L., & Isaacs, L. (2002). Attachment-based family therapy for depressed adolescents: A treatment development study. *Journal of the American Academy of Child & Adolescent Psychiatry, 41*, 1190–1196.

Eamon, M. K. (2002). Influences and mediators of the effect of poverty on young adolescent depressive symptoms. *Journal of Youth and Adolescence, 31*, 231–242.

Frank, E., & Spanier, C. (1995). Interpersonal psychotherapy for depression: Overview, clinical efficacy, and future directions. *Clinical Psychology: Science & Practice, 2*, 349–369.

Ge, X., Lorenz, R. O., Conger, R. D., Elder, G. H., & Simons, R. L. (1994). Trajectories of stressful life events and depressive symptoms during adolescence. *Developmental Psychology, 30*, 467–483.

Gotlib, I. H., & Whiffen, V. E. (1989). Depression and marital functioning: An examination of specificity and gender differences. *Journal of Abnormal Psychology, 98*, 23–30.

Graze, K. K., Nee, J., & Endicott, J. (1990). Premenstrual depression predicts future major depressive disorder. *Acta Psychiatrica Scandinavica, 81*, 201–205.

Hammen, C. (2003). Interpersonal stress and depression in women. *Journal of Affective Disorders, 74*, 49–57.

Helgeson, V. S., & Fritz, H. L. (1998). A theory of unmitigated communion. *Personality & Social Psychology Review, 2*, 173–183.

Hendrick, V., Altshuler, L. L., & Suri, R. (1998). Hormonal changes in the postpartum and implications for postpartum depression. *Psychosomatics, 39*, 93–101.

Hetherington, J. A., & Stoppard, J. M. (2002). The theme of disconnection in adolescent girls' understanding of depression. *Journal of Adolescence, 25*, 619–629.

Jack, D. C. (1991). *Silencing the self: Women and depression*. Cambridge, MA: Harvard University Press.

Jacobson, K. C., & Rowe, D. C. (1999). Genetic and environmental influences on the relationships between family connectedness, school connectedness, and adolescent depressed mood sex differences. *Developmental Psychology, 35*, 926–939.

Jacobson, N. S., Dobson, K., Fruzzetti, A. E., Schmaling, K. B., & Salusky, S. (1991). Marital therapy as a treatment for depression. *Journal of Consulting and Clinical Psychology, 59*, 547–557.

Joiner, T. E., & Katz, J. (1999). Contagion of depressive symptoms and mood: Meta-analytic review and explanations from cognitive, behavioral, and interpersonal viewpoints. *Clinical Psychology: Science and Practice, 6*, 149–164.

Jorm, A. F. (1987). Sex and age differences in depression: A quantitative synthesis of published research. *Australian & New Zealand Journal of Psychiatry, 21*, 46–53.

Josephs, R. A., Markus, H. R., & Tafarodi, R. W. (1992). Gender and self-esteem. *Journal of Personality and Social Psychology, 63*, 391–402.

Joyner, K., & Udry, J. R. (2000). You don't bring me anything but down: Adolescent romance and depression. *Journal of Health and Social Behavior, 41*, 369–391.

Kendler, K. S., & Prescott, C. A. (1999). A population-based twin study of lifetime major depression in men and women. *Archives of General Psychiatry, 56*, 39–44.

Marcotte, D., Alain, M., & Gosselin, M.-J. (1999). Gender differences in adolescent depression: Gender-typed characteristics or problem-solving skills deficits? *Sex Roles, 41*, 31–48.

McFarlane, A. H., Bellissimo, A., Norman, G. R., & Lange, P. (1994). Adolescent depression in a school-based community sample: Preliminary findings on contributing social factors. *Journal of Youth and Adolescence, 23*, 601–620.

McLeod, J. D., Kessler, R. C., & Landis, K. R. (1992). Speed of recovery from major depressive episode in a community sample of married men and women. *Journal of Abnormal Psychology, 101,* 277–286.

Melartin, T., & Isometsae, E. (2000). Psychiatric co-morbidity of major depressive disorder—a review. *Psychiatria Fennica, 31,* 87–100.

Moretti, M. M., & Wiebe, V. J. (1999). Self-discrepancy in adolescence: Own and parental standpoints on the self. *Merrill-Palmer Quarterly, 45,* 624–649.

Nolen-Hoeksema, S. (1987). Sex differences in unipolar depression: Evidence and theory. *Psychological Bulletin, 101,* 259–282.

Nolen-Hoeksema, S., & Girgus, J. S. (1994). The emergence of gender differences in depression during adolescence. *Psychological Bulletin, 115,* 424–443.

Roberts, J. E., & Monroe, S. M. (1999). Vulnerable self-esteem and social processes in depression: Toward an interpersonal model of self-esteem regulation. In T. Joiner & J. C. Coyne (Eds.), *The interactional nature of depression* (pp. 149–187). Washington, DC: American Psychological Association.

Rosenstein, D. S., & Horowitz, H. A. (1996). Adolescent attachment and psychopathology. *Journal of Consulting and Clinical Psychology, 64,* 244–253.

Ross, C. E. (2000). Neighborhood disadvantage and adult depression. *Journal of Health and Social Behavior, 41,* 177–187.

Rumstein-McKean, O., & Hunsley, J. (2001). Interpersonal and family functioning of female survivors of childhood sexual abuse. *Clinical Psychology Review, 21,* 471–490.

Sheeber, L., Hops, H., & Davis, B. (2001). Family processes in adolescent depression. *Clinical Child and Family Psychology Review, 4,* 19–35.

Silberg, J., Pickles, A., Rutter, M., Hewitt, J., Simonoff, E., Maes, H., et al. (1999). The influence of genetic factors and life stress on depression among adolescent girls. *Archives of General Psychiatry, 56,* 225–232.

Thompson, J. M., Whiffen, V. E., & Aube, J. A. (2001). Does self-silencing link perceptions of care from parents and partners with depressive symptoms? *Journal of Social and Personal Relationships, 18,* 503–516.

Watson, J. C., Gordon, L. B., Stermac, L., Kalogerakos, F., & Steckley, P. (2003). Comparing the effectiveness of process-experiential with cognitive-behavioral psychotherapy in the treatment of depression. *Journal of Consulting and Clinical Psychology, 71,* 773–781.

Weaver, T. L., & Clum, G. A. (1995). Psychological distress associated with interpersonal violence: A meta-analysis. *Clinical Psychology Review, 15,* 115–140.

Weiss, E. L., Longhurst, J. G., & Mazure, C. M. (1999). Childhood sexual abuse as a risk factor for depression in women: psychosocial and neurobiological correlates. *American Journal of Psychiatry, 156,* 816–828.

Wenninger, K., & Ehlers, A. (1998). Dysfunctional cognitions and adult psychological functioning in child sexual abuse survivors. *Journal of Traumatic Stress, 11,* 281–300.

Whiffen, V. E. (1992). Is postpartum depression a distinct diagnosis? *Clinical Psychology Review, 12,* 485–508.

Whiffen, V. E., & Clark, S. E. (1997). Does victimization account for sex differences in depressive symptoms? *British Journal of Clinical Psychology, 36,* 185–193.

Whiffen, V. E., & Gotlib, I. H. (1989). Stress and coping in maritally distressed and nondistressed couples. *Journal of Social and Personal Relationships, 6,* 327–344.

Whiffen, V. E., Judd, M. E., & Aube, J. A. (1999). Intimate relationships moderate the association between childhood sexual abuse and depression. *Journal of Interpersonal Violence, 14,* 940–954.

Whiffen, V. E., Kallos-Lilly, A. V., & MacDonald, B. J. (2001). Depression and attachment in couples. *Cognitive Therapy and Research, 25,* 577–590.

Whisman, M. A. (2001). The association between depression and marital dissatisfaction. In S. R. H. Beach (Ed.), *Marital and family processes in depression.* Washington, DC: American Psychological Association.

Whisman, M. A., & Bruce, M. L. (1999). Marital dissatisfaction and incidence of major depressive episode in a community sample. *Journal of Abnormal Psychology, 108,* 674–678.

Wichstrom, L. (1999). The emergence of gender difference in depressed mood during adolescence: The role of intensified gender socialization. *Developmental Psychology, 35,* 232–245.

Williams, S., Connolly, J., & Segal, Z. (2001). Intimacy in relationships and cognitive vulnerability to depression in adolescent girls. *Cognitive Therapy and Research, 25,* 477–496.

Substantial empirical evidence points to a preponderance of females showing and/or reporting some form of anxiety disturbance (e.g., fear, worry, anxiety) across the life span. This chapter provides an overview of the existing literature on gender differences in anxiety disturbance across the life span with respect to developmental course and etiological variables. First, we begin by reviewing empirical findings on gender differences in anxiety disturbance with studies using participants randomly selected from the population (community studies) and studies using participants who present for treatment (clinical studies). Next, we review evidence from epidemiological studies regarding the overall prevalence of individual anxiety disorders across sexes. We then consider several theoretical explanations (e.g., biological, social, and cognitive) that seek to explain how gender differences in anxiety disturbance emerge. This is followed by a brief discussion of differences across gender as a function of ethnicity. We conclude with an examination of prevention and treatment methods relevant to girls and women.

FEATURES OF ANXIETY DISTURBANCE

Fears and Worry in Girls and Women

Although distinctions have been made between fear (a response to imminent threat), worry (a preparation for future threat), and anxiety (apprehension and anticipation), they all share a similar response pattern that may lead to impairing anxiety symptoms or disorders. These response patterns typically fall under three different but interrelated components: cognitive responses (e.g., "People will laugh at me if I raise my hand"), physiological responses (e.g., increased heart rate or sweating), and behavioral responses (e.g., avoidance of social situations). An important challenge for researchers lies in distinguishing aspects of transitory fears, worries, and anxieties that differ for females and males from fears, worries, and anxieties that persist and impair functioning over different developmental periods.

Childhood and Adolescence

Research on fears in youth is based mainly on findings using the Fear Survey Schedule for Chil-

WENDY K. SILVERMAN
and RONA CARTER

Anxiety Disturbance in Girls and Women

dren (FSSC-R; Ollendick, 1983; FSSC-II; Gullone & King, 1992). The FSSC-R and FSSC-II assess youths' level of fears to various objects and situations and have yielded a similar pattern of results across studies. For example, community studies using both fear inventories show that girls self-rate a greater number of fears than boys (18 fears vs. 10 fears), as well as greater fear intensity (as indicated by selecting "a lot" vs. "some" or "a little") (see Gullone, 2000). Girls also endorse different fears than boys endorse. Specifically, girls endorse being more fearful about getting lost in a strange place, being kidnapped, snakes, getting burned, and the dark, and boys endorse being more fearful about getting an illness, getting poor grades, being invaded or attacked, and being injured (e.g., Ollendick, 1983). Despite gender differences with respect to specific types of fears, eight of the ten most frequently endorsed fears are the same for girls and boys: (a) being invaded or attacked, (b) falling from a high place, (c) a burglar breaking into the house, (d) getting burned, (e) being hit by a car or truck, (f) not being able to breathe, (g) earthquakes, and (h) death or dead people (e.g., Ollendick, 1983).

Research on worry in youth is based mainly on interview or questionnaire procedures. Community studies show that girls self-report two to three times more worries than boys as well as differences in type of worry endorsed (e.g., Muris, Meesters, Merckelbach, Sermon, & Zwakhalen, 1998; Silverman, La Greca, & Wasserstein, 1995). Specifically, girls report being more worried than boys about their performance, their appearance, and future events and boys report being more worried than girls about being punished and receiving failing grades (e.g., Muris et al., 1998).

Differences relating to gender are less well researched in clinic-based studies relative to community studies. One study using clinically anxious youth found that the prevalence and intensity of fears, as rated by the child, parent, teacher, and clinician, did not differ as a function of sex (e.g., Treadwell, Flannery-Schroeder, & Kendall, 1995). It is difficult to draw conclusions about gender differences in the fears, worries, and anxieties of clinic-referred samples (either clinically anxious samples or other types of clinical samples) given the limited amount of research that has been conducted. Further research in this area is needed.

Adulthood and Old Age

Research on fears in adults and older adults are mainly based on findings using the Fear Survey Schedule (FSS-II; Geer, 1965; FSS-III; Wolpe & Lang, 1964). The FSS-II and FSS-III assess adults' level of fears to various objects and situations and have yielded a similar pattern of results across studies. For example, community studies using the FSS-II and FSS-III show that women self-rate a greater number of fears than men as well as greater fear intensity (e.g., Liddell & Hart 1992; Liddell, Locker, & Burman, 1991). Women also endorse different fears than do men. Women endorse being more fearful than men of social situations, walking alone in the street, animals, and crowded stores and men endorse being more fearful than women of catching an illness, losing a job, and having a heart attack (e.g., Liddell et al., 1991).

Research on worry in adults and older adults is relatively limited in terms of analyzing for gender differences. The extant community studies mainly used interview or questionnaire procedures to assess frequency and content of worry; findings generally show that women report more worries than men and endorse different types of worry (e.g., Borkovec, Metzger, & Pruzinsky, 1986; Robichaud, Dugas, & Conway, 2002). Specifically, women report more worrisome thoughts about social evaluative situations (e.g., parties) and lack of confidence than men. Available data for older adults (aged 55 years or older) is even more limited, but suggest that older men and women who worry are more anxious, in poorer health, and experience more chronic illnesses relative to older men and women who do not worry (e.g., Beck, Stanley, & Zebb, 1996).

A small number of clinic-based studies with adults referred for treatment have reported gender differences with respect to fear and worry symptoms. Available data suggest that the severity and patterns of symptoms are different for women and men. For example, women receiving treatment typically endorse more panic-related symptoms and higher levels of fear than men (Pigott, 1999). Other findings show that women and men who present with generalized anxiety disorder (GAD) and panic disorder (PD) for treatment tend to display different clinical features. For example, women with GAD are more likely than men with GAD to develop co-occurring disorders, such as dysthymia (Pigott, 1999). In addition, somatization disorder is four times more likely to occur in women with PD than in men with PD (Pigott, 1999).

Summary

Gender differences are evident at normative, subclinical, and clinical levels of fear, worry, and anxiety. Further research is needed to assess specific patterns of fear, worry, and anxiety symptoms, not just number or intensity of symptoms. Relative to community-based studies, clinic-based studies on gender differences are inconsistent, particularly with respect to youth. Perhaps this inconsistency stems from differences in perceived need and willingness to seek treatment among females and males resulting in putative sex/gender differences within clinical settings (Rutter, Caspi, & Moffitt, 2003). For the most part, firm conclusions about the relation between gender and anxiety disturbance cannot be drawn; the most that can be stated is that females are more likely than males to show and/or report features of anxiety disturbance.

PREVALENCE OF ANXIETY DISORDERS

Anxiety Disorders in Girls and Women

The latest edition of the *Diagnostic and Statistical Manual of Mental Disorders* (*DSM-IV;* American Psychiatric Association, 1994; *DSM-IV-TR,* American Psychiatric Association, 2000) recognizes the following anxiety disorder diagnoses: separation anxiety disorder (SAD), specific phobia (SP), social phobia (SOP), generalized anxiety disorder (GAD), panic disorder (PD), agoraphobia, (AG) posttraumatic stress disorder (PTSD), and obsessive-compulsive disorder (OCD). Prevalence rates of anxiety disorders are derived mainly from diagnostic interview schedules, such as the Schedule for Affective Disorders and Schizophrenia for School-Age Children (K-SADS; Puig-Antich & Chambers, 1983) and using criteria from previous editions of the *DSM* (e.g., *DSM-III* or *DSM-III-R*). Epidemiological studies consistently show girls and women have higher rates of anxiety disorders than boys and men. Table 6.1 presents a sample of epidemiological studies.

Findings from table 6.1 suggest the following. First, SOP and PD appear less frequently in youth than in adults, with prevalence rates generally below 2%. Higher rates are evident in girls than boys regardless of age. Second, OCD is less prevalent among youth compared to the other anxiety disorders, with boys showing slightly higher rates than girls. Third, girls are three times more likely than boys to manifest SAD, and women are two times more likely to manifest GAD than men. Lastly, in older adults, women are more likely than men to suffer from SP, PD, and OCD.

Despite these relatively robust findings, ambiguity remains in this area of research and warrants attention. First, no clinic-based studies have systematically evaluated the influence of gender and anxiety disorders among clinical samples of anxious youths and adults. The only exception is the Treadwell et al. (1995) study, which found no significant gender differences in anxiety symptoms or diagnoses in youth referred to a childhood disorders specialty clinic. Second, available data are limited with respect to clinical characteristics, such as age at onset, severity, and duration, particularly with youth. Lastly, research examining the influence of gender on anxiety disorders across different age periods, ethnicity, and socioeconomic status is sparse.

Nevertheless, some empirical evidence does exist on a few issues relating to gender differences in anxiety disturbance. For example, there is some evidence suggesting women and men with anxiety disorders present with different clinical characteristics upon entering treatment. For example, OCD in women has a later age at onset (mean age = 25 years) than in men (mean age = 20 years), and boys are more likely than girls to develop OCD classified as early onset (before age 10) and very early onset (before age 6) (Pigott, 1999). Possible changes in rates of anxiety disorders based on development in girls and boys also are evident. For example, Cohen, Cohen, Kasen, and Velez (1993) found the average prevalence

TABLE 6.1 Prevalence (%) of Anxiety Disorders in Recent Epidemiological Studies

	N	Age	SAD	SP	SOP	OAD	GAD	PD	AG	OCD
					Anxiety Disorders					
Females										
Eaton et al. (1991)	14,436	18–96	—	14.4	2.9	—	—	2.1	7.9	—
Flint (1994)	5,702	65–90	—	6.1	—	—	—	0.2	—	0.9
Kashani and Orvaschel (1990)	210	8, 12, 17	21.0	5.7	1.0	15.2	—	—	—	—
Kessler et al. (1994)	8,098	15–54	—	15.7	15.5	—	6.6	5.0	7.0	—
Lewinsohn, Hops, Roberts, Seeley, and Andrews (1993)	1,710	14–18	5.8	2.8	2.4	1.8	—	1.1	1.1	0.3
Males										
Eaton et al. (1991)	14,436	18–96	—	7.8	2.5	—	—	0.9	3.2	—
Flint (1994)	5,702	65–90	—	2.9	—	—	—	0.0	—	0.7
Kashani and Orvaschel (1990)	210	8, 12, 17	4.8	1.0	1.0	9.5	—	—	—	—
Kessler et al. (1994)	8,098	15–54	—	6.7	11.1	—	3.6	2.0	3.5	—
Lewinsohn et al. (1993)	1,710	14–18	2.4	1.1	0.5	0.7	—	0.5	0.2	0.7

Note: SAD = separation anxiety disorder; SP = specific phobia (simple phobia); SOP = social phobia; OAD = overanxious anxiety disorder; GAD = generalized anxiety disorder; PD = panic disorder; AG = agoraphobia; OCD = obsessive-compulsive disorder.

rate for SAD in a community sample of youth was 13.1% for 10- to 13-year-old girls and 11.4% for 10- to 13-year-old boys; 4.6% for 14- to 16-year-old girls and 1.2% for 14- to 16-year-old boys; and 1.8% for 17- to 20-year-old girls and 2.7% for 17- to 20-year-old boys. These findings suggest girls are more likely than boys to have SAD, but after age 16 years prevalence rates of SAD are more evident in boys than girls. Clearly, further research is needed that can assess the diverse range of experiences or influences that may account in part for these observed gender differences within age groups.

POSSIBLE CONTRIBUTIONS TO GENDER DIFFERENCES

A range of biological, cognitive, and social theoretical explanations have been proposed concerning possible mechanisms by which girls and women become more prone to anxiety disturbance than boys and men. Most of these mechanisms have not been empirically tested, however. Studying mechanisms is important because it may provide clues to etiological processes in the development of anxiety disturbance. Research is needed to delineate these proposed mechanisms

by examining whether they serve as risk or protection within each gender. It is unlikely that there is only one factor (i.e., biological, cognitive, or social), or even a small set of factors that accounts for the emergence of gender differences in anxiety disturbance, but these proposed mechanisms are promising first steps.

Biological Processes

Genetics and Temperament

Evidence for genetic correlations between anxiety symptoms and disorders is derived from twin and adoption studies using questionnaire measures (Eley, 2001). Findings on sex or gender differences are mixed. For this reason, it is unclear whether gender or sex differences can be attributed to genetic factors, environmental factors, or both. Nor is it certain how sex or gender may modify genetic risk for anxiety (Eley, 2001). Nonetheless, these findings offer some insight into the role genes play in transmitting a general risk for anxiety, with girls and women showing higher heritability estimates than boys and men (Eley, 2001). Moreover, some evidence points to developmental variations in genetic influence. That is, girls tend to demonstrate higher heritability of anxiety symptoms in early adolescence (ages 11–13) than in late childhood (ages 8–10) or mid-adolescence (ages 14–16); and boys tend to show a decrease in heritability over time (e.g., Topolski et al., 1997). These results are in line with findings obtained with adults, although the extent to which genetic factors influence anxiety varies across anxiety disorders.

Research also has focused on the temperamental trait identified as "behavioral inhibition," the tendency to be unusually shy or to display fear and withdrawal in situations that are new or unfamiliar (Biederman, Rosenbaum, Chaloff, & Kagan, 1995). Researchers propose behavioral inhibition is a risk factor for developing anxiety disorders in children, yet little is known about sex differences in behavioral inhibition (Lonigan & Phillips, 2001). Some findings suggest girls have a slight propensity to present as behaviorally inhibited and to classify themselves more frequently as middle or high on behavioral inhibition compared to boys (Muris, Merckelbach, Wessel, & van de Ven, 1999). However, it is unclear whether behavioral inhibition poses a general risk for anxiety and/or a specific risk for girls.

Puberty

Research on biological processes demonstrates an interaction between gender and pubertal maturation in the development of anxiety symptoms and disorders. Several studies have demonstrated that early pubertal maturation in adolescent girls, not boys, may constitute a general risk factor for developing anxiety symptoms and disorders: girls who mature earlier than their peers exhibit higher rates of anxiety symptoms and disorders (e.g., Caspi & Moffitt, 1991).

Although little is known about the mechanisms by which early pubertal maturation in girls' increases the risk for anxiety, one possible explanation suggests that the early development of secondary sex characteristics (e.g., breasts) increases the risk of anxiety disturbance because it increases the likelihood that girls will confront new stressors from their peers and family before they are emotionally ready (e.g., Ge, Conger, & Elder, 1996). The assumption here is that early maturing girls faced with demanding biological and social transitions are less prepared to cope with these emotional changes and social challenges, thus making them vulnerable to develop anxiety. Research has not investigated whether the observed pubertal timing effects on anxiety in adolescent girls persist into adulthood.

Menstrual Cycle, Menopause, Pregnancy, and Postpartum Period

Research on neurotransmitter systems (e.g., locus ceruleus norepinephrine system) has provided some insights into potential biological factors that may contribute to the emergence of sex differences in anxiety disorders (Pigott, 1999). Findings suggest female gonadal hormones (estrogen, progesterone) may have a regulatory effect on the neurotransmitter systems thought to influence the production of internalizing symptoms, such as anxiety and reactions to stress (Hayward & Sanborn, 2002). Specifically, estrogen has been found to have a mood-elevating effect; whereas progesterone has been found to destabilize mood states (Pigott, 1999). Thus, the view here is that changes in estrogen and progesterone levels during the reproductive cycle and menopause may make women more vulnerable to develop anxiety.

Additionally, mild to moderate levels of anxiety have been reported over the course of pregnancy and the postpartum period; however, findings do not always coincide. There is some evidence that anxiety symptoms in expected mothers increase between the first and third trimester and decrease after birth (e.g., Shear & Oommen, 1995). Findings further demonstrate that pregnancy may be associated with the improvement of PD and that the postpartum period may be a risk for the onset and exacerbation of anxiety disorders (e.g., March & Yonkers, 2001). These findings support the notion that fluctuations in hormonal levels at different points across the life span may substantially influence the onset and course of anxiety in girls and women.

Cognitive Processes

Perceived Control and Attributional Styles

Research on perceived control and negative life events suggests girls and women with a higher sense of uncontrollability may exhibit more tendencies of learned helplessness than boys and men (e.g., Leadbeater, Blatt, & Quinlan, 1995). According to Chorpita and Barlow (1998), girls and boys who experience uncontrollable events early in life may eventually develop a propensity to perceive or process events as not being under their control. Thus, as development proceeds, individuals accumulate a history of uncontrollable experiences that influences subsequent experiences negatively across the life span. Little attention has been paid to the effects of gender on perceived uncontrollable experiences. There is some evidence, however, that girls who experience a high number of negative life events learn that their behaviors have either little or no impact on their environment. These girls are likely to develop pessimistic attributional styles (e.g., learned helplessness) (Barlow, 2003) and as such may place them at higher risk for anxiety disturbance.

Anxiety Sensitivity

Cumulative research findings have shown that anxiety sensitivity is a risk factor in the development of panic attacks and other anxiety problems (e.g., see Reiss, Silverman, & Weems, 2001). Although research is limited, there is evidence that women tend to score significantly higher on anxiety sensitivity measures than men (e.g., Stewart, Taylor, & Baker, 1997). That is, women more than men tend to believe that anxiety-related sensations, such as heart beat awareness, shortness of breath, increased heart rate, and trembling, have severe negative social, psychological, or physical consequences. This view is guided by Reiss's sensitivity theory (Reiss, 1999), which posits that these beliefs modify individuals' inherited sensitivity to anxiety. So much so that when these individuals become anxious, they worry about what is happening to their body and this worry increases their level of stress. However, it is not surprising that women tend to worry more about their anxiety symptoms, given they tend to report more fear and worry than men. Nonetheless, these elevated levels of anxiety sensitivity in women suggest potential heuristic value of studying gender differences in anxiety sensitivity.

Social Processes

Familial Factors

Family studies on anxiety suggest familial factors such as modeling of anxious behavior, over-protective child-rearing responses, and reinforcement of avoidant behavior are risk factors for anxiety (see Dadds & Roth, 2001). Gender differences with respect to these familial factors have not been analyzed in studies, however. Keenan and Shaw (1997) propose possible parental socialization practices that encourage girls to inhibit externalizing behaviors (e.g., aggression) during early childhood and, in its place, express internalizing symptoms (e.g., anxiety). Peers and teachers also participate in this socialization process by attending to and reinforcing aggressive behaviors in boys, but not girls. Support for Keenan and Shaw (1997) comes from studies that demonstrate parents are more likely to support shyness and passivity in girls than in boys (Lonigan & Phillips, 2001). Further research is needed to determine whether gender differential socialization persists throughout the life span and, if so, influence how women and men express their distress.

Additional evidence for a socialization perspective can be found in child and adult fear studies (e.g., Ginsburg & Silverman, 2000; Tucker & Bond, 1997). Findings often present a pattern consistent with gender-role orientation—that is, expressing emotions such as fear and anxiety is consistent with the feminine gender role and is inconsistent with the masculine gender role. The more assertive or instrumental traits children or adults endorse, the less likely they are to express distressing fears (e.g., Ginsburg & Silverman, 2000). This is true for both females and males, although females on average endorse fewer assertive and instrumental traits than males (Feingold, 1994). There is no way of knowing from the findings across these studies whether the gender differences in assertive and instrumental traits emerge at the same time or just before the gender differences in fear ratings. Such information might explain how being female or male could lead to gender differences in anxiety disturbance.

Summary

The biological, cognitive, and social factors discussed in this section have considerable relevance for understanding the emergence of gender differences in anxiety disturbance. The degree to which certain factors operate, or the manner in which they operate, to account for gender differences may vary, depending on the point in development at which the anxiety disturbance occurs. Some problems may be homotypic (i.e., the same) across long periods of development, whereas others are heterotypic (i.e., they undergo phenotypic changes from one developmental period to another) (Silverman & Ollendick, 1999). Of course, patterns of anxiety disturbance and its intensity also may vary systematically across situations, social contexts, and interaction partners, including teachers, parents, siblings, peers, and spouses. Thus, whether the emergence of gender differences in anxiety disturbance can be attributable to biological, cognitive, or social processes remains unclear.

PREVALENCE IN DIFFERENT ETHNIC GROUPS

There are no consistent empirical findings about the prevalence, intensity, or severity of fear, worry, and anxiety among girls and women of various ethnicities. There has been work examining the influence of ethnicity on fear ratings using youth from community and clinical samples; however, specific differences based on gender are either not reported or are inconclusive (e.g., Neal, Lilly, & Zakis, 1993; Silverman et al., 1995). Nonetheless, promising results using clinical samples warrant attention. Ginsburg and Silverman (1996) used a semistructured interview to assess prevalence, frequency, and intensity of children's worries and fears. Findings showed Hispanic/Latina girls worried more than Hispanic/Latino boys about school and performance situations; African American boys worried more than African American girls about performance situations. Another community study assessing worry in Native American children (D'Andrea, 1994) found girls reported more worries than boys, particularly moral and social worries. Boys and girls worried similarly however about personal well-being and peer relationships.

Eaton, Dryman, and Weissman (1991) reported that African American women and Hispanic/Latina women have higher rates of simple phobia (now called SP), AG, and SOP than African American men and Hispanic/Latino men; prevalence rates of other anxiety disorders are nonexistent. Similarly, prevalence rates of anxiety disorders in girls of color are lacking. The influence of ethnicity in the presentation and manifestation of anxiety disturbance needs to be considered in future research.

RECOVERY AND HEALTHY GROWTH

Prevention and Treatment

Despite the high prevalence of anxiety disturbance in girls and women, little efforts have been made to examine ways of preventing such disturbance. A range of intervention methods likely to be useful in preventing anxiety disturbance across the life span has been proposed by Spence (2001). These preventive methods attempt to target many of the cognitive (e.g., learned helplessness) and social processes (e.g., parenting style) discussed earlier, such as, coping skills training (i.e., teaching strategies to successfully handle stressful life events) and parenting skills training (i.e., reducing overprotective child-rearing responses).

Empirical studies provide evidence that cognitive behavior therapy, used in either individual or group treatment formats, is efficacious in reducing anxiety disorders (see Silverman & Berman, 2001). The evidence from these studies further suggests that the efficacy of cognitive and behavior treatment may be enhanced by involving parents (to work on managing their children's anxiety as well as the parents' own anxiety) and peers. In general, treatment outcome studies do not report gender differences based on treatment methods; however, there is one study that found treatment success varied by gender. Barrett, Dadds, and Rapee (1996) conducted a randomized clinical trial to investigate the effectiveness of cognitive-behavioral therapy (CBT) and family management training procedures with children diagnosed with an anxiety disorder. Findings indicated that girls responded significantly better than boys to the CBT + family treatment condition both at posttreatment and at the 12-month follow-up. However, given the small number of girls in each treatment condition, further research is needed before drawing firm conclusions.

CONCLUSIONS

Much remains to be discovered about the emergence of gender differences in anxiety disturbance. Throughout this chapter we have reviewed empirical evidence that highlights the importance of both clinicians and researchers to carefully consider sex and/or gender within a developmental (e.g., childhood, adolescence, adulthood) and social (e.g., family systems, school/workplace, social networks) context in efforts to understand anxiety disturbance. Although there is literature suggesting potential mechanisms that may account for gender differences, there is a paucity of empirical research studies that have examined these mechanisms. As a beginning step, studies using community and clinic-based samples are needed that compare gender differences within possible mechanisms leading to anxiety disturbance, as well as gender differences within specific risk or protective factors. Ethnic, cultural, and socioeconomic factors also need to be carefully considered in future research.

REFERENCES

American Psychiatric Association. (1994). *Diagnostic and statistical manual of mental disorders* (4th ed.). Washington, DC: Author.

American Psychiatric Association. (2000). *Diagnostic and statistical manual of mental disorders* (4th ed., text rev.). Washington, DC: Author

Barlow, D. H. (2003). *Anxiety and its disorders: The nature and treatment of anxiety and panic* (2nd ed.). New York: Guilford Press.

Barrett, P. M., Dadds, M. R., & Rapee, R. M. (1996). Family treatment of childhood anxiety: A controlled trial. *Journal of Consulting and Clinical Psychology, 64,* 333–342.

Beck, J. G., Stanley, M. A., & Zebb, B. J. (1996). Characteristics of generalized anxiety disorder in older adults: A descriptive study. *Behaviour Research and Therapy, 34,* 225–234.

Biederman, J., Rosenbaum, J. F., Chaloff, J., & Kagan, J. (1995). Behavioral inhibition as a risk factor for anxiety disorders. In J. S. March (Ed.), *Anxiety disorders in children and adolescents* (pp. 61–81). New York: Guilford Press.

Borkovec, T. D., Metzger, R. L., & Pruzinsky, T. (1986). Anxiety, worry, and the self. In L. Hartman & K. R. Blankstein (Eds.), *Perception of self in emotional disorders and psychotherapy* (pp. 219–260). New York: Plenum Press.

Caspi, A., & Moffitt, T. E. (1991). Individual differences as accentuated during periods of social changes:

The sample case of girls at puberty. *Journal of Personality and Social Psychology, 61,* 157–168.

Chorpita, B. F., & Barlow, D. H. (1998). The development of anxiety: The role of control in the early environment. *Psychological Bulletin, 124,* 3–21.

Cohen, P., Cohen, J., Kasen, S., & Velez, C. N. (1993). An epidemiological study of disorders in late childhood and adolescence: I. Age- and gender-specific prevalence. *Journal of Child Psychology and Psychiatry and Allied Disciplines, 34,* 851–867.

Dadds, M. R., & Roth, J. H. (2001). Family processes in the development of anxiety problems. In M. W. Vasey & M. R. Dadds (Eds.), *The developmental psychopathology of anxiety* (pp. 278–303). New York: Oxford University Press.

D'Andrea, M. (1994). The concerns of Native American youth. *Journal of Multicultural Counseling and Development, 22,* 173–181.

Eaton, W. W., Dryman, A., & Weissman, M. M. (1991). Panic and phobia. In L. N. Robins & D. A. Regier (Eds.), *Psychiatric disorders in America: The Epidemiological Catchment Area study* (pp. 328–366). New York: Free Press.

Eley, T. C. (2001). Contributions of behavioral genetics research: Quantifying genetic, shared environmental and nonshared environmental influences. In M. W. Vasey & M. R. Dadds (Eds.), *The developmental psychopathology of anxiety* (pp. 45–59). New York: Oxford University Press.

Feingold, A. (1994). Gender differences in personality: A meta-analysis. *Psychological Bulletin, 116,* 429–456.

Flint, A. J. (1994). Epidemiology and comorbidity of anxiety disorders in the elderly. *American Journal of Psychiatry, 151,* 640–649.

Ge, X., Conger, R., & Elder, G. (1996). Coming of age too early: pubertal influences on girls' vulnerability to psychological distress. *Child Development, 67,* 3386–3400.

Geer, J. H. (1965). The development of a scale to measure fear. *Behaviour Research Therapy, 3,* 45–53.

Ginsburg, G. S., & Silverman, W. K. (1996). Phobic and anxiety disorders in Hispanic and Caucasian youth. *Journal of Anxiety Disorders, 10,* 517–528.

Ginsburg, G. S., & Silverman, W. K. (2000). Gender role orientation and fearfulness in children with anxiety disorders. *Journal of Anxiety Disorders, 14,* 57–67.

Gullone, E. (2000). The development of normal fear: A century of research. *Clinical Psychology Review, 20,* 429–451.

Gullone, E., & King, N. J. (1992). Psychometric evaluation of a revised fear survey schedule for children and adolescents. *Journal of Child Psychology and Psychiatry, 33,* 987–998.

Hayward, C., & Sanborn, K. (2002). Puberty and the emergence of gender differences in psychopathology. *Journal of Adolescent Health, 30,* 49–58.

Kashani, J. H., & Orvaschel, H. (1990). A community study of anxiety in children and adolescents. *American Journal of Psychiatry, 147,* 313–318.

Keenan, K., & Shaw, D. (1997). Developmental and social influences on young girls' early problem behavior. *Psychological Bulletin, 121,* 95–113.

Kessler, R. C., McGonagle, K. A., Zhao, S., Nelson, C. B., Hughes, M., Eshleman, S., et al. (1994). Lifetime and 12-month prevalence of *DSM-III-R* psychiatric disorders in the United States. *Archives of General Psychiatry, 51,* 8–19.

Leadbeater, B. J., Blatt, S. J., & Quinlan, D. M. (1995). Gender-linked vulnerabilities to depressive symptoms, stress, and problem behaviors in adolescents. *Journal of Research on Adolescence, 5,* 1–29.

Lewinsohn, P. M., Hops, H., Roberts, R. E., Seeley, J. R., & Andrews, J. A. (1993). Adolescent psychopathology: I. Prevalence and incidence of depression and other *DSM-III-R* disorders in high school students. *Journal of Abnormal Psychology, 102,* 133–144.

Liddell, A., & Hart, D. (1992). Comparison between FSS-II scores of two groups of university students sampled 15 yr apart. *Behaviour Research and Theory, 30,* 125–131.

Liddell, A., Locker, D., & Burman, D. (1991). Self-reported fears (FSS-II) of subjects aged 50 years and over. *Behaviour Research and Theory, 29,* 105–112.

Lonigan, C. J., & Phillips, B. M. (2001). Temperamental influences on the development of anxiety disorders. In M. W. Vasey & M. R. Dadds (Eds.), *The developmental psychopathology of anxiety* (pp. 60–91). New York: Oxford University Press.

March, D., & Yonkers, K. A. (2001). Panic disorder. In K. Yonkers & B. Little (Eds.), *Management of psychiatric disorders in pregnancy* (pp. 134–148). New York: Oxford University Press.

Muris, P., Meesters, C., Merckelbach, H., Sermon, A., & Zwakhalen, S. (1998). Worry in normal children. *Journal of the American Academy of Child and Adolescent Psychiatry, 37,* 703–710.

Muris, P., Merckelbach, C., Wessel, I., & van de Ven, M. (1999). Psychopathological correlates of self-reported behavioural inhibition in normal children. *Behaviour Research and Therapy, 37,* 575–584.

Neal, A. M., Lilly, R. S., & Zakis, S. (1993). What are African American children afraid of? A preliminary study. *Journal of Anxiety Disorders, 7,* 129–139.

Ollendick, T. H. (1983). Reliability and validity of the revised Fear Survey Schedule for Children (FSSC-R). *Behaviour Research and Therapy, 21,* 395–399.

Pigott, T. A. (1999). Gender differences in the epidemiology and treatment of anxiety disorders. *Journal of Clinical Psychiatry, 60,* 4–15.

Puig-Antich, J., & Chambers, W. J. (1983). *Schedule for Affective Disorders and Schizophrenia for School-Age Children (K-SADS).* Pittsburgh, PA: Western Psychiatric Institute and Clinic.

Reiss, S. (1999). The sensitivity theory of aberrant motivation. In Steven Taylor (Ed.), *Anxiety sensitivity: Theory, research, and treatment of the fear of anxiety. The LEA series in personality and clinical psychology* (pp. 35–58). New York: Erlbaum.

Reiss, S., Silverman, W. K., & Weems, C. F. (2001). Anxiety sensitivity. In M. W. Vasey & M. R. Dadds (Eds.), *The developmental psychopathology of anxiety* (pp. 92–111). New York: Oxford University Press.

Robichaud, M., Dugas, M. J., & Conway, M. (2002). Gender differences in worry and associated cognitive-behavioral variables. *Journal of Anxiety Disorders, 17,* 501–516.

Rutter, M., Caspi, A., & Moffitt, T. E. (2003). Using sex differences in psychopathology to study causal mechanisms: Unifying issues and research strategies. *Journal of Child Psychology and Psychiatry, 44,* 1092–1115.

Shear, M. K., & Oommen, M. (1995). Anxiety disorders in pregnant and postpartum women. *Psychopharmacy Bulletin, 31,* 693–703.

Silverman, W. K., & Berman, S. L. (2001). Psychosocial interventions for anxiety disorders in children: Status and future directions. In W. K. Silverman & P. D. A. Treffers (Eds.), *Anxiety disorders in children and adolescents: Research, assessment and intervention* (pp. 313–334). New York: Cambridge University Press.

Silverman, W. K., La Greca, A. M., & Wasserstein, S. B. (1995). What do children worry about? Worries and their relation to anxiety. *Child Development, 66,* 671–686.

Silverman, W. K., & Ollendick, T. H. (Eds.). (1999). *Developmental issues in the clinical treatment of children.* Needham Heights, MA: Allyn & Bacon.

Spence, S. H. (2001). Prevention strategies. In M. W. Vasey & M. R. Dadds (Eds.), *The developmental psychopathology of anxiety* (pp. 325–351). New York: Oxford University Press.

Stewart, S. H., Taylor, S., & Baker, J. M. (1997). Gender differences in dimensions of anxiety sensitivity. *Journal of Anxiety Disorders, 11,* 179–200.

Topolski, T. D., Hewitt, J. K., Eaves, L. J., Silberg, J. L., Meyer, J. M., Rutter, M., et al. (1997). Genetic and environmental influences on child reports of manifest anxiety and symptoms of separation anxiety and overanxious disorders: A community-based twin study. *Behaviour Genetics, 22,* 15–26.

Treadwell, K. R. H., Flannery-Schroeder, E. C., & Kendall, P. C. (1995). Ethnicity and gender in relation to adaptive functioning, diagnostic status, and treatment outcome in children from an anxiety clinic. *Journal of Anxiety Disorders, 9,* 373–384.

Tucker, M., & Bond, N. W. (1997). The roles of gender, sex role, and disgust in fear of animals. *Personality and Individual Differences, 22,* 15–138.

Wolpe, J., & Lang, P. J. (1964). A fear survey schedule for use in behavior therapy. *Behavior Therapy and Experimental Psychiatry, 2,* 27–30.

LINDA SMOLAK

Body Image

Cellulite-reducing cream, milkshakes that lead to weight loss, and bathing suits that make you look thinner—all of these products capitalize on women's concerns about how their bodies look. Body dissatisfaction is a problem because it may lead to buying products that don't work and may even be harmful rather than using the money on things like education, political clout, or health care. More important, though, body dissatisfaction may result in dangerous weight-loss techniques, sometimes culminating in eating disorders (e.g., McKnight Investigators, 2003; Stice & Bearman, 2001; Wertheim, Koerner, & Paxton, 2001). Body dissatisfaction may also contribute to the development of depression, including the emergence of gender differences in depression during adolescence (Stice & Bearman, 2001; Wichstrom, 1999).

Body image is a complex construct and its definition and measurement have not been uniform or even consistent. First, body image can refer to general appearance or to body-shape concerns. Overall appearance satisfaction often does not differ by gender, particularly in childhood, but body-shape concerns, especially a focus on thinness, are more common among females. Second, body image can be assessed in perceptual, evaluative, or affective terms. Men and women differ in how they evaluate their weight. Overweight men are more likely than overweight women to think of themselves as normal weight while underweight women are more likely than underweight men to consider their weight to be normal (McCreary, 2002). Affective differences appear to be even larger, with women reporting more body dysphoria (Muth & Cash, 1997).

The focus of this chapter is on how girls and women feel about their body shape and weight, how they construct an image of their own bodies that is inferior to that of the cultural ideal, and how the body dissatisfaction associated with this discrepancy can be alleviated or even prevented. Body dissatisfaction is a serious problem not only because of the discomfort it causes in and of itself but also because of its relationship to eating disorders and obesity. These connections will also be explored in this chapter.

BODY IMAGE ACROSS THE LIFE SPAN

Even very young children understand that it is bad to be fat. By age 3, children have negative attitudes about fat people, with elementary schoolchildren ascribing various negative characteristics, such as laziness and unhappiness, to obese peers (Cramer & Steinwert, 1998; Tiggeman & Wilson-Barrett, 1998). Even preschoolers apply such negative stereotyping more harshly to women than to men (Turnbull, Heaslip, & McLeod, 2000). Even elementary-school-aged girls are expected to be thin, or at least not be fat. Comparable pressure on boys to achieve the muscular body ideal is not likely to begin until puberty. Thus, not only is appearance more important for adult women than for men, the pressure to meet the cultural ideal begins earlier for girls than for boys.

Not surprisingly, then, even preadolescent girls report that they are dissatisfied with their weight and want to avoid being or becoming fat (e.g., Davison, Markey, & Birch, 2003; Field et al., 1999). By age 9 or 10, approximately 40% of girls express concerns about their weight. African American girls are somewhat less worried about being fat than other girls are. However, girls are more concerned about this than boys are in all American ethnic groups that have been studied (Smolak & Levine, 2001).

While cross-sectional research suggests that body esteem decreases in girls throughout early elementary school (e.g., Gardner, Sorter, & Friedman, 1997), a recent longitudinal study found increases in body esteem from age 5 to 9 (Davison et al., 2003). The authors call for caution in interpreting these longitudinal trends, however, because of possible problems with the younger girls' understanding of the questionnaire. It is noteworthy, though, that girls in this study tended to maintain their relative ranks in terms of body esteem. This suggests that there may be a group of girls who are already on the path to body esteem and eating problems by early elementary school. This conclusion is bolstered by Davison et al.'s (2003) finding that average body dissatisfaction at ages 5 and 7 predicted dietary restraint at age 9. However, Smolak and Levine (2001), using a smaller sample, found no relationship between body esteem in first through third graders and eating problems measured two years later. They did report a relationship between body image in the fourth or fifth grade and body esteem and eating problems in middle school. The relationship of body esteem in early elementary school to later body esteem and eating problems is an important area for future research.

Girls' body esteem drops in middle school. This is concurrently related to the onset of puberty, which moves girls away from the culturally proscribed body ideal of thinness. While body esteem makes some recovery during the high school years, it continues to be lower for girls than for boys. About 60% of adolescent girls are dissatisfied with their weight and shape (e.g., Field et al., 1999). In addition, some form of disordered eating may occur in more than half of adolescent girls, though the most severe forms, such as vomiting after eating or laxative abuse, occur in less than 10% (Croll, Neumark-Sztainer, Story, & Ireland, 2002). Furthermore, women's body dissatisfaction does not seem to disappear with development (Tiggeman & Lynch, 2001).

Most women exhibiting body dissatisfaction do not, and will not, suffer from eating disorders. Anorexia nervosa (AN) and bulimia nervosa (BN) combined probably affect 5% or fewer of the postpubertal females in the United States. Even if women who are suffering but do not meet all of the *Diagnostic and Statistical Manual of Mental Disorders* (*DSM-IV-TR*) criteria are included, the total is probably 10–15% (Herzog & Delinski, 2001).

Nonetheless, body dissatisfaction is a risk factor for eating disorders and cosmetic surgery, both of which can be fatal. Body dissatisfaction certainly interferes with healthy eating. For example, concerns with being overweight can lead to calorie-restrictive dieting, which can lead to binge-eating and lowered metabolism, which may result in obesity (Field et al., 2003; Stice, Cameron, Killen, Hayward, & Taylor, 1999). Dieting is particularly dangerous in girls whose bones are still forming. Finally, body dissatisfaction may restrict the activities, such as swimming, that individual women will engage in, again contributing to obesity.

RISK FACTORS

Girls worry about their body shapes from a very early age, perhaps even earlier than we can currently effectively measure. Given this, it is difficult to separate risk factors into categories of those that *cause* body image problems versus those that *maintain* or *intensify* body image concerns in individuals. This problem is exacerbated by the fact that most of our research is done with White, middle-class adolescents and adults.

Body image problems are rooted in sociocultural factors. In reviews of body esteem, authors will sometimes list BMI (body mass index, a ratio of weight to height) or pubertal timing as "biological" risk factors. This is something of a misnomer. There is currently no evidence that biological factors, such as hormonal levels, that might accompany either obesity or pubertal timing are involved in body dissatisfaction. For example, BMI is a risk factor because of the social construction of obesity. Americans tend to associate fatness with negative characteristics, including unattractiveness. That this is a social construction is evident by the differing definitions of which body type is attractive across cultures and history (Brumberg, 1997; Smolak & Striegel-Moore, 2001).

Risk for body image problems is in rooted in three cultural messages: (a) women must be attractive to be successful in their work lives or in relationships; (b) women must be thin to be attractive; and (c) any woman can become thin, and hence attractive, if she tries hard enough. Women who reject these messages are not particularly likely to become very dissatisfied with their weight or shape. Indeed, women may need to *internalize* these cultural messages, adopting them as part of their own definition of self, in order to develop body esteem problems (Thompson & Stice, 2001).

Sources of the Messages

Girls, and women, receive messages about their bodies and how they should look from multiple sources. Girls seem to receive more consistent body ideal messages from a wider range of sources than boys do (e.g., Smolak & Levine, 2001). Research on risk factors for body dissatisfaction has focused on three sources: peers, family, and media.

Peers

Peer influence can take many forms. It can be "indirect" in that peers may model body image concerns and weight control behaviors. It can be direct in that peers may make comments to or even tease girls about their body shapes. Or it can be some combination of the two as girls engage in conversations with their friends about their own or others' bodies. Such conversations may intensify social comparison, a characteristic that may, in turn, mediate the relationship between sociocultural influences and body dissatisfaction (Shroff & Thompson, 2003).

Cross-sectional data suggest that even among elementary school girls peer teasing and modeling of weight and shape concerns are related to body dissatisfaction and concerns about weight and shape (Vander Wal & Thelen, 2000). Longitudinal studies of adolescent girls confirm such relationships. For example, Wertheim et al. (2001) found that weight-related teasing of eighth and tenth graders predicted body dissatisfaction and bulimic behaviors eight months later. The McKnight Investigators (2003) found that peer teasing about weight and peer concerns with thinness during middle school contributed to the onset of eating disorders symptoms during a three-year period.

Family Influences

The research on family influences on body image and eating problems has followed two general paths. Some researchers have examined the effects of family structure and functioning (e.g., conflict, enmeshment). Others have focused on the body and eating messages sent by family members, particularly by parents. The latter has proved to be a much more fruitful approach.

Cross-sectional research has found correlations between parental comments about a daughter's weight and shape and the girl's body dissatisfaction in children as young as elementary school (e.g., Smolak, Levine, & Schermer, 1999; Thelen & Cormier, 1995). Researchers have also found relationships between mothers' concerns about their own weight and shape and their daughters' body dissatisfaction, even when the daughters are adults (Tiggeman & Lynch, 2001). However, this relationship tends to be less consistently documented than the ones between direct parental comments or peer influences and body esteem (Smolak et al., 1999). These findings about parental influence underscore the importance of involving parents in prevention efforts.

Mass Media

Girls watch television and read fashion magazines. In one study, 49% of late elementary school, 60% of junior high, and 62% of high school girls read fashion magazines at least two to five times every month. (Field et al., 1999). Adolescent girls in another study watched television more than 21 hours per week, with about one third of these being "body image" shows, designated by the researchers as featuring the "ideal" body images for men and women (Hofschire & Greenberg, 2002).

Sheer exposure to thin women on television and in magazines is not enough to create body image problems, though it is not unrelated. Instead, personal characteristics are typically found to mediate this relationship. These may be identification with media celebrities (Hofschire & Greenberg, 2002), thin ideal internalization or social comparison (Shroff & Thompson, 2003), or an interest in using the magazines or television to gain information about body shape and appearance (Taylor et al., 1998).

Researchers have considered media influences to consist of at least awareness of the media presented thin ideal and internalization of it. Murnen, Smolak, Mills, and Good (2003) found that first through fifth grade children were aware of the media images. Girls who were more aware of the media images were also more likely to want to look like exemplars of the thin ideal (photos of famous women) and to think it was important to look that way. These responses to the images were also related to body esteem. This was not true of boys.

Thin-ideal internalization—that is, actively wanting to look like the women on television and in the movies—appears to be a particularly powerful factor in the development of body dissatisfaction. Both longitudinal and experimental research has demonstrated this relationship in adolescent girls and college-aged women (Thompson & Stice, 2001). Murnen and colleagues (2003) reported a substantial significant correlation (r (86) = −.61) between body esteem and internalization in elementary school girls.

Convergence and Synergy

It is important to reiterate that girls who are exposed to multiple sources of messages emphasizing a thin ideal seem to be especially likely to develop body image and eating problems. For example, the McKnight Investigators (2003) reported that a factor that included media modeling, peer concerns about thinness, and peer teasing about weight predicted the onset of clinically significant eating problems during adolescence.

PROTECTIVE FACTORS

Research on factors that protect against the development of body image problems is quite limited. In general, it appears that factors that give girls a non-appearance-related source of self-esteem or turn girls away from focusing on the thin-ideal may be protective. For example, participation in nonelite team sports (e.g., basketball) by high school girls has been associated with better body image (Smolak, Murnen, & Ruble, 2000). Relatedly, Geller, Zaitsoff, and Srikameswaran (2002) found that academic competencies as well as competencies related to areas other than academics (which included sports) were correlated with higher body esteem.

Murnen and colleagues (2003) reported that elementary school girls who actively rejected the media ideal for thin women showed lower internalization of the thin-ideal and better body esteem in comparison to girls who were uncertain about whether or not they liked the image. Similarly, Harrison (2000) found that first to third grade girls who are attracted to average-size female television characters rate thinness and good looks as less important than girls who do not find these average size women attractive.

These potential protective factors have not been tested in prospective or experimental designs so their role is far from clear. This is an important area for future research. Protective factors might be incorporated into prevention and intervention programs. In addition to being potentially helpful in establishing a more positive self-image, this may be a way to test the nature and extent of the relationships.

DYNAMICS OF BODY DISSATISFACTION DEVELOPMENT

Sociocultural influences clearly contribute to the development and maintenance of body image and eating problems. One could use a social learning theory explanation of these developments. Indeed, some prevention programs have relied on this theoretical perspective (Levine & Smolak, in press). Unfortunately, social learning theory ignores the gendered nature of body dissatisfaction. Gender schema theory (Bem, 1993) might also be applicable. However, little body image research has been done from this perspective and, more important, research using the Bem Sex Role Inventory shows small and inconsistent relationships between masculinity, femininity, and body image (Murnen & Smolak, 1998).

Yet gender is clearly a factor in body image and eating problems. Roughly 85–90% of AN and BN victims are female. Even in childhood, girls are four to five times more likely than boys to develop AN (Bryant-Waugh & Lask, 2002). Although boys and men are more likely to want to be muscular than girls and women are, girls and women are more likely to be dissatisfied with their weight and shape and to engage in weight reduction, even when BMI is considered (McCreary, 2002; Smolak & Levine, 2001). When body image researchers consider gender, however, they tend to treat it as a "fixed variable" (Kraemer et al., 1997), one that can not be altered. But gender is really a summary variable, one that captures a variety of experiences under one broad rubric. It is important, then, to consider what those experiences might be, how the "lived experiences" of being female shape girls' and women's construction of their bodies. Objectification theory (Fredrickson & Roberts, 1997) provides a framework for doing this to account for gender effects.

Objectification Theory

Principles

Objectification theory (Fredrickson & Roberts, 1997) begins with the argument that male and female bodies have different meanings in American culture. Men's bodies are seen as agentic and functional; women's are objects to be viewed and enjoyed. Specifically, women's bodies are supposed to be available for men's sexual pleasure. This message is so pervasive that it is evident to elementary school girls (Murnen & Smolak, 2000). Women's success in work and relationships, and even their safety and survival, is related to understanding and cooperating with this role.

This objectification of women is part of the primary role available to women in our culture. The most visible, and often the wealthiest, women are thin models and actresses. Women make less money than men in virtually every profession. Women are less visible at the highest level of American politics. Even in sports, where women have made real gains, participation carries less status and pay than it does for men.

The pervasiveness of the image and the social pressure to accept it lead women to internalize this objectification, to treat themselves as something to be looked at and evaluated. This internalization of the gaze of others leads to habitual self-monitoring to ensure that one is meeting the image (Fredrickson & Roberts, 1997). Such self-monitoring probably includes social comparison. Self-monitoring leads, in turn, to body shame and appearance anxiety, resulting in poor body esteem and eating problems.

Empirical Support

Cross-sectional research supports this theory in adolescents and adults (Slater & Tiggeman, 2002; Tiggeman & Lynch, 2001). Furthermore, experimental research, in which self-consciousness and hence self-monitoring were manipulated, also supports objectification theory (Fredrickson, Roberts, Noll, Quinn, & Twenge, 1998). In this experimental study, men and women tried on bathing suits and sweaters and then worked on math problems, supposedly while others were watching. Only women showed increased self-monitoring and body shame in the bathing suit condition.

Internalization of objectification might also be marked by self-silencing. Women who view themselves as objects rather than actors are likely to be unaware of their psychological states and so put their own interests and needs behind those of others. This is self-silencing. Research suggests that self-silencing and eating problems are positively correlated (Smolak & Munsterteiger, 2002). Furthermore, elementary school girls who are unsure how they feel about sexual harassment or media images of women have poorer body esteem (Murnen & Smolak, 2000; Murnen et al., 2003). This might be interpreted as a developing link between self-silencing and body esteem or eating problems.

Sexual Terrorism

Sometimes these messages of self-silencing and objectification are subtle, as when fat women television characters are the ones who are most frequently the target of jokes and teasing (Harrison, 2000). Other times the message that the female body is for the pleasure of males is stronger. Sheffield (1995) has argued that rape is one way that men enforce their active dominance over women. Furthermore, she suggests that there is a continuum of sexual terrorism ranging from sexual harassment to domestic violence and rape. Sexual harassment serves to remind women what could happen to them. Rape or domestic violence against one woman reminds every woman of what can happen. Sheffield terms this "terrorism" because sexual harassment and rape can happen to any woman at any time quite independently of her behavior.

Girls are much more likely to be frightened by sexual harassment than boys are (Murnen & Smolak, 2000). This is consistent with Sheffield's (1995) argument about the societal function of sexual harassment. Furthermore, girls who are frightened by sexual harassment have poorer body esteem (Murnen & Smolak, 2000). Dating violence, child sexual abuse, and rape have been associated with eating problems (Silverman, Raj, Mucci, & Hathaway, 2001; Thompson et al., 2003).

This evidence concerning sexual harassment, abuse, and rape is not conclusive. In fact, it is not likely to ever be conclusive under the increasingly demanded standard (Kraemer et al., 1997) that only experimental research can identify causal factors. Nonetheless, these are potentially important factors in understanding why body image is so heavily gendered. Future research must include these variables.

PREVENTION OF BODY IMAGE PROBLEMS

The prevention of eating disorders has become a hot area of research over the past two decades (Levine & Smolak, in press). These programs typically include a body image component; indeed, body image is sometimes the main focus of the programs. The programs usually focus on changing the individual—for example, improving body esteem by fostering a rejection of media images (Levine & Smolak, in press). Not surprisingly, such approaches have been most effective in studies where the participants are (a) sufficiently dissatisfied with their bodies to show a statistically significant improvement; and (b) cognitively mature enough to evaluate and modify their cognitive processing. Thus, to date, targeted prevention (also known as secondary prevention) with adolescents and adults has been more effective than universal prevention with children.

It is premature to suggest that we should focus only on targeted prevention. As this review has documented, the problem for body image concerns is in the ecological context in which girls and women develop and function. Females do not seem to start out with any sort of temperamental, genetic, hormonal, or neurological predispositions to judge their bodies as too fat. Instead, they receive constant and consistent messages from many sources teaching them this. Perhaps it is the environment that needs to change. Indeed, when Piran (1999) worked with an elite ballet school to change its ecology, there was a dramatic decline in the frequency of eating disorders among the students. This was an uncontrolled study so it is not definitive. Unlike most other studies, however, it did continue long enough (10 years) to actually demonstrate a prevention (as opposed to an intervention) effect. More important, it suggests that changing the ecology—the messages that girls receive from teachers and peers as well as teachers' modeling of the unacceptability of harmful behavior and comments—can help prevent girls' body image and eating problems. In addition, therapists might consider helping clients to initiate changes at school or work. Therapists might even take the initiative to work toward systemic or institutional change themselves, as part of the effort to treat eating disorders.

It will be challenging to design programs that change the developmental ecology (Levine & Smolak, in press). Evaluations of the context will be required, for example, and the program will need to be tailored to the community. This is quite different from the expert-oriented, top-down approach currently favored in prevention programs. Furthermore, the studies will have to go on long enough to actually demonstrate that the onset of dangerously poor body esteem has been prevented. Another challenge will be identifying appropriate control groups.

Despite these challenges, long-term social change is the best hope for decreasing the rate of body image problems among girls and women. Media messages, tolerance of sexual harassment, and the expectation that girls will discuss dieting over lunch all can be changed. The bonus here is that we may find that such ecological approaches reduce eating problems, including eating disorders and obesity.

REFERENCES

Bem, S. (1993). *The lenses of gender: Transforming the debate on sexual inequality.* New Haven, CT: Yale University Press.

Brumberg, J. (1997). *The body project: An intimate history of American girls.* New York: Random House.

Bryant-Waugh, R., & Lask, B. (2002). Childhood-onset eating disorders. In C. Fairburn & K. Brownell (Eds.), *Eating disorders and obesity: A comprehensive handbook* (2nd ed., pp. 210–214). New York: Guilford Press.

Cramer, P., & Steinwert, T. (1998). Thin is good, fat is bad: How early does it begin? *Journal of Applied Developmental Psychology, 19,* 429–451.

Croll, J., Neumark-Sztainer, D., Story, M., & Ireland, M. (2002). Prevalence and risk and protective factors related to disordered eating behaviors among adolescents: Relationship to gender and ethnicity. *Journal of Adolescent Health, 31,* 166–175.

Davison, K., Markey, C., & Birch, L. (2003). A longitudinal examination of patterns in girls' weight concerns and body dissatisfaction from ages 5 to 9 years. *International Journal of Eating Disorders, 33,* 320–332.

Field, A., Austin, S. B., Taylor, C. B., Malspeis, S., Rosner, B., Rockett, H., et al. (2003). Relation between dieting and weight change among preadolescents and adolescents. *Pediatrics, 112,* 900–906.

Field, A., Camargo, C., Taylor, C., Berkey, C., Frazier, L., Gillman, M., et al. (1999). Overweight, weight concerns, and bulimic behaviors among girls and boys. *Journal of the American Academy of Child and Adolescent Psychiatry, 38,* 754–760.

Fredrickson, B., & Roberts, T. (1997). Objectification theory: Toward understanding women's lived experiences and mental health. *Psychology of Women Quarterly, 21,* 173–206.

Fredrickson, B., Roberts, T., Noll, S., Quinn, D., & Twenge, J. (1998). That swimsuit becomes you: Sex differences in self-objectification, restrained eating, and math performance. *Journal of Personality and Social Psychology, 75,* 269–284.

Gardner, R., Sorter, R., & Friedman, B. (1997). Developmental changes in children's body images. *Journal of Social Behavior and Personality, 12,* 1019–1036.

Geller, J., Zaitsoff, S., & Srikameswaran, S. (2002). Beyond shape and weight: Exploring the relationship between nonbody determinants of self-esteem and eating disorder symptoms in adolescent females. *International Journal of Eating Disorders, 32,* 344–351.

Harrison, K. (2000). Television viewing, fat stereotyping, body shape standards, and eating disorder symptomatology in grade school children. *Communications Research, 27,* 617–640.

Herzog, D., & Delinski, S. (2001). Classification of eating disorders. In R. Striegel-Moore & L. Smolak (Eds.), *Eating disorders: Innovative directions in research and practice* (pp. 31–50). Washington, DC: American Psychological Association.

Hofschire, L., & Greenberg, L. (2002). Media's impact on adolescents' body dissatisfaction. In J. Brown, J. Steele, & K. Walsh-Childers (Eds.), *Sexual teen, sexual media: Investigating media's influence on adolescent sexuality* (pp. 125–149). Mahwah, NJ: Erlbaum.

Kraemer, H., Kazdin, A., Offord, D., Kessler, R., Jensen, P., & Kupfer, D. (1997). Coming to terms with the terms of risk. *Archives of General Psychiatry, 54,* 337–343.

Levine, M. P., & Smolak, L. (in press). *The prevention of eating problems and eating disorders: Theory, research, and practice.* Mahwah, NJ: Erlbaum.

McCreary, D. (2002). Gender and age differences in the relationship between body mass index and perceived weight: Exploring the paradox. *International Journal of Men's Health, 1,* 31–42.

McKnight Investigators. (2003). Risk factors for the onset of eating disorders in adolescent girls: Results of the McKnight Longitudinal Risk Factor Study. *American Journal of Psychiatry, 160,* 248–254.

Murnen, S. K., & Smolak, L. (1998). Femininity, masculinity, and disordered eating: A meta-analytic approach. *International Journal of Eating Disorders, 22,* 231–242.

Murnen, S. K., & Smolak, L. (2000). The experience of sexual harassment among grade-school students: Early socialization of female subordination? *Sex Roles, 43,* 1–17.

Murnen, S. K., Smolak, L., Mills, J. A., & Good, L. (2003). Thin, sexy women and strong, muscular men:

Grade-school children's responses to objectified images of women and men. *Sex Roles, 49,* 427–437.

Muth, J., & Cash, T. (1997). Body-image attitudes: What difference does gender make? *Journal of Applied Social Psychology, 27,* 1438–1452.

Piran, N. (1999). Eating disorders: A trial of prevention in a high risk school setting. *Journal of Primary Prevention, 20,* 75–90.

Sheffield, C. (1995). Sexual terrorism. In J. Freeman (Ed.), *Women: A feminist perspective* (pp. 1–21). Mountain View, CA: Mayfield.

Shroff, H., & Thompson, J. K. (2003). *Direct and mediational influences on body image and eating disturbances: A test of the tripartite influence model.* Unpublished manuscript.

Silverman, J., Raj, A., Mucci, L., & Hathaway, J. (2001). Dating violence against adolescent girls and associated substance use, unhealthy weight control, sexual risk behavior, pregnancy, and suicidality. *Journal of the American Medical Association, 286,* 572–579.

Slater, A., & Tiggeman, M. (2002). A test of objectification theory in adolescent girls. *Sex Roles, 46,* 343–349.

Smolak, L., & Levine, M. P. (2001). Body image in children. In J. K. Thompson & L. Smolak (Eds.), *Body image, eating disorder, and obesity in youth* (pp. 41–66). Washington, DC: American Psychological Association.

Smolak, L., Levine, M. P., & Schermer, F. (1999). Parental input and weight concerns among elementary school children. *International Journal of Eating Disorders, 25,* 263–271.

Smolak, L., & Munsterteiger, B. (2002). The relationship of gender and voice to depression and eating disorders. *Psychology of Women Quarterly, 26,* 234–241.

Smolak, L., Murnen, S. K., & Ruble, A. (2000). Female athletes and eating problems: A meta-analytic approach. *International Journal of Eating Disorders, 27,* 371–380.

Smolak, L., & Striegel-Moore, R. (2001). Challenging the myth of the golden girl: Ethnicity and eating disorders. In R. Striegel-Moore & L. Smolak (Eds.), *Eating disorders: New directions for research and practice.* Washington, DC: American Psychological Association.

Stice, E., & Bearman, S. (2001). Body-image and eating disturbances prospectively predict increases in depressive symptoms in adolescent girls: A growth curve analysis. *Developmental Psychology, 37,* 597–607.

Stice, E., Cameron, R., Killen, J., Hayward, C., & Taylor, C. (1999). Naturalistic weight-reduction efforts prospectively predict growth in relative weight and onset of obesity among female adolescents. *Journal of Consulting and Clinical Psychology, 67,* 967–974.

Taylor, C. B., Sharpe, T., Shisslak, C., Bryson, S., Estes, L., Gray, N., et al. (1998). Factors associated with weight concerns in adolescent girls. *International Journal of Eating Disorders, 24,* 31–42.

Thelen, M., & Cormier, J. (1995). Desire to be thinner and weight control among children and their parents. *Behavior Therapy, 26,* 85–99.

Thompson, J. K., & Stice, E. (2001). Thin-ideal internalization: Mounting evidence for a new risk factor for body-image disturbance and eating pathology. *Current Directions in Psychological Science, 10,* 181–183.

Thompson, K., Crosby, R., Wonderlich, S., Mitchell, J., Redlin, J., Demuth, G., et al. (2003). Psychopathology and sexual trauma in childhood and adulthood. *Journal of Traumatic Stress, 16,* 335–338.

Tiggeman, M., & Lynch, J. (2001). Body image across the life span in adult women: The role of self-objectification. *Developmental Psychology, 37,* 243–253.

Tiggeman, M., & Wilson-Barrett, E. (1998). Children's figure ratings: Relationship to self-esteem and negative stereotyping. *International Journal of Eating Disorders, 23,* 83–88.

Turnbull, J. D., Heaslip, S., & McLeod, H. A. (2000). Pre-school children's attitudes to fat and normal male and female stimulus figures. *International Journal of Obesity, 24,* 1705–1706.

Vander Wal, J., & Thelen, M. (2000). Predictors of body image dissatisfaction in elementary-age school girls. *Eating Behaviors, 1,* 105–122.

Wertheim, E., Koerner, J., & Paxton, S. (2001). Longitudinal predictors of restrictive eating and bulimic tendencies in three different age groups of adolescent girls. *Journal of Youth and Adolescence, 30,* 69–81.

Wichstrom, L. (1999). The emergence of gender differences in depressed mood during adolescence: The role of intensified gender socialization. *Developmental Psychology, 35,* 232–245.

This chapter is concerned with the most severe and persistent mental disorders among children, adolescents, and adults. The initial focus is on the disorders themselves. Concerns of females with mental illness are then discussed, including differential diagnosis and associated characteristics, specific issues among women, victimization, mothers with mental illness, and caregiving burden. Finally, some conclusions and recommendations are offered.

THE SCOPE OF THE PROBLEM

The President's New Freedom Commission on Mental Health (2002) reported that approximately 5–9% of children and adolescents in the United States have a serious emotional disturbance (SED) that significantly undermines their daily functioning in home, school, or community. The SED term encompasses certain diagnostic categories, including autism spectrum disorder, attention-deficit/hyperactivity disorder, obsessive-compulsive disorder, other severe anxiety disorders, major depressive disorder, bipolar disorder, and schizophrenia.

The commission also reported that, in a given year, about 5–7% of adults have a serious mental illness (SMI). The SMI term has traditionally been defined in terms of diagnosis, duration, and disability. Specifically, the term refers to mental disorders that carry certain diagnoses, such as schizophrenia, bipolar disorder, and major depression; that are relatively persistent; and that result in comparatively severe impairment in major areas of functioning, such as vocational capacity or social relationships. Reflecting the overlap between the SED and SMI diagnoses, *early-onset mental illness* is sometimes used when the SMI disorders occur in young people. In this chapter, the term mental illness is used to encompass severe and persistent mental disorders across the life span, unless the discussion focuses on specific age groups.

From the perspective of clinical practice, individuals with mental illness represent a large and underserved population. The prevalence figures noted previously translate into millions of children, adolescents, and adults whose mental disorders compromise their present lives and

DIANE T. MARSH

Serious Emotional Disturbance and Serious Mental Illness

imperil their future. Mental illness is the number one cause of disability in the United States (President's New Freedom Commission on Mental Health, 2002). Yet national surveys indicate that one of out every two people who need mental health treatment does not receive *any* treatment at all, and many others are poorly served (U.S. Department of Health and Human Services [USDHHS], 1999).

The lack of satisfactory—or indeed, any— treatment has devastating consequences for individuals, for their overwhelmed families, and for a society that is deprived of their gifts. Adults with SMI have a death rate from suicide and other causes of death that is significantly higher than the rate of the general population (Caldwell & Gottesman, 1990). Moreover, as many people with mental illness reside in jails and prisons as in all of our hospitals, and at least one third of the homeless are estimated to have a mental illness (Torrey, 2001).

Some high-risk segments of this population suffer a disproportionately heavy burden from mental illness. For instance, recent research findings indicate that lesbian, gay, and bisexual adults experience higher levels of morbidity, distress, and treatment use than heterosexuals; that gay and lesbian youth are more likely than heterosexual youth to attempt suicide; and that discrimination may exacerbate the mental health problems of sexual minorities (DeAngelis, 2002). Ethnic minorities, another high-risk group, have less access to mental health services and often receive a poorer quality of mental health care (USDHHS, 2001).

RECOVERY AND RESILIENCE

In fact, effective psychosocial and psychopharmacological interventions are now available for the full range of mental disorders among children, adolescents, and adults (Mueser, Bond, & Drake, 2001; Ringeisen & Hoagwood, 2002). Once thought impossible, recovery from mental illness has been documented consistently in long-term studies (e.g., Harding, Zubin, & Strauss, 1992). For example, at least one half of those who are diagnosed with schizophrenia can be expected to achieve recovery or significant improvement

(Torrey, 2001). Recovery is also manifested in the productive lives of an increasing number of recovered and recovering people who are open about their experience (e.g., Jamison, 1995).

These positive outcomes attest to the remarkable strengths demonstrated by individuals and families when confronted with mental illness. Marshaling their own powers of recuperation and renewal, they rebound from adversity, weather their crises, prevail over difficult life events, and recapture their vitality and joy. In the midst of their suffering and despair, they learn to take charge of their lives and go on to live fully and love well. Namely, they demonstrate a resilient response to the catastrophic stressor of mental illness.

The vulnerability-stress model provides a useful way of understanding these positive outcomes. The model assumes that the illness involves a vulnerability—or biological predisposition—to develop certain symptoms, and that a range of biological and psychosocial factors can interact with this vulnerability to affect the course of the illness. In fact, there is now substantial evidence that severe and persistent mental disorders are associated with alterations in brain activity, chemistry, and structure (Andreasen, 2001). Depending on the disorder, these neurobiological abnormalities may result in a range of symptoms, such as hallucinations and delusions, and of limitations, such as unusual vulnerability to stress or deficiencies in cognitive and social functioning.

A variety of risk and protective factors can interact with this biologically based vulnerability to affect the course of mental illness. Risk factors, which increase the likelihood that symptoms will worsen and that a relapse will occur, include medication nonadherence, excessive stress, interpersonal conflict, an unhealthy lifestyle, medical problems, and substance abuse (Torrey, 2001). Some risk factors are gender-related, such as the hormonal upheavals that accompany pregnancy. Postpartum mood episodes with psychotic features appear to occur in from 1 in 500 to 1 in 1,000 deliveries (American Psychiatric Association, 2000). Protective factors, which can reduce symptoms of the illness and make relapse less likely, include effective coping skills, family and social support, and medication.

Thus, the professional challenge is to assist individuals and families to maximize their resilience under calamitous circumstances, to manage their risk and protective factors, and to access effective services.

GENDER AND SERIOUS MENTAL ILLNESS

Perhaps it should come as no surprise that adults with SMI are regarded as almost genderless (Mowbray, Oyserman, Lutz, & Purnell, 1997). In fact, along with other disability groups, they are commonly defined in terms of their disability, with little attention to their other qualities, a stance that is both dehumanizing and gender-blind. Stripped of their dignity and humanity— as well as their gender—these individuals often struggle to forge a sense of identity separate from that of "mental patient."

This neglect of gender has a number of adverse consequences for women. As Mowbray (2003) has discussed, the gendered nature of mental health services has been well documented. Traditional mental health services have actually been largely male-oriented. As a result, services may ignore not only the special needs and interests of women, but may also assume a biased and unhealthy view of women's functioning, fail to incorporate a strengths-based approach, and ignore the larger context of individual lives. As she points out, these issues are very problematic for women with mental illness. Like other women, they are more affected than men by the demands and needs of others and put more emphasis on their relational environment. Yet services are unlikely to focus on their lives as wives, mothers, or family members. Moreover, because of their history of mental illness, these women are less able to operate in a mode of agency or autonomy, and their strengths are often overlooked.

Important gender differences exist in numerous domains of life functioning that are central to women's lives and psychological well-being (Cogan, 1998). Topics discussed in this section include differential diagnosis and associated characteristics, specific issues of women, victimization, mothers with mental illness, and caregiving burden. Reflecting the available literature, this discussion focuses largely on adult women with SMI; the gender-related needs of girls with SED have received almost no attention.

Differential Diagnosis and Associated Characteristics

As reported in the current edition of the *Diagnostic and Statistical Manual of Mental Disorders* (*DSM-IV-TR;* American Psychiatric Association, 2000), gender differences exist for some of the SED and SMI disorders. Autistic disorder and ADHD occur significantly more frequently in males than in females. Childhood-onset OCD is more common in boys than girls, although the disorder is equally prevalent in adults. Major depressive disorder occurs twice as frequently in adolescent and adult females as in males, although prepubertal girls and boys are equally affected. Bipolar I disorder, which is characterized by one or more manic episodes, appears to be equally common in women and men. In contrast, bipolar II disorder, which is distinguished by one or more major depressive episodes accompanied by at least one hypomanic episode, may be more prevalent in women.

A slightly higher incidence of schizophrenia has been observed in men than in women. More important is the evidence that this disorder is expressed differently in females and males. As indicated in *DSM-IV-TR*, the modal age at onset for men is between 18 and 25 years, and for women is between age 25 and the mid-30s. The distribution is unimodal among men but bimodal among women, with a second peak occurring later in life. Women typically express more affective symptomatology, paranoid delusions, and hallucinations; men tend to express more negative symptoms, such as flat affect, avolition, and social withdrawal. Some of these differences mirror social stereotypes that assume emotions are more likely to be expressed by women and suppressed by men.

According to *DSM-IV-TR*, women have better premorbid functioning than men and a better prognosis, as defined by number of rehospitalizations and lengths of hospital stay, overall duration of illness, time to relapse, response to medication, and social and work functioning. This female advantage appears to be limited to short- to medium-term outcomes; long-term outcome is similar to that of men. In fact, in later life women constitute the majority of patients over age 50 in state psychiatric facilities, and they have longer stays than younger women (Sajatovic,

Donenwirth, Sultana, & Buckley, 2000). Although the course of schizophrenia appears to be more moderate among women, it is important to note that women with SMI have a higher prevalence of comorbidity of three or more disorders and more health problems than their male counterparts (Mowbray et al., 1997).

Specific Issues of Women

Researchers have begun to describe the experiences and needs of women with SMI, which are considerably different from those of men (Ritscher, Coursey, & Farrell, 1997). One consistent finding is the importance of their relational context, which determines many of their concerns. In one study, women reported that they needed help with emotional abuse within relationships, different forms of sexual abuse, access to information about contraception, pregnancy, sexually transmitted diseases, and child custody issues (Cogan, 1998). In a series of focus groups (Chernomas, Clarke, & Chisholm, 2000), women with SMI focused on similar issues: parenting, reproductive health, relationships, getting older, multiple losses, social stigma, poverty, and limited interpersonal contacts. These women felt that the health care system focused on their illness and that they had become invisible as women. The interviewers observed that the women led marginalized and deprived lives in the pervasive shadow of their illness.

Although women with SMI share many gender-related concerns, important differences exist among subgroups of women, based on such variables as age, ethnicity, sexual orientation, income, and education. Alvidrez (1999) points to subgroup differences in instrumental barriers to mental health services, exposure to the mental health care system, family attitudes, stigma, and beliefs about causes of mental illness. Although ethnic minority disparities in access and quality of care are well established (USDHHS, 1999), gender-related subgroup differences represent a promising avenue for future research.

Victimization

Compared both to the general population and to men with SMI, women with SMI have elevated prevalence rates for all types of victimization, including physical or sexual abuse histories, current physical and sexual abuse, rape, and sexually transmitted diseases, such as human immunodeficiency virus (HIV) (Read & Fraser, 1998). In fact, Gearon and Bellack (1999) report that the prevalence rate for violent victimization among these women is almost double that of the general population (42–64% vs. 21–34%). Women with SMI also appear to be at greater risk for posttraumatic stress disorder and for revictimization as adults (Mowbray, Nicholson, & Bellamy, 2003).

These high prevalence rates are found only when researchers inquire directly about abuse (Read & Fraser, 1998). In routine clinical practice, however, mental health practitioners seldom explore histories of current or past sexual abuse among their female patients. As a result, a substantial number of patients on acute psychiatric wards have an unrecognized history of childhood sexual abuse. The consequences of this neglect may include incorrect diagnosis, inappropriate treatment, increased likelihood of hospitalization and psychoactive medication, and poor recovery (Mowbray et al., 2003). Clearly, practitioners need to ask directly whether these women have experienced abuse and to incorporate this information in their treatment plans when appropriate.

Mothers With Mental Illness

In this era of community-based care, individuals with SMI now have greater opportunities to pursue normal adult roles, including parenting. As Mowbray and her colleagues (2001) discuss, women with SMI appear to have normal fertility rates and to bear an average or above average number of children. Women are more likely to marry than men with SMI and less likely to be childless. Many of these mothers have SMI prior to their pregnancies, but about 10–15% of pregnant women develop a mental illness postpartum. As the authors note, many of these mothers begin their parenting under high-risk conditions: with single parenting, early childbearing, inadequate housing, few social and emotional supports, limited education, poverty, family strife, substance abuse, homelessness, and victimization. The children of these mothers are at increased risk of being placed in alternative setting such as foster care and of exhibiting behavior problems and mental health problems of their own.

In spite of the compelling needs of these mothers, there has been little acknowledgement of their parenting role. As with gender issues in general, however, the experiences and needs of mothers with SMI are receiving increasing attention (Brunette & Dean, 2002; Caton, Cournos, & Dominguez, 1999, Nicholson & Henry, 2003; Nicholson, Sweeney, & Geller, 1998). Mothers with SMI face the same challenges as other parents in securing financial resources, housing, medical care, transportation, and child care. In addition, these mothers must cope with an array of illness-related issues, including the presence of disabling symptoms, medication side effects, and social stigma. Inadequate parenting knowledge and skills, as well as the at-risk conditions noted previously, may also undermine their parenting ability. Compounding the problems of these mothers are biases held by legal, medical, and other professionals that question their competence as parents and that may interfere with their ability to retain custody of their children (Cogan, 1998).

In spite of the high risk of custody loss, motherhood offers women with SMI a normalizing experience that gives meaning to their lives; a constructive, nonpatient role; and strong motivation for participating in treatment and rehabilitation programs (Nicholson et al., 1998). These mothers often affirm the importance of their parenting role, attempt to avoid custody loss, and maintain contact with children who are living elsewhere (Brunette & Dean, 2002). In order to fulfill their parenting responsibilities, however, many of these mothers need comprehensive, intensive, integrated, and individualized services designed to address their personal needs, to enhance their parenting effectiveness, and to meet the needs of their children.

A contextual and individualized approach to services should include educational and supportive interventions for relatives and other adults, who often provide child care, as well as links to the foster care system (Caton et al., 1999). Although as yet there is no well-articulated foundation for evidence-based practices with this population, many

intervention opportunities exist to address the mental health, health care, family planning, parenting, residential, social, vocational, and legal needs of mothers with SMI (Brunette & Dean, 2002; Nicholson & Henry, 2003). Prevention and early intervention services can reduce the risk of poor outcomes among these vulnerable mothers and children and enhance the quality of their lives.

Caregiving Burden

Throughout history, the burden of caregiving for people with mental illness has been overwhelmingly a female one. As Lefley (1996) has discussed, family members, assuming roles for which they are unprepared and untrained, gradually learn to cope with the requirements of daily life with someone who has mental illness; to obtain services from the mental health, welfare, and medical systems; and perhaps to negotiate with the legal and criminal justice systems. She observes that, compared to fathers, caregiving mothers experience more emotional distress (anxiety, depression, fear, emotional drain); and that single caregiving mothers are particularly prone to feelings of depression, hopelessness, and burnout.

In addition to mothers, the wives, sisters, and daughters of people with mental illness are also likely to assume caregiving responsibilities (Marsh, 1998, 2001; Pickett-Schenk, 2003). Although all of these women share in the caregiving burden, each female role is associated with unique experiences, needs, and concerns (Marsh & Lefley, 2003). One reason for these differences is their divergent relationships and responsibilities within the family. In addition, the impact of mental illness is partly determined by their age at the onset of their relative's illness. Given the frequent late adolescent or early adulthood onset of schizophrenia, for instance, the illness is most likely to occur in middle adulthood for mothers, in young adulthood for wives, in adolescence for sisters, and in childhood for daughters.

When a child of any age develops mental illness, mothers generally experience a range of intense losses, both real and symbolic. As one mother wrote, "The problems with my daughter were like a black hole inside of me into which everything else had been drawn."[1] Most likely to assume roles as primary caregivers for their adult children, mothers may sacrifice their own life plans along the way. As one mother commented, "My daughter's mental illness pushed us back into parenting of the most demanding kind, probably for the rest of our lives." Almost universally, mothers are prone to feelings of guilt and responsibility, which may be intensified by professionals who espouse unsupported models of family pathogenesis or dysfunction.

Wives also have particular issues and concerns, yet these family members have received relatively little attention. An estimated 30–35% of hospitalized patients are discharged to live with their spouses, with a profound impact on their families (Mannion, 1996). One wife has written: "My husband's schizophrenia is like a third member in our marriage. It is always there. Even with medication, we still deal with his paranoia, his isolation, and his need for my full attention on a daily basis." The emotional, social, and economic losses experienced by wives are similar to those that accompany spousal bereavement. These women may feel they are no longer married to the same individual and often assume increased responsibility for parenting and other aspects of family life. Under these circumstances, wives may experience substantial conflict and guilt if they consider separation or divorce, shadowed by a sense that they have failed to live up to their marriage vows.

As children and adolescents, girls share a special vulnerability to the mental illness in their families (Marsh & Dickens, 1997). Compared with adults, these young family members are more easily overwhelmed and have fewer coping skills and psychological defenses, as well as a more limited ability to understand mental illness and to verbalize painful feelings. Young girls are more dependent on other people in their lives, placing them in a precarious position when a beloved parent or sibling suffers from mental illness. Deflected from their developmental tasks by the disruptive force of the illness, young family members may carry a legacy of "unfinished business" into their future lives. Depending on their age, the mental illness might have an adverse impact on the establishment basic trust during their earliest years, on peer relationships and academic skills during childhood, or on identity formation during adolescence. Because these young females are still developing, the illness is woven into their very sense of self, becoming *part* of them rather than something that happens to their family.

Sisters may feel they have lost both their sibling and their parents, whose energy may be consumed by the mental illness. They often feel like forgotten family members, struggling to be heard in a family that is focused on the illness. Almost inevitably, sisters feel alienated from the world of their peers, and they may deny their own needs in an effort to compensate their aggrieved parents (the "replacement child syndrome"). One woman wrote of her early years, "I became the perfect child to spare my parents more grief. But I have spent my life trying to run away from this problem. Feeling guilty and helpless, the unending sorrow for not being able to help."

Young daughters face special risks in light of the centrality of the parent-child bond. The losses of these girls may be profound, as attested by a woman who lamented "my loss of a healthy mother, a normal childhood, and a stable home." Daughters may become enveloped in their parent's psychotic system, with an adverse impact on their own mental health. Sometimes assuming a parentified role before they have finished being children, they may attempt to become ideal children to protect their fragile family. In the words of one woman, "As a child I tried desperately never to have a problem because our family had so many. So I became perfectionistic and hid my fears, concerns, and needs from everyone."

Although sisters and daughters are less likely than mothers and wives to assume caregiving roles during their early years, as adults they express considerable anxiety about caregiving. In our survey of illness-related concerns (Marsh & Dickens, 1997), almost all (94%) of the adult siblings and children mentioned caregiving for their relative, which was their top-rated concern. In middle adulthood, all of these caregiving women may be deflected from their own developmental tasks; and in late adulthood, they may find themselves with substantial responsibilities during a period of diminishing personal resources (Lefley, 1996).

CONCLUSIONS

People of all ages with severe and persistent mental illness have many unmet needs. Although by definition their mental illness results in substantial functional impairment, a majority of these vulnerable individuals are not served or are underserved by the mental health system. The first order of business, then, is to reduce the barriers to care for this population and to increase their access to effective interventions and services. People with SED and SMI need a comprehensive, humane, and responsive system of mental health care.

Second, it is essential to identify and reduce gender-related disparities in service provision. Although females and males with mental illness share many service needs, they do not always receive comparable services (Levin, Blanch, & Jennings, 1998). For women as well as men, intervention should be designed to assist them in achieving their goals, in fulfilling their potential, and in improving the quality of their lives. Yet there is evidence of service disparities that may adversely affect females. Women are more likely to receive psychotropic medication, for example, and less likely to receive vocational rehabilitation services (Mowbray et al., 2003).

Third, it is essential to address the changing needs of females throughout the life span. For instance, many young women with SED eventually require services from the adult mental health system. Yet, as Jonikas, Laris, and Cook (2003) have documented, the needs of these transitional adolescents (ages 16 to 21) are too often neglected. Appropriate targets of intervention with this age group include completion of postsecondary education, initiation of a career path, attainment of residential independence, development of intimate relationships, and the maintenance of family ties and friendships. Likewise, adult women with mental illness have specific gender-related concerns, which may center on sexuality, role and relationship issues, educational and vocational needs, past or current victimization, self-esteem, status, physical health, and substance use. For females of all ages, it is essential to incorporate contextual and strength-based assessments that can identify their personal and relational needs.

Finally, many females with mental illness also have unmet needs related to their role as mothers. They are likely to have many personal needs concerned with family planning, parenting knowledge and skills, parenting stress, child care resources, household tasks, custody issues, legal assistance, financial security, and environmental support. As parents, they also may require assistance in meeting the needs of their children for a stable and nurturing environment, socialization skills, academic success, nutritional food, health care, and perhaps mental health care.

Clearly, the development and implementation of a gender-sensitive mental health system for females of all ages with mental illness will require a substantial commitment from policy makers, administrators, and practitioners. Equally clearly, the price of *not* addressing their gendered needs will surely exact a much higher price in the present and future: for these vulnerable women, for their at-risk children, and for society at large.

NOTE

1. Quotes from family members not otherwise referenced are excerpted from research reported in Marsh (1998) and Marsh and Dickens (1997).

REFERENCES

Alvidrez, J. (1999). Ethnic variations in mental health attitudes and service use among low-income African American, Latina, and European American young women. *Community Mental Health Journal, 35,* 515–530.

American Psychiatric Association. (2000). *Diagnostic and statistical manual of mental disorders* (4th ed., text rev.). Washington, DC: Author.

Andreasen, N. C. (2001). *Brave new brain: Conquering mental illness in the era of the genome.* New York: Oxford University Press.

Brunette, M. F., & Dean, W. (2002). Community mental health for women with severe mental illness who are parents. *Community Mental Health Journal, 38,* 153–165.

Caldwell, C. G., & Gottesman, I. I. (1990). Schizophrenics kill themselves, too: A review of risk factors for suicide. *Schizophrenia Bulletin, 16,* 571–589.

Caton, C. L., Cournos, F., & Dominguez, B. (1999). Parenting and adjustment in schizophrenia. *Psychiatric Services, 50,* 239–243.

Chernomas, W. M., Clarke, D. E., & Chisholm, F. A. (2000). Perspectives of women living with schizophrenia. *Psychiatric Services, 51,* 1517–1521.

Cogan, J. C. (1998). The consumer as expert: Women with serious mental illness and their relationship-based needs. *Psychiatric Rehabilitation Journal*, 22, 142–154.

DeAngelis, T. (2002). New data on lesbian, gay and bisexual mental health. *Monitor on Psychology*, 33(2). Retrieved July 19, 2003, from http://www.apa.org/monitor

Gearon, J. S., & Bellack, A. S. (1999). Women with schizophrenia and co-occurring substance use disorders: An increased risk for violent victimization and HIV. *Community Mental Health Journal*, 35, 401–419.

Harding, C. M., Zubin, J., & Strauss, J. S. (1992). Chronicity in schizophrenia: Revisited. *British Journal of Psychiatry*, 161(Suppl. 18), 27–37.

Jamison, K. R. (1995). *An unquiet mind: A memoir of moods and madness*. New York: Knopf.

Jonikas, J. A., Laris, A., & Cook, J. A. (2003). The passage to adulthood: Psychiatric rehabilitation service and transition-related needs of young adult women with emotional and psychiatric disorders. *Psychiatric Rehabilitation Journal*, 27, 114–121.

Lefley, H. P. (1996). *Family caregiving in mental illness* (Family Caregiver Applications Series, Vol. 7). Thousand Oaks, CA: Sage.

Levin, B. L., Blanch, A. K., & Jennings, A. (Eds.). (1998). *Women's mental health services: A public health perspective*. Thousand Oaks, CA: Sage.

Mannion, E. (1996). Resilience and burden in spouses of people with mental illness. *Psychiatric Rehabilitation Journal*, 20, 13–23.

Marsh, D. T. (1998). *Serious mental illness and the family: The practitioner's guide*. New York: John Wiley & Sons.

Marsh, D. T. (2001). *A family-focused approach to serious mental illness: Empirically supported interventions*. Sarasota, FL: Professional Resource Press.

Marsh, D. T., & Dickens, R. M. (1997). *How to cope with mental illness in your family: A self-care guide for siblings, offspring, and parents*. New York: Tarcher/Putnam.

Marsh, D. T., & Lefley, H. P. (2003). Family interventions for schizophrenia. *Journal of Family Psychotherapy*, 14, 47–67.

Mowbray, C. T. (2003). Special section on women and psychiatric rehabilitation practice: Introduction and overview. *Psychiatric Rehabilitation Journal*, 27, 101–103.

Mowbray, C. T., Nicholson, J., & Bellamy, C. D. (2003). Psychosocial rehabilitation service needs of women. *Psychiatric Rehabilitation Journal*, 27, 104–113.

Mowbray, C. T., Oyserman, D., Bybee, D., MacFarlane, P., & Rueda-Riedle, A. (2001). Life circumstances of mothers with serious mental illnesses. *Psychiatric Rehabilitation Journal*, 25, 114–123.

Mowbray, C. T., Oyserman, D., Lutz, C., & Purnell, R. (1997). Women: The ignored majority. In L. Spaniol, C. Gagne, & M. Koehler, *Psychological and social aspects of psychiatric disability* (pp. 171–194). Boston: Center for Psychiatric Rehabilitation, Boston University.

Mueser, K. T., Bond, G. R., & Drake, R. E. (2001). Community-based treatment of schizophrenia and other severe mental disorders: Treatment outcomes. *Medscape General Medicine*, 3(1). Retrieved from http://www.medscape.com/viewarticle/430529

Nicholson, J., & Henry, A. D. (2003). Achieving the goal of evidence-based psychiatric rehabilitation practices for mothers with mental illness. *Psychiatric Rehabilitation Journal*, 27, 122–130.

Nicholson, J., Sweeney, E. M., & Geller, J. L. (1998). Focus on women: Mothers with mental illness: I. The competing demands of parenting and living with mental illness. *Psychiatric Services*, 49, 635–642.

Pickett-Schenk, S. A. (2003). Family education and support: Just for women only? *Psychiatric Rehabilitation Journal*, 27, 131–139.

President's New Freedom Commission on Mental Health. (2002). *Interim report to the president*. Rockville, MD: Author.

Read, J., & Fraser, A. (1998). Abuse histories of psychiatric inpatients: To ask or not to ask? *Psychiatric Services*, 49, 355–359.

Ringeisen, H., & Hoagwood, K. (2002). Clinical and research directions for the treatment and delivery of children's mental health services. In D. T. Marsh & M. A. Fristad (Eds.), *Handbook of serious emotional disturbance in children and adolescents* (pp. 33–55). New York: John Wiley & Sons.

Ritscher, J. E., Coursey, R. D., & Farrell, E. W. (1997). A survey on issues in the lives of women with severe mental illness. *Psychiatric Services*, 48, 1273–1282.

Sajatovic, M., Donenwirth, M. A., Sultana, D., & Buckley, P. (2000). Admissions, length of stay, and medication use among women in an acute care state psychiatric facility. *Psychiatric Services*, 51, 1278–1281.

Torrey, E. F. (2001). *Surviving schizophrenia: A manual for families, consumers, and providers* (4th ed.). New York: HarperCollins.

U.S. Department of Health and Human Services. (1999). *Mental health: A report of the surgeon general*. Washington, DC: Author.

U.S. Department of Health and Human Services. (2001). *Mental health: Culture, race, ethnicity-Supplement*. Washington, DC: Author.

JACQUELYN W. WHITE
and JAMES M. FRABUTT

Violence Against Girls and Women: An Integrative Developmental Perspective

Violence against women takes many forms and may be physical or psychological, with the goal of intimidation and control. Sexual violence ranges from unwanted contact to rape. Rape may be the stereotypical stranger attack, but more frequently it is verbally or physically coerced sexual intercourse by an acquaintance. According to Amnesty International (1992), rape also occurs during cultural rituals involving genital contact, arranged marriages of children, gynecological procedures (rupture of the hymen, genital mutilation, induced abortions), forced prostitution, and sexual slavery. Rape of refugees and wartime rape have also been documented. Physical violence is most frequently manifested in cases of battering and wife abuse, as well as dating violence. Violence also can be seen in cases where men isolate women and deprive them of educational and employment opportunities, and in the case of immigrant women, denial of access to their green cards. These forms of violence share in common the fact that they are frequently committed by men known to the girls and women. Unlike other crimes, they are crimes in which others, as well as the victim herself, may blame the victim for what happened. By blaming the individual victims, attention and responsibility are shifted away from the perpetrators and from the social and political contexts that contribute to violence against women.

Our perspective in this chapter examines individual behavior in context, based on the integrated contextual developmental model of White and Kowalski (1998). The model assumes that patriarchal societies accord men higher value than women and that men are expected to dominate in politics, economics, and the social world, including family life and interpersonal relationships. The model further assumes that patriarchy operating at the historical/sociocultural level affects the power dynamics of all relationships. Historical and sociocultural factors create an environment in which children learn rules and expectations, first in the family network and later in peer, intimate, and work relationships. Individual violence is understood as embedded in gendered social and cultural contexts. Power dynamics become enacted at the interpersonal level and result in the internalization of gendered values, expectations, and behaviors. Thus, cultural norms governing the use of aggression as a tool of the more powerful to subdue the weaker combine with gender inequalities to create a climate conducive to violence against women.

GENDERED VIOLENCE IN CHILDHOOD

Early childhood establishes a framework for patterns of interactions between adult women and men. The major lesson of patriarchy is learned in childhood: the more powerful individuals control the less powerful, and that power is gendered They learn that men and masculinity are (or should be) associated with power and dominance, and that victimization is also gendered—that is, boys and men can hurt girls and women. Girls are taught to be less direct in expressing aggression and regard relational aggression (i.e., verbal threats) more positively than boys, who judge physical aggression more positively. By adulthood men see anger expression as a means of reasserting control over a situation, whereas women experience it as a loss of control (Campbell, Muncer, Guy, & Banim, 1996).

Children learn very early that boys are supposed to be stronger than girls and that girls should follow boys. In particular, children receive very specific messages about aggression. For example, in same sex playgroups girls learn to use verbal persuasion, whereas boys learn to establish dominance physically. Boys establish their identity as male by defining girls as different and inferior, scorn girl-type activities, and exclude girls from their play. In fact, boys' rougher play may be one reason for same-sex segregated playgroups.

Patterns of parental punishment offer another venue for children to learn about gendered aggression and violence. Children, especially those from abusive homes, have many opportunities to learn that the more powerful person in a relationship can use aggression to successfully control the less powerful person. The majority of parents in American homes use verbal and physical aggression as disciplinary tactics. The majority of children are spanked sometime in their youth, and many are also pushed, shoved, and slapped. Parents often tolerate aggression in boys as a *masculine* behavior; thus, boys expect less parental dis-

approval than girls for aggression directed toward peers, although they are punished more harshly for aggression than are girls. The effects of parental punishment are not uniform; the sex of the child and parent affect the pattern and outcome. Paternal spanking leads to reactive (angry) aggression in both girls and boys, but only boys show unprovoked bullying aggression against others when spanked by their fathers (Lytton & Romney, 1991).

For a minority of girls and boys, the message that the more powerful can control the less powerful is also learned in a sexual context. The sexual victimization of children is an abuse of interpersonal power and a violation of trust. Most children are victimized by people they know and trust; almost 90% of children who are raped are victimized by someone known to them. Boys are more likely to be sexually abused by someone outside the family whereas girls are more likely to be sexually abused by a family member or a quasi-family member (e.g., mother's boyfriend). Betrayal of the trust vested in those who have power is central to understanding childhood sexual abuse, its consequences, and the systems that sustain it.

Vulnerability to sexual abuse emerges around age 3, with girls three times more likely than boys to be sexually abused, with no significant ethnic differences. There are an estimated 300,200 children being sexually abused annually, with 614,000 being physically abused. Birth parents (89% male) commit approximately one quarter of all sexual abuses and these abuses are most likely to result in a serious injury or impairment (National Clearinghouse on Child Abuse and Neglect, 2003).

Certain characteristics of families put a child at risk for sexual abuse. These families are often fraught with conflict and have a rigid, traditional structure in which fathers are authoritarian, punitive, and threatening and view women and children as their subordinates. Obedience and control permeate all aspects of family life. Family members are emotionally distant and open displays of affection often are absent. Victimized children often feel powerless to stop the abuse and feel they have nowhere to turn for help, comfort, and support. The child's ability to confront and refuse sexual contact is overwhelmed by the feelings of loyalty and trust that the child may have developed for the perpetrator. The adult, from his position of authority, communicates to the child that the behavior is part of an exclusive, secretive, and special relationship. The perpetrator may even come to believe and attempt to convince the child that the relationship is a mutually loving and caring one.

Childhood sexual abuse has been identified as a gateway to juvenile prostitution, defined as the use of or participation of persons under the age of 18 in sexual intercourse or other sex acts where no force is present in exchange for money, clothing, food, shelter, drugs, or other considerations (Estes & Weiner, 2001). While police statistics suggest there are between 100,000 and 300,000 juvenile prostitutes under the age of 18 (the U.S. Department of Health and Human Services has estimated 300,000), nonofficial sources place the number closer to 500,000, with females accounting for approximately two thirds of the juvenile prostitutes in this country (Flowers, 1998). The majority of juvenile female prostitutes are between the ages of 15 to 17 and enter into prostitution before age 16. Contrary to popular belief, the majority (75%) of juvenile prostitutes are from working-class and middle-class families. Three identified levels of risk factors for juvenile prostitution are *contextual* (e.g., poverty, societal responses to crimes committed against children), *situational* (e.g., history of sexual assault, gang membership, parental drug dependency), and *individual* (e.g., poor self-esteem, chronic depression).

Ethnicity and Childhood Sexual Abuse

The relationship between ethnicity and victimization is currently being studied. No statistical differences between the percentages of African American (57%) and White (67%) women reporting childhood sexual victimization have been reported (Wyatt, 1991). Similarly, 49% of the women in a Southwestern American Indian tribal community reported childhood sexual victimization (Robin, Chester, Rasmussen, Jaranson, & Goldman, 1997). Using a more restrictive definition of sexual abuse, Arroyo, Simpson, and Aragon (1997)

also found no significant differences in the prevalence of childhood sexual abuse among Hispanic (27.1%) and non-Hispanic women (33.1%).

Summary

This overview of gendered violence in childhood, with a specific focus on childhood sexual abuse, suggests that prevention efforts must be multipronged. Although survivors may remain silent as children, the abuse may resurface in adulthood with myriad negative consequences. Adult survivors may be reminded of their abuse when seeing a family member again, looking at pictures, watching a movie about incest, being sexually victimized again, or having children reach the same age as they were when they were abused. Girls and boys need opportunities to learn to play in non-gendered ways and need the skills to resolve conflicts when they arise. Parents need training to provide consequences to children in ways that do not teach and reinforce gendered patterns of aggression and violence. Children reared in warm, loving families are quite resilient to the negative impact of challenges posed by developmental transitions to school and into adolescence. These children are likely to exhibit more secure parental attachment, higher self-esteem, and greater academic success.

Protection of children from abuse is a focus of national attention in recent years. Schools are beginning to educate teachers about the signs of physical and sexual abuse. They are also beginning to teach children what is appropriate touch, that they are their own property and they have the right to say no to someone who is abusive, while encouraging children to tell a teacher, parent, or adult friend when someone touches them inappropriately (Wurtele, 2002). Doctors are being trained to identify signs of child sexual abuse in their patients and to conduct the necessary tests to verify sexual abuse. Many adult survivors also are becoming aware of their victimization and are seeking help from private therapists, support groups of other survivors, and books. Survivors report that others can help by believing their stories and by allowing them to talk about what happened and their feelings (Nelson-Gardell, 2001).

Although the memory of the abuse may not be completely forgotten, many women find ways to heal.

GENDERED VIOLENCE IN ADOLESCENCE

During adolescence, young men and women experience extreme pressure to conform to traditional gender roles. Peer influences and media images are quite powerful. Male companionship permits men to distance themselves from women except in social contexts involving "power-enhancing" or sexual opportunities. Distancing oneself socially and psychologically from anything feminine is part of establishing a masculine identity. Sexually aggressive men are likely to have a peer group that values sexual conquests at any cost (Ageton, 1983).

Media images contribute to prescriptive gendered interactions. The sexual objectification of women, as depicted in pornography, has an impact on adolescent women and men. Repeated exposure to pornography increases young men's sexual callousness toward women, desensitizes them to violence against women, and increases their acceptance of rape myths and willingness to engage in aggressive behavior toward women. Pornography consumption is an important risk factor in sexual aggression (Malamuth, 1998).

Sexualized images of women's bodies are prevalent, not only in sexually explicit materials but also in general media images (e.g., advertising). Women become the objects of men's gaze and evaluation. Western culture socializes girls to view themselves as objects for evaluation and approval by others. Moreover, the girls themselves come to internalize an observer's perspective of self and may come to evaluate their self-worth based on the responses and evaluations of others. Some women seem to believe that when they are more attractive than men, they must treat them especially well as a means of equalizing power in the relationships, but if they are less attractive than men, they can treat them poorly to compensate for their unattractiveness. Women, if less attractive than men, may reduce their expectations for good treatment. Women may also come to use men's treatment as an index of their relative attractiveness. When mistreated, they tend to blame themselves rather than men for their victimization (Holland & Eisenhart, 1990).

It appears that dating violence and sexual assault among adolescents and college students is so prevalent, in part, because the overall structure and meaning of dating in our culture give men greater power. Adolescent dating patterns follow a fairly well defined script that has not changed much over several decades. A traditional dating script is a set of rules to be followed by girls and boys that affords men greater power relative to women, although women are assumed to be responsible for "how far things go," and if things "get out of hand," it is their fault. These social scripts, often depicted in media images, may lead some women into a "relationship trap" when they feel they must put maintenance of the relationship above their own self-interests (Carey & Mongeau, 1996). Courtship has different meanings for young women and men. Whereas for most men courtship involves themes of "staying in control," for women themes typically involve "dependence on the relationship." Violence is one of the tactics used to gain control in a relationship.

Women who experience ongoing victimization often report more commitment to and love for their partner; they are less likely to end the relationship because of abuse and they allow their partner to control them. These women also report more traditional attitudes toward women's roles, justify their abuse, and tend to romanticize relationships and love. Conflict in dating relationships increases the risk for violence, and is more likely when relationships are plagued by jealousy, fighting, interference from friends, lack of time together, breakdown of the relationship, and problems outside the relationship, as well as disagreements about drinking and sexual denial.

Studies indicate that dating violence during the teen years is pervasive. It has been estimated that over three quarters of high school and college-aged youth have experienced some verbal aggression and approximately one third have experienced physical aggression (Smith, White, & Holland, 2003). The ubiquity of courtship violence among college students is apparent in that comparable rates of violence have been observed across gender, ethnic group, and type of institution of higher learning, such as private or public, religious or secular.

As men and women establish intimate relationships, dominance and violence also surface in the form of sexual aggression. Several large surveys have suggested that over half of the women by the age of 24 have experienced some form of sexual victimization, with approximately 15% experiencing acts by a man that meet the legal definition of rape, and 12% have experienced an attempted rape (Koss, Gidycz, & Wisniewski, 1987). High school women also appear to be at greater risk for rape than previously thought. A survey of 834 entering college students found that 13% reported being raped between the ages of 14 and 18, and an additional 16% reported being victims of an attempted rape (Humphrey & White, 2000). Most victims knew the perpetrator and the assaults frequently occurred in a dating context.

Several researchers have confirmed that the best predictor of victimization is past victimization. Childhood victimization typically increases the risk of adolescent victimization, which in turn increases the risk of victimization as a young adult (Humphrey & White, 2000). Additionally, childhood victimization has been related to earlier age of menarche and sexual activity that may increase the perpetrator's attraction to the victim (Vicary, Klingman, & Harkness, 1995). Women with a history of victimization may turn to alcohol as a means of coping. Prior victimization, along with drinking habits, also affects women's judgments of risk (Norris, Nurius, & Graham, 1999). Alcohol also is implicated in sexual assault in several other ways. Unfortunately, alcohol use also may make it more difficult for women to read the danger cues present in an impending assault. Also, alcohol consumption is a barrier to women's ability to resist (Norris et al., 1999), and more important, her alcohol use may suggest, erroneously, to the perpetrator that she is sexually available and/or that she will be less able to resist an assault.

Ethnicity and Sexual Assault

Dating violence and sexual assault pose additional problems among adolescents who are not White, middle class, and heterosexual. Although it is difficult for any young person to admit being victimized by a dating partner, it is especially so for ethnic minorities. The legacy of slavery and distrust of White authority figures have made it difficult for African American teens to report abusive dating relationships (Wyatt, 1991). Asian/Pacific women, too, are reluctant to disclose abuse because of cultural traditions of male dominance and reticence to discuss private relationships in public (Yoshihamana, Parekh, & Boyington, 1991). For lesbian teens, the problem is complicated by the fact that, in reporting abuse, they may have to reveal their sexual orientation, something they may not be psychologically ready to do (Levy & Lobel, 1991).

Summary

This review of violence toward teen-aged girls makes it clear that adolescence is a time of high risk for victimization, especially by male peers. There is a need for adolescents to develop conflict management and sexual negotiation skills. There are multiple levels at which efforts should be directed to combat interpersonal violence during the adolescent years: criminal justice system; school and community programming; and targeted male-based programs. First, changes in the legal system are necessary to overcome victims' reluctance to report the crime and increase the likelihood that a report will result in a conviction (Koss, Bachar, Hopkins, & Carlson, 2003). Unfortunately, judicial reforms to date have not changed societal attitudes about interpersonal violence, especially among acquainted teens.

Second, at the institutional level, experts encourage schools and universities to espouse a philosophy condemning dating and sexual violence, to develop policies, and to offer services congruent with their policies (i.e., escort services, violence prevention programming, counseling/treatment services, strict judicial procedures and punitive consequences). A third, and very promising trend, is the development of violence prevention programs developed by men and run by men for men. An interesting aspect of such programming is the focus on fraternities and athletic teams on college campuses. Community-based organizations that focus on men are also working on men taking responsibility for violence against women. The White Ribbon Campaign (http://www.undp.org/rblac/gender/mens.htm), begun in Canada, is the largest worldwide effort of men to end men's violence against women. During White Ribbon Week, beginning November 25, the International Day for the Eradication of Violence Against Women, men wear a white ribbon as a pledge to never commit violence or to remain silent about other men's violence.

VIOLENCE IN MARRIAGE AND OTHER COMMITTED RELATIONSHIPS

Patterns of interpersonal violence established during adolescence may continue in adulthood. Victimization in adolescence predicts victimization in adulthood for women (Smith et al., 2003); likewise, for men perpetration in adolescence predicts perpetration in adulthood (White & Smith, 2004). The greatest threat of violence to adult women is from their intimate partners. An estimated 2 to 3 million women are assaulted by male partners in the United States each year (21–34% of all women at some time during adulthood); at least half of these women are severely assaulted (i.e., punched, kicked, choked, beaten, threatened with a knife or gun, or had a knife or gun used on them). Further, it is estimated that 33–50% of all battered wives are also the victims of partner rape (Peacock, 1998). Studies have shown that 22–40% of the women who seek health care at clinics or emergency rooms were victims of battering (Stark & Flitcraft, 1996). Intimate violence may escalate, resulting in homicide. Approximately two thirds of family violence deaths are women killed by their male partners; current or former partners commit over half of all murders of women. Murder-suicides are almost always cases where the man kills his partner or estranged partner, sometimes his children or other family members as well, before killing himself (Stuart & Campbell, 1989).

Data from the National Violence Against Women Survey of 8,000 women and 8,000 men in the United States indicate that married/cohabiting women reported significantly more intimate partner physical assault, stalking, and rape than did married/cohabiting men. Women also reported more frequent and longer lasting victimization; fear of bodily injury, time lost from work, injuries, and use of medical, mental health, and justice system services (Tjaden & Thoennes, 1998).

Studies of abusive couples have found little evidence that battered women have certain personalities that put them at risk. Rather, abusive men are likely to have a history of alcohol abuse, to have more life stress, and to lack coping skills (Barnett & Fagan, 1993). Other characteristics include low self-esteem, a need to dominate, depression, dependency on others to meet emotional needs, and hostility toward women (Dewhurst, Moore, & Alfano, 1992). Marital conflict and witnessing violence in the family of origin are also strong predictors of continuing marital violence (Aldarondo & Sugarman, 1996).

Ethnicity and Intimate Partner Violence

Community-based surveys have found that 25% of African American women (Wyatt, 1991) and 8% of Hispanic women (Sorenson & Siegel, 1992) reported at least one physical or sexual assault experience in their lifetime. However, when norms regarding violence approval, age, and economic stressors are held constant, Kantor, Kaufman, Jasinski, and Aldarondo (1994) did not find differences between Hispanic Americans and other Americans in their odds of wife abuse. However, they did find that being born in the United States increases the risk of wife assaults by Mexican American and Puerto Rican American husbands. Importantly, they found that in any group, regardless of socioeconomic status, the presence of norms sanctioning wife assaults is a risk factor for wife abuse. For women in Israel, the West Bank, and the Gaza Strip, acceptance of patriarchal values is associated with acceptance of wife beating. Despite growth in educational and career opportunities for women in Arab countries, religious and family values condone wife abuse and provide women few avenues for escape (Haj-Yahia, 1998). Women in other countries such as Bangladesh and India also suffer from wife abuse (Fernandez, 1997).

Violence in Lesbian Relationships

Relationship abuse is not limited to heterosexual relationships. Although there have been no prevalence studies, research with convenience samples indicates that partner abuse is a significant problem for lesbian women (Lockhart, White, Causby, & Isaac, 1994). Partner abuse has been associated with issues of power and dependency in lesbian couples. For lesbians, the internalization of societal homophobic attitudes may, in part, lead to aggression against partners and reduce reporting due to threats that they may be "outed" by their partner.

Elder Abuse: Violence Toward Elderly Women

The American Association of Retired Persons (1992) produced a report identifying similarities between elder abuse and other forms of violence against women. The report identified power imbalances, secrecy and isolation, personal harm to victims, social expectations and sex roles, inadequate resources to protect victims, and the control perpetrators have over their actions. The report further suggested that life-span factors pose unique problems for elder abuse.

Elder abuse is often spouse abuse that has continued for years. One of the only random sample based surveys examining elder abuse found that in the over-65 population of Boston, 2% were the victims of physical abuse, with 58% of those being abused by a spouse and 24% by an adult child (Finkelhor & Pillemer, 1988). Victimization by adult children reflects the change in relationship dynamics as parents age. Adult children gain power and the aging parent loses power within a social context that values youth and devalues maturity. Although half the victims were men, women were much more severely injured than men. Submissiveness, self-blame, self-doubt and lack of social support mediate the effects of abuse on older women (Aronson, Thornewell, & Williams, 1995).

Even less is known about the sexual abuse of older women. This remains a taboo topic, although there is a growing recognition that the problem needs attention. Clinical evidence suggests that older women may be raped in their homes as well as in institutions (such as residential treatment facilities and nursing homes). Holt (1993), in a study of elder sexual abuse in Great Britain, reported a 6:1 ratio of female to male vic-

tims; they found that the perpetrators were more likely to be sons than husbands. Research has documented the continued long-term effects of childhood sexual abuse and domestic violence in the later years. Symptoms may include depression and revictimization. Diagnosis of symptoms related to prior abuse in the elderly is complicated by age and may result in misdiagnosis as dementia or mental illness. Additionally, one study suggests that men who sexually assault older women may suffer from more severe psychopathology and that their assaults are more brutal and motivated by anger and a need for power (Pollock, 1988).

Summary

The review of research on violence against women indicates that it is a problem across the life span. Various factors, such as a history of childhood and adolescent abuse and economic dependence on one's partner, are risk factors for abuse. Educational and economic opportunities, self-esteem, and social support have all been identified as important protective factors. The presence of community shelters for victims of domestic violence and sexual assault is critical to offering women the possibility of escape from dangerous situation and the possibility of building a new, abuse-free life.

CONSEQUENCES OF VIOLENCE AGAINST GIRLS AND WOMEN

The developmental pattern of gendered violence is mirrored in an escalation of the consequences for victims. Beginning in childhood, victimization experiences influence subsequent psychological, social, and emotional development. Sexually victimized girls suffer from several problems including impaired self-esteem, feelings of betrayal, lack of trust, and age-inappropriate sexual behavior. It is highly likely that these factors contribute to an increased risk of revictimization during adolescence. Young women who experience physical or sexual violence during adolescence are more likely to be injured and to feel surprised, scared, angry, and hurt by a partner's aggression than are men. An additional serious consequence of courtship violence is a possible increased risk of marital violence either with the same or a different partner.

Abused women are at higher risk for a range of psychological and physical health problems that may be exacerbated when violent partners prevent them from seeking appropriate health care when needed. Abused women also show a range of adverse behavioral outcomes such as suicide and substance use. Additionally, there are social and economic consequences. The abused woman's partner may limit access to household resources and control decision making, as well as the woman's employment patterns. Her educational attainment and income, as well as her participation in public life, may be restricted. The quality of life for children in the home may be compromised as well.

CONCLUSIONS

Traditionally, secrecy and myths regarding male-female relationships trivialized and/or justified male violence against women. The women's movement has done much to bring to public awareness the extent of the harm done to women by men and has prompted redefinitions that acknowledge the violence. For example, rape is no longer defined as a sexual act, sexual harassment is not accepted as standard working conditions, and wife abuse is not a legitimate way to "show the little woman who is boss"; rather, each is seen as an act by men intended to dominate and control women.

Violence against women, in its various forms, is now recognized as a public health and social problem. Hence, research has moved from focusing on individual psychopathology to identifying the sociocultural factors that contribute to such violence. Also, communities, institutions, and organizations are combating violence against women by developing interventions that not only help individuals but also promote change in values and attitudes at the societal level.

REFERENCES

Ageton, S. (1983). *Sexual assault among adolescents.* Lexington, MA: Lexington Books.

Aldarondo, E., & Sugarman, D. B. (1996). Risk marker analysis of the cessation and persistence of wife assault. *Journal of Consulting and Clinical Psychology, 64,* 1010–1019.

American Association of Retired Persons. (1992). *Abused elders or older battered women?* Special Activities Department, AARP. Washington, DC: Author.

Amnesty International. (1992). *Rape and sexual abuse: Torture and ill treatment of women in detention.* New York: Author.

Aronson, J., Thornewell, C., & Williams, K. (1995). Wife assault in old age: Coming out of obscurity *Canadian Journal on Aging, 14,* 72–88.

Arroyo, J. A., Simpson, T. L., & Aragon, A. S. (1997). Childhood sexual abuse among Hispanic and non-Hispanic White college women. *Hispanic Journal of Behavioral Sciences, 19,* 57–68.

Barnett, O. W., & Fagan, R. W. (1993). Alcohol use in male spouse abusers and their female partners. *Journal of Family Violence, 8,* 1–25.

Campbell, A., Muncer, S., Guy, A., & Banim, M. (1996). Social representations of aggression: Crossing the sex barrier. *European Journal of Social Psychology, 26,* 135–147.

Carey, C. M., & Mongeau, P. A. (1996). Communication and violence in courtship relationships. In D. D. Cahn & S. A. Lloyd (Eds.), *Family violence from a communication perspective* (pp. 127–150). Thousand Oaks, CA: Sage.

Dewhurst, A. M., Moore, R. J., & Alfano, D. P. (1992). Aggression against women by men: Sexual and spousal assault. *Journal of Offender Rehabilitation, 18,* 39–47.

Estes, R. J., & Weiner, N. A. (2001). *The commercial sexual exploitation of children in the U.S., Canada and Mexico.* Center research report of the Center for the Study of Youth Policy, University of Pennsylvania. Philadelphia. Retrieved from http://caster.ssw.upenn.edu/~restes/CSEC_Files/Complete_CSEC_020220.pdf

Fernandez, M. (1997). Domestic violence by extended family members in India. Interplay of gender and generation. *Journal of Interpersonal Violence, 12,* 433–455.

Finkelhor, D., & Pillemer, K. (1988). Elder abuse: Its relationship to other forms of domestic violence. In G. T. Hotaling and D. Finkelhor (Eds.), *Family abuse and its consequences: New directions in research* (pp. 244–254). Thousand Oaks, CA: Sage.

Flowers, R. B. (1998). *The prostitution of women and girls.* Jefferson, NC: McFarland & Company.

Haj-Yahia, M. M. (1998). Beliefs about wife beating among Palestinian women: The influence of their patriarchal ideology. *Violence Against Women, 4,* 533–558.

Holland, D. C., & Eisenhart, M. A. (1990). *Educated in romance: Women, achievement, and college culture.* Chicago: University of Chicago Press.

Holt, M. (1993). Elder sexual abuse in Britain. In C. McCreadie (Ed.), *Elder abuse: New findings and guidelines* (pp. 16–18). London: Age Concern Institute of Gerontology.

Humphrey, J. A., & White, J. W. (2000). Women's vulnerability to sexual assault from adolescence to young adulthood. *Journal of Adolescent Health, 27,* 419–424.

Kantor, G., Kaufman, Jasinski, J. L., & Aldarondo, E. (1994). Sociocultural status and incidence of marital violence in Hispanic families. *Violence and Victims, 9,* 207–222.

Koss, M. P., Bachar, K., Hopkins, C. Q., & Carlson, C. (2004). Expanding a community justice response to sex crimes through advocacy, prosecutorial, and public health collaboration: Introducing the RESTORE program. *Journal of Interpersonal Violence, 18,* 1–29.

Koss, M. P., Gidycz, C. A., & Wisniewski, N. (1987). The scope of rape: Incidence and prevalence of sexual aggression and victimization in a national sample of higher education students. *Journal of Consulting and Clinical Psychology, 55,* 162–170.

Levy, B., & Lobel, K. (1991). In B. Levy (Ed.), *Dating violence: Young women in danger* (pp. 203–208). Seattle, WA: Seal Press.

Lockhart, L. L., White, B. W., Causby, V., & Isaac, A. (1994). Letting out the secret: Violence in lesbian relationships. *Journal of Interpersonal Violence, 9,* 469–492.

Lytton, H., & Romney, D. M. (1991). Parents' differential socialization of boys and girls: A meta-analysis. *Psychological Bulletin, 109,* 267–296.

Malamuth, N. M. (1998). The confluence model as an organizing framework for research on sexually aggressive men: Risk moderators, imagined aggression, and pornography consumption. In R. G. Geen & E. Donnerstein (Eds.), *Human aggression: Theories, research, and implications for social policy* (pp. 229–245). San Diego, CA: Academic Press.

National Clearinghouse on Child Abuse and Neglect. (2003). Web material. Retrieved June 26, 2003, from http://www.calib.com/nccanch

Nelson-Gardell, D. (2001). The voices of victims: Surviving child sexual abuse. *Child and Adolescent Social Work Journal, 18,* 401–16.

Norris, J., Nurius, P. S., &Graham, T. L. (1999). When a date changes from fun to dangerous: Factors affecting women's ability to distinguish. *Violence Against Women, 5,* 230–250.

Peacock, P. (1998). Marital rape. In Bergen, R. K. (Ed.), *Issues in intimate violence* (pp. 225–235). Thousand Oaks, CA: Sage.

Pollock, N. L. (1988). Sexual assault of older women. *Annals of Sex Research, 1,* 523–532.

Robin, R. W., Chester, B., Rasmussen, J. K., Jaranson, J. M., & Goldman, D. (1997). Prevalence and characteristics of trauma and posttraumatic stress disorder in a southwestern American Indian community. *American Journal of Psychiatry, 154,* 1582–1588.

Smith, P. H., White, J. W., & Holland, L. J. (2003). A longitudinal perspective on dating violence among adolescent and college-age women. *American Journal of Public Health, 93,* 1104–1109.

Sorenson, S. B., & Siegel, J. M. (1992). Gender, ethnicity, and sexual assault: Findings from the Los Angeles Epidemiological catchment area study. *Journal of Social Issues, 48,* 93–104.

Stark, E., & Flitcraft, A. (1996). *Women at risk: Domestic violence and women's health.* Thousand Oaks, CA: Sage.

Stuart, E. P., & Campbell, J. C. (1989). Assessment of patterns of dangerousness with battered women. *Issues in Mental Health Nursing, 10,* 245–260.

Tjaden, P., & Thoennes, N. (1998). *Stalking in American: Findings from the National Violence Against Women survey.* Denver, CO: Center for Policy Research.

Vicary, J. R., Klingman, L. R., & Harkness, W. L. (1995). Risk factors associated with date rape and sexual assault of adolescent girls. *Journal of Adolescence, 18,* 289–306.

White, J. W., & Kowalski, R. M. (1998). Male violence against women: An integrative perspective. In R. G. Geen & E. Donnerstein (Eds.), *Human aggression: Theory, research, and implications for social policy* (pp. 203–228). New York: Academic Press.

White, J. W., & Smith, P. H. (2004). Sexual assault perpetration and re-perpetration: From adolescence to young adulthood. *Criminal Justice and Behavior, 31,* 182–202.

Wurtele, S. K. (2002). School-based child sexual abuse prevention. In P. A. Schewe (Ed.), *Preventing violence in relationships: Interventions across the life span* (pp. 9–25). Washington, DC: American Psychological Association.

Wyatt, G. (1991). Sociocultural context of African American and White American women's rape. *Journal of Social Issues, 48,* 77–91.

Yoshihamana, M., Parekh, A. L., & Boyington, D. (1991). Dating violence in Asian/Pacific communities. In B. Levy (Ed.), *Dating violence: Young women in danger* (pp. 84–93). Seattle, WA: Seal Press.

R H O D A O L K I N

Physical or Systemic Disabilities

It has taken a while for attention to be paid to the intersection of disability and other personal characteristics, including gender. A focus on girls and women with disabilities immediately raises two questions. Do girls and women with disabilities differ from boys and men with disabilities? And do girls and women with disabilities differ from girls and women without disabilities? The answer, in a word, is yes. The issue for this chapter is not *if*, but *how*. "How does disability affect the gendering process? How does it affect the experience of gender? . . . In what ways are the experiences of women and men with disabilities similar and different?" (Gerrschick, 2000, p. 1263).

Both gender and disability are central characteristics for a person. Gender and disability status are critical components of impression formation. But disability is viewed as such a strong central characteristic that it overshadows other characteristics. Thus, the study of people with disabilities has not considered gender until fairly recently, which is to say males with disabilities were the samples used in research.

A concept closely related to central characteristic is that of spread, which is "the power of single characteristics to evoke inferences about a person" (Wright, 1983, p. 32). Given only limited data about a person (e.g., that she has a disability), people ascribe other personality traits to that person. If the central characteristic is positive, the spread is also likely to be positive, and the reverse is true if the central characteristic is negative. If gender and disability are both central characteristics, is there overlap in the spread effects of each of these? There are similarities in the characteristics that are ascribed to each: childlike, dependent, helpless, passive. The stereotypes about women with disabilities are powerful images that devalue and disempower the person on both the basis of gender and disability. This dual minority status is a critical factor in understanding women with disabilities. Neither gender nor disability should be seen as less important in our research or clinical work.

Two social and civil rights movements have affected women with disabilities—the women's and disability rights movements. These two movements have not always been in accord. Women with disabilities long complained of being left out of the feminist movement. The stereotype of people with disabilities (weak and dependent) was the very image the women's movement was fighting against (Gill, 1996). Inclusion of disability had to wait until the women's movement began to embrace diversity as a way to be more inclusive and representative.

Another area of conflict is over reproductive rights. While both disability and women's movements sought equality in the workplace, feminists were asserting the right to be out of the home and to have reproductive choice, and women with disabilities were fighting for the right to be mothers. This conflict stems in part from the emphasis within a liberal bioethical framework on individual rights, versus the emphasis in the social model of disability on the sociopolitical structures that maintain inequality and discrimination (McLaughlin, 2003). Should society hold individual women to blame for choices that are shaped by these structures? We may not like the constricted choices within which women are forced to choose, and may decry the forces that compel her choices, but this is not the same as blaming the individual woman for her actions or for the perpetuation of discrimination (McLaughlin, 2003). Nonetheless, the area of antenatal screening is a current area of vigorous debate.

Women with disabilities and older woman share some common features, namely stigma and social invisibility (Healey, 1993). The dangers of living in a society without universal health care affect both groups. Despite their commonalities, the two groups would like to distance themselves from each other. Older woman may fear disability. Women outlive men, and are more likely to be widowed or single—an inability to care for themselves and an absence of supports and caregivers could force them into nursing homes. Younger women with disabilities likewise worry that they will be categorized with the elderly and put in nursing homes (Healey, 1993). A coalition between the two groups might seem desirable but has not occurred. The leadership of advocacy for the elderly (notably the American Association of Retired Persons) tends to be politically conservative and top down, while the leadership of the disability movement has leaned toward the liberal and been community and grass roots based. Within this context, older women with disabilities face unique challenges. Although it is more

likely that others among their peers have disabilities, they nonetheless may experience more social isolation. Natural social groups (e.g., through work or other parents of young children) are no longer extant. Limited mobility and effects of disability and age on driving abilities can make travel outside the home more difficult. And the issues of mortality and meaning that are inevitably raised by disability may be particularly salient at this stage of life.

This chapter examines several areas related to being both female and disabled. These include the rather grim demographics that are the reality for girls and women with disabilities, disability identity, risk factors, health and wellness, and lastly some considerations regarding clinical intervention with girls and women with disabilities.

DEMOGRAPHICS AND DISADVANTAGE

At somewhere between 15 and 20% of the population, people with disabilities constitute the largest minority group in the United States (McNeil, 1997). Women with disabilities (more than 28 million) outnumber men with disabilities (more than 25 million) (Nosek & Hughes, 2003). Of working age adults with disabilities, more than one third are ethnic minorities (Bernal, 1996). Of women with severe disabilities, over one third are ethnic minorities, and half of these women are single heads of households. Only 25% are married, and another 25% are single with no children (Bernal, 1996). One reason to study women with disabilities is that they are a disadvantaged but overlooked population. "It is inappropriate to compare the severity of disability-related problems faced by women to the problems faced by men. . . . More appropriately, these issues should be examined for the *ways in which* they differ, rather than *how much* they differ" (Nosek & Hughes, 2003, p. 230, emphasis in original). Indeed, "gender and disability synergistically interact to compound the stigma, prejudice, and discrimination women with disabilities face" (Olkin, 2003, p. 150).

Most empirical research has been on men with disabilities, and then predominantly on the types of disabilities incurred in war (spinal cord injury, traumatic brain injury, amputation). The initial attention to women with disabilities focused primarily on issues of reproduction, fertility, pregnancy, and labor and delivery (Nosek & Hughes, 2003). Later the issue of sexuality became the focus of attention, in part due to funding availability in that area. It is only in the last decade that serious attention has been paid the general health, well-being, and functioning of women with disabilities, thanks in large measure to early pioneers who shone the spotlight on the need for such attention (e.g., Deegan & Brooks, 1985; Fine & Asch, 1988). Two assumptions had to be overturned in order to achieve this focus (Nosek & Hughes, 2003). The first was that disability and health are at opposite ends of the spectrum. In fact, they are separate continua that overlap but are distinguishable. The second was that gender is less important than disability, and that disability can be studied outside the context of any other personal characteristics. Consideration of disability in conjunction with gender opens the door to multiple identities. The civil rights and women's movements of the sixties, the gay rights movement of the seventies, and the disability rights movement of the eighties begin to coalesce with a united message of community and identity pride.

Just as health issues and risks differ for men and women in general, so do they for men and women with disabilities (Nosek & Hughes, 2003). For example, although the top seven disabling conditions (back disorders, arthritis, cardiovascular disease, asthma, orthopedic impairment of lower extremity, mental disorders, learning disabilities, and intellectual disabilities) are the same for both genders, the order of prevalence differs. The demographics and health status of men and women with disabilities differ, and they also differ between women with and without disabilities. A comparison between women with and without disabilities (see table 10.1) and men and women with and without disabilities (see table 10.2) shows that women with disabilities fare worse than their nondisabled female or disabled male counterparts. The two stigmatized conditions of gender and disability converge for women with disabilities, such that disability further diminishes women's already devalued gender status and vice versa (Gerrschick, 2000), what Fine and Asch called "sexism without the pedestal" (1988, p. 1).

TABLE 10.1 A Comparison of Women With and Without Disabilities on Six Factors

	Women With Disabilities	Nondisabled Women
Less likely to be married	40%	64%
More likely to be living alone	35%	13%
More likely to have a high school education or less	78%	54%
Less likely to be employed	14%	63%
More likely to be living in households below poverty level	23%	10%
Less likely to have private health insurance	55%	75%

IDENTITY AND COMING OF AGE WITH A DISABILITY

The person's age at onset of disability interacts with the particulars of the disability (type, severity, and visibility). How one is expected to conform to gender expectations also varies with age at disability onset. With early disability onset, and with more pronounced disabilities, gender expectations are all but suspended as disability overshadows other personal characteristics. Under circumstances of later disability onset, gender socialization has already occurred, and the disability joins an already internalized set of gender norms. Thus the degree to which one experiences stringent gender socialization is contingent on many disability factors.

Children with early onset disabilities have both advantages and disadvantages over people with later onset of disability. Research on children born either deaf or blind indicates that although such children face social obstacles, and in some cases have fewer friends, they also display resilience and are as well-adjusted as their nondisabled peers (Olkin, 2004). But children with disabilities are usually the only person with a disability in their family, and often the only one in the classroom. Mainstreaming leads to improved academic results compared with segregation based on disability, but it can produce

TABLE 10.2 Comparison of Nondisabled and Disabled Men and Women on Seven Factors

	Men	Women
Single/Never Married		
Nondisabled	4%	3%
Disabled	4%	7%
Divorced/Separated		
Nondisabled	12%	15%
Disabled	11%	25%
Education: Did Not Graduate From High School		
Nondisabled	16%	18%
Disabled	33%	42%
Education: Attended College		
Nondisabled	47%	38%
Disabled	34%	25%
Working		
Nondisabled	91%	65%
Disabled	73%	43%
Working Full Time		
Nondisabled	88%	49%
Disabled	69%	33%
Mean Monthly Income		
Nondisabled	$2,330	$1,744
	($2,190)[a]	($1,470)[a]
Disabled	$843	$578
	($1,262)	($1,000)

Source: Data from the 1989 U.S. Census and the 1986 Harris and Associates Poll, as cited in Hanna and Rogovsky (1991).
[a]Data in parentheses cited in Nosek and Hughes (2003).

isolation from peers with disabilities, and the potential for ostracism by nondisabled peers. In two arenas, home and school, the child is faced with an absence of peers or role models with disabilities. Further, she is held to norms developed for nondisabled children, and differences due to disability often are defined as deficits. It is in this less than optimal context that girls with disabilities develop their identity.

Identity as a girl or woman with a disability involves stigma, gender interaction with disability, and the heightened importance of the body to both gender and disability. Stigmatization associated with disability is the substance of disability experience, rather than a product of it (Murphy,

1990, as cited in Gerrschick, 2000). "We have been split into good and bad selves, split from each other, and split from greater society literally through environmental impediments and symbolically through feelings of invalidity" (p. 46). However, that which has been split may be integrated. Gill (1997) has developed a model of how people with disabilities incorporate and integrate disability into their identities. She discusses integration of the self as a theme in theories of human development, one that is associated with positive mental and emotional health. Her four types of integration are:

- *Coming to feel we belong,* in which the right to inclusion in society is expected, not in spite of but with the disabilities. The onus for the mismatch between person and environment is shifted to society rather than people with disabilities.
- *Coming home,* in which integration into a disability community is achieved, and people find a commonality, connectedness, acceptance and community in a way they have not in the nondisabled world.
- *Coming together,* in which the two poles of sameness and difference (from family and from the disability community) are explored. This level of identity moves from a focus on equal rights to a view of disability as a source of value and pride. A woman may have to distance herself from the perspectives of her family and others who promulgate a medical model of disability. The woman negotiates between the disabled and nondisabled world, and hence is multicultural.
- *Coming out,* in which the goal is to be oneself, with the disability integrated into the self, in all spheres. One moves fluidly between the disability and nondisabled cultures, but is oneself in both environments.

People who incur disabilities do not go through stages of response to disability such as denial, anger, bargaining, depression, and acceptance. The stage model is a well entrenched myth. Not only has research failed to support it but, in fact, quite the opposite is the case (Olkin, 1999). It is especially important to note that depression in particular is not a necessary stage, and indeed is not the modal response to disability; most people who are born or become disabled do not get depressed. However, those who do experience a clinical depression after disability onset have a higher probability of future depression. This depression both complicates and is complicated by the disability. Therefore, depression should be routinely evaluated and aggressively treated.

RISK FACTORS

There are at least five major psychosocial problems for women with disabilities, compared to men with disabilities and to women without disabilities: depression, stress, self-esteem, social connectedness, and abuse (Nosek & Hughes, 2003). Economic privation is also a chronic problem for women with disabilities, and is connected to each of these factors.

Depression

The ratio of depression in women versus men is 2 to 1. For persons with disabilities the rate is estimated to be about three times higher than for the general population (Nosek & Hughes, 2003). Thus, women with disabilities are doubly at risk for depression, due to both gender and disability. The rate of depression for women with disabilities is about 30%, compared to 8% for nondisabled women and 26% in men with disabilities. Depression is probably the most prevalent secondary condition. But it is important to remember two aspects about depression in women with disabilities. First, the depression rate varies widely by disability type (Olkin, 2004). For example, the lifetime risk of depression in multiple sclerosis (which is more common in women than men) is 50%, which is higher than for most other disabilities. Although there is no evidence that risk of depression is any greater in people with early onset blindness or deafness, and in fact there may be less risk, there is a risk associated with later onset vision or hearing loss, compared to peers without these impairments. It is difficult to make generalizations about depression across all disabilities. The second aspect to remember about depression in women with disabilities is that depression is not the modal response to disability.

Stress

Living with a disability means living in a society that stigmatizes and devalues the person with the disability, and this creates psychological stress (Gill, 1996). This devaluation, and indeed the invisibility of disability and people with disabilities, is a chronic stressor. Women with disabilities report higher levels of stress than do men with disabilities (Nosek & Hughes, 2003). Compared to their male counterparts, women with disabilities have more financial problems, less education and employment, less access to disability benefits, and greater rates of single status. They are more likely to live in poverty, to be socially isolated, to be abused, and to have chronic health problems. A National Health Institute Survey reports that 21% of women who had at least three functional limitations experienced difficulty with day-to-day stress, compared to 2% of women with no limitations (cited in Nosek & Hughes, 2003).

Self-Esteem

It is not surprising women with disabilities experience lowered self-esteem, given the types, frequency, and severity of stressors for women with disabilities. Women are more likely to internalize the negative socialization about disability, a highly stigmatized condition. These problems are compounded because self-esteem is linked to employment status, which in turn is linked to economic resources. Therefore, self-esteem is a critical point for intervention.

Social Connection

Isolation is a problem for many women with disabilities. This refers not just to the physical isolation related to inaccessible transportation and environment but also to social isolation. For the ethnic minority woman with a disability this isolation is compounded by dual minority status. She is an outsider in her ethnic group and in her women's group (due to disability), as well as in her disability group (due to ethnicity). This isolation may contribute to the absence of demographic and research data on minority women with disabilities (Bernal, 1996).

Women who incur disabilities after marriage are four times as likely as their male counterparts to divorce. Disabled women are one third less likely to marry than are disabled men, and are older when they do marry. This higher rate of single status puts women with disabilities at economic risk. For example, they are more likely to live below the poverty level, less likely to have private health insurance, and less likely to receive social security benefits (Nosek & Hughes, 2003). Their participation in the workforce is less than that of women without disabilities or men with disabilities (see table 10.3), and their monthly earnings are similarly less (see table 10.2). Lower marriage and employment rates means that women with disabilities have fewer social contacts. Isolation is itself a risk factor for morbidity and mortality, as well as for depression, and is an important target for clinical intervention.

Abuse

Disability is not a protective factor against abuse, it is a risk factor. Children with disabilities are significantly more likely to be physically and sexually abused than nondisabled children, and the abuse is more likely to be chronic and perpetrated by a family member or attendant (Nosek & Hughes, 2003; Sobsey, Randall, & Parrila, 1997). Abuse and other types of victimization (e.g., harassment, neglect, withholding of assistance, taking of assistive devices) must be assessed for all clients with disabilities of whatever age. It is important for assessment of traditional types of

abuse, and disability-related abuse as well. Measures such as the *Abuse Assessment Screen—Disability* (McFarlane et al., 2001) can aid in detecting disability-related abuse that might otherwise be overlooked. Five factors predict with 80% accuracy whether a woman has experienced physical, sexual, or disability-related abuse in the past year: her age, education, mobility, social isolation, and depression (Nosek & Hughes, 2003).

Violence and abuse are also a cause of disability (Olkin & Pledger, 2003). Suicide attempts account for some disabilities. A study of 8,000 people over a period of 40 years found that 1.6% of cases of spinal cord injury (SCI) were caused by a failed suicide attempt (Kennedy, Rogers, Speer, & Frankel, 1999). For those 1.6% the gender ratio was equal, although a high proportion were single (49%), unemployed (42%), and parents (33%). Another study of SCI survivors in Denmark from 1953 to 1990 found that 3% of all SCI cases were due to suicide attempts (Hartkopp, Bronnum-Hansen, Seidenschnur, & Biering-Sorensen, 1998). Physical abuse may cause disability onset or exacerbation. Although no statistics are kept on this cause of disability, one study of mothers with visual impairments found that 5% of the 31 participants reported that their disability was caused by or exacerbated by family violence (Conley-Jung & Olkin, 2001). Another study involving 31 mothers with various disabilities indicated a 32% rate of violence in the family of origin, though participants did not report whether the violence was implicated in the onset or exacerbation of the disability (Cohen, 1998). It is imperative for health-care professionals to collect data about the role of family violence as a cause of disability, as the first step toward prevention.

HEALTH AND WELLNESS

The life situation of women with disabilities is complex and permeated with attitudinal, social, and economic obstacles to psychosocial well-being (Nosek & Hughes, 2003, p. 229). One obstacle is the ways in which women with disabilities are perceived as romantic partners. Physical attractiveness means being socially and sexually desirable. Disability is seen as counter to attrac-

TABLE 10.3 Participation in the Workforce, 1994

	Men	Women
No disability	89.9%	74.5%
Mild disability	85.1%	68.4%
Severe disability	27.8%	24.7%

Source: Data from McNeil (1997).

tiveness, and hence limiting to opportunities to find partners, mate, and have children. Women with disabilities are often viewed as unable to perform useful functions in society, either economically productive roles or reproduction and nurturance (Bernal, 1996; Gill, 1996). The stereotype of women with disabilities is that they are passive and recipients but not givers of care. Consistent with this stereotype, they are not expected to be workers, romantic partners, caregivers, or mothers (Gill, 1996). Unfortunately, most people indicate that they would not marry a person with a disability (DeLoach, 1994; Olkin & Howson, 1994). The disability pride movement is working to counter these notions of disability as unattractive. Still, very little is known about the dating and mating patterns of women with disabilities. Men with disabilities are more likely to marry if they are employed, and it can be surmised that the same holds true for women with disabilities as well.

The definition of disability as a social construction removes the burden of blame from women with disabilities and places it in the physical, social, economic, educational, legal, and political environment. This moves the focus off people with defects requiring cure or normalization, to a view of women with disabilities as part of a disability community and culture in which they can take pride. However, "we [women with disabilities] are finding ourselves and each other as never before. We are joining forces across the country and across generations to take our rightful place in society . . . we know our greatest power to get what we need is not by doing it alone but through cooperation and collaboration–skills that are hallmarks of the culture of both women and people with disabilities" (Gill, 1996, p. 14). The emphasis within the medical service delivery system on the medical model (burden, pain, personal tragedy) (McLaughlin, 2003) focuses attention on only the physical and medical aspects of disability. Such an emphasis ignores the sociopolitical and cultural realities of women with disabilities and the stigma that permeates every level of their lives (Gill, 1996).

Clients may prefer health professionals from the same cultural background, and achieve better outcomes (Bernal, 1996). However, ethnic minorities with disabilities encounter medical care from a like ethnic minority infrequently. African Americans, Hispanics/Latinos, and Native Americans together make up about 22% of the general population, but only 8.5% of physicians (Bernal, 1996). Women with disabilities are even less likely to encounter physicians with disabilities; medicine is a field in which people with disabilities are severely underrepresented. So too is psychology; fewer than 2% of the members of the American Psychological Association identity themselves as people with disabilities, although some unknown number of members with disabilities do not identify themselves as such. Girls and women with disabilities are unlikely to receive either medical or psychological care from someone with a disability.

Women with disabilities have difficulty gaining access to appropriate health care, although their need is great. Approximately 33% of women with at least three functional limitations rate their overall health as poor, compared to fewer than 1% of women with no limitations (Nosek & Hughes, 2003). Typical women's health problems, such as stress, hypertension, depression, smoking and weight, are more problematic when they interact with disability. Rehabilitation specialists are not trained in women's health and reproductive issues; general practitioners are not trained in disability issues and often work in offices or with equipment devices that are inaccessible. In this way, the medical care of women with disabilities splits them into their gendered selves and their disabled selves.

As people with disabilities take more control of the disability dialogue, they will become a part of key processes that impact their lives. This requires that it is people with disabilities who (a) set the research agenda and funding priorities, (b) participate in health research that is not focused on disability as well as that which is, (c) have access to research findings and assistive technologies that impact the lives of people with disabilities, and (d) encourage the voices of those who have been most invisible.

INTERVENTION

Clinical work with girls and women clients with disabilities might incorporate three areas of intervention (ideas in this section come from Olkin,

1999, 2001; Solomon, 1993; and colleagues at Through the Looking Glass[1]). The first is process: How does disability affect the process of intervention? The second is content: What should be the focus of treatment? And third, the role of the therapist: How does disability affect the role(s) of the therapist?

Regarding process, it is essential for the health professional to become comfortable with disability. It is helpful if professionals are not startled or put off by encountering a new client with a disability. Also, the pace and timing of psychotherapy may need to be adjusted to accommodate the girl or woman with a disability. Some clients (e.g., with traumatic brain injury) may need more frequent sessions, and others (e.g., someone living with multiple sclerosis) may need a slower pace to assimilate therapeutic ideas. The psychotherapist must feel free to bring up the disability even if the client does not, and know how to talk about it respectfully.

Regarding content, all of the risk factors are prime areas for treatment focus. A therapeutic case formulation incorporates disability issues into the treatment plan without unduly over- or underemphasizing their role. It can be therapeutic to provide concrete assistance (e.g., give the client the phone number of a national disability organization; provide a form to apply for paratransit; suggest useful Web sites) and may move the therapy forward into new phases. The economic realities of living with a disability often are essential to address as well. "Unless we change the tide of poverty within this population, we are not going to see an improvement in their health, health care delivery, or their abilities to afford a decent lifestyle" (Bernal, 1996, p. 61).

Regarding the role of the therapist, work outside the office is at least as important as work inside the office. This suggests being an advocate, and working for social, political and legal changes that affect the lives of people with disabilities. Girls and women with disabilities seem to bear an undue burden of society's ills—abuse, poverty, isolation, and depression. These ills are not inherent in disability, but in the stigma, prejudice and discrimination that disability incurs. Psychotherapists are limited in their abilities to help the individual without addressing the sociopolitical environment.

NOTE

1. Through the Looking Glass, 2198 Sixth St., Berkeley, CA 94710.

REFERENCES

Bernal, D. L. (1996). The perspective of ethnicity on women's health and disability: More questions than answers. In D. M. Krotoski, M. A. Nosek, & M. A. Turk (Eds.), *Women with physical disabilities: Achieving and maintaining health and well-being* (pp. 57–61). Baltimore: Paul Brookes.

Cohen, L. J. (1998). *Mothers' perceptions of the influence of their physical disabilities on the developmental tasks of children.* Unpublished doctoral dissertation, California School of Professional Psychology, Alameda, CA.

Conley-Jung, C., & Olkin, R. (2001). Mothers with visual impairments or blindness raising young children. *Journal of Visual Impairment and Blindness, 91*(1), 14–29.

Deegan, M. J., & Brooks, N. A. (Eds.). (1985). *Women and disability.* New Brunswick, NJ: Transaction Books.

DeLoach, C. P. (1994). Attitudes toward disability: Impact on sexual development and forging of intimate relationships. *Journal of Applied Rehabilitation Counseling, 25,* 18–25.

Fine, M., & Asch, A. (Eds.). (1988). *Women with disabilities: Essays in psychology, culture, and politics.* Philadelphia: Temple University Press.

Gerrschick, T. J. (2000). Toward a theory of disability and gender. *Signs, 25*(4), 1263–1268.

Gill, C. J. (1996). Becoming visible: Personal health experiences of women with disabilities. In D. M. Krotoski, M. A. Nosek & M. A. Turk (Eds.), *Women with physical disabilities: Achieving and maintaining health and well-being* (pp. 5–15). Baltimore: Paul Brookes.

Gill, C. J. (1997). Four types of integration in disability identity development. *Journal of Vocational Rehabilitation, 9,* 39–46.

Hanna, W. J., & Rogovsky, B. (1991). Women with disabilities: Two handicaps plus. *Disability, Handicap & Society, 6*(1), 49–63.

Hartkopp, A., Bronnum-Hansen, H., Seidenschnur, A. M., & Biering-Sorensen, F. (1998). Suicide in a spinal cord injured population: Its relation to functional status. *Archives of Physical Medicine and Rehabilitation, 79*(11), 1356–1361.

Healey, S. (1993). The common agenda between old women, women with disabilities and all women. *Women and Therapy, 14*(3/4), 65–77.

Kennedy, P., Rogers, B. A., Speer, S., & Frankel, H. (1999). Spinal cord injuries and attempted suicide: A retrospective review. *Spinal Cord, 37*(12), 847–852.

McFarlane, J., Hughes, R. B., Nosek, M., Groff, J., Swedlund, N., & Mullen, P. (2001). Abuse Assessment Screen–disability (AAS–D): Measuring frequency, type, and perpetrator of abuse toward women with physical disabilities. *Journal of Women's Health and Gender-Based Medicine, 10,* 861–866.

McLaughlin, J. (2003). Screening networks: Shared agendas in feminist and disability movement challenges to antenatal screening and abortion. *Disability and Society, 18*(3), 297–310.

McNeil, J. M. (1997). *Americans with disabilities, 1994–95.* Current Population Report No. P70-61. Washington, DC: U.S. Bureau of the Census.

Nosek, M. A., & Hughes, R. B. (2003). Psychosocial issues of women with physical disabilities: The continuing gender debate. *Rehabilitation Counseling Bulletin, 46*(4), 224–233.

Olkin, R. (1999). *What psychotherapists should know about disability.* New York: Guilford Press.

Olkin, R. (2001). Disability-affirmative therapy. *Spinal Cord Injury Psychosocial Process, 14*(1), 12–23.

Olkin, R. (2003). Women with disabilities. In J. C. Chrisler, C. Golden, & P. D. Rozee (Eds.), *Lectures on the psychology of women* (3rd ed., pp. 144–157). New York: McGraw-Hill.

Olkin, R. (2004). Disability and depression. In F. Haseltine (Ed.), *Women with disabilities—a comprehensive guide to care.* Philadelphia: Lippincott, Williams & Wilkins.

Olkin, R., & Howson, L. (1994). Attitudes toward and images of physical disability. *Journal of Social Behavior and Personality, 9,* 81–96.

Olkin, R., & Pledger, C. (2003). Can disability studies and psychology join hands? *American Psychologist, 58*(4), 296–304.

Sobsey, D., Randall, W., & Parrila, R. K. (1997). Gender differences in abused children with and without disabilities. *Child Abuse and Neglect, 21*(8), 707–720.

Solomon, S. E. (1993). Women and physical distinction: A review of the literature and suggestions for intervention. *Women and Therapy, 14*(3/4), 91–103.

Wright, B. (1983). *Physical disability: A psychosocial approach* (2nd ed.). New York: Harper and Row.

JANIS SANCHEZ-HUCLES
and KIMBERLY GAMBLE

Trauma in the Lives of Girls and Women

Traumatic events are commonplace and can occur in the lives of any of us. Between 70–90% of all individuals in the United States experience at least one traumatic event in their lives and a third to a half must contend with a second trauma (Breslau & Kessler, 2001; Solomon & Davidson, 1997).

An individual's history, experience, temperament, and resiliency all shape the potential impact of trauma. Although reactions can be unique and subjective, gender mediates exposure to trauma in the lives of women and girls. Women face trauma imposed by the vulnerability of inhabiting a female body. In addition, they are exposed to unique traumas in patriarchal societies that implicitly or explicitly support the subordination of women. Unequal status makes women and girls vulnerable to trauma. Each year, 20 million women have unsafe abortions, resulting in 78,000 mortalities; one in four women are abused in pregnancy; one in three are beaten or sexually coerced; 60 million girls are reported as missing due to infanticide or neglect; and 5,000 women and girls are killed by their own families due to perceived violations to the family's honor (Solomon, 2003).

Women who suffer from a traumatic event are twice as likely as men to develop problems following the experience (Kessler, Sonnega, Bromet, Hughes, & Nelson, 1995). The higher rates of help seeking for women in medical and mental health systems may reflect the gender effects of trauma. Research shows that half of all women in psychiatric hospitals were previously abused physically or sexually (Beck & van der Kolk, 1987). Following trauma, women are more likely than men to engage in self-destructive behaviors like suicide and mutilation, and they are disproportionately exposed to trauma that is severe, sustained, and repetitive.

HISTORICAL CONCEPTIONS OF TRAUMA

Although references to traumatic events have been found in literary references for more than 4,000 years, it was not until 1980 that the American Psychiatric Association introduced a formal category of posttraumatic stress disorder (PTSD). Herman (1992) has identified three eras in the conceptualization of trauma. In the late 19th century, the label of trauma was used in conjunction with "hysterical women." It was applied next to male soldiers who suffered shell shock, beginning with World War I. Only in the last 20 years has the sexual, physical, emotional, and psychological abuse of women and children been recognized as another significant source of trauma.

The American Psychiatric Association, in its *Diagnostic and Statistical Manual of Mental Disorders (DSM-IV)*, classifies PTSD as a form of anxiety disorder and defines a traumatic stressor as: "the experiencing, witnessing, or being confronted with an event or events that involve actual or threatened death or serious injury or a threat to the physical integrity of self or others and to which the person's response was one of intense fear, helplessness, or horror" (American Psychiatric Association, 1994, p. 428). Some of the clinical assessment tools used to explore trauma and PTSD include the childhood trauma questionnaire, the trauma life history, and the structured clinical interview for *DSM-III-R/DSM-IV* (Hien & Bukszpan, 1999).

The *DSM* definitions of PTSD trauma seem to apply best to large-scale and single-episode events. But more attention should be focused on the repeated and long-term effects of chronic exposure to racism, sexism, classism, homophobia, disability, religious persecution, the witnessing of violence, and assisting those who have been traumatized. In addition, what factors explain why some individuals show resilience after trauma while others develop psychopathology?

NEWER CONCEPTIONS OF TRAUMA

Not all trauma reactions meet the criteria for PTSD diagnoses. Some individuals exposed to trauma never come to the attention of professionals because they self-medicate with alcohol or drugs. Other individuals receive a primary diagnosis in the areas of affective, anxiety, eating, dissociative, somatoform, conversion, borderline, or psychotic disorders. Clinicians and researchers have developed newer conceptions of trauma in an attempt to be more attuned to the day-to-day experiences of women and girls.

Type I and II Trauma

Terr (1991) distinguishes between events that are sudden, brief, unexpected, and devastating and those that involve chronic and repeated exposure. She classified the former as type I trauma and the latter as type II. Type I traumas encompass natural disasters, accidents, and a single episode of rape or robbery. Type II traumas include multiple or long-term experiences of sexual harassment, abuse, incest, or rape and appear to engender more long-term damaging effects and a poorer prognosis for recovery. Type II symptoms include numbing, dissociation, detachment, and possible long-term cognitive, emotional, and interpersonal difficulties.

Complex PTSD and DESNOS

Complex PTSD or DESNOS (disorders of extreme stress not otherwise specified) as proposed by Herman (1992) refer to type II traumas involving interpersonal threats that are severe, sustained, and repetitive. One assessment instrument that attempts to measure the possible symptoms of complex PTSD or DESNOS is the dissociative experience scale (DES). This test assesses symptoms such as disturbances in affect, cognition, perceptual alterations, dissociation, and amnesia (Bernstein & Putnam, 1986).

Violation of Just or Safe-World Expectations

Janoff-Bulman (1992) has expanded ideas of trauma by underscoring the subjectivity of individual responses to traumatic events. Her definition of a traumatic event is one that violates an individual's expectations of a just or safe world. Trauma victims experience a shattering of their beliefs that the self is valuable, that they live in a benevolent world where people are treated with fairness, and that life is meaningful. The particular trauma may be very personal, such as a hate crime based on ethnicity, religion, sexual orientation, or sex. It may be associated with a life threatening illness, infertility, or miscarriage of a pregnancy.

Betrayal Trauma

Traumas that develop in response to violations of trust in significant relationships are defined as betrayal trauma by Freyd (1996). These relationships often involve an imbalance of power, dependence, and nurturance. The betrayal is typically sexual, physical, or emotional abuse carried out by parent and parent figures, relatives, religious figures, teachers, therapists, and other figures of power in or about the home. Freyd notes that this type of abuse can produce significant cognitive and emotional barriers for victims especially in the development of other interpersonal relationships.

Insidious Trauma and Domestic Captivity

Insidious trauma also involves sustained, repetitive, and cumulative trauma, but here the acts of trauma are aimed systematically at the less powerful by those who are in power (Root, 1996). Examples of insidious trauma include sexism, racism, systematic murder of female infants, homophobia, and religious persecution. An example of insidious trauma is the "driving while Black or Brown" racial profiling that leads minority parents to warn their adolescents of the real dangers of random traffic stops.

Other examples are the domestic violence and rape sustained by women. Historically, women were perceived to be the property of men and what occurred in the home was deemed private. Conceptions of women's complaints as "hysterical" made it more difficult for women to be taken seriously. Making formal complaints within the legal system can be even more daunting to women of color because of gender, race, or class and the beliefs that our society does not value their lives or try to protect them from harm (Sanchez-Hucles & Dutton, 1999).

Root (1996) uses the term "domestic captivity" to refer to the chronic state of vigilance that women must maintain to protect themselves in societies where they are subject to violence from partners, acquaintances, and strangers. Many girls and women are fearful of traveling alone, of being out at night, of walking in their neighborhoods, and of living in unsafe locations lest they experience violence or sexual aggression. Children and adults with physical disabilities are at higher risk for abuse and neglect (Mueser, Hiday, Goodman, & Valenti-Hein, 2003). Gay, lesbian, and transgendered individuals are at increased risk for physical violence (Franklin, 2001).

Postcolonial Syndrome

The long-lasting effects of genocide, racism, and oppression have been termed postcolonial syndrome (Duran, Duran, Brave Heart, & Yellow Horse-Davis, 1998). Groups that have been colonized or have been the targets of ethnic cleansing endure torture, rape, violence, threats, murder, displacement, theft, and disruption of their families, language, culture, and values. There is pressure on these groups to assimilate a dominant culture, and there is no legal redress for the problems that victims experience as the governments typically sanction the actions against them where they live. Colonized individuals may internalize their rage, despair, and lack of self-efficacy and develop posttraumatic stress disorders. They may also at times redirect their internalized racism against themselves or others in their group. This can lead to high rates of suicide and violence. For many men who suffer from postcolonial syndrome, women and girls become the all too easy targets as outlets of rage, despair, and frustration (Sanchez-Hucles & Dutton, 1999).

GENDER AND DEVELOPMENTAL DIFFERENCES IN TRAUMA

Women are more exposed to high-impact trauma like rape, childhood physical abuse, and neglect and they are twice as likely to receive a PTSD diagnosis (Kessler et al., 1995).

Criminal Victimization, Rape, and Abuse

Clear sex differences exist for crime victims and include the following findings (Feuer, Jefferson, & Resick, 2001): Females are more likely to experience violence at the hands of a partner or acquaintance and are at higher risk for rape, abuse, neglect, and molestation. Women account for 94% of rape victims (Kessler et al., 1995), and a recent national survey indicated that 18% of women reported a completed rape or attempted rape in their lifetime (Tjaden & Thoennes, 2000).

There are also gender differences in childhood sexual abuse. Girls are more likely rape victims than boys, with occurrence rates of 27% and 16%, respectively (Finkelhor, Hotaling, Lewis, & Smith, 1990). There are also differences in the perpetrator of the abuse. Girls are more likely than boys to suffer sexual abuse from their biological fathers (13% vs. 4.5%, respectively). In general, girls are at greatest risk from relatives, whereas boys are more likely to be the victims of strangers and friends (Feinauer, 1989).

Up to approximately the age of 12, there are no obvious sex differences associated with experiencing or observing a trauma (Pynoos et al., 1987). After the age of 12, gender mediates the impact of trauma, with females showing worse effects. This is due apparently to the greater exposure of women and girls to rape, and rape is the traumatic event most likely to result in posttraumatic stress (Kessler et al., 1995).

Symptom Expression

Gender patterns in trauma are not always clear and consistent. Feuer and her colleagues (2001) reviewed the literature on symptom expression and summarized several themes. In general, females demonstrate a greater number of symptoms following a traumatic event, and more of these symptoms are associated with the diagnostic criteria for posttraumatic stress disorder. Part of the difficulty in achieving accurate data to understand possible sex differences for the diagnosing of PTSD is the fact that most trauma follow-up studies focus on the internalizing symptoms of women rather than the externalizing symptoms of men (Heath, Bean, & Feinauer, 1996). Whereas females are encouraged to express emotions, males are reinforced for emotional inhibition (Feuer et al., 2001). Hence, girls and women are more likely than males and boys to report trauma and their symptoms. There are minimal gender differences in symptom expression prior

to the teenaged years, when there is less pressure to conform to societal stereotypes.

TYPES OF TRAUMA

Medical Trauma

It was not until 1994 that *DSM-IV* included being diagnosed with a chronic or life threatening illness as a possible antecedent for PTSD (American Psychiatric Association, 1994). This inclusion was significant as it recognized how the diagnoses and the aggressive treatment of diseases such as cancer can elicit symptoms of PTSD, such as fear, helplessness, hyperarousal, avoidance, blunted affect, and reliving of experiences. The majority of cancer patients do not meet the criteria for PTSD, as incidence rates vary from 2.5–20% (Alter et al., 1996). However, children who suffer from PTSD symptoms as a result of serious illness are at risk for developmental disruptions, and parents can be harmed by the stresses associated with the illnesses of their children. Stuber, Christakis, Houskamp, and Kazak (1996) report symptoms of PTSD in 12.5% of children two years after treatment, with mothers and fathers also evidencing PTSD symptoms at the rates of approximately 40% and 33%, respectively. Adult survivors of cancer show adverse impact in their overall quality of life, social effectiveness, and mental and physical health (Jacobsen et al., 1998). Research suggests that it is important to identify those medical patients with PTSD complications, as they may need additional interventions to avoid long-term negative consequences (Meeske, Ruccione, Globe, & Stuber, 2001).

Homicide

Although males account for the majority of all homicide victims, women are at greater risk to be killed by a spouse. Browne (1987) reports that a significant number of women who murdered their domestic partners have a long history of threats and abuse from those partners. Furthermore, they were unable to obtain protection and relief from social services.

Ritchie (1996) has coined the term "gender entrapment" to describe a cycle for many imprisoned African American women who were physically and sexually abused as children, later became involved in violent and abusive relationships with men, and became dependent on alcohol and drugs and lives of prostitution. This lifestyle of violence and abuse led to retaliatory violence toward their partners and arrests for homicide.

Spouse or Partner Abuse

Violence that occurs in the context of an intimate sexual, spousal, or cohabitation relationship is commonly referred to as spousal or domestic violence or abuse. This violence may be physical, psychological, or emotional. There are widespread beliefs that domestic violence is most prevalent among the poor. Domestic violence exists across all cultural, ethnic, and social classes; however, those with financial resources and high social status are better able to avoid detection and prosecution.

Domestic violence is the major cause of injury to females. Domestic violence incidence rates have been reported to range from 10–30% (Fagan & Browne, 1994). Although women can become violent, men are far more likely to be arrested, and women are at higher risk for injury in domestic violence. In addition, the abuse of women tends to be more severe, repetitive, and long term than violence toward men. Women are at higher risk to sustain serious injuries and hospital visits and are more at risk to be killed by their male partners than by other assailants (Sanchez-Hucles & Hudgins, 2001). People often wonder why battered women do not leave their batterers. A woman is most at risk of being killed when trying to escape from a batterer. Also, there are complex emotional, financial, and psychological dependencies that tie women to batterers.

Girls who witness domestic violence are at higher risk for aggression, withdrawal, anxiety, somatization, and suicide at that time, and even as adults are at higher risk for physical and sexual abuse and violence in their dating relationships. Women are also at risk for abuse as they become

elderly and are dependent on others for their care (Maker, Kemmelmeier, & Peterson, 1998).

War, Torture, Terrorism, and Refugee Status

Although war represents one of the most persistent examples of human violence, it is important to note the different experiences that males and females encounter. Unlike men, women are rarely the initiators of war, leaders in combat, or invited to negotiations; nevertheless, they play active roles (Bop, 2001). When females serve in the military, they are exposed to a variety of combat and hospital settings where they witness death, injuries, and destruction. They must also contend with sexual harassment and rape. Only since the Vietnam War has it been noted that women can suffer from intense emotional effects, psychiatric symptoms, and secondary traumatization when their partners have combat stress reactions and PTSD (Nelson & Wright, 1996).

Women and children are increasingly counted as war casualties, primarily as civilians but also as combatants. UNICEF has estimated that 80% of international warfare victims are women and children (Yule, Stuvland, Baingana, & Smith, 2003). It has been noted that the assault of women and girls is a central and universal component of war (Bop, 2001). Women and girls are the more invisible casualties of war because they are traumatized and terrorized in order to weaken the morale and commitment of men. The daily atrocities that females endure, such as rape, torture, captivity, and confinement, are often unreported. When the enemy brutalizes these women, they are all too frequently blamed for their traumatic treatment and are shunned by their partners and families. They may endure additional abuse from their partners. Many of these women and girls must contend with pregnancy, sexually transmitted diseases, sexual injuries, and dysfunctions and can be forced into prostitution as a result of their experiences in war (Solomon, 2003).

Torture

Most definitions of torture involve the basic elements of intentional infliction of physical or psychological pain and repression against individuals and communities. The United Nations has described torture as encompassing intentional acts of severe mental and physical pain that is designed to punish, intimidate, or obtain information or a confession (Vesti & Kastrup, 1995).

Pope (2001) has noted that women and children are at special risk for torture because of their smaller physical size relative to most men and the likelihood they will not be deemed credible reporters of their experiences. Women and girls are often tortured in retaliation for actions of their husbands or male relatives, as a ploy to intimidate or subordinate plans or as a demonstration in front of males to make them divulge information.

Terrorism

Terrorism is variously described as the use of force, violence, or intimidation to demoralize, intimidate, or control others for political reasons (Baker, 2003). Typically, terrorism is aimed at violating a sense of safety and disrupting normal routines and activities. What makes terrorism unique is that this criminal violence is directed at civilian rather than military targets to induce fear and dread (Marsella, 2004). Women can be terrorized by attacks of sexual violence, random and suicidal bombings, drive-by shootings, and psychological abuse and intimidation.

Refugees

Mothers and children account for more than 70% of the refugee population (Martin, 1994). In examining the research on mental health effects of immigration on Latino children, researchers found that acculturation has a more negative effect on women and children than men and that the resilience of children was highly correlated to the positive adaptations of mothers (Garrison, Roy, & Azar, 1999). Women and girls are at high risk for violence and abuse as they try to leave their home countries and resettle in new locations.

Sexual violations are used to intimidate females especially in cultures that highly value chastity in women. Refugees are exposed to lack of food, shelter, and health care, as well as the trauma of witnessing atrocities or not knowing the fate of loved ones. The combined losses of immigration can lead men to react by increased violence and intimidation directed at women (Sanchez-Hucles & Dutton, 1999).

RISK AND RESILIENCY FACTORS

Although many individuals are exposed to traumatic events, only a minority meet the full PTSD criteria (North, 2003). In general, the younger a girl is when subjected to trauma, the more severe the consequences. Children are not equipped with the practical, emotional, and cognitive resources to handle overwhelming challenges. Trauma can cause developmental delays and can place girls at greater risk for revictimization and PTSD (Astin, Ogland-Hand, Coleman, & Foy, 1995).

Traumas caused by other people are more devastating than those due to natural causes, and the closer the relationship between victim and victimizer, the greater the trauma. When girls are violated by a parent, teacher, relative, or religious figure, it eliminates that person as a potential resource in the young person's life that is unlikely to be filled by anyone else. In the case of sexual abuse, more severe trauma is associated with physical force, genital contact, and the involvement of an authority figure or other loved one. Children and adolescents are most vulnerable to harm as they are still developing (Browne & Finkelhor, 1986). Less socially acceptable traumas like rape, gay bashing, and hate crimes against ethnic minorities, immigrants, prostitutes, and the homeless revictimize individuals with feelings of shame, guilt and self-blame (Briere, 1997).

There are also psychosocial risk factors that impact on responses to trauma. Adverse impact is more likely if any of the following coexist: the presence of high stress before or after a trauma, psychiatric history in an individual or in close relatives, low self-esteem, living in a home with a marital disruption before adolescence, and exposure to poverty, violence, homelessness, abuse, or trauma as a child. In addition, being female or an ethnic minority contributes higher risk for both experiencing trauma and having a poorer prognosis (Briere, 1997; Friedman & Marsella, 1996).

Bonanno (2004) has noted that for some individuals, trauma has a transformative function. The majority of individuals exposed to a traumatic event experience only brief and minor disruption to functioning. Bonanno argues that resilience is more common than pathology. Some individuals emerge from trauma with a stronger sense of self-efficacy, empowerment, and coping skills; a keener appreciation of priorities in their lives; improved interpersonal relationships; and a heightened capacity to bring sense and meaning to their lives (Updegraff & Taylor, 2000).

TREATMENT

The first task of helping professionals who seek to assist individuals exposed to trauma involves assessment. Assessment of trauma entails a multidimensional approach that examines emotional, behavioral, and cognitive status, and an investigation of symptoms and developmental history (Drake, Bush, & van Gorp, 2001). Whether the diagnosis is PTSD, complex PTSD, or some other variation, clinical pictures are dominated by anxiety in one form or another. Across theoretical orientations there is agreement that it is challenging to treat women who have been exposed to trauma, as it requires clinicians with strong clinical skills, sensitivity, and empathy. No one therapeutic intervention has emerged as the definitive treatment of choice, and there are even controversies with respect to the efficacy of early interventions. For example, although stress debriefing has been widely advocated as a primary intervention for trauma victims, research indicates that this process may cause harm to individuals by stimulating depression, retraumatization, arousal, and distress, and it may interfere with natural recovery (Watson et al., 2001).

The first intervention following exposure to trauma entails providing safety, stabilization, and psychological first aid which consists of emotional support, education about typical stress reactions, and responsiveness to what the person wants and needs (Litz & Gray, 2004). Another key element of treatment is the therapeutic relationship because traumatized individuals often have issues relating to trust, betrayal, dependency, love, and hate. Emotions are often intense and challenge the stability of the therapeutic relationship, especially in cases of complex PTSD and with borderline individuals.

The treatment options most frequently employed for traumatized individuals include cognitive behavioral, psychodynamic, interpersonal, group, and pharmacological interventions. Choices of treatment must be matched to the needs of clients, their stage of trauma, the severity and type of symptoms, and their responses to interventions. In general, treatments are designed to help clients regain a sense of safety, diminish adverse symptoms, and heal the trauma by a process of reintegration and restructuring of thoughts, behaviors, and relationships (van der Kolk & McFarlane, 1996).

Treatment research suggests the greatest efficacy for cognitive behavioral techniques but most clinicians use psychodynamic and interpersonal models to treat trauma clients perhaps due to the greater emphases these approaches place on emotional regulation, dissociation, somatization, depression, reintegration, and relationship issues (van der Kolk, McFarlane & van der Hart, 1996). Clinical treatment studies have supported the efficacy of cognitive behavioral techniques such as exposure therapy, cognitive restructuring, education such as stress inoculation, and anxiety management approaches such as biofeedback and relaxation (Rothbaum & Foa, 1996).

Group therapy can also be a particularly helpful treatment; by interacting with other traumatized individuals, a victim's feelings of safety, mastery, normalization and bonding can be achieved (van der Kolk, van der Hart, & Burbridge, 2002). What remains a treatment challenge is determining the best protocol to address both the deconditioning of anxiety symptoms and the restructuring of the way trauma clients view themselves and the world to promote greater personal integrity and control (van der Kolk, McFarlane, & van der Hart, 1996).

Medications may also be used as adjuncts to psychotherapy, primarily to assist with symptoms of anxiety and depression. Two medical interventions have recently been recommended for PTSD by the Food and Drug Administration: sertraline and paroxetine (Danieli, Engdahl, & Schlenger, 2004).

Often people with trauma need long-term psychotherapy to learn to resolve issues of self-blame and guilt, and to develop appropriate boundaries and an accurate sense of reality. Trauma experts generally agree that the process of healing involves helping victims to regain a sense of safety, mourn their losses, and reconnect with others. Treatment effects should be monitored and adjusted if indicated. Increasingly, more attention is directed toward the development of holistic approaches that match victims' needs and are attentive to cultural frameworks, familial and community support, and reducing the possibility of future trauma.

REFERENCES

Alter, C. L., Pelcovitz, D., Axelrod, A., Goldenberg, B., Harris, H., Myers, B., et al. (1996). Identification of PTSD in cancer Survivors, *Psychosomatics, 37,* 137–143.

American Psychiatric Association. (1994). *Diagnostic and statistical manual of mental disorders* (4th ed.). Washington, DC: Author.

Astin, M. C., Ogland-Hand, S. M., Coleman, E., & Foy, D. W. (1995). Posttraumatic stress disorder and childhood abuse in battered women: Comparisons with maritally distressed women. *Journal of Consulting and Clinical Psychology, 63,* 308–312.

Baker, N. J. (2003). Terrorism: Another form of violence. In L. Slater, J. H. Daniel, & A. E. Banks (Eds.), *The complete guide to mental health for women* (pp. 173–176). Boston: Beacon Press.

Beck, J. C., & van der Kolk, B. (1987). Reports of childhood incest and current behavior of chronically hospitalized psychotic women. *American Journal of Psychiatry, 144,* 1474–1476.

Bernstein, E. M., & Putnam, F. W. (1986). Development, reliability, and validity of a dissociation scale. *Journal of Mental and Nervous Diseases, 174,* 727–734.

Bonanno, G. (2004). Loss, trauma, and human resilience. *American Psychologist, 59,* 20–28.

Bop, C. (2001). Women in conflict: Their gains, their losses. In S. Meintjes, A. Pillay, & M. Turshen (Eds.), *The aftermath: Women in post conflict transformation* (pp. 19–34). London: Zed Books.

Breslau, N., & Kessler, R. C. (2001). The stressor criterion in *DSM-IV* posttraumatic stress disorder: An empirical investigation. *Biological Psychiatry, 50,* 699–704.

Briere, J. (1997). *Psychological assessment of adult posttraumatic states.* Washington, DC: American Psychological Association.

Browne, A. (1987). *When battered women kill.* New York: Macmillan/Free Press.

Browne, A., & Finkelhor, D. (1986). Impact of child sexual abuse: A review of the research. *Psychological Bulletin, 99,* 66–77.

Danieli, Y., Engdahl, B., & Schlenger, W. E. (2004). The psychosocial aftermath of terrorism. In F. M. Moghaddam & A. J. Marsella (Eds.), *Understanding terrorism: Psychosocial roots, consequences, and interventions* (pp. 223–246). Washington, DC: American Psychological Association.

Drake, E. B., Bush, S. E., & van Gorp, W. G. (2001). Evaluation and assessment of PTSD in children and adolescents. In S. Eth (Ed.), *PTSD in children and adolescents* (pp. 1–31). Washington, DC: American Psychiatric Press.

Duran, E., Duran, B., Brave Heart, M., & Yellow Horse-Davis, S. (1998). In Y. Danieli (Ed.), *International handbook of multigenerational legacies of trauma* (pp. 341–354). New York: Plenum Press.

Fagan, J. A., & Browne, A. (1994). Violence between spouses and intimates: Physical aggression between women and men in intimate relationships. In A. J. Reiss, Jr. & J. A. Roth (Eds.), *Understanding and preventing violence* (Vol. 3, pp. 115–292). Washington, DC: National Academy Press.

Feinauer, L. L. (1989). Sexual dysfunction in women sexually abused as children. *Contemporary Family Therapy: An International Journal, 11,* 299–309.

Feuer, C., Jefferson, D., & Resick, P. (2001). Posttraumatic stress disorder settings. In J. Worell (Ed.), *Encyclopedia of women and gender: Sex similarities and differences and the impact of society on gender* (pp. 827–836). San Diego, CA: Academic Press.

Finkelhor, D., Hotaling, G., Lewis, I. A., & Smith, C. (1990). Sexual abuse in a national survey of adult men and women: Prevalence, characteristics, and risk factors. *Child Abuse and Neglect, 14,* 19–28.

Franklin, K. (2001). Hate crime. In J. Worell (Ed.), *Encyclopedia of women and gender: Sex similarities and differences and the impact of society on gender* (pp. 571–576). San Diego, CA: Academic Press.

Freyd, J. (1996). *Betrayal trauma: The logic of forgetting abuse.* Cambridge, MA: Harvard University Press.

Friedman, M., & Marsella, A. (1996). Posttraumatic stress disorder: An overview of the concept. In A. J. Marsella, M. J. Friedman, E. T. Gerrity, & R. M. Scurfield (Eds.), *Ethnocultural aspects of posttraumatic stress disorder: Issues, research, and clinical applications* (pp. 11–32). Washington, DC: American Psychological Association.

Garrison, E. G., Roy, I. S., & Azar, V. (1999). Responding to the mental health needs of Latino children and families through school based services. *Clinical Psychological Review, 19,* 199–219.

Heath, V., Bean, R., & Feinauer, L. (1996). Severity of childhood sexual abuse: Symptom differences between men and women. *American Journal of Family Therapy, 24,* 305–314.

Herman, J. L. (1992). *Trauma and recovery.* New York: Basic Books.

Hien, D., & Bukszpan, C. (1999). Interpersonal violence in a "normal" low income control group. *Women and Health, 29,* 1–16.

Jacobsen, P. B., Widows, M. R., Hann, D. M., Andrykowski, M. A., Kronish, L. E., & Fields, K. K. (1998). Post-traumatic stress disorder symptoms after bone marrow transplant for breast cancer. *Psychosomatic Medicine, 60,* 366–371.

Janoff-Bulman, R. (1992). *Shattered assumptions: Towards a new psychology of trauma.* New York: Free Press.

Kessler, R., Sonnega, A., Bromet, E., Hughes, M., & Nelson, C. B. (1995). Post-traumatic stress disorders in the national co-morbidity survey. *Archives of General Psychiatry, 52,* 1048–1060.

Litz, B. Y., & Gray, M. J. (2004). Early intervention in trauma for adults: A framework for first aid and secondary prevention. In B. T. Litz (Ed.), *Early Intervention for trauma and traumatic loss* (pp. 87–111). New York: Guilford Press.

Maker, A. H., Kemmelmeier, M., & Peterson, C. (1998). Long-term psychological consequences in women of witnessing parental physical conflict and experiencing abuse in childhood. *Journal of Interpersonal Violence, 13,* 574–589.

Marsella, A. J. (2004). Reflections on international terrorism: Issues, concepts, and directions. In F. M. Moghaddam & A. J. Marsella (Eds.), *Understanding terrorism: Psychosocial roots, consequences, and interventions* (pp. 11–48). Washington, DC: American Psychological Association.

Martin, S. F. (1994). A policy perspective on the mental health and psychosocial needs of refugees. In A. J. Marsella, T. Borneman, S. Ekblad, & J. Orley (Eds.), *Amidst peril and pain: The mental health and well being of the world's refugees* (pp. 69–83). Washington, DC: American Psychological Association.

Meeske, K. A., Ruccione, K., Globe, D., & Stuber, M. L. (2001). Posttraumatic stress, quality of life, and psychological distress in young adult survivors of childhood cancer. *Oncology Nursing Forum, 28,* 481–506.

Mueser, K. T., Hiday, V. A., Goodman, L. A., & Valenti-Hein, D. (2003). People with mental and physical disabilities. In B. L. Green, M. J. Friedman, J. T. de Jong, S. D. Solomon, T. M. Keane, J. A. Fairbank, et al. (Eds.), *Trauma interventions in war and peace: Prevention, practice, and policy* (pp. 129–154). New York: Kluwer.

Nelson, B., & Wright, D. (1996). Understanding and treating post-traumatic stress disorder symptoms in female partners of veterans with PTSD. *Journal of Marital and Family Therapy, 22,* 455–467.

North, C. S. (2003). Psychiatric epidemiology of disaster responses. In R. J. Ursano & A. E. Norwood (Eds.), *Trauma and disaster: Responses and management* (pp. 37–62). Washington, DC: American Psychiatric Publishing, Inc.

Pope, K. (2001). Torture. In J. Worell (Ed.), *Encyclopedia of women and gender: Sex similarities and differences and the impact of society on gender* (pp. 1141–1150). San Diego, CA: Academic Press.

Pynoos, R. S., Fredrick, C., Nader, K. Arroyo, W., Steinbergh, A., Eth, S., et al. (1987). Life threat and posttraumatic stress in school-age children. *Archives of General Psychiatry, 44,* 1057–1063.

Root, M. P. (1996). Women of color and traumatic stress in "domestic captivity": Gender and race as disempowering statuses. In A. J. Marsella, M. J. Friedman, E. T. Gerrity & R. M. Scurfield (Eds.), *Ethnocultural aspects of posttraumatic stress disorder: Issues, research, and clinical applications* (pp. 363–388). Washington, DC: American Psychological Association.

Ritchie, B. (1996). *Compelled to crime: The gender entrapment of Black battered women.* New York: Routledge.

Rothbaum, B. O., & Foa, E. B. (1996). Cognitive behavioral therapy for posttraumatic stress disorder. In B. van der Kolk, A. C. McFarlane, & L. Weisaeth (Eds.), *Traumatic stress: The effects of overwhelming experience on mind, body, and society* (pp. 491–509). New York: Guilford Press.

Sanchez-Hucles, J., & Dutton, M. (1999). The interaction between societal violence and domestic violence: Racial and cultural factors. In M. Harway and J. M. O'Neil (Eds.), *What causes men's violence against women?* (pp. 183–204). Thousand Oaks, CA: Sage.

Sanchez-Hucles, J., & Hudgins, P. (2001). Trauma in diverse settings. In J. Worell (Ed.), *Encyclopedia of women and gender: Sex similarities and differences and the impact of society on gender* (pp. 1151–1168). San Diego, CA: Academic Press.

Solomon, S. D. (2003). Introduction. In B. L. Green, M. J. Friedman, J. T. de Jong, S. D. Solomon, T. M. Keane, J. A. Fairbank, et al. (Eds.), *Trauma interventions in war and peace: Prevention, practice, and policy* (pp. 3–16). New York: Kluwer.

Solomon, S. D., & Davidson, J. (1997). Trauma, prevalence, impairments, service use and cost. *Journal of Clinical Psychiatry, 58,* 5–11.

Stuber, M. L., Christakis, D., Houskamp, B., & Kazak, A. (1996). Post-trauma symptoms in childhood leukemia survivors and their parents. *Psychosomatics, 37,* 254–261.

Terr, L. (1991). Childhood traumas: An outline and overview. *American Journal of Psychiatry, 48,* 10–20.

Tjaden, P., & Thoennes, N. (2000). *Extent, nature, and consequence of intimate partner violence* (NCJ181867). Washington, DC: National Institute of Justice and the Centers for Disease Control and Prevention.

Updegraff, J. A., & Taylor, S. E. (2000). From vulnerability to growth: Positive and negative effects of stressful life events. In J. H. Harvey & E. D. Miller (Eds.), *Loss and trauma: General and close relationship perspectives* (pp. 3–28). Philadelphia: Brunner-Routledge.

van der Kolk, B. A., & McFarlane, A. C. (1996). The black hole of trauma. In B. van der Kolk, A. C. McFarlane, & L. Weisaeth (Eds.), *Traumatic stress: The effects of overwhelming experience on mind, body, and society* (pp. 3–23). New York: Guilford Press.

van der Kolk, B. A., McFarlane, A. C., & van der Hart, O. V. (1996). A general approach to the treatment of posttraumatic stress disorder. In B. van der Kolk, A. C. McFarlane, & L. Weisaeth (Eds.), *Traumatic stress: The effects of overwhelming experience on mind, body, and society* (pp. 417–440). New York: Guilford Press.

van der Kolk, B. A., van der Hart, O., & Burbridge, J. (2002). Approaches to the treatment of PTSD. In M. B. Williams & J. F. Sommer, Jr. (Eds.), *Simple and complex post-traumatic stress disorder: Strategies for comprehensive treatment in clinical practice* (pp. 23–46). Binghamton, NY: Haworth Press.

Vesti, P., & Kastrup, M. (1995). Refugee status, torture, and adjustment. In J. R. Freedy & S. E. Hobfoll (Eds.), *Traumatic stress: From theory to practice* (pp. 213–235). New York: Plenum Press.

Watson, P. J., Friedman, M. J., Gibson, L. E., Ruzek, J. I., Norris, F. H., & Ritchie, E. C. (2001). Early intervention for trauma related problems. In R. J. Ursano & A. Norwood (Eds.), *Trauma and disaster: Responses and management* (pp. 97–124). Washington, DC: American Psychiatric Publishing, Inc.

Yule, W., Stuvland, R., Baingana, F. K., & Smith, P. (2003). In B. L. Green, M. J. Friedman, J. T. de Jong, S. D. Solomon, T. M. Keane, J. A. Fairbank, et al. (Eds.), *Trauma interventions in war and peace: Prevention, practice, and policy* (pp. 217–242). New York: Kluwer.

Women have a long history of using and abusing drugs in the United States, use that compromises their physical, psychological, and social health and development. Attention to substance abuse in women, however, is recent and still emerging. To respond effectively to the substance-abuse prevention and treatment problems of girls and women requires understanding the factors that contribute to their use and intervention approaches that address their needs.

EPIDEMIOLOGY OF DRUG USE IN WOMEN AND GIRLS

The overall prevalence of drug use by females and males from the late 1970s until the mid-1990s has generally decreased for all drugs with some yearly fluctuations (Substance Abuse and Mental Health Services Administration [SAMHSA], 2002). Although males report using both licit (e.g., alcohol and nicotine) and illicit substances (e.g., marijuana, cocaine, heroin) more than females, the gender gap in drug use has been shrinking over time (SAMHSA, 1997; Weiss, Kung, & Pearson, 2003). Starting in the early 1990s, girls and boys began increasing their use of cigarettes, alcohol, and illicit drugs, particularly marijuana, with boys still using more than girls (SAMHSA, 1997). Recent research suggests that males have more opportunity to use drugs, and if given the same opportunity, males and females are equally likely to use (Van Etten & Anthony, 1999), which may account for the rising rates in female use of drugs.

Estimates of substance use by females may differ slightly based on the data source and methodology used, but the pattern of drug use among females reported across studies is similar. The National Household Survey on Drug Abuse (SAMHSA, 2002), an annual survey of about 70,000 noninstitutionalized Americans 12 years of age and older, is the largest and most frequently used data set on drug use. Its findings show that, overall, girls and women, like boys and men, most frequently use the licit drugs of alcohol and nicotine (primarily cigarettes), followed by the illicit drugs, most frequently marijuana (accounts for about 75% of all illicit drug use), with smaller numbers of women using psychotherapeutics,

LULA A. BEATTY,
CORA LEE WETHERINGTON,
DIONNE J. JONES,
and ADELE B. ROMAN

Substance Use and Abuse by Girls and Women

cocaine, and other illicit drugs (SAMHSA, 1997). About 42.3% of the female respondents reported current use (at least once in last 30 days) of alcohol with females under 18 years of age reporting use at about the same rate of boys (17.3% for females vs. 17.2% for males). In women 18 years of age and over, alcohol is frequently used; over 50% of the women 18–34 years of age and over 45% of women over 35 years old report current use. Nearly one quarter (23.8%) of the females reported current use of a tobacco product, usually cigarettes. Misra (2001) reports that about 22 million women over 18, about one in five, and 1.5 million girls under 18 currently smoke cigarettes. Current cigarette smoking is most often reported by women in the 25–44 age range, although differences between age groups are minor (ranges from 21.5–25.7%) except for women over 65, where less than 12% report smoking.

Female users in comparison to men may differ in their drug using patterns. For example, among treatment seekers, females were found to be more likely than males to be daily users of cocaine, heroin, and sedative barbiturates (Wechsberg, Craddock, & Hubbard, 1998) and to use greater quantities of cocaine per week (Hays, Farabee, & Patel, 1999).

Factors associated with drug use in females include age, race/ethnicity, region of the country, socioeconomic status, neighborhood, perceptions of harm, drug availability, and personal trauma (SAMHSA, 1997). Girls were nearly twice as likely (10.2%) as adult women to report current illicit drug use (SAMHSA, 2002); women who currently use illicit drugs are most often aged 18–25, with rates decreasing with advancing age (Misra, 2001). Striking differences in drug use have been found among females by race/ethnicity and age particularly in the rate of drug use, drug preference, and the degree to which use becomes problematic (Leigh & Jimenez, 2002; Misra, 2001; Weiss et al., 2003). Wallace et al. (2003) examined gender and ethnic differences in substance use among adolescents in eighth, tenth, and twelfth grades over the 1976–2000 time period. The great majority of girls did not report current use of any substance although their lifetime prevalence rate (used at least once) for alcohol and cigarette use was fairly high. At all grade levels, Native American girls in comparison to other girls reported more current use of most of the substances inventoried including cigarettes, alcohol, and marijuana. Their use of marijuana in eighth grade (24.9%) was nearly double the rate for the next most frequent users of that drug, the Mexican American girls (13.8%). Asian American and African American girls were less likely to report substance use. Similarly, nearly one third (31.3%) of adult American Indian/Alaska Native women currently smoke cigarettes, a rate higher than any other racial/ethnic group of women (Misra, 2001). American Indian women in comparison to all other women also report more current use of any illicit drug while White women report more current use of alcohol and Black women report more current use of cocaine. In comparison to American Indian women, White, Black, Latina, and Asian/Pacific Islander women are, in descending order respectively, less likely to use drugs (Weiss et al., 2003).

Differences in drug use also occur within racial/ethnic groups. For example, among Asian American women, Japanese women were found to smoke more than Korean and Chinese women; and among Latina women, foreign-born Latina women were less likely to smoke than Latina women born in the United States. Moreover, other factors such as educational level seem to influence smoking, with generally more education indicating less smoking for White and Black women (Leigh & Jimenez, 2002).

Substance use is problematic when it becomes excessive (e.g., binge drinking, heavy daily drinking, heavy smoking) and interferes with everyday living and functioning, when a clinical diagnoses of dependency or addiction can be made, or when drugs are used by minors. Substance use during pregnancy is not recommended because of its potential negative impact on the fetus. About 2.8% of pregnant women use an illicit drug and more than half (54%) of pregnant women use alcohol and cigarettes (Ebrahim & Gfroerer, 2003). Research is not definitive on the interplay of factors that differentially predict drug dependency at the individual level; however, progression from initial drug use to dependence appears equally likely to occur for males and females for the most commonly used drugs, although females who report at least one nonmedical usage of a sedative, anxiolytic, or hypnotic are more likely than men to become dependent on those drugs (Anthony, Warner, & Kessler, 1994).

MENTAL HEALTH PROBLEMS, HIV/AIDS, AND OTHER CONSEQUENCES OF SUBSTANCE USE

Substance use and abuse are a primary or underlying cause of medical and social illness in the U.S. population, accounting for a significant number of preventable deaths and nearly $300 billion dollars a year in costs associated with health care and criminal justice programs (Office of National Drug Control Policy, 2001). The proportion of these dollars devoted to the care of women with substance-abuse problems is not clear; however, girls and women experience myriad problems associated with substance use similar to men and, in many ways, they suffer greater medical and emotional/psychological consequences of drug use.

Substance abuse and psychological problems are comorbid disorders, with co-occurring rates higher in females than in males. Substance-abusing women are more likely to be diagnosed with a mental health disorder, particularly depressive, personality, and anxiety disorders. Although there has been debate regarding the temporal relationship between substance use and mental health disorders, in women substance abuse most often occurs subsequent to depression and anxiety disorders, including posttraumatic stress disorder (PTSD) and eating disorders (Weiss et al., 2003). Violence-related trauma is related to substance use in women. Women in violent relationships often become depressed and use alcohol and other drugs as a way to help them cope (Wechsberg et al., 2003).

An association among substance use, other risky behaviors (e.g., early sexual involvement), and mental health problems is also evident in adolescent girls. For example, a significant relationship between problematic drug and alcohol use and posttraumatic stress was found in girls but not in boys (Lipschitz, Grilo, Fehon, McGlashan, & Southwick, 2000), and alcohol and marijuana use appeared to be a mediating factor for an association found between depressive symptoms and sexually transmitted diseases (STDs) and girls (Shrier, Harris, Sternberg, &

Beardslee, 2001). In a sample of at-risk minority adolescent females, age was found to be a differentiating factor for the initiation of substance use and other risky behaviors (Bachanas et al., 2002). Younger girls, 12–15 years old, reported more symptoms of depression and earlier initiation of sexual activities than older girls, 16–19 years old, and older girls reported more substance use and were more likely to be pregnant and to have contracted an STD than younger girls. Moreover, there was a significant association between risky sexual behavior with conduct problems and substance use for younger girls, but not for older adolescents.

Using drugs often reduces inhibitions and increases vulnerability to high-risk behaviors. Girls and women who use alcohol and illicit drugs are at increased risk of participating in unplanned and unprotected sexual intercourse, leading to a much greater likelihood of their contracting HIV/AIDS, STDS, and other diseases transmitted by intimate contact (e.g., hepatitis). Moreover, they are more likely to engage in other high-risk behaviors such as prostitution and the exchange of sex for drugs, and they are at increased risk of rape and unwanted pregnancies. Relationship dynamics (power, money, control, dependence, insecurity, and decision-making authority) influence participation in substance use, and girls and women who use drugs may find themselves in dependent and exploitative relationships with men. Women whose partners have more control over them report more substance use (Riehman, Iguchi, Zeller, & Morral, 2003), and women who feel powerless in their relationships are less likely to protect themselves against HIV exposure (Wechsberg et al., 2003).

Of the new AIDS cases among women in 2002, 21% were attributable to injection drug use (IDU) and 42% were contracted through heterosexual contact, a category that includes having sex with an injecting drug user, a bisexual male, and an HIV infected person, among others. Ethnic minorities are disproportionately affected by the HIV/AIDS epidemic in the United States. Of the AIDS cases reported to CDC in 2002 for all races, 69.8% were among ethnic minorities. African American women represented 65.2% of the AIDS cases among women, and they constituted 58.5% of new AIDS cases among women in the IDU exposure category. HIV infection rates among African American and Latina women reflect a similar pattern. African Americans and Hispanics/Latinas represented 67.1% of all new HIV infection cases reported in 2002, and 81.6% of new HIV infection cases reported for women. For African American women, heterosexual contact was the highest reported mode of exposure (34%) and IDU accounted for 9%. Similarly, for Hispanic/Latina women, heterosexual contact was the most frequently reported mode of exposure (37%), followed by IDU (15%) (Centers for Disease Control [CDC], 2002).

There are gender differences in the clinical significance of CD4+ cell counts and viral load (RNA level), major indicators of disease status. Women with the same CD4+ cell counts tend to have lower viral loads than men. Women with lower plasma RNA levels of HIV than men were found to be at risk of progression to AIDS at the same rate as men. However, women and men with similar CD4+ cell counts appeared to progress to AIDS at the same rate. Current treatment guidelines using CD4+ counts are based on male cohort studies. Research supports the use of lower HIV RNA thresholds for the initiation of antiretroviral therapy (ART) for women (Napravnik, Poole, Thomas, & Eron, 2002). Ongoing research in this area should include appropriate, proportional representation of female cohorts in treatment research studies.

Other consequences of drug use include a variety of body and cognitive functions. For example, prolonged high-level use of methamphetamine can lead to cardiac arrhythmia, shaking, stomach cramps, insomnia, paranoia, and structural changes to the brain in both males and females. Long-term alcoholism is associated with atrophy of several brain regions, with the frontal lobes and limbic structures appearing to be most vulnerable, although continued abstinence appears to reverse this effect (Netrakom, Krasuski, Miller, & O'Tuama, 1999). Sex-specific research in this area is limited, but needed. For example, placebo-controlled studies of the subjective effects of MDMA ("ecstasy") have shown that this drug produces greater subjective effects (e.g., more intense psychological effects, anxiety reactions, and hallucinogen-like effects) as well as more adverse effects and sequelae in

woman than in men (Liechti, Gamma, & Vollenweider, 2001).

Pregnancy Complications and In Utero Drug Effects

Substance use during pregnancy is associated with low birth weight, small head circumference, and preterm delivery. Excessive drinking during pregnancy can cause fetal alcohol syndrome and fetal alcohol effects, leading causes of birth defects and mental retardation in children. Tobacco use is associated with stillbirth and neonatal deaths and the risk of sudden infant death syndrome (U.S. Department of Health and Human Services [USDHHS], 2001). Moreover, substance use in pregnancy is associated with an increased risk for medical complications, including infectious diseases, with cocaine abusers especially vulnerable to abruptio placenta. These outcomes can be ameliorated by medical monitoring through routine prenatal care (Bauer et al., 2002).

Stigma Associated With Drug Use

Substance abusers are a stigmatized population, held in low regard because of presumed voluntary behaviors and lifestyles that are believed to be contrary to the morals and norms of responsible adult living. Stigmatization affects the entire community including the substance abuser, who may delay seeking treatment because of shame, embarrassment, and fear (e.g., loss of family standing and employment, criminal prosecution) and treatment providers who may view substance abusers as difficult, nonresponsive, and costly. Ritson (1999), who identified stereotypes held of drug users (e.g., problem is self-inflicted hence less worthy of help) and reasons professionals resist working with substance users, advocates training and public education as a means of changing stereotypic perceptions. Female substance abusers appear to experience stigmatization to a greater extent than males because of society's lower tolerance of deviant behavior in females, especially deviant behaviors typically associated with males and that interfere with their traditional duties as mother and wife. Women from ethnic minority populations (e.g., African American and Hispanic/Latina) that hold strong cultural, idealized views of women as mothers and culture bearers may not find their families and communities to be supportive or tolerant of them. Further, the stereotypes and disadvantage they face in the larger society may stigmatize them even more when they abuse drugs.

VULNERABILITY AND PREDICTORS OF DRUG USE AND ADDICTION IN GIRLS AND WOMEN

Drug dependence is both a psychological and a neurobiological phenomenon. Addiction is increasingly acknowledged as a brain disease, based on a body of research that shows the mechanisms of drug action in the brain as they affect neurotransmitter activity (particularly the mesolimbic dopamine system) and sometimes alter brain structure and function. These brain changes lead to the outward behavioral manifestations such as craving, withdrawal (depending on the drug), and drug-seeking behaviors commonly associated with addiction. The basic neurobiology of addiction in women has not been fully explored; however, females differ from males in some ways in their biological response to drugs. Animal studies on acquisition of self-administration of cocaine and heroin, for example, find that females self-administer sooner and in larger amounts than do males. Furthermore, the reinforcing properties of cocaine and nicotine are stronger for females than for males, and females demonstrate greater propensity to cocaine relapse than do males (Lynch, Roth, & Carroll, 2002).

Recent studies in humans indicate that both the pharmacological and behavioral actions of drugs can be affected by the menstrual cycle. A study of cocaine pharmacokinetics, for example, found that women in the follicular phase of the menstrual cycle reached peak plasma levels in a considerably shorter time (4 minutes) than did either males (8 minutes) or women in the luteal phase (6.7 minutes) (Mendelson et al., 1999). Women's smoking is also affected by the menstrual cycle, with more cigarettes smoked per day during the late luteal than during the late-to-mid

follicular phase (Snively, Ahijevych, Bernhard, & Wewers, 2000).

Cigarette smoking in women is more highly controlled by the smell and taste of a cigarette then in men (Perkins, 2001). Human studies have found that nicotine metabolism can be impaired by a natural genetic mutation. For males, this impairment acts as a protective factor resulting in considerably less cigarettes smoked per day and per week, but women's smoking is not affected by the presence or absence of this mutation (Tyndale, Pianezza, & Sellers, 1999). The predictors and risk factors associated with nicotine use and dependence often vary by gender. For example, smoking in girls is associated with stress relief, dieting, conduct disorder, and high levels of sociability (e.g., Sarigiani, Ryan, & Petersen, 1999), and parental approval (more than peer approval) of smoking (Siddiqui, Mott, Anderson, & Flay, 1999). Moreover, cigarette use is more predictive of progression to marijuana use by girls than boys (Kandel, Yamaguchi, & Chen, 1992).

Various theories have been offered to explain why people initiate drug use, including models that emphasize stress-vulnerability, relative deviance, and ecological systems. None of them have proved to be sufficient, stand-alone explanations. Research strongly suggests that drug initiation and abuse in women is related to stress, trauma, social networks, and relationships with men and family. For example, Russac and Weaver (1995), in reviewing research on substance abuse in females, found that adolescent girls who abused drugs were likely to have a parent who abused alcohol or other drugs, and addicted women were more likely than addicted men to have disturbed family backgrounds including violence and sexual abuse. Childhood sexual abuse places females at substantially greater risk than males for the development of numerous psychopathologic outcomes, especially, drug and alcohol abuse (Kendler et al., 2000). Family characteristics such as maternal substance use, insufficient parental bonding, and family dysfunction are more predictive of drug abuse in females than males (e.g., Chatham, Hiller, Rowan-Szal, Joe, & Simpson, 1999). Early pubertal maturation, both biological and psychosocial, is a high-risk factor for substance use for girls in general (Lanza & Collins, 2002). Women are more likely than men to have been introduced to drug use through sexual partners.

PREVENTION

Although drug-abuse prevention programs are cost-effective, there are not enough of them to meet the need. Effective substance abuse prevention programs are comprehensive, skill-driven (e.g., teach resistance strategies) and theory-driven, among other characteristics, and ideally are tailored to fit the gender and cultural needs of girls and women (National Institute on Drug Abuse [NIDA], 1997). Prevention programs should also target peers and address both the interpersonal underpinnings and the addiction processes that are intrinsic to chronic use, dependence, and abuse. In a review of prevention programs, Catalano, Hawkins, Berglund, Pollard, and Arthur (2002) observed that prevention programs for females should include the specific substance abuse risk factors that propel girls and women to use drugs and the protective factors that block their drug use. They recommend that prevention programs address the whole person, not be single-problem-focused, and that they be implemented early (before age 14) in order to postpone early use by girls.

Gender neutral approaches to drug abuse prevention have been the norm. There are few substance-abuse prevention programs specifically designed for girls and women. Prevention programs are usually developed for children and adolescents and are frequently school-based. Girls are included in large numbers in these programs, but their concerns and styles do not drive the programs' designs. Few prevention programs are directed to adult women, yet the epidemiologic data show that females, especially ethnic minority females, are at risk for substance abuse at later ages. Intensive efforts to halt HIV/AIDS transmission has yielded useful information and models for developing prevention strategies with women. Amaro (1995) concluded that effective HIV prevention for women must be gender specific and recognize the importance of women's connections with others, the role of male partners in their lives, their fears, and their unequal social status and power in relationships with men.

TREATMENT

Drug abuse can be successfully treated using a variety of behavioral, cognitive, and pharmacological treatment interventions, often in combination with one another. Factors that influence treatment success include availability of and access to services and treatment, competency of the treatment provider (e.g., knowledge about addiction, therapeutic skills), appropriateness of the treatment program, and client characteristics (e.g., motivation, engagement in the treatment process). Commonly employed substance abuse treatment models and techniques that have been relatively successful with men have often been less effective with women, leading researchers to investigate reasons for treatment failure in women and to develop improved treatment services for them.

Treatment models and strategies frequently do not accommodate or appropriately address the concerns and problems of women currently in or needing drug abuse treatment. Issues that affect treatment in women include current life circumstances such as social support, chronic medical conditions, and historical profiles of personal risks such as homelessness, depression and partner abuse, the influence of intimate partners on treatment engagement, and drug use (Riehman et al., 2003), and negative treatment and system experiences (Penn, Brooks, & Worsham, 2002).

Two major barriers to effective treatment with women may be inadequate attention to parenting and family responsibilities and co-occurring disorders. Women may delay or not seek treatment because they fear losing custody of their children, or they may not have someone to care for their children while they are in treatment. Child custody and care issues may be particularly salient for ethnic minority and poor women who have fewer resources for alternative child care and who are more likely to be involved with or subject to the scrutiny of public agencies. Interestingly, a finding that African American women with children in foster care were more likely to complete drug abuse treatment (Scott-Lennox, Rose, Bohlig, & Lennox, 2000) confirms both the importance of children to treatment involvement and outcome and the stage in the addiction at which treatment is sought or ordered when children have to be considered.

Women enter drug abuse treatment with high rates of psychological comorbidity, usually depression and/or anxiety disorder, and experiences of physical and sexual abuse and other forms of violent trauma. Histories of physical and sexual abuse in both men and women affect treatment engagement and outcome. Substance-abuse treatment that focuses exclusively on the drug addiction to the exclusion of the comorbid disorder (which may not be obvious in the face of addiction) will likely fail. The National Institute on Drug Abuse (NIDA, 1999) identified 13 principles of effective drug abuse treatment, several of which have particular relevance to women's treatment needs: to match treatment settings, services, and interventions to each individual's need, gender, ethnicity, and culture; to address the individual's drug use and all associated medical, psychological, social, vocational, and legal problems; and to treat co-occurring disorders in an integrated way.

Research suggests that women differ in their response to certain drug treatment therapies or strategies. For example, in smoking cessation treatment, nicotine patch gum, and spray have better outcomes in men but the nicotine inhaler is more effective in women; women are concerned about reduction of weight gain; and menstrual phase affects depressive symptomatology and withdrawal (Perkins, 2001). Women in women-only treatment versus mixed-gender treatment remain in treatment for a longer period of time and are twice as likely to complete treatment (Grella, Polinsky, Hser, & Perry, 1999); and treatment attendance and abstinence in methadone-maintained pregnant women was increased by using an escalating voucher incentive schedule compared to a non-incentive schedule (Jones, Haug, Silverman, Stitzer, & Svikis, 2001). A review of 38 studies on substance-abuse treatment programming in women examined the association among six components of substance-abuse programming purported to be instrumental in treatment effectiveness with women (i.e., child care, prenatal care, women-only programs, supplemental services, and workshops that address women-focused topics, mental health programming, and comprehensive programming) and treatment outcomes (Ashley, Marsden, & Brady, 2003). Positive associations were found between the components and successful treatment outcomes such as treatment completion, decreased use of substances, employment, HIV risk reduction, and reduced mental health symptoms. These findings suggest that widely used treatment models can be effective with women if women specific components are included in the treatment plan. Unfortunately, most treatment programs do not provide these services.

IMPLICATIONS FOR RESEARCH AND PRACTICE

Research on substance abuse in girls and women has grown and considerably advanced our understanding of the factors that lead to drug use in women and to interventions that facilitate recovery. But there are major gaps in our knowledge. Research shows, for example, that ethnic minority status and age are associated with substance-abuse risk and protection, sometimes in unexpected ways. We need more research on substance use, prevention, and treatment for ethnic minority girls and women, lesbians, and girls and women with disabilities, living in rural areas, and in correctional facilities. We need to know more about protective factors for girls and women and how they can be used to develop and improve gender-specific or gender-sensitive prevention and treatment programs. Another issue of increasing concern is the misuse of prescription drugs and other substances, especially alcohol, among older and elderly women. The abuse of substances by older, often middle-class women, is frequently hidden or shrouded in secrecy and ignored by professionals who do not expect, recognize, or screen for it.

Professionals providing substance-abuse services to girls and women must be well informed and trained about their specific problems and needs. Because of the high rates of comorbidity of substance abuse and mental health disorders in women, and the growing number of women who will present with both problems, mental health professionals must be knowledgeable about comorbidity and skilled in both the diagnosis and treatment of addiction and mental disorders in women. Similarly, substance-abuse counselors must be capable of providing mental health counseling or have a professionally trained mental health specialist available as part of the treatment staff. Professionals working in general community practices such as psychologists, social workers and primary care physicians can be particularly helpful in the screening and early identification of substance-abuse problems in their clients. Training programs for psychologists, clinical social workers, physicians, and others should include these issues in their curricula. Professional associations and service agencies also need to include these topics as part of their continuing education and staff development series.

REFERENCES

Amaro, H. (1995). Love, sex, and power. Considering women's realities in HIV prevention. *American Psychologist, 50*(6), 437–447.

Anthony, J. C., Warner, L. A., & Kessler, R. C. (1994). Comparative epidemiology of dependence on tobacco, alcohol, controlled substances, and inhalants: Basic findings from the National Comorbidity Survey. *Experimental and Clinical Psychopharmacology, 2*(3), 244–268.

Ashley, O. S., Marsden, M. E., & Brady, T. M. (2003). Effectiveness of substance abuse treatment programming for women: A review. *American Journal of Drug and Alcohol Abuse, 29*(1), 19–53.

Bachanas, P. J., Morris, M. K., Lewis-Gess, J. K., Sarett-Cuasay, E. J., Flores, A. I., Sirl, K., et al. (2002). Psychological adjustment, substance use, HIV knowledge and risky sexual behavior in at-risk minority females: Developmental differences during adolescence. *Journal of Pediatric Psychology, 27*(4), 373–84.

Bauer, C. P., Shankaran, S., Bada, H. S., Lester, B., Wright, L. L., Krause-Steinrauf, H., et al. (2002). The maternal lifestyle study: Drug exposure during pregnancy and short-term maternal outcomes. *American Journal of Obstetrics and Gynecology, 186*(3), 487–495.

Catalano, R. F., Hawkins, J. D., Berglund, M. L., Pollard, J. A., & Arthur, M. W. (2002). Prevention science and positive youth development: Competitive or cooperative frameworks? *Journal of Adolescent Heath, 31*(6 Suppl.), 230–239.

Centers for Disease Control and Prevention. (2002). *HIV/AIDS Surveillance Report, 14,* A2–A5.

Chatham, L. R., Hiller, M. L., Rowan-Szal, G. A., Joe, G. W., & Simpson, D. D. (1999). Gender differences at admission and follow-up in a sample of methadone maintenance clients. *Substance Use & Misuse, 34*(8), 1137–1165.

Ebrahim, S. H., & Gfroerer, J. (2003). Pregnancy-related substance use in the United States during 1996–1998. *Obstetrics and Gynecology, 101*(2), 374–379.

Grella, C. E., Polinsky, M. L., Hser, Y. I., & Perry, S. M. (1999). Characteristics of women-only and mixed-gender drug abuse treatment programs. *Journal of Substance Abuse Treatment, 17*(1–2), 37–44.

Hays, L. R., Farabee, D., & Patel, P. (1999). Characteristics of cocaine users in a private inpatient treatment setting. *Journal of Drug Education, 29*(2), 157–164.

Jones, E. E., Haug, N., Silverman, K., Stitzer, M., & Svikis, D. (2001). The effectiveness of incentives in enhancing treatment attendance and drug abstinence in methadone-maintained pregnant women. *Drug and Alcohol Dependence, 61*(3), 297–306.

Kandel, D. B., Yamaguchi, K., & Chen, K. (1992). Stages of progression in drug involvement from adolescence to adulthood: Further evidence for the gateway theory. *Journal of Studies on Alcohol, 53*(5), 447–457.

Kendler, K. S., Bulik, C. M., Silberg, J., Hettema, J. M., Myers, J., & Prescott, C. A. (2000). Childhood sexual abuse and adult psychiatric and substance use disorders in women: An epidemiological and Cotwin control analysis. *Archives of General Psychiatry, 57*(10), 953–959.

Lanza, S. T., & Collins, L. M. (2002). Pubertal timing and the onset of substance use in females during early adolescence. *Prevention Science, 3*(1), 69–82.

Leigh, W. A., & Jimenez, M. A. (2002). *Women of color health data book.* NIH Publication No. 02-4247. Bethesda, MD: Office of Research on Women's Health, Office of the Director, National Institutes of Health.

Liechti, M. E., Gamma, A., & Vollenweider, F. X. (2001). Gender differences in the subjective effects of MDMA. *Psychopharmacology, 154*(2), 161–168.

Lipschitz, D. S., Grilo, C. M., Fehon, D., McGlashan, T. M., & Southwick, S. M. (2000). Gender differences in the associations between posttraumatic stress symptoms and problematic substance use in psychiatric inpatient adolescents. *Journal of Nervous and Mental Diseases, 188*(6), 349–356.

Lynch, W. J., Roth, M. E., & Carroll, M. E. (2002). Biological basis of sex differences in drug abuse: Preclinical and clinical studies. *Psychopharmacology, 164*(2), 121–137.

Mendelson, J. H., Mello, N. K., Sholar, M. B., Siegel, A. J., Kaufman, M. J., Levin, J. M., et al. (1999). Cocaine pharmacokinetics in men and in women during the follicular and luteal phases of the menstrual cycle. *Neuropsychopharmacology, 21*(2), 294–303.

Misra, D. (Ed.). (2001). *The women's health data book. A profile of women's health in the United States* (3rd ed.). Washington, DC: Jacobs Institute of Women's Health and The Henry J. Kaiser Family Foundation.

Napravnik, S., Poole, C., Thomas, J. C., & Eron, J. J. (2002). Gender difference in HIV RNA levels: A meta-analysis of published studies. *Journal of Acquired Immune Deficiency Syndrome, 31*(1), 11–19.

National Institute on Drug Abuse. (1997). *Preventing drug use among children and adolescents. A research-based guide.* NIH Publication No. 99-4212. Rockville, MD: National Institute on Drug Abuse, NIH, DHHS.

National Institute on Drug Abuse. (1999). *Principles of drug addiction treatment. A research-based guide.* NIH Publication No. 99-4180. Rockville, MD: National Institute on Drug Abuse, NIH, DHHS.

Netrakom, P. Krasuski, J. S., Miller, N. S., & O'Tuama, L. A. (1999). Structural and functional neuroimaging findings in substance-related disorders. *The Psychiatric Clinics of North America, 22*(2), 313–329.

Office of National Drug Control Policy. (2001). *The economic costs of drug abuse in the United States, 1992–1998.* NCJ-190636. Washington, DC: Author.

Penn, P. E., Brooks, A. J., & Worsham, B. D. (2002). Treatment concerns of women with co-occurring serious mental illness and substance abuse disorders. *Journal of Psychoactive Drugs, 34*(4), 355–362.

Perkins, K. A. (2001). Smoking cessation in women: Special considerations. *CNS Drugs, 15*(5), 391–411.

Riehman, K. S., Iguchi, M. Y., Zeller, M., & Morral, A. R. (2003). The influence of partner drug use and relationship power on treatment engagement. *Drug and Alcohol Dependence, 70*(1), 1–10.

Ritson, E. B. (1999). Alcohol, drugs and stigma. *International Journal of Clinical Practice, 53*(7), 549–551.

Russac, R. J., & Weaver, S. T. (1995). Trends and theories concerning alcohol and other drug use among adolescent females. In R. R. Watson (Ed.), *Drug and alcohol abuse reviews. Vol. 8, Drug and alcohol abuse during pregnancy and childhood.* Totowa, NJ: Human Press.

Sarigiani, P. A., Ryan, L., & Petersen, A. C. (1999). Prevention of high-risk behaviors in adolescent women. *Journal of Adolescent Health, 25*(2), 109–119.

Scott-Lennox, J., Rose, R., Bohlig, A., & Lennox, R. (2000). The impact of women's family status on completion of substance abuse treatment. *Journal of Behavioral Health Services and Research, 27*(4), 366–379.

Shrier, L. A., Harris, S. K., Sternberg, M., & Beardslee, W. R. (2001). Association of depression, self-esteem and substance use with sexual risk among adolescents. *Preventive Medicine, 33*(3), 179–189.

Siddiqui, O., Mott, J., Anderson, T., & Flay, B. (1999). The application of Poisson random-effects regression models to the analyses of adolescents' current level of smoking. *Preventive Medicine, 29*(2), 92–101.

Snively, T. A., Ahijevych, K. L., Bernhard, L. A., & Wewers, M. E. (2000). Smoking behavior, dysphoric states and the menstrual cycle: Results from single smoking sessions and the natural environment. *Psychoneuroendocrinology, 25*(7), 677–691.

Substance Abuse and Mental Health Services Administration. (1997). *Substance use among women in the United States.* DHHS Publication No. (SMA) 97-3162. Rockville, MD: Office of Applied Studies.

Substance Abuse and Mental Health Services Administration. (2002). *Results from the 2001 national household survey on drug abuse: Volume I. Summary of national findings.* DHHS Publication No. (SMA) 02-3758. Rockville, MD: Office of Applied Studies.

Tyndale, R. F., Pianezza, M. L., & Sellers, E. M. (1999). A common genetic defect in nicotine metabolism decreases risk for dependence and lowers cigarette consumption. *Nicotine and Tobacco Research, 1*(Suppl. 2), S63–S67.

U.S. Department of Health and Human Services. (2001). *Women and smoking: A report of the Surgeon General.* Rockville MD: U.S. Department of Health and Human Services, Public Health and Human Services, Office of the Surgeon General.

Van Etten, M. L., & Anthony, J. C. (1999). Comparative epidemiology of initial drug opportunities and transitions to first use: Marijuana, cocaine, hallucinogens and heroin. *Drug and Alcohol Dependence, 54*(2), 117–125.

Wallace, J. M., Jr., Bachman, J. G., O'Malley, P. M., Schulenberg, J. E., Cooper, S. M., & Johnston, L. D. (2003). Gender and ethnic differences in smoking, drinking and illicit drug use among American 8th, 10th and 12th grade students, 1976–2000. *Addiction, 98*(2), 225–234.

Wechsberg, W. M., Craddock, S. G., & Hubbard, R. L. (1998). How are women who enter substance abuse treatment different than men? A gender comparison from the Drug Abuse Treatment Outcome Study. *Drugs and Society, 13*(1–2), 97–115.

Wechsberg, W. M., Lam, W. K. K., Zule, W., Hall, G., Middlesteadt, R., & Edwards, J. (2003). Violence, homelessness, and HIV risk among crack-using African-American women. *Substance Use and Misuse, 38*(3–6), 671–701.

Weiss, S. R., Kung, H. C., & Pearson, J. L. (2003). Emerging issues in gender and ethnic differences in substance abuse and treatment. *Current Women's Health Reports, 3*(3), 245–253.

The United States is an extremely wealthy nation. Yet poverty constitutes one of the most serious and pervasive threats to the lives and emotional well-being of women and girls in the United States. The insidious and complex stress factors associated with poverty damage women's mental and physical health, shortening the life span of many poor women. Living in poverty may also compromise a woman's capacity to protect and nurture her children. Girls growing up in poor families suffer from material deprivation and may be obligated to assume adult roles if parents are frequently away at work or debilitated by poverty-related conditions. The cycle of hardship, extreme effort, and exhaustion exact a gendered toll on women and girls who often care for others as they try to survive and pursue their own lives.

ECONOMIC REALITIES

Although corporate profits and chief executive pay have been at record levels in recent years, over 34 million Americans live below the poverty line, and a majority of these are women and children (Proctor & Dalaker, 2003). Among women who head their own households, 28.8% are poor, with even higher poverty rates among single mothers who are African American (37.4%) or Hispanic/Latina (36.4%) (Proctor & Dalaker, 2003). The United States has the highest child poverty rate among the wealthy nations (Mishel, Bernstein, & Boushey, 2003). Economic mobility for those in poverty is also lower in the United States than in other rich countries (Mishel et al., 2003).

Recent decades have been difficult ones for most working Americans, as many workers have lost health insurance, retirement benefits, and paid sick leave. Half of U.S. workers earn less than $13 an hour (Mishel et al., 2003), a wage that would provide a minimal living standard for a parent of two children who was employed full time year-round. Responding to these realities, U.S. workers now work more hours per year than workers in any of the other industrialized nations, and with fewer supports, such as subsidized child care, paid vacations, and paid parental leave (Heymann, 2000). More jobs now require work in the evening and weekend hours, when child care is particularly hard to arrange (Heymann, 2000).

DEBORAH BELLE
and LISA DODSON

Poor Women and Girls in a Wealthy Nation

Such jobs are easily lost when a parent must miss work to care for an ill child or when other child care arrangements break down.

Nor, since the U.S. government ended 60 years of guaranteed economic assistance to poor families in 1996, do poor women have many options for survival beyond their own employment. Former welfare recipients who find jobs typically earn only $6–7 an hour (Seccombe, 2000), and many are not employed or are employed only sporadically. Well-documented increases in demand at food banks and homeless shelters have resulted (Burnham, 2002; Green, 2000). Today, poor women and their children make up a large portion of the U.S. homeless population (Bassuk, Buckner, Perloff, & Bassuk, 1998) and hunger is increasingly a problem for poor women with children, especially poor women of color (Siefert, Heflin, Corcoran, & Williams, 2001).

POVERTY AND STRESS

The association between poverty and mental health problems is firmly established, and the stress processes that account for this association are increasingly well understood. Poor women experience more threatening and more uncontrollable life events than does the general population (Makosky, 1982), typically in the context of ongoing, chronic deprivation (Ennis, Hobfoll, & Schroder, 2000). Poverty increases a woman's vulnerability to violence and abuse. In one sample of low-income mothers, 83% had been physically or sexually assaulted during their lifetimes, and over a third had experienced posttraumatic stress disorder (Bassuk et al., 1998). The onset of depression has been linked to the experience of humiliating or entrapping severe life events, which are, in turn, more common among women experiencing financial hardship (Brown & Moran, 1997). Loss of material resources, or the threat of their loss, was associated with more depressed mood in low-income single women (Ennis et al., 2000). Inadequate housing, burdensome responsibilities, and other chronic conditions are even more stressful than acute crises and events (Makosky, 1982; Stansfeld, Head, & Marmot, 1998). Going hungry is a significant predictor of major depression among low-income women, controlling for background characteristics and other social and environmental risk factors (Siefert et al., 2001).

LIVING WITH BLAME

Poverty is deeply discrediting within U.S. society. Many Americans blame poverty on poor people, particularly poor women, without understanding the forces that stratify society and prevent millions from escaping poverty (Cozzarelli, Wilkinson, & Tagler, 2001). While many categories of Americans receive public aid, such as the elderly, the disabled, farmers, and college students, poor mothers who receive welfare payments are uniquely stigmatized. Welfare recipients often describe experiences of humiliation and denigration and many internalize shameful welfare-mother portraits. As one mother reported in 1992, "I would cry all the way to the welfare office and my daughter would cry with me. Once inside, I never cried, never smiled, never said nothing I didn't have to" (Dodson, 1998, p. 127). Yet some mothers understood and resisted the damage of accepting a "welfare mother" identity. A mother of two in Milwaukee in 2002 commented, "Just ignore them [the caseworkers], that's what I say. Just think of yourself someplace else and do their little thing and get out of there."

Most low-income mothers consider the protection and care of their children their overriding imperative (Jarrett & Jefferson, 2003). Poverty undermines the ability to protect children and often demands unconventional and even risky strategies to ensure children's well-being. As Edin and Lein (1997) point out, the poor mothers they studied generally wished to be employed, both to avoid the stigma of receiving welfare payments and to offer their children positive role models. Yet these mothers also realized that paid employment was hardly a solution to their economic troubles and carried serious risks for their children, including the loss of health insurance and maternal supervision. To supplement wages and welfare payments too low to support their families, mothers sometimes turned to under-the-counter or illegal work (Edin & Lein, 1997). However, breaking laws and powerful social norms is very stressful.

Poor mothers also describe the complexity of teaching their children the conventional "rights and wrongs" while also training them for life in the real world of poor America (Dodson, 1998). Poor women have such acute needs that they have little leverage when dealing with employers, landlords, and government bureaucracies. Sometimes powerful institutions and individuals simply decline to respond. Caseworkers, counselors, police officers, building managers, job training instructors, and others with power can also sexually exploit women in desperate need (Dodson, 1998). "Whenever power is particularly unbalanced, there is covert license to abuse those with the least of it, 'and who's got less power than some girl on welfare?' " (Dodson, 1998, p. 134).

Repeated experiences unsuccessfully negotiating for their own and their families' well-being, or succumbing to sexual exploitation as a precondition, can become overwhelming. Women may turn to palliative coping strategies such as self-medication with drugs or alcohol, overeating, sleeping during the day, and repressing thoughts of the problem. These behaviors, while generally viewed as pathological, may represent the only self-protection possible (Dodson, 1998). Not surprisingly, long-term economic hardship is associated with a diminished sense of efficacy (Popkin, 1990), while increases in household income, regardless of their source, are associated over time with increases in the sense of personal efficacy expressed by women who head households (Downey & Moen, 1987).

SOCIAL SUPPORTS: BENEFITS AND BURDENS

Many poor women create mutual aid networks through which they care for each other in times of stress (Higginbotham & Weber, 1992), and support from family, friends, and other network members is associated with a reduced risk of depression among low-income women (Coiro, 2001). Yet social networks can serve as conduits of stress just as they can serve as sources of social support (Belle, 1982). Network members are themselves likely to be poor and stressed and in need of assistance. Reciprocating the help that is received from network members can consume time, resources, and

energy that are already in short supply. Economically secure women can more easily extricate themselves from difficult relationships than poor women who rely on others for services they cannot afford to buy, such as child care. Kin-care options have also declined in recent years, as grandmothers, aunts, and other members of the social network are likely to be employed themselves and unable to offer regular help with child care (Roschelle, 1997).

PHYSICAL HEALTH PROBLEMS

The stresses that compromise women's mental health also damage their bodies, and poor women, especially those living in persistently poor communities, age before their time (Geronimus, 1996). During the reproductive years, African American women experience higher rates of hypertension, obesity, and diabetes than do White women. Geronimus (1996) refers to this process as "weathering," and notes that the probability among White women of surviving until the age of 65 is equal to the probability among African American women living in Harlem of surviving to age 45. (The disparity is even more marked for African American men.) It is reasonable for young African American women to have doubts about living to experience what the larger society refers to as "middle age."

CHILDREN IN POVERTY

In comparison to their middle-class peers, low-income children face an accumulation of risk factors, both physical and psychosocial, and it is such cumulative risk that best predicts psychological and physical morbidity (Saegert & Evans, 2003). Poor neighborhoods, particularly those in which African Americans are ghettoized, are characterized by inferior public services ranging from sanitation to health care to schools to recreational opportunities (Saegert & Evans, 2003). Poor children are more likely to experience inadequate prenatal care, low birth weight, birth defects, hunger and malnutrition, elevated lead levels, iron deficiency, diarrhea, colitis, and asthma (Seccombe, 2000), and poor adolescents are at elevated risk for depression, obesity, poor self-rated health, and suicide attempts (Goodman, 1999). These problems also foreshadow further serious psychological and physical debility on into adulthood.

Inflexible work schedules mean that poor parents often find it difficult to care for their ill children, visit children's schools, or supervise children in the afternoon and evening hours without losing their jobs (Heymann, 2000). Children then suffer when they cannot turn to their parents for comfort when they are ill or need help with schoolwork, and when they must spend long hours without effective adult supervision. Poor children are more likely than affluent children to be on their own for lengthy periods in the after-school hours (Halpern, 1999), and the risks of un-supervised time are greatest for low-income children and for those in dangerous neighborhoods (Belle, 1999).

Even if they can be at home with their children, economically stressed parents may be so over-worked, demoralized, and depleted that the quality of their parenting deteriorates. Financially stressed and depressed mothers are less responsive to their children, more coercive, and less consistent in setting limits (Raver, 2003). Some studies find that for poor women, employment is associated with better morale and more positive parenting styles. Yet mothers' entry into menial, low-prestige jobs was associated over time with more angry and coercive parenting, suggesting the negative implications of such jobs on family functioning (Raver, 2003).

GIRLS AS FAMILY WORKERS

When parents are away at work or psychologically unavailable, girls are likely to be drawn into demanding household responsibilities (Dodson, 1998). More than half of the poor high school girls Dodson studied contributed regular child care to their families, 80% did regular housecleaning, and half did the family laundry, typically without having a washer or dryer in the home. Thirty percent provided regular help with an ill or incapacitated relative or family member, and one in four girls routinely cooked for their families. Girls spent between 16 and 20 hours each week on this

family work, often in addition to paying jobs necessary to supplement parental earnings. They were often exhausted by the time they had a chance to begin their own schoolwork.

Many girls respond positively to the challenge of family demands with greater appreciation of their mothers' efforts, strengthened connections to younger siblings, and pride in their own extreme competence and tough-girl identities. "Ain't no Barbie dolls living around here" (Dodson, 1998, p. 81). Such girls may learn lessons about strength and about holding onto their selfhood and this may protect them to a certain degree from the silencing which affects middle-class girls (Dodson, 1998). Yet many find that their heavy responsibilities destroy opportunities to focus on their own education and development. Some are required to be family mediators and protectors when adult strength breaks down. Girls with such responsibilities take on the anxieties of caretaking in precarious circumstances, in many ways experiencing the stresses of mothering in poverty before they ever bear children of their own (Dodson & Dickert, in press).

Poor children worry about survival issues and about their own futures, and they are aware that poor people are stigmatized and devalued (Seccombe, 2000). Not surprisingly, poor children are more likely than middle-class children to suffer from depression, low self-esteem, behavioral problems, and poor school performance. Deep poverty, persistent poverty, and poverty experienced early in life are most strongly associated with decrements in academic performance, while children's mental health disadvantages increase with the length of time they spend in poverty (Seccombe, 2000).

EARLY CHILDBEARING

Poverty is associated with childbearing at earlier ages than is typical of the middle-class population, and teenage childbearing is highly stigmatized by the larger society when it occurs. To many in the middle class, childbearing by poor young people proves that they are too selfish or impulsive to delay sexual gratification, and helps to make the case that poor people deserve their own impoverishment.

Yet teenage childbearing may in some ways be an adaptive response to growing up in poor America. In impoverished African American communities, life expectancies are drastically shortened for both women and men, and serious health problems tend to arise much earlier in life, realities of which young people are quite aware (Geronimus, 1996). So rapid is the health decline that among poor African Americans, adolescent mothers experience *lower* rates of low-birth-weight babies and infant death than do mothers in their twenties. Adolescence is the healthiest time for them to have a child. Such realities can push young people to begin childbearing while their own health and that of their potential support providers remains good. Nor, without an evident educational and occupational trajectory that will be risked by early childbearing, do young people have strong incentives to wait. Many are already caring for children and managing a household. A boyfriend may seem the only available hope for a new role, a new life (Dodson, 1998).

EXPERIMENTAL RESEARCH ON POVERTY AND WELL-BEING

Most research on the psychological impact of poverty has been correlational, focusing on the statistical associations between poverty and negative psychological states. Some recent studies, however, have actively experimented or have taken advantage of natural experiments to investigate whether improvements in material conditions can lead to improvements in physical and psychological health as well. In the Moving to Opportunity program, residents of low-income public housing projects in neighborhoods of concentrated poverty were randomly assigned to low-poverty neighborhoods and enabled to move there. The low-income mothers who had been helped to move reported less depression than the control group mothers, and the children who moved experienced a dramatic decline in asthma symptoms (Goering, Feins, & Richardson, 2003).

Another recent study monitored the impact on Native American children of royalties their families received from a new casino on the Indian reservation (Costello, Compton, Keeler, & Angold, 2003). Before the opening of the casino, poor children had more psychiatric symptoms than children living above the poverty level. After the casino opened, children whose families moved out of poverty showed a significant decrease in psychiatric symptoms, particularly conduct and oppositional defiant disorders. Further analyses demonstrated that this improvement was mediated by parental supervision: parents who had moved out of poverty had more time to pay attention to their children.

WHAT HELPS?

Resistance to poverty's assaults comes in many forms. Poor girls speak of the importance of having safe spaces to talk with other girls and with respectful women of their own ethnicity who know the real conditions of low-income girlhood. Many mothers insist on telling the truth to their daughters about life, relationships, violence, and "what a girl's gotta do to get by" (Dodson, 1996). Raising daughters not to expect a life of fairness and care, some mothers truth-tell with "tongues of fire" (Lorde, 1982).

Many women find that talking with a trained clinician about old pain, recalling the troubles which haunted their earlier lives, and considering the connections between what they experienced then and their lives today makes them stronger. Counseling also helps women to raise their own children more thoughtfully, changing family patterns so that the pain is not passed on. Mental health services are hard to access without money, and many who suffer from emotional problems receive no help. Restored public funding is essential if they are to obtain the treatment they need.

Since low-wage jobs provide no economic security, poor women and girls need access to the postsecondary education that will enable them to move out of the minimum wage ghetto. A single year of college cuts minority women's poverty rate in half, and welfare recipients who have attended college report significant improvements in self-esteem and agency (Rice, 2001; Scarbrough, 2001). Ironically, welfare "reform" has foreclosed this opportunity for many women, who have been forced to leave colleges and serious vocational training programs to take dead-end jobs that will never enable them to support their families at a decent level (Scarbrough, 2001). Some states redefine work requirements to include higher education, and other states should follow these examples. Clinicians can help women to think seriously about education and career and can work with women who are struggling to succeed in these endeavors despite the difficulties.

When a woman attempts to change her life it sometimes seems as if there is a conspiracy to hold her back, particularly at first. Friends and family members may reinforce a woman's fears that going to class and leaving children is selfish. "My mother told me it was and so did their father. I kept trying to do everything at home, cook and keep everything all right so it was like I wasn't any different. But when I had to go to class, everyone made me feel bad. The kids cried, my husband told me I was not being a good wife, even my mother shook her head" (Dodson, 1998, p. 162).

To move on and seize new dreams women need the support of others who share their goals and understand the obstacles they are facing. Women in supportive programs quickly recreate social networks with each other, often across ethnic or cultural lines, as people who share struggles but are determined to succeed. In fact, holding onto the team (or class cohort) often becomes part of their credo, a recreated family loyalty. Equally important are the coaches, mentors, and teachers whom women remember as providing special help and encouragement. As one woman said, "There ain't no way I would be out here now, on my own, doing like I am doing with nobody's help" (Dodson, 1998, p. 184). Though children are an impediment to change, they are also a primary inspiration. Children's admiration and emulation of their mothers' bravery can be the greatest reward. Once they are on their way, women often pull their families, and sometimes it seems their whole neighborhood, right along with them.

With the evisceration of the social safety net and the rise of a labor market that does not provide a living wage to increasing numbers of workers, many parents cannot ensure the safety of their children. Mothers may bolster children in the face of hardship and bigotry. Children may seek out ways to sustain self-respect. Those in the caregiving professions may work harder than ever to undo the human cost of poverty and inequality.

Yet individual efforts will often be swamped by the immensity of the problem.

Political organizing is needed to fight for affordable housing and health care, living wages, and a just tax system. Revived union strength is crucial if workers are to reclaim power in their negotiations with powerful employers. Contemporary U.S. society provides a unique laboratory in which to examine the psychological consequences of poverty and economic inequality. Only economic justice will dismantle that laboratory.

REFERENCES

Bassuk, E. L., Buckner, J. C., Perloff, J. N., & Bassuk, S. S. (1998). Prevalence of mental health and substance use disorders among homeless and low-income housed mothers. *American Journal of Psychiatry, 155*(11), 1561–1564.

Belle, D. (1982). Social ties and social support. In D. Belle (Ed.), *Lives in stress: Women and depression* (pp. 133–144). Beverly Hills, CA: Sage.

Belle, D. (1999). *The after-school lives of children: Alone and with others while parents work.* Mahway, NJ: Erlbaum.

Brown, G. W., & Moran, P. M. (1997). Single mothers, poverty and depression. *Psychological Medicine, 27,* 21–33.

Burnham, L. (2002). Welfare reform, family hardship, and women of color. In R. Albelda & A. Withorn (Eds.), *Lost ground: Welfare reform, poverty, and beyond* (pp. 43–56). Cambridge, MA: South End Press.

Coiro, M. J. (2001). Depressive symptoms among women receiving welfare. *Women & Health, 32*(1/2), 1–23.

Costello, E. J., Compton, S. N., Keeler, G., & Angold, A. (2003). Relationships between poverty and psychopathology: A natural experiment. *Journal of the American Medical Association, 290,* 2023–2029.

Cozzarelli, C., Wilkinson, A. V., & Tagler, M. J. (2001). Attitudes toward the poor and attributions for poverty. *Journal of Social Issues, 57*(2), 207–227.

Dodson, L. (1996). *We could be your daughters: Girls, sexuality and pregnancy in low-income America.* Research report of the Radcliffe Public Policy Institute, Radcliffe College.

Dodson, L. (1998). *Don't call us out of name: The untold lives of women and girls in poor America.* Boston: Beacon Press.

Dodson, L., & Dickert, J. (in press). Girls' family labor in low-income households: A decade of qualitative research. *Journal of Marriage and the Family.*

Downey, G., & Moen, P. (1987). Personal efficacy, income, and family transitions: A longitudinal study of women heading households. *Journal of Health and Social Behavior, 28,* 320–333.

Edin, K., & Lein, L. (1997). *Making ends meet: How single mothers survive welfare and low-wage work.* New York: Russell Sage Foundation.

Ennis, N. E., Hobfoll, S. E., & Schroder, K. E. E. (2000). Money doesn't talk, it swears: How economic stress and resistance resources impact inner-city women's depressive mood. *American Journal of Community Psychology, 28*(2), 149–173.

Geronimus, A. (1996). What teen mothers know. *Human Nature, 7,* 323–352.

Goering, J., Feins, J. D., & Richardson, T. M. (2003). What have we learned about housing mobility and poverty deconcentration? In J. Goering & J. D. Feins (Eds.), *Choosing a better life? Evaluating the Moving to Opportunity social experiment.* Washington, DC: The Urban Institute Press.

Goodman, E. (1999). The role of socioeconomic status gradients in explaining differences in U.S. adolescents' health. *American Journal of Public Health, 89,* 1522–1528.

Green, J. (2000, June 19–July 3). Holding out. *The American Prospect,* p. 33.

Halpern, R. (1999). After-school programs for low-income children: Promise and challenges. *The Future of Children, 9*(2), 81–95.

Heymann, J. (2000). *The widening gap: Why America's working families are in jeopardy and what can be done about it.* New York: Basic Books.

Higginbotham, E., & Weber, L. (1992). Moving up with kin and community: Upward social mobility for black and white women. *Gender and Society, 6*(3), 416–440.

Jarrett, R., and Jefferson, S. R. (2003). "A good mother got to fight for her kids": Maternal management strategies in a high-risk, African American neighborhood. *Journal of Children and Poverty, 9*(1), 21–39.

Lorde, A. (1982). *Zami: A new spelling of my name.* Freedom, CA: Crossing Press.

Makosky, V. P. (1982). Sources of stress: Events or conditions? In D. Belle (Ed.), *Lives in stress: Women and depression* (pp. 35–53). Beverly Hills, CA: Sage.

Mishel, L., Bernstein, J., & Boushey, H. (2003). *The state of working America 2002–2003.* Ithaca, NY: Cornell University Press.

Popkin, S. J. (1990). Welfare: Views from the bottom. *Social Problems, 37*(1), 64–79.

Proctor, B. D., & Dalaker, J. (2003). *Poverty in the United States: 2002.* Washington, DC: U.S. Government Printing Office.

Raver, C. C. (2003). Does work pay psychologically as well as economically? The role of employment in predicting depressive symptoms and parenting among low-income families. *Child Development, 74,* 1720–1736.

Rice, J. K. (2001). Poverty, welfare, and patriarchy: How macro-level changes in social policy can help low-income women. *Journal of Social Issues, 57*(2), 355–374.

Roschelle, A. R. (1997). *No more kin: Exploring race, class, and gender in family networks.* Thousand Oaks, CA: Sage.

Saegert, S., & Evans, G. W. (2003). Poverty, housing niches, and health in the United States. *Journal of Social Issues, 59,* 569–589.

Scarbrough, J. W. (2001). Welfare mothers' reflections on personal responsibility. *Journal of Social Issues, 57*(2), 261–276.

Seccombe, K. (2000). Families in poverty in the 1990s: Trends, causes, consequences, and lessons learned. *Journal of Marriage and the Family, 62,* 1094–1113.

Siefert, K., Heflin, C. M., Corcoran, M. E., & Williams, D. R. (2001). Food insufficiency and the physical and mental health of low-income women. *Women and Health, 32*(1/2), 159–177.

Stansfeld, S. A., Head, H., & Marmot, M. G. (1998). Explaining social class differences in depression and well-being. *Social Psychiatry and Psychiatric Epidemiology, 33,* 1–9.

LILLIAN M. RANGE

Women and Suicide

Sex differences in suicide rates indicate that girls and women have strengths, and some risks, in this area. The present chapter examines these rates, and treatment, highlighting the issues specific to girls and women.

Suicide is a problem for both women and men. In 2001, a total of 30,622 people in the United States (24,672 men, 5,950 women) died by suicide (Centers for Disease Control and Prevention [CDC], 2001). Given that the population was 285 million, that number of deaths gives a death rate by suicide of 10.73 per 100,000. Practically speaking, this number means that 1 or 2 of every 100,000 people alive in 2001 died by suicide, and these deaths were more likely to be men than women, although misclassification may mean that women are not as protected from suicide as these numbers imply (Phillips & Ruth, 1993). About .01% of the population of the United States will die by suicide.

The percentages are higher on suicide thoughts and attempts. In a random-digit telephone survey of over 5,000 citizens in the United States, 5.6% reported thinking of suicide in the previous year, 2.7% reported planning their own suicide in the previous year, and .7% had attempted suicide in the previous year (Crosby, Cheltenham, & Sacks, 1999). Although only 1 person in 100,000 actually dies by suicide, about 1 person in 20 has thought about suicide in the past year.

Women and men are not at equal risk of dying by suicide. In the United States in 2001, across different cultural groups, the rate for women was only 4.10, whereas for men the rate was 18.10 (CDC, 2001). The same kind of gender gap in suicide death rate between women and men is true in most developed countries (Cutright & Fernquist, 2003), with the major exceptions of India and China, where the suicide rate is highest for young married women (Brockington, 2001). The difference in suicide death rates between women and men is striking.

Women and men are also not at equal risk for attempts. Women attempt suicide more than men (CDC, 1996). By mid adolescence, girls outnumber boys as attempters by a ratio of roughly 4:1 (Maris, Berman, & Silverman, 2000). One likely explanation is that cultural forces acting on the individual influence suicide rates.

Different cultural groups have different suicide rates. In the United States, Hispanic/Latino

Americans have a very low suicide rate, and Native Americans have about 50% higher suicide rate than the population as a whole. Among U.S. women, African American women have a very low suicide rate, and East Asian American women have the highest suicide rates of all women over the age of 65 (McKenzie, Serfaty, & Crawford, 2003). Internationally, some South and Central American and Eastern European countries report annual rates as lower than 3 per 100,000, whereas the former Soviet Union and eastern bloc countries have rates as high as over 60 per 100,000 (World Health Organization, 2004). In most countries, suicide rates are highest in men, those who are divorced or separated, unemployed, poor, and socially isolated (McKenzie et al., 2003). In terms of suicide, women in some cultural groups are at more risk than women in other cultural groups, and men generally are at more risk than women.

Paradoxically, then, women are more likely to attempt suicide, but men are much more likely to die by suicide. What is it about the impact of women's lives, options, and roles that has such a beneficial impact on their health—at least in regard to preventing them from committing suicide? Knowing their strengths and risks could help in making appropriate interventions.

STRENGTHS

Focusing on strengths is a core tenet of modern practice, so it is appropriate to focus first on the strengths of girls and women with regard to suicide.

- *Children,* in terms of probability, protect against suicide (Brockington, 2001). The protective effect appears to operate so long as an offspring lives at home, irrespective of the offspring's age (Driver & Abed, 2004). The fact that women are more likely than men to have children at home is a reflection of cultural practices in society.
- *Religion* provides some protection against suicide (McKenzie et al., 2003). In a large sample of African Americans and European Americans, orthodox religious beliefs and personal devotion were associated with beliefs that suicide is never acceptable (Neeleman, Wessely,

& Lewis, 1998). Among urban, public hospital African American adults, high religiosity/spirituality was associated with low suicide risk (Kaslow et al., 2004). Among a national sample of adolescents, frequency of prayer and importance of religion were associated with low probability of suicide thoughts or attempts (Nonnemaker, McNeely, & Blum, 2003). However, in one American and Ghanaian sample religion did not correlate with suicide (Eshun, 2003). The benefits of religion as a protection against suicide are not universal. Women's greater religious beliefs and practices than men's can convey some protection against suicide. Best practices for suicide prevention involve exploring a suicidal individual's religious beliefs and personal meanings.
- *Coping strategies* among women are often better than among men, particularly in late life. Older women may have more flexible and diverse ways of coping than older men, greater capacity and/or willingness to accommodate and adapt to situations, and greater flexibility in the capacity and/or willingness to be active, resourceful, and independent (Canetto, 1992). However, differences among women and men are greater than differences between them, so best practices would involve exploring personal coping strategies with suicidal women and men.
- *Feminine gender socialization* entails women being more willing than men to admit to having fears and anxieties (Feingold, 1994), which allows expression of emotion and help seeking. Feminine sex roles are associated with several reasons for living: survival and coping beliefs, responsibility to family, child concerns, and moral objections (Ellis & Range, 1988). These cognitive beliefs serve as some protection against suicide. Children, religion, and coping strategies convey some protection against suicide, and may all be related to feminine gender socialization.

RISKS

These strengths of girls and women that result in lower suicide rates compared to boys and men are (not entirely) counterbalanced by some risks.

- *Depression* affects 1 out of every 5 women, twice the rate found in men (Kessler, McGonagle, Swartz, Blazer, & Nelson, 1993). The gender disparity in rates of first onset of major depressive episodes begins around age 13 to 15 and lasts until approximately age 50 (Kessler et al., 1993). This depression may be women's response to a discriminatory society. In that women are less likely to die by suicide than men, their higher depression, at least in some cases, may be protective against suicide.
- *Blocked or distorted relationships,* in one view, induce suicide thoughts more often in women than in men. This view recognizes that U.S. society teaches women that their sense of meaning and value derive from mutuality of care and responsibility in relationships. Women's vulnerability to suicide, therefore, increases when they perceive their opportunity for growth within relationships to be blocked or distorted (Maris et al., 2000). This view posits that women's suicidal behavior represents a desperate plea for engagement under conditions of threat. Further, relatedness to others and social supports serve women most profoundly both as a protection against suicidal urges and as a precipitant for nonfatal suicidal behavior (Maris et al., 2000).
- *Gender role socialization,* particularly very thin body image ideals, have a toxic impact on body satisfaction and eating patterns (Thompson & Heinberg, 1999). Bulimia and anorexia are associated with suicide. In one study, about 25% of eating disordered women reported a history of suicide attempts (Corcos et al., 2002). When treating a suicidal adolescent girl, a knowledgeable therapist would examine her understanding and acceptance of society's messages, such as the pressure to be thin. When examining a suicidal individual, it is helpful to understand that men are at more risk than women, that some age and cultural groups are at more risk than others, and that some aspects of socialization can be both strengths and risk factors for women and men. However, it is im-

portant to keep in mind that every individual is unique.

INTERVENTION

Intervention for suicidal thoughts and behaviors can focus globally, at the community or societal level, or locally, at the individual or family level. Interventions at both levels can have an impact on suicide deaths.

Restricted Access to Guns

Restricted access to guns is vital in preventing suicide. Evidence from epidemiological, case control, quasi-experimental, and prospective studies is that there is a relationship between gun availability in the home and completed suicide by firearms. The risk conveyed by availability of guns may be particularly high among adolescents and young adults. Laws restricting gun possession may substantially reduce the rate of suicide in the United States. Further, because the risk is greater in the first year of gun ownership than in other years, a "cooling off" period may reduce some suicidal deaths (Brent & Bridge, 2003). Gun control laws prevent suicide among women and men.

However, from a practical point of view, it is unwise to assume that telling parents to remove of guns will work because the non-gun-owning parent typically brings the youth to treatment (Brent & Bridge, 2003). Best practice with a suicidal individual would include discussing gun ownership, conveying risks to parents, learning about the suicidal person's history of owning and using guns, and exploring the meaning of guns to all family members.

Restricted Access to Alcohol

Restricted access to alcohol may prevent suicide as well. In the United States in 1976–1999, increases in the excise tax on beer were associated with a reduced number of suicides by boys and men (but not girls and women). Suicides by men aged 20–24 related positively to the availability of alcohol and negatively to the presence of drunk driving laws. Suicides by women were unrelated to availability of alcohol, but presence of drunk driving laws reduced suicides by teenage girls (Markowitz, Chatterji, & Kaestner, 2003). Strict drunk driving laws, high excise taxes on alcohol, severe gun restrictions, and total bans on handguns are political steps that would reduce suicide among women and men.

Intervention in the Lives of Both Women and Men

Intervention, both at the political and community level, could reduce suicide. A healthy environment would encourage both women and men to pursue a variety of interests and talents, within and across gender roles (Canetto, 1992). Interventions that might reduce suicide rates for both women and men, but particularly older men, would keep them busy, give them relational experiences and responsibilities, and encourage them to ask for help (Canetto, 1992). Societal interventions to reduce suicide would authorize voices of the oppressed, and help women and men develop better coping strategies, actively seek social connections, and refute societal messages that guns are prestigious or masculine.

Interventions for suicide should focus on at-risk groups, particularly early adolescents and elderly individuals. Mid to late adolescence is a high-risk period for suicide, with suicide being the third leading cause of death in adolescence (Goldman & Beardslee, 1999). Early adolescence may be a particularly powerful time to intervene for depression because during this time the sex difference in depression emerges and depression rates rise dramatically (Gillham, 2003). Universal interventions for depression might teach strategies for coping with difficult interpersonal events. Late life is the highest risk period for suicide (McIntosh, 1992), and is another time to intervene for depression and suicide. Organized telephone checks can decrease suicide rates among elderly individuals (De Leo, Carollo, & Buono, 1995). For both women and men, adolescents and the elderly are at higher risk than other age groups.

Education

Education, particularly for youth, might reduce suicide. It is important to teach youth to be discriminating in their acceptance of mass media ideals and to develop strategies to reduce social comparisons (Shaw & Waller, 1995). In one study, psycho-educational interventions challenging acceptance of media pressures and explaining airbrushing, computer generated images, and other technology reduced appearance and weight anxiety more than standard health classes (Thompson & Heinberg, 1999). Suicide attempts among adolescent girls might decrease with interventions that promote positive redefinitions of femininity as multifaceted, help them resist pressure for thinness and attractiveness, and contrast the artificial, carefully manipulated media images with the diversity of women's sizes and shapes (Thompson & Heinberg, 1999). It can be very empowering for an adolescent girl to recognize increasingly that her despair has arisen in a context beyond her own intrapsychic difficulties, and that she can reclaim her own voice and validate her feelings and needs (Manley & Leichner, 2003). Both women and men would benefit from a healthy skepticism toward the media.

For women and men of all ages, but especially youth, suicide prevention education interventions challenge the notion that nonfatal suicidal behavior is a feminine way to cope with problems (Canetto, 1997). Suicide interventions evaluate the meaning of girls' accepting attitudes toward suicidal persons, and explore with boys and men the meanings of their focus on the right to kill oneself, while reducing the stigma of surviving a suicidal act (Canetto, 1997). For elderly individuals, suicide educational interventions convey the message that having any kind of weapon in the home is risky for suicide, and handguns are particularly dangerous (Conwell et al., 2002). Best practices for women and men who are suicidal would reinforce rules for safe gun storage.

For physicians, education about interventions should stress active listening, and should encourage all physicians, but particularly primary practice physicians, to be alert for suicide signs (see table 14.1), and for indirect clues of suicidal intent, such as vague physical complaints. In several retrospective studies, most (70%) elderly individuals

TABLE 14.1 Suicide Warning Signs

Category	Signs
Global	Specific plan
	History of suicide attempts
	History of drug or alcohol abuse
	Talk of suicide
Mood	Feeling powerless
	Depression
	Anxiety/panic attacks
	Unexplained mood change
Behavior	Withdrawal/isolation
	Final arrangements
	Unexplained behavior change
	Recent loss
	Drop in grades
	Drop in activities
	Change in eating or sleeping habits or eating disorder
	Outbursts of unusual or reckless behavior
Cognitions	Rigid thinking
	Preoccupation with death
	Feeling hopeless about future

who committed suicide visited their primary care physician in the previous month, many (>33%) within the past week (Brown, Bruce, & Pearson, 2001). In terms of suicide reduction, physicians should also be alert for depression, inasmuch as there is some epidemiological evidence that antidepressant availability reduces suicide rate (Olfson, Shaffer, & Marcus, 2003). Physicians should screen for psychiatric correlates of suicide including depression, anxiety, psychosis, and substance abuse; ask directly about suicidal thoughts, plans, behaviors, or history; investigate medical conditions associated with suicide; and search for physical or cognitive changes that may increase suicide risk (Miller & Paulsen, 1999). Further, antidepressants can relieve depression, but because of the possibility of overdose it is safer at the beginning of treatment to dispense only a week's supply (Miller & Paulsen, 1999). Physicians, as well as others with prescription authority such as psychologists and nurse practitioners, may have unique opportunities to intervene with suicidal individuals.

Media Activism

The media can protest unhealthy messages with regard to suicide and reward healthy messages. For example, after rock musician Kurt Cobain committed suicide, psychologists and other health professionals worked with the media to inform the public of resources for suicidal individuals, warn people to be sensitive to suicidal messages from friends and family, describe the painful consequences of suicide for bereaved loved ones, and overall diminish the possibility of suicidal contagion (Jobes, Berman, O'Carroll, Eastgard, & Knickmeyer, 1996). In addition, for women and men of all ages, it is important to pay attention to the power of language, including avoiding terms such as "suicide gesture" to describe suicide attempts (Miller & Paulsen, 1999). Boycotting, writing letters of complaint, writing letters to editors, and other forms of activism about the dangers (and health benefits) of the media with regard to suicide is part of a suicide prevention mandate.

Suicide prevention interventions can take a political, public health, or educational focus. These global interventions can change society and thereby reduce suicide deaths. On an individual level, some approaches such as crisis intervention and dialectic behavior therapy are established treatments for suicidal individuals. Other relevant approaches and combinations of approaches include family systems, humanistic, dynamic, and cognitive behavioral therapy. Feminist therapy is more of an approach, a framework, or a way of analyzing therapy than an actual system (Fodor, 1993). Feminist therapists are highly sensitive to issues of advocacy, power, and inherent power imbalances in therapy; they strive for an egalitarian relationship with clients and maintain a heightened awareness of power relationships so as not to abuse or restrict unduly a client's choices (Wyche & Rice, 1997). In the case of a suicidal client, the feminist therapist focuses on strengths, not deficits. Variables that may cause oppression include gender, ethnic minority status, class, age, sexual identity, and able-bodiedness (Wyche & Rice, 1997). So the feminist therapist examines how the suicidal individual's culture, history, and traditions intersect with the person's suicidal thoughts/plans/actions, in the process demystifying therapy and language. Despite the fact that the client is suicidal, the feminist therapist negotiates the pace of therapy with the client (Wyche & Rice, 1997), integrating feminist tenets into a crisis intervention, dialectic, family, or other orientation.

Crisis Intervention

Crisis intervention involves engaging the suicidal individual in a working alliance, providing structure for managing emotional turmoil, and involving family and friends (Kleespies, Deleppo, Mori, & Niles, 1998). The focus is on decreasing acute psychological disturbances rather than curing long-term personality or mental disorders (Brown, Shiang, & Bongar, 2003). The psychologist or other mental health practitioner may conduct a mental status exam (see Kleespies et al., 1998, p. 59), negotiate a no-suicide contract, and determine whether medicine and/or hospitalization are necessary. In negotiating contracts, rather than assuming that therapist and client are of equal status, which is an illusion, best practices would involve awareness of power differences inherent in the relationship (Brabeck & Brown, 1997), recognizing that the relationship is more important than the contract. Power imbalances might be especially relevant to hospitalization decisions. For example, a youth's reluctance to voice an opinion about hospitalization could be due to power imbalance in the relationship with the parent. For a suicidal individual, immediate safety is the primary concern.

Dialectic Behavior Therapy

Dialectical behavioral therapy (DBT; Linehan, 2001) is an outpatient psychotherapy approach for chronically suicidal adults with borderline personality disorder. Many suicidal individuals have borderline personalities, but others have depression, bipolar disorder, posttraumatic stress disorder, or other disorders. DBT is based on the premise that suicidal individuals lack important interpersonal, self-regulation, and distress tolerance skills, and that personal and environmental factors inhibit the use of the skills they do have,

and often reinforce inappropriate and suicidal behaviors (Linehan, 2001). DBT presumes that psychotherapy must pay attention to both skill acquisition and behavioral motivation, but it also recognizes that patients are likely to experience the therapist's focusing on change as invalidating. Therefore, DBT balances acceptance and change within the treatment as a whole and within each interaction. The therapist structures therapy targets in the following order: life-threatening behaviors, therapy-interfering behaviors, quality-of-life-interfering behaviors, and increasing behavioral skills. DBT includes four modes: structured individual or group therapy (for skills training), individual psychotherapy (for motivation and skills training), telephone coaching (for generalization), and peer consultation or supervision (for the therapist) (Linehan, 2001).

A core strategy for those who offer DBT is to search for, recognize, and reflect the current validity or sensibility of the patient. Regarding suicidal behavior, the therapist must recognize how life may not be worth living for the patient unless she makes substantial changes. Pointing out how a response was functional in the past but is not functional in the present is invalidating, not validating. The therapist presumes that the patient can make these changes (Linehan, 2001). DBT balances the immediate concerns characteristic of crisis intervention with the clinical understandings that context is critical, that the client's voice is as important as the therapist's voice, and that society often labels women as unhealthy.

Multisystemic Therapy

Multisystemic therapy (MST; Huey et al., 2003) is a family-centered, home-based intervention. MST therapists intervene primarily at the family level, empowering caregivers with the skills and resources they need to communicate with, monitor, and discipline children effectively. They assist caregivers to engage their children in prosocial activities and disengage them from deviant peers. MST therapists address individual and systemic barriers to effective parenting. To minimize self-harm, MST therapists develop a safety plan with the family that includes securing or eliminating potentially lethal methods (i.e., guns, knives, etc.), particularly those used in past attempts. MST is intensive (often daily), but also time-limited (3–6 months). At 1-year follow-up of youths approved for emergency psychiatric hospitalization, MST decreased attempted suicide (but not depression, hopelessness, or suicide thoughts) more than did hospitalization (Huey et al., 2003). Multisystemic therapy emphasizes the family context of the suicidal individual.

Existential-Constructivist Therapy

Existential-constructivist therapy is a humanistic approach that also stresses the context, as well as the meaning, of the suicidal thoughts and behaviors. The existential nature of this approach requires not a relationship between clinician and client, but an encounter between two human beings. The therapist is fully present to the client and willing to mutually and fully explore the suicidal thoughts, feelings, and behaviors as a precondition to moving forward (Rogers & Soyka, 2004). This approach presumes that the client brings internal expertise on her own life and avoids the potential distancing, marginalizing, and stigmatizing of crisis intervention (Rogers & Soyka, 2004). This humanistic approach presumes that assessment involves collaboration wherein therapist and client mutually establish goals and the client actively participates in the interpretation of assessment data (de Barona & Dutton, 1997). An existential-constructivist therapist takes a long-term approach to suicidal individuals.

CONCLUSIONS

The understanding and treatment of suicidal girls and women can focus on community or society, and activism is particularly relevant. The understanding and treatment of suicidal girls and women individuals can also focus on the person or family. In this case, what makes the most sense is not one specific therapeutic orientation, but rather multifaceted, knowledgeable, sensitive approaches tailored to the psychological and cultural needs of the individual, the family, and the community.

REFERENCES

Brabeck, M., & Brown, L. (1997). Feminist theory and psychological practice. In J. Worell & N. G. Johnson (Eds.), *Shaping the future of feminist psychology* (pp. 15–31). Washington, DC: American Psychological Association.

Brent, D., & Bridge, J. (2003). Firearms availability and suicide: Evidence, interventions, and future directions. *American Behavioral Scientist, 46*, 1192–1210.

Brockington, I. (2001). Suicide in women. *International Clinical Psychopharmacology, 16*(Suppl. 2), S7–S19.

Brown, G. K., Bruce, M. L., & Pearson, J. (2001). High-risk management guidelines for elderly suicidal patients in primary care settings. *International Journal of Geriatric Psychiatry, 16*, 593–601.

Brown, L. M., Shiang, J., & Bongar, B. (2003). Crisis intervention. In G. Stricker & T. Widiger (Eds.), *Handbook of psychology* (pp. 431–451). Hoboken, NJ: John Wiley & Sons.

Canetto, S. S. (1992). Gender and suicide in the elderly. *Suicide and Life-Threatening Behavior, 22*, 80–97.

Canetto, S. S. (1997). Meanings of gender and suicidal behavior during adolescence. *Suicide and Life-Threatening Behavior, 27*, 339–351.

Centers for Disease Control and Prevention. (1996). Morbidity and Mortality Weekly Report, *45*(8).

Centers for Disease Control and Prevention. (2001). *Web-based injury statistics query and reporting system*. Retrieved August 19, 2004, from http://www.cdc.gov/ncipc/wisqars/

Conwell, Y., Duberstein, P. R., Conner, K., Eberly, S., Cox, C., & Caine, E. D. (2002). Access to firearms and risk for suicide in middle-aged and older adults. *American Journal of Geriatric Psychiatry, 10*, 407–416.

Corcos, M., Taïeeb, O., Benoit-Lamy, S., Paterniti, S., Jeammet, P., & Flament, M. F. (2002). Suicide attempts in women with bulimia nervosa: Frequency and characteristics. *Acta Psychiatrica Scandinavica, 106*, 381–386.

Crosby, A., Cheltenham, M., & Sacks, J. (1999). Incidence of suicidal ideation and behavior in the U.S., 1994. *Suicide and Life-Threatening Behavior, 29*, 131–140.

Cutright, P., & Fernquist, R. (2003). The gender gap in suicide rates: An analysis of 20 developed countries, 1955–1994. *Archives of Suicide Research, 7*, 323–339.

de Barona, M. S., & Dutton, M. A. (1997). Feminist perspectives on assessment. In J. Worell & N. G. Johnson (Eds.), *Shaping the future of feminist psychology* (pp. 37–57). Washington, DC: American Psychological Association.

De Leo, D., Carollo, G., & Buono, M. (1995). Lower suicide rates associated with a tele-help/tele-check service for the elderly at home. *American Journal of Psychiatry, 152*, 632–634.

Driver, K., & Abed, R. T. (2004). Does having offspring reduce the risk of suicide in women? *International Journal of Psychiatry in Clinical Practice, 8*, 25–29.

Ellis, J., & Range, L. (1988). Femininity and reasons for living. *Educational and Psychological Research, 8*, 19–24.

Eshun, S. (2003). Sociocultural determinants of suicide ideation: A comparison between American and Ghanaian college samples. *Suicide and Life-Threatening Behavior, 33*, 165–171.

Feingold, A. (1994). Gender differences in personality: A meta-analysis. *Psychological Bulletin 116*, 429–456.

Fodor, I. (1993). A feminist framework for integrative psychotherapy. In G. Stricker & J. Gold (Eds.), *Comprehensive handbook of psychotherapy* integration (pp. 217–235). New York: Plenum Press.

Gillham, J. (2003). Targeted prevention is not enough. *Prevention & Treatment, 6*, n.p.

Goldman, S., & Beardslee, W. R. (1999). Suicide in children and adolescents. In D. Jacobs (Ed.), *Harvard Medical School guide to suicide assessment and prevention* (pp. 417–442). San Francisco: Jossey-Bass.

Huey, S. J., Henggeler, S. W., Rowland, M. D., Halliday-Boykins, C. A., Cunningham, P. B., Pickerel, S., et al. (2003). Multisystemic therapy effects on attempted suicide by youths presenting psychiatric emergencies. *Journal of the American Academy of Child and Adolescent Psychiatry, 43*, 183–190.

Jobes, D. A., Berman, A. L., O'Carroll, P. W., Eastgard, S., & Knickmeyer, S. (1996). The Kurt Cobain suicide crisis: Perspectives from research, public health, and the news media. *Suicide and Life-Threatening Behavior, 26*, 260–271.

Kaslow, N. J., Price, A., Wyckoff, S., Grall, M., Sherry, A., Young, S., et al. (2004). Person factors associated with suicidal behavior among African American women and men. *Cultural Diversity and Ethnic Minority Psychology, 10*, 5–22.

Kessler, R. C., McGonagle, K. A., Swartz, M., Blazer, D. G., & Nelson, C. B. (1993). Sex and depression in the National Comorbidity Survey I: Lifetime prevalence, chronicity and recurrence. *Journal of Affective Disorders, 29*, 85–96.

Kleespies, P. M., Deleppo, J. D., Mori, D. L., & Niles, B. L. (1998). The emergency interview. In P. Kleespies (Ed.), *Emergencies in mental health practice: Evaluation and management* (pp. 41–72). New York: Guilford Press.

Linehan, M. (2001). Standard protocol for assessing and treating suicidal behaviors for patients in treatment. In D. G. Jacobs, *Harvard Medical School guide to suicide assessment and intervention* (pp. 146–187). San Francisco: Jossey-Bass.

Manley, R. S., & Leichner, P. (2003). Anguish and despair in adolescents with eating disorders. *Crisis, 24*, 32–36.

Maris, R., Berman, A., & Silverman, M. (2000). *Comprehensive textbook of suicidology.* New York: Guilford Press.

Markowitz, S., Chatterji, P., & Kaestner, R. (2003). Estimating the impact of alcohol policies on youth suicides. *Journal of Mental Health Policy and Economics, 6*, 37–46.

McIntosh, J. L. (1992). Older adults: The next suicide epidemic? *Suicide and Life-Threatening Behavior, 22*, 322–332.

McKenzie, K., Serfaty, M., & Crawford, M. (2003). Suicide in ethnic minority groups. *British Journal of Psychiatry, 183*, 100–101.

Miller, M. C., & Paulsen, R. H. (1999). Suicide assessment in the primary care setting. In D. Jacobs (Ed.), *The Harvard Medical School guide to suicide assessment and prevention* (pp. 520–539). San Francisco: Jossey-Bass.

Neeleman, J., Wessely, S., & Lewis, G. (1998). Suicide acceptability in African- and White Americans: The role of religion. *Journal of Nervous & Mental Disease, 186*, 12–16.

Nonnemaker, J., McNeely, C., & Blum, R. (2003). Public and private domains of religiosity and adolescent health risk behaviors: Evidence from the National Longitudinal Study of Adolescent Health. *Social Science and Medicine, 57*, 2049–2054.

Olfson, M., Shaffer, D., & Marcus, S. C. (2003). Relationship between antidepressant medication treatment and suicide in adolescents. *Archives of General Psychiatry, 60*, 978–982.

Phillips, D. P., & Ruth, T. D. (1993). Adequacy of official suicide statistics for scientific research and public policy. *Suicide and Life-Threatening Behavior, 23*, 307–319.

Rogers, J. R., & Soyka, K. M. (2004). "One size fits all": An existential-constructivist perspective on the crisis intervention approach with suicidal individuals. *Journal of Contemporary Psychotherapy, 34*, 7–22.

Thompson, J. K., & Heinberg, L. J. (1999). The media's influence on body image disturbance and eating disorders: We've reviled them, now can we rehabilitate them? *Journal of Social Issues, 55*, 339–353.

Shaw, J., & Waller, G. (1995). The media's impact on body image: Implications for prevention and treatment. *Eating Disorders: The Journal of Treatment & Prevention, 3*, 115–123.

World Health Organization. (2004). Suicide rates (per 100,000), by country, year, and sex. Retrieved September 13, 2004, from http://www.who.int/mental_health/prevention/suicide/en

Wyche, K., & Rice, J. K. (1997). Feminist therapy: From dialogue to tenets. In J. Worell & N. G. Johnson (Eds.), *Shaping the future of feminist psychology* (pp. 57–71). Washington, DC: American Psychological Association.

Strengths and Resources

To my daughter Rebecca
Who saw in me
what I considered
a scar
And redefined it
as
a world.

—Alice Walker,
In Search of Our Mothers' Gardens
(1983, p. ix)

There's no question that ample opportunities for coping exist in the 21st century. Stress and anxiety are the norm, with terrorism and economic uncertainty at the social level, as well as developmental, personal, and interpersonal challenges at the individual level. For girls and women who are socialized today to care for others *and* to achieve, coping can have particular challenges. Being female brings with it special privileges and burdens related to social role conflicts, sexist behavior, and gendered belief systems. In this chapter, we explore the many ways girls and women cope, the common challenges they face, and the need to balance what Bakan (1969) called agency (self-efficacy) and communion (connection) in order to promote optimal growth. We review the developmental stages of women's lives, beginning in adolescence, and underline the need to enhance both agency and communion for healthy coping at each stage. We illustrate with case examples that have been altered to protect confidentiality.

PATRICIA A. BENNETT
and SUSAN H. McDANIEL

Coping in Adolescent Girls and Women

15

DEFINING COPING

Stress and *coping* are two of the most ubiquitous words in the literature of psychology. Perhaps this is why attempts to define them tend to fall at either end of the continuum: broad and vague or narrow and restricted. Richard Lazarus and Susan Folkman (1984) define coping as "constantly changing cognitive and behavioral efforts to manage specific external and/or internal demands that are appraised as taxing or exceeding the resources of the person" (p. 141). A more recent definition from the *APA Dictionary of Psychology* (VandenBos, in press) includes the importance of context and development: "Adaptation to stress. This involves the use of social and psychological resources to reduce the negative emotions and conflict caused by stress associated with changes in life." We elaborate on this definition by considering coping from a biopsychosocial perspective. This perspective recognizes that biological, psychological, and social factors are all-important components for understanding stress and coping, although the weight of each will vary according to the particular stressor.

Women are socialized to value and to care for relationships (Gilligan, 1993). Balancing agency and communion throughout the life span reflects the importance for women of all ages to cope by attending to care of the self as well as care of others. This approach highlights the importance of maintaining one's unique identity and strengthening rather than losing it through relationships. Balancing agency and communion refers to the ability to be separate yet connected.

We propose that healthy coping is reflected by the woman who prioritizes her dreams and recognizes her limits in creating a balanced lifestyle. This approach to coping depends on where one is within life-span development, within one's culture, and within a given time and space. At the extremes, either unmitigated agency or unmitigated communion, there are risks to the self such that the cost of the behavior outweighs its benefits. The autonomy of unmitigated agency guards the self against hurt by considering the needs of the self as paramount. Unmitigated agency often presents as a negative worldview and hostile attitude. It is associated with negative social interactions, psychological distress, lower self-esteem, and decreased engagement in good health behavior (Helgeson & Fritz, 1999). Clearly, the cost of unmitigated agency includes losing the contribution to coping provided by support systems, the connection and validation of close friendships, and the meaning that relationships can generate.

In contrast, unmitigated communion overfocuses on relationships. A woman's positive self-image is contingent upon the well-being of the relationship, and she may feel ineffective and disconnected from her self. Not surprisingly, unmitigated communion has been linked to low self-esteem, dependency, and psychological distress,

including depression and rumination (Fritz & Helgeson, 1998).

GENDER DIFFERENCES IN COPING: TAYLOR'S TEND AND BEFRIEND MODEL

The importance of communion to women may have a neurophysiological basis. Taylor et al. (2000) suggest that women may be primed toward relational coping for survival. The traditional model of stress and coping is the fight-or-flight response, which Taylor asserts may be more applicable to men. Instead, women may tend to their offspring and befriend others in their community to cope during stressful times. Tending and befriending have psychological and physiological bases, and both increase a woman's chance for not just survival but also growth. Tending to offspring promotes a secure mother-child attachment, which is associated with healthy child development (Carlson & Sroufe, 1995). Taylor suggests that attachment is beneficial for the mother as well. Likewise, befriending other women affords a woman the greater safety of numbers as well as access to more resources.

Taylor's model proposes that women's tendencies to use coping strategies that are focused on relational needs may be beneficial. This contrasts with other research literature, which suggests not only that problem-focused coping is better but also that men are more likely to use problem-focused coping (Tamres, Janicki, & Helgeson, 2002). The model may explain the tendency of women to use emotion-focused strategies, which generally involve a relational component. For example, discussing problems with and venting to a friend are two of the more frequently employed emotion-focused strategies. The model suggests that these coping strategies may be beneficial as they may increase the attachment response and engage social support networks.

COPING: IT'S ALL IN THE FAMILY

While the details of the relationship between gender and coping remain tentative, it is clear that coping starts within the family. Families teach the children what is stressful, how to cope with stressors, and expectations about the efficacy of coping. Parents model for their children how to manage distress and what distress is manageable. Children learn how to demonstrate their emotions and what level of emotionality is acceptable. Families develop support networks of extended family members and friends. They determine when, from whom (doctors, spiritual leaders, or friends), and for what reasons one seeks help.

Parents and family members shape coping skills by reinforcing and rewarding as well as ignoring and punishing. Children may learn that it is more effective to cope by venting, somatizing, or denying because that particular style is understood within the family. A mismatch in temperament between parent and child can impede the acquisition of coping skills. Linehan (1996) proposed that exposure to an invalidating environment can result in deficits in major areas of coping skills and in a diagnosis of borderline personality disorder.

The family's ability to teach offspring coping skills is tempered by the availability of resources. Impoverished families are not only likely to have less access to resources but also the available resources are likely to be overtaxed and of lower quality. Families dealing with multiple stressors will require greater supports but are often less able to obtain those supports. Parents who are depressed and impoverished illustrate this point. These parents often experience difficulty in spending the time and energy needed to wade through the paperwork and the systems to secure assistance.

COPING IN CONTEXT: THE IMPORTANCE OF CULTURE

Coping is acquired within the context of culture. Cultural beliefs, roles, and rituals help to shape which coping skills are considered to be useful, appropriate, and effective. Cultural values translate into different preferences for coping skills. For example, Maria, who is Costa Rican, chose her daughter's godparents carefully because godparents are important members of the support network. They are helping Maria to plan and to finance her daughter's *quinceañera* (the celebration of a girl's coming of age at 15 years old).

Falicov (2001) notes that this custom is common in Latino cultures, where extended family members and members of the support network are expected to assist with the financial and emotional needs of other family members. This contrasts with a typical middle-class White American, who might try to cope on her own with loans, rather rely on a godparent who is not related by blood.

Jones (2003) discusses how African American values translate into coping in his TRIOS theory. He proposes that the values of time, rhythm, improvisation, orality, and spirituality have been incorporated into a way of being in the world that enables African Americans to cope with daily hassles, and the ongoing and inherent stress of racism. The findings of Chapman and Mullis's (2000) comparison of coping preferences of African American and White adolescents support Jones's theory. The authors reported that African American adolescents employed close friendships, seeking spiritual support, solving family problems, developing self-reliance, and relaxing more than White adolescents, whereas White adolescents used venting and avoidance more. Of note, the authors did not find a significant relationship between coping preference and self-esteem.

Many cultures incorporate rituals as a form of communion, even while honoring an individual's agency. Imber-Black (1988) has identified five purposes of rituals: relating, identity, healing, affirming/celebrating, and expressing beliefs—all of which encourage communion. The rituals that accompany celebrations such as *quinceañera* in the Latino culture, bat mitzvahs among Jews, and Juneteenth in the African American culture reinforce the connection between individuals and their culture. These rituals symbolize the cultural values and beliefs, strengthen the network of support and belonging on multiple levels, and remind members of inherent resources and coping skills.

Racism and prejudice are sources of stress that women of color face daily. Coping with such ubiquitous stressors creates a need for additional coping resources and skills.

■ Suzanne, an African American graduate student, grew up in a predominantly White well-to-do suburb. Her parents chose to increase her skills in coping with racism by enhancing her sense of communion with her own culture. They had her join the local branch of Jack and Jill, spend vacations with her extended family in the South, and encouraged her to attend a historically Black college. Now, as one of the few women of color in her program, she is coping successfully with racism by employing similar strategies. She created an informal support network locally, maintains regular contact with family and friends, and participates in the national organization for African Americans in her field.   ■

COPING THROUGH THE LIFE SPAN: MANAGING TIMES OF TENSION BY BALANCING AGENCY AND COMMUNION

To consider development in isolation is to lose valuable information and understanding. Rather, development and, more specifically, the development of coping skills are best understood as proceeding within the overlapping spheres of family, community, society, and culture (Bronfenbrenner, 1979).

As girls develop into adolescents and then women, they face challenges that exceed, promote, and enhance their coping skills. Each stage of development brings its unique pathway for growth modified by the resources and opportunities available. Girls, adolescents, and women negotiate these choice points in order to grow. Each negotiation reflects the balance between the self and the other, and sets the stage for the decisions to follow. Communion driven by agency rather than anxiety enhances the development of a healthy self for girls and women.

While development proceeds along a chronological path, there are also unpredictable stressors that occur throughout the life span. These stressors include, for example, racism, chronic illness, and disability (McDaniel & Cole-Kelly, 2003; McDaniel, Hepworth, & Doherty, 1992), trauma (Johnson, 2002), and terrorism and war. The features of these unanticipated stressors interact with developmental challenges, adding another layer of complexity. A history of childhood sexual abuse both affects and is affected by how an individual negotiates a new developmental stage.

■ Jill, a 30-year-old lesbian White woman with cerebral palsy, used crutches longer than her doctor recommended during adolescence to please her parents who thought the crutches made her look more "normal." She recalls it took time to figure out that she was more than her disability. During college, she created a supportive network of friends, and with their encouragement she began using a motorized wheelchair. That change enabled her to expand her focus from walking to living. As an adult, she works as an advocate and has recently moved in with her partner of many years. Jill is now dealing with the effects on her intimacy and sexual relationship with her partner because of the early morning arrival of the aide who assists with her daily living skills. This dilemma, related to the stress of a chronic illness, is forcing Jill to find a way to care for herself and her relationship.   ■

ADOLESCENT GIRLS: SEPARATING WHILE REMAINING CONNECTED

The task in adolescence is to develop one's own identity, that unique sense of self that results from teens' synthesizing their thoughts, feelings, and behaviors into a coherent whole and balancing the need for independence with the need for connection. Some adolescents will value their individual identity and independence above fitting in, while others will choose social support and validation at the expense of more openly acknowledging the self.

Communion and connection play critical roles in teaching adolescents how to cope. Important relationships communicate the family's values; a secure attachment increases the likelihood that the adolescent will listen. As the adolescent's needs to belong and be safe are met, she internalizes a positive view of her self and the world, which enhances her sense of self-efficacy. Her relationships become a mirror for her self and her strengths. The adolescent then understands relationships as supports and as scaffolding that facilitate her ability to define her self (Vtogtsky, as cited in Sigelman, 1999).

The danger lies in unmitigated communion if the adolescent learns it is acceptable to lose one's self to connect with others. A daughter may watch her mother sacrifice her own wants and needs for the family and then do the same. The family may divide roles along gender lines, with females expected to do the caregiving and males, the "real work." The family may consider women to be emotional and dependent, in contrast to men being unemotional, independent, and powerful. Gendered messages are reinforced by teen magazines that suggest that girls should alter their appearances and their selves to secure a boy's attention.

Adolescent girls learn to disconnect from their selves and to wear masks that fit the occasion and the need. When the mask is reinforced, it is brought out more often and a girl's true self becomes submerged. Gilligan (1993, p. xxii) describes this developmental process as "the dissociation of girls' voices from girls' experiences" and notes that this division results in the silencing of voice both to avoid hurting others and to avoid not being heard. This process may explain research findings that indicate that adolescent girls more than boys tend to employ rumination as a coping strategy (Broderick, 1998). Broderick found that boys were more likely to use distraction strategies to decrease distress, while girls' responses were more self-focused and seemed to increase the level of distress.

Agency is also required for effective adolescent development and coping. Families teach agency by promoting independence and autonomy. They encourage the adolescent to follow her dreams without dictating the content of those dreams. They let her take risks and step in to brace her if she falls. When a family values agency, the adolescent gains a greater variety of coping skills. The risk of unmitigated agency is a family that is so distant and disengaged that the adolescent must prematurely take full care of herself. She is not afforded the benefits of her parents' learning to shape her attempts and assist her in evaluating her coping strategies. She succeeds and fails on her own, which in turn, may lead to the use of strategies that further isolate her.

One challenge that faces young women of color is managing the conflict between the values of the majority and minority cultures as they create an individual identity yet remain connected to their community.

■ Nikkia's family attended church several times a week for extended periods. Nikkia knew that faith and the church community helped her mother to become and remain sober. At the same time, she longed to go out with all of her friends. She began seeing the church as the source of her unhappiness and started to skip choir practice. This led to a confrontation with her mother and the minister, and Nikkia stopped attending church. Over time, she missed the comfort of the community but was too proud to return. Now, a young mother herself, she is considering rejoining the church.   ■

YOUNG WOMEN: CHOOSING A PATH AND A PARTNER

Young adult women must find a way to express and reinforce a budding self-identity, whether through a career, a relationship, or both. Rules, roles, and expectations from the family-of-origin help to determine the relative importance of intimacy for a woman, as well as where she should look for it. Families influence who is an acceptable partner and what is a valid career. Some families teach that finding a partner is the only meaningful activity for a young woman to engage in, while other families teach that a fulfilling career is more stable and satisfying than a partner.

Intimacy has the power to strengthen and consolidate an identity as well as to submerge and hide it. A balance between communion and agency in this stage might mean dating while in graduate school, or marrying and starting a family, or coming out with one's sexual identity. A successful balance is determined by increased self-knowledge, a growing ability to be intimate while remaining oneself, and a greater ability to act independently while maintaining connections to others.

Unmitigated communion is a particular danger at this life stage. A woman might give up her life dream to find or please her partner. She might silence herself in order to be who she believes he wants her to be, hiding her desires and wants even from her own awareness to fulfill her family's wishes. For example, Katy, who struggled with substance abuse as a teenager, describes herself as a chameleon that shifted to meet her parents' expectations. This is her way of making amends and assuaging her guilt about the pain that she caused her parents during her addiction.

■ Julie, a biracial Latina woman, sought therapy because she was silencing her true self to please her partner. The more she relied on his approval, the more distant he became. At the same time, her depression was interfering with her ability to complete her college degree. Julie began volunteering at a local business to gain experience in her field. The positive feedback that she received provided momentum for completing her schoolwork. In therapy, she examined the legacy of her history of childhood physical abuse and of her last failed relationship for her self-concept. She learned alternative coping strategies to express her needs and to manage conflict. In turn, her partner began to feel more connected to her and their relationship became stronger. Julie's increased agency enabled her to gain increased communion in her relationship.   ■

ADULT WOMEN: DEFINING AND CREATING FAMILIES OF THEIR OWN

At this stage, women and their partners decide how to form a family and what roles will be. Some women choose to create a family without a partner. Choosing roles becomes the means of implementing agency and communion within a relationship and within a family of creation. The balance itself will depend upon what each partner learned in his/her family-of-origin as well as his/her development thus far. Women decide how to define their roles as partners, mothers, friends, employees, sisters, and caregivers. Each role has a personal valence for a woman and she will select if and how to fill it, balancing of agency and communion to meet her needs.

Women help to set expectations about the acceptable level of intimacy within their families of creation. For women who are able to achieve a satisfying level of communion, their new family becomes an opportunity to increase intimacy with their partners, their children, and their selves. However, the mother who struggles with unmitigated communion may find herself rating herself by her baby's moods. She may have difficulty sorting through others' advice and try pleasing others rather than herself. She may have to forgo roles that she values in order to keep the peace in her marriage. For example, Eliza would like to be a stay-at-home mother with her first child but her boyfriend's sister has told the family that she can babysit the child while Eliza works. Eliza would like to say no but is afraid of angering family members, especially her boyfriend who thinks the offer is very generous.

Women also establish expectations around agency and independence in adulthood. Some women expect their partners to be equal partners in sharing household chores, child-raising duties, and work responsibilities. Other women prefer to divide responsibilities along traditional gender lines. A woman at this stage who struggles with unmitigated communion may wish for the same freedom that her partner has to participate in recreational activities or to sleep in, but as a woman may not feel entitled to ask for such privileges. A woman who struggles with unmitigated agency might postpone childbearing, not wanting to be saddled with the burdens of caregiving.

A common stressor that may occur during this developmental stage is infertility. Berghuis and Stanton (2002) studied 43 heterosexual couples with a failed artificial insemination attempt. They found that women who used social support seeking, emotional approach coping, and/or problem-focused coping were protected from depression. In contrast, women who used avoidant strategies were more likely to display depressive symptoms. Interestingly, when women had low or average use of emotional strategies for coping, their partners' high use of emotional approach coping can compensate and serve as a protective factor. The authors suggest that this may occur because the partners' actions convey investment and attachment to the women. Thus, this connection acts as a scaffold to promote healthier coping for women.

■ Sonia, a 37-year-old Peruvian lawyer, and her husband, a 35-year-old French college professor, experienced infertility caused by multiple factors. They attempted artificial insemination but the fetus died in the second trimester. Sonia coped with the loss of this potential child and her fertility by e-mailing supportive friends, writing poetry, and discussing the loss with her husband. She joined a pregnancy loss support group and was matched with another woman who had suffered a similar loss. She spoke regularly with this "buddy." The couple decided to discontinue fertility treatment to grieve their loss. Now, a year later, they are ready to consider adoption.   ■

WOMEN AND MIDDLE AGE: THE BALANCING ACT

At this stage of life, women's roles generally include being a family caregiver. Caregiving extends to the previous generations (parents and in-laws) and to the next generation (children), resulting in the labeling of women in this stage as the "sandwich" generation. This situation has become more common for women today as life expectancy continues to increase. For example, Beth gave up her job, which she loved, to stay at home with her active toddler and her chronically ill mother-in-law. Beth's husband was an only child and both he and Beth agreed that it was best for his mother to live with them. To cope, Beth needed to find other sources of meaning and enjoyment in her life besides her employment. She worked to elevate her needs to the same level of importance as those of other family members, and to decrease her feelings of guilt when she attended to herself.

Balancing multiple roles is critical for a woman's well-being. Barnett and Hyde (2001), in their review of the literature, report that multiple roles are beneficial in terms of physical, psychological, and relationship health. Multiple roles can increase agency and communion; however, there is also a risk of role strain, exceeding personal limits for the number of roles and the time spent in each role. The quality of the roles is an important factor in enhancing the benefits of multiple roles and decreasing the disadvantages (Barnett & Hyde, 2001). Barnett and Hyde also

highlight the importance of context and social class. Women of color may be exposed to racism and discrimination, while all women working at minimum wage jobs may work in demoralizing environments. Clearly, both of these situations decrease the quality, and therefore, the benefit of that particular role for a woman.

The research on multiple roles points to the importance of social support networks for enhanced coping. This is true as women deal with unexpected stressors such as health concerns, like breast cancer. Stanton et al. (2000) studied the coping styles of 92 women with breast cancer and found that emotional coping skills were associated with decreased distress, increased energy level, fewer medical visits, and improved self-perceptions of health status. Coping by expressing emotions was associated with improved quality of life when women rated their supports as receptive to their concerns.

Weingarten (1997) shares the story of her experience of coping with breast cancer in her book *The Mother's Voice: Strengthening Intimacy in Families*. Weingarten balanced multiple roles—wife, mother, daughter, psychologist, family therapist, and author—when she was diagnosed with cancer. In part, she copes with her illness, obligations, desires, and needs through sharing her story. As she puts words to her experience within her family, the medical system, and society-at-large, she offers examples of how she maintains agency and communion. She gives voice to the unspoken cultural pull toward unmitigated communion in the name of good mothering.

OLDER WOMEN: SHARING WISDOM WITH ONE'S COMMUNITY

The concept of communion includes the importance of spirituality, especially for older women. Spirituality reflects a connection to God, to greater meaning, or to a larger purpose. This in turn broadens the meaning of the self because communion occurs within and outside of the self. Simoni, Martone, and Kerwin (2002) suggest that spirituality enhances coping because it offers resources (such as prayer, ritual, and community), increases one's sense of control, and suggests a structure for meaning and significance. These factors promote both agency and communion.

A study of older mothers as caregivers of adults with developmental disabilities found that religious coping was associated with higher levels of caregiving satisfaction (Miltiades & Pruchno, 2002). Furthermore, African American women were more likely to use religious coping and to experience higher levels of caregiving satisfaction than were White women. The authors suggest that religion may provide a positive reframe for the experience of caregiving and place it within a broader context. In essence, religious coping may enable a woman to engage in caregiving as a form of communion, while maintaining a sense of agency.

In general, it is important that a woman be able to access her faith community as a resource, rather than as a restraint. The woman needs to be able to remain differentiated within her community in order to cope in the manner that best meets her needs and suits her style. If a woman feels the need to silence her voice because the church community might not want to hear it, then she begins to engage in unmitigated communion. For example, in more fundamentalist religions, the belief that the wife is required to honor and obey her husband might impede a woman's willingness to discuss domestic violence within the religious community.

■ Louise is a 62-year-old married African American woman. Her two adult biological children are successful professionals; however, both children have chronic medical conditions with ongoing complications. Her adoptive son has special needs and requires a group-home placement to meet those needs. Louise decreased her hours at her job in a human service agency because she felt that it was too overwhelming to work with such needy people given her family's stress level. She joined a neighborhood walking group where nobody knew her role as problem-solver. She began to prepare for her adoptive son's move and to accept that she has done what she can for him. She remains active in her church but has discontinued her membership on several boards. She noted that she interacts with the people and agencies that recognize her as human, and distances herself from those that expect her to be a self-sacrificing superhero. ■

INCREASING COPING THROUGH INCREASED AGENCY AND COMMUNION: TREATMENT, POLICY, AND RESEARCH

Clinical work, public policy, and research are all valuable forums for increasing coping skills for girls and women through the life span. Several psychotherapies have philosophical foundations that are congruent with the treatment goals of increasing agency and communion to strengthen coping. Transitional family therapy posits that families seek treatment when their current skills are not sufficient for adjusting to a transition (Seaburn, Landau-Stanton, & Horwitz, 1995). The use of a genogram to map the family's history, negotiation of transitions, and strengths provides the clinician with a contextualized understanding of the problem and the family's skills and resources. The clinician is able to reinforce and nurture existing coping skills as well as to teach coping skills that fit with the family's style and needs.

Likewise, solution-focused family therapy (De Jong & Berg, 2001; de Shazer, 1985) recognizes that families are skillful but may not be aware they already possess the coping skills needed to resolve their problems. Solution-focused family therapy uses techniques such as the Miracle Question and scaling techniques to facilitate a family's ability to implement preexisting coping skills. Interpersonal psychotherapy is a short-term therapy that focuses on relationships and helps clients to enhance their coping through improved communication, problem solving, and increased support networks (Stuart & Robertson, 2002). It has been effective with women dealing with diverse issues such as poverty, postpartum depression, and bulimia. Relational therapy is based specifically on a psychology of women that recognizes the importance of connections to women and has been applied to a range of problems including eating disorders (Tantillo, 2000).

There are also therapies that directly teach coping skills, which increase agency and communion. Many of these have a cognitive-behavioral underpinning, and the therapist takes an active stance in teaching and promoting the active use of coping skills. For example, Dialectical Behavior Therapy (Linehan, 1996) teaches coping skills in four areas: mindfulness, interpersonal effectiveness, emotion regulation, and distress tolerance. Clients learn and practice in skills training groups while individual therapy is used to troubleshoot problem areas as identified by the client's diary card. Mindfulness cognitive-based therapy teaches clients how to engage in a meditation practice and how to incorporate mindfulness skills in their daily lives to prevent recurrent depression (Segal, Williams, & Teasdale, 2001). Simonds (2001), in her therapy for women with depression, recommends an individualized approach to the development of coping skills. She teaches women to create concrete plans for relapse prevention and encourages them to engage in meaningful activities.

Often, as implied above, the therapist will act as a coach or mentor in the teaching of coping skills. The therapist can model coping skills in session, either explicitly or implicitly. The therapeutic relationship can enable the client to experience a balance of connection and autonomy. Processing interactions in session can highlight the client's typical style of interaction, as well as any shifts that may occur as the therapy progresses.

Genograms, as noted earlier, can provide a powerful picture of the balance of agency and communion in a family. Gendered patterns and cultural values become clear when the genogram is drawn. Other helpful therapeutic techniques include rituals, letters to deceased relatives, the empty chair technique, and internal family systems work. Striepe and Coons (2002) provide a detailed example of a group therapy program for Hmong women, which teaches coping skills in a manner that respects their culture and enhances their well-being.

Public policy has the potential at the larger systems level to increase or decrease adolescent girls' and women's coping skills. Public policy must address poverty, which is a risk factor for many adverse events such as depression and violence, and impedes development. Programs that provide resources, such as access to education, health care,

and employment opportunities, often need to be federally funded. Currently, programs exist across the spectrum of development; however, these programs are often on a shoestring budget and depend upon charitable donations. Such programs include enriched day-care programs, after school recreational programs, college-bound programs, adolescent mother programs, women's career centers, family-based homeless shelters, and inclusive battered women's shelters.

It is also critical that public policy support parents' care of their children. Maternity and paternity leaves enable parents to create a healthy attachment with their children. Affordable, family friendly day-care arrangements that facilitate children's development are necessary for working parents. Laws such as the Family Leave Act, which permits time off for family members to care for sick relatives and new children (whether biological, foster, or adoptive), promote effective coping. These laws are necessary to create a society that values both agency and communion for women, a state in which families matter.

Another important arena of public policy is preventive services. Programs and policies that implement early intervention often create short-term and long-term changes. Prenatal programs offer additional services for women at risk during pregnancy; these services increase coping by fostering a support system and providing education (Klerman et al., 2001). Several early intervention projects provide mentors who visit mothers and their children in the home, enhancing the mother's coping skills and support system (Wallach & Lister, 1995). This not only facilitates the biological mother's acquisition of skills through scaffolding but also models for the children a healthy balance of agency and communion.

Public policy is increasingly needed to assist for women in coping with the threat of terrorism. In the 12 months after the September 11, 2001, tragedies, large-scale studies report that 7.5–40% of adults carry diagnoses of posttraumatic stress, depression, anxiety, or stress-related somatic symptoms, with the higher percentages related to proximity to the sites (Miller & Heldring, 2004). Successful coping styles in this challenging situation include increased agency and communion through community action and response, as well as working toward increased preparedness for future problems. It is imperative that public policy support these response efforts, which are critical in reorganizing the community and providing vehicles for women and their families to cope through meaningful activism.

Research informs how we teach coping skills, it guides our interventions, and it suggests appropriate public policy. Much existing research on coping is cross-sectional in design (Somerfield & McCrae, 2000). Research that considers gender as a variable tends to compare emotion-focused and problem-focused coping skills. In general, the literature is limited and would benefit from a broader conceptual base that considers coping in context, rather than as good versus bad strategies. New research in this area should include longitudinal systemic intervention studies in areas such as coping with chronic abdominal pain or responses to genetic testing.

Whether it is demonstrated in research, clinical stories, or great literature, girls and women have a long history of coping creatively with challenges that are uniquely female, such as childbirth, and with challenges that are uniquely (in)human, such as terrorism. Strategies span the possibilities, but often include turning to relationships for nurturance. Balancing agency and a focus on self, with communion and a focus on others, helps to ensure healthy coping in a 21st century full of both opportunity and stress for women.

REFERENCES

Bakan, D. (1969). *The duality of human existence.* Chicago: Rand-McNally.

Barnett, R. C., & Hyde, J. S. (2001). Women, men, work and family: An expansionist theory. *The American Psychologist, 56,* 781–796.

Berghuis, J. P., & Stanton, A. L. (2002). Adjustment to a dyadic stressor: A longitudinal study of coping in infertile couples over an insemination attempt. *Journal of Consulting and Clinical Psychology, 70,* 433–438.

Broderick, P. C. (1998). Early adolescent gender differences in the use of ruminative and distracting coping strategies. *Journal of Early Adolescence, 18,* 173–191.

Bronfenbrenner, U. (1979). *The ecology of human development: Experiments by nature and design.* Cambridge, MA: Harvard University Press.

Carlson, E. A., & Sroufe, L. A. (1995). Contribution of attachment theory to developmental psychology. In D. Cicchetti & D. J. Cohen (Eds.), *Developmental psychopathology: Vol. 1. Theory and methods* (pp. 581–617). New York: John Wiley & Sons.

Chapman, P. L., & Mullis, R. L. (2000). Racial differences in adolescent coping and self-esteem. *The Journal of Genetic Psychology, 161,* 152–160.

De Jong, P., & Berg, I. K. (2001). *Interviewing for solutions.* Belmont, CA: Wadsworth.

de Shazer, S. (1985). *Keys to solutions in brief therapy.* New York: Norton.

Falicov, C. J. (2001). The cultural meanings of money: The case of Latinos and Anglo-Americans. *The American Behavioral Scientist, 45,* 313–328.

Fritz, H. L., & Helgeson, V. S. (1998). Distinctions of unmitigated communion from communion: Self-neglect and overinvolvement with others. *Journal of Personality and Social Psychology, 75,* 121–140.

Gilligan, C. (1993). *In a different voice: Psychological theory and women's development.* Cambridge, MA: Harvard University Press.

Helgeson, V. S., & Fritz, H. L. (1999). Unmitigated agency and communion: Distinctions from agency and communion. *Journal of Research in Personality, 33,* 131–158.

Imber-Black, E. (1988). Ritual themes in families and family therapy. In E. Imber-Black, J. Roberts, & R. A. Whiting (Eds.), *Rituals in families and family therapy* (pp. 47–83). New York: Norton.

Johnson, S. M. (2002). *Emotionally focused couple therapy with trauma survivors: Strengthening attachment bonds.* New York: Guilford Press.

Jones, J. M. (2003). TRIOS: A psychological theory of the African legacy in the American culture. *Journal of Social Issues, 59,* 217–242.

Klerman, L. V., Ramey, S. L., Goldenberg, R. L., Marbury, S., Hou, J., & Cliver, S. P. (2001). A randomized trial of augmented prenatal care for multiple-risk, Medicaid-eligible African American women. *American Journal of Public Health, 91,* 105–111.

Lazarus, R. S., & Folkman, S. (1984). *Stress, appraisal, and coping.* New York: Springer.

Linehan, M. M. (1996). *Cognitive-behavioral treatment for borderline personality disorder.* New York: Guilford Press.

McDaniel, S. H., & Cole-Kelly, K. (2003). *Gender, couples and illness: A feminist analysis of medical family therapy, feminist family therapy.* Washington, DC: American Psychological Association.

McDaniel, S. H., Hepworth, J., & Doherty, W. J. (1992). *Medical family therapy: A biopsychosocial approach to families with health problems.* New York: Basic Books.

Miller, A. M., & Heldring, M. (2004). Mental health and primary care in a time of terrorism: Psychological impact of terrorist attacks. *Families, Systems & Health, 22,* 7–30.

Miltiades, H. B., & Pruchno, R. (2002). The effect of religious coping on caregiving appraisals of mothers of adults with developmental disabilities. *The Gerontologist, 42,* 82–91.

Seaburn, D., Landau-Stanton, J., & Horwitz, S. (1995). Core techniques in family therapy. In R. Mikesell, D. D. Lusterman, & S. H. McDaniel (Eds.), *Integrating family therapy* (pp. 5–26). Washington, DC: American Psychological Association.

Segal, Z., Williams, J. M., & Teasdale, J. D. (2001). *Mindfulness-based cognitive therapy for depression: A new approach for preventing relapse.* New York: Guilford Press.

Sigelman, C. K. (1999). *Life-span human development* (3rd ed.). Pacific Grove, CA: Brooks/Cole.

Simonds, S. L. (2001). *Depression and women: An integrative treatment approach.* New York: Springer.

Simoni, J. M., Martone, M. G., & Kerwin, J. F. (2002). Spirituality and psychological adaptation among women with HIV/AIDS: Implications for counseling. *Journal of Counseling Psychology, 29,* 139–147.

Somerfield, M. R., & McCrae, R. R. (2000). Stress and coping research: Methodological challenges, theoretical advances, and clinical applications. *American Psychologist, 55,* 620–625.

Stanton, A. L., Danoff-Burg, S., Cameron, C. L., Bishop, M., Collins, C. A., Kirk, S. B., et al. (2000). Emotionally expressive coping predicts psychological and physical adjustment to breast cancer. *Journal of Consulting and Clinical Psychology, 68,* 875–882.

Striepe, M. I., & Coons, H. L. (2002). Women's health in primary care: Interdisciplinary interventions. *Families, Systems, & Health, 20,* 237–251.

Stuart, S., & Robertson, M. (2002). *Interpersonal therapy: A clinician's guide.* London: Edward Arnold Ltd.

Tamres, L. K., Janicki, D., & Helgeson, V. S. (2002). Sex differences in coping behavior: A meta-analytic review and an examination of relative coping. *Personality and Social Psychology Review, 6,* 2–30.

Tantillo, M. (2000). Short-term relational group therapy for women with bulimia nervosa. *Eating Disorders: The Journal of Treatment & Prevention, 8,* 99–121.

Taylor, S. E., Klien, L. C., Lewis, B. P., Gruenewald, T. L., Gurung, R. A. R., & Updegraff, J. A. (2000). Biobehavioral responses to stress in females: Tend-and-befriend, not fight-or-flight. *Psychological Review, 107,* 411–429.

VandenBos, G. (Ed.). (in press). *The APA dictionary of psychology.* Washington, DC: American Psychological Association.

Walker, A. (1983). Dedication, *In search of our mothers' gardens.* New York: Harcourt, Brace, Jovanovich.

Wallach, V. A., & Lister, L. (1995). Stages in the delivery of home-based services to parents at risk of child abuse: A healthy start experience. *Scholarly Inquiry for Nursing Practice, 9,* 159–173.

Weingarten, K. (1997). *The mother's voice: Strengthening intimacy in families.* New York: Guilford Press.

Much has been written about self-esteem in the past 50 years, most of it with the assumption that self-esteem is a pervasive and universal phenomenon with primarily beneficial outcomes. The emphasis has been mostly on levels of self-esteem and their accompanying correlates, with a concomitant interest in how to obtain high self-esteem. This line of research eventually fostered a practical approach in the 1980s on how to provide self-esteem to children in school-based programs (Mecca, Smelser, & Vasconcellos, 1989). No easily definable outcomes having resulted from this approach, an extensive review of the literature was undertaken in the 1990s. The surprising conclusion was that self-esteem is not discernibly related to any beneficial outcomes and that high self-esteem may not always be a good thing (Baumeister, Campbell, Kreuger, & Vohs, 2003). Most recently, the focus has shifted from self-esteem as an entity to self-esteem as a process, from self-esteem as a passive personality characteristic to self-esteem as a motive (Crocker & Park, 2004a). New theories have arisen as to the functions that self-esteem serves: as an anxiety buffer against death (Pyszczynski, Solomon, Greenberg, Arndt, & Schimel, 2004b) or social exclusion (Baumeister & Leary, 1995; Leary, Tambor, Terdal, & Downs, 1995). But the argument has been made that the pursuit of self-esteem is not a fundamental need, that it is very costly both physically and psychologically, and that perhaps pursuing self-esteem should not be a normative goal (Crocker & Park, 2004a). Before turning to these newer trends in self-esteem research and the implications for mental health, a review of the basics, especially as they relate to gender, is in order (definition, distribution over the life span, and sources of self-esteem).

OKSANA MALANCHUK
and JACQUELYNNE S. ECCLES

Self-Esteem

16

DEFINING SELF-ESTEEM

The concept of self-esteem originated with William James (1890), in which he referred to it as a person's evaluation of, or attitude toward, the self. The most prevalent definition of self-esteem views it as the extent to which an individual likes, values, and accepts himself or herself (Rogers, 1951). This differs from related constructs such as self-confidence or self-efficacy, which refers to beliefs about one's abilities to obtain desired outcomes (Bandura, 1997). Several distinctions have been made about the concept of self-esteem. Valuing and accepting oneself is considered to have both cognitive (i.e., self-knowledge) and affective (i.e., evaluative) components. Considered as a basic component of the self, it can be stable across situations (trait self-esteem) or it can be open to change and be situationally manipulated (state self-esteem) (Kernis & Waschull, 1995). Self-esteem can be global or domain-specific, and it rises and falls around its typical level in response to successes and failures in domains on which one has staked one's self-worth (James, 1890). It can also be contingency-based and fluctuate as a function of accomplishments, requiring continual validation and resulting from matching some standard or excellence or living up to some interpersonal expectations. Or it can be noncontingent or "true" self-esteem, based on intrinsic motivation which is the natural, innate tendency to explore, assimilate, and experience mastery within one's surroundings (Deci & Ryan, 1995).

DEMOGRAPHIC DISTRIBUTION OF SELF-ESTEEM ACROSS THE LIFE SPAN

While some researchers argue that the pursuit of self-esteem is a fundamental need and universal feature of human nature (Baumeister & Leary, 1995; Pyszczynski et al., 2004b), others question whether the self-esteem motive is specific to Western culture (Heine, Lehman, Markus, & Kitayama, 1999). Empirical research in the United States indicates that levels of self-esteem vary according to age, gender, and ethnicity. Self-esteem is at its highest in early childhood at ages 9 through 12; it drops sharply in adolescence (13–17); continues its decline into the college period (18–22); rises slightly in the post-college years (23–29); and then reaches a plateau in the 30s with gradual increases from then on until it declines markedly from the 60s to the 80s (Robins, Trzesniewski, Tracy, Gosling, & Potter, 2002). Both boys and girls start out high in self-esteem in early childhood, but during adolescence, girls' self-esteem drops twice as much as boys'. According to their data, this gender difference persists throughout adulthood and only narrows in old age (70s and 80s), when

women report only slightly higher levels of self-esteem than men (Robins et al., 2002).

The dramatic drop in adolescent girls' self-esteem has been noted in several studies (e.g., American Association of University Women [AAUW], 1990). But in one study this result was found to be true only for European American early adolescents who made a transition from elementary school to junior high school at the same time as they moved from sixth to seventh grade, suggesting that both school structure and ethnic culture play important roles in this developmental change (Simmons & Blyth, 1987). Drawing upon cumulative stress theory, the argument was made that the gender differences in the rate of decline in self-esteem among European American youth was an outcome of the girls' coping with two major transitions (both pubertal and school changes) at the same time. Since coping with multiple transitions is more difficult than coping with only one, these young women should be at greater risk of negative outcomes than adolescents who have to cope with only one transition (either school or pubertal changes) during this developmental period.

Indeed, a more recent study indicates that pubertal development is not the same kind of risk factor for African American females as it is for some European American females (Michael & Eccles, 2004). Separating out each ethnic group into early and on-time maturers, the researchers found that only the European American girls' self-esteem and mental health were related to their maturational rate—with the early maturing females reporting lower self-esteem and mental health and higher rates of bulimic eating patterns. Maturational rate had no relation to these outcomes among the African American females.

With the exception of early childhood, African Americans consistently report higher self-esteem than Whites or other minority groups (Robins et al., 2002; Twenge & Crocker, 2002). Until the 1970s this was considered counterintuitive as researchers had hypothesized that African Americans and members of other oppressed or stigmatized groups would have low self-esteem because they were held in low regard by others, because they were excluded from desirable occupations, or because they had fewer opportunities to control their environment (Gray-Little & Hafdahl, 2000). Using meta-analysis, Twenge and Crocker (2002) considered four distinct theoretical perspectives as to why ethnicity may play a role in self-esteem differences between groups: internalization of stigma, stigma as self-protection, ethnic identity, and cultural differences in self-concept. The cultural perspective fit best, especially since the pattern of differences by ethnicity in individualism mirrored the differences in self-esteem, with African Americans scoring highest on both. The authors caution against single-variable explanations and suggest an interactive approach involving moderator variables to more fully understand the phenomenon, as well as examining how self-esteem is constructed in different ethnic groups.

Eccles, Barber, Jozefowicz, Malanchuk, and Vida (1999) in fact compared African American and European American girls' self-perceptions in two studies, one of which was a primarily European American working-class and middle-class sample and one of which was a normative African American sample. First, in both studies, the general pattern of gender differences were much weaker, if significant at all, among the African Americans. Second, the African American females had higher self-esteem than both the European American girls and the African American males. Third, there were significant differences by ethnicity in these young women's self-perceptions that could explain the ethnic minority differences in young women's self-esteem: the African American girls had either similar or higher academic ability self concepts than the European American girls. The African American girls also had higher athletic and social self-concepts and were more satisfied with their physical attractiveness (Winston, Eccles, Senior, & Vida, 1997). Finally, unlike the evidence for the European American girls, there was no evidence of a decline in the African American girls' self-esteem over the early adolescent years. However, a subsequent study of self-esteem in later adolescence indicated a slight downward trend for African American girls in the 11th grade (Malanchuk & Eccles, 1999), indicating that their sources of self-esteem might be converging with those of European American girls. Similar comparative studies on other ethnic groups are badly needed.

SOURCES OF SELF-ESTEEM

Neither the processes underlying individual differences nor the process underlying developmental changes in self-esteem are well understood. Harter (1993) reports that there are two main sources of global self-esteem: (a) direct experiences of competence and efficacy and (b) social feedback, particularly as it is reflected in the appraisals of significant other people. These sources differ somewhat by gender. Men's self-esteem tends to be based on achievements and women's self-esteem on interpersonal connectedness (Josephs, Markus, & Tafarodi, 1992). As noted above, other researchers have focused on changes in the school environment as an important influence on the age-related changes over time (see Eccles et al., 1993; Simmons & Blyth, 1987). They have also suggested that changes in the nature of one's familial relationships during adolescence could contribute to the developmental declines in self-esteem during early adolescence (Eccles et al., 1993). Finally, the variations in the patterns of self-concepts and values discussed earlier are also likely to be relevant.

In a recent study that undertook to examine several sources of self-esteem simultaneously, researchers found that a number of factors were predictive: popularity, appearance, parent approval of peers, worries about weight, importance of schooling, self-consciousness, and concerns about sexuality (Davis-Kean, Eccles, Malanchuk, & Peck, 2004). In middle school, White girls are worried about their weight, their popularity with the same sex, and their appearance. African American girls are more concerned about their popularity with the opposite sex, their looks, being self-conscious, and worries about their weight in that order (Eccles et al., 1999). By high school, White and African American females are equally impacted by wishes to be more popular with opposite-sex peers, as well as desires to be good looking and fears about negative sex-related outcomes. Numerous other studies indicate that physical appearance is an important domain predicting to self-esteem for girls but not for boys (e.g., Harter, 1990), and to a greater extent for European American than African American girls (e.g., Simmons & Blyth, 1987).

The salience of physical appearance for the stability of young women's self-esteem is troubling. Given that both individual differences in physical appearance and the exact nature of pubertal changes in different individuals' bodies are substantially biologically determined and thus is somewhat out of the individual's control, a focus on physical attractiveness for persons who are not, or do not feel, attractive enough is likely to undermine some young women's self-esteem. It is also likely to push some young women toward extreme efforts to try to change their bodies in order to meet both real and perceived peer and societal standards. It follows that girls at this age who have a negative perception of their appearance may be at risk for developing symptoms that reflect their diminished self-esteem, such as eating disorders. And in fact, lack of confidence in one's physical appearance was one of the primary significant predictors of bulimia-related eating behaviors (Michael & Eccles, 2004).

Sources of self-esteem during the college years are similarly contingency-based: competition, family support, appearance, God's love, approval from others, school competence, and virtue (Crocker and Wolfe, 2001). In this study, White females were highest of all the subgroups on family support, appearance, and approval from others as their sources of self-esteem. African Americans were highest on God's love and lowest on approval from others. African American females were lowest on competition; African American males were lowest on appearance. All subgroups were equally impacted by virtue and school competence.

It is critical to take note of the ethnic group differences summarized above. African American adolescent females do not appear to be at greater risk than their male peers for declines in self-esteem. The reasons for this difference need to be explored for three reasons: (a) because we need to understand the sources of resilience in African American adolescent girls; (b) because understanding these differences will help us understand the nature of cultural differences between these two ethnic groups; and (c) because such studies will offer insights into the kinds of preventive interventions that might help bolster European American and African American females' self-esteem during this critical transitional period. It seems likely that cultural differences in the standards of feminine beauty are one piece of this difference but this hypothesis has not been fully studied. Other possible influences include variations in meaning of sexual maturity and in the response of both adults and peers to signs of pubertal development.

FUNCTIONS OF SELF-ESTEEM

Why do we need self-esteem and what functions does it serve? Some innovative new theories have recently emerged with compelling explanations for why we might choose to seek self-esteem. The most influential is terror management theory (Pyszczynski et al., 2004b) which argues that self-esteem serves as a buffer against death anxiety. Arguing that a biologically rooted desire for life and the uniquely human awareness of the inevitability of death lead to an existential anxiety, these theorists posit that our forefathers sought to alleviate this death anxiety by creating cultural worldviews ("humanly constructed shared symbolic conceptions of reality that give meaning, order, and permanence to existence; provide a set of standards for what is valuable; and promise some form of either literal or symbolic immortality to those who believe in the cultural worldview and live up to its standards of value," p. 436). Self-esteem thus serves as a shield against existential anxiety by giving us a sense of personal value obtained by living up to the standards of one's cultural worldview and being a contributor to a meaningful universe. That is why people are motivated to maintain high levels of self-esteem and why they defend their self-esteem when it comes under threat. While terror management theory makes a compelling argument for this evolutionary hypothesis, critics of this theory argue that some of its fundamental assumptions have not been adequately tested—specifically, that it has not been demonstrated empirically that people need self-esteem, that pursuing it is an effective means for reducing anxiety, or that death is the real issue driving the pursuit of self-esteem (Crocker & Nuer, 2004).

Another influential theory explaining why we seek self-esteem is the sociometer theory (Baumeister & Leary, 1995; Leary et al., 1995), which suggests that we have a driving need to belong and that self-esteem is a buffer against anxiety about loneliness and social rejection. This theory similarly posits that self-esteem evolved as an adaptive advantage that enhanced survival, but the function of self-esteem in this view is thought to be the monitoring of the social environment for threats to social acceptance or rejection in any given situation, with perceived social exclusion leading to feelings of low self-esteem. Thus, it is not success or failure per se that affect levels of self-esteem but how we think others will react to our achievements or limitations.

Both terror management theory and sociometer theory have difficulty explaining all of the evidence regarding self-esteem, and some argue that the propositions of each theory can be roughly translated into the concepts of the other (Leary, 2004). Another criticism of both theories is that they are primarily focused on defensive processes and do not take into account intrinsic developmental processes (Ryan & Deci, 2004). The argument here is that this approach is akin to contingent self-esteem and that true self-esteem is based on the ongoing satisfaction of needs for competence, autonomy, and relatedness.

IMPLICATIONS FOR MENTAL HEALTH

There is a large literature on the implications of having high and low self-esteem where high self-esteem is generally related to better outcomes and is assumed to have beneficial effects. (See Baumeister, 1993, 1998, for reviews.) The emphasis on self-esteem as a source of positive well-being and successes eventually led to the self-esteem movement, epitomized by the California Task Force to Promote Self-Esteem and Personal and Social Responsibility (Mecca et al., 1989), which tried to promote self-esteem in the classroom on the assumption that high self-esteem would cause many positive outcomes. Baumeister et al. (2003) criticized this view, arguing that there was no evidence supporting the claim that boosting self-esteem causes higher academic achievement, better job performance, or leadership. Rather, it seems that high but unstable self-esteem is actually related to hostility and aggression (Baumeister et al., 2003). These researchers did find that self-

esteem has a strong relation to happiness and that there were two benefits of high self-esteem: enhanced initiative and pleasant feelings.

Indeed, self-esteem has been noted as the strongest predictor of life satisfaction in the United States, outstripping all other predictors such as age, income, education, physical health, marital status, and other psychological variables (Diener, 1984). In early adolescence, it is the best predictor of gains in mental health, surpassing such indicators as depression, coping, and resilience (Peck, Davis-Kean, Schnabel, & Eccles, 2002). Furthermore, low self-esteem has consistently been shown to be related to depression and suicidal ideation (Crocker & Wolfe, 2001; Harter, 1999).

Rather than focus on level of self-esteem, Crocker and Park (2004a) argued that we should be looking at why people choose to pursue self-esteem. They conceive of self-esteem not as a passive state or personality characteristic but as a dynamic human striving. They examined what people did to achieve boosts to their self-esteem and to avoid drops in self-esteem in their daily lives and came to the conclusion that self-esteem is costly to pursue. They argued that it impedes the satisfaction of needs for competence, relatedness, and autonomy—all indicators of intrinsic or "true" self-esteem, as well as the ability to self-regulate behavior. Furthermore, it has costs to physical and mental health. Striving for self-esteem makes people feel anxious and stressed, potentially hostile, and may lead to unhealthy coping behavior or health risk behaviors, all of which have negative effects on physical health. Similarly, they found a relation between pursuing self-esteem and depression, narcissism, and anxiety.

Crocker and Park neatly summarized their critics, who argued that they overstate the case for the costs of pursuing self-esteem (Sheldon, 2004); that it is possible to strive for it in healthy ways (DuBois & Flay, 2004); and that it would be extremely difficult if not impossible for people to stop pursuing self-esteem (Pyszczynski & Cox, 2004). These critics suggested an integrative perspective that acknowledges that self-esteem buffers anxiety and is greatly influenced by social relations; they also argued that when it is based on standards that are intrinsic or well-integrated with one's core self-elements, it is especially adaptive. But, they said, this is more than likely not the case. The pursuit of self-esteem is more often based on extrinsic factors. In addition, it is unlikely that people will cease dealing with their anxieties by pursuing high self-esteem (Pyszczynski, Solomon, Greenberg, Arndt, & Schimel, 2004a).

Are we inevitably prone to striving for self-esteem? Crocker and Park (2004b) argued that a distinction should be made between having self-esteem and pursuing it. One can value and accept oneself without continually seeking confirmation from others. It is the pursuit of self-esteem that is like a bad habit that can be broken with practice. In their view, self-esteem is not a fundamental need, like competence, autonomy, or relatedness, but a goal. Its pursuit, when successful, boosts self-esteem and reduces anxiety but only for a short time (Crocker, Sommers, & Luhtanen, 2002). These authors suggested that rather than having self-esteem as a goal, people should apply a learning orientation where successes and failures are viewed as learning opportunities and that this approach more effectively reduces anxiety than can boosts to one's self-esteem. Along with others, they also reflect on achieving self-esteem through other means. That is, rather than focusing on contingent self-esteem with its emphasis on appearance or academic and other achievements, people should pursue goals that are larger than themselves. They note that it is in focusing beyond ourselves, without regard to self-esteem enhancement, that we may best satisfy ourselves (Crocker & Park, 2004b).

PRACTICAL IMPLICATIONS

If it's not advantageous to pursue self-esteem but it is desirable to have it, how might we go about helping people obtain it? Deci and Ryan (1995), combining self-determination theory and self-esteem research, have argued that it is autonomy-granting situations that initiate and maintain feelings of true self-esteem. Kernis (2003) believes that there is such a thing as optimal self-esteem, which is different from high self-esteem, and in his estimation, it is based on promoting authenticity in the individual. But

self-esteem is a developmental phenomenon and needs to be approached differently depending on the current stage of development of the individual. Mruk (1999) has indicated that by adulthood, it's not a question of developing self-esteem but of maintaining it, and he offers an intervention program for clinicians for enhancing self-esteem in adults.

Harter, who has written extensively on issues in the development of the self-concept, has recommended various intervention strategies based on the individual's stage of development—from early to late childhood and early to late adolescence, at which point the self-concept is considerably formed (Harter, 1999). She also has argued that authenticity is a key factor in developing a strong self of self-worth. We concur with her assessment that educators should promote autonomy and authenticity by giving greater voice to students by building upon the life experiences of the students, rather than on rigid adherence to academic content, thereby engaging them in the learning process. The need for empowerment through providing opportunities for their voices to be heard may be especially true for girls and young women who are faced with considerable devaluation in society and are valued more for their physical appearance than for their inner qualities. Providing an atmosphere in which girls are taken seriously by teachers, as well as their peers, will go a long way to contributing toward a more equitable society.

REFERENCES

American Association of University Women. (1990). *Shortchanging girls, shortchanging America: Full data report.* Washington, DC: Author.

Bandura, A. (1997). *Self-efficacy: The exercise of control.* New York: Freeman.

Baumeister, R. F. (Ed.). (1993). *Self-esteem: The puzzle of low self-regard.* New York: Plenum Press.

Baumeister, R. F. (1998). The self. In D. T. Gilbert & S. T. Fiske (Eds.), *Handbook of social psychology* (4th ed., Vol. 1, pp. 680–740). New York: McGraw-Hill.

Baumeister, R. F., Campbell, J. D., Kreuger, J. I., & Vohs, K. D. (2003). Does high self-esteem cause better performance, interpersonal success, happiness or healthier lifestyles? *Psychological Science in the Public Interest, 4*(1), 1–44.

Baumeister, R. F., & Leary, M. R. (1995). The need to belong: Desire for interpersonal attachments as a fundamental human motivation. *Psychological Bulletin, 117,* 497–529.

Crocker, J., & Nuer, N. (2004). Do people need self-esteem? Comment on Pyszczynski et al. (2004). *Psychological Bulletin, 130*(3), 469–472.

Crocker, J., & Park, L. E. (2004a). The costly pursuit of self-esteem. *Psychological Bulletin, 130*(3), 392–414.

Crocker, J., & Park, L. E. (2004b). Reaping the benefits of pursuing self-esteem without the costs? Reply to Dubois and Flay (2004), Sheldon (2004), and Pyszczynski and Cox (2004). *Psychological Bulletin, 130*(3), 430–434.

Crocker, J., Sommers, S., & Luhtanen, R. (2002). Hopes dashed and dreams fulfilled: Contingencies of self-worth in the graduate school admissions process. *Personality and Social Psychology Bulletin, 28,* 1275–1286.

Crocker, J., & Wolfe, C. T. (2001). Contingencies of self-worth. *Psychological Review, 108,* 593–623.

Davis-Kean, P. E., Eccles, J. S., Malanchuk, O., & Peck, S. C. (2004, November). The dark matter of self-esteem. Presentation at the Research Center for Group Dynamics Seminar, Ann Arbor, MI.

Deci, E. L., & Ryan, R. M. (1995). Human agency: The basis for true self-esteem. In M. H. Kernis (Ed.), *Efficacy, agency, and self-esteem* (pp. 31–50). New York: Plenum Press.

Diener, E. (1984). Subjective well-being. *Psychological Bulletin, 95,* 542–575.

DuBois, D. L., & Flay, B. R. (2004). The healthy pursuit of self-esteem: Comment on and alternative to the Crocker and Park (2004) formulation. *Psychological Bulletin, 130*(3), 415–420.

Eccles, J. S., Barber, B. L., Jozefowicz, D., Malanchuk, O., & Vida, M. (1999). Self-evaluations of competence, task values, and self-esteem. In N. Johnson, M. Roberts, & J. Worell (Eds.), *Beyond appearances: A new look at adolescent girls* (pp. 53–83). Washington DC: American Psychological Association.

Eccles, J. S., Midgley, C., Wigfield, A., Buchanan, C. M., Reuman, D., & MacIver, D. (1993). Development during adolescence: The impact of stage/environment fit on young adolescents' experiences in schools and families. *American Psychologist, 48,* 90–101.

Gray-Little, B., and Hafdahl, A. R. (2000). Factors influencing racial comparisons of self-esteem: A quantitative review. *Psychological Bulletin, 126,* 26–54.

Harter, S. (1990). Causes, correlates, and the functional role of global self-worth: A life-span perspective. In R. J. Sternberg & J. Kolligian, Jr. (Eds.), *Competence considered* (pp. 67–97). New Haven, CT: Yale University Press.

Harter, S. (1993). Causes and consequences of low self-esteem in children and adolescents. In R. F. Baumeister (Ed.), *Self-esteem: The puzzle of low self-regard* (pp. 87–116). New York: Plenum Press.

Harter, S. (1999). *The construction of self.* New York: Guilford Press.

Heine, S. J., Lehman, D. R., Markus, H. R., & Kitayama, S. (1999). Is there a universal need for positive self-regard? *Psychological Review, 106,* 766–794.

James, W. (1890). *The principles of psychology.* New York: Holt.

Josephs, R., Markus, H., & Tafarodi, R. (1992). Gender and self-esteem. *Journal of Personality and Social Psychology, 63,* 391–402.

Kernis, M. H. (2003). Toward a conceptualization of optimal self-esteem. *Psychological Inquiry, 14,* 1–26.

Kernis, M. H., & Waschull, S. B. (1995). The interactive roles of stability and level of self-esteem: Research and theory. In M. P. Zanna, *Advances in experimental social psychology.* San Diego, CA: Academic Press.

Leary, M. R. (2004). The function of self-esteem in terror management theory and sociometer theory: Comment on Pyszczynski et al. (2004). *Psychological Bulletin, 130*(3), 478–482.

Leary, M. R., Tambor, E. S., Terdal, S. K. & Downs, D. L. (1995). Self-esteem as an interpersonal monitor: The sociometer hypothesis. *Journal of Personality and Social Psychology, 68*(3), 518–530.

Malanchuk, O., & Eccles, J. S. (1999, April). Determinants of self-esteem in African-American and White adolescent girls. Poster presented at the biennial meeting of the Society for Research on Child Development, Albuquerque, NM.

Mecca, A. M., Smelser, N. J., & Vasconcellos, J. (Eds.). (1989). *The social importance of self-esteem.* Berkeley: University of California Press.

Michael, A., and Eccles, J. S. (2004). When coming of age means coming undone: Links between puberty and psychosocial adjustment among European American and African American girls. In C. Hayward (Ed.), *Gender differences at puberty.* New York: Cambridge University Press.

Mruk, C. J. (1999). *Self-esteem: Research, theory and practice* (2nd ed.). New York: Springer.

Peck, S. C., Davis-Kean, P. E., Schnabel, K. U., & Eccles, J. S. (2002). *Self-esteem does matter: Research on the longitudinal impact of self-esteem.* Unpublished manuscript, Ann Arbor, MI.

Pyszczynski, T., & Cox, C. (2004). Can we really do without self-esteem? Comment on Crocker and Park (2004). *Psychological Bulletin, 130*(3), 425–429.

Pyszczynski, T., Solomon, S., Greenberg, J., Arndt, J., & Schimel, J. (2004a). Converging toward an integrated theory of self-esteem: Reply to Crocker and Nuer (2004), Ryan and Deci (2004), and Leary (2004). *Psychological Bulletin, 130*(3), 483–488.

Pyszczynski, T., Solomon, S., Greenberg, J., Arndt, J., & Schimel, J. (2004b). Why do people need self-esteem? A theoretical and empirical review. *Psychological Bulletin, 130*(3), 435–468.

Robins, R. W., Trzesniewski, K. H., Tracy, J. L., Gosling, S. D., & Potter, J. (2002). Self-esteem across the lifespan. *Psychology and Aging, 17,* 423–434.

Rogers, C. R. (1951). *Client centered therapy.* Boston: Houghton Mifflin.

Ryan, R. M., & Deci, E. L. (2004). Avoiding death or engaging life as accounts of meaning and culture: Commenting on Pyszczynski et al. (2004). *Psychological Bulletin, 130*(3), 473–477.

Sheldon, K. M. (2004). The benefits of a "sidelong" approach to self-esteem need satisfaction: Comment on Crocker and Park (2004). *Psychological Bulletin, 130*(3), 421–424.

Simmons, R. G., & Blyth, D. A. (1987). *Moving into adolescence: The impact of pubertal change and school context.* Hawthorn, NY: Aldine de Gruyter.

Twenge, J. M., & Crocker, J. (2002). Race and self-esteem: Meta-analyses comparing Whites, Blacks, Hispanics, Asians, and American Indians and comment on Gray-Little and Hafdahl (2000). *Psychological Bulletin, 128,* 371–408.

Winston, C., Eccles, J. S., Senior, A. M., & Vida, M. (1997). The utility of an expectancy/value model of achievement for understanding academic performance and self-esteem in African American and European-American adolescents. *Zeitschrift Fur Padagogische Psychologie (German Journal of Educational Psychology), 11,* 177–186.

VIRGINIA E. O'LEARY
and JESHMIN BHAJU

Resilience and Empowerment

Until recently, most psychological theory and research on women's health and well-being focused exclusively on the vulnerability deficit model of girls and women (c.f., O'Leary & Flanagan, 2001). In actuarial terms, this focus appears warranted as women are more likely than men to be poor (Wyche, 2001), to have higher rates of morbidity (Landrine & Klonoff, 2001; Stanton & Gallant, 1996), to be widowed (Lopata, 1988; Wortman & Silver, 1989), and to be the victims of violence (Koss, 1990). However, the same differential distribution of challenges that puts girls and women at risk for adversity affords them the opportunity, if they are empowered (Johnson, 2001; Worell, 2001), to exhibit resilience in the face of adversity and even to thrive (O'Leary & Ickovics, 1995).

Resilience was introduced into the psychological literature relevant to children by investigators interested in identifying factors that protected those at risk for developmental psychopathology from the negative consequences of stress (c.f., Masten, 1989; Werner & Smith, 1982). Garmezy and Nuechterlein (1972) first used the concept of resilience to describe a small sample of highly competent African American children living in the ghetto who were well adjusted despite profound social and environmental challenges such as poverty, prejudice, and difficult living conditions. Luthar, Cicchetti, and Becker (2000) recently defined resilience as a dynamic process encompassing positive adaptation within the context of significant adversity (p. 543). In the early 1990s, resilience was invoked to elucidate the processes of successive challenge and compensatory recovery among the aging (Kahn, 1991). In this context, Kahn and the MacArthur Foundation Network on Successful Aging defined resilience as the ability to recover swiftly from any misfortune or challenge. As people age, they are expected to exhibit declining health and mobility. However, those who are aging successfully are able to respond positively to this challenge and to grow psychologically (Kahn, 1991).

The idea that adversity might actually provide the impetus for psychological growth, thereby enhancing life, has proved particularly appealing to advocates of the positive psychology movement spearheaded by Seligman (2002) and his colleagues (c.f., Keyes & Haidt, 2003). Paralleling the positive psychology movement, but not well integrated into it, have been theories advanced by feminist psychologists who actively rejected many of the traditional assumptions of the male dominated medical model of psychology with its emphasis on pathology (c.f., O'Leary & Ickovics, 1995; Worell & Remer, 1992, 2003; Wyche & Rice, 1997).

DEFINITIONS OF RESILIENCE

Resilience is defined by *Webster's* dictionary as "the power or ability to return to the original from, position etc., after being bent, compressed, or stretched; the ability to recover strength, spirit, good humor etc. quickly" (*Merriam-Webster*, 2003, p. 1220). The first definition comes from the physical sciences and refers to solid matter in response to direct manipulation. The second definition is more psychological; it is the definition with which most social scientists and the popular press resonate.

Despite its intuitive appeal, resilience has not been operationalized consistently in the scientific literature. Definitions have included school and social competence (Garmezy, 1983), overcoming adversity and rising above disadvantage (Rutter, 1981), the positive side of adaptation under extenuating circumstances (Masten, 1989), the capacity to cope with stress (Werner & Smith, 1982), and recently, "a dynamic process encompassing positive adaptation within the context of significant adversity" (Luthar et al., 2000, p. 543). The definition of *positive adaptation* remains elusive. Does it refer to the failure to meet criteria for a specific disorder or constellation of symptoms or something more, such as evincing positive change over time (Johnson, 2001)? Luthar and her colleagues (2000) identify six areas of concern that have been raised about the construct: (a) varying definitions and terminologies, (b) variations in functioning within different behavioral domains, (c) variations in risk experiences among those labeled resilient, (d) the constructs situational specificity, (e) a lack of theory, and (f) questions regarding the utility of the construct.

Despite these definitional and conceptual problems, the literature on resilience continues to grow (c.f., Carver, 1998; Felten, 2000; Todd & Worell, 2000; Werner-Wilson, Schindler Zim-

merman, & Whalen, 2000). Some authors have defined resilience as a set of personality traits (Al-Naser & Sandman, 2000) while others have focused on defining behaviors such as achieving success despite risk (Brodsky, 1999). Recently, Christopher (2000) used resilience to refer to a personal resource that contributes to positive outcomes. Luthar and her colleagues (2000) differentiate between resiliency—a set of personality traits—and resilience—the process of adaptation despite adversity—and identify two themes that have repeatedly emerged in the literature relevant to resilience among children. These are (a) the importance of close relationships and connections with competent adults and (b) effective schools.

MODELS OF RESILIENCE

The study of thriving grew out of a foundation of research on resilience. Researchers have described several mechanisms by which environmental and individual factors help reduce or offset the adverse effects of risk. Although different researchers have suggested different models, many researchers have given the same mechanisms different names. Garmezy, Masten, and Tellegen (1984) have identified three models used to describe the impact o f stress on the quality of adaptation: the compensatory model, the challenge model, and the protective factor or immunity versus vulnerability model.

The Compensatory Model

A compensatory factor is a variable that neutralizes exposure to risk (Garmezy et al., 1984). It does not interact with a risk factor; rather, it has a direct and independent influence on the outcome of interest. Both risk and compensatory factors contribute additively to the prediction of outcome.

Illustrative of the compensatory model of resilience is the work of Werner and Smith (1982), who conducted a landmark study of 700 native children born on the island of Kauai in 1955. Four characteristics were common to the 10% of young adults labeled resilient: an active approach toward solving life's problems; a tendency to perceive or construct their experiences positively; the ability, from infancy, to gain other people's positive attention; and a strong reliance on faith to maintain a positive view of a meaningful life. Thus, Werner and Smith identified compensatory factors that either lowered risk initially or ameliorated risk throughout development.

The Challenge Model

The challenge model of resilience is one in which a stressor is treated as a potential enhancer of successful adaptation, providing that it is not excessive. In this model, too little stress is not challenging enough and too much results in dysfunction. Moderate levels of stress, however, provide a challenge that, when overcome, strengthens competence. If the challenge is successfully met, it helps prepare the individual for the next difficulty. Rutter (1987) referred to this process as "inoculating." If efforts to meet the challenge are not successful, the individual may become increasingly vulnerable to risk.

For example, mild childhood traumas appear to help adult women handle depression if their childhood stress was handled well and instilled a sense of resourcefulness. Using a life-course analysis, Forest (1996) found that women who had experienced stressful events during childhood (e.g., death of a loved one or changes in family structure due to divorce) were less likely to respond with depressive symptoms to distress-provoking situations in adulthood (e.g., divorce, death of a spouse, or major illness). In the case of resilience, protection develops not through the evasion of risk but in successfully engaging it (Rutter, 1987).

The Protective Factor Model

A protective factor is a process that interacts with a risk factor to reduce the probability of a negative outcome. It moderates the effect of exposure to risk. Rutter (1987) described a protective mechanism as an interactive process that helps identify "multiplicative interactions or synergistic affects in which one variable potentates the effect of another" (p. 106).

In the course of a series of longitudinal studies referred to as Project Competence, Garmezy and his colleagues (1984) have found that competent children have higher IQ scores and better cognitive abilities related to social know-how and are members of families with greater stability, better parenting quality, and higher socioeconomic status (Masten, 1989). It may be that higher IQ, income, and stable parenting promote resilience.

The protective model of resilience is different from the compensatory model or the challenge model in that it operates indirectly to influence outcomes. It should be noted, however, that the three models, though different, are not mutually exclusive (Zimmerman & Arunkumar, 1994).

To promote our understanding of human strength and adaptation, resilience must represent more than a semantic shift from the negative pole to the positive pole of the risk continuum. Rutter (1987) described four functions of resilience: to reduce risk impact, to reduce negative chain reactions, to establish and maintain self-identity and self-efficacy, and to enhance opportunities. The emphasis on protective processes that affect adjustment following confrontation with risk raises important questions regarding the nature of reliance. Indeed, the successful negotiation of risk differentiates resilience from vulnerability.

OUTCOMES OF CHALLENGE: RESILIENCE AS THRIVING

O'Leary and Ickovics (1995) suggested that when individuals are confronted with challenge, they may respond in one of three ways: survive, recover, or thrive. Figure 17.1 is a schematic representation of the process of challenge and outcome for a single hypothetical stressor. Each alternative represents a potential psychological outcome in response to a specific challenge.

In figure 17.1, "Survival" (line A) implies that an individual continues to function, albeit in an impaired fashion—For example, a breast cancer patient who sits quietly at home waiting to die despite the fact that every indication suggests her lumpectomy plus radiation was effective and her prognosis is good. The psychological conse-

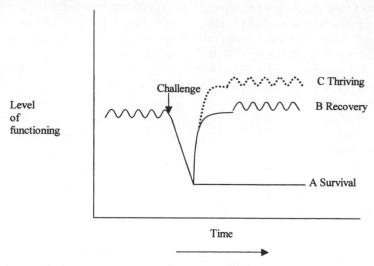

FIGURE 17.1 Outcomes of challenge: potential consequences for a single hypothetical stressor.

quence of the event was so debilitating that recovery is not possible. "Recovery" (line B) indicates a return to baseline. After the decrement associated with an initial challenge, the individual is able to return to previous levels of functioning. For example, following rehabilitation from a mild stroke, an individual may be able to carry on with life much in the same way as before. "Thriving" (line C) represents the ability to go beyond the original level of psychosocial functioning, to grow vigorously, to flourish. Through the interactive process of confronting and coping with a challenge, a transformation occurs. The individual does not merely return to a previous state but, rather, grows beyond it and in the process adds value to life. It is this conception of thriving that differentiates this model of resilience from prior formulations. Thriving may be manifested in three domains; behaviorally, cognitively, and emotionally. Thriving is transformative. It is contingent upon a fundamental cognitive shift in response to challenge. Challenge provides the opportunity for change because it forces individuals to confront personal priorities and to reexamine their sense of self. For such transformation to occur the challenge must be profound, an event such as facing a life-threatening illness, a severe traumatic accident or victimization, a great loss, or an existential crisis-events that shake the foundation of one's life, calling into question

one's sense of purpose, meaning, or identity. The construct of resilience in psychology has been essentially homeostatic, emphasizing an inherent human capacity to recover from adversity and restore equilibrium of functioning (Bonanno, 2004). In contrast, O'Leary and Ickovics's (1995) conception of thriving represents a value-added construct. Understanding the concept and process can provide an important basis for theoretical development, empirical research, and clinical intervention.

Determinants of Thriving

Given the complexity of this process, thriving must be multidetermined. The individual and social factors that may be important determinants of health, prevention, recovery, and maintenance have been identified (for review see, e.g., Adler & Matthews, 1994). However, few investigators have explored factors associated with moving beyond homeostasis in response to challenge. Individual and social resources have been found to play a role in thriving (O'Leary & Ickovics, 1995).

Individual Resources

Personality factors such as hardiness, coping, and a sense of coherence have been theoretically and empirically linked to disease and health (Friedman, 1990, 1991). Personality factors are most often linked to thriving. For example, Siegel (1986) wrote about the exceptional cancer patients with whom he worked, pointing to their ability to mobilize personal resources in their struggles. More recently, Florian, Mikulincer, and Taubman (1995) found that hardy individuals are more confident and better able to use active coping and available social support, rendering them more able to deal with distress when they experience it. Other individual difference variables that have been identified as potentially important in promoting thriving include self-enhancement (Bonanno, Rennicke, Dekel, & Rosen, in preparation), repressive coping (Bonanno & Field, 2001; Bonanno, Noll, Putman, O'Neill, & Trickett, 2003), and positive emotion (Fredrickson, Tugade, Waugh, & Larkin, 2003).

Cognitive resources are also critical to thriving. Cognition influences how individuals perceive risks and how they subsequently deal with it. Cognitive factors such as threat appraisal, perceived personal risks, generalized expectancies for good versus bad outcomes, and self-efficacy may all be critical personal resources. The significance of finding meaning in the challenge is a theme that reoccurs in the literature pertinent to thriving. For example, Folkman and her colleagues found that even in their darkest moments, many caregivers to AIDS patients find positive meaning in the context of caring for their sick partners (Folkman, Chesney, & Christopher-Richards, 1994).

Meaning

O'Leary, Alday, and Ickovics (1998) reviewed a number of current psychological models of change and growth in an effort to identify the antecedents and correlates of positive change resulting from negative events. Of the eight models they reviewed in detail, six identified meaning making, or appraisal, as critical to growth. However, the conceptual and operational formulations employed in these models vary greatly. Recently, Acquirre (2004) has reviewed this literature distinguishing between meaning as a coping activity or process (meaning making or meaning reconstruction), while other research examines meaning as an outcome of the process of adjustment (e.g., meaningfulness or increased existential awareness). For example, Park and Folkman's (1997) transactional model of coping with aversive life events delineates the functions of meaning in the processes through which people cope with stressful events. They conceptualize meaning as perceptions of significance and distinguish between two types of meaning, global and situational. Global meaning refers to an abstract, generalized form of meaning comprising an individual's enduring beliefs and valued goals. It influences a person's understanding of the past, present, and future as it encompasses her or his fundamental assumptions and expectations about the world. Alternatively, situational meaning denotes a more specific type of meaning created through the interaction between a given situation and the individual's global meaning. Situational meaning is composed of appraisal of meaning, the search for meaning, and meaning as an outcome. The search for meaning refers to actual coping processes employed in stressful situations, particularly those in which loss has occurred, such as bereavement. According to Park and Folkman (1997), a fundamental function of the meaning-making process entails reappraisal of meaning in which an individual attempts to diminish the disparity between the situational meaning of an event and the existing global meaning. Thus, "reappraisal processes transform appraised meaning and global meaning either by modifying the meaning of an event to make I consistent with preexisting beliefs and goals or by modifying relevant beliefs and goals to accommodate the event, or both" (p. 125). The cognitive strategies used to change situational meaning may include attribution processes, compensatory self-enhancement, downward comparisons, and developing new perspectives on the situation. Likewise, individuals may change their global meaning by revising their global beliefs or altering their fundamental goals. Rumination occurs if the reappraisal of meaning does not diminish incongruence between situational and global meaning. In this event, fixation in this cycle of reappraisal may occur, rendering the individual powerless to engage the challenge effectively without assistance.

EMPOWERMENT

Most of what is known about those who are resilient in the face of adversity and grow is based on studies of individuals who have confronted challenge and both access and utilize the individual and social resources necessary to thrive. One critical determinant of the ability to utilize these resources is engaging directly with the challenging event. Engagement may occur "naturally"— that is, the individual may be predisposed to stand and face threatening events, or it may be fostered through therapeutic intervention in which the individual is empowered to acquire a sense of control over her behavior, feelings, thoughts, and development (Worell & Remer, 1992). People who are empowered have a proactive approach to life and understand the factors that hinder or enhance their efforts to resolve issues and to obtain desired outcomes (Lee, 1989). Given their (low) status in society, women are often among the groups, including ethnic minorities, children, the homeless, the elderly, and the physically and mentally disabled, recognized and/or designated as oppressed or disempowered. Moving individuals or groups from their disempowered status toward empowerment is contingent upon providing them with a sense of control and promoting in them a feeling of self-efficacy or self-competence (Bandura, 1997).

According to Ozer and Bandura (1990), perceived self-efficacy is manifested in a belief in one's capacities to mobilize the motivation, cognitive resources, and courses of action necessary to exercise control over events. Such beliefs are essential to ensure the perseverance essential to successfully confront or engage challenge.

A number of studies provide evidence for the role of empowerment as requisite for personal and social change (Bandura, 1989; Rappaport, Swift, & Hess, 1984; Ratcliff, 1984). For example, Ozer and Bandura (1990) found that personal empowerment is a critical determinant of the ability to control and prevent sexual abuse. Women who participated in a mastery-modeling program in which they mastered the physical skills necessary to defend themselves successfully against unarmed sexual assailants became significantly more confident in their abilities to cope with problematic social situations and to control their own negative cognitions. Based on these results, Ozer and Bandura contend that an effective means of developing a resilient sense of efficacy is through mastery experiences. According to them, performance successes build a sense of personal efficacy, whereas performance failures undermine it. Thus, mastery can be regarded as a key component of empowerment. And mastery can be acquired through intervention.

Empowerment has become one of the recent therapeutic approaches to enhance an individual's ability to successfully deal with adversity. One of the key characteristics of feminist approaches to therapy is empowerment. Anchored in its belief systems, empowerment feminist therapy is based upon four principles: (a) personal and social identities are interdependent, (b) the personal is political, (c) egalitarian relationships, and (d) valuing the female perspective (Worell & Remer, 2003). The goal of feminist therapy is to validate a woman's experience and acknowledge her right to make decisions affecting her own life. The goal of this therapy is to work on personal empowerment, to help women to become more independent and assertive about attaining goals and achieving change and psychological growth. This goal can be attained by working on the client's ability to control her own life and by making changes that would have positive consequences for her well-being and circumstances (Worell & Remer, 1992, 2003). The therapeutic process involves exploring various coping skills in the face of external and internal stressors and mobilizing external and internal resources. Internal resources are individual resources such as personality traits like hardiness, self-appraisal, and self-efficacy, and external resources are social support and other external resources.

In empowerment-focused therapy, a primary goal of intervention would be to encourage and support the individual to engage in the issue, rather than avoid it. According to Ozer and Bandura (1990), individuals tend to avoid activities and situations they believe exceed their coping capabilities, but readily undertake activities and select social environments they judge themselves capable of handling. In empowerment-focused therapy, the relationship between the therapist and the client centers on discovering assertive and functional ways of expressing personal power and strong emotions such as anger. Self-esteem is enhanced by highlighting the client's unique contributions, strengths, and achievements. The therapist provides opportunities for constant evaluation and feedback of change and growth. In this way, the client becomes aware of external forces that limit her freedom as well as forces that can be mobilized to extend it (Worell & Remer, 1992, 2003).

A diagrammed representation of how empowerment-focused intervention may foster resilience is presented in figure 17.2. This model illustrates that in the presence of an adverse life situation a woman is provided with an opportunity for growth and change. However, adverse situations in life are not always perceived as opportunities. It is our assumption that individuals who are able to face the challenge and overcome the adversity are the ones who are able to recognize and mobilize internal and external resources. They are resilient. However, those individuals who are not able to cope with the challenges life presents may be able to overcome the situation with the help of therapeutic intervention. As mentioned earlier, the goal of the therapy would be to empower such individuals by the means of increasing their self-efficacy, which in turn will strengthen their beliefs in their capability to mobilize motivation, cognitive resources, and courses of action needed to exercise control over the given events (Ozer and Bandura, 1990).

Social cognitive theorists assert that self-efficacy provides control over potentially threat-ening events (Bandura, 1989). Therefore, individuals who believe in their perceived coping capabilities do not cave in when faced with an adverse situation. However, those individuals who believe they cannot manage threats experiences high level of anxiety (Ozer & Bandura, 1990). Such individuals succumb to the situation and tend to dwell on their coping deficiencies and view many facets of the environment as dangerous, resulting in impaired level of functioning (Ozer & Bandura, 1990). Intervention with such individuals will focus on changing their negative cognitions about the self and emphasize learning skills that will aid them in increasing their capability to cope with threatening situations—for example, learning self-defense for women.

Empowerment provides the individual with the ability to choose how she wishes to respond to the external world, within her own cultural contexts and restraints by clarifying the line between internally and externally controlled life events. Those who are empowered can take actions to control potentially threatening situations and solve problems. As a result, they are able to develop new positive behaviors, attitudes, and motivation to assume control to actualize appropriate choices (Washington & Moxley, 2003). They can identify and effectively utilize the resources available and have the confidence necessary to pursue resources that are currently not available but which might be accessed over time, given the appropriate strategy. As individuals are empowered, either naturally or through therapeu-

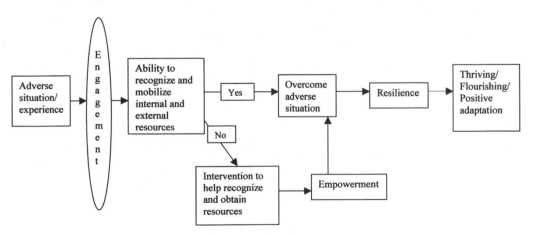

FIGURE 17.2 Model of two possible routes to resilience and thriving.

tic intervention they become resilient in the face of adversity.

REFERENCES

Acquirre, M. (2004). *Thriving after bereavement: The role of meaning.* Unpublished manuscript, Auburn University.

Adler, N. E., & Matthews, K. (1994). Health psychology: Why do some people get sick and some stay well? *Annual Review of Psychology, 45,* 229–259.

Al-Naser, F., & Sandman, M. M. A. (2000). Evaluating resiliency patterns using the ER89: A case study from Kuwait. *Social Behavior and Personality, 28,* 505–514.

Bandura, A. (1989). Human agency in social cognitive theory. *American Psychologist, 44,* 1175–1184.

Bandura, A. (1997). *Self-efficacy: The exercise of control.* New York: W. H. Freeman.

Bonanno, G. A. (2004). Loss, trauma, and human resilience. *American Psychologist, 59*(1), 20–28.

Bonanno, G. A., & Field, N. P. (2001). Examining the delayed grief hypothesis across five years of bereavement. *American Behavioral Scientist, 44,* 798–806.

Bonanno, G. A., Noll, J. G., Putman, F. W., O'Neill, M., & Trickett, P. (2003). Predicting the willingness to disclose childhood sexual abuse from measures of repressive coping and dissociative experiences. *Child Maltreatment, 8,* 1–17.

Bonanno, G. A., Rennicke, C., Dekel, S., & Rosen, J. (in preparation). *Self-enhancement and resilience among survivors of the September 11th terrorist attack on the World Trade Center.*

Brodsky, A. E. (1999). "Making it": The components and process of resilience among urban, African-American, single mothers. *American Journal of Orthopsychiatry, 69*(2), 148–160.

Carver, C. (1998). Resilience and thriving: Issues, models and linkages. *Journal of Social Issues, 54,* 245–266.

Christopher, K. A. (2000). "Determinants of psychological well-being in Irish immigrants": Response. *Western Journal of Nursing Research, 22,* 143.

Felten, B. S. (2000). Resilience in a multicultural sample of community-dwelling women older than age 85. *Clinical Nursing Research, 9,* 102–123.

Florian, V., Mikulincer, M., & Taubman, O. (1995). Does hardiness contribute to mental health during a stressful real-life situation? The roles of appraisal and coping. *Journal of Personality and Social Psychology, 68,* 687–695.

Folkman, S., Chesney, M. A., & Christopher-Richards, A. (1994). Stress and coping in caregiving partners of men with AIDS. *Psychiatric Clinics of North America, 17,* 35–53.

Forest, K. B. (1996). Gender and the pathways to subjective well-being. *Social Behavior & Personality, 24,* 19–34.

Fredrickson, B. L., Tugade, M. M., Waugh, C. E., & Larkin, G. R. (2003). What good are positive emotions in crisis? A prospective study of resilience and emotion following the terrorist attacks on the United States on September 11th, 2001. *Journal of Personality and Social Psychology, 84,* 365–376.

Friedman, H. S. (Ed.). (1990). *Personality and disease.* New York: John Wiley & Sons.

Friedman, H. S. (1991). *The self-healing personality: Why some people achieve health and others succumb to illness.* New York: Henry Holt.

Garmezy, N. (1983). Stressors of childhood. In N. Garmezy & M Rutter (Eds.), *Stress, coping and the development in children* (pp. 43–48). New York: McGraw-Hill.

Garmezy, N., Masten, A. S., & Tellegen, A. (1984). The study of stress and competence in children: A building block for developmental psychopathology. *Child Development, 55,* 97–111.

Garmezy, N., & Nuechterlein, K. (1972). Invulnerable children: The fact and fiction of competence and disadvantage. *American Journal of Orthopsychiatry, 42,* 328–329.

Johnson, D. J. (2001). *Exploring women's power and resilience: Beyond symptom reduction.* Unpublished dissertation, University of Kentucky.

Kahn, R. L. (1991, March). Retention, resilience, and enhancement: Components of vitality throughout the life course. Course paper presented at the meeting of the MacArthur Foundation Successful Aging Program, San Francisco.

Keyes, C. L. M., & Haidt, J. (Eds.). (2003). *Flourishing: Positive psychology and the life well lived.* Washington, DC: American Psychological Association.

Koss, M. P. (1990). The women's mental health research agenda: Violence against women. *American Psychologist, 45,* 374–380.

Landrine, H., & Klonoff, E. A. (2001). Health and health care: How gender makes women sick. In J. Worell (Ed.), *Encyclopedia of women and gender* (Vol. 1, pp. 577–592). San Diego, CA: Academic Press.

Lee, J. (1989). *Group work with the poor and oppressed.* New York: Haworth.

Lopata, H. Z. (1988). Support systems of American urban widowhood. *Journal of Social Issues, 44,* 113–128.

Luthar, S. S., Cicchetti, D., & Becker, B. (2000). The construct of resilience: A critical evaluation and guidelines for future work. *Child Development, 71,* 543–562.

Masten, A. S. (1989). Resilience in development: Implications of the study of successful adaptation for developmental psychopathology. In D. Cicchetti (Ed.), *The emergence of a discipline: Rochester symposium on developmental psychopathology* (Vol. 1, pp. 261–294). Hillsdale, NJ: Erlbaum.

Merriam-Webster's Collegiate Dictionary (2003). (11th ed.). Boston: Merriam-Webster.

O'Leary, V. E., Alday, C. S., & Ickovics, J. R. (1998). Models of life change and posttraumatic growth. In R. G. Tedeschi & L. Crystal (Eds.), *Posttraumatic growth: Positive changes in the aftermath of crisis* (pp. 127–151). Mahwah, NJ: Erlbaum.

O'Leary, V. E., & Flanagan, E. H. (2001). Leadership. In J. Worell, (Ed.), *Encyclopedia of women and gender* (Vol. 2, pp. 645–656). San Diego, CA: Academic Press.

O'Leary, V. E., & Ickovics, J. R. (1995). Resilience and thriving in response to challenge: an opportunity for a paradigm shift in women's health. *Women's Health: Research on Gender, Behavior and Policy, 1*(2), 121–142.

Ozer, E. M., & Bandura, A. (1990). Mechanisms governing empowerment effects: A self-efficacy analysis. *Journal of Personality and Social Psychology, 58*(3), 472–486.

Park, C., & Folkman, S. (1997). Meaning in the context of stress and coping. *Review of General Psychiatry, 1*, 115–144.

Rappaport, J., Swift, C., & Hess, R. (Eds.). (1984). *Studies in empowerment: Steps toward understanding and action.* New York: Haworth.

Ratcliff, R. E. (Ed.). (1984). *Research in social movements, conflicts and change* (Vol. 6). Greenwich, CT: JAI Press.

Rutter, M. (1981). Stress, coping, and development: Some issues and some questions. *Journal of Child Psychology and Psychiatry, 22*, 323–356.

Rutter, M. (1987). Psychosocial resilience and protective mechanisms. *American Journal of Orthopsychiatry, 57*, 316–331.

Seligman, M. E. P. (2002). *Authentic happiness.* New York: Free Press.

Siegel, B. (1986). *Love, medicine, and miracles: Lessons learned about self-healing from a surgeon's experience with exceptional patients.* New York: Harper & Row.

Stanton, A. L., & Gallant, S. J. (Eds.). (1996). *Psychology of women's health: Progress and challenges in research and application.* Washington, DC: American Psychological Association.

Todd, J. L., &. Worell, J. (2000). Resilience in low-income, employed, African American women. *Psychology of Women Quarterly, 24*(2), 119–128.

Washington, O. G. M., & Moxley, D. P. (2003). Promising group practices to empower low-income minority women coping with chemical dependency. *American Journal of Orthopsychiatry, 73*(1), 109–116.

Werner, E. E., & Smith, R. S. (1982). *Vulnerable but invincible: A study of resilient children.* New York: McGraw-Hill.

Werner-Wilson, R. J., Schindler Zimmerman, T., & Whalen, D. (2000). Resilient response to battering. *Contemporary Family Therapy: An International Journal, 22*, 161–188.

Worell, J. (2001). Feminist interventions: Life beyond symptom reduction. *Psychology of Women Quarterly, 25*, 334–343.

Worell, J., & Remer, P. (1992). *Feminist perspectives in therapy: An empowerment model for women.* New York: John Wiley & Sons.

Worell, J., & Remer, P. (2003). *Feminist perspectives in therapy: Empowering diverse women* (2nd ed.). New York: John Wiley & Sons.

Wortman, C. B., & Silver, R. C. (1989). The myths of coping with loss. *Journal of Consulting and Clinical Psychology, 57*, 349–357.

Wyche, K. (2001). Poverty and women in the United States. In J. Worell and P. Remer (Eds.), *Encyclopedia of women and gender* (Vol. 2, pp. 837–846). New York: Academic Press.

Wyche, K. F., & Rice, J. K. (1997). Feminist therapy: From dialogue to tenets. In J. Worell and N. G. Johnson (Eds.), *Shaping the future of feminist psychology: Education, research, and practice* (pp. 57–71). Washington, DC: American Psychological Association.

Zimmerman, M. A., & Arunkumar, R. (1994). Resiliency: Implications for schools and policy. Social Policy Report. *Society for Research in Child Development, 8*, 1–18.

Since the Second World War, the psychological study of human emotions and mental health has focused primarily on negative moods and pathological states, rather than on positive ones (Seligman & Csikszentmihalyi, 2000). Recognizing this imbalance, researchers have been showing increased empirical interest in topics such as positive emotions, human strengths, and normative functioning. Yet a focus on negative and maladaptive behavior continues to persist. For example, entering "depression" as a keyword into PsycINFO, a popular search engine for the psychological sciences, yields well over 85,000 entries. The same search using "positive affect" as a keyword generates a comparatively paltry 4,000 results and "happiness" only about 2,000 results. Although researchers may never lose the undoubtedly natural and valuable inclination to study what is wrong with human behavior, they should not overlook the equally important question, "What is right with human behavior?" After all, the vast majority of individuals, including girls and women, report positive feelings most of the time (Diener & Diener, 1996).

One of the domains of this long-overdue and more optimistic approach is the study of subjective well-being (SWB). SWB, which is commonly termed "happiness" or "well-being" by the layperson, concerns people's day-to-day feelings and evaluations of their lives. With this in mind, the central goals of this chapter are to broadly define what is meant by SWB, to describe the central findings in this field, to provide a perspective of SWB as it relates to the unique lives of girls and women, and, finally, to briefly discuss the mechanisms by which women can increase their personal SWB levels.

THE DEFINING CHARACTERISTICS OF SUBJECTIVE WELL-BEING

As mentioned previously, SWB is a construct that turns the spotlight away from dissatisfaction with life and undesirable emotional states, such as anxiety and stress, to satisfaction with life, happiness, and desirable emotional states, such as joy and excitement. SWB is defined as comprising both cognitive (judgmental) and affective (emotional) components (Diener, Suh, Lucas, &

SONJA LYUBOMIRSKY
and RENE DICKERHOOF

Subjective Well-Being

18

Smith, 1999). The cognitive component consists of a person's judgments of her satisfaction with life in general, as well as judgments about specific areas of her life (e.g., marital satisfaction or satisfaction with education). The affective component, on the other hand, involves both a person's pleasant and unpleasant moods or emotions. Thus, a woman who judges herself to be very satisfied with life overall and who experiences frequent pleasant or positive emotional states, while experiencing infrequent unpleasant or negative emotional states, can be said to harbor high SWB. In contrast, a woman who is generally dissatisfied with her life and who experiences relatively few pleasant or positive emotional states, while experiencing many unpleasant or negative emotional states, may be said to have low SWB.

Several other defining characteristics of SWB should be noted. The first characteristic relates to the uniqueness and importance of the evaluator's perspective—that is, the perspective of the person whose well-being is being judged. Thus, well-being is assessed by the target individual, and not by some objective measure, such as a physiological indicator or the report of a clinician or peer (Diener & Diener, 1998). This being the case, it is possible (although unlikely) for an individual with high SWB, who feels very satisfied and happy, to meet clinical criteria for a psychiatric disorder. At the same time, SWB cannot always be equated with superior functioning. Whereas authors such as Virginia Woolf and Sylvia Plath made significant contributions to the world through their writing, neither of these women could be said to have had a high level of well-being. Therefore, SWB is neither an adequate assessment of psychological mental health nor a reliable indicator of who will or will not be a productive member of society, but it does provide us with a very important piece of the well-being puzzle—namely, the respondent's point of view.

Another distinctive characteristic of SWB is that it is experienced unconsciously and continuously (Diener & Lucas, 2000). Every individual, at any particular moment in time, is experiencing some type of emotion. These states are usually maintained just outside of the realm of awareness and, indeed, must be called to a person's attention when a particular mood is being assessed. However, once a person is made aware

of her emotional states, a measure of her well-being can presumably be acquired anytime and anywhere. Furthermore, the study of SWB is characteristically concerned with long-term evaluations of a person's life (Diener & Diener, 1998). Researchers in this field do not just want to know only how a woman feels at any given moment; they want to know how she feels over a more reliable span of time. This distinction is important, because an assessment of well-being made during a particular moment in time (e.g., immediately after a tense conflict with her husband) may be entirely atypical of a woman's aggregated self (e.g., she may be upbeat and easy-going most of the time).

THE MEASUREMENT OF SUBJECTIVE WELL-BEING

The construct of SWB is typically measured with self-report scales. The consensus among researchers is that, while not entirely unbiased, self-reports of SWB are generally valid (Diener & Lucas, 2000; Sandvik, Diener, & Seidlitz, 1993). For example, three commonly used scales that measure SWB—the Satisfaction With Life Scale (SWLS; Diener, Emmons, Larsen, & Griffin, 1985), the Positive Affect and Negative Affect Schedule (PANAS; Watson, Clark, & Tellegen, 1988), and the Psychological Well-Being Scale (PWB; Ryff, 1989)—have all been found to display excellent psychometric properties (Pavot & Diener, 1993; Ryff & Keyes, 1995; Watson et al., 1988). The SWLS, which assesses the cognitive component of SWB, asks participants to rate the extent to which they agree with the following items: (a) In most ways, my life is close to my ideal; (b) The conditions of my life are excellent; (c) I am satisfied with my life; (d) So far I have gotten the important things I want in life; and (e) If I could live my life over, I would change almost nothing. In contrast, the PANAS, used to assess the affective component of SWB, comprises 10 positive and 10 negative emotions that describe the self (e.g., enthusiastic, inspired, distressed, upset). Respondents are asked to indicate the extent to which they have recently felt these emotions on a scale from 1 (i.e., very rarely or not at all) to 5 (i.e., very often).

Finally, a third commonly used measure of well-being, the PWB scale, assesses both cognitive and affective aspects of subjective well-being and can be used to show that women can differ in their levels of well-being in particular life domains. Based on a theory-driven conceptualization of well-being, this 84-item measure taps six dimensions of SWB found to characterize positive psychological functioning: autonomy, environmental mastery, personal growth, positive relations with others, purpose in life, and self-acceptance. Sample items on each of these scales include, "People rarely talk me into doing things I don't want to do" (autonomy), "In general, I feel I am in charge of the situation in which I live" (mastery), "I feel like I get a lot out of my friendships" (growth), "Most people see me as loving and affectionate" (relations), "I have a sense of direction and purpose in life" (purpose), and "In general, I feel confident and positive about myself" (self-acceptance). Respondents select the degree to which they disagree or agree with each item on a scale from 1 to 6.

The assumption behind these and other self-report measures of SWB is that the respondent—the person making the judgment—is uniquely situated to provide a useful and accurate report of her cognitive and affective life experience. Yet, while it is intuitive that the respondent is in the best position to report on her private, internal emotions, this "subjectivist" perspective has been criticized for its potential biases (Freund, 1985). Of course, biases in self-report measurement are not specific to the study of well-being. Whenever self-reports are used, growing concern and pressure exist to adopt a wider variety of methodologies, such as observer/peer reports and physiological assessments. The primary concern regarding error in the measurement of SWB is related to response biases—for example, the effects on well-being ratings of a woman's current mood (e.g., due to a cloudy vs. sunny day, or a particularly stressful vs. fulfilling day at work) or of social desirability (e.g., the wish to appear normal, healthy, and happy). However, many studies have found that neither current mood nor social desirability have discernible effects on well-being measurement (Diener, Sandvik, Pavot, & Gallagher; 1991; Kozma & Stones, 1988). In light of these findings, and given the fact that self-report measures are both practical and economically feasible for use in research, it is wise to continue employing them in conjunction with additional non-self-report assessment tools (Diener & Larsen, 1993). Such supplementary measures might include experience sampling (e.g., obtaining multiple evaluations of a woman's well-being over a single day, week, or month; see Larsen, Diener, & Emmons, 1986) and observational study of affective expressions (e.g., using judges to assess the sincerity of women's smiles in yearbook pictures; see Harker & Keltner, 2001).

THE CORRELATES OF SUBJECTIVE WELL-BEING

What characterizes people who have high levels of well-being versus those who have low levels of well-being? The first review of the correlates of happiness and SWB was conducted over 35 years ago (Wilson, 1967). This preliminary investigation made several bold yet premature statements about what variables are related to well-being. According to Wilson, "The happy person emerges as a young, healthy, well-educated, well-paid, extraverted, optimistic, worry-free, religious, married person with high self-esteem, high job morale, modest aspirations, of either sex, and of a wide range of intelligence." Since this initial review, researchers still have not determined the characteristics of the happy individual definitively; however, they have discovered that this conclusion was not entirely correct. For example, although Wilson proposed that income is important to well-being, a large body of research now indicates that money is not necessarily the root of happiness (Diener & Biswas-Diener, 2002; Myers, 2000). In one oft-cited study supporting this conclusion, researchers found that a group of lottery winners were not any happier than a group of non-lottery winning controls (Brickman, Coates, & Janoff-Bulman, 1978). Furthermore, among a sample of 49 very rich people, wealthy individuals were only slightly happier than the average American (Diener, Horwitz, & Emmons, 1985).

Additional studies have also revealed that once a person's basic human needs have been met (as they commonly are in industrialized nations), wealth and SWB are only trivially correlated with one another (Argyle, 1999; Inglehart, 1990). Furthermore, gender has been shown to moderate the effect of income on well-being. For example, Adelmann (1987) found that income was positively correlated with happiness for men, but not for women. Likewise, among a sample of married women, earnings did not affect a woman's likelihood of depression; however, among married men, income directly decreased the odds of becoming depressed (Ross & Huber, 1985). Such findings suggest that money may be relatively more likely to bring satisfaction and well-being to men because men are still more likely to assume the role of breadwinner and, as such, rely on their salaries to support their families. Yet, even given this result, it would appear that the commonsense perception that "money can buy happiness" is not typically borne out in the empirical findings, although many factors must be considered (e.g., a nation's economic growth status) before definitive conclusions can be drawn.

In addition to the lack of evidence supporting a strong link between income and well-being, another variable whose association to SWB appears to have been overstated is health. Although past research suggested that happier people are more healthy, more recent studies have not replicated this finding. First, the positive correlation between health and SWB seems to hold up only when the respondent rates his or her own health subjectively (Okun & George, 1984). When a physician's ratings of an individual's health are used, the correlation between health and SWB is found to be much smaller. Whereas a strong case has been made for the importance of using subjective assessments of well-being ("Shouldn't the respondent know best how happy she is?"), the same case for subjective assessments of *physical* health may not be so easily defended ("*Should* a patient's assessment of her physical health be considered over a doctor's?").

Along with the mixed findings concerning the relation of well-being to income and health, an association between well-being and age has also not been upheld since Wilson's 1967 review. Whereas, in the past, researchers believed that younger individuals are typically happier than older individuals, a brief overview of the current literature reveals that the young are not necessarily the happiest people after all (Charles, Reynolds, & Gatz, 2001; Diener & Suh, 1998).

What about ethnicity and well-being? Although this variable was left out of Wilson's initial review, many studies have focused on the question of whether or not an individual's ethnicity is correlated to her SWB. Within the United States, for example, Whites are almost always found to be happier than their African American counterparts (Aldous & Ganey, 1999). Furthermore, a sample drawn from South Africa (Moller & Schlemmer, 1989) demonstrated that happiness could be ordered from White participants (who were the "happiest") to Indians, to "Coloreds," and then, finally, to Blacks. These findings are not particularly surprising, given the benefits known to be associated with majority group affiliation. Indeed, the primary explanation as to why Whites are generally more subjectively happy than ethnic minorities is that these minorities typically have less education, less income, and less access to desirable jobs (Argyle, 1999). After controlling for these variables, the effect of ethnicity on well-being becomes fairly weak (Veenhoven et al., 1994).

Although many of the original claims about the links between SWB and other variables have since been found to be erroneous, a few findings continue to withstand the test of time. One example is the link between well-being and personality. That is, individuals with high levels of SWB have still consistently been found to be relatively more extraverted and optimistic, to have higher self-esteem, and to be less neurotic (Diener & Lucas, 2000). Extraversion, optimism, and high self-esteem have all been shown to positively correlate with pleasant affect, whereas neuroticism has been shown to positively correlate with unpleasant affect. Further, life satisfaction, the cognitive component of SWB, has been found to be correlated with self-esteem across many Western nations (Diener & Larsen, 1993).

Another one of Wilson's (1967) conclusions that appears to have been accurate was the assertion that gender has no effect on a person's well-being. Can it truly be the case that women are no less happy than their male counterparts given the androcentric world in which they live? Although this notion challenges what is commonly understood about women and their historical role in nearly all societies, much empiri cal work continues to report that gender is unrelated to well-being (Francis, 1999), and some studies have even found that women are happier than men (Aldous & Ganey, 1999). Along with the appealing and intuitive belief that younger people should be happier than older people, the question of whether or not women are actually as happy or happier than men will be the focus of the remainder of this chapter.

THE SUBJECTIVE WELL-BEING OF WOMEN

Throughout history, women have faced a broad spectrum of discrimination, ranging from the once commonly held belief that females are intellectually inferior to males, to the still prevalent objectification of women in all types of media. In addition to battling these ever-present sexisms, on a global level, women continue to make less money than men; women experience greater poverty and lack of power in their families and communities; women endure violence specific to their gender; and women are more likely to suffer a variety of poor reproductive and mental health outcomes, such as unwanted pregnancy, unsafe abortion, maternal mortality, and sexually transmitted disease (Murphy, 2003). Indeed, the 1995 Human Development Report commissioned by the United Nations Development Programme (UNDP, 1995) stated that, "In no society do women enjoy the same opportunities as men." Given these facts, it seems intuitive that women should not be as happy overall as men. Yet research on well-being has consistently found that not only are women as happy as their male counterparts (Francis, 1999), but in some samples they appear to be slightly happier (Aldous & Ganey, 1999).

One explanation for the lack of gender differences in well-being applies more broadly to understanding why many demographic variables (e.g., income, gender, ethnicity, education, etc.) are not strongly correlated with SWB. Researchers have attempted to account for such findings by referring to the concept of hedonic adaptation (Diener et al., 1999). The process of adaptation involves an initial reaction—either positive or negative—to new life circumstances (e.g., moving to a desirable new location or becoming un-

employed); however, over a period of time, individuals become habituated to these new circumstances and ultimately return to their baseline level of well-being. One study, for example, revealed that paraplegics and quadriplegics experienced high levels of unpleasant affect immediately after their initial paralysis; but, a mere two months later, these same individuals showed more pleasant than unpleasant affect (Silver, 1982). Furthermore, Brickman and colleagues' (1978) study of the well-being of lottery winners versus nonwinners suggested that even extremely desirable events can ultimately produce adaptation. Although participants in this study had recently won between $50,000 to $1 million, they were only slightly more satisfied with their lives than nonwinners. Along these lines, perhaps because demographic status is typically stable throughout life, an adult would have long since adapted to the effects on her well-being of being young or old, female or male, and Black or White (Inglehart, 2002). Thus, it may be the case that adult women have adapted to the disadvantages of being female by the time of childhood or adolescence and, consequently, show no effects of these disadvantages on well-being through the course of their lives. This argument explains why exposure to a set of distinctive life stressors (e.g., gender discrimination and inequality) appears to have little to no effect on women's well-being.

However, although it is plausible that women have simply adapted early on to many of the societal drawbacks of being female, this notion cannot account for one robust finding in the literature—that is, that not only are women equally as happy or more happy than men, but they are also twice as likely as men to be diagnosed with clinical depression (Nolen-Hoeksema, 1987). Given this paradoxical result, the question arises, "How can women be both more depressed and happier than men?" Hedonic adaptation cannot adequately explain these apparently divergent findings. A more persuasive account is provided in research on "affect intensity," defined as a person's degree of response to emotion-provoking stimuli (Larsen & Diener, 1987). Interestingly, people who experience high levels of negative affect have been found also to experience high levels of positive affect (Fujita, Diener, & Sandvik, 1991; Larsen & Diener, 1987). Thus, it is conceivable that an individual can simultaneously report both depressive affect and high levels of well-being. For example, in one study, researchers demonstrated that, while women are no happier than men, they are significantly more affectively intense than men (Fujita et al., 1991). Thus, the finding that women are twice as susceptible to depression as men is not necessarily inconsistent with the finding that women are also as happy or happier than men. That is, women may be both more depressed and happier than men because they experience both positive and negative emotions more intensely. Alternatively, men may simply be relatively more emotionally inhibited. Further research is needed to clarify the mechanisms by which affect intensity accounts for gender differences in well-being, as well as in depression.

WOMEN'S SUBJECTIVE WELL-BEING ACROSS THE LIFE SPAN

As noted previously, early research on well-being and age reported that younger people were generally happier than older people (Wilson, 1967), a result that is consistent with most people's expectations. After all, one need only turn on a television to capture a glimpse of Western youth-obsessed culture. For example, plastic surgery, which essentially attempts to recover an individual's youth, is more popular than ever and many pop stars' careers (e.g., Britney Spears and Mandy Moore) now peak before they are even old enough to drink legally. Meanwhile, at least in the United States, a continued devaluation and disinterest in older Americans persists (Inglehart, 2002). Given these facts, one is surprised to learn that cross-sectional research has found negligible age differences in well-being (Diener & Suh, 1998). Furthermore, evidence that older people may be happier than younger people is now growing (Charles et al., 2001). Why might older women and men be happier than younger women and men, given the media's overt message that youth is so desirable? One explanation, based in socioemotional selectivity theory, proposes that older people are essentially emotionally wiser— that is, they learn to structure their lives and to pursue goals that increase positive emotions

(Carstensen, 1995). As Lang and Heckhausen (2001) note, individuals are happy and satisfied to the extent that they believe they can successfully master the goals and tasks of their everyday life.

Some researchers have focused on studying how positive and negative affect change over the life course (Charles et al., 2001). For example, do older people experience more positive emotions and fewer negative emotions than younger people, or is it the reverse? With regard to positive emotions, the evidence is mixed—sometimes studies show that positive affect increases across the life span (Mroczek & Kolarz, 1998), while other studies show that positive affect decreases with age (Diener & Suh, 1998) or does not change at all (Barrick, Hutchinson, & Deckers, 1989). Given these results, little overall evidence exists to indicate definitive age differences in the experience of positive emotions (Charles et al., 2001).

With regard to negative emotions, the empirical evidence has been more decisive. The general finding is that negative affect is reported less frequently by older persons than by younger persons (Charles et al., 2001; Gross et al., 1997), although this effect may reverse around the age of 60 (Diener & Suh, 1998). Interestingly, just as gender differences in affect intensity have been used to explain why women report both more depression and possibly more happiness than men, age differences in affect intensity have been used to explain why older persons may sometimes express both less positive and less negative affect than younger persons. For example, one study showed that emotional intensity decreases somewhat as people age (Diener, Sandvik, & Larsen, 1985). Furthermore, challenging the possibility that such findings may be a result of a cohort effect, a longitudinal analysis indicated that both positive and negative affect are reduced across individuals' lives (Charles et al., 2001). In this study, negative affect decreased continuously with age, while positive affect remained relatively stable among the young and middle-aged, decreasing only slightly among the oldest group. It may be that, as people grow older, they adapt to life's ups and downs, and this adaptation results in a smaller range of high and low emotional responses. Further research is needed to better understand how well-being changes as people move from youth into old age. This research is particularly relevant to women, whose estimated life expectancy in the last decade has been about 79 years, from 5.5 to 7 years longer than that of men (National Center for Health Statistics, 2002). In any case, at present, the outlook is considerably more optimistic for older individuals than once thought. One can no longer assume that youth is the key to happiness and, as people grow older, this is certainly something in which they can take comfort.

ENHANCING WOMEN'S SUBJECTIVE WELL-BEING

As mentioned previously, positive psychological functioning and well-being were not always of focal interest to students of human behavior. However, as this tide changes, researchers are beginning to ask not only, "What characterizes a happy individual?" but more applicably, "How can people be made happier?" Initially, many psychologists believed that a woman with low SWB might be doomed to accept her unhappy fate. One reason for such pessimism about the possibility of boosting well-being is the assumption of a genetically determined set point for happiness. That is, many researchers accept the notion that each person has a characteristic level of happiness to which they will inevitably return, regardless of changing circumstances or any effort to the contrary. This concept has been supported by evidence suggesting that the heritability of well-being may be as high as 80% (Lykken & Tellegen, 1996). Another reason that many researchers are pessimistic about people's ability to actively increase happiness is the notion of hedonic adaptation. As discussed previously, hedonic adaptation suggests that gains in SWB will be temporary because humans quickly adapt to new positive life circumstances. This adaptation is thought to cause initial increases in happiness to dissipate once the novelty of a positive circumstantial change wears off.

Yet, even though a woman's level of SWB may be highly heritable and prone to adaptation, new research is beginning to provide empowering evidence that women can increase and maintain their personal psychological well-being—through their own physical and mental efforts. For example, maintaining an exercise program has been repeatedly shown to have a positive impact on peoples' moods (Arent, Landers, & Etnier, 2000). Additionally, studies that have induced participants to practice particular intentional activities with effort and commitment have demonstrated that such activities as regularly counting one's blessings (Emmons & McCullough, 2003), committing systematic acts of kindness (Lyubomirsky, Sheldon, & Schkade, 2003), engaging in daily thoughtful self-reflection (Sousa & Lyubomirsky, 2003), and practicing optimistic thinking (King, 2001) can boost people's happiness levels. Furthermore, it appears that setting and achieving "self-concordant" life goals (i.e., goals that match one's interests and values) can help to increase well-being as well (Sheldon, Kasser, Smith, & Share, 2002). These and other research programs are suggesting that increasing women's SWB is not only possible but readily accessible to most people who are willing and able to put forth the effort. Women either unwilling or unable to improve their well-being may be those experiencing negative life circumstances (e.g., recent layoff, divorce, or unpleasant living quarters) or those habitually engaged in self-destructive, self-denigrating, or maladaptive practices (e.g., drug abuse, excessive self-criticism, or obsessive rumination); these individuals must address their pressing problems to immediately relieve their depression or unhappiness before attempting to bolster their happiness levels from the neutral to the positive range.

CONCLUSIONS

The purpose of this chapter was fourfold. We began by introducing the concept of subjective well-being and discussed how SWB is characterized and measured in the literature. Next, we briefly reviewed a number of variables that correlate with well-being. The remaining portions of the chapter were dedicated to three subtopics. The first, an overview of how well-being is related to gender, discussed the finding that women are often as happy or happier than men while being twice as likely as men to be depressed. An explanation for this seemingly paradoxical, but robust, finding was provided. The second topic, a summary of how well-being changes across the life span, addressed another surprising result—namely, that well-being often appears to increase as women and men grow older. This research challenges commonly held notions that the quality of one's life will be reduced with age. Finally, we broached the topic of how to increase women's SWB. Although there may be limitations to this emerging line of research, initial attempts to increase well-being via effortful, intentional activities (e.g., expressing gratitude, committing kind acts, pursuing valued goals) have been promising in samples of relatively healthy, nondepressed individuals.

Given the complicated and unique life circumstances that girls and women have faced for centuries, it is important to understand how they subjectively view the quality of their lives and how they experience positive and negative emotions. All in all, the study of SWB is showing that many women are happy, contented individuals. It is a testament to female resiliency that, in spite of numerous life obstacles, injustices, and prejudices, women—and especially older women—appear to be just as happy and satisfied as men.

REFERENCES

Adelmann, P. K. (1987). Occupational complexity, control, and personal income: Their relation to psychological well-being in men and women. *Journal of Applied Psychology, 72,* 529–537.

Aldous, J., & Ganey, R. F. (1999). Family life and the pursuit of happiness: The influence of gender and race. *Journal of Family Issues, 20,* 155–180.

Arent, S. M., Landers, D., M., & Etnier, J. L. (2000). The effects of exercise on mood in older adults: A meta-analytic review. *Journal of Aging and Physical Activity, 8,* 407–430.

Argyle, M. (1999). Causes and correlates of happiness. In D. Kahneman, E. Diener, & N. Schwartz (Eds.), *Well-being: The foundations of hedonic psychology* (pp. 353–373). New York: Russell Sage Foundation.

Barrick, A. L., Hutchinson, R. L., & Deckers, L. H. (1989). Age effects on positive and negative emotions. *Journal of Social Behavior and Personality, 4,* 421–429.

Brickman, P., Coates, D., & Janoff-Bulman, R. (1978). Lottery winners and accident victims: Is happiness relative? *Journal of Personality and Social Psychology, 36,* 917–927.

Carstensen, L. L. (1995). Evidence for a life-span theory of socioemotional selectivity. *Current Directions in Psychological Science, 4,* 151–156.

Charles, S. T., Reynolds, C. A., & Gatz, M. (2001). Age-related differences and change in positive and negative affect over 23 years. *Journal of Personality and Social Psychology, 80,* 136–151.

Diener, E., & Biswas-Diener, R. (2002). Will money increase subjective well-being? A literature review and guide to needed research. *Social Indicators Research, 57,* 119–169.

Diener, E., & Diener, C. (1996). Most people are happy. *Psychological Science, 7,* 181–185.

Diener, E., & Diener, M. B. (1998). Happiness: Subjective well-being. In H. S. Friedman (Ed.), *Encyclopedia of mental health* (pp. 311–321). San Diego, CA: Academic Press.

Diener, E., Emmons, R. A., Larsen, R. J., & Griffin, S. (1985). The satisfaction with life scale. *Journal of Personality Assessment, 49,* 71–75.

Diener, E., Horwitz, J., & Emmons, R. A. (1985). Happiness of the very wealthy. *Social Indicators, 16,* 263–274.

Diener, E., & Larsen, R. J. (1993). The experience of emotional well-being: Stabilities in the global assessment of emotion. In M. Lewis & J. M. Haviland (Eds.), *Handbook of emotion* (pp. 405–415). New York: Guilford Press.

Diener, E., & Lucas, R. E. (2000). Subjective emotional well-being. In M. Lewis & J. M. Haviland-Jones (Eds.), *Handbook of emotions* (2nd ed., pp. 325–337). New York: Guilford Press.

Diener, E., Sandvik, E., & Larsen, R. J. (1985). Age and sex effects for emotional intensity. *Developmental Psychology, 21,* 542–546.

Diener, E., Sandvik, E., Pavot, W., & Gallagher, D. (1991). Response artifacts in the measurement of subjective well-being. *Social Indicators Research, 24,* 35–56.

Diener, E., & Suh, E. M. (1998). Subjective well-being and age: An international analysis. In K. W. Schaie & M. P. Lawton (Eds.), *Annual review of gerontology and geriatrics: Vol. 17. Focus on emotion and adult development* (pp. 304–324). New York: Springer.

Diener, E., Suh, E. M., Lucas, R. E., & Smith, H. E. (1999). Subjective well-being: Three decades of progress. *Psychological Bulletin, 125,* 276–302.

Emmons, R. A., & McCullough, M. E. (2003). Counting blessings versus burdens: An experimental investigation of gratitude and subjective well-being in daily life. *Journal of Personality and Social Psychology, 84,* 377–389.

Francis, L. J. (1999). Happiness is a thing called stable extraversion: A further examination of the relationship between the Oxford happiness inventory and Eysenck's dimensional model of personality and gender. *Personality and Individual Differences, 26,* 5–11.

Freund, M. (1985). Toward a critical theory of happiness: Philosophical background and methodological significance. *New Ideas in Psychology, 3,* 3–12.

Fujita, F., Diener, E., & Sandvik, E. (1991). Gender differences in negative affect and well-being: The case for emotional intensity. *Journal of Personality and Social Psychology, 61,* 427–434.

Gross, J. J., Carstensen, L. L., Pasupathi, M., Tsai, J., Goetestam, S. C., & Angie, Y. C. (1997). Emotion and aging: Experience, expression, and control. *Psychology and Aging, 12,* 590–599.

Harker, L., & Keltner, D. (2001). Expressions of positive emotions in women's college yearbook pictures and their relationship to personality and life outcomes across adulthood. *Journal of Personality and Social Psychology, 80,* 112–124.

Inglehart, R. (1990). *Culture shift in advanced industrial society.* Princeton, NJ: Princeton University Press.

Inglehart, R. (2002). Gender, aging, and subjective well-being. *International Journal of Comparative Sociology, 43,* 391–408.

King, L. A. (2001). The health benefits of writing about life goals. *Personality and Social Psychology Bulletin, 27,* 798–807.

Kozma, A., & Stones, M. J. (1988). Social desirability in measures of subjective well-being: Age comparisons. *Social Indicators Research, 20,* 1–14.

Lang, F. R., & Heckhausen, J. (2001). Perceived control over development and subjective well-being: Differential benefits across adulthood. *Journal of Personality and Social Psychology, 81,* 509–523.

Larsen, R. J., & Diener, E. (1987). Emotional response intensity as an individual difference characteristic. *Journal of Research in Personality, 21,* 1–39.

Larsen, R. J., Diener, E., & Emmons, R. A. (1986). Affect intensity and reactions to daily life events. *Journal of Personality and Social Psychology, 51,* 803–814.

Lykken, D., & Tellegen, A. (1996). Happiness is a stochastic phenomenon. *Psychological Science, 7,* 186–189.

Lyubomirsky, S., Sheldon, K. M., & Schkade, D. (2003). *Pursuing happiness: The architecture of sustainable change.* Manuscript submitted for publication.

Moller, V., & Schlemmer, L. (1989). South African quality of life: A research note. *Social Indicators Research, 21,* 279–291.

Mroczek, D. K., & Kolarz, C. M. (1998). The effect of age on positive and negative affect: A developmental perspective on happiness. *Journal of Personality and Social Psychology, 75,* 1333–1349.

Murphy, E. M. (2003). Being born female is dangerous for your health. *American Psychologist, 58,* 205–210.

Myers, D. G. (2000). The funds, friends, and faith of happy people. *American Psychologist, 55,* 56–67.

National Center for Health Statistics. (2002). *National Vital Statistics Reports.* Retrieved July 20, 2003, from http://www.cdc.gov/nchs/about/major/dvs/mortdata.htm

Nolen-Hoeksema, S. (1987). Sex differences in unipolar depression: Evidence and theory. *Psychological Bulletin, 101,* 259–282.

Okun, M. A., & George, L. K. (1984). Physician and self-ratings of health, neuroticism and subjective well-being among men and women. *Personality and Individual Differences, 5,* 533–539.

Pavot, W., & Diener, E. (1993). Review of the satisfaction with life scale. *Psychological Assessment, 5,* 164–172.

Ross, C. E., & Huber, J. (1985). Hardship and depression. *Journal of Health and Social Behavior, 26,* 312–327.

Ryff, C. D. (1989). Happiness is everything, or is it? Explorations on the meaning of psychological well-being. *Journal of Personality and Social Psychology, 57,* 1069–1081.

Ryff, C. D., & Keyes, C. L. M. (1995). The structure of psychological well-being revisited. *Journal of Personality and Social Psychology, 69,* 719–727.

Sandvik, E., Diener, E., & Seidlitz, L. (1993). Subjective well-being: The convergence and stability of self-report and non-self-report measures. *Journal of Personality, 61,* 317–342.

Seligman, M. P. E., & Csikszentmihalyi, M. (2000). Positive psychology. *American Psychologist, 55,* 5–14.

Sheldon, K. M., Kasser, T., Smith, K., & Share, T. (2002). Personal goals and psychological growth: Testing an intervention to enhance goal attainment and personality integration. *Journal of Personality, 70,* 5–31.

Silver, R. L. (1982). *Coping with an undesirable life event: A study of early reactions to physical disability.* Unpublished doctoral dissertation, Northwestern University, Evanston, IL.

Sousa, L., & Lyubomirsky, S. (2003). *The medium is the message: The costs and benefits of thinking, writing, and talking about life's triumphs and defeats.* Manuscript submitted for publication.

United Nations Development Programme. (1995). *The human development report.* Oxford: Oxford University Press.

Veenhoven, R., et al. (1994). *World database of happiness: Correlates of happiness.* Rotterdam: Erasmus University.

Watson, D., Clark, L. A., & Tellegen, A. (1988). Development and validation of brief measures of positive and negative affect: The PANAS scales. *Journal of Personality and Social Psychology, 54,* 1063–1070.

Wilson, W. (1967). Correlates of avowed happiness. *Psychological Bulletin, 67,* 294–306.

VANESSA L. McGANN
and JANICE M. STEIL

The Sense of Entitlement: Implications for Gender Equality and Psychological Well-Being

The sense of entitlement is defined as a set of attitudes about what a person feels she or he has a right to expect from others. As such, it is viewed as key to the perception of unfair treatment and the motivation to seek change. Because of its link to social justice, entitlement has been a central construct in attempts to understand the gendered asymmetries of social life and in the search to identify both the problems and facilitators associated with recent efforts to achieve gender equality.

GENDERED ASYMMETRIES

Since the 1970s, the opportunities and achievements of women and girls have expanded dramatically. Unlike 30 years ago, women now receive the majority of associate's, bachelor's, and master's degrees, constitute almost half (47%) of the paid labor force, and are increasingly visible across all spheres of economic and public life. Equally dramatic are the shifts in women's relationships at home. Women's increased labor force participation, including the participation of those who are married and mothers of young children, has made the dual-earner family the modal family in America. As well, dual-earner families now have the highest median incomes, and this is increasingly due to the economic contributions of employed wives. Indeed, almost 30% of these women now earn more than their spouses, and this has brought increasing expectations of greater work sharing at home.

Despite the advances, women have yet to achieve outcomes equal to those of men. While young women represent the majority of the student body, and receive the majority of degrees in university undergraduate and master's programs, women remain underrepresented at the highest levels. Women receive only 41% of doctoral degrees and represent less than 20% of tenured full professors (Reid & Zalk, 2001). Women also reap fewer returns on their educational investments. In 2001, the median income of a woman with an associate's degree was less than that of a man with only a high school education ($31,194 vs. $33,037, respectively; U.S. Census Bureau, 2003). Women who are employed full time earn only 79 cents relative to every dollar earned by a comparable man

(Institute for Women's Policy Research, 2004); and women constitute only 5% of the top earning corporate officers at Fortune 500 companies. Indeed, "women earn less than men in all ethnic groups, across all educational categories, across the life cycle, within detailed occupational categories, as well as across male-dominated and female-dominated occupations" (Gutek, 2001, pp. 1197–1198).

This pattern of progress, but not to equality, is repeated across all spheres—public and private—including relationships at home. In the 1970s, for example, mothers performed two thirds more household work and one third more child care than fathers. Today, by contrast, wives perform one quarter more of the household work and child care, respectively (Bond, Galinsky, & Swanberg, 1998). Wives also seem to do vastly more of the emotion and interaction work that relationships require, including initiating talk, communicating feelings, and confiding innermost thoughts and feelings (Newman, Steil, & Novak, 2003). Thus, asymmetries persist. Employed wives continue to do a disproportionate share of household work, child care, and relationship work, and report less choice over their involvement in these activities than their husbands do (Larson, Richards, & Perry-Jenkins, 1994).

WOMEN'S LACK OF GRIEVANCE

Yet women do not seem proportionately aggrieved. A survey of 345 female and male full-time workers, matched on three levels of occupational prestige, found that women were underpaid relative to men in comparable positions but reported themselves no less satisfied with their pay, their jobs, or their treatment than their more highly paid male colleagues (Crosby, 1982). Other studies, conducted in both the United States and Canada, showed that even when controlling for academic major and career aspirations, college women reported significantly lower income expectations across all points of their careers. And, when a nationally representative sample of Canadian workers were asked "What was the income you deserved (in the previous year) all things considered?" women reported that they deserved significantly less money than men thought they de-

served. Again, this was the case even when relevant factors such as age, education level, and job characteristics were held constant (Desmarais & Curtis, 1997a, 1997b).

Evidence from laboratory studies is equally compelling. Callahan-Levy and Messe (1979) asked women and men to work on a task for a fixed amount of time and then to pay themselves for the work they did. Women paid themselves significantly less money and reported less money as fair pay than did men. Brenda Major and her colleagues replicated and expanded this self-pay paradigm, finding that when women and men were given a fixed amount of pay and asked to do as much work as they thought was fair for the amount of money they were paid, women worked significantly longer, did more work, completed more correct work, and worked more efficiently than did men (Major, McFarlin, & Gagnon, 1984).

Neither women nor men are oblivious to these differences. Among the employed, both women and men report that women, in general, are paid less than men; and both women and men participants in laboratory studies expect that men will pay themselves more than women. Still, women report themselves as no less satisfied than men. Crosby (1982) characterized these findings as the "paradox of the contented female worker" and wondered whether women's lack of grievance over pay inequities extends to inequalities at home. To a large extent it does. Despite the gendered asymmetries in husbands' and wives' contributions to housework and child care, the majority of women and men report the division of labor at home as fair. African American and White women report the division of labor as less fair than Hispanic women, and women overall report the division of labor as less fair than men. Yet the differences between women and men are small, and there is little to no difference between full-time homemaker wives and wives who are employed (Sanchez & Kane, 1996).

THE SENSE OF ENTITLEMENT

Entitlement Defined

Seeking to better understand the persistence of the inequalities both at home and at work, as well as women's lack of proportional grievance over these inequalities, a number of scholars have focused on the role of a sense of entitlement—as both a facilitator of and a barrier to social change. Defined as a set of attitudes about what a person feels he/she has a right to and can expect from others, the sense of entitlement signifies claims to legitimate rights and highlights the societal obligation to respect and enforce these rights (Nadkarni, Steil, Malone, & Sagrestano, 2003). Thus, the sense of entitlement is viewed as key to the perception of unfair treatment and the motivation to seek change.

Gender Differences in Entitlement

Extensive theorizing has focused on the degree to which society's differential socialization of women and men, and differential valuing of gendered attributes and behaviors, produces gender differences in the sense of entitlement. Clinical scholarship argues that women are socialized to be nurturing caretakers whose priority is to others' needs first and to value connections above achievement (Chodorow, 1978). Thus, they argue that for women, nurturing, expressiveness, and relationship work come to be valued above independent strivings, competition, and agency. Men, by contrast, are lauded for concentrating on their own needs in order to become independent, successful, and achievement oriented. Thus boys and men are rewarded for being self-reliant, confident, and adventurous; girls and women for being nurturing, responsible, deferential, and concerned for others' welfare. These differences, it is argued, result in a lower sense of entitlement in women than men. Indeed, Jack (1991) argues that it is men's entitlements and women's lack of entitlement that contribute to relationship interactions that often lead to women's depression.

Social psychologists argue that gender differences in entitlement emanate from differences in status ascribed to various social groups, as well as to the differences in rights and responsibilities associated with different social roles. From the social psychological perspective, gendered expectations beginning early in family life, and the division of labor along gendered lines, affects the expectations and beliefs that women and men

hold regarding both their capacities and their opportunities (Okin, 1989). Beginning at an early age, boys receive larger allowances than girls, and "boys' chores" are rewarded with higher wages than "girls' chores." The pattern continues as college women earn less in their summer jobs than college men, and those areas of employment in which women predominate, such as nursing and teaching, tend to be lower paid than those such as airline piloting and the law, in which men predominate.[1] Thus, girls learn at an early age that women's work is valued less than men's and that it is normative for women to be paid less than men. Similarly, studies of family work show that boys are allowed to spend more time in leisure activities than girls; and girls are asked to spend more time in household tasks and child care and to undertake a greater share of family work than boys. As these gendered patterns become internalized they provide normative referents as to what one can expect and feel entitled to. According to Major (1994), these gendered differences in the sense of entitlement are then reinforced by a pattern of restricted comparisons in which women compare their expectations and outcomes to their own past experiences and those of similar, primarily same-sex others. Thus, to the extent that women work in low-paying jobs, and see other women in similar jobs as their most relevant comparison, a low sense of entitlement will be maintained and they will report themselves as satisfied with their outcomes. In a parallel vein, women who see the responsibilities of the home and relationships as women's work, and compare their relationships, their outcomes, and their lives to those of other women, will tend to be satisfied and believe they are faring better than most.

Adolescence

While gendered expectations begin early in life, they intensify at adolescence as the pressure to engage in gender appropriate behavior heightens. Thus, at adolescence, one sees increasing divergence between girls and boys in several important domains (O'Sullivan, Graber, & Brooks-Gunn, 2001). Girls begin to believe that they would be better at female-dominated rather than male-dominated occupations, girls begin to take fewer math courses, and those girls with exceptional ability become less likely than their male counterparts to pursue majors in science or engineering (Eccles, 1994). Girls become less happy with themselves and experience a decline in self-esteem (Basow & Rubin, 1999). As well, depression rates that were similar for boys and girls in childhood begin to increase at a fourfold rate for girls (Lewinsohn, Hops, Roberts, Seeley, & Andrews, 1993). Interestingly, this seems to be less true for girls of African American descent than it is for girls of any other ethnic group. Thus, it is noteworthy that stereotypes of African Americans depict males and females as more similar to each other in terms of expressiveness and competence than do the stereotypes of other ethnic groups and many believe this is a source of resilience. By contrast, Hispanic culture expectations of females are influenced by the traditional cultural values of *marianismo* that honors self-sacrifice and nurturance. Traditional gender-role expectations are also pronounced for Asian American women where the culture emphasizes harmonious interpersonal relationships, interdependence, mutual obligations and loyalty, and according to some, women are expected to be particularly passive and subservient (Basow & Rubin, 1999). Despite variations within ethnic groups, then, pressures to accommodate to gendered expectations seem to intensify at adolescence in ways that are not always functional for girls.

Adolescence is also the time of burgeoning romantic and sexual relationships. Here, young women are faced with a series of important challenges, including how to make active and safe choices about sexual behaviors of all kinds, how to develop a sense of entitlement to their own pleasure and desire, and how to develop a sense of agency grounded in their own bodies (Tolman, 1999). As a number of investigators have pointed out, rates of contraceptive use in the United States are lower than those of other Western nations and the rate of adolescent pregnancy is higher (O'Sullivan et al., 2001). As well, dating violence during the teen years is pervasive, with as many as 35% of female and male students surveyed reporting at least one episode (White, 2001). In these contexts, "femininity" has been deemed an "unsafe sexual strategy" (Holland, Ramazanoglu, Scott, Sharpe, & Thomson, 1992).

Specifically, passivity, deference to male partners, perceiving others' needs and desires as more important than one's own, and suppression of one's own instrumental traits including independence and agency are inconsistent with both women's safety and their pleasure. Indeed, it seems that the pressures of gender-role conformity peak at adolescence and diminish young women's sense of entitlement at a time when they need it most.

GENDER DIFFERENCES IN ENTITLEMENT: EMPIRICAL EVIDENCE

The 1980s and 1990s

Over the last 15 years, research on the sense of entitlement has focused on three questions: Are there differences in women's and men's sense of entitlement, as both social psychological and clinical theories suggest? If differences in the sense of entitlement exist, are they related to a pattern of restricted comparisons, specifically a preference for comparisons to same-sex others? Is there a relationship between women's entitlement levels and women's satisfaction with lower outcomes? Findings suggest that the answers to these questions are yes, yes, and yes.

Consistent with the findings reported earlier in this chapter, studies conducted with college students showed that, in the absence of social comparisons, women consistently paid themselves less than their male counterparts (Major, 1994). Findings also provided evidence of a preference for both women and men to compare their outcomes to the outcomes of similar others, particularly same-sex, same-job others. Women college students were more likely to ask for information about the self-pay levels of other women, and women who were employed full time were more likely to say they compared their pay and their promotions to those of other women rather than to men (Major, 1994; Steil & Hay, 1997). Yet, among college students, the preference for same-sex comparisons was ameliorated for women assigned to typically male tasks, and among full-time employed workers, women in prestigious and male-dominated positions were more likely to compare to both women and men than to women exclusively (Major, 1994; Steil & Hay, 1997). Finally, women who made comparisons to the highest achievers and to men (who were over-represented in the high achieving positions), achieved higher salaries and more prestigious positions, and expressed less satisfaction with the status quo than women who compared primarily to other women (Steil & Hay, 1997; Zanna, Crosby, & Lowenstein, 1987). In sum, research conducted in the 1980s and 1990s strongly supported social psychological representations of sex differences in the sense of entitlement and the importance of a sense of entitlement to the attainment of more equal outcomes for women both at home and at work.

But a number of fundamental issues remained unexplored. Clinical theory suggests that a low-ered sense of entitlement is associated with tradi-tional female characteristics such as nurturance and communality. Others, however, suggest that it is the absence of traditionally male characteris-tics that is key (Whitley, 1984). From this perspec-tive, both women and men who measure high on masculine-associated traits such as agency should evidence higher levels of entitlement than those who measure low on these traits, whereas entitlement levels should be unrelated to traits typically viewed as feminine. Also ignored were is-sues of socioeconomic class and ethnicity. Yet, to the extent that values relevant to rights and obliga-tions vary across cultures, so should the sense of entitlement. Members of cultures that emphasize independence and individual rights over inter-dependence and social obligation should report higher levels of entitlement than those who are socialized to put others first. And what of the many other issues relevant to women and girls' psychological well-being? Moving beyond issues of pay equity and work sharing at home, what is the nature of the relationship between entitle-ment and depression? And what of issues of voice, of vitality, of healthy and safe sexuality?

Entitlement and Depression

At least three positions have been posed relative to the relationship of entitlement and depres-sion. Writing from a clinical perspective, Jack (1991) argues that women's socialization to de-fine themselves through relationships leads them to feel that they are not entitled to ask to have their own needs filled, nor to feel that their own needs are legitimate. This lack of entitlement in relationships leads to a loss of voice, a loss of self, and ultimately to depression. Steil (1997), writing from the perspective of the justice literature, ar-gued that a low sense of entitlement leads to women's lack of grievance over inequality. Yet, according to Steil, the literature clearly shows that women in unequal relationships pay sig-nificant costs in terms of their psychological well-being, including increased fatigue, low self-esteem, and dysphoria. Others, however, have argued that a low sense of entitlement can serve a protective function (Major, 1993). From this per-spective, when change is unattainable, a sense of entitlement leading to dissatisfaction with the status quo only fosters dysfunctional anger and discontent. In such situations, those who are dis-advantaged avoid comparisons with advantaged others so as to minimize psychological distress. Thus, subordinated groups learn to accept injus-tices as a way of surviving and a low sense of en-titlement facilitates coping (Miller, 1986). Under what conditions, then, does an enhanced sense of entitlement encourage voice, unfettered strivings, and a desire for change? Under what conditions, if any, are lower levels of entitlement functional?

Finally, in all of the studies conducted during that period, there was no measure of entitlement. Thus, rather than directly assessing respondents' sense of entitlement, entitlement levels were in-ferred from women's levels of self-pay and ex-pressed satisfaction with their outcomes relative to others.

The Entitlement Attitudes Scale

To address this gap, Steil and her colleagues de-veloped a 17-item Entitlement Attitudes Scale (EAS; Nadkarni et al., 2003). The scale consisted of two weakly related but qualitatively different di-mensions. One dimension, labeled "self-reliance/self-assurance" (SRSA), seemed similar to social psychological representations of entitlement as necessary to being an emotionally healthy person able to attain and safeguard legitimate rights. The other factor, labeled "narcissistic expectations/

self-promotion" (NESP), was more closely aligned with clinical representations of a non-reality-based sense of entitlement consisting of grandiose ideas of one's rights without consideration of the rights and feelings of others.

Consistent with social psychological representations, in samples of both African American and White women, SRSA was positively associated with self-esteem, positively associated with greater decision making (say, in relationships), and negatively associated with both depression and self-silencing in relationships (McGann, 2000; Nadkarni et al., 2003; Vinograde, 2001). As well, and consistent with predictions, among married women, higher levels of SRSA were associated with higher levels of sexual assertiveness and greater sexual satisfaction (Kahn, 2001).

In studies with large samples, males scored higher on SRSA than did females. Yet tests of the predictive ability of gender-related attributes showed that respondents' agency, or capacity to independently and confidently get things done, was a better predictor of SRSA than was respondent sex. Further, SRSA was unrelated to respondents' communality or sensitivity and concern for others. Findings also supported the notion that entitlement levels may vary by ethnicity. Consistent with predictions, Asians scored lower on SRSA than did non-Hispanic Caucasians and African Americans (Nadkarni et al., 2003).

To date, studies of the relationship between entitlement and issues of social class have been extremely limited. Yet, in one of the first systematic assessments of the relationships among entitlement level, sex of social comparison, and work sharing in a sample of professional (faculty) and nonprofessional (staff) women, higher levels of entitlement were reported by faculty, who made more frequent comparisons to men and enjoyed more equal sharing of the work at home than did staff. As well, when asked the reasons for their choice of comparison other, faculty members were more likely to report issues of equality ("Because I want to ensure that we split the housework 50–50") and fairness ("He could be doing some of the work I'm doing") as their reasons for choosing to compare to their male partners. In contrast, staff members were almost twice as likely to use positive role models ("Her house is always ready for guests, neat and ready to entertain") and three times as likely to use similarity ("She works full time also") as reasons for choosing to compare primarily to other females, primarily their mothers, sisters, and friends (Newman et al., 2003).

CONCLUSIONS

Over the last three decades, there has been significant interest in the sense of entitlement as an important precondition to the perception of unfair treatment. During that time, empirical studies focused primarily on women's lower levels of a healthy sense of entitlement relative to men and the extent to which this leads to continuing gender inequalities both at home and at work. Empirical work, over that same period, supported assertions that entitlement differences are maintained by women's and men's preference for comparing their outcomes to others of the same sex. Yet the findings also suggest that differences in the sense of entitlement can be ameliorated if differential socialization of women and men regarding their capacities and opportunities are eliminated, and girls, as well as boys, are encouraged to compare to the standard setters, or highest achievers, whether female or male.

Women's socialization to the role of nurturing caretaker is often viewed as the source of a lowered sense of entitlement, resulting in a loss of self-advocacy and effective voice in relationships. Recent studies, however, consistently show that a healthy sense of entitlement is unrelated to women's nurturing qualities. Rather, lower levels of entitlement are associated with lower levels of instrumentality. Thus, it is not that women need to relinquish their concern for others but, rather, that they need to be supported in maintaining their own sense of agency so as to develop a healthy balance between concern for others and concern for self.

What, then, are the clinical implications of these findings? While empirically unanswered questions remain, it seems clear that a sense of entitlement is necessary to being an emotionally healthy person who can effectively assert her rights and seek change. Entitlement, then, becomes a lens through which clinicians and clients can examine themes of anger, self-esteem, and growth. Indeed, women in abusive relationships, marital distress, and career crisis can all be seen as struggling to varying degrees with entitlement issues. The extent to which women feel they matter, whom they choose to compare to, and how they conceptualize just treatment for themselves become pivotal issues. Using the perspective of entitlement, clinicians can help girls and women to understand these issues as a foreground of their struggles in pursuing change, rather than allowing them to remain as an invisible background that maintains the status quo.

As clinicians, we can investigate on an individual level how entitlement varies across contexts and across roles. How is the sense of entitlement affected by marriage, motherhood, and divorce, as well as women's diverse professional roles? How does the sense of entitlement expand or diminish over the life span? How does entitlement function for women and girls of different ethnicities, from different family structures and varied economic opportunities?

Thus, while much has been learned over the last three decades, fundamental questions remain as we seek to better understand how best to develop and support a healthy sense of entitlement, one that facilitates women's and girl's ability to approach life with a healthy zest, ready and able to claim their full share of its bounty and vicissitudes in the 21st century.

NOTE

1. More than 90% of nurses and 80% of elementary teachers are women who earn $49,840 and $44,080 annually (based on median annual income). Over 90% of pilots and 70% of lawyers are men who earn over $100,000 annually. Since the 1970s, however, the number of women lawyers has increased threefold.

REFERENCES

Basow, S. A., & Rubin, L. R. (1999). Gender influences in adolescent development. In N. G. Johnson, M. C. Roberts, & J. Worell (Eds.), *Beyond appearance: A new look at adolescent girls* (pp. 25–52). Washington, DC: American Psychological Association.

Bond, J. T., Galinsky, E., & Swanberg, J. E. (1998). *The 1997 study of the changing workforce.* New York: Families and Work Institute.

Callahan-Levy, C. M., & Messe, L. A. (1979). Sex differences in the allocations of pay. *Journal of Personality and Social Psychology, 37,* 433–446.

Chodorow, N. J. (1978). *The reproduction of mothering.* Berkeley: University of California Press.

Crosby, F. J. (1982). *Relative deprivation and working women.* New York: Oxford University Press.

Desmarais, S., & Curtis, J. (1997a). Gender and perceived pay entitlement: Testing for effects of experience with income. *Journal of Personality and Social Psychology, 72*(1), 141–150.

Desmarais, S., & Curtis, J. (1997b). Gender differences in pay histories and views on pay entitlement among university students. *Sex Roles, 37*(9/10), 623–642.

Eccles, J. S. (1994). Understanding women's educational and occupational choices: Applying the Eccles et al. model of achievement-related choices. *Psychology of Women Quarterly, 18,* 585–609.

Gutek, B. (2001). Working environments. In J. Worell (Ed.), *Encyclopedia of women and gender* (pp. 1191–1204). San Diego, CA: Academic Press.

Holland, J., Ramazanoglu, C., Scott, S., Sharpe, S., & Thomson, R. (1992). Pressure, resistance, empowerment: Young women and the negotiation of safer sex. In P. Aggleton, P. Davies, & G. Hart (Eds.), *AIDS: Rights, risk and reason* (pp. 142–162). Washington, DC: Falmer Press.

Institute for Women's Policy Research. (2004, October). *Fact sheet. The gender wage ratio: Women's and men's earnings.* IWPR Publication No. C350 updated. Washington, DC: Author. Retrieved from http://www.iwpr.org/pdf/c350updated.pdf

Jack, D. C. (1991). *Silencing the self: Women and depression.* New York: Harper Perennial.

Kahn, A. (2001). Entitlement and sexuality: An exploration of the relationship between entitlement level and female sexual attitudes, behaviors, and satisfaction. *Dissertation Abstracts International,* UMI No. 3003516, *62*(2-B), 1086.

Larson, R., Richards, M., & Perry-Jenkins, M. (1994). Divergent worlds: The daily emotional experience of mothers and fathers in the domestic and public spheres. *Journal of Personality and Social Psychology, 6,* 1034–1046.

Lewinsohn, P. M., Hops, H., Roberts, R. E., Seeley, J. R., & Andrews, J. A. (1993). Adolescent psychopathology: I. Prevalence and incidence of depression and other *DSM-III-R* disorders in high school students. *Journal of Abnormal Psychology, 102,* 133–144.

Major, B. (1993). Gender, entitlement and the distribution of family labor. *Journal of Social Issues, 49,* 141–159.

Major, B. (1994). From social inequality to personal entitlement: The role of social comparisons, legitimacy appraisals, and group membership. In M. Zanna (Ed.), *Advances in experimental social psychology* (pp. 293–355). San Diego, CA: Academic Press.

Major, B., McFarlin, D., & Gagnon, D. (1984). Overworked and underpaid: On the nature of gender differences in personal entitlement. *Journal of Personality and Social Psychology, 47*, 1399–1412.

McGann, V. (2000). *Entitlement and depression: An exploration of differences between the sexes and among women.* Doctoral dissertation, Adelphi University (UMI No. 9970474).

Miller, J. B. (1986). *Toward a new psychology of women* (2nd ed.). Boston: Beacon.

Nadkarni, L., Steil, J., Malone, J., & Sagrestano, L. (2003). *The sense of entitlement: The development of a self-report scale.* Manuscript submitted for publication.

Newman, A., Steil, J., & Novak, A. (2003, May). *Entitlement and work sharing in contemporary relationships: A social comparison perspective.* Poster session presented at the meetings of the American Psychological Society, Atlanta, GA.

Okin, S. M. (1989). *Justice, gender and the family.* New York: Basic Books.

O'Sullivan, L. F., Graber, J., & Brooks-Gunn, J. (2001). Adolescent gender development. In J. Worell (Ed.), *Encyclopedia of women and gender* (pp. 55–68). San Diego, CA: Academic Press.

Reid, P. T., & Zalk, S. R. (2001). Academic environments: Gender and ethnicity in higher education. In J. Worell (Ed.), *Encyclopedia of women and gender* (pp. 29–42). San Diego, CA: Academic Press.

Sanchez, L., & Kane, E. (1996). Women's and men's constructions of perceptions of housework fairness. *Journal of Family Issues, 17*, 358–387.

Steil, J. (1997). *Marital equality: Its relationship to the well-being of husbands and wives.* Thousand Oaks, CA: Sage.

Steil, J., & Hay, J. (1997). Social comparison in the workplace: A study of 60 dual-career couples. *Personality and Social Psychology Bulletin, 23*, 427–438.

Tolman, D. L. (1999). Female adolescent sexuality in relational context: Beyond sexual decision making. In N. G. Johnson, M. C. Roberts, & J. Worell (Eds.), *Beyond appearance: A new look at adolescent girls* (pp. 227–246). Washington, DC: American Psychological Association.

U.S. Census Bureau. (2003). *Historic income tables.* Washington, DC: Author. Retrieved July 31, 2003, from http://www.census.gov/hhes/income/histinc/p24.html

Vinograde, D. (2001). Black and white heterosexual women's marital and same-sex best friend relationships, and the contributions of entitlement, relationship equality and relationship intimacy to well-being. *Dissertation Abstracts International, 61*(9-B), 5010. (UMI No. 9988058.)

White, J. (2001). Aggression and gender. In J. Worell (Ed.), *Encyclopedia of women and gender* (pp. 81–94). San Diego, CA: Academic Press.

Whitley, B. (1984). Sex-role orientation and psychological well-being: Two meta-analyses. *Sex Roles, 12*(1/2), 207–225.

Zanna, M. P., Crosby, F., & Lowenstein, G. (1987). Male reference groups and discontent among female professionals. In B. Gutek & L. Larwood (Eds.), *Women's career development* (pp. 28–41). Thousand Oaks, CA: Sage.

The topic of self-care and balance among women continues to gain popularity within the literature and media, yet these practices remain rare. Women know that self-care is important, yet it is frequently compromised when the realities of daily life force them to make decisions about how to distribute time and energy, sustain relationships, and meet commitments. Barriers to self-care can be identified easily. Trying to negotiate work demands, household obligations, child care, familial needs, illnesses, and ailments, or deal with economic constraints, life changes or traumas, safety issues, and environmental constraints makes self-care seem impractical. Less easily recognized, however, are the reasons and ways to incorporate self-care into daily practice. Nevertheless, taking time for self-care, in spite of looming responsibilities, creates balance and fosters health. Balance is not achieved by trying to handle more or work faster and harder. In general, balance is realized through meaningful work (paid and unpaid), satisfying relationships and personal rejuvenation.

DEFINING SELF-CARE

Self-care includes the activities women undertake with the intention to promote, ensure, or restore psychological and physical health; to prevent, manage, or recover from disease, injury, or trauma; or to achieve a sense of well-being. Self-care is a multidimensional concept in which psychological and physical well-being are interdependent and lead to enhanced quality of life and a sense of fulfillment (Cameron & Leventhal, 2003; Johnson, 1991). Self-care activities must be defined and discovered individually. What one woman classifies as self-care may be what another identifies as stressful. For example, sports participation may be relaxing for some, but the competitive tenor may be too stressful for others. Self-care incorporates multiple components, including physical, emotional, intellectual, spiritual, social, relational, and safety and security areas of function. This chapter addresses each of these domains by providing a definition, critical issues and research, and self-care activities. Although these domains are presented as distinct categories of self-care, they are not mutually

CAROL WILLIAMS-NICKELSON

Balanced Living Through Self-Care

20

exclusive; one activity might meet a number of self-care needs.

Physical Self-Care

As one of the most widely researched self-care practices, physical self-care concerns fitness, nutrition, preventive medical care, early intervention, and treatment (Cameron & Leventhal, 2003). Fitness includes all aspects of physical activity, and it need not interfere with one's life, as many inactive women believe it will (Kjelsas, Augestad, & Gotestam, 2003). Exercise is a type of physical activity that consists of planned and structured movement done for pleasure and fitness. But physical activity should be conceptualized broadly to include a range of movement, not just structured exercise. The positive relationship between physical activity and emotional well-being among girls, younger women, and older women is well documented. Regular exercise reduces depression (Faulkner & Biddle, 2004), contributes to successful aging (Resnick & Nigg, 2003), ameliorates the effects of maltreatment and deprivation on children (Lederman & Osofsky, 2004), reduces stress (Ensel & Lin, 2004), improves self-concept and body image (Stoll & Alfermann, 2002), reduces symptoms of premenstrual syndrome (Rapkin, 2003), and improves the quality of life for women with chronic illnesses (Gandhi, DePauw, Dolny, & Freson, 2002).

Nutritional aspects of self-care include eating regular meals that limit fat and sugar and contain a variety of fruits, vegetables, proteins, and grains; and avoiding tobacco and excessive alcohol use. These basic fitness and nutrition principles are among the major factors influencing risks of morbidity and mortality in the United States (Berrigan, Dodd, Troiano, Krebs-Smith, & Barbash, 2003).

Obesity is associated with several chronic diseases, and its increasing prevalence is a major public health concern. It is a major factor in several noncommunicable diseases—for example, diabetes and cardiovascular disease. Obesity also increases the risk of many types of cancer, gallbladder disease, musculoskeletal disorders, and respiratory ailments (Hartl, 1997). In 1999, research by Mokdad et al., showed the prevalence of obesity increased from 12.0% in 1991 to 17.9% in 1998. Residents in all states, in both sexes, across ages, ethnicity, and educational levels, experienced steady rises in obesity, regardless of smoking status. The largest increase was found in 18–29-year-olds (7.1–12.1%), individuals with some college education (10.6–17.8%), and Hispanic/Latinos (11.6–20.8%). Many experts agree that the principal causes of the accelerating obesity problem are sedentary lifestyles and high-fat, energy-dense diets (Berrigan et al., 2003). Some of the psychological ramifications of obesity include feelings of low self-worth in girls (Zametkin, Zoon, Klein, & Munson, 2004) and women (Matz, Foster, Faith, & Wadden, 2002), social rejection due to weight stigmatization (Puhl & Brownell, 2003), and employment discrimination (Polinko & Popovich, 2001). Women may buffer the effects of obesity prejudice by altering their own perceptions of weight appropriateness to participate in a range of physical, social, and career activities (Chang, Christakis, & Chang, 2003).

Research from the Centers for Disease Control and Prevention shows fewer than 30% of ethnic minority women in the United States obtain moderate activity in amounts sufficient to derive health benefits (Finkelstein, Fiebelkorn, & Wang, 2004). According to Karla Henderson and Barbara Ainsworth (2003), more than half of all women lead sedentary lives, and among women of color this percentage is even higher, although there is insufficient information about the health needs of ethnic minority women. In girls, the onset of early puberty is linked with higher smoking rates and an increase in sedentary lifestyle, as well as acceleration in the development of unhealthy exercise and diet habits (Simon, Wardle, Jarvis, Steggles, & Cartwright, 2003). Women can integrate physical activity and healthy eating habits into daily life with minimal disruption and effort.

Emotional Self-Care

Emotional self-care concerns the identification, acceptance, and expression of a range of feelings. Women differ widely in how they interpret and manage emotional experiences. Although women might label themselves as experiencing similar emotions, they do not necessarily feel or act the same. Women often camouflage or ignore their feelings because they believe some feelings are unacceptable, or they simply do not have the time or motivation to explore the physiological, situational, and cognitive qualities of their emotions (Roysamb, Tambs, Reichborn-Kjennerud, Neal, & Harris, 2003). Because research shows clear links between emotions and health, it is important for women to understand and address feelings (Frederickson, 2000).

If not managed properly, anger, anxiety, isolation, and depression can be debilitating or destructive. Chronic anger and anxiety may lead to increased susceptibility to a range of diseases. For instance, anger can reduce the pumping efficiency of the heart and has been associated with higher incidence of heart attacks (Frederickson, 2000). Although anxiety may be a normal reaction to stress and can serve a useful purpose, without a legitimate focus it can trigger the onset of illness and affect recovery in women (Roysamb et al., 2003). Social isolation, the subjective sense of being cut off from people and having no one to turn to, may lead to depression, and it doubles the chances of sickness or death. Isolation is as significant to mortality rates as smoking, high blood pressure, high cholesterol, obesity, and lack of physical exercise (Casper, 2000).

Sex differences in depression begin to emerge in adolescence, with girls exhibiting higher vulnerabilities to depression (Simon et al., 2003). In addition to a tendency to suppress feelings such as anger and dissatisfaction, women perceive emotional loss more frequently than men; such occurrences may range from a single traumatic loss to frequent losses of emotional connectedness in the relationships women value so highly. Women suffer more depression, anxiety, and eating disorders than men. The explanation for this gender gap lies in a combination of complex biological, genetic, psychological, and social factors (Cameron & Leventhal, 2003). However, Johnson (1991) suggests that women are socialized to be more vulnerable to depression, based on a tendency to focus more on others' satisfaction rather than understanding and satisfying their own wishes, needs, and emotions.

The ability to recognize and show feelings is essential to women's health. Women can use im-

agery and self-talk to foster a sense of emotional mastery and bolster immunity (Cameron & Leventhal, 2003). When upset, angry, or sad, women must find outlets for those feelings, such as talking to a trusted friend or family member. If the feelings are persistent and intrude on daily life, help from a psychologist or other mental health professional may be necessary. Recording feelings may help women identify, express, and work through emotions. Many people find the creative expression of feelings through various forms of art to be healing and rejuvenating—for example, drawing, painting, sewing, cooking, landscaping, floral arranging, or playing music. Meditation and relaxation can also help girls and women become more aware and comfortable with a range of emotions.

Spiritual Self-Care

Spiritual self-care includes an ongoing search for meaning and understanding in life and what may extend beyond. It involves the exploration and expression of beliefs and values that are shaped by experience. Spirituality may be manifested through religion, but religion is not synonymous with spirituality (McCormick, 1994). It may be expressed also through connections to nature and the world, and may be characterized as an individual sense of purpose.

In his seminal work on the psychology of religion, Clark (1958) defined religion as "the inner experience of the individual when he senses a Beyond, especially as evidenced by the effect of this experience on his behavior when he actively attempts to harmonize his life with the Beyond" (p. 22). Others have distinguished between religion and spirituality, suggesting that religion has an institutional connotation, involves the practice of rituals, adherence to dogma, and attendance at services (Conger, 1994). Still others describe spirituality as more related to life's deeper motivations and an emotional connection to God or a force beyond oneself (Roof, 1993).

The meaning of spirituality and religion in women's lives is highly variable and subjective, yet a considerable body of research suggests that it is helpful to a majority of American women (Taylor, Chatters, Jayakody, & Levin, 1996). Brown

(2000) found that African American women used their religious beliefs to enhance their ability to cope with medical problems. Other research reports that the use of prayer and increased spiritual and religious activity are associated with higher self-esteem, greater personal happiness, higher life satisfaction, higher sense of control, and fewer depressive symptoms (Blaine & Crocker, 1995).

Because the preponderance of evidence generally indicates a positive association between spirituality or religion and the health and well-being of women, spiritual self-care strategies such as meditation (or prayer for women of faith) may be useful. Meditation is a calm and focused process that takes various forms among diverse cultural and religious traditions. Meditative states have been induced in dance, song, relaxation, and prayer in spiritual or religious worship (Blaine & Crocker, 1995). Transcendental meditation is a tool for personal growth and is commonly used by clinicians who employ a mind-body approach to treating psychological disorders and other conditions; this includes applications for homeless and addicted women (Plasse, 2001). But a calm and relaxed state of being can also be self-induced through a series of muscle relaxation exercises, focused awareness on deep and rhythmic breathing, and visualization techniques, such as imagining oneself lying on the beach, floating on a cloud, or visiting a peaceful location.

Spiritual self-care may be facilitated through participation organized religion, joining a spiritual community, taking a comparative-religions course, visiting different houses of worship, or investigating new religious movements as a woman seeks to understand her place in the universe and feel connected to a larger purpose. Spiritual experiences can also be facilitated by visiting geographic areas of natural beauty, attending performing arts events, visiting museums, or watching the sun rise or set.

Intellectual Self-Care

Intellectual self-care involves regular opportunities to engage in critical thinking and inquiry to expand knowledge and stimulate the mind. In its most simple form, this kind of self-care involves an abiding interest in ideas, learning, thinking, and creativity.

Intelligence is a multifaceted and well-studied area of psychology. Many of its connotations and constructs have remained intertwined with the techniques developed for its measurement. Binet and colleagues (1912) developed the first test to measure intellectual behavior in children, thought to be manifested in such abilities as reasoning, imagination, judgment, and adaptability. Others expanded Binet's early notions of intelligence by identifying components of intellect and additional methods of measurement. For instance, the Wechsler Intelligence Scales (now more widely used) yield verbal and performance quotients for both children and adults (Groth-Marnat, 2001). Likewise, Raymond Cattel defined crystallized intelligence as the ability to utilize facts and fluid intelligence as the ability to solve novel problems creatively (Brennan, 1997).

In 1983, a theory of multiple intelligences was advanced by Gardner to provide practical definitions of intelligence that pair cognitive skills with culturally valued activities. These types of intelligences include verbal, mathematical/logical, musical, spatial, kinesthetic/body control, intrapersonal (self-understanding), and interpersonal (social understanding). Most recently, Goleman (1998) coined the term *emotional intelligence,* which involves personal and social competence. Personal competence refers to emotional awareness, accurate self-assessment, self-confidence, self-control, trustworthiness, conscientiousness, adaptability, innovation, drive for achievement, commitment, initiative, and optimism. Social competence refers to how one handles relationships through empathic understanding and helping others, a service orientation, appreciation of diversity, and political awareness. It also includes social adeptness such as the ability to influence others, communicate openly and convincingly, manage conflict, lead and inspire others, initiate and manage change, build relationships, collaborate, cooperate, and work with groups. Because intelligence is a broad concept, there are many activities for meeting intellectual needs, such as occupational or career development, awareness of current events, or creative arts participation.

Social Self-Care

Social self-care pertains to regular emotional investment in relationships outside of the immediate family. It includes establishing, nurturing, and expanding social networks and friendships through community involvement, group affiliation, and contribution to collective causes. Friendships, and especially those with other women, may provide emotional support, companionship, reciprocity, and assistance in problem solving.

The 2001 Harvard Medical School's Nurses' Health Study (Hankinson, Colditz, Manson, & Speizer, 2001) showed that friendships among women play an important role in enhancing health and quality of life. The study concluded that the lack of at least one good confidante is as detrimental to a woman's health as smoking or obesity. Taylor and colleagues' (2000) research suggests that the hormone oxytocin may be one of the driving forces behind the formation and maintenance of close social bonds because it enhances the ability to nurture and be nurtured. When women release oxytocin in response to stress, the hormone causes women to establish and sustain friendships with other women and tend to children, rather than triggering the innate fight-or-flight response, as once thought. As these befriending and tending behaviors increase, more oxytocin is released, which further buffers stress and produces a calming effect.

Self-in-relation theory postulates that women organize their sense of identity, find existential meaning, achieve a sense of coherence and continuity, and are motivated, in the context of relationships (Jordan, Kaplan, Miller, Stiver, & Surrey, 1991). Over the course of women's lives, friendships with other women become increasingly important, particularly as women move into middle age and face changes and challenges such as illness, divorce, the empty nest, and parents' deaths (Shapiro, 2001).

Relational Self-Care

Relational self-care concerns the establishment, development, and strengthening of relationships with life partners, spouses, children, parents, and extended family. In the hustle of everyday life, families may neglect to talk regularly and partners may begin to take each other for granted or ignore their health.

Research shows that the quality of daily interactions among family members impacts one's construction of health, talk about health, participation in health-care systems, enactment of healthy or unhealthy behaviors, and health status (Bylund & Duck, 2004). People expect to live longer, are reinforced for their healthy habits and improve current health when they report high levels of familial emotional support, mediated by the perception that one has someone to call on when one is sick or in need (Ross & Mirowsky, 2002).

Safety and Security Self-Care

Self-care for safety and security involves personal, environmental, and financial planning. It includes taking precautions to feel safe and comfortable in your home and community. Understanding personal finances, obtaining health insurance, and taking steps to ensure a comfortable financial future are critical, yet often overlooked aspects of self-care.

Too often, safety and security issues are addressed only when a threat, breach of safety, or trauma occurs. People avoid checking their smoke detectors until they find, through an emergency, that they are inoperable. People may be careless about locking car or house doors until they are burglarized. Women may avoid taking a self-defense class until frightened or assaulted. Some women do not learn about their household budget or long-term financial issues until faced with separation, divorce, children's college education costs, or the death of a spouse (Miller & Iris, 2002).

TRACKING SELF-CARE

Writing or keeping a journal are common methods used for tracking and changing behavior. Food diaries, feelings and experiences journals, exercise calendars, and even health diaries used to monitor treatment regimens (Keleher & Verrinder, 2003), have been prescribed by a number of health-care providers and used regularly by patients with good results. Combining all of these elements into a self-care journal may be a simple way to chronicle and monitor self-care activities. Some women may find it difficult or time-consuming at first, but after a few months of careful attention to each self-care domain, new habits form. The maintenance of the self-care journal may become less important than the continuation of the personalized activities.

Bandura and Locke (2003) found that establishing and believing that you can accomplish personal goals enhances motivation, performance, and ultimate goal attainment. Writing about self-care can give women the opportunity to self-reflect, record and review accomplishments, increase self-commitment, and set goals. Because research shows that women prefer to concentrate on positive aspects of health, self-care records should focus on the presence of healthy behaviors, not the avoidance of destructive behaviors (Kjelsas et al., 2003). In a study of messages related to eating and exercise, college women found a focus on healthy eating and lifestyle more enjoyable, personally relevant, and interesting compared to a focus on problematic eating and lifestyles, which they found to be anxiety-provoking, fear-inducing, and less helpful to their overall health and well-being (Sanderson & Holloway, 2003).

Table 20.1 provides a sample self-care tracking method that may be modified and completed based on an individual's self-care preferences. The most important aspect of tracking self-care is to assure that activities are completed regularly in each domain. Self-care is a multidimensional construct. There is no singular correct method to achieve balance and foster self-care. The most effective strategies will be unique and personal for every woman and her circumstances.

PRINCIPLES OF BALANCED LIVING

In unusual situations, many women can manage a multitude of responsibilities for a short time. But maintaining the necessary level of mental and physical acuity to balance many activities well for an extended duration is impossible. Juggling is a coping mechanism women may use when time is tight and seemingly nothing can be postponed. As long as they are rested and reflexes are sharp, it works. But they quickly tire and skills decline when women must respond to multiple demands over time. The following principles can help women develop a framework to stop juggling, rebalance life in a more gratifying and sustainable pattern, and free up time for self-care activities.

- *Focus.* The ability to focus on a discrete task without interruption for a specified period of time and then switch full attention to another task is critical. Likewise, one must learn to focus on a particular activity in certain protected environments. This requires limit-setting.
- *Delegate.* Responsibilities may be offloaded to free up time and energy. Many women erroneously believe that they must seize all opportunities to get ahead. The ability to let go of some control and say no is vital.
- *Consolidate.* Women should build and rely on a support network to aid efficiency. For instance, regular exercise with others creates the benefit of social contact and the chance to deepen friendships.
- *Technology.* New machines and methods may be utilized to add flexibility and to gain control over a full schedule. Banking, paying bills, and filing tax returns online can streamline these routine transactions.
- *Simplify.* Women should reduce nonessential activities and habits. Perfectionism is antithetical to simplicity, yet many are driven to be superwomen.

Living the principles of a balanced life by spending an hour or two per week on the things that matter most helps women manage stress, maintain responsibilities, and engage in self-care. Overdue for replenishment, but feeling pressured for time, women often respond by returning to patterns like juggling that place their health at risk. Accustomed to focusing on others to the exclusion of self, the thought of self-care may seem foreign. Balance is a difficult skill to master, although learning to successfully balance

TABLE 20.1 Self-Care Tracking

Self-Care Tracking		Week (Place a check or hash marks on days activity performed)						
Domains	Activity (List)	Sunday	Monday	Tuesday	Wednesday	Thursday	Friday	Saturday
Physical								
Emotional								
Spiritual								
Intellectual								
Social								
Relational								
Safety/security								
Daily totals								
Weekly grand total								

Journal

self-care with life responsibilities increases efficiency, maintains productivity, reduces stress, and leads to healthy living.

REFERENCES

Bandura, A., & Locke, E. A. (2003). Negative self-efficacy and goal effects revisited. *Journal of Applied Psychology, 88*(1), 87–99.

Berrigan, D., Dodd, K., Troiano, R. P., Krebs-Smith, S. M., & Barbash, R. B. (2003). Patterns of health behavior in U.S. adults. *Preventive Medicine, 36*(5), 615–623.

Binet, A., Simon, T., & Town, C. H. (1912). *A method of measuring the development of the intelligence of young children.* Lincoln, IL: Courier.

Blaine, B., & Crocker, J. (1995). Religiousness, race, and psychological well-being: Exploring social psychological mediators. *Personality and Social Psychology Bulletin, 21*(10), 1031–1041.

Brennan, J. F. (1997). *History and systems of psychology.* New Jersey: Prentice-Hall.

Brown, C. M. (2000). Exploring the role of religiosity in hypertension management among African Americans. *Journal of Health Care for the Poor and Underserved, 11*(1), 19–32.

Bylund, C. L., & Duck, S. (2004). The everyday interplay between family relationships and family members' health. *Journal of Social & Personal Relationship, 21*(1), 5–7.

Cameron, L. D., & Leventhal, H. (2003). Self-regulation, health, and illness. In L. D. Cameron, & H. Leventhal (Eds.), *The self-regulation of health and illness behaviour.* London: Routledge.

Casper, M. L. (2000). *Women and heart disease: An atlas of racial and ethnic disparities in mortality* (2nd ed.). Morgantown: Office for Social Environment and Health Research, West Virginia University.

Chang, V. W., Christakis, N. A., & Chang, V. W. (2003). Self-perception of weight appropriateness in the United States. *American Journal of Preventive Medicine, 24*(4), 332–339.

Clark, W. H. (1958). *The psychology of religion.* New York: Macmillan.

Conger, J. A. (1994). *Spirit at work: Discovering the spirituality in leadership.* San Francisco: Jossey-Bass.

Ensel, W. M., & Lin, N. (2004). Physical fitness and the stress process. *Journal of Community Psychology, 32*(1), 81–101.

Faulkner, G., & Biddle, S. J. H. (2004). Exercise and depression: Considering variability and contextuality. *Journal of Sport & Exercise Psychology, 26*(1), 3–18.

Finkelstein, E. A., Fiebelkorn, I. C., & Wang, G. (2004). State-level estimates of annual medical expenditures attributable to obesity. *Obesity Research, 12,* 18–24.

Frederickson, B. L. (2000). Cultivating positive emotions to cultivate health and well-being. *Prevention and Treatment.* Retrieved March 27, 2004, from http://www.journals.apat.org/prevention/volume3/pre0030001a.html

Gandhi, N., DePauw, K. P., Dolny, D. G., & Freson, T. (2002). Effect of an exercise program on quality of life of women with fibromyalgia. *Women & Therapy, 25*(2), 91–103.

Gardner, H. (1983). *Frames of mind: The theory of multiple intelligences.* New York: Basic Books.

Goleman, D. (1998). *Working with emotional intelligence.* New York: Bantam Books.

Groth-Marnat, G. (2001). The Wechsler intelligence scales. In A. S. Kaufman & N. L. Kaufman (Eds.), *Specific learning disabilities and difficulties in children and adolescents: Psychological assessment and evaluation.* New York: Cambridge University Press.

Hankinson, S. E., Colditz, G. A., Manson, J. E., & Speizer, F. E. (Eds.). (2001). *Healthy women, healthy lives: A guide to preventing disease from the landmark nurses' health study.* New York: Fireside.

Hartl, G. (1997). Obesity epidemic puts millions at risk from related diseases. *World Health Organization Press Release.* Retrieved April 10, 2004, from http://www.who.int/archives/inf-pr-1997/en/pr97-46.html

Henderson, K. A., & Ainsworth, B. E. (2003). A synthesis of perceptions about physical activity among older African American and American Indian women. *Journal of Public Health, 93*(2), 313–317.

Johnson, K. (1991). *Trusting ourselves: The complete guide to emotional well-being for women.* New York: Atlantic Monthly Press.

Jordan, J. V., Kaplan, A. G., Miller, J. B., Stiver, I. P., & Surrey, J. L. (1991). *Women's growth in connection: Writings from the stone center.* New York: Guilford Press.

Keleher, H. M., & Verrinder, G. K. (2003). Health diaries in a rural Australian study. *Qualitative Health Research, 14*(3), 435–443.

Kjelsas, E., Augestad, L. B., & Gotestam, K. G. (2003). Exercise dependence in physically active women. *European Journal of Psychiatry, 17*(3), 145–155.

Lederman, C. S., & Osofsky, J. D. (2004). Infant mental health interventions in juvenile court: Ameliorating the effects of maltreatment and deprivation. *Psychology, Public Policy, & Law, 10*(1–2), 162–177.

Matz, P. E., Foster, G. D., Faith, M. S., & Wadden, T. A. (2002). Correlates of body image dissatisfaction among overweight women seeking weight loss. *Journal of Consulting & Clinical Psychology, 70*(4), 1040–1044.

McCormick, D. W. (1994). Spirituality and management. *Journal of Managerial Psychology, 9*(6), 5–8.

Miller, A. M., & Iris, M. (2002). Health promotion attitudes and strategies in older adults. *Health Education and Behavior, 29*(2), 249–267.

Mokdad, A. H., Serdula, M. K., Dietz, W. H., Bowman, B. A., Marks, J. S., & Koplan, J. P. (1999). The spread of the obesity epidemic in the United States, 1991–1998. *Journal of the American Medical Association, 282*(16), 1519–1522.

Plasse, B. R. (2001). A stress reduction and self-care group for homeless and addicted women. *Social Work With Groups, 24*(3–4), 117–133.

Polinko, N. K., & Popovich, P. M. (2001). Evil thoughts but angelic actions: Responses to overweight job applicants. *Journal of Applied Social Psychology, 31*(5), 905–924.

Puhl, R., & Brownell, K. D. (2003). Ways of coping with obesity stigma: Review and conceptual analysis. *Eating Behaviors, 4*(1), 53–78.

Rapkin, A. (2003). A review of treatment of premenstrual syndrome and premenstrual dysphoric disorder. *Psychoneuroendocrinology, 28,* 39–53.

Resnick, B., & Nigg, C. (2003). Testing a theoretical model of exercise behavior for older adults. *Nursing Research, 52*(2), 80–88.

Roof, W. C. (1993). *A generation of seekers: The spiritual journeys of the baby boom generation.* San Francisco: HarperCollins.

Ross, C. E., & Mirowsky, J. (2002). Family relationships, social support and subjective life expectancy. *Journal of Health & Social Behavior, 43*(4), 469–489.

Roysamb, E., Tambs, K., Reichborn-Kjennerud, T., Neal, M. C., & Harris, J. R. (2003). Happiness and health: Environmental and genetic contributions to the relationship between subjective well-being, perceived health, and somatic illness. *Journal of Personality and Social Psychology, 85*(6), 213–228.

Sanderson, C. A., & Holloway, R. M. (2003). Who benefits from what? Drive for thinness as a moderator of responsiveness to different eating disorder prevention messages. *Journal of Applied Social Psychology, 33*(9), 1837–1861.

Shapiro, P. G. (2001). *Heart to heart: Deepening women's friendships at midlife.* Berkeley, CA: Berkeley Publishing Group.

Simon, A. E., Wardle, J., Jarvis, M. J., Steggles, N., & Cartwright, M. (2003). Examining the relationship between pubertal stage, adolescent health behaviours and stress. *Psychological Medicine, 33*(8), 1369–1379.

Stoll, O., & Alfermann, D. (2002). Effects of physical exercise on resources evaluation, bodyself-concept and well-being among older adults. *Anxiety, Stress, & Coping, 15*(3), 311–319.

Taylor, R. J., Chatters, L. M., Jayakody, R., & Levin, J. S. (1996). Black and white differences in religious participation: A multisample comparison. *Scientific Study of Religion, 35*(4), 403–410.

Taylor, S. W., Klein, L. C., Lewis, B. P., Gruenewald, T. L., Gurung, R. A. R., & Updegraff, J. A. (2000). Female responses to stress: Tend and befriend, not fight or flight. *Psychological Review, 107*(3), 411–429.

Zametkin, A. J., Zoon, C. K., Klein, H. W., & Munson, S. (2004). Psychiatric aspects of child and adolescent obesity: A review of the past 10 years. *Journal of the American Academy of Child & Adolescent Psychiatry, 43*(2), 134–150.

This chapter is organized around a simple premise: Sexuality is an integral component of psychological health. This claim is anchored in both theoretical and empirical scholarship. In 1986, the World Health Organization (WHO) issued a report that stated: "Sexuality influences thoughts, feelings, actions and interactions and thereby our mental and physical health" (Coleman, 2002). In 1994, the International Conference on Population and Development in Cairo declared that sexual health should be considered an important part of a person's physical and psychological well-being (Lottes & Adkins, 2003). Similarly, in 2001, the U.S. Surgeon General issued *A Call to Action to Promote Sexual Health and Responsible Sexual Behavior,* in which he proposed that sexuality goes beyond the physical aspects and includes emotional, mental, and interpersonal components as well (Satcher, 2001).

These positions reinforce a view that sexual health is inextricably bound to both physical and mental health over an individual's entire life span. To elucidate the relationships between sexuality and girls' and women's psychological health, we first explain the importance of viewing sexuality through a gendered lens and also clarify the meaning of sexuality and sexual health. We then review three arenas of research on women's sexuality that highlight the intersection of positive sexuality and psychological health: (a) mental and emotional health, (b) physical health, and (c) relational health. Finally, we describe recent attempts to apply existing knowledge in ways that promote sexual health among a range of groups.

GENDER, SEXUAL HEALTH, AND CULTURAL CONTEXT

When we consider sexuality and related topics, gender immediately surfaces as a primary feature. While it is fairly obvious that sex differences at the biological level help to explain some variation in sexual behavior and health, it is important to keep in mind that our bodies are not simple, deterministic systems ruling our sexual lives (Rossi, 1994). Socialization, personal experience, culture, and historical and political contexts are all part of the mix of our developing sexuality. In Western cultures, and in most cultures around

LUCIA F. O'SULLIVAN,
M. C. McCRUDDEN,
and DEBORAH L. TOLMAN

To Your Sexual Health! Incorporating Sexuality Into the Health Perspective

the world, girls and women's sexuality have been given short shrift, understood most often in the context of relationships to men. Instead of being seen as active sexual beings who have sexual desires and preferred sexual outcomes of their own, girls and women are often viewed as objects of male sexual attention and control.

In line with this perspective, researchers have found a nearly universal double standard that gives men greater sexual freedom and rights of sexual determination (Jackson & Cram, 2003). Conventional sexual standards require that women be sexually submissive, reluctant to engage in sexual interactions with men, but acquiescent to a primary and sole male sexual partner (O'Sullivan & Byers, 1992). This double standard inhibits women's sexual health practices because the characteristics of being socially desirable are in direct contradiction to the characteristics of being prepared and safe (Crawford & Popp, 2003). Across cultures and time, girls and women are actively discouraged from exploring their sexuality, seeking pleasure, or seizing their right to sexual expression and health. In some cultures, terrorizing tactics are used to prevent and punish perceived violation of these sexual standards. While never explicitly named as methods of social control, practices that suppress women's sexuality range from female genital mutilation and public death by stoning to high rates of physical, emotional, and sexual violence and coercion (Basile, 2002). Even today, young adolescent girls in Western urban cultures face sexual harassment, public denigration, and social isolation when they are perceived to have strayed from the restrictive parameters of appropriate sexual behavior (O'Sullivan & Meyer-Bahlburg, 2003).

It is important to bear in mind that women's and girls' sexual health can be compromised by gender inequality that is not specifically sexual in nature. Lack of education and limited financial and physical freedoms ultimately serve to strengthen the sexual double standard and diminish women's ability to make healthy or desirable choices. Because women have lower social status than men, they are often forced into positions of social, interpersonal and economic vulnerability that make it more difficult for them to access the treatment and support needed to safeguard their health (Amaro, Raj, & Reed,

2001). Marginalized women, such as ethnic minority, immigrant, impoverished, and sexual-minority women, are particularly vulnerable to positions of compromised access and powerlessness.

DEFINING SEXUAL HEALTH AND WELL-BEING

In 1975, WHO advanced the discourse on sexual health by defining it as: "The integration of the physical, emotional, intellectual and social aspects of sexual being in ways that are enriching and that enhance personality, communication and love" (Coleman, 2002). This conception of sexual health includes freedom of sexual expression, sexual pleasure and satisfaction, control over one's sexual and reproductive behavior, access to sexual information and health professionals, and freedom from abuse, fear, shame, guilt, false beliefs, and other psychological factors inhibiting sexuality. More recently, WHO expanded its concept of sexual health to include "the ongoing process of physical, psychological, and sociocultural well being in relation to sexuality" (Lottes, 2000).

Despite such comprehensive formulations at the theoretical level, in practice, conceptions of women's sexual health are more narrowly defined. Sexual health is often understood as the absence of suffering, dysfunction, or disease and is centered largely on reproductive aspects. Concepts of pleasure and desire have been largely avoided in favor of public or individual health concerns. Before the HIV/AIDS epidemic, research on sexuality was dominated by work addressing women's experiences of sexual coercion and girls' fertility-related behavior, particularly unwanted teenage pregnancy. While the use of these more constrained characterizations of sexual health have often produced useful and important work and services, they nonetheless serve to reinforce cultural narratives about women's sexualities that are ultimately inadequate and disempowering. While we cannot ignore the large body of research that has grown out of this more negative perspective of female sexual health, we have integrated it with the literature characterizing the more positive relationships between sexuality and psychological health for girls and women.

MENTAL AND EMOTIONAL HEALTH

There are a number of challenges inherent in any attempt to document the role that sexuality plays in girls' and women's mental and emotional well-being. One problem is the variety of ways to measure psychological health. In addition, studies on sexuality and well-being are relatively rare and they often exclude or underrepresent ethnic minority groups and those in nonheterosexual relationships. Finally, most of the work is correlational, which prevents us from drawing definitive conclusions about causality. Thus, we do not know if psychological health contributes to sexual health, if sexual health contributes to psychological health, or if there is a third factor that links them. At present, we lack the well-designed longitudinal studies that would make it possible to pull apart the multitude of factors that contribute to the experience of health and sexuality. As a result of these difficulties, the conclusions that can be drawn from the research are necessarily limited in strength and scope. In addition, a great deal of the research involving ethnic minority or other disenfranchised groups focus on problem outcomes, not normative experiences or healthy development. But, fortunately, there are number of things we do know and can summarize in some form here.

Studies indicate that sexuality is a central feature of women's lives, one that is linked to psychological health and life satisfaction. In a recent multiethnic study of midlife women, over two thirds of women indicated that sex was moderately to extremely important in their lives (Cain et al., 2003). Measures of quality of life are associated with sexual enjoyment and response, regardless of age or orientation (Apt, Hurlbert, Pierce, & White, 1996). In keeping with this finding, women with sexual dysfunctions score lower on quality of life measures compared to those with no sexual dysfunctions (McCabe, 1997). Associations between positive sexuality and quality of life have been found among all ages, including adolescents and the elderly (Dello Buono et al., 1998; McCabe & Cummins, 1998). Psychological

health is positively associated with measures of sexual pleasure, such as sexual satisfaction, orgasm frequency and consistency (Bancroft, Loftus, & Long, 2003; Brody, 2003). A longitudinal study of 500 heterosexual couples found that sexual desire, sexual satisfaction, and sexual frequency for women were associated with a range of psychological benefits (Hyde, DeLamater, & Hewitt, 1998). In an international study of sexuality and quality of life among elderly people, positive ratings of sexual activity and interest were associated with life satisfaction (Dello Buono et al., 1998). Positive sexuality and sexual experiences are also important components of life satisfaction among adolescents (McCabe & Cummins, 1998).

Research also indicates that happiness is positively associated with sexuality. In a study across five European countries, sex was found to be one of the four main causes of joy (Scherer, Walbott, & Summerfield, 1986). In the most comprehensive survey to date of sexual behavior in the U.S. population (the National Health and Social Life Survey; NHSLS), a greater frequency of sex was positively associated with being happy among women, whereas little or no sex was associated with being unhappy (Laumann, Gagnon, Michael, & Michaels, 1994). In addition, women who always or usually experienced orgasm during sexual interactions with their partner were substantially happier than were those who usually did not or never experienced orgasm. Researchers are also identifying the mechanisms by which sexual activity and mood interact. There is evidence that orgasm raises levels of certain hormones, such as oxytocin, which is associated with positive emotional and psychological states (Angier, 1999). In essence, this body of research has established that having pleasurable sexual experiences is related to a happy and satisfying life.

As one would expect, the association between mood and sexuality holds for negative emotions as well. Depressed mood is linked to lower sexual desire, lower frequency of intercourse, and lower sexual satisfaction and pleasure (Danaci, Oruc, Adiguezel, Yildirim, & Aydemir, 2003). Depression is also associated with higher levels of sexual problems, such as inhibited orgasm, sexual aversion, and sexual pain problems (Frohlich & Meston, 2002). A variety of mental health problems, ranging from anxiety and personality disorders to simple stress, are associated with elevated risk of sexual problems (Figueira, Possidente, Marques, & Hayes, 2001; Heiman, 2002). At the same time, positive ratings of sexual activity and interest for women are associated with an absence of depression and anxiety (Dello Buono et al., 1998).

A view that sexuality is linked to psychological dysfunction is demonstrated, with some controversy, by the inclusion of sexual dysfunctions in the *Diagnostic and Statistical Manual of Mental Disorders*, Fourth Edition (*DSM-IV*). *DSM-IV* female sexual dysfunctions include low levels of desire, inadequate arousal, lack of orgasm, and genital pain associated with sexual intercourse (Heiman, 2002). Although it is important that disturbances in women's sexuality are recognized as real problems that deserve attention, such medical classification of women's sexual complaints have potentially serious negative consequences (Tiefer, 2001b). Some contend that women's sexual distress may reflect other kinds of problems that medical labels and treatments can obscure, such as economic stress, relationship difficulties, or past sexual abuse (Kashak & Tiefer, 2002). Caution is warranted in applying sexual dysfunction labels because they inherently attempt to define what is normal and what is not. In doing this, we run the risk of stigmatizing or pathologizing women whose sexualities are different from the "norm" (Nicolson & Burr, 2003). In addition, some argue that the *DSM* classification system is based on a triphasic model of sexual response that assumes women's sexual responses mimic those of men. Thus, it may be inappropriate or erroneous to utilize the *DSM-IV* in evaluating female sexual function (Sugrue & Whipple, 2001).

As sexual health and psychological health appear intricately connected, those who face additional obstacles to their psychological well-being may be at increased risk for sexual problems. For example, lesbian and bisexual women are likely to endure to some greater or lesser extent social environments characterized by stigma, prejudice, and discrimination, which leads to strain, reduced quality of life, and coping difficulties (Meyer, 2003). In a nationally representative sample, homosexual minority women at midlife reported greater prevalence of generalized anxiety disorder compared to heterosexual women (Cochran, Sullivan, & Mays, 2003). Others have found higher rates of mood and anxiety disorders among sexual minority groups compared to their heterosexual counterparts (Sandfort, de Graaf, Bijl, & Schnabel, 2001). As expected, there are signs that having a positive lesbian/gay/bisexual identity and rejecting negative stereotypes about sexual orientation are associated with higher levels of psychological well-being (Luhtanen, 2003).

PHYSICAL HEALTH

Although they have yet to be clearly established, the pathways by which physical and sexual health interact are likely multiple, complex, and interrelated. Not surprisingly, sexual health is affected by physical health. Factors associated with good physical health, such as high levels of activity and energy, also serve as significant predictors of sexual satisfaction (McCabe & Taleporos, 2003). According to the NHSLS findings, people with poor physical health were somewhat more likely to have no sexual partners than were those with fair to excellent health (Laumann et al., 1994). Researchers have found that individuals with more severe physical impairments experience lower levels of sexual esteem and satisfaction compared to those with mild or no impairments (McCabe & Taleporos, 2003).

Sometimes, physical changes are linked to sexual health directly through biological mechanisms that affect the sex organs or less directly by physical symptoms, such as pain or fatigue. Other times a change in sexual health is more likely caused by the emotional, cognitive, or interpersonal effects of physical change. For example, a physical problem may contribute to lowered self-esteem, depression, and social withdraw, thus reducing opportunities for sexual development and expression.

A variety of specific physical health conditions are known to affect sexual functioning. Diabetes, blood pressure abnormalities, cardiovascular disease, epilepsy, Parkinson's disease, Alzheimer's disease, smoking, and multiple sclerosis are all associated with sexual problems (Heiman, 2002; Ross, 2002). In general, diseases of the neurological, vascular, and endocrine systems can all seriously impair sexual functioning, as can cancers. More specifically, strokes, brain injuries, and spinal-cord injuries have the potential to decrease sexual health (Sipski, 2002). In general, any illness or physical trauma that affects physical capabilities and mobility can have a negative impact. Treatments for different ailments can also compromise sexual health, especially drugs used to treat high blood pressure, cancer, and certain depression. Similarly, recreational drugs, such as barbiturates, narcotics, marijuana, alcohol, and even tobacco, can impair sexual functioning (Peugh & Belenko, 2001).

Natural physical changes associated with the process of aging may have an impact on sexual health. In some people, aging coincides with chronic illness and alterations of the body that affect sexual frequency and satisfaction. The decline in the production of estrogen that occurs during menopause is associated with several changes in the vagina, including thinning of the vaginal lining, that can make intercourse more difficult and uncomfortable (DeLamater & Friedrich, 2002).

However, it is important to note that these changes do not preclude having an active and satisfying sexual relationship in later life. In fact, sexual dysfunctions among women tend to decrease with age (Heiman, 2002). Cultural attitudes regarding midlife development likely have a greater impact on experiences than physical changes alone. White women often fear reaching menopause, as it represents a loss of attractiveness and value in society, whereas African American often view menopause as a normal, even welcome, part of life (Sampselle, Harris, Harlow, & Sowers, 2002). Fact, distress over midlife changes associated with menopause is significantly higher among White women than all other major ethnic groups in the United States (Bromberger et al., 2001). Little is known about whether lesbians may experience an increased risk of disease relative to heterosexual women, because aging lesbians constitute "an invisible minority" (Barker, 2004, p. 53). However, higher stress levels due to many years of discrimination and homophobia could be a factor yielding higher rates of stress-related behaviors, such as smoking and substance abuse, all of which have a detrimental impact on physical health (Barker, 2004).

RELATIONAL HEALTH

Sexual behavior most often occurs within the context of key relationships. Consequently, there are links between sexual health and "relational health." For example, both the physical and emotional dimensions of sexual satisfaction are related to the level of commitment within a relationship. The NHSLS found that an exclusive sexual relationship was associated with the highest rates of positive feelings, including pleasure, satisfaction, desire, and excitement (Laumann et al., 1994). Similarly, higher levels of sexual satisfaction were found among married women as compared to those who are cohabiting or single (Waite & Joyner, 2001). Women who had only one sexual partner in the past 12 months reported being happier than those who report no partners or more than one partner (Laumann et al., 1994). These findings suggest that sexual health for women may be more likely within the context of a loving, committed relationship.

Predictably, sexual health is also associated with general relationship satisfaction. Women who report high relationship satisfaction tend to report high levels of sexual satisfaction, desire, and frequency of sexual activity and orgasm (DeJudicibus & McCabe, 2002). Higher levels of relationship satisfaction and commitment are associated with higher sexual satisfaction (Sprecher, 2002). Longitudinal studies of relationship development indicate that the relationships of couples experiencing sexual dysfunctions or sexual dissatisfaction are more likely to break up than those not experiencing these problems (Rostosky, Galliher, Welsh, & Kawaguchi, 2000). These findings suggest that sexual satisfaction serves as a useful index at times of relationship satisfaction, and vice versa.

Unfortunately, the negative aspects of a relationship can also have an effect on health. Most obviously, sexual abuse and assault can compromise sexual and psychological health. Women who have been subjected to sexual coercion or abuse report higher rates of drug abuse, unhappiness, depression, and other mental problems (Roosa, Reyes, Reinholtz, & Angelini, 1998). They also suffer increased rates of sexual dysfunction and decreased levels of sexual well being (Oeberg, Fugl-Meyer, & Fugl-Meyer, 2002). Thus, the conceptual and theoretical links between psychological and sexual health are reinforced further.

IMPROVING SEXUAL HEALTH

History is replete with examples of attempts to modify women's, and especially girls,' sexual behavior in the interests of medical, psychological, social, and public health, yet few if any acknowledge the importance of enhancing positive sexuality in ways that reinforce healthy choices rather than curtailing expression and experience. Despite the evidence demonstrating that sexual health and psychological health are intricately linked, for the most part interventions have not adopted this view. For instance, a variety of interventions have been designed to reduce what has been called "the dreaded trilogy" of adolescent unprotected sex, pregnancy, and childbearing (Kirby, 2002). Such interventions tend to emphasize abstinence (without defining what that is) and just "saying no." The possibility that these decision pathways may have negative psychological consequences for adolescent girls and their development (Tolman, 2002) has not been explored because of the "missing discourse of desire" (Fine, 1988). There are countless HIV/AIDS interventions that focus almost exclusively on delaying indefinitely the onset of first sexual intercourse and reducing unprotected sexual intercourse occasions. Most are ineffective in promoting healthy outcomes, especially in the long term, and few provide the tools required to integrate health into their lives.

It is clear, however, which factors can be useful in terms of promoting sexual health. Researchers analyzed current sex education programs and derived 10 components. These include: talking about sex, culture and sexual identity, sexual anatomy and functioning, sexual health care and safer sex, challenges to sexual health, body image, masturbation and fantasy, positive sexuality, intimacy and relationships, and spirituality (Bean, Bockting, Rosser, Miner, & Coleman, 2002). These aspects are notably absent from almost all sex education programs available today (Kirby, 2002). U.S. policies and attitudes regarding adolescent sexuality have been focusing on sexual risks without taking into account the position of sexuality as a major and positive dimension of human development. Responsible public health policy should rely on scientific evidence of what works rather than emotional and moral views alone to truly counter risk behavior through education and health interventions (Ehrhardt, 1996).

There is a wealth of therapies designed over the years to improve sexual functioning, working from a deficit or dysfunction model. Few models exist solely to promote sexual functioning and experience. There is some speculation, however, that the field of sex therapy is stagnating while the field of couples therapy is expanding. Moreover, in recent years, sexual functioning has been increasingly narrowly construed by pharmaceutical companies as physical detriments (Kashak & Tiefer, 2002), obscuring the broader personal, social and cultural contexts that are critical for understanding both sexual health and psychological well-being. Tiefer (2001a) has argued that this perspective is harmful because it reduces sexuality to a mechanized, superficial arena appropriate for quick-fix, biomedical intervention. Sexual dysfunctions are complexly determined and intricately related to psychosocial dimensions of an individual's life (Heiman, 2002). Inadequate education, fatigue from overwork, and financial strain are all linked to higher levels of sexual dysfunction (Heiman, 2002; Laumann et al., 1994; Tiefer, 2001a,b). Outcome research indicates that there is little difference in the proliferation of methods and techniques designed to treat sex disorders—they are all fairly effective for the most part, across diagnoses, orientations, and ethnic groups (Donahey & Miller, 2000). Interestingly, generalization from couples therapy to sexual functioning is greater than generalization from sex therapy to couples functioning. To be effective and to advance women's needs and interests, comprehensive improvement of women and girls' sexual health must go beyond individual women's bodies to address the circumstances of their lives. Too often, however, these factors are neglected or overlooked altogether.

CONCLUSIONS

We have summarized the relatively small body of research that addresses the connections between women's sexual health and psychological well-being. More positive conceptions of girls' and women's sexuality will yield salient and useful research and treatment. Recognition of the diversity of experiences and circumstances in such efforts is vital for producing and providing information and care that will make a difference. A broad conception of sexual health needs to be at the core of these efforts. Researchers, educators, therapists, families, and policy makers can and must acknowledge how psychological health, physical health, sexual health, and relational health continuously interact within and between individuals in a dynamic, integrated system that has the potential to improve the health both of individuals and of our society.

REFERENCES

Amaro, H., Raj, A., & Reed, E. (2001). Women's sexual health: The need for feminist analyses in public health in the Decade of Behavior. *Psychology of Women Quarterly, 25,* 324–334.

Angier, N. (1999). *Woman: An intimate geography.* New York: Anchor Books.

Apt, C., Hurlbert, D. F., Pierce, A. P., & White, L. C. (1996). Relationship satisfaction, sexual characteristics and the psychosocial well-being of women. *The Canadian Journal of Human Sexuality, 5,* 195–210.

Bancroft, J., Loftus, J., & Long, J. S. (2003). Distress about sex: A national survey of women in heterosexual relationships. *Archives of Sexual Behavior, 32,* 193–208.

Barker, J. C. (2004). Lesbian aging: An agenda for social research. In G. Herdt & B. D. Vries (Eds.), *Gay and lesbian aging: Research and future directions* (pp. 29–72). New York: Springer.

Basile, K. C. (2002). Prevalence of wife rape and other intimate partner sexual coercion in a nationally representative sample of women. *Violence & Victims, 17,* 511–524.

Bean, B. B. E., Bockting, W. O., Rosser, B. R. S., Miner, M., & Coleman, E. (2002). The Sexual Health Model: Application of a sexological approach to HIV prevention. *Health Education Research, 17,* 43–57.

Brody, S. (2003). Concordance between women's physiological and subjective sexual arousal is associated with consistency of orgasm during intercourse but not other sexual behavior. *Journal of Sex & Marital Therapy, 29,* 15–23.

Bromberger, J. T., Meyer, P. M., Kravitz, H. M., Sommer, B., Cordal, A., Powell, L., et al. (2001). Psychologic distress and natural menopause: A multiethnic community study. *American Journal of Public Health, 91,* 1435–1442.

Cain, V. S., Johannes, C. B., Avis, N. E., Mohr, B., Schocken, M., Skurnick, J., et al. (2003). Sexual functioning and practices in a multi-ethnic study of midlife women: Baseline results from SWAN. *The Journal of Sex Research, 40,* 266–276.

Cochran, S. D., Sullivan, J. G., & Mays, V. M. (2003). Prevalence of mental disorders, psychological distress, and mental services use among lesbian, gay, and bisexual adults in the United States. *Journal of Consulting and Clinical Psychology, 71,* 53–61.

Coleman, E. (2002). Promoting sexual health and responsible sexual behavior: An introduction. *The Journal of Sex Research, 39,* 3–6.

Crawford, M., & Popp, D. (2003). Sexual double standards: A review and methodological critique of two decades of research. *The Journal of Sex Research, 40,* 13–26.

Danaci, A. E., Oruc, S., Adiguezel, H., Yildirim, Y., & Aydemir, O. (2003). Relationship of sexuality with psychological and hormonal features in the menopausal period. *West Indian Medical Journal, 52,* 27–30.

DeJudicibus, M. A., & McCabe, M. P. (2002). Psychological factors and the sexuality of pregnant and postpartum women. *The Journal of Sex Research, 39,* 94–103.

DeLamater, J. & Friedrich, W. N. (2002). Human sexual development. *The Journal of Sex Research, 39,* 10–14.

Dello Buono, M., Zaghi, P. C., Padoani, W., Scocco, P., Urciuoli, O., Pauro, P., et al. (1998). Sexual feelings and sexual life in an Italian sample of 335 elderly 65 to 106-year-olds. *Archives of Gerontology & Geriatrics,* (Suppl. 6), 155–162.

Donahey, K. M., & Miller, S. D. (2000). Applying a common factors perspective to sex therapy. *Journal of Sex Education & Therapy, 25,* 221–230.

Ehrhardt, A. A. (1996). Our view of adolescent sexuality: A focus on risk behavior without the developmental context. *American Journal of Public Health, 86,* 1523–1525.

Figueira, I., Possidente, E., Marques, E., & Hayes, K. (2001). Sexual dysfunction: A neglected complication of panic disorder and social phobia. *Archives of Sexual Behavior, 30,* 369–377.

Fine, M. (1988). Sexuality, schooling and adolescent females: The missing discourse of desire. *Harvard Educational Review, 58,* 29–53.

Frohlich, P., & Meston, C. (2002). Sexual functioning and self-reported depressive symptoms among college women. *The Journal of Sex Research, 39,* 321–325.

Heiman, J. R. (2002). Sexual dysfunction: Overview of prevalence, etiological factors, and treatments. *The Journal of Sex Research, 39,* 73–78.

Hyde, J. S., DeLamater, J. D., & Hewitt, E. C. (1998). Sexuality and the dual-earner couple: Multiple roles and sexual functioning. *Journal of Family Psychology, 12,* 354–368.

Jackson, S. M., & Cram, F. (2003). Disrupting the sexual double standard: Young women's talk about heterosexuality. *British Journal of Social Psychology, 42,* 113–127.

Kashak, E., & Tiefer, L. (Eds.). (2002). *A new view of women's sexual problems.* Binghamton, NY: Haworth Press.

Kirby, D. (2002). Effective approaches to reducing adolescent unprotected sex, pregnancy, and childbearing. *The Journal of Sex Research, 39,* 51–57.

Laumann, E. O., Gagnon, J. H., Michael, R. T., & Michaels, S. (1994). *The social organization of sexuality: Sexual practices in the United States.* Chicago: University of Chicago Press.

Lottes, I. L. (2000). New views on sexual health: The case of Finland. In I. Lottes & O. Kontula (Eds.), *New perspectives on sexual health* (pp. 7–28). Helsinki: The Population Research Institute of the Family Federation of Finland.

Lottes, I. L., & Adkins, C. W. (2003). The construction and psychometric properties of an instrument measuring support for sexual rights. *The Journal of Sex Research, 40,* 286–295.

Luhtanen, R. K. (2003). Identity, stigma management, and well-being: A comparison of lesbians/bisexual women and gay/bisexual men. *Journal of Lesbian Studies, 7,* 85–100.

McCabe, M. P. (1997). Intimacy and quality of life among sexually dysfunctional men and women. *Journal of Sex & Marital Therapy, 23,* 276–290.

McCabe, M. P., & Cummins, R. A. (1998). Sexuality and quality of life among young people. *Adolescence, 33,* 761–773.

McCabe, M. P., & Taleporos, G. (2003). Sexual esteem, sexual satisfaction, and sexual behavior among people with physical disability. *Archives of Sexual Behavior, 32,* 359–369.

Meyer, I. H. (2003). Prejudice, social stress, and mental health in lesbian, gay, and bisexual populations: Conceptual issues and research evidence. *Psychological Bulletin, 129,* 674–697.

Nicolson, P., & Burr, J. (2003). What is "normal" about women's (hetero)sexual desire and orgasm?: A report of an in-depth interview study. *Social Science & Medicine, 57,* 1735–1745.

Oeberg, K., Fugl-Meyer, K. S., and Fugl-Meyer, A. R. (2002). On sexual well-being in sexually abused Swedish women: Epidemiological aspects. *Sexual and Relationship Therapy, 17,* 329–342.

O'Sullivan, L. F., & Byers, E. S. (1992). College students' incorporation of initiator and restrictor roles in sexual dating interactions. *The Journal of Sex Research, 29,* 435–446.

O'Sullivan, L. F., & Meyer-Bahlburg, H. F. L. (2003). African American and Latina inner-city girls' reports of romantic and sexual development. *Journal of Social & Personal Relationships, 20,* 221–238.

Peugh, J., & Belenko, S. (2001). Alcohol, drugs and sexual function: A review. *Journal of Psychoactive Drugs, 33,* 223–232.

Roosa, M. W., Reyes, L., Reinholtz, C., & Angelini, P. J. (1998). Measurement of women's child sexual abuse experiences: An empirical demonstration of choice of measure on estimates of incidence rates and of relationships with pathology. *The Journal of Sex Research, 35,* 225–233.

Ross, M. W. (2002). Sexuality and health challenges: Responding to a public health imperative. *Journal of Sex Research, 39,* 7–9.

Rossi, A. S. (1994). *Sexuality across the life course.* Chicago: University of Chicago Press.

Rostosky, S. S., Galliher, R. V., Welsh, D. P., & Kawaguchi, M. C. (2000). Sexual behaviors and relationship qualities in late adolescent couples. *Journal of Adolescence, 23,* 583–597.

Sampselle, C. M., Harris, V., Harlow, S. D., & Sowers, M. (2002). Midlife development and menopause in African American and Caucasian women. *Health Care for Women International, 23,* 351–363.

Sandfort, T. G. M., de Graaf, R., Bijl, R. V., & Schnabel, P. (2001). Same-sex sexual behavior and psychiatric disorders: Findings from the Netherlands mental health survey and incidence study (NEMESIS). *Archives of General Psychiatry, 58,* 85–91.

Satcher, D. (2001). *The Surgeon General's Call to Action to Promote Sexual Health and Responsible Sexual Behavior.* Washington, DC: U.S. Department of Health and Human Services.

Scherer, K. R., Walbott, H. G., & Summerfield, A. B. (1986). *Experiencing emotion.* Cambridge: Cambridge University Press.

Sipski, M. L. (2002). Central nervous system based neurogenic female sexual dysfunction: Current status and future trends. *Archives of Sexual Behavior, 31,* 421–424.

Sprecher, S. (2002). Sexual satisfaction in premarital relationships: Associations with satisfaction, love, commitment, and stability. *The Journal of Sex Research, 39,* 190–196.

Sugrue, D. P., & Whipple, B. (2001). The consensus-based classification of female sexual dysfunction: Barriers to universal acceptance. *Journal of Sex and Marital Therapy, 27,* 221–226.

Tiefer, L. (2001a). A new view of women's sexual problems: Why new? Why now? *The Journal of Sex Research, 38,* 89–96.

Tiefer, L. (2001b). The selling of "female sexual dysfunction." *Journal of Sex and Marital Therapy, 27,* 625–628.

Tolman, D. (2002). *Dilemmas of desire: Teenage girls talk about sexuality.* Cambridge, MA: Harvard University Press.

Waite, L., & Joyner, K. (2001). Emotional and physical satisfaction with sex in married, cohabiting, and dating sexual unions: Do men and women differ? In E. O. Laumann & R. T. Michael (Eds.), *Sex, love, and health in America: Private choices and public polices* (pp. 239–269). Chicago: University of Chicago Press.

An emphasis on giving to others and putting others first has long been considered a part of the traditional gender-role message for women in this culture. This gender-role message has both positive and negative consequences. While there are many satisfactions to be gained from helping others, in its exaggerated traditional form, giving to others may lead to depression and loss of self (Hare-Mustin, 1983). Many women are so busy giving to others that they have no time for themselves. By contrast, balanced forms of giving (for example, as in the case of feminist mentoring) typically involve reciprocal relationships in which both giving and receiving are experienced, leading to more satisfying interchanges. Giving is also something that women can do across the life span. For example, women, teens, and even quite young girls can give as a sign of power and strength to others and a signal to themselves of well-being. Even very young children can help their mothers with simple household tasks and can build pleasure in their sense of competence. Many elderly women continue to be able to give, despite infirmity. Giving can involve many kinds of resources, such as time, skills, money, another pair of hands, expertise, a willing ear, an attitude of responsiveness, and generosity. It involves the self perception that one has something of value to give. Giving is also consistent with the cultural values of many communal groups (such as certain Asian or African cultures), where providing for the group's well-being is of more importance than is focusing on individual needs.

This chapter considers common definitions of giving and reviews empirical findings about the characteristics of those who give (specifically, the relationship between gender and giving). The chapter also examines the impact of gender-role socialization on learning to give, examines the positive and negative effects of giving, and concludes with solutions for a healthier balance.

DEFINITIONS OF GIVING AND ALTRUISM

Giving as a formal activity comes primarily from the field of philanthropy. Charitable contributions in the United States are reported to exceed

MICHELE HARWAY
and ROBERTA L. NUTT

Women and Giving

$50 billion annually and over 80 million people volunteer more than 20 billion hours of their time annually helping others (Batson, 1995). Used colloquially, the term "giving" has encompassed a variety of ways of helping others, including both concrete and abstract manifestations. Within psychology, giving has been studied within the purview of research on altruism, helping, empathy, and prosocial behavior. Because these terms are closely related, we consider each concept as it impacts the construction of giving in this chapter.

In the century and a half since the term was coined by August Comte (1851/1875), altruism has been studied from a variety of perspectives. More recently, Batson (1991) indicated that "Altruism is a motivational state with the ultimate goal of increasing another's welfare" (p. 6). Discussions in the professional literature have revolved around whether altruism involves self-sacrifice, whether it can ever include self-benefit, and how it differs from egoism. According to Batson, two variables need to be considered to examine altruism: the outcomes of giving (that is, whether it serves primarily to relieve another's suffering or to receive self-benefits) and the nature of the motive (whether egoism or altruism are intended or unintended consequences). Thus when relieving someone else's suffering is the ultimate goal, then the behavior is considered to be altruistic.

Altruism has also been examined in relation to the concepts of empathy and helping. Batson (1995) noted that "feeling empathy for a person in need evokes altruistic motivation to help that person" (p. 373) and "leads to increased helping of that person" (p. 356). That is, Batson noted that empathy leads to helping when compassion and other related emotions are aroused. The process may involve four factors: perception of another in need, adopting the perspective of the person in need, being willing to help someone to whom one is attached, and the internal response of empathic emotion. There may be two different types of emotions evoked by perceiving someone in need: these are personal distress and empathy (Batson, Fultz, Schoenrade, & Paduano, 1987). Empathy in children has been linked to perspective taking and to helpfulness (based on teacher rating; Litvack-Miller, McDougall, & Romney, 1997) and lack of empathy to a variety of antisocial behaviors.

WHO GIVES?

Social psychologists have also explored what factors may be related to the likelihood of responding altruistically and have speculated about the existence of an altruistic personality. There may be several personality variables associated with a general predisposition to help (Staub, 1974). For example, Staub suggests that "people with a prosocial orientation, may under conditions which still need to be further specified, be willing to endure greater sacrifices and to give up more of their self-interest for the sake of others" (p. 36). Altruism or an altruistic personality is described by Rushton (1980), who claimed that some individuals are consistently more willing to help others and that "there is a 'trait' of altruism" (p. 66). Altruism is assumed to be a universal phenomenon cutting across ethnic and racial groups.

Gender and Giving

Gender has been described as a key factor in the desire to help others (Batson, 1991). In exploring the link between gender and altruistic behavior, several studies link gender, empathy, and helping behavior. When nursery schoolchildren were shown slides or told stories to elicit different emotions, girls reacted more empathically to the protagonists portrayed in the slides and stories than did boys (Hunt, 1990). When fifth and sixth graders were asked to reach out to hospitalized children, girls wrote more letters, made more toys, and donated more gift certificates than did boys (Hunt, 1990). In peer ratings of altruism among fifth graders, girls were also rated as more altruistic by their peers than were boys, but boys were more often selected by both sexes for "masculine items" while girls were selected more often for "feminine" and gender-neutral items (Zarbatany, Hartmann, Gelfand, & Vinciguerra, 1985). In contrast, Carr (2000) found that both genders helped at relatively high rates in his study of undergraduate students.

In support of the importance of gender-role socialization on helping behavior, there is some evidence that by adulthood, men are more willing to help in risky or physically strenuous situations whereas women are more likely to help in situations thought to require "the female touch" (Hunt, 1990). Studies suggests that men help more with car trouble (West, Whitney, & Schnedler, 1975) or with carrying laundry (Dovidio, 1993), whereas women are more willing to help fold the laundry. Masculine helping traits include being daring, forceful, and directed toward anyone who is deserving, while feminine helping traits include being nurturing, supportive, and directed primarily to family and friends (Eagly & Crowley, 1986). A number of other studies (Otten, Penner, & Waugh, 1988) demonstrated that women are more willing to help with emotional support and informal counseling on personal problems than are men. In studies of emergency aid, where men have generally been shown to help more than women, women are more likely to help than are men when the person in need is a friend (McGuire, 1994).

HOW IS GIVING LEARNED?

Girls and women learn to be givers, caretakers, and self-sacrificing through a variety of socialization sources. Three major theoretical paradigms have typically been used to explain gender-role development: social learning theory utilizing traditional classical and operant conditioning as well as observation (Bandura, 1986), cognitive development theory in which children learn the rules for their gender's behavior and adopt a gender identity (Cowan & Hoffman, 1986), and social role theory (Eagly, 1987), which carries gender typing into adulthood. Girls are reinforced for giving, observe giving in adult women around them, and learn that girls and women are supposed to be nice and helpful.

The messages for girls and women to be giving, caretaking, and self-sacrificing come from a number of sources. Parents and other family members are usually the source of the earliest expectations (Golombok & Fivrish, 1994). Mothers expect girls to be better behaved than boys and parents continue to demonstrate gender stereotyped beliefs about their children from birth onward (Karraker, Vogel, & Lake, 1995). Mothers model gender-appropriate roles for their daughters and expect their children to engage in similar behavior (Weisner, Garnier, & Loucky, 1994). Par-

ents also send children messages about expected behavior via the decor of their rooms and the toys they provide (Miller, 1987), with dolls for girls sending clear messages about caregiving and nurturing. Chores assigned to girls and boys also differ, with girls' chores involving caregiving tasks such as cleaning, meal preparation, caring for younger siblings, and laundry (Antill, Goodnow, Russell, & Cotton, 1996). Similarly, books chosen for children by parents or other sources often depict girls as helpers rather than leaders. Girls generally appear in supporting or helping roles and are seldom independent and brave (Odean, 1997).

Children's peer groups are another source of gender role influence. Children from the ages of 2 or 3 until middle childhood prefer to play with children of the same sex (Powlishta, 1995). Same-sex peers have been shown to have a powerful influence and tend to reinforce gender appropriate behavior (Goodenough, 1990).

All forms of media (television, radio, newspapers, music, magazines, advertisements, etc.) predominantly show women and men, girls and boys in stereotypic roles with stereotypic personality and behavior (Davis, 1990). Women are frequently portrayed as caretakers, servers, mothers (Olson & Douglas, 1997), and helpers (Signorielli, 1989). The effect of media presentations on attitudes is well documented (Abrams, 2003).

Schools and teachers have also been considered as sources of gender-role socialization and bias, with Meece (1987) calling teachers the "hidden carriers of society's gender role stereotyping" (p. 58). Teachers have been observed to treat girls and boys differently and female teachers have modeled traditional gender roles such as being supportive and helpful (Sadker & Sadker, 1994).

Finally, a number of religions have had a stereotypic gender-role influence on children and adults (Wilson & Musick, 1995). Women are frequently taught that their roles are nurturing and supportive and family-based (Carmody, 1989). For example, scriptural references to women are often misinterpreted to mean helpmate, or server to men (Mollenkott, 1984). Even though feminist scholars may dispute the patriarchal interpretation of the text, be it Bible, Koran, or Torah, many organized religions have treated women as in the service of their husbands (Hekmat, 1997).

EFFECTS OF GIVING

The effects on women for behavior seen as giving, be it helping, altruism, mentoring, caretaking, or any prosocial action, can be either positive or negative in that it can create good feelings about the self that raise esteem or it can deplete personal energy and resources. The value of the behavior depends upon levels of satisfaction derived, the context (where? for whom?), and the personal cost of the activity.

The positive aspects of giving are well documented in the psychological literature (Batson, 1991; Schroeder, Penner, Dovidio, & Piliavin, 1995). In fact, one group of researchers explained helping or altruism by developing the empathic joy hypothesis (Smith, Keating, & Stotland, 1989), meaning that helping gives the helper joy or good feelings about the act. Being helpful to others can both give the helper feelings of pleasure and worth and increase self-esteem (Nadler & Fisher, 1986).

One of the "most fundamental roles to the image of women is that of caregiver, especially of children . . . [and also] partners, parents, friends, and neighbors, or through volunteer work" (Yoder, 2003, p. 179). Hence, a woman with traditional values can find satisfaction in fulfilling her assigned role, plus she may well be praised by others for being "a good woman"—a measure of recognition. Volunteer work has often been viewed as a way to make a contribution to society (Clary & Snyder, 1999) and has been strongly encouraged by families, churches, politicians, etc., particularly for women. Nurturing others, both children and adults, promotes growth and development for the helper by satisfying needs for altruism, which yields feelings of satisfaction and contribution (Donelson, 1984). While research has demonstrated overlap between women and men in helping behaviors (as described earlier), varying greatly by context (Eagly, 1987; Eagly & Crowley, 1986), most cultures still expect women to be responsible for family and other caregiving, even as they add new roles to their lives (Kuchner, 1999). These expectations can extend to caring for elderly parents and in-laws after children have grown and left the home (Kuchner, 1999).

The negative effects of giving for women occur when the giving becomes self-sacrifice, depletes the resources of the giver, and creates loss of self. For example, although nurturing and caring for children can give women pleasure from feeling they are doing something of great social value, the demands of children and loss of freedom and personal space can create frustration and dissatisfaction (Thompson & Walker, 1989). Duffy (1991) coined the term "conflict of nurturance" to describe the conflict she observed in women in caring for others at the cost of attending to their own needs. Long-term effects of lack of self-care include: loss of self-awareness, the development of distrust of self, the silencing of personal voice or self-expression, and depression (Duffy, 1991). In her classic article on women and mental health, Rachel Hare-Mustin (1983) wrote "that the demands of traditional sex roles lead to more problems for women than men. Certain aspects of women's sex roles may influence the development of mental illness, such as . . . behaving to satisfy a male partner . . . and other-directedness" (p. 595).

The concept of self-silencing may be part of the negative effects of giving if behaving to satisfy traditional roles causes the woman to lose her voice and therefore her self-identity. In developing a scale to measure silencing of self in women, Jack (1991), labeled one of her four subscales as "care as self-sacrifice." Items of this subscale support the belief that success in interpersonal relationships requires consistently putting the needs of others before one's own (Miller & Stiver, 1997). Self-silencing has been hypothesized to contribute to lowered self-esteem, self-alienation, and depression (Dill & Anderson, 1999; Jack, 1991). In the 1980s, the term *codependency* was applied to women to describe this self-harming overconcern for the needs of others, which Cowan, Bommersbach, and Curtis (1995) have demonstrated to be related to feeling less powerful and less in charge of life. Codependency is damaging to women because it is agentic, or instrumental traits more typically found in males (rather than communal and expressive traits) that are related to high self-esteem (Blackman & Funder, 1996). Women are expected to give their husbands and others in their lives emotional support—listen to problems and try to help, yielding a situation of high demands and little control—creating stress that fosters depression (Barnett & Baruch, 1987).

FINDING BALANCE

Since not all forms of giving are deleterious to a woman's mental health and self-esteem, what is key to the ability to continue doing so without negative consequences? Giving must be balanced with activities that replenish women's psychic batteries. Feminist mentoring, described below, is an example of how a one-sided giving relationship can be transformed into one in which giving and receiving are mutual. Following the description of feminist mentoring, other examples of activities that may help women attain balance are proposed.

Feminist Mentoring: An Example of the Positive Effects of Giving

Mentoring relationships that focus on the reciprocal nature of the mentoring arrangement and its impact on the mentor as well as the mentee have been labeled feminist mentoring (Harway, 2001). This type of mentoring, which is characterized by mutuality, respect, collaboration, awareness of power relationships, and giving voice to the mentee, is not necessarily gendered, nor do participants necessarily have to consider themselves feminists to participate. Feminist mentoring relationships have several characteristics that contribute to their having a positive impact on the giver as well as on the recipient. Because they place great value on collaborative endeavors and on mutual respect for each person's knowledge and feelings, the giver is as likely as the recipient to receive benefits from the relationship. Feminist mentoring relationships are nonhierarchical, and as a result the mentee is encouraged to express her perspective. Feminist mentoring relationships are built on a belief in the importance of relationships. Also important to these types of mentoring interactions is an analysis and understanding of the impact of power politics in the workplace, in the mentoring relationship itself, and in the surrounding culture.

One of the most important aspects of feminist mentoring is that the mentor receives as much as she gives. Some of what the mentor receives is a collegial relationship that the mentor might other-wise lack (for example, if she is working in a White male-dominated environment). The mentor also benefits from the assistance the mentee may provide with tasks that the mentor is unable or unwilling to do, thereby increasing the mentor's productivity. Mentees may also develop creative professional ideas that contribute to both the mentor and the mentee's professional development. There is much to learn also from a mentee, learning which may not necessarily relate to the workplace but may come from areas of expertise or personal strengths unique to the mentee. Along with the opportunity to provide the support that she herself may not have received, the mentor may benefit from the appreciation, respect, and friendship that the mentee provides. Thus, feminist mentoring relationships represent one type of an ideal giving relationship.

On the cautionary side, women often are expected to do more than their share of mentoring. Although they may want to do such mentoring, it can be to the detriment of their productivity in other areas. This is also often true for prospective mentors of color. However, come time for promotion, it is still the worker's productivity that counts most for advancement (e.g., research and writing in academic settings; Creamer, 1998). Herein lies another example of the downside of giving for women. When feminist mentors who are also women, they may have difficulty with the reciprocal nature of the feminist mentoring relationship because they are socialized to give and to put their own needs aside. Mentors must therefore carefully monitor their own reactions and behavior and strive for balance in the mentoring relationship. The model provided by feminist mentoring is a collaborative one that can be useful to maintaining a balanced give and take relationship in many different contexts (for example, in mentoring inner city youngsters).

Attaining Balance in Other Ways

Women have much to gain by putting themselves in situations in which they receive focused attention. For example, women can attain balance by participating in psychotherapy or pursuing degrees in higher education, they are recipients of others' giving.

Individual psychotherapy provides a woman with a dedicated period to focus on herself and her needs. Because of the nature of the psychotherapeutic relationship, a woman client has no responsibility to take care of or give to the therapist. Thus, involvement in such a relationship over the long term can help her refocus her caregiving tendencies to her own needs. In a group therapy setting a woman may learn the impact that an exaggerated need for caregiving may have on her and on others. She may also learn the importance of achieving balance by observing other women who give until it hurts. She may realize in psychotherapy the importance of "putting on her own oxygen mask first" (Harway & Carlson, 1994). The quoted statement refers to the message given on all passenger planes that in the case of an emergency, when oxygen is necessary, individuals must put on their own oxygen mask in order to remain sufficiently functional to be able to help others survive. Similarly, women in therapy learn the importance of nourishing themselves in order to be able to continue giving to others. Therapy with a mental health professional who is knowledgeable about gender-role socialization and who is willing to guide a woman in a focused questioning of traditional gender roles also may contribute to realigning the give-receive balance. Finally, a woman can take the time to seek out help for herself, which provides a powerful message that she deserves some time focused uniquely on herself.

Pursuing higher education is another important act of balance for a woman. Many women abandoned early plans to obtain an education when they married or had children. Choosing to pursue educational opportunities later in life is a powerful entitlement statement for women. Doing so may require adjustments in the family, as Mom may not be as available to do traditional domestic chores while she is in school. Her lack of availability may require a reorganization of priorities both on her part and on the part of her family members. After an initial period of adjustment, most families are likely to thrive as individual members grow from learning new responsibilities and skills.

Finally, becoming involved in political advocacy can provide balance and satisfying involvement that helps a woman replenish and restore.

By becoming active in social issues that will ultimately impact other women and herself, a woman's giving needs are channeled in socially desirable and influential ways.

REFERENCES

Abrams, L. (2003). Contextual variations in young women's gender identity negotiations *Psychology of Women Quarterly, 27*, 64–74.

Antill, J. K., Goodnow, J. J., Russell, G., & Cotton, S. (1996). The influence of parents and family context on children's involvement in household tasks. *Sex Roles, 34*, 215–236.

Bandura, A. (1986). *Social foundations of thought and action: A social cognitive theory.* Englewood Cliffs, NJ: Prentice-Hall.

Barnett, R. C., & Baruch, G. K. (1987). Social roles, gender, and psychological stress. In R. C. Barnett, L. Biener, & G. K. Baruch (Eds.), *Gender and stress* (pp. 122–143). New York: Free Press.

Batson, C. D. (1991). *The altruism question: Toward a social-psychological answer.* Hillsdale, NJ: Erlbaum.

Batson, C. D. (1995). Prosocial motivation: Why do we help others? In A. Tesser (Ed.), *Advanced social psychology.* Boston: McGraw-Hill.

Batson, C. D., Fultz, C., Schoenrade, P. A., & Paduano, A. I. (1987). Critical self reflection and self perceived altruism: When self-reward fails. *Journal of Personality and Social Psychology, 55*, 594–602.

Blackman, M. C., & Funder, D. C. (1996). Self-esteem as viewed from the outside: A peer and gender perspective. *Journal of Social Behavior and Personality, 11*, 115–126.

Carmody, D. L. (1989). *Women and world religions.* Nashville, TN: Abingdon.

Carr, D. A. (2000). The effects of individual differences and situational influences on goal-directed prosocial motivation. *Dissertation Abstracts International: Section B: The Sciences & Engineering, 61*(4-B), October 2000, 2269.

Clary, E. G., & Snyder, M. (1999). The motivations to volunteer: Theoretical and practical considerations. *Current Directions in Psychological Science, 8*, 156–159.

Comte, I. A. (1851/1875). *System of positive policy* (Vol. 1). London: Longmans, Green & Co.

Cowan, G., Bommersbach, M., & Curtis, S. R. (1995). Codependency, loss of self, and power. *Psychology of Women Quarterly, 19*, 221–236.

Cowan, G., & Hoffman, C. D. (1986). Gender stereotyping in young children: Evidence to support a concept learning approach. *Sex Roles, 14*, 211–224.

Creamer, E. G. (1998). Assessing faculty publication productivity: Issues of equity. ERIC DIGEST, ERIC Clearinghouse on higher education: Washington, DC [BBB15669], George Washington University,

Washington, DC, Graduate School of Education and Human Development [BBB32577].

Davis, D. M. (1990). Portrayals of women in prime-time network television: Some demographic characteristics. *Sex Roles, 23*, 325–332.

Dill, D., & Anderson, C. A. (1999). Loneliness, shyness, and depression: The etiology and interrelationships of everyday problems in living. In T. Joiner & J. C. Coyne (Eds.), *The interactional nature of depression: Advances in interpersonal approaches* (pp. 93–125). Washington, DC: American Psychological Association.

Donelson, E. (1984). *Nurture.* Philadelphia: Westminster Press.

Dovidio, J. F. (1993, October). Androgyny, sex roles, and helping. Paper presented at the meeting of the Society of Experimental Social Psychology, Santa Barbara, CA.

Duffy, V. J. (1991). *The conflict of nurturance for women: Implications for self-esteem and depression.* Doctoral dissertation, University of Rochester.

Eagly, A. H. (1987). *Sex differences in social behavior: A social role interpretation.* Hillsdale, NJ: Erlbaum.

Eagly, A. H., & Crowley, M. (1986). Gender and helping behavior: A meta-analytic review of the social psychological literature. *Psychological Bulletin, 100*, 283–308.

Golombok, S., & Fivrish, R. (1994). *Gender development.* Cambridge: Cambridge University Press.

Goodenough, R. G. (1990). Situational stress and sexist behavior among young children. In P. R. Sanday & R. G. Goodenough (Eds.), *Beyond the second sex* (pp. 225–252). Philadelphia: University of Pennsylvania Press.

Hare-Mustin, R. T. (1983). An appraisal of the relationship between women and psychotherapy: 80 years after the case of Dora. *American Psychologist, 38*, 593–601.

Harway, M. (2001). Mentoring and feminist mentoring. In J. Worell (Ed.), *The encyclopedia of women and gender: Sex similarities and differences and the impact of society on gender* (pp. 743–748). San Diego, CA: Academic Press.

Harway, M., & Carlson, K. (1994, March). The impact of motherhood on midcareer professional women Paper presented at the Midwinter Meeting of Divisions 29, 42 and 43, Scottsdale, AZ.

Hekmat, A. (1997). *Women and the Koran.* Amherst, NY: Prometheus Books.

Hunt, M. (1990). *The compassionate beast: What science is disclosing about the humane side of humankind.* New York: William Morrow.

Jack, D. C. (1991). *Silencing the self: Women and depression.* Cambridge, MA: Harvard University Press.

Karraker, K. H., Vogel, D. A., & Lake, M. A. (1995). Parents' gender-stereotyped perceptions of newborns: The eye of the beholder revisited. *Sex Roles, 33*, 687–701.

Kuchner, J. F. (1999). The sandwich generation: Women's roles as multi-generational caregivers. In C. Forden, A. E. Hunter, & B. Birns (Eds.), *Read-*

ings in the psychology of women: Dimensions of the female experience (pp. 231–241). Boston: Allyn & Bacon.

Litvack-Miller, W., McDougall, D., & Romney, D. M. (1997). The structure of empathy during middle childhood and its relationship to prosocial behavior. *Genetic Social and Genetic Psychology Monographs, 123*, 303–324.

McGuire, A. M. (1994). Helping behaviors in the natural environment: Dimensions and correlates of helping. *Personality and Social Psychology Bulletin, 20*, 45–56.

Meece, J. L. (1987). The influence of school experiences on the development of gender schemata. *New Directions for Child Development, 38*, 57–73.

Miller, C. L. (1987). Qualitative differences among gender-stereotyped toys: Implications for cognitive and social development in girls and boys. *Sex Roles, 16*, 473–488.

Miller, J. B., & Stiver, I. P. (1997). *The healing connection: How women form relationships in therapy and in life.* Boston: Beacon Press.

Mollenkott, V. R. (1984). *The divine feminine: The biblical imagery of God as female.* Lavergne, TN: Crossroad.

Nadler, A., & Fisher, J. D. (1986). The role of threat to self-esteem and perceived control in recipient reactions to help: Theory development and empirical validation. In L. Berkowitz (Ed.), *Advances in experimental social psychology* (Vol. 19, pp. 81–123). New York: Academic Press.

Odean, K. (1997). *Great books for girls.* New York: Ballantine.

Olson, B., & Douglas, W. (1997). The family on television: Evaluation of gender roles in situation comedy. *Sex Roles, 36*, 409–427.

Otten, C. A., Penner, L. A., & Waugh, G. (1988). What are friends for: The determinants of psychological helping. *Journal of Social and Clinical Psychology, 7*, 34–41.

Powlishta, K. K. (1995). Gender bias in children's perceptions of personality traits. *Sex Roles, 32*, 17–28.

Rushton, J. P. (1980). *Altruism, socialization and society.* Englewood Cliffs, NJ: Prentice-Hall.

Sadker, M., & Sadker, D. (1994). *Failing at fairness: How America's schools cheat girls.* New York: Scribner's.

Schroeder, D. A., Penner, L. A., Dovidio, J. F., & Piliavin, J. A. (1995). *The psychology of helping and altruism.* New York: McGraw-Hill.

Signorielli, N. (1989). Television and concepts about sex roles: Maintaining conventionality and the status quo. *Sex Roles, 21*, 341–360.

Smith, K. D., Keating, J. P., & Stotland, E. (1989). Altruism reconsidered: The effect of denying feedback on a victim's status to empathetic witnesses. *Journal of Personality and Social Psychology, 57*, 641–650.

Staub, E. (1974). Helping a distressed person: Society, personality and stimulus determinants. In L.

Berkowitz (Ed.), *Advances in experimental social psychology* (Vol. 7, pp. 293–341). New York: Academic Press.

Thompson, L., & Walker, A. J. (1989). Women and men in marriage, work, and parenthood. *Journal of Marriage and the Family, 51,* 845–872.

Weisner, T. S., Garnier, H., & Loucky, J. (1994). Domestic tasks, gender equalitarian values and children's gender typing in conventional and nonconventional families. *Sex Roles, 30,* 23–24.

West, S. G., Whitney, G., & Schnedler, R. (1975). Helping a motorist in distress: The effects of sex, race and neighborhood. *Journal of Personality and Social Psychology, 31,* 691–698.

Wilson, J., & Musick, M. (1995). Personal autonomy in religion and marriage: Is there a link? *Reviews of Religious Research, 37,* 3–18.

Yoder, J. D. (2003). *Women and gender: Transforming psychology* (2nd ed.). Upper Saddle River, NJ: Prentice-Hall.

Zarbatany, L., Hartmann, D. P., Gelfand, D. M., & Vinciguerra, P. (1985). Gender differences in altruistic reputation: Are they artifactual? *Developmental Psychology, 21,* 97–101.

Our ability to maintain relationships is a critical aspect of our humanity. Being a friend, committing to an intimate relationship, and caring for and about others are all-important aspects of our relational capacity and sources of strength and resiliency. Of course, individuals differ in the degree to which they are relational. Some are highly relational and construct their selves as embedded in social relations; that is, they do not see themselves as existing apart from their relationships with others. Relational people may be more or less affiliative; they may seek the company of others often or seldom. In contrast, others tend to be more nonrelational and see themselves as separate from others. For them, the individual self is defined less in relation to others and more in terms of what one does as an autonomous being.

In this chapter we examine theories about the relational nature of individuals and the empirical evidence that supports the theoretical claims. We review the research on women's familial, romantic, and platonic relationships throughout the life span and examine the ways in which women's relationships do and do not differ from men's relationships. Finally, we provide a case study that examines the role of relationships in the lives of one particular group of women, Latinas. We end with some recommendations for service providers.

MARY M. BRABECK
and KALINA M. BRABECK

Women and Relationships

PERSPECTIVE ONE: WOMEN'S RELATIONSHIPS ARE INTRAPSYCHICALLY FORMED AND UNIVERSAL

The first person with whom the infant has a relationship is the mother. Since Freud (1925/1961), this observation has led to a number of psychodynamic views of the critical role of the mother-infant relationship. Psychodynamic theorists claim that this relationship is crucial in determining how we form other human relationships. For most infants, the father enters the psychological world much later than the mother and is, therefore, not involved in the most primitive emotional stages of the developing infant. Most psychodynamic theorists also have claimed that there are important differences between mother-daughter and mother-son relationships. As a consequence, girls and women are more attached, first to their relationships with mothers and later to relationships in general, than boys and men. A brief discussion of some key ideas from psychodynamic theorists follows.

Karen Horney (1937) claimed that the origins of neuroses lie, not in the frustration of instincts as Freud had argued, but in negative childhood relational experiences, such as having an uncaring parent. Horney saw a vulnerable child in need of parental warmth, protection, love, and nurturance. She recognized the importance of unconditional parental care for children as unique beings, so that they may be free to discover who they are without risking the loss of parental love. Horney assumed that female heterosexuality and the wish for motherhood were instinctual for girls and women and that the maternal drive was what accounted for differences between women and men. However, this is not to say that society played no role in shaping girls and women, or boys and men. Horney saw the mother-child relationship as embedded within the familial and cultural context.

Nancy Chodorow (1978) began her explanation of relational differences between women and men with the observation that, across cultures and across times, women, not men, are primary caregivers during infant years. Her theory was an attempt to explain this gendered division of labor. She claimed that a mother's relationship with her female infant was fundamentally different from her relationship with her male infant and this affected the psychological development of girls and boys. In early infancy, Chodorow argued, two sides of the infant's ego or self developed simultaneously. The first was the self in relationship, the sense that we exist in relationship to and with others. The second was the self in separation, the sense that we exist as a separate self. She called the former a "relational ego" and the latter an "autonomous ego."

During the earliest years, infant girls and boys both begin with a close sense of being in relationship with the mother, but differences emerge as the autonomous or separate sense of self develops. The mother experiences a sameness with her daughter but a difference from the infant boy. Her identification with the son is more relatively distant, which facilitates the development of his autonomous self. Because she identifies more with the daughter, a girl's relational self is more developed, but her autonomous self suffers.

Around age 5, Chodorow argued, the autonomous and relational selves are further differentiated. Boys, in order to become identified as male, psychologically repress the mother in order to identify with the father; this also represses their relational needs and capacities. The girl does not need to reject the mother in order to attain her female gender identity and her relational ego is further developed but her autonomous ego is never as strong as a boy's. As a result, Chodorow claimed, women continue to seek the close relationship of their own infancy by becoming mothers. Because typically mothers and fathers are differently involved and invested in the infant, this pattern of development of desires and capacities are re-created generation after generation. This pattern, for Chodorow, will be changed only when men become as involved and invested in parenting infants as are women.

WOMEN AND THE ETHIC OF CARING: JEAN BAKER MILLER AND CAROL GILLIGAN

Jean Baker Miller (1976) presented a feminist analysis of our patriarchal society and how it has influenced women's lives and their relationality. Miller (1976) and colleagues from the Stone Center disagreed with Chodorow's notion of the relational and autonomous egos and argued that the there is only one ego and it is, at core, a relational ego. Development, the Stone Center theorists claimed, is the process of becoming a self in relationship. They argued that over time the relational self becomes more complex and more elaborated. Moreover, they asserted that women have a greater capacity for relationships than men. However, Miller claimed that in devaluing women, society also devalued the traits associated with women. Thus, caring for others, mutual engagement, and relational values are diminished in a sexist society. This results in women's greater tendency to experience difficulties with depression, anxiety, anger, and work inhibition. Women's relationships, argued the Stone Center theorists, are both a source of fulfillment and a source of greater pain for women more than men.

Like both Chodorow and Miller, Carol Gilligan (1982) theorized that women are more relational than men. She argued that differences in moral orientation (care ethic vs. justice ethic) reflect differences in one's self (relational self vs. individualistic self). Gilligan claimed that girls' and women's experiences of inequality and subordination which characterize their lives create a moral self grounded in human connections and characterized by concerns with relationships. For relational people, she argued, moral issues arise when relationships are threatened, at which point the ethic of care is invoked to resolve moral dilemmas. Gilligan and Miller celebrate that which they see as the essential "feminine" self and the feminine values associated with what they characterize as "the feminine voice." The "feminine voice," claimed Gilligan, "emerges with great clarity, defining the self and proclaiming its worth on the basis of the ability to care for and protect others" (1982, p. 79). This different moral voice develops because women "define their identity through relationships of intimacy and care" (p. 164). For Gilligan, the male "I" was defined in separation (p. 161). Gilligan writes, "Instead of attachment, individual achievement rivals the male imagination and great ideas or distinctive activity defines the standard of self-assessment and success" (p. 163).

PERSPECTIVE TWO: WOMEN'S RELATIONALITY AS SOCIAL CONSTRUCTION

There are a number of preconceptions about gender differences in relationality. Most middle-class girls and women are expected to be exceptionally nurturing, empathic, and altruistic, and girls and women expect these qualities of themselves. Women are more likely to enter "helping" professions, such as nursing and social work (Schroeder, Penner, Dovidio, & Piliavin, 1995). Girls and women are more frequently sought for emotional support from both males and females, and have a reputation among teachers, peers, and parents for being more helpful and empathic.

Claims about gender differences in relationality go far back in history. The view that (White) women are innately relational, and therefore

"good mothers," was known as the "Cult of True Womanhood" (Brabeck, 1996). Nineteenth-century beliefs about gender differences provided the basis for assigning men and women to separate spheres (Lott, 1981). The separate spheres argument was built on the notion that the male sphere of work and achievement was suited for independent and autonomous selves, while the female sphere of the private home and relationships was intended for relational, nurturing selves. The idea that women are "relational" has been used to convince women that they are "naturally" caring and therefore should keep out of men's territories of agency and competence. The consequence of propagating this idea was that women's presumed special traits were used to deny them education and to justify poor pay and gender segregation in the work force (Lott, 1981). Feminist researchers have attempted to show that gender differences in personality, if they exist at all, are attributable to differences in socialization and amenable to change (Lott, 1981).

Researchers such as Gilligan and Miller drew attention to the inadequacy of the masculine, competitive, aggressive, autonomous model and sought a new norm that celebrated the alternative, feminine virtues. Gilligan made a major contribution to moral development theory by drawing attention to beneficence, the moral principle that requires us to consider the welfare of others in deciding on a course of action. Yet inherent in Gilligan and Miller's argument was the assumption that gender differences do exist; this leads to the question, What is the evidence for differences in care and relationality? Research that includes both females and males concludes that both sexes can and do use both care and justice orientations (Bebeau & Brabeck, 1987). It appears that the topic of concern, (e.g., an issue about a friendship, care for child, etc.), and not the person's gender, is associated with care reasoning. Moreover, despite popular assumptions, gender differences in regards to empathy and nurturance appear to be found primarily in self-report studies (Brabeck, 1989).

Some researchers (e.g., Crawford & Unger, 2004; Snodgrass, 1985) have suggested that women have become relational as a result of being marginalized in society. Because they lacked power as individuals, women had to join with others to maximize their chances of gaining access to that which men had by virtue of their relatively more powerful status. For example, Snodgrass (1985) found that when power is experimentally manipulated, the lack of power (not gender) leads people to know more about the persons who have power over them; she likens this information seeking to "women's instinct" or ability to be sensitive to what others are feeling and thinking.

WOMEN'S RELATIONSHIPS THROUGHOUT THE LIFE SPAN: WHAT THE RESEARCH TELLS US

Whether relationality is an inherent aspect of who we are or a socially constructed orientation, relationships are integral parts of women's lives. Women's connections to others can sometimes be problematic and many struggle with the conflict between doing what is best for themselves and doing what is best for another person, like a parent, friend, or spouse (Eccles, 2001). Yet relationships are also sources of strength, happiness, and fulfillment in women's lives. This section reviews the research on women's relationships with their families, their friends, and their romantic partners.

Relationships Within the Family

Perhaps the most significant and life-changing relationship for a woman is the relationship between herself and her child. With motherhood comes intense and sometimes conflicting emotions; a new mother may feel unprecedented love and connection, but also the weight of being responsible for another's life. While motherhood brings great additions to women's lives, it also entails significant losses. For example, as a woman is increasingly defined in terms of her relationship to her child, she may lose the sense of her own separate identity. Mourning this loss of one's "old," more autonomous self is not sanctioned by our Western society (Nicolson, 1993) and women may feel guilty and abnormal if they experience what is, in fact, a very common postpartum response.

Crawford and Unger (2004) recognized that motherhood results in a "large, significant, and permanent change" in a woman's life situation and identity (p. 352). Moreover, motherhood can bring intense feelings of love, competence, and achievement. Motherhood also requires that children and mothers recognize the limitations of love and care and the limitations of a world that typically does not provide adequate support for mothers or their children. Indeed, we live in a society where "mother blaming" (Caplan, 1989) is practiced with growing frequency and mothers are deemed responsible for the psychological well-being of their children. Finally, Crawford and Unger (2004) noted that the mother-child relationship constantly changes as the mother and the child grow older: "Throughout the process, the mother moves from meeting physical needs to meeting intellectual ones; emotional demands remain a constant" (p. 353). We, the mother-daughter coauthors of this chapter, can certainly attest to the validity of this statement.

Economics, Sexual Identity, Age, and Motherhood

Some groups of mothers—for example, single mothers and lesbian mothers—face unique obstacles in child rearing. Single mothers are more likely to live in poverty than married mothers, particularly if they are women of color (Steil, 2001). While most single mothers have jobs, finding good, affordable child care is problematic, particularly if women are raising their children in high-risk environments (Jackson, 1997). Despite these obstacles, single mothers are just as satisfied with motherhood as married mothers and may in fact have unique strengths. One study identified flexibility, spirituality, having many "mothers," and an increased sense of community as notable strengths among woman-headed African American families (Randolph, 1995).

One in six lesbian women is a mother and faces obstacles like discrimination, isolation from other mothers, and economic hardships because they don't have the earning potential of men (Crawford, 1987). Research suggests that lesbian mothers raise their children in similar ways as do heterosexual mothers, and that there is no difference in the psychological adjustment of their children. Research reviews have found no detrimental effects of lesbian parenting on children's psychological adjustment or gender-role development, and yet lesbians typically face a fifty-fifty chance of losing their children in custody battles (Falk, 1993).

As the adult child changes, so too does the middle-aged mother. Despite the popular conception of the "empty nest syndrome," research shows that middle-aged mothers whose children left home tend to be about as happy or even slightly happier than middle-aged mothers who have at least one child at home (Johnston-Robledo, 2000). This is not to suggest that middle-aged mothers stop missing their relationship with children but, rather, that the relationships change as mothers begin to reshape their lives around new interests and activities (Johnston-Robledo, 2000).

Middle age is sometimes called the "sandwich generation," a reference to middle-aged women's dual responsibilities to take care of their children and their aging parents. Daughters are about three times more likely to become caretakers for an elderly parent in poor health than are men (Canetto, 2001). Daughters are also more likely to also report that caregiving causes stress; however, many women report this is a satisfying relationship.

In older age, women's familial roles shift as they likely become grandmothers and perhaps widows as well. Grandmothers interact with their grandchildren through activities and babysitting, as well as through mentoring and providing advice regarding what is morally and socially responsible (Morgan & Kunkel, 2001). Grandmother relationships tend to be especially important in Black, Latino, and Native American families. Loneliness can be a challenge in later life, as women, who on average live longer than men, lose spouses, partners, and friends (Bedford & Blieszner, 2000) and struggle to maintain social connections with their community, and combat feelings of isolation, and depression.

WOMEN'S FRIENDSHIPS

Research suggests that women of all ages are more likely than men to have close friends, confide personal information to friends, and have a more diverse circle of friends (Adams, 1997). This

is not surprising, given that girls are more socialized to value friendship than are boys (Crawford & Unger, 2004). However, research indicates that the gender differences in males' and females' intimate relationships are not enormous (Zarbatany, McDougall, & Hymel, 2000) and both report the same degree of satisfaction with same-sex friendships (Crick & Rose, 2000). Both sexes report the important elements of friendship are trust, loyalty and conversations (Way, 1998). For women and men, intimacy in friendship entails self-disclosure, emotional expressiveness, communication skills, unconditional support, and trust; women, but not men, also report the importance of physical contact with friends (Wright, 1998). Women may value self-disclosure in friendships more than men (Dindia & Allen, 1992) and receive greater training in emotional communication, an important factor in maintaining relationships.

Adolescent girls appear to spend more time with friends than boys do, have smaller groups of friends, and expect more kindness, loyalty, commitment, and empathy from friends (Brown, Way, & Duff, 2000). Moreover, girls report a more intense and wider array of emotions in their friendships than do boys, experiencing their friendships as stronger and more emotionally rewarding, but also as more stressful. Patterns of friendships may vary across cultural and class lines. White, middle-class girls seem to experience the most difficulty in their friendships with other girls (i.e., deal with more issues of competition and jealousy; Brown et al., 2000). While friendships may be sources of great strength and enjoyment in women's lives, women may also struggle between being connected to and interdependent with their friends to the point of ignoring their own needs. This struggle may be reconciled through friendships that do not compromise one's own integrity for the sake of others.

ROMANTIC RELATIONSHIPS AND MARRIAGE

Unfortunately, many girls learn about how they are supposed to act in romantic relationships from the media's gender-stereotyped images (Brown et al., 2000). Girls' and women's magazines emphasize the "necessity" of having a boyfriend and provide the reader detailed instructions for how to change herself—through dieting, hair styles, clothing, behavior, etc. (Rennells, 2001). Teenage romances can have positive and negative impact on girls' lives. On the one hand, teenage girls may spend so much of their time dreaming about, thinking about, and planning for a boyfriend that their time for other activities (i.e., academics, sports, and family time) may become limited. Once she has a boyfriend, a teenage girl may arrange her life around him, helping him with his homework, attending his sports events, spending time with his friends (Holland & Eisenhart, 1990). On the other hand, when a girl's boyfriend respects and values her, the relationship can help each of them explore questions about identity, self-worth, and long-term relationships (Collins & Sroufe, 1999). Adolescent females and males both value personal characteristics of their ideal romantic partner (i.e., being nice and funny). However, boys emphasize physical attractiveness, while girls are more likely to emphasize personal characteristics (i.e., being supportive and intimate; Feiring, 1996). Media messages about what is valued in girls and boys help shape these attitudes. Teenage romances may be especially problematic for lesbians, who rarely see positive images of lesbians in the media and who risk discrimination. However, a romantic relationship is, for many lesbians, a milestone in the coming-out process (Schneider, 2001).

Adult women are especially likely to report that their romantic relationships are based on friendship; women are also more likely than men to report experiencing positive emotions in relationships, (i.e., commitment, satisfaction), as well as more negative emotions (i.e., hurt, loneliness; Sprecher & Sedikides, 1993). Men are more likely than women to say that their spouses understand them and bring out their best qualities, and women are more likely to report feeling responsible for making sure the relationship is going well (O'Mahen, Beach, & Banawan, 2001). However, research suggests much similarity in how women and men define their romantic relationships. Women and men are more likely to be satisfied with their romantic relationships if they are based on friendship and if their partners can

express their emotions (Sternberg, 1998). For both, the most essential features of romantic relationships are trust, caring, honesty, and respect. While in general, women may engage in more self-disclosure than men, in romantic relationships there are similar patterns of self-disclosure (Hatfield & Rapson, 1993). Romantic relationships continue to be important in the lives of older women, although society frequently dismisses them as undesirable sexual partners.

In choosing lifelong partners, women and men both appear to employ similar criteria (i.e., honesty, good personality, and intelligence). For adult men, physical attractiveness is more important than for women. Women tend to prefer men whom they perceive as altruistic, as opposed to dominant and strong (Jensen-Campbell, Graziano, & West, 1995). Evolutionary psychologists suggest that men prefer young, attractive, healthy women because they are most likely to be fertile, while women look for stable men whom they can depend on (Buss, 1998). Feminists object to this explanation, citing research that a woman's attractiveness is unrelated to her fertility and that both men and women are interested in long-term relationships. Moreover, they warn that the evolutionary approach implies that gender differences are large and inevitable, and therefore may be used to justify that men should have more power. Many feminists favor the social-roles explanation of different gender patterns in choosing romantic partners (i.e., the observation that women and men have different roles, are socialized differently, and experience different opportunities and disadvantages in society; Eagly & Wood, 1999). In marital relationships, women continue to bear the brunt of housework and child care, even when both partners work for pay. Unbalanced sharing of domestic work is consistent across cultural and ethnic groups (Hossain & Roopmarine, 1993).

Lesbian women want many of the same qualities in romantic partners and mates (i.e., dependability and good personality) as heterosexual women do (Peplau & Spalding, 2000) and couples report being happier if both partners contribute equally to decision making and housework (Peplau & Spalding, 2000). Satisfaction with the relationship is much the same for lesbians as for heterosexual couples and gay couples; breakup patterns and emotional aftermath are also similar (Peplau & Beals, 2001). However, some legal issues that create barriers to heterosexual partners breaking up relationships (i.e., children, property, and divorce) may be less relevant for lesbian couples.

WOMEN AND MULTIPLE SUBGROUPS: A CASE STUDY OF LATINAS' RELATIONSHIPS

Clearly, women are influenced by their culture, ethnicity, disability, sexual orientation, and a host of other individual differences. In this section we examine the role of culture in women's relationships by examining relationships within the Latina pan-ethnicity. One caveat is in order: The "iron rule" (Gilbert & Scher, 1999) of gender differences is the notion that intragroup differences *within* sexes always exceed intergroup differences *between* sexes. This rule applies to ethnic differences as well. Caution must be taken in making generalizations about a cultural or pan-ethnic group, particularly when that group includes numerous religions, countries of origin, languages, traditions, and ethnicities. What is presented here is meant to provide a research-based perspective on the relationship experiences of a particular group of women, Latinas. It is, however, not meant to describe every person of Latin American/Spanish descent living in the United States. We include this section to make the point that there are differences among subgroups of women in the role of relationships in women's lives.

Latina/Latino culture is often described as collectivistic and interdependent, and relationships are given great emphasis (Brabeck, 1996). Certain Latino cultural values (i.e., *familismo, personalismo,* and *respeto*) reinforce the importance of relationships. *Familismo* refers to strong feelings of reciprocity, loyalty, and solidarity among family members (Santiago-Rivera, Arredondo, & Gallardo-Cooper, 2002). It is expressed through placing the family ahead of individual interest and development, living near extended family, and being responsible and obligated to the family. Latino psychological well-being has been found to be related to family involvement (Raymond &

Rhoads, 1980) and being unable to fulfill the role as mother and wife and is strongly linked to depression among Latinas (Vega, Kolody, & Valle, 1986). *Personalismo* involves the building and valuing of interpersonal relationships (Santiago-Rivera et al., 2002), while *respeto* refers to the high regard that exists among family and community members, especially for authority figures and the elderly. These values underscore the importance of relationships in the lives of many Latinos, both men (Latinos) and women (Latinas).

Within the "traditional" Latino family, the father is the provider and authority figure, while the mother is the principal figure in the home, caring for children, supporting her husband, passing on traditions, and keeping the family together (Santiago-Rivera et al., 2002). Some empirical evidence suggests that Latinas tend to be less egalitarian in their gender-role attitudes than European Americans (Harris & Firestone, 1998). Traditional gender roles are thought to be reinforced by the cultural scripts of *machismo*, which demands that a man be assertive, hyper-masculine, and physically powerful, and *marianismo*, the mandate that a women should be sexually pure, self-sacrificing, and deferent to others' needs. A Latina may be especially concerned for and responsive to the needs of her children, and motherhood may be a particularly important source of her identity.

However, some researchers argue that Latino spousal or partner relationships do not display the degree of male dominance and female subordination that many assume (Montoya, 1996). Research indicates that most Latino couples have an egalitarian division of household tasks, and that women and men actually tend to share decision making (Cromwell & Cromwell, 1978). Interestingly, however, even when Latinas and Latinos engage in nontraditional roles, they may continue to hold *machista* attitudes and to believe that the man should be the primary breadwinner and the woman should be the central parental figure (Davis & Chavez, 1985).

A number of scholars argue that cultural interpretations of Latino gender roles within families and Latino family life may obscure the role of sociostructural factors, ethnicity, culture, and gender, as shapers of family life (Baca Zinn & Eitzen, 1996). Extended kinship networks may operate as mechanisms of social exchange and support among Latinos, particularly for women, who gain access, through such networks to resources that are not available elsewhere (i.e., child care, housing, and employment). Reliance on family for support may be a coping strategy for Latino individuals who are marginalized by U.S. society and is best understood in view of the structural conditions with which Latino families cope, rather than solely in terms of cultural values (Harris & Firestone, 1998). Similarly, Latinas' characteristic responsiveness to others' needs and role as family caretaker should be considered within the context of the universality of women's subordination as well as societal attributions of women of color as resilient in the face of all odds.

In addition to familial relationships, relationships within the community appear important to Latinas' mental health and well-being (Vega et al., 1986) Community relationships may be an important source of emotional and material strength and support for Latinas. Access to women's networks may be an invaluable resource particularly for immigrant women.

CONCLUSIONS

For almost a century, psychologists have asserted that relationships are part of the human experience and are sources of great psychological support and resilience. Clearly, our Western society emphasizes the role of relationships in the lives of women, and women themselves speak of the importance of family, friends, and spouses in a satisfying life. Yet empirical evidence suggests that women's relationality may be socially constructed and its importance may be overemphasized in women's lives, to the detriment of developing personal autonomy and identity.

The information we have presented has important implications for counseling women. Counselors and psychotherapists must recognize the importance of relationships in women's lives and not minimize the distress experienced when a female client's relationships are threatened or ruptured. Those who counsel girls and women should understand relationships as strengths in women's lives and as sources of support, coping, and resiliency. This understanding, however,

should be balanced with a critical lens to ensure that clients' relationships are based on mutual respect and caring, and that women are not sacrificing their own needs for the sake of others. Psychologists should be wary of popular views of women as essentially nurturing and relational; these views may lead them to overemphasize these qualities in their female clients, while they underemphasize the development of "masculine or agentic" traits, such as independence and assertiveness. Psychologists are encouraged to foster both communal and agentic traits in their clients, and to bear in mind the empirical evidence that indicates the many individual differences that qualify general claims of gender differences in relationships. Finally, those in the helping professions ought to pay attention to the many contextual factors that affect a person's relationship, regardless of sex. To further our comprehension of how to better help our clients, understanding how to foster more mutual, satisfying relationships that enhance human development ought to continue to be a focus of psychological study.

REFERENCES

Adams, R. C. (1997). Friendship patterns among older women. In J. M. Coyle (Ed.), *Handbook on women and aging* (pp. 400–417). Westport, CT: Greenwood Press.

Baca Zinn, M., & Eitzen, D. S. (1996). *Diversity in families* (4th ed.). New York: HarperCollins.

Bebeau, M., & Brabeck, M. M. (1987). Integrating care and justice in professional education: A gender perspective. *Journal of Moral Education, 16,* 189–203.

Bedford, V. H. & Blieszner, R. (2000). Older adults and their families. In D. H. Demo, K. R. Allen, & M. A. Fine (Eds.), *Handbook of family diversity* (pp. 216–232). New York: Oxford University Press.

Brabeck, M. M. (Ed.). (1989). *Who cares? Theory, research and educational implications of the ethic of care.* New York: Praeger.

Brabeck, M. M. (1996). The moral self, values and circles of belonging. In K. F. Wyche & F. J. Crosby (Eds.), *Women's ethnicities: Journeys through psychology* (pp. 145–165). Boulder, CO: Westview Press.

Brown, L. M., Way, N., & Duff, J. F. (2000). The others in my I: Adolescent girls' friendships and peer relations. In N. G. Johnson, M. C. Roberts, & J. Worell (Eds.), *Beyond appearance: A new look at adolescent girls* (pp. 205–225). Washington, DC: American Psychological Association.

Buss, D. M. (1998). The psychology of human mate selection: Exploring the complexity of the strategic repertoire. In C. Crawford & D. L. Krebs (Eds.), *Handbook of evolutionary psychology* (pp. 405–429). Mahwah, NJ: Erlbaum.

Canetto, S. S. (2001). Older adult women: Issues, resources, and challenges. In R. K. Unger (Ed.), *Handbook of the psychology of women and gender* (pp. 183–197). New York: John Wiley & Sons.

Caplan, P. J. (1989). *Don't blame mother.* New York: Harper & Row.

Chodorow, N. (1978). *The reproduction of mothering.* Berkeley: University of California Press.

Collins, W. A., & Sroufe, L. A (1999). Capacity for intimate relationships: A developmental construction. In W. Furman, B. B. Brown, & C. Feiring (Eds.), *The development of romantic relationships in adolescence* (pp. 125–147). New York: Cambridge University Press.

Crawford, M., & Unger, R. (2004). *Women and gender: A feminist psychology.* Boston: McGraw-Hill.

Crawford, S. (1987). Lesbian families: Psychological stress and the family-building process. In Boston Lesbian Psychologies Collective (Ed.), *Lesbian psychologies* (pp. 195–214). Urbana: University of Illinois Press.

Crick, N. R., & Rose, A. J. (2000). Toward a gender-balanced approach to the study of social-emotional development: A look at relational aggression. In P. H. Miller & E. K. Scholnick (Eds.), *Toward a feminist developmental psychology* (pp. 151–168). New York: Routledge.

Cromwell, V., & Cromwell, R. (1978) Perceived dominance in decision-making and conflict resolution among Anglo, Black, and Chicano couples. *Journal of Marriage and the Family, 40,* 749–759.

Davis, S. K., & Chavez, V. (1985). Hispanic households. *Hispanic Journal of Behavioral Sciences, 7,* 317–332.

Dindia, K., & Allen, M. (1992). Sex differences in self-disclosure: A meta-analysis. *Psychological Bulletin, 112,* 106–124.

Eagly, A. H., & Wood, W. (1999). The origins of sex differences in human behavior: Evolved dispositions versus social roles. *American Psychologist, 54,* 408–423.

Eccles, J. S. (2001). Achievement. In J. Worell (Ed.), *Encyclopedia of women and gender* (pp. 43–53). San Diego, CA: Academic Press.

Falk, P. J. (1993). Lesbian mothers: Psychosocial assumptions in family law. In D. C. Kimmel (Ed.), *Psychological perspectives on lesbian and gay male experiences* (pp. 420–436). New York: Columbia University Press.

Feiring, C. (1996). Concepts of romance in 15-year-old adolescents. *Journal of Research on Adolescents, 6,* 181–200.

Freud, S. (1925/1961). Some psychical consequences of the anatomical distinction between the sexes. In J. Strachey (Ed.), *The standard edition of the complete psychological works of Sigmund Freud* (Vol. 19, pp. 243–258). London: Hogarth Press.

Gilbert, L. A., & Scher, M. (1999). *Gender and sex in counseling and psychotherapy.* Boston: Allyn & Bacon.

Gilligan, C. (1982). *In a different voice: Psychological theory and women's development.* Cambridge, MA: Harvard University Press.

Harris, R. J., & Firestone, J. M. (1998). Changes in predictors of gender role ideologies among women: A multivariate analysis. *Sex Roles, 38,* 239–252.

Hatfield, E., & Rapson, R. L. (1993). *Love, sex, and intimacy: Their psychology, biology, and history.* New York: HarperCollins.

Holland, D. C., & Eisenhart, M. A. (1990). *Educated in romance: Women, achievement, and college culture.* Chicago: University of Chicago Press.

Horney, K. (1937). *The neurotic psychology of our time.* New York: W. W. Norton.

Hossain, Z., & Roopmarine, J. L. (1993). Division of household labor and childcare in dual-earner African-American families with infants. *Sex Roles, 29,* 571–584.

Jackson, A. P. (1997). Effects of concerns about child care among single, employed black mothers with preschool children. *American Journal of Community Psychology, 25,* 657–673.

Jensen-Campbell, L. A., Graziano, W. G., & West, S. G. (1995). Dominance, prosocial orientation, and female preferences: Do nice guys really finish last? *Journal of Personality and Social Psychology, 68,* 427–440.

Johnston-Robledo, I. (2000). From postpartum depression to the empty nest syndrome: The motherhood mystique revisited. In J. C. Chrisler, C. Golden, & P. D. Rozee (Eds.), *Lectures on the psychology of women* (2nd ed., pp. 128–147). Boston: McGraw-Hill.

Lott, B. (1981). A feminist critique of androgyny: Toward the elimination of gender attributions for learned behavior. In C. May & N. M. Henley (Eds.), *Gender and nonverbal behavior* (pp. 171–180). New York: Springer-Verlag.

Miller, J. B. (1976). *Toward a new psychology of women.* Boston: Beacon Press.

Montoya, L. J. (1996). Latino gender differences in public opinion. *Hispanic Journal of Behavioral Sciences, 18,* 255–276.

Morgan, L., & Kunkel, S. (2001). *Aging: The social context* (2nd ed.). Thousand Oaks, CA: Pine Forge Press.

Nicolson, P. (1993). Motherhood and women's lives. In D. Richardson & V. Robinson (Eds.), *Thinking feminist: Key concepts in women's studies* (pp. 201–224). New York: Guilford Press.

O'Mahen, H. A., Beach, S. R. H., & Banawan, S. F. (2001). Depression in marriage. In J. H. Harvey & A. Wenzel (Eds.), *Close romantic relationships* (pp. 299–319). Mahwah, NJ: Erlbaum.

Peplau, L. A., & Beals, K. P. (2001). *Lesbians, gay men, and bisexuals in relationships.* In J. Worell (Ed.), *Encyclopedia of women and gender* (pp. 657–666). San Diego, CA: Academic Press.

Peplau, L. A., & Spalding, L. R. (2000). The close relationships in lesbians, gay men, and bisexuals. In C. Hendrick & S. S. Hendrick (Eds.), *Close relationships* (pp. 111–123). Thousand Oaks, CA: Sage.

Randolph, S. M. (1995). African American children in single-mother families. In B. J. Dickerson (Ed.), *African American single mothers* (pp. 117–145). Thousand Oaks, CA: Sage.

Raymond, J., & Rhoads, D. (1980). The relative impact of family and social involvement on Chicano mental health. *American Journal of Community Psychology, 8,* 557–569.

Rennells, J. (2001). *The focus of the content of teen magazines.* Unpublished manuscript, SUNY Geneseo.

Santiago-Rivera, A. L., Arredondo, P., & Gallardo-Cooper, M. (2002). *Counseling Latinos and la familia: A practical guide.* Thousand Oaks, CA: Sage.

Schneider, M. S. (2001). Toward a reconceptualization of the coming-out process for adolescent females. In A. R. D'Augelli & C. J. Patterson (Eds.), *Lesbian, gay, and bisexual identities* (pp. 71–96). New York: Oxford University Press.

Schroeder, D. A., Penner, L. A., Dovidio, J. F., & Piliavin, J. A. (1995). *The psychology of helping and altruism.* New York: McGraw-Hill.

Snodgrass, S. (1985). Women's intuition: The effect of subordinate role on interpersonal sensitivity. *Journal of Personality and Social Psychology, 49,* 146–155.

Sprecher, S., & Sedikides, C. (1993). Gender differences in perceptions of emotionality: The case of close heterosexuals. *Sex Roles, 28,* 511–530.

Steil, J. M. (2001). Marriage: Still "his" and "hers"? In J. Worell (Ed.), *Encyclopedia of women and gender* (pp. 403–410). San Diego, CA: Academic Press.

Sternberg, R. J. (1998). *Cupid's arrow: The course of love through time.* New York: Cambridge University Press.

Vega, W., Kolody, B., & Valle, J. R. (1986). The relationship of marital status, confidant support, and depression among Mexican American women. *Journal of Marriage and the Family, 48,* 597–605.

Way, N. (1998). *Everyday courage: The lives and stories of urban teenagers.* New York: New York University Press.

Wright, P. H. (1998). Toward an expanded orientation to the study of sex differences in friendship. In D. J. Canary & K. Dindia (Eds.), *Sex differences and similarities in communication* (pp. 41–63). Mahwah, NJ: Erlbaum.

Zarbatany, L. McDougall, P., & Hymel, S. (2000). Gender-differentiated experiences in the peer culture: Links to intimacy in preadolescence. *Social Development, 9,* 62–79.

KAREN FRASER WYCHE

Healthy Environments for Youth and Families

24

The literature on environmental contexts that are supportive of healthy behavioral and psychological outcomes does not focus on girls and women. The focus is primarily on age, rather than gender, or age and gender. It is a developmental literature with a macro, rather than a micro, focus. It examines where families live and how parenting, marital quality, work, family structure, or other family factors are conducive to helping rear children. Emphasis is on understanding developmental changes and commonalities, processes by which healthy environments are established and maintained, cultural values evolve, and contextual variation is expressed in life situations. There is a consistent finding that family environment continues to be of crucial importance from childhood through adolescence and into young adulthood (Vandervalk, Spruijt, De Goede, Meeus, & Mass, 2004). Emphasized also are factors distal to the individual such as community contexts (Cocking, 1994). Information provided by this body of work will enable readers to extrapolate from this literature toward understanding the processes of creating healthy environments for girls and women.

Various theoretical frameworks are proposed to identify protective factors that assist individuals and families with survival and adaptation in society. These frameworks focus on positive outcomes to study healthy environments, but are vague in how healthy environments are operationally defined. There is an assumption of positive social behavior and good emotional health that may differ across cultures. For researchers who look at micro-level variables, the operational definitions of outcomes are clearer, for it is easier to design a study looking at structural rather than process variables. For example, one can design a study to assess positive or negative gender identity and parenting practices in two-parent married couples with girl children. The results from such a study could provide an operational definition of healthy environments based on positive gender identity. In this example, the researcher has made the decision regarding the definition. Other definitions are part of the legal system. There the attempt is to establish a definition of healthy environments for children by trying to assess what is in the best interest of the child based on psychological functioning of children in dysfunctional family environments (Benjet, Azar,

& Kuersten-Hogan, 2003). However, this is not a precise definition. Researchers who focus on macro-level factors assume there are multiple ways healthy environments can be conceptualized and defined. They are interested in the process by which this may occur and in what contexts. For them the ecological context is fluid and ever-changing. Hence, the reader should keep these assumptions in mind while reading the chapter.

THEORETICAL FRAMEWORKS

Several theoretical models help elucidate how the process of living in a family may promote healthy outcomes for family members. These models or frameworks focus on macro components to understand children's development within families and the interactions they have in the larger society. These frameworks or theories specify causal mechanisms and are developmental in orientation. They examine the ways children living with adults are nested within various environmental contexts to obtain healthy outcomes as they grow into adulthood. Parents act as facilitators within and outside family processes to shape healthy child outcomes. The process is fluid, not static, and is difficult to test empirically. Emphasis is on healthy outcomes for children in general, rather than specifically by sex of the child. Parental influences are primarily those of mothers when the sex of the parent is studied. In general, parenting practices are considered proximal effects and child adjustment as distal effects.

Life-cycle models (e.g., Erikson, Freud, Kohlberg, Piaget, Mahler, etc.) describe family development as linear and sequential. Emphasized are the developmental tasks at each stage such as marriage, birth of children, child rearing, last child leaving home, empty-nester couples, retirement, and death of spouse creating the end of marriage. These models are time and culture bound and are insufficient for studying today's families (Germain, 1994). For example, today's adult children may live in the family home for a longer time than previous generations, divorced and widowed persons remarry, and retirement is no longer mandatory at a specific age, creating a workforce that continues working beyond age

65. Social class and cultural issues also influence what families deem as appropriate gender-role behaviors for youth as they age within each culture. In addition, there are different types of family structures (lesbian, gay, single, childless by choice).

Life-course models were developed in response to the limitations of the life-cycle models. Life-course models recognize the influence of culture, physical and social environments, and diversity of family types. Belsky (as cited in Baharudin & Luster, 1998) proposes that individual differences in parenting are multiply determined. Influences are dependent on the characteristics of the parent, the child, and the context in which the parent-child relationship is evolving. These contextual factors can be family income, family structure, and/or marital quality. He predicts that the supportive care results from parents who have manageable levels of stress, social supports, and perceive their child as not difficult to parent. Specific parent characteristics that may influence this process are psychological issues of self-esteem and depression. This model is directional. Factors that affect parenting behaviors result in parenting outcomes that impact the child's development both in behavioral domains such as gender roles and in cognitive aspects such as self-esteem. These ecological or environmental factors can be divided into proximal and distal correlates of parenting (Meyers & Battistoni, 2003). The proximal variables are considered by researchers to be current social and emotional functioning of parents (i.e., self-esteem, social support, and the presence of violence or abuse in the relationship, substance abuse). The distal predictor variables are historical and relate to the parent's own history of childhood abuse. While intuitively one may assume that parental childhood physical and sexual abuse would create negative child-rearing behaviors among adolescent mothers, the research findings are equivocal. Some studies find direct significant findings and others do not (Meyers & Battistoni, 2003).

A more expansive conceptualization of healthy environments is found in ecology models. These models help us understand the ways that development can be shaped by various pathways. These include the characteristics of family, kin networks, the community, and the interactions among them. As ecodevelopmental models, they recognize that individuals are nested in families and families in communities (J. Szapocznik, personal communication, June 29, 2004). Hence, any notion of healthy environments for children and families is derived from this interactive-process-oriented focus. Several theorists espouse an ecological framework (i.e., Bronfenbrenner, Garcia-Coll, and Rutter). While there are distinctions among them, the commonality is that what constitutes healthy environments is understood by studying youth in various family structures within environments—an interactive, not a direct process. Little attention is paid to the sex of youth and few empirical studies report sex differences. While parents are studied, most typically it is the mother.

Rutter (2002) and colleagues (Rutter, Pickles, Murray, & Eaves, 2001) proposed a model that emphasizes the flexibility of development, the possibility of emotional and behavioral change from childhood through adulthood, and the significance of the environmental context over the life course. Rutter's extensive research on children living in adverse environments has consistently found that some children are able to overcome hostile environmental influences. These children are able to interact both temperamentally and behaviorally in ways to deal with the environmental stressors. He hypothesizes that these children may have a predisposition toward genetic variation in vulnerability as well as suitable temperament to maneuver these situations. They have an adult who is strict but loving. This could be a parent, a relative, or a nonrelative such as a teacher or neighbor. These youth develop positive self-esteem and acquire coping skills despite the environmental deprivation.

Bronfenbrenner's ecological model is perhaps the best known, and provides distinctions between various levels of relationships (Bronfenbrenner, 1993). The paradigm posits that human development occurs through organism-environment interaction along the life course. It is visible in the successive interplay between environmental contexts that differ from the family at home, to systems interacting with the home (i.e., work or school), to system-to-system interactions all impacting on the development of individuals within the family. He proposes a descriptive taxonomy to look at how social context interacts with individuals to influence child development. There are multiple levels of these social contexts, all of which interact within the cultural and historical framework in which they exist. These systems go from simple to complex interactions.

The first, the microsystem, is an ongoing, face-to-face relationship between the child and the other people in the home. Developmental outcomes are shaped by this person-context model. For example, children in families of color who experience high marital conflict at home have poorer psychological well-being than those children in homes where marriage is harmonious (McLoyd, Cauce, Takeuchi, & Wilson, 2000). The mesosystem is the next higher structure of the environment. It is defined as relationships between two or more settings or microsystems that an individual occupies such as home and work, or school and home. Positive developmental outcomes are expected to the extent that the roles and regularities of the two microsystems are congruent with one another. For example, in single-parent African American families, parental monitoring of their child's school work is a positive outcome for youth in school (Brody, Dorsey, Forehand, & Armistead, 2002). Both the mesosystem and the microsystem are concerned with developmental influences in environments in which the developing person is actually present and able to interact directly with persons in their immediate situation. However, some environmental contexts are such that direct interaction is not possible. This is the exosystem, the next structure of the environment. Here, there are linkages and processes between two or more settings, but the youth is not present. For example, parents who experience stressful work environments may find this stress spills over at home into the parenting role in a negative way (Dilworth, 2004). In this example, the child does not go to the parent's workplace, but the workplace of the parent influences the parenting role, the marital relationship, and the home climate. The last system is the macrosystem. It consists of the cultural beliefs, values, and ideologies that shape the form of the micro, meso, and exosystems. For example, cultural norms regarding gender socialization might affect the linkage between the type of maternal employment and attitudes regarding women's work, family social support, and the number of hours worked. In all of these systems (micro, meso, exo, and macro) environmental interactions influence the development of youth in families.

Some ecological models, such as Garcia Coll and colleagues' (1996), focus specifically on how being a member ethnic minority group can influence developmental outcomes for youth. She argues that the centrality of culture and ethnicity need to be addressed. In making this argument she goes beyond the previously discussed ecology models to look at one's social location as an ethnic minority person in American society. These personal characteristics result in societal experiences of racism, prejudice, oppression, discrimination, and segregation. They are viewed as a normal part of minority youth's interaction with society and contain both micro and macro factors. The micro factors are individual child and family variables that influence development such as sex-role stereotyping. The macro factors are associated with minority status and community context (includes schools, neighborhoods, and health care) and are impacted directly by multiple forms of segregation (residential, economic, social) and culture. The result is either supporting or inhibiting of healthy child development. For example, racial minority adolescent females who experience strategic parental ethnocultural and racial socialization are able to develop positive self-identity (Way, 1995).

Intergenerational systems theory is another way to examine the relationship between family functioning and individual positive mental health outcomes (Whittaker & Robitschek, 2001). This focus is on the uniqueness of the family system and not, as in ecological theory, on how the family interacts with or is embedded with other systems in the environment Intergenerational systems theory hypothesizes that family influences are shaped by family-level variables such as communication, conflict, problem solving, and differentiation of family members from each other. For child-rearing families, good communication provides members with a feeling of being heard and understood and is hypothesized to create a family atmosphere where the children feel secure in expressing increasingly independent thoughts and feelings. Low-conflict families foster good communication and problem-solving skills within the family unit (Dilworth, 2004; McLoyd et al., 2001). Good problem solving helps differentiate family roles and relates to healthy family functioning toward promoting intimacy and expressions of individuality. On the surface this seems a culturally constrained view, biased toward middle-class Euro-American norms. However, one can hypothesize that children reared in environments that are healthy learn how to communicate in culturally appropriate ways, structured by age and gender norms within their culture to negotiate their world and move from childhood to adolescence to adulthood.

STUDIES ON HEALTHY ENVIRONMENTS

The research on healthy environments is not large. As a discipline, psychology has tended to focus more on negative individual differences and problematic outcomes in youth and families than on positive aspects. As a result, the healthy environments literature is scattered among several areas of research that can inform our understanding of this complex area. These areas are discussed below.

Family Structure

Studies on family structure typically use a mother's marital status, or compare biological-parent families to stepfamilies at one point in time rather than assessing changes over time in family structure. Large-scale national data sets of family surveys are common. These have the advantage of being more representative of the U.S. population than is possible in small-scale studies, are available for public use by researchers, and provide cross-sectional analyses of factors contributing to family environments and child outcomes (Manfried et al., 2002). The most common of these data sets is the National Longitudinal Survey of Youth (NLSY). The original sample size of 63,000 youth between ages 14 to 21 who were born to primarily low-income and African American and Latina mothers has been assessed every two years since 1986 (Carlson & Corcoran, 2001).

Typical studies using this data set assess family structure and economic status, child socialization, family stress, characteristics of the child and the mother, and mother's psychological well-being. Although the children in these studies can live in single or two-parent families, the mother is usually the target person of interest for the study (Carlson & Corcoran, 2001). Often these studies are interested in child outcomes in the behavioral or cognitive domains. So, for example, Carlson and Corcoran report in their study of 7- to 10-year-olds that family structure doesn't influence behavior problems in children when socioeconomic status is controlled. Rather, mothers who score in the depression range on standardized tests have children who exhibit more behavioral problems compared to nondepressed mothers.

Other researchers using the NLSY data have found that quality maternal parenting for their school-aged children (ages 6–8 and no sex differences) was related to the mother's age at the time of the child's birth, the presence of a spouse or partner in the household, and the intellectual and educational level of the mother (Baharudin & Luster, 1998). Not surprisingly, mothers who delay childbearing, and thus are older, provide better quality child care than adolescent mothers.

Another large survey of family structure is the National Longitudinal Survey of Adolescent Health. It is a study of approximately 90,000 parents and adolescents in grades 7 through 12 who have been followed from 1994 to 1996 by in-home interviews and assessments of family, peers, and school factors (Resnick et al., 1997). Using this data set, Manning and Lamb (2003) report that teens (no sex differences) living with biological married parents report better psychological well-being than those living with cohabiting stepparents and/or single unmarried mothers. This is primarily because of better socioeconomic circumstances in two parent families. Those teens with the cohabiting stepparents had the lowest school grades and more problem behaviors than the teens in the other living arrangements. Resnick et al. (1997) analyzed this data set and found that adolescents who perceive that their parents expect school attainment and whose parents are available to them with time, have higher healthy behaviors (lack of substance and alcohol abuse and delayed sexual behavior) than those whose parents don't deliver these messages. More important, those homes where there is access to guns, alcohol, tobacco, and illicit substances have adolescents who are more likely to have an increased risk for suicidality, substance use, and interpersonal violence experiences.

The National Survey of America's Families has been used to study family structure (Brown, 2004). This survey tracks differences in life circumstances in a broad range of economic, social, and health-care topics. The survey contains representative data from almost 45,000 families (none with members over age 65) and over 100,000 people over the entire distribution of income levels. These families came from 13 selected states. Brown used this data set to examine the relationship between family structure and child well-being as defined as social and psychological functioning. She selected families with children ages 6–11 and 12–17, focusing on age, not gender-related influences on family structure. The results indicate that young children experience fewer behavioral problems and better emotional health and school engagement if they live with two married biological parents as opposed two biological cohabiting families. However, economic resources mediated this such that when family finances were low or insufficient for family needs, children experienced less well-being behaviorally, emotionally, and at school. The pattern for families of adolescents is different. Lack of economic resources and type of family structure was not related to adolescent well-being. In all family types, adolescents had less well-being than the younger children.

Extended family parenting is important in positive child outcomes. The involvement of grandmothers in helping to rear children has been associated with positive child outcomes in ethnic minority families (Wyche, 1998). Also in single-mother families, among African American and Latina adolescent mothers, external household caregivers have been viewed as providing invaluable assistance in child care and in providing cultural continuity when relatives provide care. (Johnson et al., 2003). However, some literature indicates that high levels of grandmother support for African American and Latina adolescent mothers may result in lower quality parenting (McLoyd et al., 2000), and nurturance (Meyers &

Battistoni, 2003). The reasons aren't clear. Do grandmothers increase their support when they perceive the adolescent as incapable of being a "good" mother, or do they not allow the adolescent to develop a mother role for other reasons?

Lesbian and gay families are rarely studied from an ecological perspective. Fitzgerald (1999) reviewed studies on child rearing by gay parents between the years 1972 and 1997. Her findings are that children of lesbian and gay parents have positive socioemotional and behavior development. More current research is needed in this area, especially since gay and lesbian parents are actively adopting and having biological children. For those who adopt we do not know if there is a preference for girl children.

Marriage and Divorce

Partner status is one way healthy environments are studied. The quality and stability of the parents' marriage is related to the emotional adjustment of the adolescent. Youth living with parents in low conflict and higher well-being families have fewer problems than those from divorced and married but psychologically distressed families (Vandervalk et al., 2004). The sex of the child seems to be related to divorce for some White middle-class families where families of girls divorce more than those with boys (Hetherington, 2003). Studies of young and adolescent children from divorced families show both short- and long-term emotional effects. Divorce leads to problems with parental support, monitoring and discipline, parent-child relationships, financial resources, maternal depressive symptoms, and general spillover of problems associated with divorce to the parenting role (Vandervalk et al., 2004). Age and gender differences in reaction to divorce and marital distress are inconsistent. When sex effects are found, boys are more likely to have externalizing problems such as delinquency and aggression and girls more internalizing problems such as depression and anxiety. Younger children may continue to exhibit the effects into adolescence. The research does indicate that parents in stable marriages are able to provide more emotional support to their chil-

dren than are parents in divorced or separated couples (Vandervalk et al., 2004).

Hetherington's (2003) studies provide one of the few opportunities to examine longitudinal effects of divorce, albeit with White, middle-class families where the mother had child custody. Overall, her results indicate that after two to three years children adapt to their new lives if there is no continued stress. Compared to nondivorced families, divorced parents are more problematic in their parenting. Mothers are more authoritarian and controlling and fathers more permissive in monitoring of children's behaviors, and fathers spend less time with their daughters compared to their sons. As adults, women of divorced parents are more likely to accept divorce as an option for an unhappy marriage, but not to act on this belief out of financial and family responsibility concerns. Women of divorced parents who selected responsible and emotionally stable husbands helped to stabilize their marriages compared to those who chose the opposite type of husband.

It is clear that marital distress is related to many negative child development outcomes such as psychological distress, externalizing behavior, reduced life satisfaction, lower academic competence and reduced self-regulation (McLoyd et al., 2000). While there are no consistent patterns of ethnic differences in the way marital conflict is exhibited, those families with extended family networks seem to provide a protection against the negative psychosocial effects of the parental conflict (Johnson et al., 2003). This mediation effect is referred to as the attenuation hypothesis, a speculation that racial minority children may be less susceptible to the effects of parental marital conflict than White children. Clinically the implications are that family structures for racial minority families in marital distress should include assessing kin and extended social networks that serve as protective forces in the lives of children.

Work

Working parents in dual-wager-earner marriages have been studied as to spillover (Dilworth, 2004). *Spillover* is defined as the means by which behaviors, attitudes, and experiences in one environment spill over and affect another environment that an individual occupies on a daily basis. In large national studies of workers, aspects of positive spillover are greater family satisfaction and less conflict for mothers with older, compared to younger, children and marital satisfaction. Positive spillover is shown to occur between work and family environments and serves to promote better parenting and psychological functioning for working spouses. Mothers of young children and with low marital satisfaction experience negative spillover that is associated with adverse outcomes including depression, poor physical health, and alcohol use in dual-wage-earner marriages. This situation creates negative home environments for children. Unfortunately, the focus of this work is primarily on mothers with less information about the role of fathers or the influences by sex on children.

Emotional work is another way to study married couples (Strazdins & Broom, 2004). It is defined as efforts to understand others, to improve their well-being, and to maintain family harmony. Emotional work is the cost of caring within families and is related to positive feelings, closeness, and regulation of negativity among family members. Findings of this literature are that women carry the burden of maintaining and creating emotional work. Women and men have different experiences in giving and receiving support in social and work relationships, but women care more for others in the family. When the marital relationship is harmonious, there is a decrease in women's psychological distress and depression. Women who provide high levels of emotional work in marriage have an increase in marriage conflict and a greater risk for depression compared to those who provide lower levels of emotional work. Thus the outcome for children is a home environment that is not harmonious.

Types of Parenting

These studies look at the association between family interaction patterns at the parent-child level of relationship (such as parental control or concern) and the systemic level of family cohesion, conflict, or harmony. Also, there is literature regarding parenting attitudes that are associated with maternal and child functioning. This literature focuses on mothers, rather than the couple (Meyers & Battistoni, 2003).

Mothers who reported harsh parenting as children, negative attitudes toward life, and unrealistic developmental expectations about their young children have more negative attitudes about their own children (Daggett, O'Brien, Zanolli, & Peyton, 2000). Hostile parenting of first- and second-grade children can be mediated by neighborhoods with high social cohesion—a sense of shared community values (Silk, Sessa, Sheffield-Morris, Steinberg, & Avenevoli, 2004). Mothers who utilize an authoritative style of parenting that includes democratic, warm, receptive, rational, controlling, and demanding behaviors are more satisfied with parenting than those who use an authoritarian parenting approach (Arendell, 2000).

Many studies of mothers are on adolescent parents. Their visibility and availability to researchers make them a focus in the research on problematic parenting. Findings from these studies are primarily of parenting attitudes and their association with maternal and child functioning. The preponderance of studies use the proximal correlates of parenting in the following variables. Adolescent mothers with good self-esteem are less likely to use physical punishment, have knowledge of developmental milestones, are emphatic toward their infants, and are aware that their children are individuals. Conversely, adolescent mothers with low self-esteem are more likely to view their children as objects to satisfy their own personal needs (Meyers & Battistoni, 2003). Social support provided by others is found to foster resiliency in youth (Rutter et al., 2001). When given a choice, adolescents will pick parental social support over peers, but the findings as to the sex of the parent and child are not clear. Some studies report mothers and daughters are more intimate than sons and fathers, and father support is positive for protecting against suicide in males and females, but mothers have been the primary parent of focus in this literature (Tarver, Wong, Neighbors, & Zimmerman, 2004).

There is a consistent finding that children experience a protective environment when there is a secure supportive attachment to parents and a home atmosphere that fosters respect for all family members. Thus family support relates to positive attachment (Tradd & Greenblatt, 1990).

Also in early adolescence, the more positive the parent-adolescent relationship, the greater the warmth and less conflict in both mother and father's relationship with their daughters and sons (Belsky, Jaffee, Caspi, Moffitt, & Silva, 2003). This relationship appears to extend into adolescence and young adulthood, when measurements of affectional solidarity are obtained from families with young adolescents who are followed into young adulthood. These intergenerational relationships are less positive when children are in conflictual parental relationships (Belsky et al., 2003), but we know little about gender differences compared to age effects.

Father absence has been studied in relation to early sexuality in girls. From an ecological perspective, father absence is one of the many factors that can undermine the quality of the family environment. His absence becomes associated with at-risk factors (divorce, lower standard of living, conflictual family relationships, erosion of parental monitoring, etc.) and early sexual activity in daughters. However, the research evidence indicates that the processes involved with youth sexuality are interactive and not clear (Ellis et al., 2003). That is, father-daughter processes, father-mother relationships, exposure to stepfathers, etc., are all factors that interact in ways that we do not understand to produce early sexual activity.

Depression

There is a well-established relation between poverty and women's mental health (Wyche, 2001, 2003). When families are studied, it is usually mothers with young children. The findings are clear that, by age 2, children who live in families with low socioeconomic status score lower on standardized tests of IQ and other cognitive abilities compared to children with higher incomes (Petterson & Albers, 2001). Children of depressed mothers have problems in the areas of behavior, social interactions, motor skills, and cognitive development. There is mixed evidence that affluence buffers the negative effects of maternal depression for either preschool girls or boys (Petterson & Albers, 2001).

Parenting risk on the basis of psychiatric diagnosis has been a focus in the legal literature (Benjet et al., 2003). A psychiatric diagnosis alone is not enough to predict risk in parenting, and the sex of the parent or child is important in a case-by-case analysis rather than by looking only at mothers and daughters. There are multiple interactive factors seen as important in a child's environment (e.g., parental support, advocacy, partner stability, or extended family involvement). A notion of continued risk along the life course is a linear concept and an "at-risk" paradigm. This does not seem the best model for making decisions as to the "best" environments for children to reside in when the parent has psychological problems. (Benjet et al., 2003).

Neighborhoods

The literature on neighborhoods is about characteristics of neighborhoods and developmental outcomes for children. The research indicates that families are instrumental in determining how urban environments impact their children's lives. However, it is difficult to understand the precise pathways through which families influence their relationship between the neighborhood and the subsequent child outcomes, or what the unmeasured neighborhood and family effects may be (Burton & Jarrett, 2000).

In a review of studies of neighborhood effects on child and adolescent development, Leventhal and Brooks-Gunn (2000) summarize the main findings. Family behaviors that are helpful to children are moving from a problematic neighborhood to better one with higher income residents. Neighborhoods with resources such as learning, recreational, social, educational, and employment opportunities have positive influences on family and children's outcomes. Families in high-resource neighborhoods are more likely than those in low-resource neighborhoods to enroll their adolescents in and take them to organized neighborhood group programs. These neighborhoods have norms that monitor and control residents' behavior in accordance with socially accepted practices. Conformity is maintained by the residents who abide by the stated (i.e., no littering) and unstated (no public drunkenness) rules.

Carter and McGoldrick (1999) refer to the multicontextual aspects of communities that foster social connections. These include face-to-face interactions between individuals as friends and neighbors and involvement with governmental, nonprofit, religious, and educational institutions in the community. Opportunities exist for volunteer work and involvement in school, recreational, or cultural groups. There is a sense of pride in the community with residents actively engaging in neighborhood or community improvement. However, many families are, for economic reasons, unable to change neighborhoods. At-risk neighborhoods are economically deprived and are associated with adverse mental health, criminal and delinquent behavior, and early sexuality and fertility in adolescents (Leventhal & Brooks-Gunn, 2003; Wyche, 2001). Residence in low-income and/or high-risk neighborhoods gives families two choices. Either they succumb to the dysfunction of the neighborhood or they cope in adaptive ways. Some adaptations are having extended-kin networks that assist children in maintaining safety (i.e., accompanying them to activities in and out of the neighborhood, providing a check-in system of phone contact), having flexibility in family role assignments, and regular family routines with youths assigned to domestic and households tasks. This process is interactive and multileveled.

Leventhal and Brooks-Gunn (2003) discuss that the literature supports nurturing, activist and strategic parenting practices that are aimed at providing a healthy environment for their children. Parents are advocates at school and in community organizations. A good example can be found in a study of the relationships among parental practices, school policies and practices, and child outcomes in elementary school-aged children. This study found that African American children of single mothers had good social-emotional and psychological adjustment when families had high levels of monitoring, good mother-child relationships, and a classroom process characterized by organization, rule clarity, predictability, and affirming teaching (Brody et al., 2002). Parents and families monitor youth's behavior (friends, curfews, where they were going, how they dressed, etc.) and stress academic performance. There are clear boundaries between the parent and the youth. That is, the roles are not blended or unclear. In addition these families see themselves as socially mobile although they live in these problematic neighborhoods.

CONCLUSIONS

In this chapter, I proposed that to understand healthy environments for girls, women, youth, and families we must look at an ecological perspective. This is one that emphasizes the process of growth, development, and environmental factors as interactive and ongoing. This macro focus gives us a way to contextualize how youth and parents move from the family to the outside world. The research gives us some understanding of the process by which this occurs and provides applications for understanding girls and women in these processes. Certainly we need more studies of the role of women in the process of creating healthy environments for their daughters and within differing family and cultural situations. Finally, neighborhoods and communities seem good places to begin this work, since girls and women exist in these societal structures moving in and out to go to school and work. Such a research agenda is long term and complex. In my opinion, the fluidity of environments and the supportive factors in them cannot be captured without this agenda.

REFERENCES

Arendell, T. (2000). Conceiving and investigating motherhood: The decade's scholarship. *Journal of Marriage and the Family, 62*(4), 1192–1207.

Baharudin, R., & Luster, T. (1998). Factors related to the quality of the home environment and children's achievement. *Journal of Family Issues, 19*(4), 375–401.

Belsky, J., Jaffee, S., Caspi, A., Moffitt, T., & Silva, P. (2003). Intergenerational relationships in young adulthood and their life course, mental health, and personality correlates. *Journal of Family Psychology, 17*(4), 460–471.

Benjet, C., Azar, S., & Kuersten-Hogan, R. (2003). Evaluating the parental fitness of psychiatrically diagnosed individuals: Advocating a functional-contextual analysis of parenting. *Journal of Family Psychology, 17*(2), 238–251.

Brody, G., Dorsey, S., Forehand, R., & Armistead, L. (2002). Unique and protective contributions of parenting and classroom processes to the adjustment of African American children living in single-parent families. *Child Development, 73*(1), 274–286.

Bronfenbrenner, U. (1993). The ecology of cognitive development: Research models and findings. In R. Wozniak & K. Fisher (Eds.), *Development in context* (pp. 3–44). Hillsdale, NJ: Erlbaum.

Brown, S. (2004). Family structure and child well-being: The significance of parental cohabitation. *Journal of Marriage and the Family, 66*(2), 351–468.

Burton, L., & Jarrett, R. (2000). In the mix, yet on the margins: The place of families in urban neighborhoods and child development research. *Journal of Marriage and the Family, 62*(11), 1114–1135.

Carlson, M., & Corcoran, M. (2001). Family structure and children's behavioral and cognitive outcomes. *Journal of Marriage and the Family, 63*(3), 779–792.

Carter, B., & McGoldrick, M. (1999). *The expanded family life cycle: Individual, family, and social perspective.* Needham Heights, MA: Allyn & Bacon.

Cocking, R. (1994). Ecologically valid frameworks of development: Accounting for continuities and discontinuities across contexts. In P. M. Greenfield & R. Cocking (Eds.), *Cross-cultural roots of minority child development* (pp. 393–10). Hillsdale, NJ: Erlbaum.

Daggett, J., O'Brien, M., Zanolli, K., & Peyton, V. (2000). Parent's attitudes about children: Associations with parental like histories and child-rearing quality. *Journal of Family Psychology, 14*(2), 187–199.

Dilworth, J. (2004). Predictors of negative spillover from family to work. *Journal of Family Issues, 25*(2), 241–261.

Ellis, B., Bates, J., Dodge, K., Fergusson, D., Horwood, L., Petit, G., et al. (2003). Does father absence place daughters at special risk for early sexual activity and teen age pregnancy? *Child Development, 74*(3), 801–821.

Fitzgerald, B. (1999). Children of lesbian and gay parents: A review of the literature. *Marriage and Family Review, 29*(1), 57–75.

Garcia Coll, C., Crnic, K., Lamberty, G., Wasik, B. H., Jenkins, R., & Garcia, H., et al. (1996). An integrative model for the study of developmental competencies in minority children. *Child Development, 67*, 1891–1914.

Germain, C. (1994). Emerging conceptions of family development over the life course. *Families in Society, 75*(5), 259–263.

Hetherington, M. (2003). Intimate pathways: Changing patterns in close personal relationships across time. *Family Relations, 52*, 318–331.

Johnson, D., Jeager, E., Randolph, S., Cauce, A. M., Ward, J., & National Institute of Child Health and Human Development Early Child Care Research Network. (2003). Studying the effects of early child care experiences on the development of children of color in the U.S.: Toward a more inclusive research agenda. *Child Development, 74*(5), 1227–1244.

Leventhal, T., & Brooks-Gunn, J. (2000). The neighborhoods they live in: The effects of neighborhood residence on child and adolescent outcomes. *Psychological Bulletin, 126*(2), 309–337.

Leventhal, T., & Brooks-Gunn, J. (2003). Children and youth in neighborhood contexts. *Current Directions in Psychological Science, 12*(1), 27–34.

Manfried, H. M., van Dulmen, M., Grotevant, H., Dunbar, N., Miller, B., Bayley, B., et al. (2002). Connecting national survey data with *DSM-IV* criteria. *Journal of Adolescent Health, 31*(6), 475–481.

Manning, W., & Lamb, K. (2003). Adolescent well-being in cohabiting married and single-parent families. *Journal of Marriage and the Family, 65*(4), 878–894.

McLoyd, V., Cauce, A. M., Takeuchi, D., & Wilson, L. (2000). Marital processes and parental socialization in families of color: A decade review of research. *Journal of Marriage and the Family, 62*(4), 1070–1093.

Meyers, S. A., & Battistoni, J. (2003). Proximal and distal correlates of adolescent mothers' parenting attitudes. *Journal of Applied Developmental Psychology, 24*(1), 33–49.

Petterson, S., & Albers, A. (2001). Effects of poverty and maternal depression on early child development. *Child Development, 72*(6), 1794–1831.

Resnick, M. D., Bearman, P. S., Blum, R. W., Bauman, K. E., Harris, K. M., Jones, J., et al. (1997). Protecting adolescents from harm: Findings from the National Longitudinal Study on adolescent health. *Journal of the American Medical Association, 278*(10), 823–832.

Rutter, M. (2002). Nature, nurture and development from evangelism through science toward policy and practice. *Child Development, 73*(1), 1–21.

Rutter, M., Pickles, A., Murray, R., & Eaves, L. (2001). Testing hypotheses on specific environmental causal effects on behavior. *Psychological Bulletin, 127*(3), 291–324.

Silk, J., Sessa, F., Sheffield-Morris, A., Steinberg, L., & Avenevoli, S. (2004). Neighborhood cohesion as a buffer against hostile maternal parenting. *Journal of Family Psychology, 18*(1), 135–146.

Strazdins, L., & Broom, D. (2004). Acts of love (and work): Gender imbalance in emotional work and women's psychological distress. *Journal of Family Issues, 25*(3), 356–378.

Tarver, D., Wong, N., Neighbors, H., & Zimmerman, M. (2004). The role of father support in the prediction of suicidal ideation among Black adolescent males. In N. Way & J. Chu (Eds.), *Adolescent boys:*

Exploring diverse cultures of boyhood (pp. 145–163). New York: NYU Press.

Tradd, P. V., & Greenblatt, E. (1990). Factors in coping and stress resistency. In L. Arnold (Ed.), *Childhood Stress* (pp. 34–44). New York: John Wiley & Sons.

Vandervalk, I., Spruijt, E., De Goede, M., Meeus, W., & Mass, C. (2004). Marital status, marital process, and parental resources in predicting adolescent's emotional adjustment. *Journal of Family Issues, 25*(3), 291–317.

Way, N. (1995). "Can't you see the courage, the strength I have?" Listening to adolescent girls speak about their relationships. *Psychology of Women Quarterly, 19,* 107–128.

Whittaker, A., & Robitschek, C. (2001). Multidimensional family functioning: Predicting personal growth initiative. *Journal of Counseling Psychology, 48*(4), 420–427.

Wyche, K. F. (1998). Let me suffer so my kids won't: African American mothers living with HIV/AIDS. In C. Garcia Coll, J. L. Surrey, & K. Weingarten (Eds.), *Mothering against the odds: Diverse voices of contemporary mothers* (pp. 173–189). New York: Guilford Press.

Wyche, K. F. (2001). Poverty and women in the United States. In J. Worell (Ed.), *Encyclopedia of women and gender* (pp. 837–846). San Diego, CA: Academic Press.

Wyche, K. F. (2003). Poverty and women's mental health. In L. Slater, J. Daniels, & A. Banks (Eds.), *The complete guide to mental health for women* (pp. 185–189). Boston: Beacon.

The goal is to encourage the client to criticize not herself but to "engage in the world from a critical perspective."

—Marcia Westkott (1986), p. 202

Psychotherapy is a powerful and positive resource for women and girls who are hurting, needing a lifeline, or seeking clarity on their life experiences and options. Through psychotherapy, girls and women can learn new behaviors, solve problems, confront traumas, and come to terms with events that left them feeling confused or uncertain. This chapter first addresses the basic aspects of the psychotherapeutic relationship and what makes it a worthwhile activity. It then addresses more specifically what is important for psychotherapy to be effective for girls and women, several areas of particular concern to them for which psychotherapy is useful, and important factors to consider in selecting a therapist.

LUCIA ALBINO GILBERT
and LISA K. KEARNEY

The Psychotherapeutic Relationship as a Positive and Powerful Resource for Girls and Women

25

WHAT IS PSYCHOTHERAPY?

Psychotherapy is primarily an interpersonal, confidential treatment based on psychological principles (Garfield, 1980; Wampold, 2001). It involves a professionally trained psychotherapist and a client who seeks assistance for resolving ongoing problems in living, dealing with a mental disorder, or managing other difficulties (Worell & Remer, 2003). Psychotherapy can take place with individuals, couples, and families, or with groups whose members have similar concerns. It occurs in many settings, ranging from hospital and community clinics and college counseling centers to the private offices of psychologists, social workers, professional counselors, and psychiatrists. Psychotherapy is remedial when the treatment is designed to remove or ameliorate distress associated with a client's presenting problems or disorders; it is preventive or empowering when it focuses on new skill development related to life experiences such as parenting, death of a loved one, loss of a job, or living with a chronic illness.

Thus, psychotherapy is helpful for a wide range of people and a wide range of problems (Lambert, 2004). A large-scale survey by *Con-*

sumer Reports (1995) found that approximately one third of individuals and families surveyed sought help for emotional problems. Most of the 2,900 respondents who had sought therapeutic assistance reported benefiting from the psychotherapy and being satisfied with the treatment they received. Cumulative controlled research on the outcomes of psychotherapy indicates that the average treated client is better off than 80% of untreated subjects (Lambert & Barley, 2002).

The field of psychotherapy is characterized by a variety of philosophical and theoretical viewpoints and distinct approaches—psychodynamic, behavioral, cognitive, feminist, humanistic, and family systems, among others. Most psychotherapists, however, ascribe to an eclectic orientation in which they integrate aspects of various theoretical viewpoints into their practice (Garfield, 1980; Kopta, Lueger, Saunders, & Howard, 1999; Lambert, 1992). In one study, most of the psychotherapists who identified with an eclectic orientation reported the use of psychodynamic, cognitive, and behavioral approaches in their treatment of clients (Jensen & Bergin, 1990). Those identified with a feminist orientation also embrace a range of theoretical viewpoints, including cognitive, behavioral, psychodynamic, and humanistic approaches (Gilbert, 1992).

Whatever the specific approach they use, psychotherapists strive to establish a therapeutic alliance, set treatment goals, provide clients a rationale for the treatment they receive, and plan for termination. Moreover, most psychotherapists bring a broad base to their therapeutic work; they modify their conceptual scheme to take into account the concepts and background clients bring to therapy. In general, treatment is more effective when its rationale is consistent with the worldview, assumptions, attitudes, and values of the clients who are being assisted (Frank & Frank, 1991).

Overall, the various psychotherapeutic approaches produce similar benefits for their clients and are generally equivalent in their effectiveness (Lambert, 2004; Wampold, 2001). That is, a very large part of what is helpful for clients is shared across the different approaches to treatment. That shared or common factor across the various therapeutic modalities and treatments is associated with the therapeutic relationship, the topic of this chapter.

The therapeutic relationship involves two individuals, the therapist and what s/he brings to the developing relationship, and the client and what s/he brings to the relationship. Positive outcomes for the client are associated with both therapist and client variables. For example, the therapist's warmth and empathy, and the client's expectancies about psychotherapy and ability to trust in the therapist, are associated with positive outcomes for the client (Beutler et al., 2004; Garfield, 1994). Effective psychotherapy requires the active engagement and participation of both the client and the therapist.

In the remainder of the chapter, we address factors that promote an effective therapeutic relationship for women and girls and facilitate their improved coping, growth, well-being, and resilience.

BASIC DIMENSIONS OF AN EFFECTIVE PSYCHOTHERAPEUTIC RELATIONSHIP

What makes the various approaches to psychotherapy effective is inextricably tied to a common set of personal and professional dimensions. Factors especially important to effective treatment are the relationship that develops between the therapist and the client, the trust the client places in the therapist, the client's openness to change, and the ability of the therapist to assist the client in the areas in which help is sought. The therapist's ability to assist a particular client is dependent upon knowledge and expertise in the areas of the client's concern, knowledge of what brings about lasting psychotherapeutic change, and the ability to practice in accordance with the ethical and legal codes of the profession.

Carl Rogers was among the first of the early theorists to espouse a therapeutic relationship whose characteristics were warmth and responsiveness of the therapist and a permissive climate in which the feelings of the client could be freely expressed. Rogers believed that successful therapy "would mean that the therapist has been able to enter into an intensely personal and subjective relationship with this client—relating not as a scientist to an object of study, not as a physician expecting to diagnose and cure, but as a person to a person" (Rogers, 1961, p. 184). According to Rogers, a client in such a relationship would gain understanding of a newly experienced self and make constructive behavioral changes in accordance with this newly experienced self.

A large body of research (Norcross, 2002) now supports Rogers's theory, including his belief in the centrality of the therapeutic relationship in bringing about positive outcomes for clients. Core aspects of the therapeutic relationship include the role of the therapist as an interested, informed, and understanding collaborator, trust in the client for making changes and choosing goals that the client identifies as personally important, and the working alliance that develops between the therapist and the client (Frank & Frank, 1991; Garfield, 1980).

A key part of the therapist's role is to provide accurate, empathic understanding—to sense the world as seen and experienced by the client. Also central is the therapist's ability to communicate that understanding to the client in a nonjudgmental way, with genuineness and respect for the client's experience. Thus, the therapist is a real person who is collaboratively involved in the helping relationship, not simply a mirror or blank screen (Patterson, 1974). This mutual involvement extends to ways the therapist and client work together to establish agreed-upon therapeutic expectations and goals.

The therapeutic working alliance refers to the quality and strength of the collaborative relationship that develops between the client and therapist. According to Horvath and Bedi (2002), "alliance involves a sense of partnership in therapy between the therapist and client, in which each participant is actively committed to their specific and appropriate responsibilities in therapy, and believes that the other is likewise engaged in the process" (p. 40). Components of the therapeutic working alliance include the client's affective relationship with the therapist, the client's motivation and ability to accomplish work collaboratively with the therapist, the therapist's active engagement in the therapeutic process, and the consensus and commitment that emerges between them about the goals of therapy and how they can be accomplished.

Frank and Frank (1991) described the importance of an emotionally safe relationship with a psychotherapist who clients believe can provide help and engender their trust. The goals, direction, and pace of the therapy are developed within a collaborative process in which clients are viewed as the experts on their own lives and experiences. The therapist provides new learning experiences, engages clients emotionally, works with clients to enhance self-efficacy, and provides opportunities to practice new learning within a safe relationship. The creation of a safe environment for female clients is especially crucial to their well-being, healing, and growth, and is a topic to which we return in the next section.

WHAT MAKES FOR EFFECTIVE PSYCHOTHERAPY FOR WOMEN AND GIRLS

Effective psychotherapy for women and girls requires placing their concerns and the therapeutic relationship within the larger sociocultural context, valuing women and their contributions, and knowing the current research on the psychology of women and gender. In this section we first discuss the importance of context, which includes gender as well as considerations of culture, ethnicity, and sexuality. We then address the importance to the psychotherapeutic relationship of valuing women and having knowledge about the psychology of women and gender. We conclude by providing several brief examples of the importance of these values and knowledge in psychotherapeutic treatment.

Placing Clients' Concerns Within Their Larger Sociocultural Context

Using the psychotherapeutic relationship "to engage in the world from a critical perspective" is important to understanding and dealing with the conflicts and difficulties experienced by women and building their strengths and resilience (Westkott, 1986). Women's psychological health and disorders are often linked to the social context of their lives, particularly to conditions that maintain women in subordinate positions. Social inequality has effects on power, social identity, and emotional processes. Discrimination based on gender, for example, is a significant contributor to women's experience of distress (e.g., Landrine, Klonoff, Gibbs, Mannings, & Lund, 1995), as is discrimination based on ethnic minority status (Phinney, 1996), or sexual orientation (Fassinger, 1991).

Understanding Gender

Many chapters of the *Handbook* describe the critical framework provided by gender theories and processes in understanding women's psychological development and health. Indeed, if any one factor is central to women's and girls' development it would be gender. Sex (being a women or a man biologically) distinguishes human individuals. Gender is not simply biological sex, however. A woman or man is not born with gender. One learns how to become a woman or a man, and that highly complex social psychological process and what it entails vary across cultures and historical periods (Gilbert & Scher, 1999). Contrary to conventionally held views, women and men are more similar than they are different (Swann, Langlois, & Gilbert, 1999); the sexes clearly are not opposites.

Gender pertains to what we assume is true or will be true of someone who is born biologically female or male. Gender concerns personal and societal beliefs, stereotypes, and ingrained views about the fundamental nature of women and men. Such views are created and maintained through interpersonal interactions, formal and informal institutional practices, and other complex processes within the societal and cultural environment (Deaux & LaFrance, 1999). For example, the assumptions that women provide the care in relationships and that love is what women do best and most need from men is at the heart of patriarchal views of womanhood, as are assumptions of men's well-being being dependent on women's care.

Understanding gender and gender processes is central to effective therapy with women and girls. Women and girls who seek therapeutic assistance often experience symptoms that reflect the costs of an aversive or unhealthy environment, and they cope the best they can, given their situation. Thus, effective psychotherapy explores possible links between the concerns individual women bring to therapy and the particular features of their lives (Marecek, 2001). A presenting problem such as poor work performance evaluations or low self-confidence, for example, may be associated with an employment context in which women's contributions are differentially valued from men's. Therapists use knowledge about gender processes to explore with their clients possible connections between their symptoms and the larger context of their lives. The ongoing therapeutic process of recognizing unhealthy situations, building on strengths, and affirming self-knowledge assists clients in identifying, confronting, and effectively dealing with current issues and future difficulties (Worell & Remer, 2003).

Central to an understanding of gender with female clients is an understanding of power in relationships, a topic discussed in other chapters of the *Handbook*. Psychotherapists have unique power and privilege vis-à-vis their clients and ideally do not use their authority and position with female clients to recreate conventional gender dynamics based on traditional gender roles.

Historically women were positioned differently from men in terms of the power they had to define their own lives (Heilbrun, 1988). Conventional socialization practices encouraged women to look to others, especially strong male others, to make decisions about what was best for them. Within a safe therapeutic environment, girls and women are able to explore their own self-definitions and needs with the assistance of the therapist. Effective psychotherapists strive to develop a collaborative and nonauthoritarian therapeutic relationship based on mutual respect and on knowledge about the psychology of women and gender. As already mentioned, the creation of a safe environment for female clients is especially crucial to their well-being, healing, and growth.

Psychotherapists who are able to establish a therapeutic working alliance based on mutuality and collaboration positively affect psychotherapy as a powerful and positive resource for female clients. Research indicates that psychotherapists who hold less traditional views of gender roles promote greater therapeutic change and satisfaction among female clients than those holding more traditional views (Beutler et al., 2004; Gilbert & Scher, 1999).

Understanding Ethnicity

Understanding ethnicity is also important to the development of an effective therapeutic alliance in psychotherapy. Ethnicity includes the cultural values, attitudes, and behaviors that may distinguish ethnic groups; the subjective sense of ethnic identity that may be held by group members; and the experiences associated with ethnic minority status, including powerlessness, discrimination, and prejudice (Phinney, 1996). Although relatively few studies have specifically examined the effectiveness of psychotherapy with ethnic minorities, the available research indicates the usefulness of culturally sensitive treatments (Beutler et al., 2004). Therapist-client ethnic matching is an example of culturally sensitive treatment that has been found to be effective for less acculturated ethnic minority clients (Sue & Lam, 2002).

Wyche (2001) describes the cultural competence needed for psychotherapy with women of color. One core competence is understanding that the worldviews of women of color are based on multiple identities of gender, culture, and ethnicity. Culturally skilled psychotherapists are also aware of their own cultural assumptions, biases, stereotypes, and the limitations of their backgrounds in understanding clients' concerns. They monitor their biases so as to not impose their values on their female clients, value their clients' definition of their problems, and use culturally relevant solutions that build on their clients' existing strengths.

Understanding Sexualities

Heterosexism and homophobia are additional contextual processes that shape the lives of girls and women. Heterosexism is a belief in the inherent superiority of heterosexuality. Homophobia comprises irrational fears, intolerance, and, in its most severe form, hatred of people who are lesbian or gay. This type of prejudice leads to persistent beliefs in negative stereotypes about lesbians, and supports discriminating actions against these groups in areas such as jobs, housing, and child custody. Some lesbian women and gay men may internalize negative stereotypes about what it means to be homosexual; some may develop a degree of self-hatred or low self-esteem, a form of internalized homophobia.

Fassinger and Richie (1997) describe the competencies important for psychotherapy with lesbian, bisexual, and transgender women. Effective therapists have examined their own heterosexist attitudes and their possible homophobia; they understand the social oppression, invisibility, and isolation clients may experience; and they are knowledgeable about the social, political and legal realities of their clients' lives, including knowledge of community resources that might be available to provide additional support and assistance. Although the research is still quite limited, client-therapist matching on sexual orientation appears to be important, especially for clients seeking assistance for issues related to their sexual orientation (Fassinger, 1991; Sue & Lam, 2002).

Knowing the Current Research on the Psychology of Women and Gender

Since its beginning in the 1960s, research on the psychology of women and gender has contributed a large body of scholarship and information about women's lives. Valuing women and their contributions has been central to the wide range of research areas studied. This scholarly work challenged outdated theories of women's development and studied topics of importance and concern to women, including the social relations between women and men. As a result, psychology developed new theoretical perspectives about women and their health based on the study of women within the context of their life experiences. For example, early theories assumed that girls' and women's intrapsychic needs and conflicts brought on their real or imagined sexual abuse, while contemporary theories view female sexual abuse as a violation of trust and a misuse of adult power (Herman, 1981; Westkott, 1986).

Research on the psychology of women and gender has had an enormous influence on psychotherapeutic practice (Crawford & Unger, 2004). Areas of new knowledge are detailed in the *Handbook*'s many chapters. Examples include illuminating the importance of female-related values such as altruism, cooperation, and affiliation; clarifying the meaning of consent to sex; making visible the prevalence and consequences of childhood sexual abuse and domestic violence; and broadening the study of women to include areas such as career development and work-family issues.

The *Handbook*'s earlier chapters on problems and risks for women and girls, and its later chapters on phases of development within the life span, all focus on areas informed by the psychology of women in which psychotherapy is known to be effective. These areas include mood and anxiety disturbance; body image issues and eating disorders; serious psychological disorders; sexual, physical, and emotional abuse; physical illness and disability; trauma; intimate relationships; work-family balance; midlife issues; and later life transitions.

This wide range of areas for which psychotherapy can be of assistance to women reflects the health foundation of this *Handbook,* which is grounded in biopsychosocial and cultural perspectives. These perspectives consider biological, sociocultural, economic, and psychological factors in understanding and treating issues girls and women might bring to psychotherapy.

Depression, discussed at length in other chapters, provides a good example. It is not unusual for female clients experiencing depression to receive a combination of medication and psychotherapy. Depression co-occurs with a range of psychological and medical problems (Nolen-Hoeksema & Keita, 2003). Sexual abuse, for instance, may be a cause of depression, while chronic fatigue may be a cause or a consequence. In addition, a large body of research indicates that biological factors do not necessarily directly cause depression in women, but they contribute to vulnerability or function as stressors that precipitate depression. A case in point is menopause. A recent review of depression and menopause concluded that some women in menopausal transition appear vulnerable to depression; however, their depressed mood state was also significantly related to psychosocial factors unrelated to menopause (Avis, 2003).

Psychological and sociocultural factors such as cognitive style, social and economic conditions, and presumptions about women's and men's roles and responsibilities are known moderators of women's depressive mood states (McGrath, Keita, Strickland, & Russo, 1990; Nolen-Hoeksema & Keita, 2003). The most widely studied psycho-

therapy for depression is cognitive-behavioral therapy, which helps clients alter maladaptive thoughts, beliefs, and behaviors. Its effectiveness is well established, especially with less severely depressed or dysfunctional individuals (Kopta et al., 1999). Although not as widely studied, interpersonal therapy is also effective in the treatment of depression. Interpersonal therapy helps clients gain an understanding of their interpersonal problems and develop adaptive strategies for dealing with others.

Examples of Psychotherapeutic Areas of Concern to Women Informed by the Research on the Psychology of Women and Gender

We close this section of the chapter by describing how research on the psychology of women and gender has informed the psychotherapeutic treatment of girls and women. The areas selected as illustrations from the perspective of psychotherapeutic treatment are considered more broadly elsewhere in the *Handbook*.

The three areas we consider briefly are rape, body image, and work and family life. These serve as particularly good examples. They reflect areas in which research on the psychology of women and gender has significantly contributed to making girls' and women's concerns more visible, as well as providing the knowledge needed to bring about change. While these areas may not be what always bring women and girls to psychotherapy, they well illustrate the central role of research on the psychology of women and gender to effective psychotherapy.

Rape

Scholarship on the psychology of women has been instrumental in the illumination of a previously hidden form of rape now known as "acquaintance rape" or "date rape," as well as the reframing of rape from blaming women for what happened to them to viewing assailants as perpetrators of violence and as responsible for their actions. Response to the experience of rape may be described as posttraumatic distress disorder in some cases. Most effective treatments for posttraumatic distress disorder involve some type of exposure to the traumatic event (Wampold, 2001). Examples of treatment approaches include cognitive-behavioral therapy and stress management training, in which a sense of safety and control is rebuilt before exposure to the memory of the trauma.

Research in the area of rape also led to the identification of women's freedom from fear of rape as an important preventive goal. Many women live with a fear of rape, a fear that limits their activities and behaviors and may affect how they perceive men (Rozee, 2000). One approach for prevention is participating in self-defense and resistance training. A growing body of research indicates that women who resist rape, and are less fearful, are less likely to get raped and experience less deleterious psychological and physical aftereffects (Rozee & Koss, 2001). A second approach to prevention involves women discussing women's fear of rape with male friends and family members as a way of engaging men in strategies for changing the cultural climate surrounding rape (Rozee, 2000). Research on gender processes discussed elsewhere in the *Handbook* describes how women and men inadvertently contribute to problem areas such as women's fear of rape and issues associated with body image or work and family by internalizing stereotypic views about gender and then acting in accordance with those views.

Body Image

Research on the psychology of women and gender has illuminated the role of societal messages and images in setting unrealistic and unhealthy standards for women's beauty and attractiveness (Gilbert & Thompson, 1996) and the identification of multiple causal models for understanding eating disorders and body image (Marecek, 2001). The "culture of thinness" model links women's eating problems to societal standards for women's beauty and heterosexual attractiveness. Other models consider eating problems as a means of gaining empowerment (e.g., Bordo, 1993) or as a means of coping with life and relationship stressors (e.g., Thompson, 1995).

Eating disorders typically emerge in adolescence and early adulthood when young women are dealing with peer group pressures, negotiat-

ing their sexuality, and separating from their families within the larger context of societal messages and images about how they should look. Involving parents in prevention or treatment efforts with their adolescent daughters to reduce body image dissatisfaction is recommended (Kazdin, Siegal, & Bass, 1990). Being aware of the vulnerability to disordered eating during adolescence is extremely important; early recognition of possible difficulties with disordered eating is associated with more effective outcomes from psychotherapeutic treatment (Stein et al., 2001).

Cognitive-behavior therapy has been the primary form of psychotherapy used in treating binge eating disorders, and there is substantial evidence to support its effectiveness for the reduction of binge eating and purging behaviors, improvement in perceptions of body image, and decreased stress (Stein et al., 2001). This approach focuses on reframing problematic cognitions and attitudes about eating, shape, and weight within the context of cultural views of thinness.

In addition to cognitive-behavior therapy, interpersonal therapy appears to be effective for the treatment of bulimia (Apple, 1999). It focuses on the client's problematic relationships rather than her bulimic symptomatology. By focusing on relationship patterns with respect to role transitions, role disputes, and interpersonal deficits, interpersonal therapy targets what it considers to be the underlying stressors rather than the eating symptoms. Exploring the relational context is thought to help clients to avoid future setbacks and recognize current gains.

Issues Associated With Dual-Earner Family Life

Understanding women's occupational work and its relation to their family life has been central to the emerging scholarship on women and gender. Women and men both combining occupational work and family life is quite common (Barnett & Hyde, 2001; Gilbert, 1993; Gilbert & Rader, 2001). In fact, the dual-earner family is the normative family form in the United States. A large body of research indicates that engaging in family and work roles is beneficial for women, as reflected in indices of physical health, mental health, and relational health (Barnett & Hyde, 2001).

This relatively new norm of women and men engaging in family and work roles is accompanied by practical, psychological, and relationship issues for which women may seek educational, preventive, or therapeutic assistance. Women and their partners in dual-earner families may seek assistance in how to negotiate relationships and family responsibilities, develop sources of personal and social support, deal with conflict with their partners, or counter stereotypic views and societal barriers to their integrating work and family roles. Issues of who is entitled to what within relationships remain a struggle as women and their partners deal with their own gender socialization and the expectations placed on them by others about their work and family responsibilities. Women may need to grapple with their own internalized societal mandates of the male partner being more successful occupationally and earning more, and the female partner providing more nurturance and care within the family. Conflicts in these areas can result in depression, stress, and relationship difficulties.

If relationship issues are the most salient, couples therapy is effective for improving communication, lowering conflict, and negotiating more egalitarian roles (Sexton, Alexander, & Mease, 2004). As with individual therapy, the strength of the therapeutic alliance and the cooperation between therapist and client are associated with positive outcomes for clients (Butler & Wampler, 1999). Three approaches to couple's therapy are well studied and have been found to be effective. Behavioral marital therapy targets increasing caring behavior, communication/problem solving, and decreasing punitive behaviors. Emotionally focused couples therapy focuses on the emotional experiences of the partners and their patterns of interaction, while cognitive behavioral couples therapy focuses on changing cognitive distortions in areas of conflict.

Regardless of the approach taken, effective psychotherapy takes into account the changing roles of women and men and is informed about the current research on work and family. Effective therapists understand what facilitates and what hinders role sharing by partners. Discussions of how to best accomplish role sharing within the relationship are considered within the context of a couple's external constraints and realities and each partner's values and preferences.

External constraints are factors over which one tends to have less direct control. These include partners' work schedules, employers' work/life policies, child-care availability and quality, and conditions at work. Conditions at work, for example, have been identified as key predictors of life-quality indicators for both women and men. Having a demanding job and job insecurity are associated with low life quality, while having a supportive supervisor is positively linked to life quality outcomes (Moen & Yu, 2000).

Partners' values and preferences include such factors as the importance of shared parenting, beliefs about how family decisions are made, and views of career involvement and advancement. Across studies, effective work-family balance generally clusters into six general partnership themes: shared housework, mutual and active involvement in child care, joint decision making, equal access to and influence over finances, value placed on both partners' work/life goals, and shared emotional work (Zimmerman, Haddock, Current, & Ziemba, 2003).

SELECTING A PSYCHOTHERAPIST

In seeking a psychotherapist, it is important to inquire about the therapist's education, training, and experience with different kinds of presenting problems and populations. It may also be helpful to ask about the approaches that guide the treatment process. It is important for women to feel free to choose a therapist with whom they feel they can work. Parents often select therapists for their daughters, but it is still important that the daughter feel comfortable with the choice of therapist. A wide range of treatment approaches provides similar beneficial effects, making the person of the therapist more important in most cases than the particular therapeutic approach used. Women are to be encouraged to find a therapist with whom they are comfortable and to choose a therapist according to their own criteria (Gilbert & Scher, 1999). Recommendations by friends with similar attitudes or cultural background or referrals by professionals who are knowledgeable about the client's concerns are advisable.

Because the psychotherapeutic relationship is so personal and private, and clients enter the relationship seeking assistance, the psychotherapist takes the responsibility of informing clients about the nature and boundaries of the psychotherapeutic relationship. The effectiveness of psychotherapy resides in the relationship totally focusing on the needs and growth of the client. The therapist cannot be the personal friend, sexual partner, employer, supervisor, or business partner of her or his clients. Sexual intimacies with a therapist and other forms of dual relationships are unethical and violate the principles of an effective therapeutic relationship (American Psychological Association, 2002).

The psychotherapist also takes responsibility for providing clients with information that allows them to make informed decisions about their therapy and for supplying them with a contract that outlines the therapist's expectations (e.g., fees, length of sessions, and relationship boundaries). In addition, the therapist takes responsibility for informing clients of their rights with regard to challenging therapists who practice outside their areas of competence or violate the boundaries of the therapeutic relationship, and informing them as to where the client can file ethical complaints. Empowering the client is at the heart of good psychotherapy.

CONCLUSIONS

To summarize and conclude, psychotherapy has shown itself over time to be a powerful and positive resource in the lives of girls and women. Through effective psychotherapeutic relationships in which they are heard and valued by their therapist, women and girls can make changes that increase their well-being and improve their ability to recognize the cultural and societal influences in their lives. By understanding the unique biopsychosocial context of women's lives, psychotherapy provides girls and women an opportunity to both heal past wounds and build on their capacities to create even healthier and stronger lives.

REFERENCES

American Psychological Association. (2002). Ethical principles of psychologists and code of conduct. *American Psychologist, 57,* 1060–1073.

Apple, R. F. (1999). Interpersonal therapy for bulimia. *Journal of Clinical Psychology, 55,* 699–713.

Avis, N. E. (2003). Depression during the menopausal transition. *Psychology of Women Quarterly, 27,* 91–100.

Barnett, B. C., & Hyde, J. S. (2001). Women, men, work, and family: An expansionist theory. *American Psychologist, 56,* 781–796.

Beutler, L. E., Malik, M., Alimohamed, S., Harwood, R. M., Talebi, H., Noble, S., et al. (2004). Therapist variables. In M. J. Lambert (Ed.), *Bergin and Garfield's handbook of psychotherapy and behavior change* (pp. 227–306). New York: John Wiley & Sons.

Bordo, S. (1993). *Unbearable weight: Feminism, Western culture, and the body.* Berkeley: University of California Press.

Butler, M. H., & Wampler, K. S. (1999). Couple-responsible therapy process: Positive proximal outcomes. *Family Process, 38,* 27–54.

Consumer Reports. (1995, November). Mental health: Does therapy help? pp. 734–739.

Crawford, M., & Unger, R. (2004). *Women and gender* (rev. ed.). New York: McGraw-Hill.

Deaux, K., & LaFrance, M. (1999). Gender. In D. Gilbert, S. T. Fiske, & G. Lindzey (Eds.), *Handbook of social psychology* (Vol. 1, pp. 788–827). New York: McGraw-Hill.

Fassinger, R. E. (1991). The hidden minority: Issues and challenges in working with lesbian women and gay men. *The Counseling Psychologist, 19*(2), 157–176.

Fassinger, R. E., & Richie, B. S. (1997). Sex matters: Gender and sexual orientation in training for multicultural competency. In D. B. Pope-Davis & H. L. K. Coleman (Eds.), *Multicultural counseling competencies: Assessment, education and training, and supervision* (pp. 83–110). Thousand Oaks, CA: Sage.

Frank, J. D., & Frank, J. B. (1991). *Persuasion and healing: A comparative study of psychotherapy* (3rd ed.). Baltimore: Johns Hopkins University Press.

Garfield, L. (1980). *Psychotherapy: An eclectic approach.* New York: John Wiley & Sons.

Garfield, S. L. (1994). Research on client variables in psychotherapy. In A. E. Bergin & S. L. Garfield (Eds.), *Handbook of psychotherapy and behavior change* (4th ed., pp. 191–228). New York: John Wiley & Sons.

Gilbert, L. A. (1992). Gender and counseling psychology: Current knowledge and directions for research and social action. In S. D. Brown & R. W. Lent (Eds.), *Handbook of counseling psychology* (2nd ed., pp. 383–416). New York: John Wiley & Sons.

Gilbert, L. A. (1993). *Two careers/one family: The promise of gender equality.* Beverly Hills, CA: Sage.

Gilbert, L. A., & Rader, J. (2001). Current perspectives on women's adult roles: Work, family, and life. In R. K. Unger (Ed.), *Handbook of the psychology of women and gender* (pp. 156–169). New York: John Wiley & Sons.

Gilbert, L. A., & Scher, M. (1999). *Gender and sex in counseling and psychotherapy.* Boston: Allyn & Bacon.

Gilbert, S., & Thompson, J. K. (1996). Feminist explanations of the development of eating disorders: Common themes, research findings, and methodological issues. *Clinical Psychology: Science and Practice, 3,* 183–202.

Heilbrun, C. G. (1988). *Writing a women's life.* New York: Ballantine.

Herman, J. L. (1981). *Father-daughter incest.* Cambridge, MA: Harvard University Press.

Horvath, A. O., & Bedi, R. P. (2002). General elements of the therapy relationship. In J. C. Norcross (Ed.), *Psychotherapy relationships that work* (pp. 37–70). New York: Oxford University Press.

Jensen, J. P., & Bergin, A. E. (1990). The meaning of eclecticism: New survey and analysis of components. *Professional Psychology: Research and Practice, 21,* 124–130.

Kazdin, A. E., Siegal, T. C., & Bass, D. (1990). Drawing upon clinical practice to inform research on child and adolescent psychotherapy: A survey of practitioners. *Professional Psychology: Research and Practice, 21,* 189–198.

Kopta, S. M., Lueger, R. J., Saunders, S. M., & Howard, K. I. (1999). Individual psychotherapy outcome and process research: Challenges leading to greater turmoil. In J. T. Spence, J. M. Darley, & D. J. Foss (Eds.), *Annual review of psychology* (pp. 441–471). Palo Alto, CA: Annual Review.

Lambert, M. J. (1992). Psychotherapy outcome research: Implications for integrative and eclectic therapists. In J. C. Norcross & M. R. Goldfried (Eds.), *Handbook of psychotherapy integration* (pp. 94–129). New York: Basic Books.

Lambert, M. J. (Ed.). (2004). *Bergin and Garfield's handbook of psychotherapy and behavior change.* New York: John Wiley & Sons.

Lambert, M. J., & Barley, D. E. (2002). Research summary on the therapeutic relationship and psychotherapy outcome. In J. C. Norcross (Ed.), *Psychotherapy relationships that work* (pp. 17–32). New York: Oxford University Press.

Landrine, H., Klonoff, E., Gibbs, J., Mannings, V., & Lund, M. (1995). Physical and psychiatric correlates of gender discrimination: An application of the Schedule of Sexist Events. *Psychology of Women Quarterly, 19,* 473–492.

Marecek, J. (2001). Disorderly constructs: Feminist frameworks for clinical psychology. In R. K. Unger (Ed.), *Handbook of the psychology of women and gender* (pp. 303–316). New York: John Wiley & Sons.

McGrath, E., Keita, G. P., Strickland, B. R., & Russo, N. F. (Eds.). (1990). *Women and depression: Risk factors and treatment issues.* Washington, DC: American Psychological Association.

Moen, P., & Yu, Y. (2000). Effective work/life strategies: Working couples, work conditions, gender, and life quality. *Social Problems, 47,* 291–326.

Nolen-Hoeksema, S., & Keita, G. P. (2003). Women and depression. *Psychology of Women Quarterly, 27,* 89–142.

Norcross, J. C. (2002). Empirically supported therapy relationships. In J. C. Norcross (Ed.), *Psychotherapy relationships that work* (pp. 3–16). New York: Oxford University Press.

Patterson, C. H. (1974). *Relationship counseling and psychotherapy.* New York: Harper & Row.

Phinney, J. S. (1996). When we talk about American ethnic groups, what do we mean? *American Psychologist, 51,* 918–927.

Rogers, C. R. (1961). *On becoming a person.* Boston: Houghton Mifflin.

Rozee, P. (2000). Freedom from fear of rape: The missing link in women's freedom. In J. Chrisler, C. Golden, & P. Rozee (Eds.), *Lectures in the psychology of women* (2nd ed., pp. 255–260). New York: McGraw-Hill.

Rozee, P. D., & Koss, M. P. (2001). Rape: A century of resistance. *Psychology of Women Quarterly, 25,* 295–311.

Sexton, T. L., Alexander, J. F., & Mease, A. L. (2004). Levels of evidence for the models and mechanisms of therapeutic change in family and couple therapy. In M. J. Lambert (Ed.), *Bergin and Garfield's handbook of psychotherapy and behavior change* (pp. 590–646). New York: John Wiley & Sons.

Stein, R. I., Saelens, B. E., Dounchis, J. Z., Lewczyk, C. M., Swenson, A. K., & Wilfey, D. E. (2001). Treatment of eating disorders in women. *The Counseling Psychologist, 29*(3), 695–732.

Sue, S., & Lam, A. G. (2002). Cultural and demographic diversity. In J. C. Norcross (Ed.), *Psychotherapy relationships that work* (pp. 401–421). New York: Oxford University Press.

Swann, W. B., Jr., Langlois, J., & Gilbert, L. A. (Eds.). (1999). *Sexism and stereotypes in modern society: The gender science of Janet Taylor Spence.* Washington, DC: American Psychological Association.

Thompson, B. W. (1995). *A hunger so wide and deep.* Minneapolis: University of Minnesota Press.

Wampold, B. E. (2001). *The great psychotherapy debate: Models, method, and findings.* Hillsdale, NJ: Erlbaum.

Westkott, M. (1986). *The feminist legacy of Karen Horney.* New Haven, CT: Yale University Press.

Worell, J., & Remer, P. (2003). *Feminist perspectives in therapy: Empowering diverse women* (2nd ed.). New York: John Wiley & Sons.

Wyche, K. F. (2001) Sociocultural issues in counseling women of color. In R. K. Unger (Ed.), *Handbook of the psychology of women and gender* (pp. 330–342). New York: John Wiley & Sons.

Zimmerman, T. S., Haddock, S. A., Current, L. R., & Ziemba, S. (2003). Intimate partnership: Foundation to the successful balance of family and work. *American Journal of Family Therapy, 31,* 107–124.

Phases of Development Within the Life Span

Children and Adolescents: Awakenings

"It's a girl!" or "It's a boy!" are likely to be the first three words spoken at the birth of a baby. These words typically signal two different patterns of expectations, treatment, and eventual behavior—for example, whether the newborn will have a pink or blue blanket, or a sports-themed or flowery room. Thus, gender development begins at birth. Indeed, given the increasing frequency with which expectant parents learn the sex of their fetus, gender development may begin even before birth. In this chapter, we examine patterns of gender development and how aspects of gendered traits and behavior contribute to psychological well-being. First, however, we must examine what we mean by the term "gender."

GENDER AS A MULTIDIMENSIONAL CONSTRUCT

Our binary conceptions of gender (male/female, masculine/feminine) are deeply flawed. Rather than all people being easily divided into two groups with contrasting personality and behavioral styles (e.g., feminine females and masculine males), people actually develop complex patterns of traits, behaviors, identities, and sexualities.

Although we frequently use *sex* and *gender* interchangeably, it may be helpful to think of *sex* as referring to biological markers, such as chromosomes or genitalia. *Gender,* in contrast, refers to the social meaning of this biological variable, as well as to an individual's identification with these meanings (*gender identity*) and/or conformity to these meanings and behaviors (*gender typing* and *gender role conformity*). These aspects of an individual are related, of course, but they are not isomorphic. For example, a person born with a double X chromosome and a uterus, clitoris, and vagina will be "sexed" as female. But depending upon her development, she may or may not identify as female. If she doesn't identify as female, she might be diagnosed with *gender identity disorder* (a controversial diagnosis) and later be considered *transgendered*. Even if she identifies as female, she may develop many possible combinations of traits and behaviors (*gender typing;* Bem, 1993). In the United States, if she develops predominantly expressive and nurturant (communal) traits, she would be gender-typed as *fem-*

SUSAN A. BASOW

Gender Role and Gender Identity Development

inine. If, however, she develops predominantly active and instrumental (agentic) traits, she would be gender-typed as *masculine*. But people also can develop both sets of traits (*androgynous*), or neither set of traits (i.e., they can be *gender aschematic*). In fact, although women tend to have stronger communal traits than do men, most women are not stereotypically feminine.

Based on these variations, there are at least eight possible sex/gender combinations (two sexes, four gender typings). But biological sex isn't binary, either. Given the 1.7% of births that are of individuals whose biological markers are not clearly male or female (*intersex;* Fausto-Sterling, 2000), there actually are at least 12 sex/gender combinations. When you add variations in sexual orientation (homosexual, heterosexual, bisexual), you have at least 36 sex/gender/sexual orientation combinations (e.g., female, androgynous, heterosexual; or female, "feminine," lesbian). Thus, gendered reality is much more complex than those first words pronounced about a newborn.

Some theorists argue that gender is not something individuals "have," but rather something we "do" within a specific social context in interaction with others (Deaux & Stewart, 2001). We are constantly constructing gender by how we dress, move, and act; we can perform gender differently in different situations at different times with different people. The seemingly fixed nature of gender is an illusion we construct to hide a more fluid process. A binary system of gender also hides the power differential embedded in gender roles, with males and all things associated with them as having more power and status in most societies than females and all things associated with them.

Since the meaning of gender is socially constructed, there are cultural variations in how femininity is defined. Meanings of gender vary across race, ethnicity, class, and urbanization (e.g., Abrams, 2003). Whereas *femininity* among U.S. women typically precludes such traits as assertiveness and self-confidence, such meanings are more typical of White than Black Americans, and of college students in the 1970s than the 1990s (Twenge, 1997). For most African Americans and current college students, such traits are not gender-typed as masculine. Using 1970s standards, then, these populations contain more

gender-balanced (i.e., androgynous) than "feminine" females. Thus, the stereotypic communal nonagentic female is a minority type among a significant percentage of the female population.

A further complexity with respect to gender is that it can refer to many things: knowledge of cultural stereotypes, identification, personality traits, and/or behavior. People can and do learn the gender stereotypes without necessarily behaving stereotypically. Similarly, people may behave in gender-"appropriate" ways without possessing a stereotypical gender identification or stereotypic personality traits.

Whether as an identity or as a performance, gender develops and changes over time. We need to examine these developmental patterns relating to gender knowledge, identification, traits, and behavior.

PATTERNS OF GENDER DEVELOPMENT

Gender Knowledge

Given the pervasive gender messages a newborn receives, from the actual words addressed to them, to the colors surrounding them, to the way people hold and talk to them, it is not surprising that children learn gender distinctions very early. In the first year of life, infants can distinguish between males and females, and by the second year, they show some knowledge of gender associations (e.g., female faces go with female voices) and gendered toy preferences (see Bussey & Bandura, 1999).

Language, especially gender labeling, allows children to understand what interests, activities, behaviors, clothes, occupations, etc., "belong" with each sex. Boys are expected to look and act "masculine"; girls are expected to look and act "feminine." These associations are acquired through observation, reactions from others to their own behaviors, and direct instruction, and vary across cultures and subcultures (Bussey & Bandura, 1999). U.S. mainstream culture tends to do a great deal of gender labeling, from colors (pink is for girls, blue is for boys), to accessories (barrettes are for girls, short hair is for boys), to activities (playing house is for girls, playing ball is for boys), to occupations (child care is for girls, truck driving is for boys). By age 4, children tend to disapprove of gender-discordant activities, such as a girl playing with a truck or a boy playing with a doll.

Gender Identification

With language (18–24 months) comes the self-understanding that a child is either a girl or a boy. During the first five years, children learn a great deal about what girls and boys are supposed to do. However, given the concrete nature of children's thinking during these years, they still haven't grasped the permanency of gender or its connection to a specific adult reproductive role. For example, a young child might say a boy is a girl if he wears a barrette, or that a girl could grow up and be a daddy. Once children move beyond concrete thinking and understand the constancy of gender (which occurs between ages 5 and 7), children display stronger gender identification and make even stronger attempts at gender conformity.

Researchers working with intersex children (those born with unclear biological markers of maleness or femaleness) typically advise assigning these children to a particular gender well before 24 months so that gender identification is not impaired (Money & Ehrhardt, 1972). This advice has been contested less on the basis of a critical period for preliminary gender identification than on the need for only two sex categories with its concomitant press for surgical alterations of the body (Fausto-Sterling, 2000). Because so few intersex children are allowed to develop without surgical interventions, we know little about how necessary a two-category gender system is to a child's mental health. We do know, however, that such surgeries can be emotionally and physically traumatic (e.g., Coventry, 2003). These findings suggest we rethink the need for such surgeries, at least on infants.

Different psychological theories provide different explanations for the development of gender identity but most target ages 5–7 as the critical period. Psychodynamic theories emphasize the importance of identifying with the same-sex parent, which occurs through complex and unconscious processes (Chodorow, 1978; Freud, 1933/1965). Problems with gender identity later in

life would be attributed back to some problem in the early parent-child relationship.

In contrast, most current theories emphasize the importance of cognitive processes. One of the first, Kohlberg's (1966) cognitive-developmental theory, stresses the importance of a child's cognitive changes in modulating the meaning of gender. Until a child understands that gender is a fixed aspect of their identity, they don't fully identify with one particular gender. But once they do attain gender identification, they focus intently on conforming to their understanding of gender. Bem's (1993) gender schema theory emphasizes how cultural messages can shape a child's understanding of gender such that by age 7, most children have a cognitive schema through which they sort incoming information according to its gender "appropriateness." Those with a strong gender schema are most likely to notice gender messages and adapt their behavior to conform to cultural norms. These are the individuals most likely to be gender-typed as either feminine or masculine. In contrast, those with a weak gender schema, or without a gender schema at all, may not pay much attention to gender messages and may not adapt their behavior to gender norms. These gender-aschematic people are more likely to be gender-typed as androgynous or undifferentiated.

Perhaps the most comprehensive theory of gender development and differentiation is the social cognitive theory put forward by Bussey and Bandura (1999). This theory views gender development as a result of the reciprocal interaction among personal (e.g., gender-linked conceptions), behavioral (e.g., gender-linked activity patterns), and environmental (e.g., social reactions to behavior) factors.

According to Bussey and Bandura (1999), we learn gender from three sources: modeling (what significant people transmit to us by their own behavior regarding gender-related values, attitudes, and actions), experience (what consequences follow our performance of gender-linked behavior), and direct instruction (what we are told about what girls/women should do, wear, etc.). For example, a girl might see females on television being subordinate to males, she might learn that she gets negative reactions from her peers when she tries to take charge on the playground, and she might be told directly that girls should be "ladylike" and not "bossy." Each person's experience is both complex and unique, so we shouldn't be surprised that many people receive conflicting messages about the meaning of gender. These inconsistencies can create stress for children who are trying to figure out "the rules" for behavior.

Because of cognitive limitations, young children tend to have simplistic views of gender and to believe that one aspect determines all others. Before gender constancy develops (at about age 5), children tend to think gender is something you can change with a change of clothes and hairstyles unless they've learned that genitalia define female/male differences (Bem, 1989). During the time gender constancy develops, children are particularly rigid regarding gendered behavior. It is not uncommon for a 6-year-old girl to insist on wearing dresses, even if her mother never wears dresses and prefers her to wear pants because "girls wear dresses." Once gender constancy exists and gender identification has occurred (typically after age 7), children tend to look even more attentively at what same-sex models are doing and to associate primarily with same-sex others. It's as if a child says to herself, "Well, now that I'm a girl for life, let me take seriously what it is that girls do."

Gendered Traits and Behaviors

Children begin learning the traits and behaviors that "go" with each sex from the minute they are born, but show individual differences in their gender performance depending upon the models they encounter, direct gender messages they receive about how girls and boys should be and behave, and reactions to their behavior. In general, girls in U.S. society show greater flexibility with respect to gender conceptualizations and behavior performance than boys (Bauer, Liebl, & Stennes, 1998; Blakemore, 2003). This greater flexibility may be because in U.S. society there is a wider range of acceptable behavior for girls than boys (for example, although girls can either wear pants or dresses, boys can only wear pants). It may also be because the lower status of the female role makes female behavior less closely attended to or regulated, at least until puberty. Another theory is that the active presence of real women in the early lives of girls gives children more complex models of female behaviors than boys (Chodorow, 1978). Whatever the reason, girls' greater flexibility may allow them to acquire a wider range of traits (both communal and agentic) and behaviors than boys, although the communal traits may be more stressed.

From age 7 to pre-puberty, children tend to have gender-typed traits (Hall & Halberstadt, 1980), play in same-sex groups, and attend more closely to same-sex models (Maccoby, 1998). Such a division is typically both directly and indirectly encouraged. For example, teachers may divide boys and girls into two competing groups for activities. If a child attempts to cross gender lines, she may experience disapproval from both her same-sex and her other-sex peers. Furthermore, she may have few models of peers or adults who engage in non-gender-stereotypic roles and behaviors. Finally, she may find playing with similar others more comfortable and enjoyable, since she already has acquired gender-based behavior patterns, such as using language to resolve conflicts rather than force. As a result of growing up in two very different "social worlds," gendered behaviors get strengthened. Girls and boys thus frequently enter puberty with very different patterns of interests, attitudes, communication patterns, and play styles.

The time around puberty is a time of gender intensification, as both girls and boys struggle to learn and adapt to the gendered norms of adulthood (Hill & Lynch, 1983). Gender takes on new meaning as sexual feelings increase. For most teens, performing gender now incorporates ways of being attractive to the other sex and preparing for adulthood. Future work and family roles become salient. Girls become more oriented toward interpersonal goals, especially attracting a mate, and become less career oriented than boys. As a result, high school girls enroll in significantly fewer higher level mathematics, science, and computer courses than their male peers (Eccles, 1987).

For girls, ages 10–13 often represent a "crossroads" (Brown & Gilligan, 1992), a time when a girls' journey toward self-development is challenged and potentially derailed. Cultural messages about the meaning of being a woman may require girls to silence their own voices and adopt a more subordinate style, more appealing to boys and men. For White girls, this may mean becoming less assertive, less confident, more concerned with one's appearance, more dissatisfied with one's body, and more restricted behaviorally. Hispanic girls in particular may have their behavior more closely monitored, as concerns about sexuality and maintaining virginity come to the fore. African American girls may encounter expectations of sexual promiscuity by parents and peers. All girls become more subject to sexual harassment from males (Abrams, 2003).

Given these pressures, it is perhaps not surprising that the incidence of depression and eating disorders increases dramatically, especially in White girls after puberty, and that many report they are less happy than they once were (Nolen-Hoeksema & Girgus, 1994; Wichstrom, 1999). The increase in depression can be attributed to dissatisfaction with weight and the attainment of a mature female body, the increased importance of feminine sex role identification, a ruminative coping style, and previous experience of sexual abuse. African American girls tend to show a more resilient pattern, perhaps because their models of womanhood are less the very thin young sex objects in the media and more the outspoken strong women in their community. A strong ethnic identity appears helpful in resisting the negative effects of idealized femininity (Abrams, 2003). For example, being proud of one's heritage as an African American or Latina may cause these girls to actively resist or reject ideals of female passivity or body dissatisfaction.

Sexual identity issues become prominent during adolescence as individuals learn more about their desires. Virtually all children are steered toward heterosexuality (Rich, 1983) and many start exploring those feelings during adolescence. Although more young women exhibit sexual agency than in the past, most still also experience "dilemmas of desire," wherein their burgeoning awareness of their own sexual desires collides with the cultural view of female sexuality as passive and female sexual behavior as stigmatized (Tolman, 2002). For non-heterosexual females, there may be even more concerns. A common trajectory is for an individual to experience some sense of being different from same-sex peers before adolescence, followed by a period of sexual identity confusion during adolescence. After this

confusion, during which heterosexual relationships may be entered, lesbians typically assume a gay identity and develop a positive view of that identity (Frable, 1997). Females seem to come to an awareness of their same-sex attraction later than males, and their sexual identity development seems to be a more fluid process throughout the life span (Peplau, 2003). For example, it is not unusual for women to "come out" in their 30s or 40s after a heterosexual marriage, or even for self-avowed lesbians to later develop a heterosexual relationship. Bisexuals appear to self-identify later than lesbians and gay men (Frable, 1997). This flexibility regarding sexuality may be related to the generally greater flexibility of the female gender role than the male in U.S. culture, or it may be related to different pathways of sexual development. In any case, a positive gay identity seems critical for good mental health, something the social stigma against homosexuality makes difficult.

Although most writers on gender development consider gender to be relatively fixed before or shortly after puberty, those with a more constructionist orientation argue that the performance of gender continues to change throughout the life span (Deaux & Stewart, 2001). Our sense of being female expands and shifts as we take on additional life roles. For example, when a woman becomes a mother for the first time, that identity may become most central. Indeed, some argue that the adult roles we assume shape our performance of gender such that anyone who cares for young children actually becomes more nurturant and empathic, and anyone in leadership roles becomes more assertive and dominant. This social role theory (Eagly, 1987) suggests that many of the gendered behavior patterns we see in adulthood are a result of different social roles rather than a precursor of assuming such roles. Thus, throughout the life span, we are constantly negotiating our gender identity in different social roles and situations.

PSYCHOLOGICAL EFFECTS OF GENDER ROLE AND GENDER IDENTITY DEVELOPMENT

Although conventional wisdom suggests that it is important for girls and boys to have a clear gender identity, to be heterosexual, and to conform to cultural gendered norms, the research results paint a different picture. Generally speaking, those individuals who possess both the stereotypical masculine traits of instrumentality and assertiveness, as well as the stereotypical feminine traits of nurturance and expressiveness (that is, gender-aschematic individuals), seem to have the most behavioral flexibility in both work and interpersonal relationships. There also is evidence that individuals with egalitarian attitudes toward gender roles and/or who are not strictly gender conforming are more likely to have higher self-esteem and better mental health and relationships than individuals with more traditional attitudes and conforming behavior. Furthermore, there is considerable evidence that individuals who identify as gay, lesbian, or bisexual are as psychologically healthy as individuals who identify as heterosexual. Feeling comfortable with one's own gender does, however, seem to be important for psychological health. Let's look at these four aspects—gender typing, gender role behavior, sexual identity, and gender identity—individually.

Gender Typing

Research since the 1970s consistently finds that individuals with strong instrumental active traits (masculine and androgynous individuals) have higher self-esteem and less anxiety and depression than individuals low in such traits (Basow, 1992; Broderick & Korteland, 2002). Because traditional socialization of girls typically neglects or discourages such traits, especially among White Americans, these girls and women tend to have higher rates of depression and anxiety and lower self-esteem than their male counterparts. Thus traditional gender typing in girls typically is not good for their mental health.

On the other hand, individuals with strong nurturant expressive traits (feminine and androgynous individuals) demonstrate better communication skills, such as decoding nonverbal cues, and report greater relationship satisfaction (Basow, 1992). Because traditional socialization of females typically encourages such traits, girls and women tend to be advantaged in this area. Indeed, women are often considered to be "re-

lationship experts," although relationship skills are more tied to communal traits than to biological sex. People low on such traits, more likely to be male than female, may have difficulty expressing their feelings, potentially impairing the degree of intimacy in their relationships and increasing the risk of stress-related physical disorders.

Thus, traditionally gender-typed individuals are prone to different types of problems. Highly feminine individuals may be more at risk for low self-esteem, anxiety, and depression while highly masculine individuals may be more at risk for stress-related disorders and unsatisfactory relationships. Gender-balanced or androgynous individuals appear most likely to avoid a wide range of psychological, relational, and physical problems (Woodhill & Samuels, 2003). It appears to be a good sign, then, that college women are becoming increasingly gender-balanced.

Gender Role Conformity: Behavior and Attitudes

Children acquire their attitudes about "appropriate" gendered behavior from their parents as well as society at large. Those with egalitarian attitudes (who believe that women and men are equal and should share the social roles of child care and employment) tend to have better adjustment and mental health, higher self-esteem, and more satisfactory personal relationships than individuals who believe in traditional gender roles (that men should be dominant and that women and men should do different activities; Bussey & Bandura, 1999). Children in homes with egalitarian parents, as well as those raised by single parents, tend to be the most egalitarian in their own attitudes, with girls tending to be more egalitarian than boys.

In terms of gender-role conformity, boys tend to be more conforming than girls and more rigid in enforcing gendered norms. There is no question that children who conform to traditional gender-role expectations have an easier time in peer interactions, starting in preschool and peaking during adolescence (Bussey & Bandura, 1999). But such social acceptance may come at the price of stifling one's own needs and desires (Brown & Gilligan, 1992; Heilman, 1998) and, for girls, increasing risk of developing body dissatisfaction and eating disorders (Martz, Handley, & Eisler, 1995). The majority of girls, especially White middle-class girls, are dissatisfied with their bodies and more than half of fifth grade girls are on diets. African American girls are more resistant to body dissatisfaction, probably because they are using different models of female attractiveness, but they too can succumb if they lack a strong ethnic identity and adopt the ultra-slim media image as their ideal (Abrams, 2003).

Girls who conform to the traditional female gender role also tend to neglect adequate career preparation. Although girls and boys perform similarly in the early grades, by junior high, girls (as well as their parents) believe girls have less talent for math and begin to avoid such classes and related activities (Eccles, 1987). Just reminding women of their gender may cause them to perform more poorly on college-level math tests than if their gender (and its related stereotype of math inadequacy) were never invoked (Steele, 1997).

In adulthood, gender conformity is less mandated although frequently still rewarded by peers. But nonconforming individuals typically can find similar others with whom to socialize: for example, other women in nontraditional careers or other women who have chosen not to have children. Still, most women choose female-dominated professions, especially if they view themselves as highly feminine (Matsui, Ikeda, & Ohnishi, 1989). The outcome is that women employed full time earn only 75% of what men earn, since traditional female occupations tend to be low in pay and status. Even women in nontraditional occupations earn less than their male peers due to societal stereotypes and the "glass ceiling."

Although there still is a prevailing expectation that mothers with young children will stay home to care for them, most mothers (55%) of infants are in the labor force, as well as three out of four mothers with children older than one year (2000 U.S. Census). The major stress for these women is the expectation that, regardless of their work involvement, they are responsible for home and child care as well. Although husbands have increased their participation in these activities, women still do more, even if they work full time (Basow, 1992). Traditional gender-role ideology may make it difficult for some women to demand more spouse participation and for some men to give it. These women tend to be most stressed by their dual workloads. In contrast, egalitarian marriages, in which the husband and wife truly share responsibilities, tend to be the most satisfying to both partners. On the whole, despite the stresses of juggling work and family responsibilities, employed mothers, especially those who are satisfied with their jobs, tend to be happier and more satisfied than stay-at-home mothers, perhaps because they have more potential sources of satisfaction (Barnett & Rivers, 1996).

Sexual Orientation

Many people still think of nonheterosexual individuals as pathological, yet research during the last 30 years confirms that the psychological well-being of heterosexuals, homosexuals, and bisexuals is indistinguishable from each other (Peplau & Garnets, 2000). Although being gay or lesbian can be very stressful for individuals whose family and peers are unaccepting, the stress and distress come from the lack of social support, not from one's sexual orientation. Individuals who have "come out" and/or who have a positive gay identity tend to have better mental health than those who feel negatively about themselves and/or who fear disclosing their sexual orientation (Frable, 1997). Studies of lesbian, gay, and heterosexual couples find no differences in relationship satisfaction, although lesbian couples tend to be the most egalitarian and have the highest intimacy levels of all couples (Kurdek, 1994).

Gender Identity

As we have seen, gender is not a fixed identity but a multidimensional construct, one sensitive to changing cultural and temporal contexts. As such, although individuals may carry with them a continuing sense of being either female or male throughout their lives, the meanings attached to those terms may vary dramatically over time and across situations. A young girl who identifies as female may know that women typically wear makeup, marry, and have children, yet when she grows up she may expand the meaning of being female to include being strong and agentic, having a female partner, and working as a police officer. Engaging in nontraditional occupations or behaviors, or possessing nonstereotypic traits, does not lessen her identification with being female. In this way, gender identity is separate from the possession of particular traits and behaviors or a particular sexual orientation. It also is not a static "thing" but a constantly negotiated process (Deaux & Stewart, 2001).

Viewing gender identity as a fixed aspect of identity is problematic for individuals whose gendered sense of self is at variance with their biological sex. Children who have "a strong and persistent cross-gender identification" and who have "persistent discomfort with his or her sex or sense of inappropriateness in the gender role of that sex" might be classified as having a gender identity disorder (GID; American Psychiatric Association, 2000, p. 581). Although not meant to describe children whose play is at variance with conventional gendered norms, such behaviors may precipitate a psychiatric referral, especially if the child is a boy since cross-gender behavior is much less tolerated in boys than girls. In the majority of cases, children outgrow the diagnosis, although they are more likely to identify as homosexual or bisexual in adolescence and adulthood than their non-GID peers. At least this is the case for males; unfortunately, there is little data on the course of GID in females. The ratio of girls to boys with GID is 1:5, which may relate to the greater flexibility of gender-role behavior and identity in girls than in boys. A minority of both sexes appear to grow into adulthood with the diagnostic criteria intact; these individuals might eventually identify as transsexuals and seek sexual reassignment surgery to transform their body so that it matches their gender identification. The distress of feeling like one was born in the "wrong" body is intense, and such individuals typically have a difficult adolescence and adulthood until they come to

terms with either a transgendered or transsexual identity (Feinberg, 1993). Many of the problems arise from the social rejection (often accompanied by verbal and physical abuse) of those who do not fit neatly into U.S. society's binary gender system. Whether there would be the same number of individuals having sexual reassignment surgery in a culture where gender identity and gender role conformity were more flexible is open to debate (e.g., Rottnek, 1999).

CONCLUSIONS

One of the implications of the complexities of gender role and gender identity development is with respect to the socialization of children. Strict gender typing and gender role conformity do not seem most advantageous to children, and children who have strong gender schemas are not as behaviorally flexible as those less schematic for gender. Children vary in terms of their individual temperaments, aptitudes, and interests, but they do not vary primarily by gender. Allowing children to develop to their maximum potential with a full range of human traits and behaviors is likely to result in healthiest and most productive children and adults.

Learning that the difference between females and males relates to potential reproductive roles should allow children to develop a healthy gender identity without restricting their behavior when it comes to toys, colors, activities, and occupations. If we accept that gays, lesbians, and bisexuals can be as healthy and happy as heterosexuals, we might be more concerned about reducing the homophobia they are likely to encounter and less on trying to change them. Schools in particular can potentially become a site for "stopping the performance" (Heilman, 1998) by fostering healthy complete identities for both girls and boys. Learning to resist unhealthy cultural mandates regarding gender is imperative for promoting fully functioning adults.

Our society as a whole needs to be more open with respect to varieties of gender expression and not punish people who do not fit neatly into the binary boxes of masculine/heterosexual/male and feminine/heterosexual/female. Only by broadening our notions of gender will we have a society where individuals can truly flourish and achieve their maximal psychological health.

NOTE

Appreciation goes to Karen Mandel for her assistance with this chapter.

REFERENCES

Abrams, L. S. (2003). Contextual variations in young women's gender identity negotiations. *Psychology of Women Quarterly, 27,* 64–74.

American Psychiatric Association. (2000). *Diagnostic and statistical manual of mental disorders* (4th ed., text rev.). Washington, DC: Author.

Barnett, R. C., & Rivers, C. (1996). *She works/he works: How two-income families are happy, healthy, and thriving.* Cambridge, MA: Harvard University Press.

Basow, S. A. (1992). *Gender: Stereotypes and roles* (3rd ed.). Pacific Grove, CA: Brooks/Cole.

Bauer, P. J., Liebl, M., & Stennes, L. (1998). Pretty is to dress as brave is to suitcoat: Gender-based property-to-property inferences by 4-1/2-year-old children. *Merrill-Palmer Quarterly, 44,* 355–377.

Bem, S. L. (1989). Genital knowledge and gender constancy in preschool children. *Child Development, 60,* 649–662.

Bem, S. L. (1993). *The lenses of gender: Transforming the debate on sexual inequality.* New Haven, CT: Yale University Press.

Blakemore, J. E. (2003). Children's beliefs about violating gender norms: Boys shouldn't look like girls, and girls shouldn't act like boys. *Sex Roles, 48,* 411–419.

Broderick, P. C., & Korteland, C. (2002). Coping style and depression in early adolescence: Relationships to gender, gender role, and implicit beliefs. *Sex Roles, 46,* 201–213.

Brown, L. M., & Gilligan, C. (1992). *Meeting at the crossroads: Women's psychology and girls' development.* Cambridge, MA: Harvard University Press.

Bussey, K., & Bandura, A. (1999). Social cognitive theory of gender development and differentiation. *Psychological Review, 106*(4), 676–713.

Chodorow, N. (1978). *The reproduction of mothering: Psychoanalysis and the sociology of gender.* Berkeley: University of California Press.

Coventry, M. (2003). The tyranny of the esthetic: Surgery's most intimate violation. In E. Disch (Ed.), *Reconstructing gender: A multicultural anthology* (3rd ed., pp. 204–212). Boston: McGraw-Hill.

Deaux, K., & Stewart, A. J. (2001). Framing gender identities. In R. K. Unger (Ed.), *Handbook of the psychology of women and gender* (pp. 84–97). New York: John Wiley & Sons.

Eagly, A. H. (1987). *Sex differences in social behavior: A social role interpretation.* Hillsdale, NJ: Erlbaum.

Eccles, J. (1987). Gender roles and women's achievement-related decisions. *Psychology of Women Quarterly, 11,* 135–172.

Fausto-Sterling, A. (2000). *Sexing the body: Gender politics and the construction of sexuality.* New York: Basic Books.

Feinberg, L. (1993). *Stone butch blues.* Ithaca, NY: Firebrand Books.

Frable, D. E. (1997). Gender, racial, ethnic, sexual, and class identities. *Annual Review of Psychology, 48,* 139–162.

Freud, S. (1933/1965). Femininity. In J. Strachey (Ed. and Trans.), *New introductory lectures on psychoanalysis* (pp. 112–135). New York: Norton.

Hall, J. A., & Halberstadt, A. G. (1980). Masculinity and femininity in children: Development of the Children's Personal Attributes Questionnaire. *Developmental Psychology, 16,* 270–280.

Heilman, E. E. (1998). The struggle for self. *Youth & Society, 30*(2), 182–208.

Hill, J. P., & Lynch, M. C. (1983). The intensification of gender-related role expectations during early adolescence. In J. Brooks-Gunn & A. C. Petersen (Eds.), *Girls at puberty: Biological and psychosocial perspectives* (pp. 201–228). New York: Plenum Press.

Kohlberg, L. (1966). A cognitive-developmental analysis of children's sex-role concepts and attitudes. In E. E. Maccoby (Ed.), *The development of sex differences* (pp. 82–173). Stanford, CA: Stanford University Press.

Kurdek, L. A. (1994). The nature and correlates of relationship quality in gay, lesbian, and heterosexual cohabiting couples. In B. Greene & G. M. Herek (Eds.), *Lesbian and gay psychology* (pp. 113–155). Thousand Oaks, CA: Sage.

Maccoby, E. E. (1998). *The two sexes: Growing up apart, coming together.* Cambridge, MA: Belknap Press.

Martz, D. M., Handley, K. B., & Eisler, R. M. (1995). The relationship between feminine gender role stress, body image, and eating disorders. *Psychology of Women Quarterly, 19,* 493–508.

Matsui, T., Ikeda, H., & Ohnishi, R. (1989). Relations of sex-typed socialization to career self-efficacy expectations of college students. *Journal of Vocational Behavior, 35,* 1–16.

Money, J., & Ehrhardt, A. A. (1972). *Man and woman, boy and girl: The differentiation and dimorphism of gender identity from conception to maturity.* Baltimore: John Hopkins University Press.

Nolen-Hoeksema, S., & Girgus, J. S. (1994). The emergence of gender differences in depression during adolescence. *Psychological Bulletin, 115,* 424–443.

Peplau, L. A. (2003). Human sexuality: How do men and women differ? *Psychological Science, 12,* 37–40.

Peplau, L. A., & Garnets, L. D. (Eds.). (2000). Women's sexualities: New perspectives on sexual orientation and gender. *Journal of Social Issues, 56,* 181–192.

Rich, A. (1983). Compulsory heterosexuality and lesbian existence. In A. Snitow, C. Stansell, & S. Thompson (Eds.), *Powers of desires: The politics of sexuality* (pp. 177–205). New York: Monthly Review Press.

Rottnek, M. (Ed.). (1999). *Sissies and tomboys: Gender nonconformity and homosexual childhood.* New York: New York University Press.

Steele, C. M. (1997). A threat in the air: How stereotypes shape the intellectual identities and performance of women and African-Americans. *American Psychologist, 52,* 613–629.

Tolman, D. L. (2002). *Dilemmas of desire: Teenage girls talk about sexuality.* Cambridge, MA: Harvard University Press.

Twenge, J. M. (1997). Changes in masculine and feminine traits over time: A meta-analysis. *Sex Roles, 36,* 305–325.

Wichstrom, L. (1999). The emergence of gender differences in depressed mood during adolescence: The role of intensified gender socialization. *Developmental Psychology, 35,* 232–245.

Woodhill, B. M., & Samuels, C. A. (2003). Positive and negative androgyny and their relationship with psychological heath and well-being. *Sex Roles, 48,* 555–565.

Today, perhaps more so than ever, interest in the integration of girls' and women's psychological and physical health is valued and recognized as an important area of study. Within this context, the purpose of this chapter is to describe the interplay of physical and psychosocial factors in girls' development, and to encourage readers to consider this interplay in interactions with pre-adolescent and adolescent girls. The chapter is not comprehensive, but rather focuses on examples to illustrate key ways that girls' physical and psychosocial functioning are interrelated. The issues illustrated complement materials described in other chapters of this book.

The first section sets the stage by highlighting common psychological issues that are especially pertinent to understanding girls' functioning. The second section focuses on common, normative events in girls' development and highlights the interplay of physical and psychosocial functioning in these contexts; in contrast, the third section focuses on nonnormative events in girls' lives that also illustrate the interrelatedness of physical and psychosocial functioning. Throughout these sections, the implications of research for health professionals are discussed.

ANNETTE M. LA GRECA,
ELEANOR RACE MACKEY,
and KAREN BEARMAN MILLER

The Interplay of Physical and Psychosocial Development

27

SEVERAL KEY ISSUES FOR GIRLS

Over the years, there has been considerable interest in the study of sex differences. Although there are obvious physical differences between girls and boys, evidence for sex differences in psychological functioning is less clear (see Shaffer, 1996). Nevertheless, several themes have emerged in research on sex differences. This section describes a few key themes that may be especially pertinent for understanding the interplay of girls' psychological and physical functioning. These themes focus on: (a) emotional sensitivity and expressivity; (b) activity level; (c) concerns about weight and appearance; and (d) expressions of emotional distress.

According to Shaffer (1996), from early childhood on, girls in comparison to boys have been found to be more emotionally expressive, to rate themselves higher in nurturance and empathy, to report more intense emotions, and to feel more comfortable expressing their emotions. Perhaps because of their sensitivity, girls are more attuned to others' impressions of them, and express more concerns about what others think of them than do boys (La Greca & Lopez, 1998). Girls cope with stressful life events by seeking support and reassurance from family and friends, and also may be concerned about the repercussions of life events for their interpersonal relations (Frydenberg & Lewis, 1991).

Another common sex difference pertains to activity level. From infancy on, girls are less physically active than boys and this difference is especially pronounced in adolescence. For example, the Youth Risk Behavior Surveillance Survey, administered by the Centers for Disease Control and Prevention (2002), revealed that 73% of adolescent boys, but only 57% of adolescent girls, participated in vigorous physical activity on a regular basis. Adolescent boys were significantly more likely than girls to play on sports teams (61% of boys; 50% of girls), or participate in strengthening activities (e.g., push-ups, sit-ups; 63% of boys; 45% of girls). Thus, girls may be less likely to use physical activities as a way of coping with stressors than boys, and may have more difficulty than boys should they develop a condition that requires regular exercise.

Emphasis on physical appearance, weight, and body shape is another salient area for girls. U.S. culture is replete with messages that suggest girls and women should be thin and physically attractive. As a result, from the elementary school years on through adulthood, girls and women express more concerns about their physical appearance than do boys and men. For example, weight concerns and dieting are common even

among third grade girls (Robinson, Chang, Haydel, & Killen, 2001), and many girls are unhappy with their body shape and weight (Field et al., 1999). Girls' preoccupation with body weight and appearance is an important factor in the interplay between girls' physical and psychological functioning, as physical conditions that adversely affect girls' weight or appearance may have negative psychological repercussions. Also, girls may engage in health-risk behaviors, such as smoking, just to maintain or lose weight (Stice & Shaw, 2003).

Finally, research on psychosocial adjustment suggests that from childhood on, girls are less likely than boys to be physically aggressive (Shaffer, 1996; Verhulst et al., 2003), but are more likely to report feelings of "internal distress," such as fears and worries, or feelings of anxiety (e.g., Epkins, 2002). By early adolescence, sex differences become apparent for rates of depressive disorders, which are substantially higher in girls than boys (e.g., Angold, Costello, & Worthman, 1998). Recent statistics from the Centers for Disease Control and Prevention (2002) indicate that adolescents girls are significantly more likely than adolescent boys to report feeling sad or hopeless almost every day (35% of girls; 22% of boys), and are more likely to have considered attempting suicide in the prior 12-month period (24% of girls; 14% of boys). Such findings indicate that "internalized distress" is a common psychosocial problem for girls, and thus should be anticipated in girls' reactions to adverse life events or to psychological or physical stressors.

NORMATIVE INFLUENCES

In the normal course of girls' lives, there is a significant interplay between their physical and psychosocial domains. There are several specific contexts that affect many girls: common problems in physical development, the transition phase of puberty, participation in athletic activities; reactions to family stress; and weight and body concerns. In most cases, it is difficult to disentangle the "cause" and "effect," as the linkages between physical and psychological functioning may be bi-directional. Nevertheless, awareness of the psychological-physical interplay is important.

Common Physical Problems

Many children experience some physical problems in childhood. Nearly 4 million people under age 18 wear braces to correct dental malformations (American Association of Orthodontics, 2003), and 25% of children wear glasses to correct poor vision (American Academy of Ophthalmology, 2003). Problems with acne are common and affect an estimated 85% of adolescents and young adults (Hanna, Sharma, & Klotz, 2003).

Because of girls' concerns about physical appearance, common physical problems, such as wearing braces or glasses, may affect girls' self-esteem and contribute to feelings of anxiety or depression. Acne is prevalent in adolescence, a time of heightened social pressures. It is related to several indicators of internal distress in girls, such as depression, anxiety, and lower self-esteem (Hanna et al., 2003). Girls who place a high degree of importance on appearance may be especially vulnerable to these potential negative consequences of physical differences.

Puberty

Puberty is one of the most important, normative, physical transitions for girls, and has far-reaching effects from late childhood through mid-adolescence. Puberty typically begins between the ages of 9 and 13, and most girls handle this transition very well. However, for some young girls, the transition through puberty is associated with increased rates of depression (Angold et al., 1998).

The physical and hormonal changes of puberty appear to exacerbate girls' high levels of concern about their body image and physical appearance. Girls' breast development is related to a more positive body image, whereas increases in follicle stimulating hormone (which stimulates the release of eggs from the ovary) is related to decreases in body image (Slap, Khalid, Paikoff, Brooks-Gunn, & Warren, 1994). The transition through puberty also is related to greater internalization of the "thin ideal" and this increased internalization cannot be explained by other factors, such as age or awareness of the ideal (Hermes & Keel, 2003). Thus, the changes girls undergo in puberty may affect their self-concept, mood, and body image.

An important question is *why* the transition through puberty, particularly with regard to hormonal changes, is related to increased rates of depression in girls. Puberty increases girls' levels of oxytocin, a hormone that stimulates affiliative needs and behaviors; in turn, this increased need for affiliation may lead to depression in girls when affiliative needs are not met (Frank & Young, 2002). Further complicating the picture is the fact that peer affiliations change rapidly during adolescence. This instability in close relationships can interact with affiliative needs and contribute to feelings of depression or dysphoria in girls.

The *timing of puberty* also influences girls' psychological well-being, especially when girls transition through puberty earlier than their peers. Early puberty has been linked with a number of psychosocial problems, including depression, phobic disorders, subclinical bulimia, substance abuse, disruptive behavior, low self-esteem, poor coping skills, low support from friends and family, suicide attempts, tobacco use, and perceptions of being overweight (Graber, Lewinsohn, Seeley, & Brooks-Gunn, 1997; Killen et al., 1997).

The link between *early* puberty and poorer psychological functioning probably occurs because girls who appear to be older than they really are face greater challenges in interpersonal, peer, and family situations. At the same time, they may lack the emotional maturity and coping skills needed to deal with challenging situations (Ge, Conger, & Elder, 1996). In addition, early-maturing girls become involved in dating relationships at an early age and are more likely to engage in problem behaviors, such as smoking, drinking, or substance use (Ge et al., 1996). Alternatively, girls who experience puberty later than their peers seem to be protected from some of the distress and negative outcomes of peers who experience puberty early or on-time (Ge et al., 1996).

The transition through and timing of puberty are prime examples of how physical functioning may affect girls' psychological health. Overall, puberty represents a potentially difficult physical transition for girls that may contribute to increased concerns about appearance and weight, increased symptoms of depression, and lower self-esteem. Psychosocial and behavioral problems are especially prominent for girls who go through this physical transition earlier than their peers. Despite these challenges, most girls successfully cope with the transition of puberty and do not develop behavioral or psychosocial difficulties as a result.

Physical Exercise

Many girls actively participate in sports and other physical activities. Girls' participation in exercise or sports is related to more positive mental health, such as higher levels of self esteem (Butcher, 1989). In addition, Moore, Glickman, Kuttler, and La Greca (2001) found that adolescent girls who affiliated with the "jock" peer crowd in their high school reported higher self-esteem, lower levels of depression and social anxiety, and higher levels of perceived romantic appeal and social support than did other girls. "Jock" girls also engaged in less risky sexual behavior than their male counterparts (La Greca & Moore, 2002).

On the other hand, girls who participate in *certain* sports may be at risk for eating problems. A recent meta-analysis revealed that among adolescent girls, athletes and nonathletes did not differ with respect to eating problems (Smolak, Murnen, & Ruble, 2000). However, girls and young women who were involved in elite sports (e.g., involving high levels of competition) and certain physical activities that encourage a thin physique (e.g., ballet, cheerleading, aerobics instruction) displayed higher levels of eating problems (bingeing, severe dieting) and greater body dissatisfaction than non-athletes. In contrast, girls who participated in nonelite, nonlean sports had *lower* levels of eating problems and *less* body dissatisfaction than nonathletes.

Such data suggest that *other aspects* of the sports' culture (e.g., pressures from parents or coaches, demands of the sport) contribute to eating problems in some girls (Smolak et al., 2000). Sports participation, without the emphasis on lean body image or high levels of competition, generally shows a positive mental health benefit for girls.

Family Stress

All families experience some stress. In fact, 80% of couples may have seriously considered divorce at some point in their marriage (Sabatelli & Chadwick, 2000). High rates of divorce and separation mean that many youth undergo significant family disruption.

Several lines of research have found linkages between family stress and girls' physical functioning. For example, girls who experience a change from a two-parent home to a single-mother home, or who are in continuous single-mother households, are more likely to transition through puberty at an earlier age than girls in stable two-parent homes (Ellis, McFadyen-Ketchum, Dodge, Pettit, & Bates, 1999). Moreover, girls who have greater conflict with their mothers and feel less support from them tend to enter puberty earlier (Kim & Smith, 1998). In contrast, girls with more positive family interactions and those who experience greater positivity and affection from their fathers tend to transition through puberty later (Ellis et al., 1999; Graber, Brooks-Gunn, & Warren, 1995).

Family stress and divorce both have been related to poor physical health for adolescent girls, including high rates of headaches, fatigue, and backaches (Spruijt, DeGoede, & Vandervalk, 2001). In addition, high amounts of family stress increase the likelihood of adolescent substance use (Farrell & Barnes, 2000).

In summary, family-related stress is associated with a number of physical and psychological repercussions for girls. This is especially the case when stressors occur during late childhood (as girls transition through puberty) and during adolescence.

Weight Concerns and Smoking

Adolescent girls' weight concerns and body dissatisfaction play a role in the initiation and maintenance of cigarette smoking (Camp, Klesges, & Relyea, 1993). Many girls believe that smoking can help control appetite and weight, and report smoking for this reason. In fact, female gender and "restrictive" eating behaviors predict the use of smoking as a weight control method (Camp et al., 1993).

In general, high levels of body dissatisfaction, dieting, problematic eating habits, and fear of weight gain are all predictive of girls' smoking behaviors (e.g., Austin & Gortmaker, 2001). In fact, dieting and weight concerns *double* girls' risk of beginning to smoke, in comparison with girls who do not report weight concerns or dieting attempts (Austin & Gortmaker, 2001). In addition, the use of smoking as an active weight-control method is the single best variable that differentiates girls who smoke regularly from girls who only experiment with smoking (Robinson, Klesges, Zbikowski, & Glaser, 1997).

Smoking and the use of extreme weight-loss strategies seem to go hand in hand for many adolescent girls. This is worrisome because extreme weight-loss strategies, as well as smoking, adversely influence physical health.

Summary and Implications

Girls' physical and psychological well-being are intertwined. Physical characteristics such as weight and appearance, and physical changes such as puberty, affect girls' psychological functioning. Conversely, girls' psychological functioning and family stress affect aspects of physical functioning, such as the timing of puberty, extreme dieting, and smoking. It is essential, therefore, for health care professionals to recognize these interrelationships in order to prevent physical or psychological difficulties from arising and to enhance both physical and psychological functioning.

For instance, it is important to be aware that common physical problems (e.g., braces, acne) may have a significant psychological impact for girls. Girls may benefit psychologically from medical treatments that can improve their appearance, but in the short term girls may also need assistance to cope better with teasing by peers or worries about their attractiveness.

Health-care professionals who deal with girls during the transition through puberty may benefit from trying to gain a *comprehensive* picture of girls' functioning. What stressors do girls' encounter? Do they have concerns about weight and body image? Have they developed any early patterns of substance use (i.e., smoking, drinking)? What social supports are available to them? It is vital to be attuned to the timing and stage of puberty in girls and to ensure that girls receive additional social support from family, peers, and health-care providers during this normal but potentially difficult transition period.

It may be useful to encourage girls to engage in certain activities, such as sports, which enhance their body image and self-esteem, or other activities that make good use of their physical and psychosocial capabilities (e.g., playing an instrument, singing in a choir, Girl Scouts, hospital volunteer, etc.). At the same time, it is important that health-care professionals be aware that girls who are involved in highly competitive sports or activities that demand a slim physique are more likely to encounter difficulties with body satisfaction and problematic eating behaviors.

Health-care professionals might also bear in mind that girls' reports of significant somatic complaints or early substance use may reflect family, peer, or school stressors. By asking girls about their family life and any significant sources of stress, as well as sources of support, health professionals can identify potential problems early on and help girls to develop positive solutions.

Finally, because depression and eating disorders disproportionately affect adolescent girls, health-care providers who work with adolescents should know the signs of depression and of eating problems. This knowledge is essential so that prevention, early identification, and treatment can be provided. It is especially useful to have a member on the health-care team who is knowledgeable about adolescent issues.

NONNORMATIVE INFLUENCES: CHRONIC DISEASE AS AN EXAMPLE

Nonnormative factors also influence the interplay of girls' physical and psychological health. Physical problems, such as a chronic or life-threatening disease, may have psychological consequences. By the same token, girls' common concerns about appearance and interpersonal relations may affect the way they manage a disease or its treatment. Chronic disease is a prime example of a nonnormative event that plays a key role in the interplay between girls' physical and psychosocial functioning.

A chronic illness is one that lasts for a substantial period of time or has repercussions that may be debilitating for a long period of time. Epidemiological studies estimate that between 10 and 20% of children and adolescents have one or more chronic illnesses (Gortmaker & Sappenfield, 1984). The two most common chronic illnesses in childhood are asthma (110 cases per 1000; Centers for Disease Control/National Center for Health Statistics, 1998) and diabetes (1.7 cases per 1000; Centers for Disease Control and Prevention, 2004).

Recent medical advances have drastically reduced the risks of life-threatening complications of chronic illness and, thus, youth with severe disease conditions have a substantially increased life expectancy. However, there are increasing concerns about the psychosocial adaptation and quality of life of youth with chronic disease conditions.

Most children and adolescents with chronic illnesses do not display psychological problems, although there is substantial variability among youngsters' in terms of their adjustment (Lavigne & Faier-Routman, 1993). Youth with chronic diseases are two to four times as likely to have a psychiatric diagnosis during childhood and adolescence than youth without chronic illnesses (Kliewer, 1997). Various aspects of an illness, such as physical limitations, complex medical regimens, disruptions in socialization activities, increased dependency, and high rates of school absences, may contribute to adjustment problems (Bennett, 1994).

Depressive Symptoms

Some girls with chronic conditions report higher levels of depression (Burke & Elliott, 1999) and more negative attitudes toward their illness than do boys (Heimlich, Westbrook, Austin, Cramer, & Devinsky, 2000). However, girls do not *consistently* report more depression than boys; these sex differences appear to be most apparent for youth with asthma, recurrent abdominal pain, and sickle cell disease (Bennett, 1994). The nature of these illnesses may play a role, especially the

pain and uncertainty of the illness episodes. Also, chronic conditions that lead to progressive decrements in physical functioning may contribute to depressive symptoms (Katon, 2003). When depressive symptoms occur, it is cause for serious concern because depressive symptoms can adversely affect health habits (e.g., smoking, drinking, lifestyle) and create *additional* health problems (Katon, 2003).

Girls' negative attitudes toward having a chronic condition also may be related to depression. For example, adolescent girls with epilepsy report more negative attitudes toward their illness than boys with epilepsy (Heimlich et al., 2000).

Dating and Peer Relations

The physical aspects of a chronic disease or its management may affect girls' social functioning. On the positive side, girls' tendency to seek support from family and friends when under stress (e.g., Frydenberg & Lewis, 1991) may contribute to girls' higher levels of social support for chronic conditions (La Greca et al., 1995).

On the other hand, the presence of a chronic disease may exacerbate adolescent girls' worries about social acceptance or perceived attractiveness to the opposite sex. For example, one study (DiGirolamo, Quittner, Ackerman, & Stevens, 1997) examined the types of stressors reported by adolescent boys and girls who had a serious, chronic illness (cystic fibrosis). The girls mentioned significantly more problem situations than boys, especially with respect to the categories of friends (e.g., being excluded or treated differently by friends because of their disease), and dating/pubertal development (e.g., concerns about being attractive to opposite sex; embarrassment about slow pubertal development). Thus, girls with chronic disease conditions may be especially concerned about how their disease affects their personal relationships.

Chronic conditions may also affect girls' social participation. For example, one study (Meijer, Sinnema, Bijstra, Mellenbergh, & Wolters, 2000) found that girls with chronic illnesses were involved in fewer social activities than boys. Chronic conditions that impose physical limitations may lead girls to withdraw from social activities and, as a result, restrict their contacts with close friends. In comparing girls with asthma and without asthma, Kitsantas and Zimmerman (2000) found the girls with asthma were less physically fit and reported less self-efficacy about their lung functioning during physical activities, which limited their social participation.

Eating Disorders

Certain chronic conditions are associated with girls' disordered eating. In particular, illnesses associated with weight gain and/or dietary restrictions may heighten girls' vulnerability to disordered eating behaviors, especially around the time of puberty when girls often focus on their body image (Striegel-Moore, 1993).

Disordered eating behavior appears to be more prevalent among adolescent girls with type 1 diabetes than among girls without diabetes (Jones, Lawson, Daneman, Olmstead, & Rodin, 2000). The onset of type 1 diabetes is usually characterized by rapid weight gain, which may exacerbate girls' common concerns about weight and body image. As many as 30% of girls with type 1 diabetes report having eating disorders or subclinical eating problems (insulin omission for weight loss, binge eating; Rydall, Rodin, Olmstead, Devenyi, & Daneman, 1997). Eating problems in adolescent girls with diabetes may persist for years and lead to serious medical complications, such as retinopathy and chronic hyperglycemia (Rydall et al., 1997). Thus, it is important for health-care professionals working with girls with diabetes, or other conditions that may affect body weight or diet, to evaluate girls' body image and eating attitudes, and to consider these issues in planning their treatment.

Disease Management

In general, girls report fewer problems with disease management and receive more support for their disease management than boys. For example, girls with diabetes report more support from their friends for their diabetes care than do boys with diabetes (La Greca et al., 1995). However, the demands of managing a chronic disease may present a challenge for girls, especially if the disease management could adversely affect girls' physical appearance. For example, steroid medication is often associated with side effects that include bloating and weight gain. Not surprisingly, adherence to steroid medication regimens (such as for renal disease) has proved to be especially difficult for adolescent girls, who are concerned about their appearance and body image (Korsch, Fine, & Negrete, 1978). Such concerns have led to serious and even life-threatening nonadherence for girls.

In cases where exercise is a key component of successful disease management, girls who have low levels of physical activity may be prone to problems. For example, girls' low levels of physical activity may compromise their physical health if they have asthma (Kitsantas & Zimmerman, 2000) because exercise is an important factor in lung functioning. Regular, intensive physical exercise also is helpful for regulating glucose levels in youth with type 1 diabetes. However, adolescent girls typically are less physically active than boys (Centers for Disease Control and Prevention, 2002), and this inactivity may contribute to girls' greater problems with disease management.

CONCLUSIONS

Most girls with chronic illnesses adjust well to their condition, although some disease-related factors may place girls at risk for adjustment problems. Such risk factors include conditions or treatments that interfere with girls' personal relationships and social participation, the presence of physical side effects that affect physical appearance, treatments that promote weight gain or have dietary restrictions, and conditions that have unpredictable or painful episodes, or lead to a deterioration in physical functioning.

Health-care professionals working with youth who have chronic illnesses must recognize the social challenges that girls encounter. Girls may perceive that their illness puts a strain on friendships, dating activities, and other social relations. In such cases, girls are faced with the stress of complying with their treatment regimen at the expense of their personal relations, or adhering to medical recommendations at the expense of their social participation. Awareness of girls' social concerns can help health care professionals assist girls in making appropriate treatment adjustments to benefit both their physical and mental health. It is important for health professionals to evaluate girls' concerns about the social implications of their illness/treatment and to encourage girls to draw upon their friendships and other close relationships for support.

As a practical example, health professionals can encourage girls' close friends and family members to provide tangible and emotional support (La Greca et al., 1995). They also may encourage girls to educate their friends about their illness and its physical effects. It is especially important to understand girls' *perceptions* of supportive behaviors, as children and adolescents vary considerably in the behaviors they perceive as supportive (La Greca et al., 1995).

In addition, health professionals may consider using treatments that are not likely to have significant social repercussions. If available, medications that do not induce hair loss, weight gain, or other potentially stigmatizing side effects, could be considered, even on a trial basis. By avoiding social problems, girls' physical adjustment and regimen adherence may both benefit.

Because many illnesses have an unpredictable course, or affect girls' appearance, girls may become depressed or develop negative attitudes toward their illness. Thus, health professionals may wish to consider ways to enhance girls' sense of control and predictability of disease symptoms. For example, health-care professionals might encourage girls to use a journal to keep track of events that precipitate symptoms/problems. In this way, girls may take action to avoid certain events or learn to expect a certain chain of events and prepare themselves (e.g., carry medications to school or sporting events, lie down when experiencing certain physical sensations). Efforts to help girls deal with any disease-related changes in physical appearance are also advisable. Health professionals can enhance girls' self-esteem through illness support groups, individual psychotherapy, or increasing family support (or other sources of support).

Finally, as noted earlier in this chapter, it is important for health-care professionals to be aware of the key signs of depression and eating problems, so that early identification and intervention is possible. This is especially critical because both depressive symptoms and eating problems may lead to problematic health behaviors (e.g., smoking, substance use, lack of exercise) that may further compromise girls' physical and mental health.

REFERENCES

American Academy of Ophthalmology. (2003). Children's eye health and safety. Retrieved January 25, 2005, from http://www.medem.com/medlb/article_detaillb.cfm?article_ID=ZZZKHI7CI5D&sub_cat=117

American Association of Orthodontics. (2003). Braced for a century: Orthodontists mark centennial of dentistry's oldest, largest specialty. Retrieved January 25, 2005, from http://www.braces.org/history/

Angold, A., Costello, E. J., & Worthman, C. M. (1998). Puberty and depression: The roles of age, pubertal status and pubertal timing. *Psychological Medicine, 28,* 51–61.

Austin, S. B., & Gortmaker, S. L. (2001). Dieting and smoking initiation in early adolescent girls and boys: A prospective study. *American Journal of Public Health, 91*(3), 446–450.

Bennett, D. S. (1994). Depression among children with chronic medical problems: A meta-analysis. *Journal of Pediatric Psychology, 19,* 149–169.

Burke, P., & Elliott, M. (1999). Depression in pediatric chronic illness. *Psychosomatics, 40,* 5–17.

Butcher, J. E. (1989). Adolescent girls' sex role development: Relationship with sports participation, self-esteem, and age at menarche. *Sex Roles, 20,* 575–593.

Camp, D. E., Klesges, R. C., & Relyea, G. (1993). The relationship between body weight concerns and adolescent smoking. *Health Psychology, 12,* 24–32.

Centers for Disease Control/National Center for Health Statistics. (1998). New asthma estimates: Tracking prevalence, health care, and mortality. Retrieved January 25, 2005, from www.cdc.gov/nchs/products/pubs/pubd/hestats/asthma/asthma.htm

Centers for Disease Control and Prevention. (2002). Youth risk behavior surveillance—United States, 2001. *Morbidity and Mortality Weekly Report, 51,* 1–63.

Centers for Disease Control and Prevention. (2004). *Epidemiology of type I and type II diabetes mellitus among North American children and adolescents.* Retrieved January 28, 2005, from http://www.cdc.gov/diabetes/projects/cda2.htm

DiGirolamo, A. M., Quittner, A. L., Ackerman, V., & Stevens, J. (1997). Identification and assessment of ongoing stressors in adolescents with a chronic illness: An application of the behavior-analytic model. *Journal of Clinical Child Psychology, 26,* 53–66.

Elium, J., & Elium, D. (1994). *Raising a daughter: Parents and the awakening of a healthy woman.* Berkeley, CA: Ten Speed Press.

Ellis, B. J., McFadyen-Ketchum, S., Dodge, K. A., Pettit, G. S., & Bates, J. E. (1999). Quality of early family relationships and individual differences in the timing of pubertal maturation in girls: A longitudinal test of an evolutionary model. *Journal of Personality and Social Psychology, 77,* 387–401.

Epkins, C. C. (2002). A comparison of two self-report measures of children's social anxiety in clinic and community samples. *Journal of Clinical Child and Adolescent Psychology, 31,* 69–79.

Farrell, M. P., & Barnes, G. M. (2000). Family stress and adolescent substance abuse. In P. C. McKenry & S. J. Price (Eds.), *Families and change: Coping with stressful events and transitions* (pp. 208–229). Thousand Oaks, CA: Sage.

Field, A. E., Cheung, L., Wolf, A. M., Herzog, D. B., Gortmaker, S. L., & Colditz, G. A. (1999). Exposure to the mass media and weight concerns among girls, *Pediatrics, 103,* E36.

Frank, E., & Young, E. (2002). Pubertal changes and adolescent challenges: Why do rates of depression rise precipitously for girls between ages 10 and 15 years? In E. Frank (Ed.), *Gender and its effects on psychopathology* (pp. 85–102). Washington, DC: American Psychiatric Press.

Frydenberg, E., & Lewis, R. (1991). Boys play sports and girls turn to others: Age, gender, and ethnicity as determinants of coping. *Journal of Adolescence, 16,* 253–266.

Ge, X., Conger, R. D., & Elder, G. H. (1996). Coming of age too early: Pubertal influences on girls' vulnerability to psychological distress. *Child Development, 67,* 3386–3400.

Gortmaker, S., & Sappenfield, W. (1984). Chronic childhood disorders: Prevalence and impact. *Pediatric Clinics of North America, 31,* 3–18.

Graber, J. A., Brooks-Gunn, J., & Warren, M. P. (1995). The antecedents of menarcheal age: Heredity, family environment, and stressful life events. *Child Development, 66,* 346–359.

Graber, J. A., Lewinsohn, P. M., Seeley, J. R., & Brooks-Gunn, J. (1997). Is psychopathology associated with the timing of pubertal development? *Journal of the American Academy of Child and Adolescent Psychiatry, 36,* 1768–1776.

Hanna, S., Sharma, J., & Klotz, J. (2003). Acne vulgaris: More than skin deep. *Dermatology Online Journal, 9,* 8.

Heimlich, T. E., Westbrook, L. E., Austin, J. K., Cramer, J. A., & Devinsky, O. (2000). Brief report: Adolescents' attitudes toward epilepsy: Further validation of the Child Attitude Toward Illness Scale (CATIS). *Journal of Pediatric Psychology, 25,* 339–345.

Hermes, S. F., & Keel, P. K. (2003). The influence of puberty and ethnicity on awareness and internalization of the thin ideal. *International Journal of Eating Disorders, 33,* 465–467.

Jones, J. M., Lawson, M. L., Daneman, D., Olmstead, M. P., & Rodin, G. (2000). Eating disorders in adolescent females with and without type 1 diabetes: Cross sectional study. *British Medical Journal, 10,* 1563–1566.

Katon, W. J. (2003). Clinical and health services relationships between major depression, depressive symptoms, and general medical illness. *Biological Psychiatry, 54,* 216–226.

Killen, J. D., Wilson, D. M., Hammer, L. D., Litt, I. F., Kraemer, H. C., Haydel, F., et al. (1997). Psychiatric risk associated with early puberty in adolescent girls. *Journal of the American Academy of Child and Adolescent Psychiatry, 36,* 255–262.

Kim, K., & Smith, P. K. (1998). Childhood stress, behavioural symptoms and mother-daughter pubertal development. *Journal of Adolescence, 21,* 231–240.

Kitsantas, A., & Zimmerman, B. J. (2000). Self-efficacy, activity participation, and physical fitness of asthmatic and nonasthmatic adolescent girls. *Journal of Asthma, 37,* 163–174.

Kliewer, W. (1997). Children's coping with chronic illness. In S. A. Wolchik & I. N. Sandler (Eds.), *Handbook of children's coping: Linking theory and intervention. Issues in clinical child psychology* (pp. 275–300). New York: Plenum Press.

Korsch, B. M., Fine, R. N., & Negrete, V. F. (1978). Noncompliance in children with renal transplants. *Pediatrics, 61,* 872–876.

La Greca, A. M., Auslander, W. F., Greco, P., Spetter, D., Fisher, E. B., & Santiago, J. V. (1995). I get by with a little help from my family and friends: Adolescents' support for diabetes care. *Journal of Pediatric Psychology, 20,* 449–476.

La Greca, A. M., & Lopez, N. (1998). Social anxiety among adolescents: Linkages with peer relations and friendships. *Journal of Abnormal Child Psychology, 26,* 83–94.

La Greca, A. M., & Moore, H. W. (2002, April). *Peer crowd affiliation and adolescent sexual behavior.* Presented at the biennial meeting of the Society for Research in Adolescence, New Orleans, LA.

Lavigne, J. V., & Faier-Routman, J. (1993). Correlates of psychological adjustment to pediatric physical disorders: A meta-analytic review and comparison with existing models. *Journal of Developmental and Behavioral Pediatrics, 14,* 117–123.

Meijer, S. A., Sinnema, G., Bijstra, J. O., Mellenbergh, G. J., & Wolters, W. (2000). Peer interaction in adolescents with a chronic illness. *Personality and Individual Differences, 29,* 799–813.

Moore, H. W., Glickman, A., Kuttler, A., & La Greca, A. M. (2001, April). *Adolescent girls' peer crowd af-*

filiation: Relations to social-psychological adjustment. Presented at the biennial meeting of the Society for Research in Child Development, Minneapolis, MN.

Robinson, L. A., Klesges, R. C., Zbikowski, S. M., & Glaser, R. (1997). Predictors of risk for different stages of adolescent smoking in a biracial sample. *Journal of Consulting and Clinical Psychology, 65,* 653–662.

Robinson, T. N., Chang, J. Y., Haydel, K. F., & Killen, J. D. (2001). Overweight concerns and body dissatisfaction among third-grade children: The impacts of ethnicity and socioeconomic status. *Journal of Pediatrics, 138,* 181–187.

Rydall, A. C., Rodin, G. M., Olmstead, M. P., Devenyi, R. G., & Daneman, D. (1997). Disordered eating behaviors and microvascular complications in young women with insulin-dependent diabetes mellitus. *New England Journal of Medicine, 336,* 1849–1854.

Sabatelli, R. M., & Chadwick, J. J. (2000). Marital distress: From complaints to contempt. In P. C. McKenry and S. J. Price (Eds.), *Families and change: Coping with stressful events and transitions* (pp. 22–45). Thousand Oaks, CA: Sage.

Shaffer, D. R. (1996). *Developmental psychology: Childhood and adolescence* (4th ed.). Pacific Grove, CA: Brooks/Cole.

Slap, G. B., Khalid, N., Paikoff, R. L., Brooks-Gunn, J., and Warren, M. P. (1994). Evolving self-image, pubertal manifestations, and pubertal hormones: Preliminary findings in young adolescent girls. *Journal of Adolescent Health, 15,* 327–335.

Smolak, L., Murnen, S. K., & Ruble, A. E. (2000). Female athletes and eating problems: A meta-analysis. *International Journal of Eating Disorders, 27,* 371–380.

Spruijt, E., DeGoede, M., & Vandervalk, I. (2001). The well-being of youngsters coming from six different family types. *Patient Education and Counseling, 45,* 285–294.

Stice, E., & Shaw, H. (2003). Prospective relations of body image, eating, and affective disturbance to smoking onset in adolescent girls: How Virginia slims. *Journal of Consulting and Clinical Psychology, 71,* 129–135.

Striegel-Moore, R. H. (1993). Etiology of binge eating: A developmental perspective. In C. G. Fairburn & G. T. Wilson (Eds.), *Binge eating: Nature, assessment, and treatment* (pp. 144–172). New York: Guilford Press.

Verhulst, F. C., Achenbach, T. M., van der Ende, J., Erol, N., Lambert, M. C., Leung, P. W. L., et al. (2003). Comparisons of problems reported by youths from seven countries. *American Journal of Psychiatry, 160,* 1479–1485.

There is ample research showing that by adolescence, girls—compared with boys—are likely to report greater concern about their appearance and behavior and to have lower self-esteem and career aspirations. In addition, they are less likely to speak out in class, challenge others, or express angry feelings. It appears that by this stage in life, many girls have internalized cultural messages that their worth lies mainly in being seen as physically attractive, sociable, modest, and docile.

For researchers, clinicians, and educators concerned with the detrimental effects of such gender differences on girls' psychological health and development, important questions are how and why these differences emerge. Years of exposure to stereotyped and distorted depictions of females in magazines, television, movies, and popular music certainly contribute to the gender role conceptions that adolescent girls develop. In addition, factors within the school environment, particularly during the middle school and high school years, may amplify those cultural messages. However, the process of learning about what it means to be female begins long before the middle school years. There is substantial evidence that "education" about gender role behavior and identity begins in the earliest months of life and continues through childhood and adolescence, conveyed by parents to their children in the course of everyday interaction within the family environment.

Parents can affect gender roles in ways that are both direct and overt and more indirect and subtle. Direct ways include the verbal transmission of cultural gender norms, such as telling sons that boys don't cry and telling daughters that it is unladylike to swear or sit with their legs apart. They also include teaching, assigning, or encouraging activities that are regarded as gender appropriate within a particular culture, such as fathers teaching sons to hunt or do household repairs and mothers encouraging daughters to help in the kitchen or earn money by babysitting. Indirect messages, on the other hand, are often below the level of awareness. One way they are conveyed is through modeling; in everything mothers and fathers do in the family, they are providing prototypes of female and male behavior. Another way is through the frequency and

PHYLLIS BRONSTEIN

The Family Environment: Where Gender Role Socialization Begins

quality of parent-child interaction—how much time parents spend with daughters versus with sons, what kinds of activities they engage in with each, and how attentive, supportive, instructive, or restrictive they may be with each in different situations. Although some parents, in an attempt to counterbalance traditional gender role expectations in the culture, may buy gender-neutral or even cross-gender toys for their children and teach their sons to cook and their daughters to use the lawn tractor, the indirect communication of gender role messages is much harder to monitor and modify. This chapter focuses on those indirect messages because, starting from the first months of life, they are likely to be pervasive throughout childhood and adolescence and to shape children's self-perceptions and gender identity in ways that neither parents nor children recognize.

GENDER ROLE MODELING WITHIN THE FAMILY

Parental roles and behaviors to some extent have a biological basis. Because only women can lactate, over the course of history they have been the primary providers of sustenance for infants and young children, and as cultures developed this responsibility extended to include broader homemaking tasks. In contrast, fathers, freed from the demands of child care and household work, could devote themselves to providing additional resources for the family by such activities as hunting, fishing, farming, or paid employment (Hrdy, 1999).

Cross-Cultural Perspectives on Parental Roles

This historical condition extends to the present day; around the world, whether in industrial urban centers or remote tribal villages, mothers are viewed as primary caretakers. Although they may have child-care helpers—for example, co-wives in polygynous societies, grandmothers in extended family households, husbands in nuclear family households, or paid workers such as babysitters, au pairs, nursemaids, or nannies—

essentially, mothers have the prime responsibility for meeting their children's physical and emotional needs and teaching them life skills and norms for social behavior. Fathers, on the other hand, have been found to be relatively uninvolved in child rearing. In cultures as diverse as Cameroon, China, and Brazil, and among Mexican Americans in the United States, fathers have traditionally been viewed as emotionally distant disciplinarians, whose main role is to provide economic support for the family (Engle & Breaux, 1998). Studies examining fathers' roles across many cultures have found that in almost all of them, they did not have ongoing, close relationships with infants or young children (Barry & Paxson, 1971; Munroe & Munroe, 1992).

These traditional family-role divisions would seem to model very specific and limited gender role options for children. However, with technological growth and increased educational and career opportunities in many countries, traditional family roles may be changing. For example, among tribal groups in Nigeria, Ghana, and the Ivory Coast, anthropologists found such advances to be associated with more egalitarian husband-wife relations and fathers' greater involvement with children, in a manner that showed more warmth and acceptance and less restrictiveness and discipline than was customary in traditional families (Werner, 1979).

Parental Roles in the United States

Married Households

In the United States, women's employment outside the home has increased dramatically over the past 40 years, with the percentage of employed married mothers going from 28 to 71% (U.S. Bureau of the Census, 1999). However, despite changes in ideology generated by the women's movement and media accounts of family-oriented fathers taking on more responsibilities in the home, research findings suggest that mothers with full-time employment still do the major share of household work (Coltrane, 1996; Risman, 1998). It appears that despite changing occupational roles for women and parents' wishes for more egalitarian sharing of child care and housework, traditional gender role definitions exert a strong pull (Cowan & Cowan, 1992). Thus, whereas girls may see that their mothers can be wage-earners who may have interesting career opportunities in the outside world, they also see that homemaking and child care remain primarily women's work.

Still, there is evidence that changes in parental roles may be having some effect on children's gender role concepts. Mothers' employment outside the home has been found to be associated with children's less gender-stereotyped concepts and girls' less gender-stereotyped preferences, beliefs, attitudes, and behaviors (Powlishta, Sen, Serbin, Poulin-Dubois, & Eichstedt, 2001; Ruble & Martin, 1998). As well, mothers' less traditional behavior in interacting with their husbands (e.g., less initiating compromise and stating husbands' feelings) was associated with adolescent girls' nontraditional gender role attitudes (Werrbach, Grotevant, & Cooper, 1992). Fathers' nontraditional family-role behavior has been found to be associated with young children's lower awareness of gender stereotyping, adolescents' greater approval of future nontraditional roles for themselves, and girls' less stereotyped concepts of parental roles (Ruble & Martin, 1998), as well as children's tendency to express gender-atypical emotions (Brody, 1999). In addition, girls whose parents had egalitarian marital roles were found to maintain a high level of achievement in math and science over the transition to seventh grade, compared with girls from traditional families whose grades declined in those subjects (Updegraff, McHale, & Crouter, 1996). Furthermore, girls who rated their parents' marital roles as more egalitarian and themselves as more masculine tended to report lower levels of depressive symptoms than did girls with more traditional parents or lower masculinity scores (Obeidallah, McHale, & Silbereisen, 1996).

Alternative Family Configurations

Perhaps the greatest changes in traditional parental roles can be seen in some alternative family configurations, and there is evidence to suggest that parental modeling in these families may have an effect on children's gender role development. Weisner, Garnier, and Loucky (1994) found lower levels of gender stereotyping among children living in nonconventional family situations compared with those living in married-couple families. Hetherington (1987) found that girls living in divorced mother-only households had more power and were assigned more responsibilities than girls living in nondivorced two-parent households, and Hilton and Haldeman (1991) found that girls in single-mother families performed both traditionally female and traditionally male household work roles more often than did boys or parents in one- and two-parent households. Although these role differences may have been necessitated by fathers' absence and mothers' employment, they may also have reflected the combined roles of breadwinner and homemaker that the mothers were modeling. On the other hand, Clarke-Stewart and Hayward (1996) found that girls living with mothers only reported more traditionally feminine attitudes and those living with fathers only reported more traditionally masculine ones, and Downey and Powell (1993) found that girls in father-only households showed higher academic achievement and had higher educational expectations than did their counterparts in mother-only households.

Lesbian and Gay Families

Variations in the traditional gender-based definition of parental roles can be found in lesbian and gay two-parent families. In lesbian families, both parents have been found to invest equal time in household work. Also, although biological mothers have been found to be more involved in child care and nonbiological mothers to spend more time in paid employment, lesbian couples have been found to share parenting more equally than do heterosexual couples; furthermore, within lesbian families, children were found to be better adjusted and parents more satisfied when child care was shared more equally (Patterson, 1995).

Regarding other outcomes for children, Green, Mandel, Hotvedt, Gray, and Smith (1986) found that daughters of lesbians were more likely to make more traditionally masculine choices in toys, clothes, activities, type of play, and career aspirations than were daughters of heterosexual mothers; further, girls whose mothers were active in lesbian or feminist organizations were more likely to aspire to traditionally masculine occupations. As well, Hoeffer (1981) found that daughters of lesbians rated themselves higher on adventuresomeness and leadership than did daughters of heterosexual mothers. Thus, the differences that have been found are in the direction of greater gender role flexibility—in particular, more assertive and instrumental behavior—for daughters of lesbian mothers, which has been found in other research to be associated with higher self-esteem and psychological well-being (Lott, 1994). However, other studies comparing preferences or aspects of personality and adjustment found no differences between children of gay and lesbian parents and children of heterosexual parents. Nor have differences been found between those groups on the likelihood of children identifying as lesbian or gay (Patterson, 1995).

Similar patterns of shared household and child-care responsibilities have also been found in gay two-father families, along with greater satisfaction with the division of labor than was reported by heterosexual couples (Patterson, 1995). Although there is little research available about these families, studies of gay fathers in general suggest that they may be more nurturing, less concerned with economic providing, more reasoning and consistent in limit setting, more democratic in family decision making, and more receptive to children's feelings than heterosexual fathers tend to be (Green & Bozett, 1991). Overall, it appears that both lesbian and gay parents may be providing more flexible and egalitarian gender-role models for their children than are provided in heterosexual-parent families.

U.S. Cultural Variations in Parental Roles

Within diverse cultural groups in the United States, parental roles frequently reflect norms that hark back to the culture of origin. For example, Latino families may show traditional gender role divisions of labor, as well as male dominance and female subordination in family decision making. However, there is also substantial evidence to suggest that marital and parenting roles in Mexican American families have become much more egalitarian, particularly as a result of women's employment outside the home, and

that fathers are more involved and less authoritarian with their children than had generally been assumed (Mirandé, 1988). Asian American families have tended to retain traditional roles, with women expected to be nurturing, family-oriented, and home-centered, and men expected to be dominant, strong, stoic, and family-oriented but also worldly (Chan, 2003). African American families often include extended-kinship relationships, which may reflect origins in African tribal life; relatives and community members often play a role in child rearing, providing care, protection, guidance, and discipline. Also, because of social and economic factors, African American women have historically been wage-earners (Staples, 1985), and currently, 60% of African American children live in households with no father present (U.S. Bureau of the Census, 1999). Thus, traditional majority-culture models of parental roles are not very representative of African American families.

Parents' Interactions With Children: Further Modeling of Gender Role Behaviors

Overall, the research reviewed here suggests that the family roles parents play do affect children's gender role concepts. Children whose mothers are available only on weekday evenings and weekends, or whose fathers are readily available for housework and child care, are likely to have different notions of appropriate gender role behavior compared with those from more traditional families. However, there is also a more specific way that parental modeling may contribute to gender role socialization. Beginning in infancy and continuing through each stage of development, mothers and fathers are providing gender-role models in their day-to-day verbal and nonverbal interactions with their children.

Parental Behaviors in the Infancy Period

A substantial amount of research has found differences between mothers' and fathers' behaviors with infants. Not only do mothers, across many cultures, spend much more time with infants than fathers do, but compared with fathers, they spend a greater proportion of their time in caregiving, whereas fathers spend a greater proportion of their time in playful and sociable activities (Bronstein, 1988). Further, fathers' style of play looks very different from that of mothers. Studies with infants ranging from 2 weeks to 2½ years of age have found that fathers were more likely to engage them in tactile, arousing, unpredictable play, often involving limb movements or bouncing and lifting; mothers, on the other hand, tended more to engage them in soothing, nontactile, and verbal interaction, and when physical play was involved, it was usually more contained and predictable, as in toy shaking, peek-a-boo, and pat-a-cake (Parke, 1995). Other studies have found mothers to be more verbal, sociable, and affectionate with infants, and to be more responsive to infants' cues of interest and attention (Bronstein, 1988).

Thus, within their first few years, infants in United States, families may be receiving different messages about adult female and male behavior. They may see that mothers are more often present—taking care of their bodily needs, being attentive and responsive, and offering a soothing kind of play. They may also see that fathers are not there as often, and that when they are present, they initiate more stimulating, unpredictable play and are less responsive to the baby's cues. These early differences in parental behavior would seem to represent the beginnings of gender role socialization. However, it is important to note that such differences are culturally influenced. For example, studies in England and India have shown patterns similar to those found in the United States, but studies in Sweden and Israel have shown no clear differences between mothers' and fathers' tendencies to engage in play or in the kinds of play initiated (Parke, 1995).

Parental Behaviors During the Early Childhood Years

Similar patterns of parental behavior have also been found in research on young children. In a naturalistic study that looked at parents and children in playground settings in three European countries, Best, House, Barnard, and Spicker (1994) found that in each country, mothers showed more caregiving behaviors than fathers did, and

French and Italian fathers played more with their children than mothers did—although the opposite play pattern emerged for German parents. Studies of parent-child interaction during the preschool years, generally involving task, teaching, and structured play situations, found that fathers engaged children in active, physical play more than mothers did, whereas mothers were more likely than fathers to engage children with objects such as toys or books (Parke, 1995) and to be more cooperative, supportive, and affiliative (Leaper, 2000). In addition, Leaper (2000) found that fathers were more likely than mothers to be more dominant and assertive with their children—for example, giving directions and commands and expressing disagreement.

Parental Behaviors in Middle Childhood and Adolescence

U.S. studies of parenting behavior with older children and adolescents have produced results that seem consistent with those found with younger children. Both girls and boys have reported experiencing more involvement, closeness, emotional nurturance, and affection—and also more rule enforcement and discipline—from mothers than from fathers (Paulson, Hill, & Holmbeck, 1991; Starrels, 1994). In contrast, fathers of adolescents have been found to play a more instrumental role in family interaction, in ways that may foster autonomy and task accomplishment (Collins & Russell, 1991). Similar findings have emerged in studies in Mexico, Australia, and other cultures. They found that mothers, compared with fathers, interacted more frequently and were more involved and responsive with children (Brooks & Bronstein, 1996; Mackey & Day, 1979) and more involved in caregiving (Brooks & Bronstein, 1996; Russell & Russell, 1987). In contrast, fathers engaged in more playful interaction and explained things more to their children (Brooks & Bronstein, 1996).

Finally, Leaper, Anderson, and Sanders (1998) examined a large number of observational studies of parents' verbal interaction with children who ranged in age from infancy through adolescence. They found that mothers were more talkative with their children and that they used more supportive language—though also more negative language—than fathers did. Fathers, on the other hand, provided more cognitively oriented, instrumental interaction in the form of asking questions and giving information and directives.

In sum, gender-based patterns of parenting, evident during the infancy period, seem to persist throughout childhood and adolescence. The model that children see in the home of female (compared with male) behavior typically involves spending more time with children, providing for their physical needs, offering emotional support and closeness, being responsive to their wishes and opinions, and engaging with them in settled activities such as reading. The model that children see of male behavior typically includes less overall time spent with children and less involvement in their lives, with interactions characterized by playfulness, physical activity, assertiveness, and the encouragement of cognitive development, particularly by explaining, giving directives, problem solving, and asking for information. Thus, despite changes in beliefs about gender roles over the past 40 years, along with women's entry into the workplace and opportunities in many traditionally male domains, things may not have changed very much within the family environment. The qualities modeled by mothers can be viewed as admirable and worth emulating; social connectedness and emotional support are factors conducive to positive social development and psychological health. However, girls may come to feel that the qualities modeled more by their fathers are less accessible and appropriate for them, which may ultimately undermine their confidence and limit their aspirations for achievement, leadership, and career attainment.

PARENTS' DIFFERENTIAL INTERACTIONS WITH GIRLS AND BOYS

Parents also contribute to the gender role socialization of their children through their differential treatment of girls and boys. Several initial reviews, which included numerous self-report studies and focused mostly on early childhood and on mothers only, concluded that parents made few distinctions (e.g., Lytton & Romney, 1991). However, a closer examination of mainly observational studies from infancy through adolescence

suggests that there are in fact consistent patterns of differences in parents' behaviors to girls and boys, particularly by fathers.

Parents With Infants and Toddlers

For both fathers and mothers, the sex of the infant appears to affect their interactions. In a review of father-child interaction studies, Bronstein (1988) reported that with both younger and older infants, fathers of daughters (compared with fathers of sons) tended to show lower levels of interest and involvement—specifically less frequent feeding, diapering, touching, looking, vocalizing, responding, and playing. This is consistent with findings that fathers to a much greater degree than mothers have shown a preference for having male children. In addition, fathers of sons tended to engage in more physical, arousing play and to encourage more visual, fine-motor, and locomotor exploration, whereas fathers of daughters encouraged more vocal behavior. In studies of mothers with infants, those with daughters have been found to be more emotionally responsive (Fagot, 1995), talkative, supportive (Leaper et al., 1998), and receptive to the expression of emotion (Bronstein, 1988) than were those with sons. Further, Fagot and Hagan (1991) found that both parents reacted more positively to girls than to boys when they attempted to communicate and less positively when they were aggressive.

Thus the picture of parenting behavior that has emerged from research on infants and toddlers shows strong evidence of girls' gender role socialization. Parents seem to be encouraging daughters' emotional closeness, communication, and expression of nonaggressive feelings, which may foster the kind of relational orientation that characterizes the traditional female role in most cultures. However, there may also be some less positive consequences. Fathers' lack of vigorous physical play with daughters may convey a message that girls are more delicate, and that it is not appropriate for them to develop their physical strength or confidence and enthusiasm about their physical abilities. Fathers' less frequent encouragement of girls' visual and physical exploration may convey the cultural message that being curious, adventuresome, and independent are not appropriate female traits. Finally, the fact that girls tend to receive less interested attention from fathers may provide a very early cultural message that females are less inherently interesting and admirable than males are.

Parents With Young Children

Parents' gender-differentiated behaviors in the early childhood years seem consistent with those found in during infancy and toddlerhood. For example, a number of studies have found that parents (particularly fathers) of daughters were less likely to emphasize cognitive development (Block, 1983; Brody, 1999) and more likely to interact positively and sociably than were parents of sons. In addition, several studies found that parents discussed anger less with daughters than with sons and tried to inhibit daughters' expression of anger (Brody, 1999), and that parents responded negatively to girls'—and positively to boys'—assertive behaviors (Kerig, Cowan, & Cowan, 1993).

Parents With Older Children and Adolescents

Similar differences in parents' behavior to girls and boys have been found from middle childhood through adolescence. In a number of mainly U.S. studies, across a wide age range of children, mothers were found to be more talkative, supportive, and closer to daughters than to sons (Leaper et al., 1998), although the opposite pattern has been found in some cultures (Whiting & Edwards, 1988). Related to greater closeness, however, are findings that mothers tend to be more intrusive and to grant less autonomy to daughters than to sons (Brody, 1999) and also to be more directive toward girls than toward boys, whether in laboratory task performance or observations in the home (Leaper et al., 1998). This is consistent with findings that across numerous cultures, mothers have been found to assign more tasks to girls than to boys, and to expect more help from girls in household work and caring for younger siblings (Whiting & Edwards, 1988)—which presumably would involve a sub-stantial amount of direction giving. In contrast, fathers of older children and adolescents, as in studies with infants and young children, have been found to be less close to daughters, showing lower levels of interested attention, intellectual involvement, and mutual activity than was found with sons (Bronstein, 1988; Starrels, 1994). In addition, parents have been found to interrupt girls more than boys (Brooks & Bronstein, 1996) and to respond more positively to girls than to boys for communicating feelings and acting dependent (Russell & Russell, 1987).

In sum, the differences in parents' behaviors to girls and boys that were seen in infancy and early childhood show a continuity through middle childhood and adolescence. Mothers across many cultures socialize their daughters for obedience and responsibility, providing training and rehearsal for a traditional female domestic and interpersonal role. In addition, by giving more directives and limiting autonomy, mothers of daughters may be communicating to them that they are less able to take charge, solve problems, and take action on their own, and that it is more appropriate to leave those behaviors to the domain of men. Fathers of school-age children and adolescents continue to show less interested attention to daughters, do fewer activities with them, and make less effort to promote their cognitive/intellectual development. This lesser degree of paternal involvement may limit girls' opportunities to develop abilities in more traditionally male domains, while also amplifying the cultural message that females are less worthy of attention.

IMPLICATIONS FOR PSYCHOLOGICAL HEALTH

The findings discussed in this chapter provide ample evidence that gender role socialization occurs within the family environment, as part of the everyday interaction between parents and children. Although there is little research available that specifically links this process to psychological health, evidence can be extrapolated from the more general literature on parenting and child adjustment in a several key areas.

Emotional Closeness and Dependency

A very large body of child-rearing research over the past 50 years has provided convincing evidence that mothers' supportiveness and warmth foster social competence and positive psychological functioning in children and adolescents. Thus the finding that girls are more likely than boys to receive this kind of maternal attention suggests a mental health advantage for girls, conveyed through the mother-daughter relationship. However, one possible disadvantage is that the higher levels of empathy, altruism, and connectedness that mothers impart to girls may socialize them for the kind of traditional, constrained female role described by Miller (1976), in which women learn to ignore their own needs and to seek fulfillment in life through attempting to meet the needs of others.

Related to mothers' encouraging closeness and connection with daughters is the tendency for parents to foster daughters' dependency and limit their development of autonomy. Short-term effects related to such practices have included girls' greater sense of passivity and dependence and more negative emotional displays and externalizing behaviors (Brody, 1999). In the absence of more extensive research in this area, long-term negative effects on girls' and women's sense of self-efficacy and self-worth as well on as their goals, life expectations, and achievement, can only be surmised. However, lower levels of traditionally masculine personality traits—in particular, self-efficacy and instrumentality—have been found by numerous researchers to be linked to depressive symptoms in adolescents and young adults (Obeidallah et al., 1996). Thus it seems likely that socializing young girls to be dependent on others' authority, guidance, and support rather than fostering confidence in their own ability to manage in life may plant early seeds for the later emergence of depression.

The Expression and Suppression of Emotion

Parents' receptivity to children's expression of emotions has been found to be related to children's higher levels of emotional expressiveness, self-esteem, social competence, and psychological adjustment; in addition, there is substantial evidence linking emotional expressiveness to better mental and physical health (Brody, 1999; Bronstein, Fitzgerald, Briones, Pieniadz, & D'Ari, 1993). Thus the fact that parents encourage overall emotional expressiveness more from girls than from boys may give girls an advantage in the areas of social development and psychological and physical well-being.

However, parents tend to inhibit girls from expressing anger. It is not surprising, then, that in many studies women have been found to express sadness and hurt rather than anger in response to negative events, and to ruminate more when they are upset, which tends to prolong depression. Brody (1999) has speculated that because women tend more to avoid the expression of anger, they may be more likely to blame negative events on situational factors rather than on another person—and such factors may seem more difficult to control, which may lead to feelings of hopelessness, anxiety, and depression. Examining the expression of emotion in late adolescence, Fox (2000) found that girls who tended to feel angry but did not express it also reported that they did not show their true feelings in intimate relationships, and that this kind of self-silencing was associated with higher levels of depression. Prohibitions against expressing anger may also lead girls and women to direct angry feelings toward themselves rather than toward others, which would help explain why, across a wide age range, internalizing has been found to be higher for females and externalizing higher for males.

In conclusion, the indirect, day-to-day gender role messages that many girls receive within the family environment confer important advantages, but also limitations. Empathy, altruism, caregiving, and connectedness are key ingredients of a meaningful life, and essential aspects of societal functioning—but so are adventuresomeness, achievement, and leadership. It is beneficial neither to individuals nor to society as a whole to assign one set of values and behaviors to one sex and a different set to the other. Despite an increased awareness in the United States and other Western cultures of the detrimental effects of gender stereotyping, many parents continue to foster behaviors and self-perceptions in children that are consonant with traditional gender role norms. It is important to understand how this process occurs, so that the family environment can become a place that promotes optimum development for all children. Educators and mental health professionals who work with families can provide information and guidance about the impact of gender role socialization, so that parents may become more aware of the gender-role models and messages they provide for their daughters.

REFERENCES

Barry, H., & Paxson, L. M. (1971). Infancy and early childhood: Cross-cultural codes 2. *Ethnology, 10,* 466–508.

Best, D. L., House, A. M., Barnard, A. E., & Spicker, B. S. (1994). Parent-child interactions in France, Germany, and Italy. *Journal of Cross-Cultural Psychology, 25,* 181–193.

Block, J. H. (1983). Differential premises arising from differential socialization of the sexes: Some conjectures. *Child Development, 54,* 1335–1354.

Brody, L. (1999). *Gender, emotion, and the family.* Cambridge, MA: Harvard University Press.

Bronstein, P. (1988). Father-child interaction: Implications for gender-role socialization. In P. Bronstein & C. P. Cowan (Eds.), *Fatherhood today: Men's changing role in the family* (pp. 107–124). New York: John Wiley & Sons.

Bronstein, P., Fitzgerald, M., Briones, M., Pieniadz, J., & D'Ari, A. (1993). Family emotional expressiveness as a predictor of early adolescent social and psychological adjustment. *Journal of Early Adolescence, 13,* 448–471.

Brooks, T., & Bronstein, P. (1996, March). *A cross-cultural comparison of mothers' and fathers' behavior to girls and boys.* Presented at the biennial meeting of the Society for Research on Adolescence, Boston.

Chan, C. S. (2003). Psychological issues of Asian Americans. In P. Bronstein & K. Quina, *Teaching gender and multicultural awareness: Resources for the psychology classroom* (pp. 179–193). Washington, DC: American Psychological Association.

Clarke-Stewart, A. K., & Hayward, C. (1996). Advantages of father custody and contact for the psychological well-being of school-age children. *Journal of Applied Developmental Psychology, 17,* 239–270.

Collins, W. A., & Russell, G. (1991). Mother-child and father-child relationships in middle childhood and adolescence: A developmental analysis. *Developmental Review, 11,* 99–136.

Coltrane, S. (1996). *Family man: Fatherhood, housework and gender equity.* New York: Oxford University Press.

Cowan, C. P., & Cowan, P. A. (1992). *When partners become parents: The big life change for couples.* New York: Basic Books.

Downey, D. B., & Powell, B. (1993). Do children in single-parent households fare better living with same-sex parents? *Journal of Marriage and the Family, 55,* 55–71.

Engle, P. L., & Breaux, C. (1998). Fathers' involvement with children: Perspectives from developing countries. Society for Research on Child Development, Ann Arbor, MI. *Social Policy Report, 12*(1).

Fagot, B. I. (1995). Parenting boys and girls. In M. H. Bornstein (Ed.), *Handbook of parenting* (Vol. 1, pp. 163–183). Mahwah, NJ: Erlbaum.

Fagot, B. I., & Hagan, R. (1991). Observations of parent reactions to sex-stereotyped behaviors: Age and sex effects. *Child Development, 62,* 617–628.

Fox, B. (2000). *Pathways to self-silencing and depression in late adolescence: A longitudinal study.* Unpublished doctoral dissertation, University of Vermont.

Green, G. D., & Bozett, F. (1991). Lesbian mothers and gay fathers. In J. C. Gonsiorek & J. D. Weinrich (Eds.), *Homosexuality: Research implications for public policy* (pp. 197–214). Newbury Park, CA: Sage.

Green, R., Mandel, J. B., Hotvedt, M. E., Gray, J., & Smith, L. (1986). Lesbian mothers and their children: A comparison with solo parent heterosexual mothers and their children. *Archives of Sexual Behavior, 7,* 175–181.

Hetherington, E. M. (1987). Family relations six years after divorce. In K. Pasley & M. Ihinger-Tolman (Eds.), *Remarriage and stepparenting: Current research and theory* (pp. 185–205). New York: Guilford Press.

Hilton, J. M., & Haldeman, V. A. (1991). Gender differences in the performance of household tasks by adults and children in single-parent and two-parent, two-earner families. *Journal of Family Issues, 12,* 114–130.

Hoeffer, B. (1981). Children's acquisition of sex-role behavior in lesbian mothers' families. *American Journal of Orthopsychiatry, 51,* 536–643.

Hrdy, S. B. (1999). *Mother nature: A history of mothers, infants, and natural selection.* New York: Pantheon Books.

Kerig, P. K., Cowan, P. A., & Cowan, C. P. (1993). Marital quality and gender differences in parent-child interaction. *Developmental Psychology, 29,* 931–939.

Leaper, C. (2000). Gender, affiliation, assertion, and the interactive context of parent-child play. *Developmental Psychology, 36,* 381–393.

Leaper, C., Anderson, K. J., & Sanders, P. (1998). Moderators of gender effects on parents' talk to their children: A meta-analysis. *Developmental Psychology, 34,* 3–27.

Lott, B. (1994). *Women's lives: Themes and variations in gender learning* (2nd ed.). Pacific Grove, CA: Brooks/Cole.

Lytton, H., & Romney, D. M. (1991). Parents' differential socialization of boys and girls: A meta-analysis. *Psychological Bulletin, 109,* 267–296.

Mackey, W. C., & Day, R. D. (1979). Some indicators of fathering behaviors in the United States: A cross-cultural examination of adult male-child interaction. *Journal of Marriage and the Family, 4,* 287–298.

Miller, J. B. (1976). *Toward a new psychology of women.* Boston: Beacon Press.

Mirandé, A. (1988). Chicano fathers: Traditional perceptions and current realities. In P. Bronstein and C. P. Cowan (Eds.), *Fatherhood today: Men's changing role in the family* (pp. 93–106). New York: John Wiley & Sons.

Munroe, R. L., & Munroe, R. H. (1992). Fathers in children's environments: A four culture study. In B. S. Hewlett (Ed.), *Father-child relations: Cultural and biosocial contexts* (pp. 213–230). New York: de Gruyter.

Obeidallah, D. A., McHale, S. M., & Silbereisen, R. K. (1996). Gender role socialization and adolescents' reports of depression: Why some girls and not others? *Journal of Youth and Adolescence, 25,* 775–785.

Parke, R. D. (1995). Fathers and families. In M. H. Bornstein (Ed.), *Handbook of parenting* (Vol. 3, pp. 27–63). Mahwah, NJ: Erlbaum.

Patterson, C. J. (1995). Lesbian and gay parenthood. In M. H. Bornstein (Ed.), *Handbook of parenting* (Vol. 3, pp. 255–274). Mahwah, NJ: Erlbaum.

Paulson, S. E., Hill, J. P., & Holmbeck, G. N. (1991). Distinguishing between perceived closeness and parental warmth in families with seventh-grade boys and girls. *Journal of Early Adolescence, 11,* 276–293.

Powlishta, K. K., Sen, M. G., Serbin, L. A., Poulin-Dubois, D., & Eichstedt, J. A. (2001). From infancy through middle childhood: The role of cognitive and social factors in becoming gendered. In R. K. Unger (Ed.), *Handbook of the psychology of women and gender* (pp. 116–132). New York: John Wiley & Sons.

Risman, B. (1998). *Gender vertigo: American families in transition.* New Haven, CT: Yale University Press.

Ruble, D. N., & Martin, C. L. (1998). Gender development. In W. Damon (Ed.) & N. Eisenberg (Vol. Ed.), *Handbook of child psychology* (5th ed., Vol. 3, pp. 933–1016). New York: John Wiley & Sons.

Russell, G., & Russell, A. (1987). Mother-child and father-child relationships in middle childhood. *Child Development, 58,* 1573–1585.

Staples, R. (1985). Changes in Black family structure: The conflict between family ideology and structural conditions. *Journal of Marriage and the Family, 47,* 1005–1013.

Starrels, M. E. (1994). Gender differences in parent-child relations. *Journal of Family Issues, 15,* 148–165.

Updegraff, K. A., McHale, S. M., & Crouter, A. C. (1996). Gender roles in marriage: What do they mean for girls' and boys' school achievement? *Journal of Youth and Adolescence, 25,* 73–88.

U.S. Bureau of the Census. (1999). *Statistical abstract of the United States: 1998* (119th ed.). Washington, DC: U.S. Government Printing Office.

Weisner, T. S., Garnier, H., & Loucky, J. (1994). Domestic tasks, gender egalitarian values and children's gender typing in conventional and nonconventional families. *Sex Roles, 30,* 23–54.

Werner, E. E. (1979). *Cross-cultural child development: A view from the planet Earth.* Monterey, CA: Brooks/Cole.

Werrbach, G. B., Grotevant, H. D., & Cooper, C. R. (1992). Patterns of family interaction and adolescent sex role concepts. *Journal of Youth and Adolescence, 21,* 609–623.

Whiting, B. B., & Edwards, C. P. (1988). *Children of different worlds: The formation of social behavior.* Cambridge, MA: Harvard University Press.

Although the focus of this chapter is on girls' learning and academic achievement, there is always an assumed or implied comparison—that is, how well and what are girls learning relative to whom or to what groups—with the obvious comparison being boys of similar ages and backgrounds. We cannot interpret female cognitive development without at least some reference to male cognitive development for points of comparison. Whether we choose to emphasize similarities or differences, we need to know how girls and boys are faring as we prepare them for adult life.

What are girls and boys learning at school? Of course, the answer includes arithmetic, reading, spelling, and the other subjects that are commonly listed on elementary school report cards, but curricular content is only one of many lessons learned in those critical years between the start of kindergarten and transition into middle school (or junior high school) and beyond. Children are also learning important life skills—following directions, sitting quietly, sharing, and understanding a variety of social roles, including the roles of students and teachers, girls and boys, bigger children and younger children, classroom aide, and principal. They learn that some of these roles are rigid; for example, they cannot be the teacher. Some role transgressions will be punished—for example, they cannot boss the bigger school bullies. And some roles have considerable overlap, depending on time and context—for example, girls and boys can play baseball together at school, but after school, baseball games may be restricted to single-sex play. These lessons are learned in school along with geography, fractions, and other academic areas. Two important questions for research psychologists are, How does role learning co-occur with subject learning? Are there subtle or explicit messages about academic achievement that differ for girls and boys?

DIANE F. HALPERN

Girls and Academic Success: Changing Patterns of Academic Achievement

SCHOOL ACHIEVEMENT: ARE SCHOOLS FAILING GIRLS OR BOYS?

The so-called battle of the sexes, a staple in the repertoire of many comedians, is being fought in elementary school classrooms and playgrounds. Popular-press writers advance different social agendas by declaring that schools are waging a "war against boys" (Sommers, 2000) or, alternatively, that "schools shortchange girls" (American Association of University Women, 1992). What and how well are girls and boys learning in school? Are they learning that academic disciplines are sex-typed, or are schools encouraging children to think about academic subjects as sex-neutral and encouraging all children to develop to their full potential? Many people are uncomfortable with questions like these because there is a pervasive dislike for studies about differences, at least in part because of legitimate concerns that results will be misused to support a misogynist political agenda. But questions about differences are important because we cannot take action to correct inequities if we refuse to look at group differences on outcomes measures. Censorship, even self-censorship, only ignores potential problems. Critics of questions about differences have sometimes countered that research should only focus on the similarities between girls and boys and between women and men because similarities cannot be misused or misinterpreted. Of course, all research occurs in a sociopolitical context that guides the questions we ask and the way we interpret results, but it is the best method available for determining the similarities and differences between groups. Girls and boys are both similar *and* different—it is a false dichotomy to ask if they are similar *or* different. The more interesting questions concern the ways in which they are similar and different, and the contexts and reasons for the findings. We cannot study similarities or differences separately, so no conclusion about similarities could be made if we did not also allow for the possibility that there are differences. It is not scientific analyses of complex issues that cause prejudice; biases for or against males or females flourish best in the absence of data and not because of them.

There are few topics in psychology or education that are as politically explosive as the similarities and differences between girls and boys in academic achievement/ability measures. The deceptively simple question about the comparative academic success for girls and boys has an equally simple answer, "It depends." In an article I wrote almost 15 years ago, I answered the many questions about sex-related differences in achievement/ability tests with the quip, "What you see depends on where you look," an answer that is as true today as it was way back in the last century (Halpern, 1989). In general, schools are happier places for girls than boys, with many fewer girls exhibiting behavior problems or failing classes. Girls are completing high school at a higher rate than boys, with completion rates that differ widely as a function of race/ethnicity (Jacobs, 2002). The high drop-out rates for African American and Hispanic males, especially in large, urban areas, suggest that male students of color should be a primary focus of school reform efforts if we want to create an equitable society and that achievement differences between the rich and poor swamp those that vary by sex.

There are many academic indicators that show *no* difference in the academic achievement of boys and girls, but there are also measures that show large and consistent differences favoring girls and still others that show large and consistent differences favoring boys. *The size and direction of the sex difference depends on what and how you measure.* The emerging picture of girls' and boys' success in school is complicated, but it is consistent across time and place, suggesting that the differences are systematic and not due to random variance.

THE SEESAW NATURE OF ACHIEVEMENT AND ABILITY TESTS

When psychologists and educators compare girls and boys (or men and women), the differences or lack of differences that are found apply to group means or averages. Of course, no single individual is average, and differences based on means cannot be used to make predictions about the success or failure of any individual. There are high-achieving females and males on all cognitive measures, and there is *no* support for simple-minded conclusions like "girls cannot do math" or "boys cannot write poetry." Additionally, group differences that are found in any sociohistorical context (e.g., 21st-century industrialized societies) could disappear, increase, or decrease in the future. Differences are not deficiencies, nor are they immutable "facts" tied to members of any group. People vary along multiple dimensions, so readers are urged not to look for "winners" and "losers" when considering average group differences.

On average (a phrase that I will repeat often to ensure that readers never forget that the data apply to group averages not individuals), girls get higher grades in school and tend to get higher scores on tests that are closely related to topics that are taught in school (e.g., how to multiply fractions or conduct an experiment). Achievement tests are designed to measure what and how much is learned in school and thus, like school grades, are closely aligned with school curricula. Standardized achievement tests show that females are better at spelling, and females are consistently and substantially better, on average, on tests of literacy, spelling, writing, and information (general knowledge; National Center for Education Statistics [NCES], 2003). A writing test was recently added to the PSAT (a test that is taken by college-bound high school juniors to identify Merit scholars and for other academic programs). The addition of the writing test substantially increased the number of females awarded prestigious Merit scholarships, a benefit that would not have occurred if researchers refused to look for sex differences in PSAT scores. Psychologists who have argued that the female advantage on verbal abilities is small usually have not included those verbal abilities where females show the largest advantages— writing, speaking, retrieval of word knowledge from long-term memory, and speech articulation tasks (e.g., tongue twisters; Halpern, 1997).

By contrast, aptitude and ability tests are designed to identify those individuals who are most likely to benefit from future instruction rather than index what has already been learned, so aptitude or ability tests have more general types of questions that do not match any particular school curricula and thus can be used across school districts with widely differing curricula. Consider, for example, international test data that cannot reflect any single course of instruction. U.S. and international studies show that females are substantially outscoring males in measures of reading literacy, with significant differences in every one of the 35 countries where the Program for International Student Assessment (PISA) was administered to fourth graders. Although the mathematics and science achievement tests were administered in fewer countries, there seems to be no consistent advantage for either boys or girls

in mathematics at fourth grade with a general advantage for boys in science at fourth grade. These data are depicted in figure 29.1.

Comparable measures for older children are shown in figure 29.2, where reading literacy scores for 15-year-olds show large and consistent advantages for girls. The mathematics and science achievement data in figure 29.2 came from international comparisons of eighth graders (approximately 13 to 14 years old). Boys are scoring higher than girls on both of these measures in all but a few countries, but the mathematics data are not as strong as the science data and neither provides the same convincing picture as the female advantage in reading literacy, with many of the differences in mathematics failing to achieve statistical significance.

The PISA data are not unusual. Numerous other national and international studies show similar patterns of results (e.g., Third International Math and Science Study [NCES, 1998, 2000], National Assessment of Educational Progress [1999], and others reviewed in Halpern [2000] and Willingham and Cole [1997]). International comparisons like the PISA data are important because they show the consistency of sex differences on academic measures across industrialized societies. Although the size of the difference in the test scores varies among countries, the overall pattern of male and female scores remains impressively the same. On average, girls are achieving much higher than boys on reading literacy; boys are achieving higher than girls on mathematics achievement, but the differences are smaller than those found with reading literacy. Science achievement suggests the same developmental trend as the other measures, with larger effect sizes for the older children. Thus, what is changing throughout childhood is a major question for researchers in this area.

DEVELOPMENTAL TRAJECTORIES THROUGH CHILDHOOD

Many of the differences between boys and girls that are found in school grades and test scores emerge early in life and vary in size as children develop. The ability to learn and use language shows a female advantage within the first two

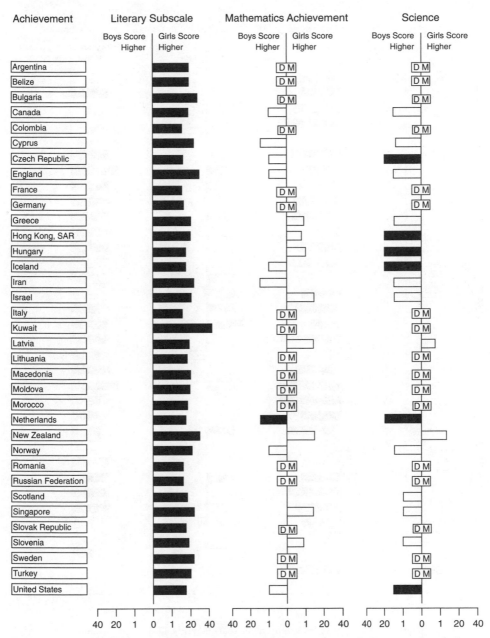

FIGURE 29.1 Gender differences in achievement: fourth-grade students. The literacy subscale data are from the PIRLS 2001 Report (International Association for the Evaluation of Education Achievement, n.d.-a); the mathematics and science data are from the TIMSS Study (International Association for the Evaluation of Education Achievement, n.d.-b). The metric shown is Cohen's *d,* which provides an effect size measure in standard deviation units. It is equal to the difference between the two means divided by the pooled standard deviation. Shaded box = gender difference significantly different at .05; open box = gender difference not significantly different; "DM" box = data missing.

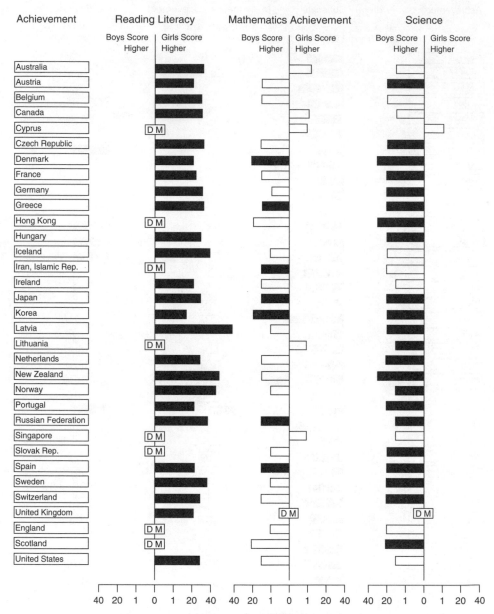

FIGURE 29.2 Gender differences in achievement: 15-year-old and eighth-grade students. The reading literacy data are for 15-year olds. They come from the PISA Report (Organisation for Economic Co-operation and Development, n.d.). The mathematics and science data are from the TIMSS Study (International Association for the Evaluation of Education Achievement, n.d.-b). The metric shown is Cohen's *d*, which provides an effect size measure in standard deviation units. It is equal to the difference between the two means divided by the pooled standard deviation. Shaded box = gender difference significantly different; open box = gender difference not significantly different; "DM" box = data missing.

years of life (e.g., Huttenlocher, Haight, Bryk, Seltzer, & Lyons, 1991), and from approximately age 5 on, girls have a consistent advantage on many (but not all) verbal learning tasks (Kramer, Delis, Kaplan, O'Donnell, & Prifitera, 1997). In grade 8, for example, two thirds of the highest scoring students on the language tests were female. Results from the Differential Aptitude Test of Spelling also shows a significant female advantage, $d = .38$ to .50 (Stanley, Benbow, Brody, Dauber, & Lupkowski, 1992).

It also seems that boys have a large and consistent advantage, beginning early in life, in using visuospatial information. Tests that require maintaining and transforming a visuospatial image (e.g., a map or visual image of a molecular shape, for example) show very large sex differences favoring boys and men. Clear sex differences have been found in preschoolers, probably as early as these skills can be assessed reliably, in spatial transformation (requiring either rotational or nonrotational operations; Levine, Huttenlocher, Taylor, & Langrock, 1999), and in the copying of a three-dimensional model using Legos (McGuinness & Morley, 1991).

Tests of mathematical ability show advantages for girls in the early primary school years when mathematics consists of computational knowledge and speed, then usually show little or no sex difference through the rest of the end of the primary school years, and then show a male advantage when the mathematical concepts are more spatial in nature, such as geometry and topology, which are taught in the higher secondary school grades (Hyde, Fennema, & Lamon, 1990). Despite the finding that boys score higher on tests of mathematics that are less closely tied to school curriculum, girls are performing as well as or better than boys on achievement tests and achieving higher grades in math classes. Girls are outperforming boys by an average of a half-grade across all subject areas (Barker, 1997). Better school performance for girls has led to college enrollments that now exceed those of boys (over 60% of college enrollments), climbing to half of all medical and law school enrollments (U.S. Bureau of the Census, 2001). These data have been the focus of numerous recent newspaper headlines: "Community Colleges Start to Ask, Where Are the Men? 151 Women Receive Associate De-

grees for Every 100 Men" (Evelyn, 2002); "Gender Gap Dogs Nation's Vet Schools: Nearly 75 Percent of Students Are Women" (MacGillis, 2001), and the objectionable and erroneous headline, "Girls Not Wired for Science, Author Claims" (Swainson, 2002). The female advantage in higher education is clearly seen in figure 29.3.

As shown in figure 29.3, there has been a steady trend for females to complete colleges at rates than are higher than those for their male counterparts, a fact that is having major implications for female participation in all aspects of the workforce.

TAILS (TALES) OF DISTRIBUTIONS

The data presented thus far have been based on comparisons of mean differences, but girls and boys have a range or distribution of scores. There are not equal numbers of girls or boys in the tails of the distributions (extremely low or high scores). Boys suffer disproportionately from several disorders that cause mental retardation, so there are more males in the low-ability tail of distributions. There are also more males in the right-hand, or high-scoring, tail of the distributions, with the differences in male to female ratios increasing as the scores increase. Thus, differences in scores of mathematics and verbal tests are small in the midrange of the distribution, where most of the scores are found, with few differences among high school students (i.e., in the general population) and increasingly larger differences on college and graduate/professional school aptitude tests (Willingham & Cole, 1997). Analyses have shown that the female-male differences do not disappear when the males and females are equated for the number of mathematics courses they have taken or when the female and male names are changed to test for bias in the way tests are graded (Baird, 1998). In an extensive analysis of many different tests, Willingham and Cole (1997) concluded that, relative to girls, boys show gains in math concepts, social science, geopolitical studies (geography and history/political science), and natural sciences from grade 4 through grade 12. Girls show gains relative to boys in these grades in writing and language use, and girls maintain their earlier

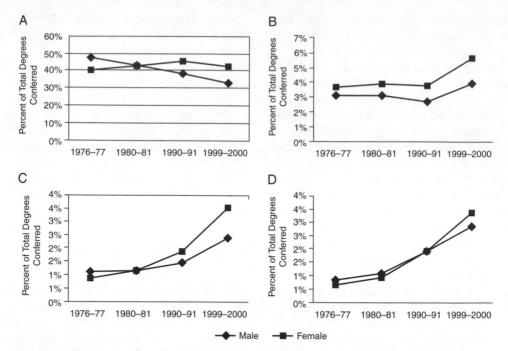

FIGURE 29.3 Degrees conferred by race and gender. (A) Bachelor's degrees conferred to White non-Hispanics by gender. (B) Bachelor's degrees conferred to African Americans by gender. (C) Bachelor's degrees conferred to non-Hispanics by gender. (D) Bachelor's degrees conferred to Asian/Pacific Islanders by gender. Source: U.S. Department of Education, National Center for Education Statistics, Higher Education General Information Survey (HEGIS) (n.d.).

advantage in reading, mathematical computations, and vocabulary. These conclusions are based on test results from millions (literally) of children and summarize findings from hundreds of individual studies.

Some psychologists have theorized that because girls tend to excel on achievement tests that are more closely aligned to context that is taught in school, boys and girls may learn in different ways. Kimball (1989) hypothesized that girls' learning is more rote than boys' learning (i.e., best for information learned in school), and girls' learning is assessed best with familiar problems, but this theory ignores the fact that writing is a highly creative act involving novel topics, and girls perform particularly well on writing tests. Other theories designed to explain why boys and girls have different (average) patterns of achievement depending on the type of test also overlook the fact that the differences are not easy to categorize. Girls' preference for cooperative learning activities and boys' preferences for more competitive ones cannot explain

the finding that girls and boys learn in a variety of types of classrooms and that differences are found as a function of the type of test that is used to assess learning and not in the type of learning activities used in classrooms.

THE BIOPSYCHOSOCIAL MODEL IN WHICH CAUSE AND EFFECT ARE CIRCULAR

What is happening in school and other contexts that can explain why girls and boys have different average performances on selected tests and other assessments? The tired old nature versus nurture model of behavior is wrong because it rests on another false dichotomy, the assumption that nature and nurture can act independently. The biopsychosocial model is based on the premise that even simple distinctions like dividing variables into biological and psychosocial (i.e., environmental) categories are impossible. Consider, for example, the fact that there are differences and similarities in girls' and boys' brains (e.g., Gur et al., 1999). The differences and similarities in brain structures could have been caused, enhanced, or decreased by environmental stimuli, so data showing that the brain is sexually dimorphic are reflective of both nature and nurture. It is now well documented that brain size and structures remain plastic throughout life (Nelson, 1999; Stefan, Kunesch, Cohen, Benecke, & Classen, 2000). Contemporary researchers have used brain-imaging techniques to show changes in cortical representations that occurred after specific experiences. What individuals learn influences neural structures like dendritic branching and cell size; brain architectures, in turn, support certain skills and abilities, which may lead us to select additional experiences. The interface between experience and biology is seamless. Biology and environment are as inseparable as conjoined twins who share a common heart. A biopsychosocial framework provides a more integrated way of thinking about the inextricable processes that influence brain structures and behaviors. Some psychologists and others have suggested that the term *biopsychosocial* be re-

placed by *psychobiosocial* so as not to imply that biology is a primary determinant of the complex interplay of these influences that make each of us a unique reflection of these multiple influences, but thus far the terminology has not been widely accepted.

The biopsychosocial model replaces a continuum anchored at its ends by nature and nurture with a continuous feedback loop where learning is conceptualized as both a biological and an environmental phenomenon. Each individual is predisposed by his or her biology to learn some skills more readily than others, and everyone selects experiences in ways that are biased by prior learning histories and beliefs about appropriate behaviors for females and males. Similarly, many stereotypes about male and female differences reflect real group differences, and by learning and endorsing them, individuals may also be selecting environments that increase or decrease these differences. A schematic diagram of the biopsychosocial model is depicted in figure 29.4.

An exciting area of recent research has shown the importance of the unconscious effects of

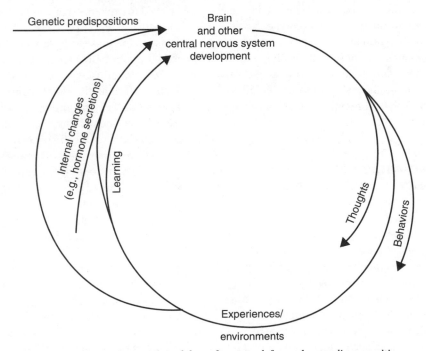

FIGURE 29.4 A biopsychosocial model as a framework for understanding cognitive sex differences. It replaces the older idea of nature versus nurture with a circle that shows the way biological and psychosocial variables exert mutual influences on each other. Reprinted from Halpern (2000).

stereotypes on thought and performance. There are many examples of the way an individual's beliefs can alter a wide range of biological systems, including hormone secretions, motor responses, breathing rates, and digestion, just to name a few. Experimenter or teacher expectations can unconsciously influence how learners respond to situations. Medical researchers are well aware of these two types of effects, which is why double-blind, placebo-controlled, cross-over studies are the "gold standard" for medical research. Recent work by Steele and his colleagues (1997) has extended these principles to explain how beliefs about the cognitive abilities of different groups can cause or contribute to group differences on tests of academic achievement. According to Steele, when group membership (male or female or racial group, for example) is made salient at the time a cognitive test is being administered, commonly held beliefs about the performance of one's group are activated. Test-takers are "threatened" by these beliefs out of the concern that they will conform to their group's negative stereotype. Stereotype threat will affect test performance only when the group membership is made salient, the test that is being taken is relevant to one's group (e.g., the stereotype that females are not as good in mathematics as males), test performance is important to the individuals taking the test, and the test is at a level of difficulty that the additional burden of defending against a perceived threat would cause a performance decrement.

ACADEMIC MOTIVATION— EXPECTANCY × VALUES MODELS

Any discussion of academic achievement needs to consider the central importance of academic motivation. Values and expectations play a role in determining the outcome of learning tasks, such as mathematical problem solving (Eccles, 1994). Expectancy models begin with the simple premise that individuals will work harder and longer on tasks when they expect to be able to achieve a goal (in this case, to solve a math problem) than when they believe that they will not be able to achieve a goal. Thus, when girls and boys believe that hard work will be rewarded with successful

outcomes, they will persist at a task. These expectations translate into actual differences in success because learners are obviously more likely to solve a problem if they persist in working on it than if they quit as soon as they encounter difficulty. In this way, positive expectancy leads to better skills and better skills lead to greater confidence, and so on. There is a huge literature on achievement motivation that supports this sort of feedback loop. It is important to remember that all academic knowledge and skills are learned—often through persistence and hard work.

APPLICATIONS FOR PARENTS, TEACHERS, COUNSELORS, AND GIRLS

What is the take-home message for parents, teachers, and others who care about the academic success of girls? Here are important points to keep in mind:

1. Although there are average differences on many measures of academic achievement, no child is average. Average differences cannot be used to explain, excuse, or predict the performance of any child or adult. Never accept or use as an excuse or explanation about individual performance a statement like, "Girls are X." No girl is average, and all of the research on academic achievement is about averages. Every girl can improve with effort, and expectancy theories explicitly explain how the belief that one can succeed by working hard will motivate the hard work for success.

2. There is no evidence to support claims that girls or boys are smarter. Boys and girls have different average scores on different measures; some show an advantage for girls and some show an advantage for boys, but average scores on intelligence tests have no meaning in the day-to-day life of girls who are working to do well in school and at home. You are too smart to be arguing about the intelligence of girls. As long as girls are achieving in school, staying healthy, and doing well in other areas of life, these are empty arguments. Stay focused on what is important.

3. Girls are achieving at higher rates in school at all levels and in all subjects, including sub-

jects in which they obtain lower scores on aptitude/ability tests (e.g., advanced mathematics). Test content and type are important in determining whether boys or girls show higher average (group) performance. Girls need more activities that involve development of spatial skills, which includes more leisure activities with spatial games on the computer and tinker toy-type games that develop visual spatial skills.

4. Average differences cannot be explained with simple nature versus nurture dichotomies. A biopsychosocial model that recognizes the reciprocal relationships among many types of effects is needed. Avoid giving the message that girls are "naturally" good at writing or poor at reading maps—especially given the changes in the types of careers women have been entering in large numbers in the last few decades. The fast changes in occupational choices show that simple biological explanations for career choices in the past are simply wrong.

5. Teachers, counselors, parents, and others can and should guard against stereotyped messages that can occur in texts and other materials and the multiple messages from the media and others. Under some circumstances, internalized stereotyped beliefs can affect academic performance. Watch for inadvertent use of stereotypes and point them out. I objected when a local elementary school principal created different top prizes for girls and boys in sixth grade. Girls were given stuffed animals and boys were given walkie-talkies; neither had a choice as to which prize they could select.

6. I am often asked about the advisability of separate classes for girls. There are no cognitive data to support the idea that girls and boys should be educated in segregated classes. The principles that all children use to learn are the same—everyone benefits from sound educational practices. Some children will take longer to learn some concepts and tasks than others because people are variable, but the variability between boys and girls is considerably smaller than the variability found among girls or boys. Cooperative classroom practices are good practices for everyone; similarly,

everyone would benefit from some competition if we are preparing for the adult world.

7. All of the academic tasks discussed in this chapter are learnable and all children can learn (with the exception of extremely retarded children, a group that was not considered in this chapter). We need to send a clear message to all girls that they can learn difficult concepts with hard work and good learning support, and we need to give them the support for learning that they need.

8. Children's interests depend on their developed abilities and their past experiences. A variety of successful learning experiences will improve academic motivation and performance. Be sure that girls experience success at learning and that feedback includes useable information that guides future learning.

9. As a society, we need all types of skills and abilities. There is no justification for restricting the development of any child because she is a girl. We will be a richer society if we respect individual differences without constraining choices.

NOTE

Some authors prefer to use the term *gender* when referring to female and male differences that are social in origin and *sex* when referring to differences that are biological in origin. In keeping with the psychobiosocial model that is advocated in this paper and the belief that these two types of influences are interdependent and cannot be separated, only one term is used in this chapter. *Sex* is used without reference to the origin of any observed differences or similarities and is not meant to imply a preference for biological explanations. These terms are often used inconsistently in the literature.

REFERENCES

American Association of University Women. (1992). *How schools shortchange girls: The AAUW report.* New York: Marlowe.

Baird, J.-A. (1998). What's in a name? Experiments with blind marking in A-level examinations. *Educational Research, 40,* 191–202.

Barker, B. (1997). Girls' world or anxious times: What's really happening at school in the gender war? *Educational Review, 49,* 221–228.

Eccles, J. S. (1994). Understanding women's educational and occupational choices: Applying the Eccles et al. model of achievement-related choices. *Psychology of Women Quarterly, 18,* 585–609.

Evelyn, J. (2002, June 28). Community colleges start to ask, where are the men? 151 women receive associate degrees for every 100 men who do. *The Chronicle of Higher Education,* p. A32.

Gur, R. C., Turetsky, B. I., Matsui, M., Yan, M., Bilker, W., & Hehett, P. (1999). Sex differences in brain gray and white matter in healthy young adults: Correlations with cognitive performance. *The Journal of Neuroscience, 19,* 4065–4072.

Halpern, D. F. (1989). The disappearance of cognitive gender differences: What you see depends on where you look. *American Psychologist, 44,* 1156–1158.

Halpern, D. F. (1997). Sex differences in intelligence: Implications for educations. *American Psychologist, 52,* 1091–1102.

Halpern, D. F. (2000). *Sex differences in cognitive abilities* (3rd ed.). Mahwah, NJ: Erlbaum.

Huttenlocher, J., Haight, W., Bryk, A., Seltzer, M., & Lyons, T. (1991). Early vocabulary growth: Relation to language input and gender. *Developmental Psychology, 27,* 236–248.

Hyde, J. S., Fennema, E., & Lamon, S. J. (1990). Gender differences in mathematics performance: A meta-analysis. *Psychological Bulletin, 107,* 139–153.

International Association for the Evaluation of Education Achievement. (n.d.-a). PIRLS 2001 report. Retrieved from http://www/iea.nl/Home/Studies/PIRLS2001/pirls2001.html

International Association for the Evaluation of Education Achievement. (n.d.-b). Trends in Mathematics and Science Study 2003 (TIMSS). Retrieved from http://www.iea.nl/Home/Studies/Current_Studies/TIMSS2003/timss2003.html

Jacobs, B. A. (2002). Where the boys aren't: Noncognitive skills, returns to school and the gender gap in higher education. *Economics of Education Review, 21,* 589–598.

Kimball, M. M. (1989). A new perspective on women's math achievement. *Psychological Bulletin, 105,* 198–214.

Kramer, J. H., Delis, D. C., Kaplan, E., O'Donnell, L., & Prifitera, A. (1997). Developmental sex differences in verbal learning, *Neuropsychology, 11,* 577–584.

Levine, S. C., Huttenlocher, J., Taylor, A., & Langrock, A. (1999). Early sex differences in spatial skill. *Developmental Psychology, 35*(4), 940–949.

MacGillis, A. (2001, December 31). Gender gap dogs nation's vet school: Nearly 75 percent of students are women, leading some to predict far-reaching changes in the profession. *The Baltimore Sun.* Retrieved June 29, 2002, from http://web.lexis-nexis.com/universe

McGuinness, D., & Morley, C. (1991). Sex differences in the development of visuo-spatial ability in preschool children. *Journal of Mental Imagery, 15,* 143–150.

National Assessment of Educational Progress. (1999). *NAEP trends in academic progress.* U.S. Department of Education.

National Center for Education Statistics. (1998). *Pursuing excellence: A study of U.S. twelfth-grade mathematics and science achievement in international context* (NCES 98-049). Washington, DC: U.S. Government Printing Office.

National Center for Education Statistics. (2000). *Pursuing excellence: Comparisons of international eighth-grade mathematics and science achievement from a U.S. perspective, 1995 and 1999* (NCES 2001-028). Washington, DC: U.S. Government Printing Office.

National Center for Education Statistics. (2003). *International comparisons in fourth-grade reading literacy: Findings from the progress in international reading literacy study (PIRLS) of 2001.* (NCES 2003-073). Washington, DC: U.S. Government Printing Office. Retrieved May 6, 2003 from http://nces.ed.gov

Nelson, C. A. (1999). Neural plasticity and human development. *Current Directions in Psychological Science, 8*(2), 42–45.

Organisation for Economic Co-operation and Development. (n.d.). PISA report. Retrieved from http://www.pisa.oecd.org/pisa/rad.htm

Sommers, C. (2000). *The war against boys: How misguided feminism is harming our young men.* New York: Simon & Schuster.

Stanley, J. C., Benbow, C. P., Brody, L. E., Dauber, S., & Lupkowski, A. (1992). Gender differences on eighty-six nationally standardized aptitude and achievement tests. In N. Colangelo, S. G. Assouline, & D. L. Ambroson (Eds.), *Talent development, Vol. 1: Proceedings from the 1991 Henry B. and Jocelyn Wallace National Research Symposium on Talent Development* (pp. 42–65). Unionville, NY: Trillium Press.

Steele, C. M. (1997). A threat in the air: How stereotypes shape intellectual identity and performance. *American Psychologist, 52,* 613–629.

Stefan, K., Kunesch, E., Cohen, L. G., Benecke, R., & Classen, J. (2000). Induction of plasticity in the human motor cortex by paired associative stimulation. *Brain, 123,* 572–584.

Swainson, G. (2002, January 10). Girls not wired for science, author claims. *Toronto Star.* Retrieved June 29, 2002, from http://web.lexis-nexis.com/universe

U.S. Bureau of the Census. (2001). *Statistical abstract of the United States: 2001* (121st ed.). Washington, DC: Author.

U.S. Department of Education, National Center for Education Statistics, Higher Education General Information Survey. (n.d.). "Degrees and Other Formal Awards Conferred" surveys, and Integrated Postsecondary Education Data System (IPEDS) "Completions" surveys. Retrieved May 27, 2003, from http://nces.ed.gov/

Willingham, W. W., and Cole, N. S. (1997). *Gender and fair assessment.* Hillsdale, NJ: Erlbaum.

JUDITH L. MEECE
and KATHRYN SCANTLEBURY

Gender and Schooling: Progress and Persistent Barriers

30

Since the enactment of Title IX of the Elementary and Secondary Education Act in 1972, much has been written about the schooling experiences of girls in America's schools. Reports leading up to this legislation documented numerous barriers that inhibited women's access to vocational, athletic, and educational programs. Title IX legislation was designed to be a comprehensive federal mandate to address gender inequities at all levels of schooling, from admission policies to career education. Over the last three decades, unprecedented changes in women's level of educational participation and achievement have been observed. For the first time in U.S. history, women today are earning more college degrees than are men, and a record number of women are earning law, medical, and business degrees. However, numerous reports suggest that significant disparities in girls' schooling experiences exist, especially when differences are examined by socioeconomic status, geographic location, ethnicity, and/or disability (American Association of University Women [AAUW], 1998a).

The focus of this chapter is the elementary and secondary school years, when school attendance is compulsory. The research review is also limited to schooling experiences within the United States, although there are many rich accounts of girls' schooling experiences in other countries (see Kenway, Willis, Blackmore, & Rennie, 1998). The chapter begins with a look at how schools may affect girls' development through reinforcing traditional gender roles. Subsequent sections examine how schools facilitate or hinder girls' academic achievement, career development, and emotional well-being.

DO SCHOOLS REINFORCE GENDER STEREOTYPES?

Schools, from the way they are organized to the types of behaviors that are encouraged and reinforced, play a key role in shaping children's gender role conceptions, beliefs, and social identities. Evidence suggests that schools expose young people to feminine and masculine images that are more rigid and more polarized than those held by the wider society (Ruble & Martin, 1998).

Staffing Patterns

Schools are an important context for observing and learning about the adult world, and gender-related staffing patterns characterize most elementary, middle, and secondary schools. In this regard, children learn important lessons about power, authority, and gendered expertise. Today, 80 percent of teachers are women but only 40 percent of school principals are female (National Center for Education Statistics [NCES], 2001). In school, women are more likely to perform traditional gender roles such as caring for young children, putting on Band-Aids, and preparing food. In contrast, men manage the school and staff, coach sports, and fix things. By observing staffing patterns at school, children may also learn that men and women have different areas of expertise. A majority of high school foreign language, humanities, business education, and English teachers are female, whereas only half of math and science teachers are female (Weiss, Banilower, McMahon, & Smith, 2001).

Curricular Materials

Approximately 80% of children's time at school involves textbooks, films, videotapes, and computer software. Textbooks today are less gender biased than they were 30 years ago, and publishers have made considerable progress to include female characters and perspectives (AAUW, 1998a). Yet evidence suggests that male characters continue to outnumber female ones in basal readers and mathematics materials and textbooks rarely represent the diversity of students who are their readers (Fleming, 2000). Girls are also still placed in stereotypic roles such as passive observers; whereas males continue to be represented as active, assertive, and adventurous (Davis & McDaniel, 1999). Additionally, subtle wording of texts, such as women were *given* the right to vote, can also reinforce a passive view of women. Also, very few texts discuss key social or historical events from a female perspective, thereby limiting female voices in these texts.

Classroom Interaction Patterns

Research also suggests that classroom interactions are differentiated along gender lines. A disproportionate number of boys' interactions with teachers involve criticism, remediation, and other forms of behavioral control; whereas girls tend to be singled out as the model student because they are neat, responsible and quiet (Sadker & Sadker, 1994). Other research suggests that questioning and feedback patterns are also gender-differentiated. When asking complex, abstract, or open-ended questions, teachers call on boys more frequently than girls (Altermatt, Jovanovic, & Perry, 1998). Compared with girls, boys also receive more acknowledgement, approval, encouragement, criticism, and corrective feedback in response to their answers.

Gender-differentiated classroom interaction patterns appear to be more pronounced in stereotypically male sex–typed school subjects, such as mathematics and science, but these patterns are not consistently found across studies (Altermatt et al., 1998). Other evidence suggests that gender differences are more pronounced in whole class instruction. Girls tend to take a more active role in classrooms where individualized or cooperative learning is the primary mode of instruction. Evidence also suggests that gender-differentiated patterns may be due to the fact that boys initiate more interactions with their teachers than do girls (Altermatt et al., 1998). Whether these teacher-student interactions reflect teacher responsivity or positive bias toward boys, the patterns serve to reinforce traditional gender role stereotypes of male dominance, authority, and competence.

Sports Participation and Extracurricular Activities

Since the introduction of Title IX, girls' participation in school-sponsored sports and athletic programs has increased significantly. Whereas less than 7% of high school athletes were women in 1971, this figure increased to 42% by 2001 (National Coalition for Women and Girls in Education, 2002). Evidence also suggests that participation rates across ethnic groups are about equal; however, low socioeconomic status can limit girls' access to physical activity and sport (AAUW, 1998a). While more girls are participating in a greater array of sports than ever before, evidence suggests that high school sports continue to be male dominated. The U.S. Department of Education reports that twice as many 12th-grade boys as girls participate in an interscholastic or individual sport (NCES, 1998).

Compared with sports participation, extracurricular activities are highly sex differentiated. A greater number of girls than boys play in the school band or orchestra, work on the school newspaper or yearbook, participate in school government, and perform school or community service. While girls' participation in pep clubs and cheerleading has decreased in recent years, their participation in traditionally male activities, such as computer and science clubs, has not changed (AAUW, 1998a). In general, extracurricular activities, more than sports, tend to reinforce traditional areas of gender competence and skills.

SCHOOLING, ACADEMIC ACHIEVEMENT, AND CAREER DEVELOPMENT

Women today are entering the labor force in unprecedented numbers, and they have made significant progress toward gaining access to postsecondary education. Despite increases in educational attainment, wage gaps between male and female workers persist, and are larger for women of color (Fleming, 2000). In this section, we examine the role of schools in contributing to girls' future career options and opportunities.

Girls' Academic Achievement

Title IX legislation helped to remove many barriers for girls' participation in mathematics and science. Whereas high school girls were far less likely than boys to take advanced mathematics and science classes in the 1980s, gender differences in course taking patterns are less evident today. Overall, girls are just as likely as boys to take algebra, geometry, calculus, biology, and chemistry (Coley, 2001). Additionally, the percentage of girls taking Advanced Placement (AP) classes in mathematics and science has increased significantly

over the last decades. The one exception to this pattern is high school physics, which continues to be dominated by boys (Coley, 2001).

On standardized tests, girls' achievement varies for different subjects. Across all cultural and ethnic groups, girls receive higher scores, when compared to boys, on standardized tests of reading and writing (Coley, 2001). In mathematics, girls' performance on the National Assessment of Educational Progress (NAEP) improved significantly over the last decades (NCES, 2004). In contrast to these findings, girls' performance on standardized tests in science is less positive. The most recent NAEP revealed significant gender differences, favoring boys, at fourth and eighth grade for White non-Hispanic/Latino students. Gender gaps in performance also were significantly higher in 2002 than in 1996. In addition, girls continue to lag behind boys on college entrance tests such as the SAT or ACT (chapter 29, this volume). Ethnic differences in subtest scores of the SAT further show discrepancies within gender. Asian and non-Hispanic White girls outperform Native American, Hispanic/Latina, and African American girls (National Council for Research on Women [NCRW], 1998).

When grades are used as the standard of achievement, a different picture emerges. Overall, girls tend to earn higher grades in school in all or almost all subjects than do boys (chapter 29, this volume). In addition, girls tend to exceed boys in class ranks and academic honors, although boys surpass girls in awards for mathematics and science competitions (Dwyer & Johnson, 1997).

Girls' Access to Technology in Schools

As computer technology becomes increasingly prevalent in the workplace, concerns have been raised about the emerging "digital divide" in schools (Cooper & Weaver, 2003). During the elementary school years, girls and boys appear to be equally interested in computers at school, although there may be out-of-school differences in computer usage and experience. By high school, however, fewer girls than boys enroll in computer classes and take AP Computer Science Tests. School-related inequities in computer training are generally attributed to male-oriented computer software and classes that feature competition, stereotypically masculine content (e.g., sports, space travel, etc.), computer mechanics, and few female characters or role models. Girls tend to show a greater interest in computer activities at school when they are used as learning, artistic, and communication tools (AAUW, 2000). Girls are likely to be "left behind on the road to technology proficiency," unless educators attend to gender differences in learning preferences and styles (Cooper & Weaver, 2003, p. ix).

Vocational Education and Career Preparation in School

Along with access to computer technology, young women's access to vocational and career preparation programs at school can shape their future employment and economic opportunities. Compared to other areas, such as mathematics, vocational education remains strongly gender-stereotyped. Approximately, 7% of the students in traditional male vocational education programs, such as plumbing, electricity, or carpentry, are female. Furthermore, studies of School-to-Work initiatives of the 1990s, which provided federal funds to eliminate sex bias in vocational education, indicated little change in these sex-differentiated patterns (AAUW, 1998a).

Girls' Leaving and Dropping Out of High School

Another factor that can dramatically limit girls' vocational and economic opportunities is obtaining a high school diploma. In general, high school dropout statistics are lower for girls than boys. Nationally, across ethnic group lines and geographic regions, 28% of girls and 36% of boys drop out of high school (Swanson, 2002). National statistics are often misleading because they do not include data for those students returning to complete a Graduate Equivalency Diploma (GED). However, national statistics do show that if a girl does drops out of high school there is a smaller chance that she will return, compared with a boy (AAUW, 1998a). A girl's chances of

dropping out increases if she is Hispanic/Latina, African American, Native American, or struggling academically. Although school dropout can have short-term benefits for some girls, young women who drop out of high school are more likely to become pregnant at a young age and to experience economic hardships (NCRW, 1998).

SCHOOLING AND EMOTIONAL WELL-BEING

Schooling experiences affect more than the academic and career development of youth. Schools can have a powerful influence on a young person's sense of self, ethnic identity, interpersonal relations, and psychological well-being. In this regard, schooling experiences can have profound and lasting consequences for adulthood.

Forming a Sense of Competence

Competency perceptions are integrally tied to academic motivation, achievement, school adjustment, and occupational choices. By early elementary school, gender differences in competency perceptions are evident and reflect traditional sex-role stereotypes. In general, girls tend to rate their verbal, reading, and social abilities higher than their abilities in math, physical science, and sports, whereas boys tend to show the opposite patterns (Eccles, Barber, Jozefowicz, Malenchuk, & Vida, 1999). Gender differences appear, even though boys and girls may do equally well as boys in these academic areas.

Do schooling experiences play a contributing role in these gendered patterns? To date, the research evidence is inconclusive. Although classroom interaction patterns may be differentiated along gender lines, findings concerning gender differences in teachers' expectations for achievement are mixed. Whereas earlier studies suggested that teachers held higher achievement expectations for boys than girls, especially in the areas of mathematics and science (Kahle & Meece, 1994), recent reviews of teacher beliefs provide no clear patterns of gender-related differences in teacher expectations (Li, 1999). Gender differences in teacher expectancies depend on grade level, student ability, subject matter, and schooling context. However, when gender differences are found, there is some evidence to suggest that girls may be more suggestible to teacher expectancy effects than are boys (Jussim, Eccles, & Maddon, 1996).

Schooling and Self-Esteem

Although girls may develop a strong sense of competency in some academic areas, numerous studies and reports highlight the difficulties they face in maintaining a strong sense of self-worth as they progress in school. Gilligan and her colleagues have written extensively about the sharp declines in girls' self-esteem in adolescence when they experience a "loss of voice" and lose confidence in themselves (Gilligan & Brown, 1992). Similarly, a 1990 AAUW survey showed that adolescent girls reported much lower self-regard (e.g., "I am happy with myself") than elementary school girls. This difference in self-esteem, although present, was less marked for African American girls (AAUW, 1992).

It is not yet clear how schools may contribute to changes in girls' self-esteem. Consistent with the "losing voice" hypothesis, girls tend to have a lower level of participation than boys in classrooms, which may lead girls to accept a quieter and secondary role in the classroom. Girls, as well as their teachers, may equate this lower participation with a lack of confidence. However, to date, there is limited empirical support for this hypothesis. In a sample of high school students, Harter (1997) found no general decline in girls' level of voice, as defined by their perceived ability to state opinions, share information, or express thoughts and feelings in classroom situations. Instead, they found that the level of voice girls reported depended on their perceptions of support for making their opinions known to others.

The transition to middle or junior high school can lead to declines in self-esteem for some girls. Simmons and Blyth's (1987) landmark studies of school transitions showed that girls' self-esteem decline from sixth to seventh grade as they change school environments. These declines are due to the multiple changes girls experience in early adolescence, including the onset of puberty, dating relations, and new school environments. However, not all girls experience these changes. African American girls, on the average, do not experience the same declines in self-esteem during early adolescence, possibly because they tend to respond more positively to their physical changes. For European American girls, strong self-concepts with regards to academics, athletics, peers, and physical appearance may help to offset negative changes in self-esteem during early adolescence. Of these self-perceptions, a positive body image is very important for European American girls (Eccles et al., 1999).

Forming an Ethnic Identity

The multiple influences of class, ethnicity, and gender impact girls' identity and their schooling experiences. For girls from the nondominant culture, school represents a place and time where girls develop transcultural identities (Davidson, 1996). For example, African American girls often have multiple ideologies that impact their identities. They are influenced first by cultural norms and expectations that value "White" and "male" as the norm and define other social groups as "other." Additionally, African American girls are influenced by their own culture. For example, African American mothers expect their daughters to attain autonomy, to develop self-reliance, and to become resourceful (Collins, 1998). These qualities can create conflict for girls in school environments where the dominant White culture expects girls to be quiet, compliant, and helpful. In contrast, parents of Latina and Asian girls generally expect their daughters to be obedient, responsible, dependent, and submissive (Weiler, 2000). These attributes are more consistent with the gendered expectations at school, and those girls assimilate into school structures more easily than their African American peers.

In general, there is very little information on how girls' ethnic identities influence their attitudes toward learning and schooling (Williams, Davis, Cribbs, Saunders, & Williams, 2002). Most studies, to date, have focused on cultural and ethnic differences in academic attitudes and achievement. African American girls are more likely than their male peers to earn a higher GPA, to finish high school, to attend college, and to enter white-collar careers (Weiler, 2000). In contrast, Latina girls, especially ones who are economically disadvantaged, are less likely to extend their studies past high school, but rather move into low-paying positions and full-time domestic duties. For Latina girls of Dominican and South American descent, school represents a vehicle for upward social mobility and economic stability (Weiler, 2000).

Forming a Sexual Identity

Girls continue to struggle with mixed messages from the school environment regarding their sexuality. On the one hand, girls are expected to dress in a manner that enhances their physical attributes and sexual appeal. However, girls who become sexually active or promiscuous may face social ridicule and ostracism when these behaviors are not consistent with peer group or school norms. Additionally, schools fail girls in substantive and useful sex education classes. Sex education classes are typically focused on delivering facts—for example, the names of sexually transmitted diseases, watching films on hygiene—with no discussions focused on understanding sexual desire or girl's agency with regards to her sexuality (Murray, 1996). In a study of sex education classes, Fine (1993) described four ways in which sexuality is presented in schools: (a) violence; (b) victimization; (c) individual morality; and (d) discourse of desire. Each of these discourses, according to Fine, have negative consequences for girls, including fear, blame, victim ideology, and repression of sexual desires. Moreover, girls learn little about body changes, sexually transmitted diseases, sexual abuse, and pregnancy prevention other than abstinence.

Additionally, most schools promote married heterosexuality as the norm over other sexual practices and preferences. Lesbian girls and bisexual youth report high instances of verbal and sexual harassment (Kosciw, 2004). While gay boys are more likely to be physically assaulted than lesbians, on most categories, bisexual students reported the highest occurrences of harassment and assault of their persons and/or property during school hours (Kosciw, 2004). Overall, lesbian girls are more likely to miss school because of feeling unsafe. Eighty-four percent of lesbian, gay, bisexual, or transsexual (LGBT) youth reported that their peers harassed them with sexist and homophobic remarks while in the presence of school faculty and 42% of students reported that faculty did not intervene (Kosciw, 2004).

Peer Relations and Girls' Emotional Well-Being at School

Peer relations play a very important role in girls' social and emotional development. As just described, many girls experience a negative peer culture at school. In the AAUW report *Hostile Hallways* (1993), 85% of girls and 76% of boys reported experiencing some form of harassment in their middle or high school. In a more detailed study of the AAUW data, Hand and Sanchez (2000) reported that girls and boys experience different forms of harassment. Girls are more likely to experience physical sexual harassment, such as inappropriate touching, forced kissing, pulled clothes, or being cornered, whereas boys experienced more verbal abuse. In addition, girls tend to respond more negatively than boys to peer harassment. Girls who were harassed at school reported negative changes in their school attendance, grades, self-confidence, and class participation. They also reported feeling less safe at school and changed their behavior at school to avoid being harassed again (AAUW, 1993).

Most of the reported harassment occurred in schools' public spaces—the hallways, classrooms, and cafeterias—places where adults had a responsibility to protect students. Stein (1995) suggests that the lack of overt intervention provides boys with tacit approval of harassment that reinforces and reproduces society's gendered power differential. Unless more actively and openly addressed by school officials, peer harassment will continue to limit and undermine girls' schooling experiences.

ARE SINGLE-SEX SCHOOLS THE ANSWER?

Single-sex educational programs for girls are expected to rise over the next few years due to new federal guidelines easing restrictions imposed by

Title IX legislation, which prohibited single-sex education other than that for sex education, contact sports, remedial classes, and singing. For girls, single-sex educational programs are generally permissible as a vehicle to improve their achievement in traditionally male content areas, such as mathematics, science, and technology, where girls tend to be historically underrepresented. Unfortunately, published research supporting the improved achievement of girls in single-sex educational programs is rather sparse and mixed (AAUW, 1998b).

Some evidence suggests that single-sex programs have a positive influence on confidence, educational and career aspirations, and self-esteem (AAUW, 1998a). In these settings, girls view their classrooms as conducive to learning and choose friends who are academically oriented. Single-sex programs also foster less stereotypical views of mathematics and science. However, only a handful of studies have reported higher achievement for girls in single than coeducational programs, and these studies have not adequately controlled for differences in teacher qualifications, class size, and student background characteristics (AAUW, 1998b). Thus, it is not clear that achievement improvements are due to factors unique to single-sex schooling. Additionally, few studies to date have examined the long-term impact of single-sex schooling on girls' development.

CONCLUSIONS

This chapter has highlighted the many ways schools affect girls' development, from the types of learning opportunities they receive to the social interactions they experience. Current research and reports provide a mixed view of girls' schooling experiences. On the one hand, the focus on gender equity in mathematics, science, and athletic programs has increased girls' participation in those areas. Achievement gaps in mathematics achievement are disappearing, and more young women than ever before are continuing their education beyond high school. On the other hand, recent reports indicate serious gaps in girls' access to careers in science and technology. Girls of color and low socioeconomic status are most likely to be left behind in an increasingly technological labor market. It is estimated that 70% of all jobs today require technological skills (Schoenfeld, 2002). Furthermore, reports indicate that little has changed in terms of the gender norms of schools. Girls receive mixed messages concerning their abilities and behaviors, and they risk ostracism or social ridicule if they should deviate from expected gender norms. Girls who are loud, "sassy," or assertive run the risk of disciplinary action. Lastly, the large number of girls who witness or experience violence or harassment in school settings is particularly disturbing.

Concerns have also been raised about the increased invisibility of girls in national policy focused on education. As noted above, single-sex educational programs are proliferating with very little research to guide those efforts. Major curriculum reforms in mathematics and science have been underway for over a decade, yet few studies have examined how these curricular reforms are benefiting girls from different ethnic, geographic, or socioeconomic backgrounds. A recent federal law, the No Child Left Behind (NCLB) Act, is likely to become a major policy document impacting schools at the start of the 21st century. However, as Kahle (2003) noted, the NCLB legislature ignored gender in the reporting of achievement and performance outcomes. States are mandated to provide annual reports of academic achievement by almost every social category *but* gender. In addition, the educational advances of girls and women over the last three decades have not gone unchallenged. Citing data documenting boys' declining achievement and status in school, some critics have argued that efforts to help girls have harmed boys (Pollock, 1998; Sommers, 2000). It is not yet clear how this growing concern about boys' achievements and well-being at school will transform the schooling experiences of girls.

In this schooling context, girls will need strong advocates to keep gender equity a priority at every level of reform. Girls need caring mentors who will listen to their concerns and honor their voices. Girls thrive in school environments that (a) depict females from various cultures in a variety of roles, (b) provide opportunities of leadership, (c) encourage awareness of cultural and gender issues, and (d) connect learning to their future and lives outside of schools. Schools need counseling programs that encourage girls to take advanced mathematics and science classes at the AP or honors levels. Schools need to collect and track academic achievement and course enrollment by gender, ethnicity, and socioeconomic status to identify gaps between and within gender groups. To address gaps in computer technology, school professionals need to advocate for intervention programs that increase girls' participation in this area. The especially high dropout rate for poor and Hispanic/Latina girls needs to be targeted and reduced. Finally, schools have been slow to respond to reports on sexual and peer harassment. It is therefore important for school professionals to make the enforcement of sexual harassment and school violence policies a priority in their schools.

NOTE

The authors are grateful for assistance of Samantha Burg and Jason Painter in the preparation of this manuscript.

REFERENCES

Altermatt, E. R., Jovanovic, J., & Perry, M. (1998). Bias or responsivity? Sex and achievement-level effects on teachers' classroom questioning practices. *Journal of Educational Psychology, 90*(3), 516–527.

American Association of University Women. (1992). *The AAUW report: How schools shortchange girls.* Washington, DC: Author.

American Association of University Women. (1993). *Hostile hallways: The AAUW survey on sexual harassment in America's schools.* Washington, DC: Author.

American Association of University Women, Educational Foundation. (1998a). *Gender gaps: Where schools still fail our children.* Washington, DC: Author.

American Association of University Women, Educational Foundation. (1998b). *Separated by sex. A critical look at single-sex education for girls.* Washington, DC: Author.

American Association of University Women, Educational Foundation. (2000). *TechsSavy: Educating girls in the new computer age.* Washington, DC: Author.

Coley, R. J. (2001). *Differences in the gender gap: Comparisons across racial/ethnic groups in education and work.* Princeton, NJ: Educational Testing Service.

Collins, P. H. (1998). *Fighting words: Black women and the search for justice.* Minneapolis: University of Minnesota Press.

Cooper, J., & Weaver, K. D. (2003). *Gender and computers. Understanding the digital divide.* Mahwah, NJ: Erlbaum.

Davidson, A. (1996). *Making and molding identity in schools: Student narratives on race, gender and academic engagement.* Albany: State University of New York Press.

Davis, A., & McDaniel, T. (1999). You've come a long way—or have you? Research evaluating gender portrayal in recent Caldecott-winning books. *Reading Teacher, 57,* 532–536.

Dwyer, C., & Johnson, L. (1997). Grades, accomplishments, and correlates. In W. Willingham & N. Cole (Eds.), *Gender and fair assessment* (pp. 127–156). Mahwah, NJ: Erlbaum.

Eccles, J. Barber, B., Jozefowicz, D., Malenchuk, O., & Vida, M. (1999). Self-evaluations of competence, task values, and self-esteem. In N. Johnson, M. Roberts, & J. Worell (Eds.), *Beyond appearance. A new look at adolescent girls* (pp. 53–84). Washington, DC: American Psychological Association.

Fine, M. (1993). Sexuality, schooling, and adolescent females: The missing discourse of desire. In L. Weis & M. Fine (Eds.), *Beyond silenced voices: Class, race, and gender in United States schools* (pp. 75–100). New York: State University of New York Press.

Fleming, P. (2000). Three decades of educational progress and continuing barriers for women and girls. *Equity and Excellence in Education, 33*(1), 74–79.

Gilligan, C., & Brown, L. M. (1992). *Meeting at the crossroads: Women's psychology and girls' development.* Cambridge, MA: Harvard University Press.

Hand, J., & Sanchez, L. (2000). Badgering and bantering: Gender differences in experiences of, and reactions to, sexual harassment among U.S. high school students. *Gender & Society, 14*(6), 718–746.

Harter, S. (1997). The development of self-presentation. In W. Damon (Ed.) & N. Eisenberg (Vol. Ed.), *Handbook of child psychology: Vol. 3. Social, emotional, and personality development* (pp. 553–618). New York: John Wiley & Sons.

Jussim, L., Eccles, J., & Maddon, S. (1996). Social perceptions, social stereotypes, and teacher expectations: Accuracy and the quest for powerful self-fulfilling prophecy. In L. Berkowitz (Ed.), *Advances in experimental social psychology* (pp. 281–388). New York: Academic Press.

Kahle, J. B. (2003). *Will girls be left behind? Gender differences and accountability.* Willystine Goodsell Award Paper, Annual Meeting, American Educational Research Association Annual Meeting, Chicago.

Kahle, J. B., & Meece, J. (1994). Research on gender issues in the classroom. In D. Gabel (Ed.), *Handbook of research in science teaching and learning* (pp. 542–576). Washington, DC: National Science Teachers Association.

Kenway, J., Willis, S., Blackmore, J., & Rennie, L. (1998). *Answering back: Girls, boys and feminism in schools.* New York: Routledge.

Kosciw, J. G. (2004). *The 2003 National Climate Survey: The school-related experiences of our nation's lesbian, gay, bisexual and transgendered youth.* New York: GLSEN.

Li, Q. (1999). Teacher beliefs and gender differences in mathematics: A review. *Educational Research, 41,* 63–76.

Murray, V. (1996). Inner city girls of color: Unmarried, sexually active non-mothers. In B. J. Leadbeater & N. Way (Eds.), *Urban girls: Resisting stereotypes, creating identities* (pp. 272–290). New York: New York University Press.

National Center for Education Statistics. (1998). *Condition of education.* Washington, DC: U.S. Department of Education, Office of Education and Improvement.

National Center for Education Statistics. (2001). *Condition of education.* Washington, DC: U.S. Department of Education, Office of Education and Improvement.

National Center for Education Statistics. (2004). *Mathematics 2003 major results.* Washington, DC: U.S. Department of Education, Institute of Educational Sciences. Retrieved January 25, 2004, from http://nces.ed.gov/nationsreportcard/mathematics/

National Coalition for Girls and Women in Education. (2002). *Title IX at 30.* Washington, DC: Author.

National Council for Research on Women. (1998). *The girls report. What we know & need to know about growing up female.* New York: Author.

Pollock, W. (1998). *Real boys.* New York: Henry Holt.

Ruble, D., & Martin, C. L. (1998). Gender development. In W. Damon (Ed.) & N. Eisenberg (Vol. Ed.), *Handbook of child psychology: Vol. 3: Social, emotional, and personality development* (pp. 933–1016). New York: John Wiley & Sons.

Sadker, M., & Sadker, D. (1994). *Failing at fairness: How America's schools cheat girls.* New York: Scribner's.

Schoenfeld, A. (2002). Making mathematics work for all children. *Educational Researcher, 31*(1), 13–25.

Simmons, R., & Blyth, D. (1987). *Moving into adolescence. The impact of pubertal change and school context.* Hawthorne, NY: Aldine de Gruyter.

Sommers, C. H. (2000). *The war against boys. How misguided feminism is harming our young men.* New York: Simon & Schuster.

Stein, N. (1995). Sexual harassment in school: The public performance of gendered violence. *Harvard Educational Review, 65,* 145–162.

Swanson, C. (2002). *Who graduates? Who doesn't? A statistical portrait of public high school graduation: Class of 2001.* Washington, DC: Urban Institute.

Weiler, J. (2000). *Codes and contradictions: Race, gender, identity, and schooling.* Albany: SUNY Press.

Weiss, I., Banilower, E., McMahon, K., & Smith, P. (2001). *Report of the 2000 national survey of science and mathematics education.* Chapel Hill, NC: Horizon Research.

Williams, T. R., Davis, L. E., Cribbs, J. M., Saunders, J., & Williams, J. (2002). Friends, family, and neighborhood: Understanding academic outcomes of African-American youth. *Urban Education, 37,* 408–431.

There's no denying that peers are very important to an adolescent girl: a best friend who knows her deepest secrets, a clique of friends who provide her with a sense of belonging and a shared identity outside of her family, an athletic team that enhances her skills and offers experiences in group coordination and shared accomplishment. The adolescent world often seems to revolve around the peer group. It is no surprise, then, that the peer group plays a critical role in the psychological and physical health of teenage girls. Peer relationships can be the best of times for some girls and the worst of times for others. Whether peers will enhance or cause harm to a teenage girl's development depends on the characteristics of the girls and boys with whom she spends her time and on the quality of those relationships.

This chapter begins with an overview of research on peers, first as sources of support and strength and second as sources of stress for adolescent girls. In both cases, studies show an impact of peers on girls' emotional and psychological well-being. For example, we discuss a form of behavior known as "relational aggression," in which a girl damages or threatens to damage someone else's relationships or social standing—for instance through the spreading of gossip. Research shows that this form of aggression is harmful not only to the victim but also to the aggressor. We review the limited available research on programs designed to reduce relational aggression by focusing on the instigators, and interventions aimed at helping their victims by involving supportive peers.

The chapter then shifts gears to consider the influence of peers on girls' physical health. We review research suggesting that the attitudes and behaviors of friends can increase or decrease health risks by shaping adolescents' use of substances, their sexual behavior, and other health behaviors. Finally, we expand our scope beyond the peer group to the larger communities in which girls live, focusing on the impact that organizations and supportive adults outside of the family can have on a girl's healthy development. The chapter closes with a discussion of future directions for research, particularly research that might lead to the development of interventions and social policies that enhance the health and well-being of adolescent girls.

BRIDGET M. REYNOLDS
and RENA L. REPETTI

Adolescent Girls' Health in the Context of Peer and Community Relationships

PEERS AS SOURCES OF STRENGTH

As we move from childhood to adolescence, intimacy, loyalty, and trust become increasingly important aspects of our friendships. In their interactions with friends, adolescents share more of their personal thoughts and feelings and show more emotional reciprocity and understanding than do younger children. Some evidence indicates that this trend is more apparent in female friendships than in male friendships (Rubin, Bukowski, & Parker, 1998). In fact, intimacy, which is often defined as the ability to share one's thoughts and feelings with a friend, has been described as a central characteristic of girls' friendships (Brown, Way, & Duff, 1999). Thus, friendships provide adolescent girls with the opportunity to express their thoughts and emotions and to receive valuable support in coping with them.

During adolescence, girls spend a substantial amount of their time interacting with peers. In fact, it has been shown that both female and male high school students spend approximately one third of their waking hours with peers, not including time spent in the classroom (Rubin et al., 1998). This amount of time is particularly noteworthy because it represents twice the amount of time spent with parents and other adults. Indeed, in some domains friends equal or surpass parents as sources of support and advice. For example, it has been found that peers provide girls with a greater proportion of emotional help than do parents in day-to-day matters (Frey & Rothlisberger, 1996). Moreover, teenage girls report a greater number of supportive friends than supportive adults, perceive more support from their friends, and are more satisfied with support from friends than with support from adults (Colarossi, 2001). The importance of friends as sources of social support among teens is not only true in the United States. In a study conducted in the Netherlands, it was found that early adolescents perceive the most support from their parents, but that older adolescents perceive their best friends as being equally supportive as parents (Scholte, van Lieshout, & van Aken, 2001). Clearly, as girls mature during adolescence, friends become increasingly important sources of social support and companionship.

Research generally shows that having positive peer relationships is linked with better psychological adjustment among adolescents (Rubin et al., 1998). For example, more support from peers is associated with lower levels of depressed affect, fewer thoughts of suicide, and higher levels of self-esteem (Boyce-Rodgers and Rose, 2002). Peer support also appears to buffer the effects of low parental support. Adolescents who are the recipients of negative parenting are at risk for a range of maladaptive outcomes (Repetti, Taylor, & Seeman, 2002). Positive peer relationships might serve as a protective factor for these at-risk adolescents. In one study, the link between negative parenting, such as poor supervision and unilateral parental decision making, and adolescent externalizing behavior (e.g., getting into fights or being disobedient at school) was mitigated among individuals who had good relationships with their peers (Lansford, Criss, Pettit, Dodge, & Bates, 2003). Thus, peer relationships can provide adolescents with important sources of strength and support and may provide some adolescents with positive experiences that are lacking in their relationship with their parents. Supportive peer relationships can be a buffer in times of stress and can lead to greater self-esteem. However, peer relationships are not always supportive and esteem-enhancing. The following section discusses the stresses and strains that are associated with problematic peer relationships.

PEERS AS SOURCES OF STRESS

We know that problems in peer relationships are related to a broad array of adjustment difficulties in childhood and adolescence (Repetti, McGrath, & Ishikawa, 1999). The correlates range from academic failure to delinquent behavior, to symptoms of depression, anxiety, and low self-esteem. The research literature addressing the kinds of problems children and adolescents experience in their peer relationships has developed along several distinct paths. One line of research investigates the correlates associated with being aggressive toward peers. This literature suggests that aggressive children are more likely than nonaggressive children to be disliked or rejected by their peers and that this type of peer rejection is associated with a number of adjustment problems (Rubin et al., 1998). Another line of research has focused on the consequences of being targeted for peer aggression. The literature in this area shows that the victims of peer aggression are also at risk for a variety of psychological difficulties (Hawker & Boulton, 2000). Until quite recently, researchers failed to investigate these topics specifically among females. In the following sections, we will describe recent advances in the study of peer aggression and victimization by focusing on a type of behavior known as "relational aggression" in the research literature. This behavior is often assumed to be characteristic of female peer groups.

The Perpetrators of Relational Aggression

Few studies have investigated the types of behavior that can lead to problems in girls' peer relationships, despite evidence that such relationships are critically important in adolescence. Indeed, research has focused primarily on the behavioral patterns characteristic of boys who are disliked by their peers. For example, among children and adolescents, physical aggression is the most commonly cited predictor of peer rejection (Rubin et al., 1998). Because boys are more physically aggressive than girls (Maccoby, 1998), early work on the topic of peer rejection focused almost exclusively on males. More recently, however, researchers have begun to study the predictors and consequences of peer rejection specifically among females (Crick & Grotpeter, 1995). For example, Crick (1996) identified a relational form of aggression that predicted increased peer rejection over the course of a school year among preadolescent girls. This type of behavior, termed relational aggression, involves harming others through actual or threatened damage to peer relationships. Examples include threatening not to be friends with someone unless that person does what the aggressor wishes or excluding someone from a peer group as a means of retaliation. Most of the research on relational aggression to date has focused on middle-to-late childhood. The findings suggest that relationally aggressive girls are not only perceived negatively by the broader peer group but also have problematic relationships with their mutual friends

(Crick & Grotpeter, 1995; Grotpeter & Crick, 1996). This is cause for concern, particularly because positive peer relationships and friendships are important sources of social support for girls. Although little is known about relational aggression in adolescence, it appears that relationally aggressive teenage girls experience adjustment problems similar to those reported by younger children (Prinstein, Boergers, & Vernberg, 2001; Werner & Crick, 1999).

Most of the research on relational aggression and victimization has been conducted within the United States; however, some support exists for cross-cultural generalizability. For example, researchers working in Indonesia found that children and adolescents, particularly females, there made extensive reference to relationally aggressive behaviors when asked to describe disliked peers (French, Jansen, & Pidada, 2002). In a study of Italian children and preadolescents, relational aggression was associated with concurrent peer rejection and a decrease in peer acceptance over the course of a school year for both girls and boys (Tomada & Schneider, 1997). Thus, it appears that relational aggression may be a significant part of children and adolescents' interpersonal lives across cultures and may represent a widespread risk factor for social maladjustment.

Debate exists within the literature regarding gender differences in the use of relational aggression. Researchers originally thought that relational aggression is more commonly used by girls than it is by boys (Crick & Grotpeter, 1995). Indeed, there exists a popular stereotype that girls are more likely than boys to engage in these types of cruel and "catty" relational conflicts. However, recent findings have challenged this pervasive stereotype; relational aggression has been shown to occur at about the same rate among male and female peer groups (Paquette & Underwood, 1999; Prinstein et al., 2001). Thus, although the concept of relational aggression was first developed to investigate problems among female peer groups, it appears that both girls and boys manifest this aggressive behavioral pattern.

The Victims of Relational Aggression

The targets of relational aggression are referred to in the research literature as "victims." Although the literature linking peer victimization to psychological maladjustment has focused largely on the victims of physical aggression, recent studies have uncovered similar associations between relational victimization and social-psychological maladjustment among preadolescent and adolescent girls (Crick & Grotpeter, 1996; Paquette & Underwood, 1999). For example, victims of relational aggression report greater levels of loneliness, depression, social anxiety, and social avoidance than do their nonvictimized peers (Crick & Grotpeter, 1996; Crick & Nelson, 2002). In research conducted in Australia, adolescent girls reported feeling confused, experiencing a loss of self-confidence, and being anxious about future relationships following an experience of relational victimization (Owens, Shute, & Slee, 2000). Because relational aggression is damaging to friendships and inclusion within a peer group, and because females are characterized by relational interaction and close friendship (Maccoby, 1998), being targeted for relational aggression might be particularly distressing for females. Recent findings have supported this notion. In one study, girls and boys reported experiencing relational victimization at about the same frequency, but girls were more likely than boys to recall specific incidents of relational victimization and to report more negative thoughts and feelings following such incidents. Moreover, the frequency of experiencing relational victimization was more strongly related to low self-worth among girls than it was among boys (Paquette & Underwood, 1999).

INTERVENTIONS

Given the importance of peer relationships, intervention and prevention programs that help adolescent girls form and maintain positive social bonds can go a long way toward enhancing their well-being. Many intervention programs have been developed to enhance peer relationships; however, few of them focus specifically on relational aggression. Because the perpetrators and the victims of relational aggression experience significant social and psychological adjustment difficulties, it is important to develop and implement empirically supported programs that can reduce the occurrence of relational aggression.

However, the literature on relational aggression is in its infancy and there has been little research on this topic. Most of the programs designed to help aggressors change their behavior have focused on physical aggression. One research team, however, has developed an intervention program designed specifically for relationally aggressive girls (Leff, Goldstein, Angelucci, Cardaciotto, & Grossman, in press). The goals of this program are to decrease relationally aggressive girls' tendency to make hostile attributions about their peers' intentions and to increase levels of prosocial behavior. The first of these goals is based on the premise that relationally aggressive individuals tend to attribute negative intent to others in ambiguous provocation situations and that such attributions increase the likelihood of behaving aggressively (Crick, 1995). This intervention program is certainly a commendable first step; however, no data have yet been reported evaluating its success. Moreover, since this program was designed for use with African American elementary school girls, we do not know how well it will generalize to children in other ethnic groups and at different ages. The time is now for psychologists to turn their attention to developing and empirically evaluating programs to reduce relational aggression among adolescents from a wide variety of groups.

At the other end of the spectrum should be interventions to help the victims of relational aggression. Programs have not been designed specifically for this purpose; however, interventions have been developed to address peer victimization more generally. Most are based on the premise that peers are important sources of social support and might serve as buffers in times of stress. Befriending programs, for example, train students to provide care and support for peers who are victimized. This involves teaching students to offer victims companionship in activities, engage in active listening, and learn assertiveness and leadership skills in order to offer direct support to distressed peers (Cowie, Naylor, Chauhan, & Smith, 2002). Research has shown that adolescents without friends are more likely to be victimized than adolescents with friends (Boulton, Trueman, Chau, Whitehead, & Amatya, 1999); therefore, programs that encourage students to offer friendship and support to victimized peers might be particularly effective in mitigating the potential negative effects of relational victimization. Other types of intervention programs involving peer support include mediation, mentoring, and counseling. The goal of mediation, or conflict resolution, is to defuse conflicts among students by taking a "no blame" approach. This approach is designed to help participants come away from the process with a sense that they have reached a resolution that is fair for all parties. Mentoring involves an experienced role model who helps his or her distressed peers develop problem-solving skills, while counseling involves someone who is trained by a qualified professional to develop a broad array of peer counseling skills. In a study designed to evaluate the effects of a school-based peer support system, it was found that adolescent females generally had more knowledge than their male peers about the system itself, who the supporters were, and how to contact them (Cowie et al., 2002). Although only a small percentage of victimized students actually utilized the support system, a great majority of the participants perceived the system to be useful or very helpful. This is promising news and should serve as an impetus to develop and evaluate more peer intervention programs. Because relational victimization is very subtle and likely to go undetected by school personnel, peer intervention programs might be particularly useful in this domain.

THE ROLE OF PEERS IN HEALTH RISK AND HEALTH ENHANCEMENT BEHAVIORS

The increasing autonomy associated with adolescence can be exhilarating as girls find that they have greater freedom to decide how, and with whom, to spend their time. However, the activities of teenage girls in our society can, and often do, include behaviors that pose serious threats to their health. Cigarette smoking, drug and alcohol abuse, and risky sexual behaviors are problems that threaten the health of teenage girls both in the short and long term. The impact of these behaviors is magnified by the fact that habits and lifestyles set in place during the teenage years often persist into adulthood. Why do some girls develop a healthy lifestyle—for example one that

includes exercise, a healthy diet, avoidance of substances, and safe sexual behavior—while others engage in behaviors that pose health risks? There are obviously many contributing factors, such as a girl's personality and the attitudes and behaviors that she has observed growing up in her family (Repetti et al., 2002). In addition, because the influence of peers, as compared to parents or other adults, increases during this period, psychologists have been interested in the contribution that the peer group makes in shaping the health behaviors of teenagers. The role of peers is especially salient because the impulsive behaviors that pose the greatest health risks for teens typically take place in the context of the peer group.

Cigarette Smoking and Substance Use

We know that teenagers emulate the behaviors that they observe in their peers, in part to facilitate their own acceptance within the group. So it is not surprising that the smoking behavior of friends predicts an adolescent's own use of cigarettes. One longitudinal study followed a large group of 14–17-year-olds for six months. The investigators found that teens whose friends smoked at the start of the study were more likely to smoke (or to smoke more), and those with friends who did not smoke were less likely to smoke (or to smoke less) six months later (Biglan, Duncan, Ary, & Smolkowski, 1995).

Somewhat more surprising are research findings indicating that a more intense involvement with the peer group, in general, is associated with an increased use of cigarettes, alcohol, and other substances. One study assessed the degree to which a teen was oriented toward her peers by asking questions such as whether she turns to her peers or to her parents when she has problems. The researchers found that the adolescents who were more strongly oriented toward their peers also used more substances. Interestingly, a teen's peer orientation completely mediated the effect of maternal nonresponsiveness on substance use (Bogenschneider, Wu, Raffaelli, & Tsay, 1998). In other words, teens whose parents were less warm and available were more likely to use substances such as tobacco, beer, wine, and marijuana. However, the evidence suggested that the peer group played a critical role in the way that the parent-child relationship influenced a teen's use of these substances. Teenage girls (and boys) who had troubled relationships with their mothers became more oriented toward their peers, which in turn led to greater substance use. Once again we see evidence suggesting that the influence exerted by the teen peer group is intertwined with characteristics of the family. Here a poor parent-child relationship seemed to drive adolescents toward a more intense focus on the peer group and greater risk of substance use. In research mentioned above, supportive relationships with peers buffered the impact of poor parenting (Lansford et al., 2003).

Risky Sexual Behaviors

Although most girls become sexually active during the teenage years, their adoption of safe sex behaviors (e.g., fewer partners, use of condoms) varies quite a bit. Some of that variability can be accounted for by the behavior of their peer group. Research suggests that friends influence the sexual behavior of teenage girls—in particular their use of safe sex behaviors and the delay of their sexual debut, both of which reduce the risk of pregnancy and serious health problems, such as sexually transmitted diseases and HIV infection. Researchers have found that the sexual activity of teenage girls is similar to the sexual behavior, or at least the *perceived* sexual behavior, of their friends. For example, in a study of 300 African American 9–15-year-olds living in public housing, the perceived behavior of friends (i.e., their sexual activity and condom use) was positively associated with the rate at which the sexual activity of girls (and boys) progressed with age and the degree to which condom use was maintained with age (Romer et al., 1994). The sexual behavior of preadolescents and adolescents seemed to mirror the behavior of their friends. Those who believed that their friends were sexually active and did not use condoms were more likely to become sexually active at an early age and were less likely to use condoms themselves. Other studies also indicate that both girls and boys whose friends are not sexually active are more likely to delay first

intercourse (Whitbeck, Yoder, Hoyt, & Conger, 1999). Thus, as with cigarette smoking, we find similarity in the sexual behaviors and practices of friends.

Research studies suggest, however, that there is more involved here than mere imitation of one specific class of behaviors. Having friends who engage in any number of antisocial behaviors seems to increase the chances that a girl will engage in risky sexual behavior. Friendships with teens who are delinquent, aggressive, or who abuse substances, increases the likelihood that an adolescent girl will have an early sexual debut, become pregnant, and engage in high-risk sexual behaviors (Scaramella, Conger, Simons, & Whitbeck, 1998; Whitbeck et al., 1999). There is some suggestion in the research literature that associating with troubled peers is linked to more risk-taking behavior in general, and that risk taking simply extends to include risky sexual activity (Scaramella et al., 1998). In contrast, having friends who aspire to more prosocial goals is associated with delay of first sexual intercourse (Whitbeck et al., 1999).

Health Enhancement Behaviors

There is other evidence suggesting that the attitudes and behavior of friends can go a long way toward helping teenage girls stay healthy. One group of researchers has examined a wide variety of health-enhancing behaviors, such as maintaining a healthy diet, getting regular exercise and adequate sleep, good dental hygiene, and regular seatbelt use (Jessor, Turbin, & Costa, 1998). They find that having friends who model conventional behavior, such as getting good grades in school and being involved with their families and community, is associated with the adoption of more of these healthy practices. Another study showed how the support and encouragement of friends can help teens maintain a healthy lifestyle. The investigators followed a group of children who were treated for obesity when they were between the ages of 6 and 12. Ten years after treatment, they examined the participants' weight and lifestyle. Two correlates of better long-term weight regulation were having a friend who discouraged bad eating and participating in exercise with a roommate (Epstein, Valoski, Wing, & McCurley,

1994). In this study, the health attitudes and behaviors of friends facilitated weight regulation among adolescents and young adults who had been obese as children.

Research clearly points to a close correspondence between the health practices and risky behaviors of adolescents and their friends. Of course, friends are not randomly assigned to teenage girls. A girl chooses to spend her time with peers who appeal to her and who are accepting and encouraging of her friendship. We know that a correlation between the health-risk and health-enhancing behaviors of girls and the characteristics and behaviors of their friends does not represent a one-way direction of influence. Peers do exert an influence, but girls also seek out friends whose attitudes and behaviors are attractive to them.

ADOLESCENT GIRLS' COMMUNITY RELATIONSHIPS

As influences outside the family become increasingly important during adolescence, girls' social worlds expand to include new contexts of interaction. Community members, such as coaches, guidance counselors, teachers, and other nonfamily adults become valuable sources of support as adolescents develop increasing independence from their parents. Unfortunately, there has been very little research on adolescent girls' sense of community or their experiences in the larger community.

Strong community connections might help adolescents become resilient and develop adaptive coping skills. Some research suggests that adolescents living in cohesive communities that provide many social and emotional resources engage in fewer risk behaviors and enjoy better mental health (Call et al., 2002). In many communities, organizations have been developed to provide adolescents with the opportunity for social interaction and support. Such organizations include religious and musical groups, sports teams, and after-school programs. Service learning, which involves performing voluntary service in the community under the guidance of supportive adults, is one type of activity designed to enhance adolescents' sense of community cohe-

siveness. Service learning is intended to provide adolescents with a constructive role to fill, to enhance their self-esteem and social adjustment, and to reduce feelings of alienation from peers and the community (Call et al., 2002). When a girl joins a community organization, she has the opportunity to meet and interact with a diverse group of peers. Moreover, she becomes acquainted with adults in the community who can be important sources of emotional support. Girls also report learning practical skills in community organizations, such as time allocation and the ability to set and achieve reasonable goals (Dworkin, Larson, & Hansen, 2003). Thus, community activities can help adolescent girls strengthen their social bonds and develop a wider range of social resources and competencies.

CONCLUSIONS

The research discussed in this chapter highlights the important role that peers and the community play in the health and development of adolescent girls. However, every question that is addressed by research prompts new questions. For example, studies of peers sometimes uncover complex interactions between peer and family relationships, intriguing findings that raise new questions. What are the circumstances that drive some teens with inadequate or nonsupportive parents toward peers and substance use, but drive others to supportive friends who buffer them from the negative consequences of poor family relationships? What are the characteristics of close friendships that provide teenage girls with the kind of support that helps them through difficult times, and what are the characteristics of friendships that fail to do so? Better information about the qualities of teenage girls' relationships with peers is needed in order to understand how friendships act to enhance or harm well-being.

Given the importance of peer relationships for girls' healthy development, it is critical to understand how girls form and maintain social bonds that are supportive. Recent research on relational aggression points to one of the ways that those social bonds can be threatened. We could find no research on the motivations for this form of social aggression. In what ways do adolescents believe that they benefit by damaging others' relationships? The attributions made by relationally aggressive teens and by their victims represent a promising avenue for research, in part because cognitions can be an effective point for intervention. Currently there is an inadequate knowledge base to guide the design of interventions that repair and improve the peer relationships of teenage girls. Investigations exploring both the positive and the negative aspects of teens' social interactions and relationships will ultimately suggest strategies that can be used to help girls form and keep friendships that promote their health and development.

Why do some teens have friendships with peers who model attitudes and behaviors that are prosocial and health-enhancing, while others spend their time with peers who engage in risky and health-threatening behaviors? Part of the answer clearly lies in a child's personality and family rearing environment. However, we do not know the degree to which similarities in smoking, substance abuse, and sexual behaviors between adolescents and their friends are due to the initial formation of social groups consisting of like-minded members versus the tendency of adolescents to conform to the behavioral norms of their peer group. Disentangling the various individual and social processes that result in similarities in the health behaviors of friends is critical to the development of interventions to reduce risky behaviors during adolescence. A better understanding of peer influence on health behaviors may also inform social policies that encourage healthy behavioral norms among adolescents.

Finally, we found very little research on the ways that the larger community contributes to the health and well-being of adolescent girls. We suspect that, as with the peer group, neighborhood organizations and adults outside of the family can play an especially important role for girls whose relationships at home are troubled. Studies of the conditions under which communities succeed and the conditions under which they fail to serve this type of compensatory function can help to inform social policy. For example, research can direct policy makers toward the development and placement of resources in communities so that they are readily available to, and are likely to be used by, the girls who need them most.

REFERENCES

Biglan, A., Duncan, T. E., Ary, D. V., & Smolkowski, K. (1995). Peer and parental influences on adolescent tobacco use. *Journal of Behavioral Medicine, 18*(4), 315–330.

Bogenschneider, K., Wu, M., Raffaelli, M., & Tsay, J. C. (1998). Parent influences on adolescent peer orientation and substance use: The interface of parenting practices and values. *Child Development, 69*(6), 1672–1688.

Boulton, M. J., Trueman, M., Chau, C., Whitehead, C., & Amatya, K. (1999). Concurrent and longitudinal links between friendship and peer victimization: Implications for befriending interventions. *Journal of Adolescence, 22*, 461–466.

Boyce-Rodgers, K., & Rose, H. A. (2002). Risk and resiliency factors among adolescents who experience marital transitions. *Journal of Marriage and Family, 64*, 1024–1037.

Brown, L. M., Way, N., & Duff, J. L. (1999). The others in my I: Adolescent girls' friendships and peer relations. In N. G. Johnson, M. C. Roberts, & J. Worell (Eds.), *Beyond appearance: A new look at adolescent girls* (pp. 205–225). Washington, DC: American Psychological Association.

Call, K. T., Riedel, A. A., Hein, K., McLoyd, V., Petersen, A., & Kipke, M. (2002). Adolescent health and well-being in the twenty-first century: A global perspective. *Journal of Research on Adolescence, 12*, 69–98.

Colarossi, L. G. (2001). Adolescent gender differences in social support: Structure, function, and provider type. *Social Work Research, 25*, 233–241.

Cowie, H., Naylor, P., Chauhan, L. T. P., & Smith, P. K. (2002). Knowledge, use of and attitudes toward peer support: A 2-year follow-up to the Prince's Trust survey. *Journal of Adolescence, 25*, 453–467.

Crick, N. R. (1995). Relational aggression: The role of intent attributions, feelings of distress, and provocation type. *Development and Psychopathology, 7*, 313–322.

Crick, N. R. (1996). The role of overt aggression, relational aggression, and prosocial behavior in the prediction of children's future social adjustment. *Child Development, 67*, 2317–2327.

Crick, N. R., & Grotpeter, J. K. (1995). Relational aggression, gender, and social-psychological adjustment. *Child Development, 66*, 710–722.

Crick, N. R., & Grotpeter, J. K. (1996). Children's treatment by peers: Victims of relational and overt aggression. *Development and Psychopathology, 8*, 367–380.

Crick, N. R., & Nelson, D. A. (2002). Relational and physical victimization within friendships: Nobody told me there'd be friends like these. *Journal of Abnormal Child Psychology, 30,* 599–607.

Dworkin, J. B., Larson, R., & Hansen, D. (2003). Adolescents' accounts of growth experiences in youth activities. *Journal of Youth and Adolescence, 32,* 17–26.

Epstein, L. H., Valoski, A., Wing, R. R., & McCurley, J. (1994). Ten-year outcomes of behavioral family-based treatment for childhood obesity. *Health Psychology, 13,* 373–383.

French, D. C., Jansen, E. A., & Pidada, S. (2002). United States and Indonesian children's and adolescents' reports of relational aggression by disliked peers. *Child Development, 73,* 1143–1150.

Frey, C. U., & Rothlisberger, C. (1996). Social support in healthy adolescents. *Journal of Youth and Adolescence, 25,* 17–31.

Grotpeter, J. K., & Crick, N. R. (1996). Relational aggression, overt aggression, and friendship. *Child Development, 67,* 2328–2338.

Hawker, D. S. J., & Boulton, M. J. (2000). Twenty years' research on peer victimization and psychosocial maladjustment: A meta-analytic review of cross-sectional studies. *Journal of Child Psychology and Psychiatry, 41*(4), 441–455.

Jessor, R., Turbin, M. S., & Costa, F. M. (1998). Protective factors in adolescent health behavior. *Journal of Personality & Social Psychology, 75,* 788–800.

Lansford, J. E., Criss, M. M., Pettit, G. S., Dodge, K. A., & Bates, J. E. (2003). Friendship quality, peer group affiliation, and peer antisocial behavior as moderators of the link between negative parenting and adolescent externalizing behavior. *Journal of Research on Adolescence, 13,* 161–184.

Leff, S. S., Goldstein, A. B., Angelucci, J., Cardaciotto, L., & Grossman, M. (in press). Using a participatory action research model to create a school-based intervention program for relationally aggressive girls—the Friend to Friend program. In J. Zins, M. Elias, & C. Maher (Eds.), *Handbook of prevention and intervention in peer harassment, victimization and bullying.* Glos, UK: Hawthorn Press.

Maccoby, E. E. (1998). *The two sexes: Growing up apart, coming together.* Cambridge, MA: Harvard University Press.

Owens, L., Shute, R., & Slee, P. (2000). "Guess what I just heard!": Indirect aggression among teenage girls in Australia. *Aggressive Behavior, 26,* 67–83.

Paquette, J., & Underwood, M. (1999). Gender differences in young adolescents' experiences of peer victimization: Social and physical aggression. *Merrill-Palmer Quarterly, 45,* 242–266.

Prinstein, M. J., Boergers, J., & Vernberg, E. M. (2001). Overt and relational aggression in adolescents: Social-psychological adjustment of aggressors and victims. *Journal of Clinical Child Psychology, 30,* 479–491.

Repetti, R. L., McGrath, E. P., & Ishikawa, S. S. (1999). Daily stress and coping in childhood and adolescence. In A. J. Goreczny & M. Hersen (Eds.), *Handbook of pediatric and adolescent health psychology* (pp. 343–360). Needham Heights, MA: Allyn & Bacon.

Repetti, R. L., Taylor, S. E., & Seeman, T. E. (2002). Risky families: Family social environments and the mental and physical health of offspring. *Psychological Bulletin, 128,* 330–366.

Romer, D., Black, M., Ricardo, I., Feigelman, S., Kaljee, L., Galbraith, J., et al. (1994). Social influences on the sexual behavior of youth at risk for HIV exposure. *American Journal of Public Health, 84*(6), 977–985.

Rubin, K. H., Bukowski, W., & Parker, J. G. (1998). Peer interactions, relationships, and groups. In N. Eisenberg (Ed.), *Handbook of child psychology* (Vol. 3, pp. 619–700). New York: John Wiley & Sons.

Scaramella, L. V., Conger, R. D., Simons, R. L., & Whitbeck, L. B. (1998). Predicting risk for pregnancy by late adolescence: A social contextual perspective. *Developmental Psychology, 34*(6), 1233–1245.

Scholte, R. H. J., van Lieshout, C. F. M., & van Aken, M. A. G. (2001). Perceived relational support in adolescence: Dimensions, configurations, and adolescent adjustment. *Journal of Research on Adolescence, 11,* 71–94.

Tomada, G., & Schneider, B. H. (1997). Relational aggression, gender, and peer acceptance: Invariance across culture, stability over time, and concordance among informants. *Developmental Psychology, 33,* 601–609.

Werner, N. E., & Crick, N. R. (1999). Relational aggression and social-psychological adjustment in a college sample. *Journal of Abnormal Psychology, 108,* 615–623.

Whitbeck, L. B., Yoder, K. A., Hoyt, D. R., & Conger, R. D. (1999). Early adolescent sexual activity: A developmental study. *Journal of Marriage and the Family, 61*(4), 934–946.

NIVA PIRAN and ERIN ROSS

From Girlhood to Womanhood: Multiple Transitions in Context

32

This chapter examines, through a feminist lens, the research and theories in several domains relating to the transition from girlhood to womanhood. Four major biases, reflecting the dominant research and theoretical trends, are noted in the chapter. First, in Western cultures, the transition from girlhood to womanhood is typically seen as stretching from puberty to early adulthood (around legal voting age of 18). In contrast, other cultures view this transition as the time when an adolescent woman is expected to fulfill the social role of a woman. Second, the research conducted on adolescent women tends to include mainly middle-class White girls. The impact of social diversity, especially the intersections of ethnocultural, social class, geographical site, sexual orientation, immigration status, and disability, is rarely examined. Third, research tends to examine the period of adolescence as a whole, or just segments of time within this range, thereby limiting knowledge to shifts within this period; in particular, the shift from late adolescence to adulthood is rarely studied. Fourth, researchers have tended to examine problem behaviors and disrupted development rather than constructive developmental processes and resilience. Despite these dominant trends in existing research, the chapter aims to take a critical look at development in context while examining two interrelated domains, the body and the self.

THE BODY

Critical social perspectives on the domain of the body, both a personal and social domain, can serve as a lens to understand girls' and adolescent women's body-anchored experiences. According to these perspectives, girls' and women's personal experiences of their bodies, as well as their practices toward their bodies, are anchored in and shaped by complex social systems (Bordo, 1993). Moreover, since the body is both a personal and a social domain, critical social perspectives highlight the centrality of the body as a medium through which individuals learn, mainly unconsciously, about their social position, worth, and rights (Foucault, 1979). The disciplining of female bodies, through restrictions on physical freedom, appetite, or desire, is central to maintain the systems of privilege and prejudice, such as patriarchy and discrimination against ethnic minorities (e.g., Bartky, 1988; Bordo, 1993). It is therefore understandable that the transition from girlhood to womanhood, associated with intense physical changes, is affected by society's meanings and social attitudes toward a girl's and a woman's body.

Puberty—Physiological Changes

Puberty is a universal characteristic of adolescence. It is a time of extensive and rapid growth as the body reaches physical maturation. For girls, puberty typically occurs between the ages of 10 and 15 (Malina & Bouchard, 1991). While on average puberty takes three to four years to be completed, for some girls it can happen in as little as 18 months, while for others it can take up to five years. Female puberty tends to begin with the early stages of breast development, often referred to as "budding." Along with breast development, girls experience a growth spurt, which peaks on average at age 11.5. Shortly thereafter, pubic hair develops. Over the course of puberty, girls gain weight in the form of body fat, and their bodies change shape as the hips become fuller and thighs become more rounded. Girls in the United States typically reach menarche around the age of 12. Internally, the uterus and vagina are growing. As with all aspects of adolescent development, there is a wide variation among individuals in terms of the order and timing of events.

Subjective Responses to Puberty

Studies conducted in North America have documented marked ambivalence in girls' reactions to their changed bodies. For example, girls may vacillate between attempts to minimize their breasts and to make them appear larger through strategic clothing choices (Rekers, 1992). While menstruation is generally viewed as a normal part of growing up, many girls hold negative feelings about it, believing it to be embarrassing, bothersome, or disgusting (Williams, 1983). Girls may simultaneously be relieved to have reached this developmental marker and desire to put off the associated hassles and anticipated negative effects, such as cramps (Brooks-Gunn & Ruble, 1983). There is a tendency among some girls to limit communication about menstruation; hence, for these girls, menstruation is associated with a greater disconnect from significant others, in particular fathers and male friends, and to a lesser degree female friends and mothers. However, girls who have a trusted adult, who can openly and respectfully communicate about the processes of puberty and sexuality, feel more comfortable with their changing bodies and learn about positive self-care (Brooks-Gunn & Ruble, 1983; Piran, Carter, Thompson, & Pajouhandeh, 2002).

Variations in adolescents' subjective reactions and social adjustments to puberty have been studied, mainly in relation to the timing of pubertal development. Early-maturing girls tend to have a negative body and self-image and decreased feelings of attractiveness and social desirability, while early-maturing boys are more likely to have a positive body image and increased feelings of attractiveness, and are often assigned leadership positions among peers (Archibald, Graber, & Brooks-Gunn, 1999).

Body Image and Body-Anchored Practices in Adolescent Women

It has been repeatedly documented that, for girls, puberty is associated with the development of a negative body image and that this discontent gets accentuated throughout adolescence, staying as a "normative" source of stress for adult women (Rodin, Silberstein, & Striegel-Moore, 1984). Negative body image has been linked to the development of eating disorders and depression (see chapter 7, this volume). Research suggests that Asian, Hispanic, and White girls show a greater body dissatisfaction than African American girls (e.g., Wildes, Emery, & Simons, 2001).

The development of a disrupted connection with the body during adolescence is expressed through multiple body-anchored practices. Studies reveal patterns of disordered eating among adolescent girls that worsens throughout the period. These disordered eating patterns include: food restrictions, binges, and the use of diet pills and purging in about 70%, 35%, 12%, and 8% of women, respectively, ages 13–18 (Grunbaum et al., 2002). The rates of alcohol, drug, and cigarette use have been increasing among young women over recent decades, with the age of initiation dropping (Amaro, Blake, Schwartz, & Flinchbaugh, 2001). Substance abuse in particular has been linked to the wish to maintain low body weight, improve self-image, gain social acceptance, reduce stress, or express defiance. While concerns about weight and high stress were important factors in initiating smoking, the sources of that stress varied. For example, among young African American women, exposure to racism was related to the onset of smoking (Guthrie, Young, Williams, Boyd, & Kintner, 2002).

Patterns of sexual involvement reflect another domain of disrupted connection with the body. While 42.9–64% of North American high school adolescent girls have had intercourse, contraception use was poor, with only 51% of sexually active girls reporting use of a condom and only 21% use of birth control pills (Grunbaum et al., 2002). Negotiating contraceptive use has been found to be difficult for adolescent women, increasing their risk of pregnancies and sexually transmitted diseases (Cantor & Sanderson, 1998). Not only do adolescent women engage sexually without protection, but they also often engage without the experience of desire (Fine, 1988; Tolman, 1999). Research, therefore, suggests that a considerable number of adolescent women engage in body-related practices that indicate a disrupted connection to their bodies.

Body-Anchored Disruption in Context

Girls' and young women's ambivalent subjective responses to owning a mature woman's body and the varied expressions of disrupted body practices can be understood in relation to multiple adverse social forces, which include: sexual harassment and violations, objectification of women's bodies, systems of prejudice and discrimination, and the social expectations of women (Piran, 2001; Piran et al., 2002). All these factors combine to make it more challenging for girls to go through and complete the process of physical maturation with a strong and positive connection with their bodies and with a sense of embodied power, desire, joy, safety, and self-care.

Sexual Harassment and Violations

Sexual harassment has been found to have damaging effects on young women, disrupting body and self-image; instilling body-anchored fear, disdain, and shame; and leading to withdrawal or even school dropout (Larkin, Rice, & Russell, 1996). Sexual harassment is commonly experienced with increased intensity and frequency as girls undergo pubertal changes. Studies report rates of sexual harassment that vary within the range of 45% and 83% (American Association of University Women [AAUW], 1993) for girls ages 11–16. Sexual harassment is perpetrated not only by peers but also by teachers and other school staff, often in public places and in the presence of others (AAUW, 1993). Larkin et al. (1996) describe the vulnerability of girls to sexual harassment due to their developing bodies and to the perceived social power gained in having a male date. Dating violence, similar to sexual harassment, is a common problem in North America, with reports ranging between 33 and 70% (Vicary, Klingaman, & Harkness, 1995; see also chapters 9 and 38, this volume). Dating violence and sexual harassment lead to the young woman's experiencing her newly acquired woman's body as a site of social and personal vulnerability, fear, and shame, and they disrupt a young woman's positive connection with her developing body. Sexual harassment and dating violence have been linked to eating disorders, self-harm, and substance abuse. Studies suggest that girls and young women with a positive body and self-image feel safe from these violations.

Prejudicial Treatment and Discrimination

Exposure of adolescents and young women to prejudicial treatment and discrimination such as from weightism, sexism, or racism, by which people often use the body as a medium for their expressions, has been found to lead to a negative body image and self-image. To date, ample research data supports the causal link between exposure to weightist prejudice by parents and peers and the development of disordered eating patterns in girls and young women (e.g., Stice, 2002). However, data are being accumulated that suggest also the disruptive influence on body esteem of discriminatory practices related to other prejudicial systems, such as sexism and racism (Piran, 2001; Piran et al., 2002). Indeed, Piran and her associates (2002), and Silverstein and his associates (e.g., Silverstein & Blumenthal, 1997), suggest that the experience of gender equity at home yields a more positive experience of the body and the self. Similarly, a participatory action study in a school revealed that school-wide changes to empower girls led to greater gender equity and a reduction in negative body image and eating disorders (Piran, 2001).

Objectification of Women's Bodies

In their description of the objectification theory, Fredrickson and Roberts (1997) have delineated the disruptive impact of the persistent patriarchal gaze through which women learn to view themselves. Girls, especially when they reach puberty, learn to see themselves through an objectifying and sexualizing lens, and are denied the potential enjoyment of their physical selves and fully experience their subjectivity. Concurrent with the process of puberty, girls learn that their female bodies fall short of the idealized image of American beauty and hence are inevitably and shamefully flawed, requiring life-long monitoring and repair through diet, exercise, make-up, and clothing choice. The internalization of the all-American beauty ideal exerts an adverse impact on girls' self-image (Stice, 2002). In samples of African American, Hispanic American, and White American women., the incorporation of the American beauty ideal was found to be predictive of a negative body image and of disordered eating patterns. Sexual objectification may also vary among ethnoculturally diverse groups, with associated adverse impacts. While young White women may be presented as sexual objects, but stripped of their sexual desires, young African American women may be stereotyped as animals or savage women with untamed sexuality (Fredrickson & Roberts, 1997; Tolman, 1999). Piran and colleagues (2002) have found in a qualitative study that young women who described relative freedom from objectifying experiences while growing up had positive connections with their bodies. The experience of physical competence— for example, through engagement in sports and related activities that de-emphasize appearance and enhance functional aspects of the body— has been found repeatedly to enhance positive body esteem (e.g., Marsh, Richards, Johnson, Roche, & Tremayne, 1994).

Social Construction of Women

In the transition from girlhood to womanhood, girls are exposed to many constraining social constructions of womanhood that specifically target the body domain. For example, images of idealized women involve constraining one's appetites and desires. In a series of studies, Tolman (e.g., 1999) described adolescent women's internalizations of the social suppression and denigration of female sexual desire that leads to ambivalence toward sexual desire (see also chapter 21, this volume). Other constraining social expectations for women involve, for example, the discouragement of self-nurturance or of taking up too much physical space (Bartky, 1988). On the other hand, girls' resistance to such limits and discriminatory social expectations enhances their well-being. Likewise, resistance to confining gender-based expectations (e.g., Steiner-Adair, 1986), to racial discrimination (Smith, 1991), and to economic discrimination (Brown, 1998) is associated with enhanced well-being. Models that embody resistance and nurture in girls are crucial in this regard.

THE SELF

Experiences of the body and self are inextricably related and are both contextualized within and affected by the hierarchical power structures and dominant discourses in everyday life. The same social forces that support or disrupt girls' experiences in the body domain as they mature also strengthen or disrupt the experiences of the self.

Developmental Aspects of the Self During Puberty

Multiple psychosocial tasks have been associated with the transition from girlhood to adulthood. These tasks occur in the domains of the self in terms of identity and self-concept, relational shifts, and school and career choices. The nature of these processes and the experiences embedded in these transitions, as well as the reactions to these processes, can be understood only within their social context.

Shifts in Self Organization in Adolescents

Adolescence is characterized as a time when individuals begin to explore the psychological characteristics of the self and examine the ways they fit into their social world. While Erikson (1968) described the adolescent identity crisis as occurring during the early to mid-teenage years, research suggests that this identity work continues late into adolescence as well as into early adulthood. In the transition from childhood to adolescence, individuals begin to develop more abstract characterizations of themselves, examining personal beliefs and standards (Harter, 1999). In middle adolescence, self-concepts become more consonant, in that adolescents' descriptions of themselves reflect greater self-consistency. In addition, adolescents do not only evaluate themselves globally but also consider distinct dimensions such as academics, social relations, athletics, appearance, and moral conduct.

Self-Concept

Quantitative and qualitative studies have repeatedly documented an erosion of self-confidence in girls during the ages of 11–15 (AAUW, 1991). These changes have been typified by a drop in self-esteem and an increase in depression. The gender difference in the rates of adult depression can often be traced to developments in early adolescence. The challenges to self-esteem, mood, and body image that affect women of all ages often are initiated in early adolescence.

Qualitative studies of the experience of the self have documented deep conflicts in girls and adolescent women about the validity of their experiences and perceptions (Brown, 1998). These "thick" descriptions of self experiences have made it possible to move beyond quantitative accounts of the significant drop in girls' self-esteem with the onset of puberty. The studies have revealed a process of retrenchment whereby many who had demonstrated a strong sense of self in

preadolescence go on to renounce and devalue their feelings, thoughts, beliefs, and perceptions during early adolescence. Clinicians in the early to mid-20th century, such as Freud or Deutsch, described this disruption as normative, as do contemporary researchers of female development, who recount how adolescent girls go underground or appear to give up their own authority (e.g., Brown, 1998). These silencing processes have been associated with dysphoria, eating disorders, and engagement in behaviors that puts girls at risk, such as drinking and driving, unprotected sex, or sex without desire (Tolman, 1999). Similar to experiences that adversely affect the experiences of the body, the experience of the self is affected by exposure to violations and prejudice. The social constructions of femininity, particularly the pressures to embody the White middle-class notion of femininity, have an adverse impact on the experience of the self during and following adolescence (Brown, 1998). Inherently constraining, this notion of femininity is particularly discrepant from the life experiences of women adolescents who hold a different social location—for example, a different social class, ethnicity, or sexual orientation.

While some girls go through a crisis during adolescence, other girls retain their voice, their positive self-regard, and their determination to succeed. Different factors come into play in a positive transition from girlhood to womanhood. These include equitable treatment at home (Silverstein & Blumenthal, 1997) and at school (Piran, 2001); nurturance of a critical voice and perspective in peer and adolescent-adult relationships (Brown, 1998; Smith, 1991); a sense of physical safety (Larkin et al., 1996); positive relationships and role modeling (Fine, 1988; Piran et al., 2002); and participation in empowering experiences (Piran, 2001).

The Experience of Relationships

One of the major developmental tasks of adolescence is to establish an identity with and close relationships outside of the family unit. Both clinical and research literature (Steinberg, 2001) suggests that earlier descriptions emphasizing a process of separation and detachment from relationships during adolescence do not represent adolescence in general or women's development in particular. Regarding contacts with the family, there is a tendency during adolescence to use negotiation to develop more egalitarian relationships. The concept of individuation does not place separation over connectedness, but allows for the development of an individual identity in the context of ongoing emotionally and psychologically significant family relationships (Archibald et al., 1999). Generally, as a girl's adolescence progresses, less time is spent at home. Nevertheless, maintaining positive and supportive emotional connections with the family is important and has been associated with more positive self-esteem and lower frequency of eating disorders or substance abuse. Further, being provided with relevant physiological, practical, and validating information and advice related to menstruation, sexual desire, and dating relationships, within the context of a trusting relationship with an adult, strengthens an adolescent woman's ability to stay connected to her body in a positive way (Piran et al., 2002).

In North American societies, as adolescents transition into young adulthood, they often leave home and set up a separate existence apart from the family. But this process may not apply to some Asian countries or to other communities, for example, where young adults continue to live with their parents. Among adolescent and young women in particular, it is the experience of self-governance (making own decisions, doing things for oneself) that marks separation from family rather than emotional or physical detachment. In a qualitative study, Daigneault (1999) found that both daughters and mothers supported the process of moving away, but wanted to maintain their relationship. Daughters were taking legacies, in the form of objects, skills, and values, with them from their mothers and grandmothers. They were also emphasizing the qualities of strength characterized by the women in their families.

Peers, as well as the media, are considered to exert greater influence during adolescence, even though this influence has been found to be mediated by connections to the nuclear family (Steinberg, 2001). Peers influence adolescents in both positive and negative ways—for example, in terms of body image, academic achievement, and substance abuse. Adolescents and their friends are often similar, not only because they influence each other but also because they choose friends with similar behaviors, attitudes, and identities. In later adolescence, they become less rigid in their expectations for "normal" behavior and more tolerant of individual differences among their peers.

There is also a move from involvement with larger gender-cohesive groups to smaller, more deeply connected, and often mixed-gender groups. For heterosexual adolescents, this also represents dating relationships. The majority of adolescents engage in dating behaviors, with 90% of boys and females reporting having dates before their 17th birthday. Furman (2002) notes that this pattern differs for gay, lesbian, and bisexual youth, who are less likely to have engaged in same-sex intimate relationships because of possible stigma and limited opportunities to meet similar others. Ideally, with the progression from early to late adolescence, these relationships with peers become more intimate in terms of self-disclosure and trust. However, the progression may be disrupted by experiences of dating violence or inequitable relationships. Also, while most literature about adolescence describes the disruption in girls' friendships with the onset of heterosexual dating, research has suggested that female friendships continue to be very important and that adolescent women work to defuse jealously and establish norms and consensus that allow them to face outside challenges (Eder, 1993).

School, Training, and Career

Several groundbreaking reports have documented ways in which schools shortchange girls through inequitable treatment, at the intersections of gender, ethnicity, social class, and other social factors (e.g., AAUW, 1993). These experiences affect well-being, graduation rates, and career choices. In many schools, teachers clearly communicate lesser expectations for girls in the fields of math and sciences. Communication of these views can range from openly sexist and demeaning comments about girls' academic abilities to more subtle forms of bias. Guidance counselors, for example, tend to question gender-atypical class choices. It is of note that, similar to their own mothers and in addition to their school work, adolescent daughters fill in household labor gaps and do more chores at home compared with their brothers (Benin & Edwards, 1990). In contrast, more task sharing was found in egalitarian homes. Despite the adverse impact of gender inequity, women in the United States are at least as likely as men to graduate from high school (National Center for Education Statistics, 1999). White students are more likely to complete high school, with 93.6% of White students, 88.2% of African American students, and 62.8% of Hispanic students obtaining a high school diploma, respectively (National Center for Education Statistics, 1999). The job market has little to offer those who do not complete high school, however. The first jobs of high school dropouts are likely to be part-time, temporary, or day-laborer jobs with low pay, low security, and no benefits.

Obtaining a postsecondary education is becoming increasingly crucial for young people entering today's workforce. Students with only a high school education typically find themselves with low-paying, unstable jobs or in jobs that Western society considers subadult. Yet despite the obvious benefits of postsecondary education, many students are unable to pursue college-level education. For many, the cost of higher education is prohibitive. A recent survey found that 32.3% of U.S. Whites aged 25–29 had a bachelor's degree or better, compared to only 15.8% of African American and 10.4% of Hispanics, respectively (National Center for Education Statistics, 1999). Even though women were more likely to hold a bachelor's degree, men were still more likely to continue their education and obtain advanced degrees.

The move from school to work is often a difficult one for young women. North American countries generally do not provide an educational system that facilitates this transition, making it a relatively turbulent time for young people. Some have suggested the need to strengthen the connections between school and work and to provide more occupationally relevant credentials. Few young women today expect to be supported as a homemaker by an employed spouse to whom they will be married for a lifetime and, as a result, most young women plan to pursue some sort of career. This can be difficult, however, as North

American countries still largely operate as though the "traditional family" of husband working and wife at home predominates (Mortimer & Larson, 2002). As a result, there are few guidelines to help young women make occupational choices and develop the necessary work-family balance. Many young women express optimism about their abilities to manage work and family, holding expectations for high-status employment in the future without having to sacrifice the homemaker role (Rich & Golan, 1992). Research suggests, however, that adolescents generally still select careers along gender lines, though adolescent women also pursue nontraditional careers, such as in the domains of math and science (Rich & Golan, 1992). In 1995, more than 70% of women in the United States were employed in one of six occupations: secretary, bookkeeper, registered nurse, cashier, elementary school teacher, and waitress (see Lips, 1997). In general, female-dominated jobs pay less and offer fewer opportunities for advancement than male-dominated occupations. In one study of high school students across 20 schools in England, less than 10% of girls wished to pursue a career in a male-dominated field, with only 3% of girls stating they would like to work as a scientist, accountant, economist, pilot, or firefighter, or be in the armed forces or work with computers (Warrington & Younger, 2000). It is, therefore, of interest to examine the factors that facilitate pursuit of nontraditional careers. These women were found to be career oriented, experience self-agency, have mothers (or other women mentors) with higher levels of education or professional attainment, and have parents who encourage their professional pursuits (Davey & Stoppard, 1993).

ENHANCING RESILIENCE AND CONSTRUCTIVE TRANSFORMATIONS

This section details facilitative conditions to enhancing the well-being of adolescent women in their transition from girlhood to womanhood.

- *Amplifying resistant/critical voices.* As diverse girls experience the intensification of limiting social conditions and stereotypes at puberty and beyond, their reactions, observations, perceptions, and critiques need to be validated and amplified. Their naming and critical analyses of the inequitable conditions that are shaping their personal experiences will keep the wealth of their feelings and observations available to them as a guide for empowering decisions and actions in relation to the more immediate and larger social milieu (Brown, 1998; Piran et al., 2002).

- *Relational critical forums and groups.* The nourishment of adolescent women's critical voices can occur in multiple relational forums. Relationships with family members, friends, teachers, mentors, and others—typified by gender equity, support, and acceptance—are found to carry a facilitative and protective value. A particular role has been accorded to conscious-raising groups that can be conducted either in or outside of schools. In such groups, as MacKinnon (1989) describes, "through socializing women's knowing, [consciousness-raising] transforms it, creating a shared reality that clears a space in the world within which women can begin to move" (p. 101). Consciousness-raising groups have been conducted on different topics, such as body experience (Piran, 2001), sexual harassment (Larkin et al., 1996), and depression (Ross, Ali, & Toner, 2004). These groups facilitate the development of a critical voice, are a catalyst for social change and empowerment, and provide social support.

- *Mentoring.* The power of mentoring offered by an adult relies on the quality of the relationship and the mentee's experience in some commonality with the mentor. Casey and Shore (2000) highlight the particular role women mentors can be in schools by encouraging adolescents to excel academically, including in the fields of math and science. Mentors can be part of the familial social milieu of youth or can be part of an official program. Klaw and Rhodes (1995) report the importance of natural mentors in the lives of pregnant and parenting African American adolescents in terms of mood and of pursuing career goals. Reis and Díaz (1999) also found that economically disadvantaged urban, high-achieving girls found supportive adults important to their success.

- *Systemic change.* Positive body and self experiences are centrally linked to the experience of social equity and power (Brown, 1998; Piran, 2001). Social action to transform inequitable social systems, at all levels, is central to enhancing the well-being of women. For example, implementing and enforcing anti-harassment policies in schools is essential. Adolescents who speak against harassment in their schools will feel empowered and positive self-esteem if the school then enforces such policies (Piran, 2001) but will feel disempowered and unsafe if the school does not follow through with such policies (Orenstein, 1994). All systems should be examined for expressions of prejudice and equity, starting with the family and sibling unit, through various peer and school systems, to larger social systems.

- *Competence.* A sense of efficacy, competence, and agency is a central aspect of well-being and should be encouraged in adolescent women, including personal, social, academic and professional spheres. An example of this principle is the emphasis on involvement in nonobjectifying team sports and, through that, the importance of body functionality and movement over appearance. Similarly, emphasizing skills and personal abilities over appearance equips young women with a sense of agency and protects them from objectifying body-related messages (e.g., Parker et al., 1995). Sanctioning and providing relevant information regarding women's desire and agency in the sexual domain liberates women's ownership of their bodies. Supporting the development of skills in all domains facilitates the well-being of adolescent women. Generally, parental and peer support and acceptance enhances adolescents' self-esteem. Recognizing the coping and resistance elements in behaviors that can put teens at risk, such as eating disorders or smoking, validates their experiences and strengths (MacDonald & Wright, 2002). Adolescent women who have successfully engaged in social transformations, such as implementing anti-harassment policies in their schools or banning the publication of advertisements demeaning to women, have found these experiences to be validating and empowering (Piran, 2001).

- *Research.* Research on the transition from girlhood to womanhood has to be expanded in different ways. While research has examined the impact of multiple adverse pressures on the bodies and self-domains on girls and young women, more research is needed into the conditions that facilitate a positive connection with the maturing body, on positive self-esteem, and on obtaining a sense of agency in relation to social institutions. Examination is also needed into the maturation of adolescent women from diverse backgrounds in terms of social class, ethnocultural group membership, and other social variables. Further, research is needed into the changes that characterize the process of adolescence to young adulthood.

CONCLUSION

The transition from girlhood to womanhood is complex, and its study informs not only the normative processes of girls' development but also the culture at large. Study of the interactions between maturing girls and their diverse social contexts reveals both adverse and facilitative conditions. The well-being of young women relies on experiences of equity, on relationships of mutuality, and on the development of positive body image and self-esteem, skills, and a sense of agency. Its success relies on our ability as a society to listen to, be informed by, and be changed by the knowledge embedded in adolescent women's lives.

REFERENCES

Amaro, H., Blake, S. M., Schwartz, P. M., & Flinchbaugh, L. J. (2001). Developing theory-based substance abuse prevention programs for young adolescent girls. *Journal of Early Adolescence, 21,* 256–293.

American Association of University Women. (1993). *Hostile hallways: The AAUW survey on sexual harassment in America's schools.* Washington, DC: Author.

Archibald, A. B., Graber, J. A., & Brooks-Gunn, J. (1999). Associations among parent-adolescent relationships, pubertal growth, dieting, and body image in young adolescent girls. *Journal of Research on Adolescence, 9*(4), 395–415.

Bartky, S. L. (1988). Foucault, femininity, and the modernization of patriarchal power. In I. Diamond & L. Quinby (Eds.), *Feminism & Foucault: Reflections on resistance* (pp. 61–86). Boston: Northeastern University Press.

Benin, M. H., & Edwards, D. (1990). Adolescents' chores: The difference between dual and single earner families. *Journal of Marriage and the Family, 52,* 361–373.

Bordo, S. (1993). *Unbearable weight: Feminism, Western culture, and the body.* Berkeley: University of California Press.

Brooks-Gunn, J., & Ruble, D. N. (1983). The experience of menarche from a developmental perspective. In J. Brooks-Gunn & A. Peterson (Eds.), *Girls at puberty* (pp. 155–178). New York: Plenum Press.

Brown, L. M. (1998). *Raising their voices: The politics of girls' anger.* Cambridge, MA: Harvard University Press.

Cantor, N., & Sanderson, C. A. (1998). The functional regulation of adolescent dating relationships and sexual behavior. In J. Heckhausen & C. S. Dweck (Eds.), *Motivation and self-regulation across the lifespan* (pp. 185–215). Cambridge: Cambridge University Press.

Casey, K. M. A., & Shore, B. M. (2000). Mentors' contributions to gifted adolescents' affective, social, and vocational development. *Roeper Review, 22,* 227–230.

Daigneault, S. D. (1999). Legacies and leaving home. *Professional School Counseling, 3,* 65–73.

Davey, F. H., & Stoppard, J. M. (1993). Some factors affecting the occupational expectations of female adolescents. *Journal of Vocational Behavior, 43,* 235–250.

Eder, D. (1993). Romantic and sexual teasing among adolescent girls. In D. Tannen (Ed.), *Gender and conversational interaction.* New York: Oxford University Press.

Erikson, E. (1968). *Identity, youth, and crisis.* New York: Norton.

Fine, M. (1988). Sexuality, schooling, and adolescent females. *Harvard Educational Review, 58*(1), 29–53.

Foucault, M. (1979). *Discipline and punish: The birth of the prison.* New York: Vintage Books.

Fredrickson, B. L., & Roberts, T.-A. (1997). Objectification theory: Toward understanding women's lived experiences and mental health risks. *Psychology of Women Quarterly, 21,* 173–206.

Furman, W. (2002). The emerging field of adolescent romantic relationships. *Current Directions in Psychological Science, 11,* 177–180.

Grunbaum, J. A., Kann, L., Kinchen, S. A., Williams, B., Ross, J. G., Lowry, R., et al. (2002). Youth risk behavior surveillance. *Morbidity & Mortality Weekly Report, 51,* 1–64.

Guthrie, B. J., Young, A. M., Williams, D. R., Boyd, C. J., & Kintner, E. K. (2002). African American girls' smoking habits and day-to-day experiences with racial discrimination. *Nursing Research, 51,* 183–190.

Harter, S. (1999). *The construction of the self: A developmental perspective* (pp. 59–88). New York: Guilford Press.

Klaw, E. L., & Rhodes, J. E. (1995). Mentor relationships and the career development of pregnant and parenting African-American teenagers. *Psychology of Women Quarterly, 19,* 551–562.

Larkin, J., Rice, C., & Russell, V. (1996). Slipping through the cracks: Sexual harassment, eating problems, and the problem of embodiment. *Eating Disorders, 4,* 5–26.

Lips, H. M. (1997). *Sex and gender: An introduction* (3rd ed.). London: Mayfield.

MacDonald, M., & Wright, N. E. (2002). Cigarette smoking and the disenfranchisement of adolescent girls: A discourse of resistance? *Health Care for Women International, 23,* 281–305.

MacKinnon, C. A. (1989). *Towards a feminist theory of the state.* Cambridge, MA: Harvard University Press.

Malina, R. M., & Bouchard, C. (1991). *Growth, maturation, and physical activity.* Champaign, IL: Human Kinetics.

Marsh, H. W., Richards, G. E., Johnson, S., Roche, L., & Tremayne, P. (1994). Physical self-description questionnaire. *Journal of Sport and Exercise Psychology, 16,* 270–305.

Mortimer, J. T., & Larson, R. W. (2002). Macrostructural trends and the reshaping of adolescence. In J. T. Mortimer & R. W. Larson (Eds.), *The changing adolescent experience* (pp. 1–17). Cambridge: Cambridge University Press.

National Center for Education Statistics. (1999). *Education statistics.* Washington, DC: Author.

Orenstein, P. (1994). *Schoolgirls.* New York: Doubleday.

Parker, S., Nichter, M., Nichter, M., Vuckovic, N., Sims, C., & Ritenbaugh, C. (1995). Body image and weight concerns among African American and white adolescent females: Differences that make a difference. *Human Organization, 54,* 103–114.

Piran, N. (2001). Re-inhabiting the body from the inside out: Girls transform their school environment. In D. L. Tolman & M. Brydon-Miller (Eds.), *From subjects to subjectivities: A handbook of interpretive and participatory methods* (pp. 218–238). New York: New York University Press.

Piran, N., Carter, W., Thompson, S., & Pajouhandeh, P. (2002). Powerful girls: A contradiction in terms? Young women speak about the experience of growing up in a girl's body. In S. Abbey (Ed.), *Ways of knowing in and through the body: Diverse perspectives on embodiment* (pp. 206–210). Welland, Ontario, Canada: Soleil.

Reis, S. M., & Díaz, E. (1999). Economically disadvantaged urban female students who achieve in schools. *The Urban Review, 31,* 31–54.

Rekers, G. A. (1992). Development of problems of puberty and sex roles in adolescence. In C. E. Walker & M. C. Roberts (Eds.), *Handbook of clinical child psychology* (2nd ed., pp. 555–564). New York: John Wiley & Sons.

Rich, Y., & Golan, R. (1992). Career plans for male-dominated occupations among female seniors in religious and secular high schools. *Adolescence, 27,* 73–86.

Rodin, J., Silberstein, L., & Striegel-Moore, R. (1984). Women and weight: A normative discontent. In T. Sonderegger (Ed.), *Psychology and gender* (pp. 267–307). Lincoln: University of Nebraska Press.

Ross, E., Ali, A., & Toner, B. (2004). Investigating issues surrounding depression in adolescent girls across Ontario: A participatory action research project. *Canadian Journal of Community Mental Health, 22,* 55–68.

Silverstein, B., & Blumenthal, E. (1997). Depression mixed with anxiety, somatization, and disordered eating: Relationship with gender-role-related limitations experienced by females. *Sex Roles, 36,* 709–724.

Smith, B. J. (1991). Raising a resister. In C. Gilligan, A. G. Rogers, & D. Tolman (Eds.), *Women, girls & psychotherapy: Reframing resistance* (pp. 137–148). New York: Harrington Park Press.

Steinberg, L. (2001). Adolescent development. *Annual Review of Psychology.* Retrieved May 15, 2003, from http://www.findarticles.com/cf_dis/m0961/2001_Annual/73232704/print.jhtml

Steiner-Adair, C. (1986). The body politic. *Journal of American Academy of Psychoanalysis, 14*(1), 95–114.

Stice, E. (2002). Risk and maintenance factors for eating pathology: A meta-analytic review. *Psychological Bulletin, 128,* 825–848.

Tolman, D. (1999). Female adolescent sexuality in relational context. In N. G. Johnson, M. C. Roberts, & J. Worell (Eds.), *Beyond appearance: A new look at adolescent girls* (pp. 227–246). Washington, DC: American Psychological Association.

Vicary, J. R., Klingaman, L. R., & Harkness, W. L. (1995). Risk factors associated with date rape and sexual assault of adolescent girls. *Journal of Adolescence, 18,* 289–306.

Warrington, M., & Younger, M. (2000). The other side of the gender gap. *Gender and Education, 12,* 493–508.

Wildes, J. E., Emery, R. E., & Simons, A. D. (2001). The roles of ethnicity and culture in the development of eating disturbance and body dissatisfaction: A meta-analytic review. *Clinical Psychology Review, 21,* 521–551.

Williams, L. R. (1983). Beliefs and attitudes of young girls regarding menstruation. In S. Golub (Ed.), *Menarche* (pp. 139–148). Lexington, MA: DC Heath.

Adults: Balancing

Although it used to be assumed that women's careers were not as important as men's because they occupied only short periods of the adult woman's life span, societal changes over the last 40 or 50 years have led to increased employment for women outside the home. Women's careers have become an increasingly important part of most women's lives and, as we now see, critically important for their mental health.

Women now constitute a significant portion of the labor force in the United States and, conversely, the vast majority of U.S. women work outside the home. In the year 2000, three fifths of women were employed. Of those aged 25–44, 75% were employed. Sixty percent of women with children under the age of one year (12 months) are employed. The odds that a woman will work outside the home during her adult life are over 90%. Consequently, paid employment (vs. work inside the home) is now the rule, not the exception. There is *no* category of women for whom the majority is not employed outside the home.

Not surprisingly, the most common family life style today is the "dual-earner" family (Gilbert, 2002). As described by Gilbert and by Barnett and Hyde (2001), we now have "work/family role convergence" whereby both work and family are considered important in the lives of both women and men, and where many if not most workers prefer the two roles equally. We know in fact that careers are important to women as well as men.

NANCY E. BETZ

Women's Career Development

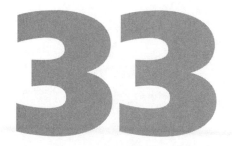

WHY CAREERS ARE IMPORTANT TO WOMEN

Women, like men, need a variety of major sources of satisfaction in their lives; as once stated by Freud (according to Erikson, 1950), the psychologically well-adjusted human being is able "to love and to work" effectively. Both women and men need the satisfactions of interpersonal relationships, with family and/or friends, but also the satisfaction of achievement in the outside world. We now have evidence that women, like men, need to utilize their abilities and talents in productive work and that multiple roles are "good" for people.

The evidence is strong that homemakers who do not have other outlets for achievement and productivity are highly susceptible to psychological distress, particularly as children grow and leave home. For example, of the women in the Terman studies of gifted children, when followed up in their 60s (Sears & Barbie, 1977), the women who reported the highest levels of life satisfaction were the employed women. Least satisfied with their lives were those who had been housewives all of their adult lives. The most psychologically disturbed women were those with exceptionally high IQs (above 170) who had not worked outside the home. It seems fairly clear that women with high intelligence who had not pursued meaningful careers outside the home have suffered psychological consequences for that failure.

In a related vein, there is also strong evidence that multiple roles—that is, those of both worker and family member—are important to women's mental and physical health (Barnett & Hyde, 2001). Most research finds that even though multiple roles are time-consuming, they are protective against depression (Crosby, 1991) and facilitate positive mental health. There are several hypotheses as to why multiple roles are beneficial for women (Barnett & Hyde, 2001). These are as follows: (a) when more than one role is important in one's life, stress or disappointment in one domain can be "buffered" by success or satisfaction in another role; (b) the added income of a second job/career can reduce the stress of being the sole breadwinner and can, in fact, provide an economic "lifeline" when one spouse or partner becomes unemployed—in difficult economic times characterized by high unemployment and corporate downsizing or collapse, two incomes can be virtually life-saving; (c) jobs provide an additional source of social support, which increases well-being (Barnett & Hyde, 2001).

PROBLEMS IN WOMEN'S LABOR FORCE PARTICIPATION

Although women now work in overwhelming numbers, the nature of their work continues to be located in traditionally female occupations and to be less well paid than that of men. Even though women have made much progress in entering traditionally male-dominated professions such as medicine and law, where half the enter-

ing students are women, the occupational world still has many areas of extreme sex segregation. For example, over 90% of preschool, kindergarten, elementary, and middle school teachers, dental hygienists, secretaries, child-care workers, cleaners and servants, nurses, and occupational and speech therapists are women (U.S. Department of Labor, Bureau of Labor Statistics, 2003).

In contrast, women remain seriously underrepresented in scientific and technical careers and high-level positions in business, government, education, and the military. For example, women earn fewer than 20% of the bachelor's degrees in fields such as engineering and physics and fewer than 10% of the graduate degrees in engineering (Kuh, 1998). High technology offers some of the fastest growing and well-paid occupational fields, yet women represent only about 10% of engineers, 30% of computer systems analysts, and 25% of computer programmers (U.S. Department of Labor, Bureau of Labor Statistics, 2003). Women were 8% of physicists and astronomers, 7% of air traffic controllers, 5% of the truck drivers, 4% of pilots, and 3% of firefighters.

Women continue to be paid less for full-time employment. Overall, women make 72.7% as much as men, when both are employed full time. The income gap is greater for middle-aged and older workers than it is for young workers and is greater for white women compared to African American or Hispanic women. And in considering women's lower income, it is essential to note that women cannot assure they will be taken care of by a husband. Today the average marriage lasts seven years (Harvey & Pauwels, 1999), and 20% of children live in a single-parent home. There are 12 million single-parent households, most of them headed by women. Women are much more likely to be widowed than men, and women represent 75% of the elderly poor, a percentage much greater than their representation (59%) among the elderly. The odds that a woman will have to care for herself financially during adult life are high, and failure to prepare her for this likelihood with high-quality education and/or training can have tragic consequences.

In summary, career pursuits will play a major role in most women's lives, so it is imperative that professionals help them make career choices that they find fulfilling, satisfying, and economically sufficient. Yet women are still choosing a smaller range of traditionally female, lower paid careers and are making substantially less money than men, even when employed full time. In the sections to follow I will briefly mention barriers to choice and barriers to equality, and I will follow the discussion of barriers with mention of supportive factors.

BARRIERS TO WOMEN'S CAREER CHOICES

Some of these barriers are socialized ones—that is, socialized belief systems or behavior patterns that lead women themselves to avoid certain career fields. Factors that will be mentioned herein are math anxiety and avoidance, low self-efficacy, problems with our educational system, and multiple-role concerns.

Math: The Critical Filter

The critical importance of a sound mathematics background for entrance to many of the best career opportunities—for example, those in engineering, scientific and medical careers, computer science, business, and the skilled trades—is now generally agreed upon (Chipman & Wilson, 1985). Women, who are significantly overrepresented among those lacking in this background, are thus faced with a major barrier to their career development and career options.

Sells (1982) elaborated the vital importance of math preparation for both career options and future earnings. Four full years of high school math are vital to surviving the standard freshman calculus course, now required for most undergraduate majors in business administration, economics, agriculture, engineering, forestry, health sciences, nutrition, food and consumer sciences, and natural, physical, and computer sciences. Only the arts and humanities do not now require a math background. Further, Sells (1982) showed a strong relationship between college calculus background and both starting salaries and employers' willingness to interview a student for a given job. Mathematics is important even for non-college-degree technical and trades occupations (U.S. Department of Labor, 2000). As so well stated by Sells (1982), "Mastery of mathe-

matics and science has become essential for full participation in the world of employment in an increasingly technological society" (p. 7).

Given the importance of math background to career options rather than to "choices" by default, females' tendency to avoid math coursework becomes one of the most serious barriers to their career development. Further, it is fairly clear now that it is lack of math background, rather than lack of innate ability, that is to blame for females' poorer performance on quantitative aptitude and mathematics achievement tests (e.g., Chipman & Wilson, 1985). Thus, a critical issue is females' avoidance of math. Educational and counseling interventions capable of helping young women to be full participants in an increasingly technological society may be among the most crucial strategies in attempts to broaden women's career choices.

Self-Efficacy Expectations

Bandura's (1997) concept of self-efficacy expectations refers to our beliefs that we can successfully complete specific tasks or behaviors. For example, an individual may perceive herself as able (or unable) to solve algebraic equations, fix a flat tire, or care for an infant. Low self-efficacy expectations are postulated by Bandura (1997) to lead to avoidance behavior, to interfere with performance, and to lead to a tendency to give up when faced with discouragement or failure. In the context of careers, *approach behavior* describes what we will try, while *avoidance behavior* refers to things we will not try. It thus influences what educational courses and majors and what career options we will attempt, versus those we will avoid. The self-efficacy expectations on performance can affect such behaviors as performance on the tests necessary to complete college coursework or the requirements of a job training program. Finally, persistence may be essential for long-term pursuit of one's goals in the face of obstacles, occasional failures, and dissuading messages from the environment—for example, gender- or ethnicity-based discrimination or harassment.

There is now over 20 years of research (see Betz & Hackett, 1997) allowing some generalities about career-related self-efficacy expectations in women. In education or job content domains, college women tend to score lower than college men on domains having to do with math, science, computer science and technology, mechanical activities, and outdoor and physical activities. Women tend to score higher on self-efficacy in social domains of activity. Note that these differences are consistent with stereotypic patterns of gender socialization. The gender differences have been found in recent research as well (Betz et al., 2003). And since self-efficacy has been found to play a significant role in career choice and occupational membership (Betz et al., 2003), these lower self-efficacy beliefs can be expected to limit women's self-perceived career options.

Multiple-Role Concerns

Fitzgerald, Fassinger, and Betz (1995) note that "the history of women's traditional roles as homemaker and mother continue to influence every aspect of their career choice and adjustment" (p. 72), typically by placing limits on what can be achieved. Women today may not be viewing this as an either/or choice, but they *do* plan careers mindful of how they will integrate these with home and family.

One unfortunate implication of the perceived overload caused by career and family priorities is that women for whom husband and children are a high priority tend to downscale their career aspirations relative to other women and to men. In Arnold and Denny's (Arnold, 1995) sample of high school valedictorians, the girls—but not the boys—showed steady decrements in aspirations and also in self-esteem after college. The stronger the home/family priorities, the more precipitous the decline in both aspirations and self-esteem. Farmer, in her 1997 longitudinal study of Midwestern high school students, reported that a large number of young women who were interested in science choose to pursue nursing because they thought it would fit well with having and rearing children or with being a single or divorced head of household. Men made no such compromises. From Farmer's sample of women (high school students in 1980), career motivation was inversely related to homemaking commitment. Thus family-role considerations limit women's investment in the occupational world.

Although the relationship of marital/familial status to women's career development has been weakening, as we have witnessed tremendous increases in workforce participation among women in all marital and parental categories, the relationship of marital/parental status to career attainment and commitment is still very strong. Studies have shown inverse relationships between being married and/or number of children and every measurable criterion of career achievement (see Betz & Fitzgerald, 1987, for a comprehensive review). This inverse relationship is not true among men: highly achieving men are at least as likely (if not more so) as their less highly achieving male counterparts to be married and to have one or more children.

Barriers in the Educational System

It is difficult to overestimate the importance of education to career development and achievement. The nature and level of obtained education are importantly related to subsequent career achievements and to adult socioeconomic status and lifestyle. All workers, men and women, earn more with increasing levels of education. For example, Latinos with a college education earn 82% more than do Latinos with a high school diploma (National Center for Education Statistics, 2002). In general, educational preparation is a major gate for occupational entrance. Education creates options, while lack of education closes them; without options, the concept of choice itself has no real meaning. Thus, the decisions an individual makes concerning his or her education, both the level and the major areas of study, will be among the most important career decisions he or she ever makes. Further, success in the educational programs chosen will be critical to successful implementation of career decisions.

Studies commissioned by the American Association of University Women (AAUW, 1999) and a major review done by Sadker and Sadker (1994) document the continuing disadvantaged position of girls in our educational system. Researchers concluded that girls receive less attention from teachers than do boys. Gender harassment in schools is increasing, and curriculum and texts ignore or marginalize the contributions of girls and women. This research and that by Brody (1997) have convincingly documented a decline in self-esteem among girls, but not boys, from elementary to middle and high school—for example, 55% of elementary school girls agreed with the statement "I am good at a lot of things," but this percentage declined to 29% in middle school and 23% in high school. Only girls who pursued math and science courses and who participated in sports maintained their self-esteem over this time period (AAUW, 1999). When young women enter college, the educational environment may continue to be unsupportive or even hostile. Sexual harassment, being discouraged from classroom participation, and lack of support and mentoring can affect women in any major, but these and other subtle or direct messages that "she doesn't belong" are particularly true in fields such as engineering and the physical sciences.

Supports to Career Choices

Just as unsupportive environments can serve as barriers to women, supportive environments can be very helpful. One of the most crucial areas of support is that from families, especially parents and older relatives, and this has been found true for women of all racial/ethnic groups. Studies by Fisher and Padmawidjaja (1999) and Pearson and Bieschke (2001), among others, have found parental support and availability to be very important in the career aspirations and achievements of women of color as well as White women.

A number of other studies have found maternal employment, particularly in nontraditional career fields, is related to daughters' higher career aspirations (e.g., Betz & Fitzgerald, 1987). Gomez and colleagues (2001) found that although Latino high achievers came from families where traditional gender roles were emphasized, most also had nontraditional female role models—for example, their mothers were nontraditionally employed or, if homemakers, held leadership roles in community organizations. On the other hand, Hackett and colleagues (1989) reported findings suggesting the importance of support from a male family member in girls' pursuit of nontraditional career fields. Many women pursuing nontraditional career fields relied heavily on male

mentors (Betz, 2002) since no female mentors were available in their environment.

In addition to supportive family and mentors, much previous research has shown the importance of personality factors such as instrumentality, internal locus of control, high self-esteem, and a feminist orientation on women's career achievements (Fassinger, 1990). *Instrumentality* refers to a constellation of traits that were previously called "masculinity" but were seen in actuality to reflect a collection of characteristics having to do with independence, self-sufficiency, and the belief that one is in control of one's life. Thus, positive factors related to support and mentoring from others and a personality characterized by high self-esteem and self-efficacy and a sense of self-sufficiency and independence can help women reach their career goals.

WOMEN OF COLOR: SPECIAL CONCERNS

The disadvantages facing women in the labor force are accentuated for women of color, who have often been described as facing the double jeopardy of both gender and ethnic discrimination (Gomez et al., 2001). Women of color are employed at rates comparable to those of White women, but they earn less than do White women or minority men. Lesbians and physically disabled women also earn less than heterosexual White women (Yoder, 1999).

African American women have achieved higher educational and occupational levels and have had more options than have African American men, but African American women have also often been found in menial jobs such as maids and nannies at a rate exceeding that of White women and still make less money than do either White women or African American men (DeVaney & Hughey, 2000). Since they are the most likely group to be supporting a child or children alone, this creates special hardship.

Latinos currently represent the largest minority group in the United States—32.8 million, or 12.5% in the 2000 census. The achievement of Latino men and Latina women in terms of both educational and occupational levels achieved lags well behind that of other U.S. minorities except for Native Americans (Bowman, 1998). Mexican American women lag behind other women of Hispanic ethnicity in college completion rates; they also lag behind Latino men who earned poorer grades in college.

Asian American women are somewhat more likely than other groups of women to be found in occupations emphasizing math or technology, but they are still predominately found in traditionally female fields and, like other groups of women, earn less money than men. Finally, Native American women, including Native Hawaiians, are almost entirely invisible (Bowman, 1998) and are the most occupationally disadvantaged and most likely unemployed of any group of women. Clearly, the career development needs of women of color must receive more attention.

EXTERNAL BARRIERS TO EQUALITY

Eliminating the barriers of discrimination and sexual harassment has long been discussed as crucial in women's attempt to attain equality in the workplace (see Fassinger, 2002). Although outright gender discrimination is against the law, informal discrimination continues to exist (Fitzgerald & Harmon, 2001). For example, although women may be allowed to enter a male-dominated workplace, it may be made clear to them, overtly or more subtly, that they are not welcome. Actions ranging from overt verbal harassment to simply being ignored and receiving no social support from colleagues can make a work environment unpleasant, and less obvious forms of discrimination in pay, promotions, and job perquisites continue as well (Fitzgerald & Harmon, 2001).

The importance of promotions is related to the continuing existence of the glass ceiling, a term that refers to the barriers based on attitudinal or organizational bias that prevent women from advancing in an organization. This situation affects the small number of women at top levels of management (Yoder, 1999). Nevertheless, the Department of Labor appointed a Federal Glass Ceiling Commission, which concluded that there still existed a corporate ceiling, in that only 3–5% of senior corporate leadership positions are held by women—far fewer than their representation in the overall labor force (Federal Glass Ceiling Commission, 1995, pp. 68–69).

Another barrier to women in nontraditional careers is that of being a token—that is, someone whose gender or ethnicity (or both) constitutes less than 15% of her work group. Tokens experience stress, social isolation, heightened visibility, and accusations of role violations ("you don't belong here"). Research on women of color who are double tokens, such as the African American women firefighters studied by Yoder and Aniakudo (1997), shows that these women faced insufficient instruction, coworker hostility, overly close and punitive supervision, lack of support, and stereotyping—an unwavering message of exclusion and a hope that they would fail (Yoder & Aniakudo, 1997).

Sexual harassment also continues to be a major problem in the workplace, with serious consequences for both women and organizations. Sexual harassment is described in detail by authors such as Norton (2002). Research now distinguishes two categories of sexual harassment: quid pro quo harassment and hostile environment harassment. *Quid pro quo harassment* refers to situations in which an employee is asked to give in to a supervisor's sexual demands in exchange for pay, a promotion, or continued employment, with the implied threat of loss of raise or promotion, or loss of employment, if the employee refuses to comply. *Hostile environment harassment* refers to instances where the employee is subject to sexual innuendo, sexist or sexually oriented comments, physical touching, or sexually oriented posters or cartoons in the work area. The issue here is making women workers sex objects; they are at work to make a living and advance their careers, and sexual harassment can seriously interfere with those aims.

Although responses to sexual harassment are beyond the scope of this chapter, suffice it to say that this is a major barrier to women's equality in the workplace. Research has shown decreases in job satisfaction and organizational commitment, job withdrawal, increased symptoms of anxiety and depression, and higher levels of stress-related illness as responses to sexual harassment (Norton, 2002). Clearly these are mental health as well as economic issues and can seriously compromise job performance and job satisfaction.

Another of the persistent conditions affecting women's equality in the workplace is that although their work force participation has increased dramatically, their work at home has not decreased. Women are now expected to cope with two full-time jobs, one outside and the other inside the home. Instead of "having it all," women are "doing it all" (Fitzgerald & Harmon, 2001, p. 215). Research suggests that few men view parenting and homemaking as their responsibility—they are primarily available to "help out" (Farmer, 1997). Yoder (1999) summarizes data showing that employed women in married couples do 33 hours of household chores weekly, compared to 14 for their husbands; this constitutes 70% of the workload for women and 30% for men, and does not even include child care. With child care, these women are working a full-time job at home in addition to what they are doing at work.

Resources and structures that could assist women in managing these multiple roles are lacking in many organizations. Organizational policies providing for subsidized child or elder care, paid family leave, flextime, job sharing, and telecommuting could greatly ease the burdens of women simultaneously managing home, family, and careers (Fitzgerald & Harmon, 2001). The United States is still the only developed country in the world without a national child-care policy and one that has no systematic means of addressing the serious problems of elder care (Fitzgerald & Harmon, 2001).

Supports for Career Adjustment

Richie et al., in their study of highly achieving African American and White women, title their article "Persistence, Connection, and Passion" (1997, p. 133), and this title well summarizes some of the supports for women's achievement of their career goals. These might also be viewed as strengths of women that enable them to surmount the barriers they confront. Persistence is critical to succeeding in the face of obstacles, and strong self-efficacy expectations, self-esteem, and a strong sense of purpose are also essential. The characteristics of instrumentality discussed previously—that is, the sense of being in control of one's own life and destiny, of being agentic, able to *act* on one's own behalf—are also important to persistence.

Related to both self-efficacy and instrumentality is access to personal coping strategies. Gomez et al. (2001) found coping strategies especially important to their highly achieving Latinas, as did Richie et al. with highly achieving African Americans and White women. They list "flexibility, creativity, reframing and redefining challenges, barriers, or mistakes, maintaining a balanced perspective in understanding how racism and sexism may affect careers, developing support networks, and developing bicultural skills where applicable" (Richie et al., 1997, p. 298) as essential.

Connection refers to the absolutely essential part played by support from family and peers/friends in women's persistence in reaching goals. There is ample literature documenting the importance of family, including spouse and children, friends both at work and outside work, and mentors. And this importance has been shown for women of color as well as for White women. As a few examples, Gilbert and Gomez et al. (2001) discuss the crucial role of supportive spouses in managing both career and home and family responsibilities. Richie et al. (1997) emphasized the importance of interconnectedness with others in the continuing high achievement of both African American and White women. Connection may also be facilitated by a feminist orientation, which gives women a sense of a community. Feminist orientation has consistently been shown to be a facilitative factor in women's career achievements (e.g., Fassinger, 1990).

Finally, *passion* is for some women loving what they do, and for others, feeling that they have made a difference in the world (Gomez et al., 2001). For some women, this is the sense of a life's calling. Although not all people, women or men, are lucky enough to have such a passion for their work, helping people find that passion is a worthy goal of professionals.

SUPPORTIVE INTERVENTIONS

The following are suggestions for professionals interested in helping women fully utilize their abilities and interests in making their career choices. Following that are ideas that may help employed women negotiate the barriers to their equality and satisfaction in their workplace

1. Encourage high-quality and extensive education and/or training. Don't overlook the importance of technical schools, two-year and community colleges, and the military for excellent training and education.
2. Adopt the rule that you can't take too much math. Encourage young women to stay in math coursework as long as possible. Math background opens options and prevents others from being eliminated by default.
3. When in doubt, stress decisions that eliminate the fewest options—staying in school and staying in math do this.
4. Focus on a woman' self-efficacy expectations with respect to various areas of educational and career pursuits. Question her feelings of inadequacy if she has never had experiences in the area; help her develop her competencies rather than sharing her assumption that she "can't do it."
5. See yourself as a facilitator of new learning experiences for the girl or woman, so that she can fully develop all her capabilities, including those in gender-nontraditional areas.
6. Explore her outcome expectations and concerns about barriers to her goal pursuits with the idea of helping her develop coping mechanisms and coping self-efficacy.
7. Assess the role of culture and ethnicity in a young woman's planning and help her make decisions respectful of both her individual capabilities and talents and her cultural values.

For employed women, discrimination, sexual harassment, tokenism, lack of support, and sheer overload from two, rather than one, full-time jobs are major causes of decrements in *both* performance and satisfaction. A few general guidelines may be useful for the counselor.

1. Help women at work develop support systems.
2. Help change the system as it pertains to flexible work schedules and family leave policies (ideally which allow leave for adoption as well as childbearing and for elder care, and which assume that men are as willing to be responsible for those they love as are women).
3. Help token women (especially women of color) find support, often by widening the net that is cast (for example, creating a support group of all the women in the College of Sciences vs. just the two in chemistry class).
4. Teach women to expect full participation in homemaking and child rearing from their husbands or partners. Teach men that it is their responsibility, and also to their benefit, to participate fully in home and family life and work.
5. Help women develop effective cognitive and behavioral coping strategies, as discussed earlier in the section on supports for career adjustment.
6. Make sure that women have information pertaining to grievance procedures in cases of discrimination or sexual harassment.

CONCLUSIONS

The potential rewards for women of selecting and managing a satisfying career can be great. It is hoped that this chapter provides ideas that will be useful to counselors seeking to help women utilize their strengths and develop coping strategies to face the challenges of achieving their career goals.

REFERENCES

American Association of University Women. (1999). *Gender gaps: Where schools still fail our children.* New York: Marlowe and Company.

Arnold, K. D. (1995). *Lives of promise: What becomes of high school valedictorians.* San Francisco: Jossey-Bass.

Bandura, A. (1997). *Self-efficacy: The exercise of control.* New York: W. H. Freeman.

Barnett, R. C., & Hyde, J. S. (2001). Women, men, work, and family: An expansionist theory. *American Psychologist, 56,* 781–796.

Betz, N. E. (2002). Women's career development: Weaving personal themes and theoretical constructs. *The Counseling Psychologist, 30,* 467–481.

Betz, N. E., Borgen, F., Rottinghuas, P., Paulsen, A., Halper, C., & Harmon, L. (2003). The Expanded Skills Confidence Inventory: Measuring basic domains of vocational activity. *Journal of Vocational Behavior, 62,* 76–100.

Betz, N. E., & Fitzgerald, L. F. (1987). *The career psychology of women.* New York: Academic Press.

Betz, N. E., & Hackett, G. (1997). Applications of self-efficacy theory to the career development of women. *Journal of Career Assessment, 5,* 383–402.

Bowman, S. L. (1998). Minority women and career adjustment. *Journal of Career Assessment, 6,* 417–431.

Brody, J. E. (1997, November 4). Girls and puberty: The crisis years. *New York Times,* p. B8.

Chipman, S. F., & Wilson, D. M. (1985). Understanding mathematics course enrollment and mathematics achievement: A synthesis of the research. In S. F. Chipman, L. R. Brush, & D. M. Wilson (Eds.), *Women and mathematics: Balancing the equation* (pp. 275–328). Hillsdale, NJ: Erlbaum.

Crosby, F. J. (1991). *Juggling: The unexpected advantages of balancing home and family.* New York: Free Press.

DeVaney, S. B., & Hughey, A. W. (2000). Career development of ethnic minority students. In D. A. Luzzo (Ed.), *Career counseling with college students* (pp. 233–252). Washington, DC: American Psychological Association.

Ehrhart, J. K., & Sandler, B. R. (1987). *Looking for more than a few good women in traditionally male fields.* Washington, DC: Project on the Status and Education of Women.

Erikson, E. (1950). *Childhood and society.* New York: Norton.

Farmer, H. S. (1997). *Diversity and women's career development.* Thousand Oaks, CA: Sage.

Fassinger, R. E. (2002). Hitting the ceiling: Gendered barriers to occupational entry, advancement, and achievement. In L. Diamant & J. Lee (Eds.), *The psychology of sex, gender, and jobs.* (pp. 21–46). Westport, CT: Praeger.

Fassinger, R. F. (1990). Causal models of career choice in two samples of college women. *Journal of Vocational Behavior, 36,* 225–240.

Federal Glass Ceiling Commission. (1995). *Report on the glass ceiling for women.* Washington, DC: U.S. Department of Labor.

Fisher, T. A., & Padmawidjaja, I. (1999). Parental influences on career development perceived by African American and Mexican American college students. *Journal of Multicultural Counseling and Development, 27,* 136–152.

Fitzgerald, L. F., Fassinger, R. E., & Betz, N. (1995). Theoretical advances in the study of women's career development. In W. B. Walsh & S. H. Osipow (Eds.), *Handbook of vocational psychology* (2nd ed., pp. 67–110). Mahwah, NJ: Erlbaum.

Fitzgerald, L. F., & Harmon, L. W. (2001). Women's career development: A postmodern update. In F. L. T. Leong & A. Barak (Eds.), *Contemporary models in vocational psychology* (pp. 207–230). Mahwah, NJ: Erlbaum.

Gilbert, L. A. (2002, August). *Changing roles of work and family.* Paper presented at the meeting of the American Psychological Association, Chicago.

Gomez, M. J., Fassinger, R. E., Prosser, J., Cooke, K., Mejia, B., & Luna, J. (2001). Voices abriendo caminos (Voices forging paths): A qualitative study of the career development of notable Latinos. *Journal of Counseling Psychology, 48,* 286–300.

Hackett, G., Esposito, D., & O'Halloran, M. S. (1989). The relationship of role model influences to the career salience and educational and career plans of college women. *Journal of Vocational Behavior, 35,* 164–180.

Harvey, J. H., & Pauwels, B. G. (1999). Recent developments in close relationships. *Current Directions in Psychological Science, 8,* 93–95.

Kuh, C. V. (1998, November). *Data on women doctoral level scientists and universities.* Paper presented at National Invitational Conference on Women in Research Universities, Harvard University and Radcliffe College.

National Center for Education Statistics. (2002). *The condition of education 2002.* NCES 2000-025. U.S. Department of Education. Washington, DC: U.S. Government Printing Office.

Norton, S. (2002). Women exposed: Sexual harassment and female vulnerability. In L. Diamant & J. Lee (Eds.), *The psychology of sex, gender, and jobs* (pp. 82–103). Westport, CT: Praeger.

Pearson, S. M., & Bieschke, K. (2001). Succeeding against the odds: An examination of familial influences on the career development of professional African American women. *Journal of Counseling Psychology, 48,* 301–309.

Richie, B. S., Fassinger, R. E., Lenn, S. G., Johnson, J., Prosser, J., & Robinson, S. (1997). Persistence, connection, and passion: A qualitative study of the career development of highly achieving African-American-Black and White women. *Journal of Counseling Psychology, 44,* 133–148.

Sadker, M., & Sadker, D. (1994). *Failing at fairness: How our schools cheat girls.* New York: Touchstone.

Sears, P. S., & Barbie, A. H. (1977). Career and life satisfaction among Terman's gifted women. In J. C. Stanley, W. George, & C. Solano (Eds.), *The gifted and creative: Fifty year perspective* (pp. 72–106). Baltimore: Johns Hopkins University Press.

Sells, L. (1982). Leverage of equal opportunity through mastery of mathematics. In S. M. Humphreys (Ed.), *Women and minorities in science* (pp. 7–26). Boulder, CO: Westview.

U.S. Department of Labor. (2000). *Occupational outlook handbook.* Washington, DC: U.S. Government Printing Office.

U.S. Department of Labor, Bureau of Labor Statistics. (2003). *Facts on women workers.* Washington, DC: Author.

Yoder, J. (1999). *Women and gender: Transforming psychology.* Upper Saddle River, NJ: Prentice-Hall.

Yoder, J., & Aniakudo, P. (1997). "Outsider within" the firehouse. *Gender and Society, 11,* 324–341.

The need for connection, the pull toward intimacy, the awareness of "belonging" to or with one or more other people, is a cornerstone of what it means to be human. Baumeister and Leary (1995) proposed that "human beings have a pervasive drive to form and maintain at least a minimum quantity of lasting, positive, and significant interpersonal relationships" (p. 497) that involve frequent and pleasant interactions that are also stable, ongoing, and reciprocally supportive. Although this "belongingness hypothesis" applies to both women and men, women particularly manifest a desire for and an ability to achieve and sustain connection. At least within certain parameters, the establishment of positive connections/social bonds should be related to positive emotional and physical outcomes, and the loss of such bonds related to negative outcomes of various kinds (Baumeister & Leary, 1995). Presumably, that is why love and intimacy are so rewarding, and breakup, divorce, and loss are so punishing.

The current chapter presents some of the factors and processes involved with the development, maintenance, and dissolution of one particular kind of social bond: the romantic relationship. Although friendship is mentioned in passing, romantic relationships are the primary focus. The chapter sketches the "life" of a romantic relationship, beginning with basic attraction. Although most of the issues addressed affect both men and women in relationships, the chapter concentrates on women's perspectives, noting phenomena that are particularly characteristic (or uncharacteristic) of women.

SUSAN S. HENDRICK

Love, Intimacy, and Partners

34

ATTRACTION AND RELATIONSHIP DEVELOPMENT

Theories of Attraction

How do we become attracted to a relationship partner? How does the dating process begin? A sample of psychological and sociological theories speaks to this question. General reinforcement theories, including operant conditioning (where a response/behavior is followed by a reinforcement) and classical conditioning (where a stimulus is followed by a response) provide the basis for exchange theory, a theory of the marketplace adapted to the study of interpersonal relationships (e.g., Blau, 1964). Some of the basic tenets of exchange theory include *rewards* (a reinforcement or gratification), *costs* (punishments or foregone rewards), and *outcomes* (rewards minus costs). Byrne (1969) proposed that attraction toward another person is determined by the relative outcomes (rewards minus costs) in dealing with that person. Based on extensive couple research, Gottman (e.g., 1994) proposed that couples should not fall below a ratio of five positives (i.e., rewards) to one negative (i.e., cost) if they wish their relationship to remain both positive and stable.

Another influential theory of attraction, largely initiated by Byrne (1971), is that of similarity leading to attraction, or "birds of a feather flock together." The more similar two people are on a variety of characteristics, the more likely they are to be attracted to each other. Although similarity is only one aspect of broader patterns of human relating, the attraction–similarity relationship has appeared for such constructs as self-esteem and various personality attributes such as how people view the world.

Similarity is not unrelated to balance theory (e.g., Heider, 1958), which stresses that humans like symmetry or balance in their relationships. For example, if a woman loves both her husband and her best friend, it is helpful if those two persons relate positively or at least do not relate negatively. A relational process called *attitude alignment* (Davis & Rusbult, 2001) supports the basic ideas of balance theory. This perspective proposes "that individuals experience discomfort when they discover that their attitudes are inconsistent with those of a close partner and are motivated to change their attitudes to achieve congruence with the attitudes of the partner" (p. 65). Attitude alignment reflects elements of both balance theory and similarity theory.

Do opposites attract? Common wisdom says that they do, but research has better supported similarity than complementarity. Felmlee (1998) has conducted research on what she calls "fatal attractions," or the case in which the qualities that draw us toward another person initially are the very qualities that later drive us apart. It appears that when a partner is both very dissimilar to oneself and is extreme and nonnormative in that difference, the result may be a fatal attraction resulting in a breakup.

Influences on Attraction

Both personal and environmental factors can influence attraction. Personal attributes such as physical appearance are powerful attractors in all cultures, but have been studied most extensively in Western cultures (Hatfield & Sprecher, 1986) and include facial features, body build, skin, hair, posture, and so on. Although evolutionary psychologists have emphasized research findings in which women are less concerned about a potential partner's physical attractiveness and more concerned about the partner's earning potential than are men (e.g., Buss & Barnes, 1986), social structural theories ascribe such findings to men's greater power in most societies and women's resulting need to seek resources (via a male partner; e.g., Eagly & Wood, 1999). Men, however, have the luxury of seeking attractiveness in a partner.

Physical appearance is presented to the world through body language. Body language includes such things as facial expressiveness, body lean, and even hairstyle, clothing, and jewelry. Desirable characteristics in general, the ability to communicate, and even reciprocity of social attraction (Vittengl & Holt, 2000) are also important to attraction.

Proximity is a major environmental influence on attraction. If people are brought together by family or friends, or occupy the same "space," whether at work, school, or in the neighborhood, they are likely to interact more frequently and perhaps become attracted to each other (Hendrick, 2004). As Western society becomes increasingly multicultural, interracial/interethnic friendships and dating will become more frequent. Some research indicates that such friendship relationships may be evaluated more positively than such dating relationships (Garcia & Rivera, 1999), but evaluations should improve as multicultural dating relationships become more common.

Relationship Development

Attraction is important in initiating a relationship, but before a relationship can mature into dating, courtship, and enduring partnership, the relationship must progress and mature. Self-disclosure, one form of verbal communication, is important as relationships begin and develop

(Derlega, Metts, Petronio, & Margulis, 1993). Through sharing oneself—one's background and history as well as one's hopes, dreams, and fears—people can become intimate with one another. Indeed, self-disclosure is one of three foundational characteristics of intimate interaction (the others are positive emotion and feeling understood by one's partner), according to Prager (2000).

Trust is another key factor in relationship development, and according to Boon (1994), is an "expectation that a partner is intrinsically motivated to take one's own best interests into account" (p. 88). Trust has an intrapersonal aspect, in that a woman may have a general tendency to be trusting (or mistrusting), and an interpersonal aspect, in that she may trust or mistrust a specific person. Trust is exceedingly important to relationship development, and honesty is valued in a partner. Broken trust, which occurs in the event of infidelity, for example, is difficult to repair and is likely to be an important focus in couples' counseling after an affair.

As partners move forward in their relationship, commitment of various kinds develops also. Johnson and his colleagues (Johnson, Caughlin, & Huston, 1999) pointed out that personal commitment (a general intention toward a partner), structural commitment (experiencing barriers to dissolving the relationship), and moral commitment (feeling a moral obligation to stay in the relationship) are all important forms of commitment. Indeed, level of commitment, mutuality of commitment, and trust are all important to a well-functioning relationship (Drigotas, Rusbult, & Verette, 1999). And commitment seems similarly important across ethnic and racial groups. For example, both Hispanic and Anglo couples were similar in such things as their perceived family influences, attitudes toward marriage, trust, and commitment to wed (Umana-Taylor & Fine, 2003). As a relationship develops, long-term partnering becomes more likely.

PARTNERING: LOVE AND INTIMACY

Forms of Partnering

As partners move from dating and courting to becoming long-term partners, their relationship may assume one of several forms. The most predominant form of partnering is heterosexual marriage, and the majority of people will marry at some point in their lives. Marriage is the relationship form most widely studied and written about, and even within marriage, there is diversity, including interreligion, interethnic, and interracial marriage. In addition, remarriage is a marital form that has increased dramatically in recent decades. Estimates are that approximately one out of three children in the United States will at some time be part of a remarried family (Ganong & Coleman, 2000). Remarried families are often compared to intact nuclear families and found "wanting" in some respect, but in fact, remarriage is its own form of long-term relationship. Women in remarried families have been particularly subject to negative stereotypes, never more explicit than in children's fairy tales, where wicked stepmothers abound (e.g., *Hansel and Gretel, Cinderella, Snow White*). Because women have traditionally been assigned the role of tending the relationship (whether romantic or more broadly familial), women are typically the bearers of blame when relationships exhibit flaws (Hendrick, 2001). But there are upsides to remarriage for women, such as greater equality in decision making, due to greater maturity and more relationship experience (Ganong & Coleman, 2000).

Cohabitation is another form of long-term relationship, and it is on the increase (Seltzer, 2000). For some couples, cohabitation is a precursor to marriage, but for other couples, it is the primary relationship form. Rates of cohabitation are rising for both younger couples and older ones (Seltzer, 2000), with the latter often choosing the option of cohabitation rather than marriage in order to avoid legal complexities, potential changes in retirement benefits, and so on. Cohabitation is more accepted in some countries than in others, and even within the United States, there is substantial geographic variation in the legal rights of "domestic partners" (Seltzer, 2000).

Cohabitation is the only long-term relationship form available to most same-sex romantic couples. Legal marriage is largely unavailable to them at the current time, though such rights for same-sex couples appear to be increasing (Stacey & Biblarz, 2003). Although estimates of the percentage of women who identify themselves as lesbian or bisexual vary, Laumann and his colleagues (Laumann, Gagnon, Michael, & Michaels, 1994) found that 1.5% of women identified as lesbian, and 3% of men identified as gay male. These are likely to be underestimates, due to society's relative lack of support for homosexual persons and same-sex partnerships. Research indicates many similarities between same-sex couples and heterosexual ones in terms of courtship patterns, though lesbian couples are more likely to incorporate friendship into their dating "script" than are gay male or heterosexual couples (Peplau & Spaulding, 2000). Power is more equitably distributed in lesbian couples than in heterosexual couples, and bringing into the relationship children from a previous relationship actually increases power for a lesbian partner (Huston & Schwartz, 1995). Both positive (e.g., satisfaction) and negative (e.g., jealousy) relationship characteristics are notably similar between same- and other-sex couples. Rates of breakup, however, are higher for lesbian and gay, as well as cohabiting couples, perhaps owing to fewer barriers to breakup and less societal support for relationship continuation.

Another type of long-term relationship that is not explored in the current chapter but that is extremely important to women's well-being is friendship, particularly friendship with other women. As noted elsewhere, "the emotional communities that women sustain in turn sustain women" (Hendrick, 2001, p. 642). This type of relationship can be extremely nurturing. For an extended discussion of this topic, see Fehr (1996).

Love, Intimacy, and Related Processes

As attraction leads into the development of a romantic relationship, love and intimacy become increasingly significant.

Love

Love is central to most romantic relationships. Both conceptualizing and measuring love are complex endeavors, which surprises those who assume that love is unidimensionally or universally defined. Although the focus here is on romantic love, it is important to acknowledge the many different forms that love can take: love for partners, love for children, love for parents and other dear family members, love for friends, and so on. Romantic love, particularly, is a many-splendored thing. It has been variously viewed as an evolutionary mechanism designed to promote pair bonding and species survival (Buss, 1988), a social and cultural construction (Eagly & Wood, 1999), and a mechanism for personal growth (Aron & Aron, 1996).

Although passionate love is thought by some scholars (e.g., Jankowiak & Fischer, 1992) to be nearly universal, both passionate, emotionally intense love, and companionate, quietly devotional love, appear to be related to relationship satisfaction for couples of varying ages (Hendrick & Hendrick, 1993; Sprecher & Regan, 1998). A proponent of a multidimensional approach to romantic love, Sternberg (1986) has proposed that the components of intimacy, passion, and commitment, in varying proportions, constitute eight different types of love, ranging from liking (which is primarily intimacy) to consummate love (which contains all three components).

Another multidimensional approach is the love-styles research based on Lee's original work (1973) and developed further by the Hendricks (e.g., Hendrick & Hendrick, 1986). This research proposes that people have love styles, as surely as they have personality styles or interaction styles. The six major love styles are as follows: Eros (intense, passionate love), Ludus (game-playing love), Storge (friendship-based love), Pragma (practical love), Mania (dependent, possessive love), and Agape (altruistic love). These six styles have been measured by the Love Attitudes Scale, which has a 42-item long version (Hendrick & Hendrick, 1986) and a 24-item short form (Hendrick, Hendrick, & Dicke, 1998).

Research on the love styles has related love to aspects of personality, communication, and so on, and has shown interesting similarities and differences between women and men (Hendrick & Hendrick, 1995). Women have often been higher on Storge, Pragma, and Mania, thus describing themselves as more oriented to friendship, practicality, and possessiveness in their love orientations. On the other hand, they are less endorsing of Ludus and thus come out squarely against game-playing love. Women have sometimes been characterized as more romantic than men, and indeed women are for the most part the consumers of romantic novels, movies, etc. When the genders differ on passionate love (Eros), however, sometimes women are the more passionate ones, and sometimes men are more passionate. Interestingly, women typically rate themselves as less altruistic (Agape) in their love styles than men rate themselves as being (Hendrick et al., 1998).

Love-styles research in dating couples showed that women's altruistic love (measured by Agape) and their passionate love (measured by Eros) were positively and significantly related to men's relationship satisfaction, whereas men's altruistic and passionate love were unrelated to women's satisfaction (Hendrick, Hendrick, & Adler, 1988). Women's relationship-tending abilities thus appear to make a difference to men. And the love styles show strong similarities across ethnic groups, such as Mexican American and Anglo couples (Contreras, Hendrick, & Hendrick, 1996). Broader measures of relational well-being such as commitment, satisfaction, general happiness, how well one's partner matched one's "ideal partner," and so on also showed similarities between African American and White couples (e.g., Ruvolo & Veroff, 1997). Love styles are viewed as attitudes rather than as personality characteristics and may vary across relationships and within relationships across the life span.

The Love Attitudes Scale is useful in couples' counseling because it gives partners a common language with which to understand their similarities and differences in the love arena.

Sexuality

Although women's sexuality is discussed in detail elsewhere in this volume, it deserves mention in the context of relationships. While not all romantic love relationships involve sexual relating, and not all sexual relating involves romantic love, the two often coexist. Women are less inclined than men to view social interactions in sexual terms (Cupach & Metts, 1991) and may thus sometimes miss the social cues that they are being interpreted sexually by men. Women's inclination to view the "person" rather than the sexual implications in a situation is congruent with recent theorizing about women's "sexual plasticity." It has

been suggested (Baumeister, 2000) that women are more sexually flexible than men, showing more variation in sexual behavior across time, lower attitude-behavior consistency, and greater responsiveness to social pressures and norms. Peplau (2001) entertained ideas about women's plasticity in terms of its meaning within the context of human relating. She noted that women, more than men, seem capable of sexual variation in terms of partner choice, with women's attraction to men and to other women as "part of a much broader pattern in which sexual behavior serves diverse social and emotional functions among both primates and humans" (Peplau, 2001, p. 12). Other theory and research supports this perspective (e.g., Diamond, 2003). As Bem (1993) observed, " my sexuality does not mesh with the available cultural categories . . . of heterosexual, homosexual, and bisexual. . . . Although some of the (very few) individuals to whom I have been attracted . . . have been men and some have been women, what those individuals have in common has nothing to do with either their biological sex or mine—from which I conclude, not that I am attracted to both sexes, but that my sexuality is organized around dimensions other than sex" (p. vii).

Intimacy

Intimacy can be conceptualized as a feeling of intense closeness, trust, and so on, but Prager (2000), who has written widely about intimacy, has chosen to frame it in interactional or behavioral terms as "intimate behavior" that leads to "intimate experience." In Prager's view, romantic partners enact behaviors that bring them closer together and create the context of "intimate experience," composed of self-disclosure, positive emotion, and feeling understood by one's partner (Prager, 2000). Over time, intimate experiencing will presumably lead to a truly intimate relationship. Although intimacy can be measured in different ways—for example, by measuring Prager's three components separately—the recently developed Interaction Record Form for Intimacy (IRF-I; Prager & Buhrmester, 1998) offers a more global measure of intimate experiencing.

In addition to comprising several characteristics, intimacy is the culmination of a dynamic process that occurs at several levels and in multiple contexts (Prager, 2000). For example, the *individual context* includes the personalities, family histories, and so on of the respective relational partners. The *relational context* involves such aspects as reciprocity of self-disclosure and responsiveness to the partner. The *social network context* concerns family and friends, who may influence strongly the success or failure of a relationship. The *sociocultural context* refers to the larger society, which may impact partners through their ethnic or racial roots, or through economic events (e.g., a recession) or political events (e.g., war) that may influence a couple in their movement toward intimacy. Finally, the *immediate context* includes whether the partners live close to each other or far apart, whether they have sufficient time to devote to the relationship, and so on. An example of how a specific context can influence relationships occurs on the social network and sociocultural levels, where partners must "navigate between the dyad and their respective families and between the dyad and their respective cultural/ethnic groups" (Gaines & Liu, 2000, p. 104).

One of Prager's aspects of intimacy deserves particular attention, since self-disclosure, or communication more broadly, is one of the most important components of an intimate relationship. Although a detailed discussion of disclosure is beyond the scope of this chapter, several points are worth noting. Self-disclosure, discussed earlier in the context of attraction and relationship development, is a verbal sharing of the self that allows intimacy to increase. It can consist of information related to the outside world, to the self, or to the relationship. Disclosing is an evolving and transformative process, in which disclosure can deepen a relationship, and the deepening relationship can feed back to foster self-disclosure (Derlega et al., 1993; Dindia, 1997). It is a dialectical process, however, in that it is normal for partners (and relationships) to move between greater disclosure and greater privacy (Altman, Vinsel, & Brown, 1981).

Nonverbal communication such as eye contact and facial expressions (types of body language, discussed earlier) are powerful means of communication. Although both verbal and nonverbal communication are important, if the two modes of communication are discrepant, nonverbal modes are more likely to be believed (Keeley & Hart, 1994). "Nonverbal behaviors are indicative of quality communication. Research indicates that people pay close attention to nonverbal behaviors as indicators of the health of their relationships" (Keeley & Hart, p. 161).

The sheer "event" of communication is not necessarily all that is important, however, because communication can be positive or negative. In cross-cultural research with couples, Halford, Hahlweg, and Dunne (1990) noted that "the most outstanding feature of unhappy couples is their inability to terminate negative interaction, particularly in nonverbal communication. . . . In contrast, happy couples manage to deescalate such a process or refrain from starting it at all" (p. 499). And unhappy partners tend to be both more confident about yet less accurate in their communication with one another (Noller & Venardos, 1986). Thus, unhappy couples are more negative, stubborn, and inaccurate in their communication. Ultimately, deficits in communication, as well as other negative relationship processes, can move a relationship toward breakup or divorce.

RELATIONSHIP LOSS

Breakup

The loss of a relationship may come in the form of breakup or divorce. (Bereavement is discussed in chapter 42.) The impact of breakup may be underestimated because the ties are not legal, and the external signs of involvement (e.g., children, property) are less evident. Nevertheless, breakup can hurt deeply.

There are many causes of breakup, but Duck (1982) grouped these causes into three larger categories. These include *preexisting doom* (where partners are ill-suited from the beginning) or *mechanical failure/process loss* (where partners do negative things such as show hostility or ignore each other, or fail to enact positive behaviors such as clear communication and effective conflict resolution). The third category, *sudden death*, encompasses behaviors such as infidelity or some other form of significant betrayal. Break-up is not a single event but rather a process that occurs over time and may involve several cycles of moving toward or away from actual breakup.

The emotional toll of breakup depends on both intrapersonal factors (e.g., someone's attachment style, whether someone perceives relationship alternatives) and interpersonal factors (e.g., level of perceived closeness to the partner, satisfaction, commitment). Thus someone with a secure attachment style, who feels capable of attracting another partner, and who is unsatisfied with the relationship, is less likely to experience breakup distress than is someone who is anxiously attached, fearful of remaining alone, and who is very satisfied with the relationship (Frazier & Cook, 1993; Sprecher, Felmlee, Metts, Fehr, & Vanni, 1998). Interestingly, degree of distress at time of breakup was not particularly related to emotional recovery several months later, and variables such as higher self-esteem and greater social support were linked to better recovery (Frazier & Cook). An even more complex type of breakup that has potentially deeper and longer aftereffects is divorce.

Divorce

Although the divorce rate in the United States may have leveled off in recent years (Teachman, Tedrow, & Crowder, 2000), it continues to have a major social impact. How do two people who begin their relationship in joy and hope get to the point of severing that relationship?

There are a number of explanations for divorce, ranging from the broadly theoretical "selection perspective" (e.g., Amato, 2000), which proposes that people who have personality problems or some other kind of personal defect are more likely to get divorced, to the identification of particular behaviors that corrode relationships, such as criticism, contempt, defensiveness, and stonewalling (Gottman, 1994). Longitudinal research by Huston and his colleagues (Huston, Caughlin, Houts, Smith, & George, 2001) showed that aspects of couple interaction that were apparent during courtship predicted later happiness as well as relationship continuation or dissolution. Both positive and negative interactions are

important, as underlined by Gottman and Levenson (2000). Following married couples over time, these researchers found that negative emotion displayed fairly early in a marriage predicted *early* divorce (7.4 years following marriage, on average), whereas the lack of *positive* emotion displayed fairly early predicted *later* divorce (13.9 years following marriage, on average).

Divorce is a difficult and complex process that "benefits some individuals, leads others to experience temporary decrements in well-being that improve over time, and forces others on a downward cycle from which they might never fully recover" (Amato, 2000, p. 1282). Though women and men are both affected by divorce, women particularly are affected by reduced income, additional child-care responsibilities, and so on. In terms of recovery from divorce, all the usual sensible self-care strategies apply (e.g., nutrition, sufficient rest, exercise, social support), and in addition, "Remarriage is one of the most positive actions a divorced person can take, since emotions, economics, and parenting are all likely to improve when one has a supportive partner" (Hendrick, 2004, p. 178). Due very likely to the complexities of remarriage, however, divorce rates are higher for remarriages than for first marriages.

Relationship loss is a profound experience, but it does not seem to deter women from reconnecting and forming new relationships.

CONCLUSIONS

Humans have a need to belong, to connect with one another, and this is especially true for women. Women and men are similar in how they become attracted to a partner, and they rely on similar characteristics (e.g., commitment) to deepen their relationships. Women, however, may be more sexually flexible in partner choice and may love a partner based more on the partner's personal characteristics and less on the partner's sex. Love and intimacy are important to women in many of their close relationships, not just their romantic ones, and communication is often an important vehicle for women's relating to others. Women, like men, suffer when a relationship is lost through breakup or divorce, and in fact women suffer disproportionately after divorce in terms of economic welfare. Yet women may achieve particular benefits from remarriage, due to greater equality between remarried partners.

For women who counsel other women—either formally or informally—it is imperative to understand and validate the need for connection, even when that connection must be limited or broken in order to ensure a woman's personal well-being. An abusive family of origin, a lifeless marriage, an adult child who is irresponsible and/or substance-abusing—all may need to be distanced or even relinquished, but not without some feelings of profound loss. And as old relationships are let go, the space will emerge in which new ones can be created. The need to belong will be stronger for some women than for others, of course; women are first individuals. But love, intimacy, and partnering will be central to the lives of most women and should be cherished.

REFERENCES

Altman, I., Vinsel, A., & Brown, B. B. (1981). Dialectic conceptions in social psychology: An application to social penetration and privacy regulation. In L. Berkowitz (Ed.), *Advances in experimental social psychology* (Vol. 14, pp. 107–160). New York: Academic Press.

Amato, P. R. (2000). The consequences of divorce for adults and children. *Journal of Marriage and the Family, 62,* 1269–1287.

Aron, E. N., & Aron, A. (1996). Love and expansion of the self: The state of the model. *Personal Relationships, 3,* 45–58.

Baumeister, R. F. (2000). Gender differences in erotic plasticity: The female sex drive as socially flexible and responsive. *Psychological Bulletin, 126,* 347–374.

Baumeister, R. F., & Leary, M. R. (1995). The need to belong: Desire for interpersonal attachments as a fundamental human motivation. *Psychological Bulletin, 117,* 497–529.

Bem, S. L. (1993). *The lenses of gender.* New Haven, CT: Yale University Press.

Blau, P. M. (1964). *Exchange and power in social life.* New York: John Wiley & Sons.

Boon, S. D. (1994). Dispelling doubt and uncertainty: Trust in romantic relationships. In S. Duck (Ed.), *Dynamics of relationships* (pp. 86–111). Thousand Oaks, CA: Sage.

Buss, D. M. (1988). Love acts: The evolutionary biology of love. In R. J. Sternberg & M. L. Barnes (Eds.), *The psychology of love* (pp. 100–117). New Haven, CT: Yale University Press.

Buss, D. M., & Barnes, M. (1986). Preferences in human mate selection. *Journal of Personality and Social Psychology, 50,* 559–570.

Byrne, D. (1969). Attitudes and attraction. In L. Berkowitz (Ed.), *Advances in experimental social psychology* (Vol. 4, pp. 35–89). New York: Academic Press.

Byrne, D. (1971). *The attraction paradigm.* New York: Academic Press.

Contreras, R., Hendrick, S. S., & Hendrick, C. (1996). Perspectives on marital love and satisfaction in Mexican American and Anglo couples. *Journal of Counseling and Development, 74,* 408–415.

Cupach, W. R., & Metts, S. (1991). Sexuality and communication in close relationships. In K. McKinney & S. Sprecher (Eds.), *Sexuality in close relationships* (pp. 93–110). Hillsdale, NJ: Erlbaum.

Davis, J. L., & Rusbult, C. E. (2001). Attitude alignment in close relationships. *Journal of Personality and Social Psychology, 81,* 65–84.

Derlega, V. J., Metts, S., Petronio, S., & Margulis, S. T. (1993). *Self-disclosure.* Newbury Park, CA: Sage.

Diamond, L. M. (2003). What does sexual orientation orient? A biobehavioral model distinguishing romantic love and sexual desire. *Psychological Review, 110,* 173–192.

Dindia, K. (1997). Self-disclosure, self-identity, and relationship development: A transactional/dialectical perspective. In S. Duck (Ed.), *Handbook of personal relationships: Theory, research and interventions* (2nd ed., pp. 411–426). New York: John Wiley & Sons.

Drigotas, S. M., Rusbult, C. E., & Verette, J. (1999). Level of commitment, mutuality of commitment, and couple well-being. *Personal Relationships, 6,* 389–409.

Duck, S. (1982). A topography of relationship disengagement and dissolution. In S. Duck (Ed.), *Personal relationships 4: Dissolving personal relationships* (pp. 1–30). New York: Academic Press.

Eagly, A. H., & Wood, W. (1999). The origins of sex differences in human behavior. *American Psychologist, 54,* 408–423.

Fehr, B. (1996). *Friendship processes.* Thousand Oaks, CA: Sage.

Felmlee, D. H. (1998). "Be careful what you wish for . . .": A quantitative and qualitative investigation of "fatal attractions." *Personal Relationships, 5,* 235–253.

Frazier, P. A., & Cook, S. W. (1993). Correlates of distress following heterosexual relationship dissolution. *Journal of Social and Personal Relationships, 10,* 5567.

Gaines, S. O., Jr., & Liu, J. H. (2000). Multicultural/multiracial relationships. In C. Hendrick & S. S. Hendrick (Eds.), *Close relationships: A sourcebook* (pp. 96–108). Thousand Oaks, CA: Sage.

Ganong, L. H., & Coleman, M. (2000). Remarried families. In C. Hendrick & S. S. Hendrick (Eds.),

Close relationships: A sourcebook (pp. 155–168). Thousand Oaks, CA: Sage.

Garcia, S. D., & Rivera, S. M. (1999). Perceptions of Hispanic and African-American couples at the friendship or engagement stage of a relationship. *Journal of Social and Personal Relationships, 16*, 65–86.

Gottman, J. (1994). *Why marriages succeed or fail.* New York: Simon & Schuster.

Gottman, J. M., & Levenson, R. W. (2000). The timing of divorce: Predicting when a couple will divorce over a 14-year period. *Journal of Marriage and the Family, 62*, 737–745.

Halford, W. K., Hahlweg, K., & Dunne, M. (1990). The cross-cultural consistency of marital communication associated with marital distress. *Journal of Marriage and the Family, 52*, 487–500.

Hatfield, E., & Sprecher, S. (1986). *Mirror, mirror . . . The importance of looks in everyday life.* Albany: SUNY Press.

Heider, F. (1958). *The psychology of interpersonal relations.* New York: John Wiley & Sons.

Hendrick, C., & Hendrick, S. S. (1986). A theory and method of love. *Journal of Personality and Social Psychology, 50*, 392–402.

Hendrick, C., Hendrick, S. S., & Dicke, A. (1998). The Love Attitudes Scale: Short Form. *Journal of Social and Personal Relationships, 15*, 147–159.

Hendrick, S. S. (2001). Intimacy and love. In J. Worell (Ed.), *Encyclopedia of women and gender* (Vol. 1, pp. 633–643). San Diego, CA: Academic Press.

Hendrick, S. S. (2004). *Understanding close relationships.* Boston: Allyn & Bacon.

Hendrick, S. S., & Hendrick, C. (1993). Lovers as friends. *Journal of Social and Personal Relationships, 10*, 459–466.

Hendrick, S. S., & Hendrick, C. (1995). Gender differences and similarities in sex and love. *Personal Relationships, 2*, 55–65.

Hendrick, S. S., Hendrick, C., & Adler, N. L. (1988). Romantic relationships: Love, satisfaction, and staying together. *Journal of Personality and Social Psychology, 54*, 980–988.

Huston, M., & Schwartz, P. (1995). The relationships of lesbians and of gay men. In J. T. Wood & S. Duck (Eds.), *Under-studied relationships: Off the beaten path* (pp. 89–121). Thousand Oaks, CA: Sage.

Huston, T. L., Caughlin, J. P., Houts, R. M., Smith, S. E., & George, L. J. (2001). The connubial crucible: Newlywed years as predictors of marital delight, distress, and divorce. *Journal of Personality and Social Psychology, 80*, 237–252.

Jankowiak, W. R., & Fischer, E. F. (1992). A cross-cultural perspective on romantic love. *Ethnology, 31*, 149–155.

Johnson, M. P., Caughlin, J. P., & Huston, T. L. (1999). The tripartite nature of marital commitment: Personal, moral, and structural reasons to stay married. *Journal of Marriage and the Family, 61*, 160–177.

Keeley, M. P., & Hart, A. J. (1994). Nonverbal behavior in dyadic interactions. In S. Duck (Ed.), *Dynamics of relationships* (pp. 135–162). Thousand Oaks, CA: Sage.

Laumann, E. O., Gagnon, J. H., Michael, R. T., & Michaels, S. (1994). *The social organization of sexuality: Sexual practices in the United States.* Chicago: University of Chicago Press.

Lee, J. A. (1973). *The colors of love: An exploration of the ways of loving.* Don Mills, Ontario, Canada: New Press.

Noller, P., & Venardos, C. (1986). Communication awareness in married couples. *Journal of Social and Personal Relationships, 3*, 31–42.

Peplau, L. A. (2001). Rethinking women's sexual orientation: An interdisciplinary, relationship focused approach. *Personal Relationships, 8*, 1–19.

Peplau, L. A., & Spaulding, L. R. (2000). The close relationships of lesbians, gay men, and bisexuals. In C. Hendrick & S. S. Hendrick (Eds.), *Close relationships: A sourcebook* (pp. 111–123). Thousand Oaks, CA: Sage.

Prager, K. J. (2000). Intimacy in personal relationships. In C. Hendrick & S. S. Hendrick (Eds.), *Close relationships: A sourcebook* (pp. 229–242). Thousand Oaks, CA: Sage.

Prager, K. J., & Buhrmester, D. (1998). Intimacy and need fulfillment in couple relationships. *Journal of Social and Personal Relationships, 15*, 435–469.

Ruvolo, A. P., & Veroff, J. (1997). For better or for worse: Real-ideal discrepancies and the marital well-being of newlyweds. *Journal of Social and Personal Relationships, 14*, 223–242.

Seltzer, J. A. (2000). Families formed outside of marriage. *Journal of Marriage and the Family, 62*, 1247–1268.

Sprecher, S., Felmlee, D., Metts, S., Fehr, B., & Vanni, D. (1998). Factors associated with distress following the breakup of a close relationship. *Journal of Social and Personal Relationships, 15*, 791–809.

Sprecher, S., & Regan, P. C. (1998). Passionate and companionate love in courting and young married couples. *Sociological Inquiry, 68*, 163–185.

Stacey, J., & Biblarz, T. J. (2003). (How) does the sexual orientation of parents matter? In C. Burack & J. J. Josephson (Eds.), *Fundamental differences: Feminists talk back to social conservatives* (pp. 27–64). Lanham, MD: Rowman & Littlefield.

Sternberg, R. J. (1986). A triangular theory of love. *Psychological Review, 93*, 119–135.

Teachman, J. D., Tedrow, L. M., & Crowder, K. D. (2000). The changing demography of America's families. *Journal of Marriage and the Family, 62*, 1234–1246.

Umana-Taylor, A. J., & Fine, M. A. (2003). Predicting commitment to wed among Hispanic and Anglo partners. *Journal of Marriage and Family, 65*, 117–139.

Vittengl, J. R., & Holt, C. S. (2000). Getting acquainted: The relationship of self-disclosure and social attraction to positive affect. *Journal of Social and Personal Relationships, 17*, 53–66.

LINDA J. BECKMAN

Women's Reproductive Health: Issues, Findings, and Controversies

In recent years health organizations, professionals, and policy makers have concurred that reproductive issues for women extend beyond fertility and pregnancy. The World Health Organization has defined reproductive health to include mental, physical, and social well-being in all areas involving the reproductive system including sexual health (Murphy, 2003). Thus, reproductive health issues for women are broadly defined to include fertility and infertility, contraception, abortion, unintended pregnancy, maternal mortality and morbidity, pregnancy loss, healthy sexual development, sexual satisfaction, sexually transmitted infections including HIV, depression and other psychological symptoms related to reproductive events, sexual abuse, physical violence from sexual partners, access to reproductive health services, and cultural and gender inequities that limit certain groups' reproductive health. Moreover, gender inequities including greater male control and decision-making power in intimate relationships may prevent women from exercising autonomy over sexual and reproductive events, thus limiting their reproductive rights and often compromising their reproductive health (Murphy, 2003).

Given the breadth of topics that are subsumed under the rubric of reproductive health, this chapter can discuss only a limited number. Selected topics include fertility and unintended pregnancy, contraception, abortion, infertility, and postpartum psychological health. These topics were chosen either because they are of concern to most women of childbearing age (e.g., contraception) or the rates are significant, they raise complicated ethical issues, and they affect the psychological well-being of women who experience them (e.g., infertility).

By far, most of the research on reproductive health focuses on physical and psychological problems. Therefore, it is important to acknowledge that most women desire to have children and identify childbearing as an important life goal. Adult women who desire children experience pregnancy and becoming a mother as rewarding and derive many important benefits from these life experiences. Women who freely choose a reproductive outcome generally express satisfaction with that choice and experience positive psychological health. Moreover, most women are resilient and cope successfully with stressful reproductive occurrences such as infertility or unwanted pregnancy.

UNINTENDED PREGNANCY

Close to half of all pregnancies in the United States and one third worldwide are unintended. (Henshaw, 1998). Despite declines in unintended pregnancy rates in recent years, the United States continues to have high pregnancy rates for both adolescent and adult women compared to most other Western industrialized nations. Most likely, these high rates are partially due to ambivalent attitudes toward sexuality.

Unintended pregnancies have a number of possible outcomes including a live birth, stillbirth, induced abortion, or miscarriage. Pregnancy, birth, and abortion rates differ among ethnic groups for both adolescent and adult women. For instance, African American women's rates of pregnancy, births, and abortion are higher than those among Whites. The most prevalent outcomes of pregnancy are a live birth or an induced abortion.

Unintended and Unwanted Births

Not all unintended births are unwanted. Some women who unintentionally get pregnant desire to have the child once they find out they are pregnant. Other pregnancies that are initially unwanted may become wanted if a woman's life circumstances change—for example, she and the father of the child wed, or she reassesses and rearranges her life options. Yet the birth of a child, whether the pregnancy was intended or unintended, wanted or unwanted, may affect women's psychological well-being. Major issues involve the psychological effects of unwanted births on women, whether motherhood is particularly difficult for adolescents, and mood disturbances that are prevalent in many women during the postpartum period.

Unwanted Births and Psychological Well-Being

It is surprising that there are so few studies of the effects of unwanted childbearing on the physical and psychological health of the mother. Studies of the possible consequences of unwanted births have primarily investigated the effects on mother-child interactions and infant health. Those that longitudinally assess the health of the mother provide moderate support for the contention that mothers with unwanted children have higher rates of depression and lower rates of psychological well-being. For instance, Barber and her colleagues, using data from a 31-year longitudinal survey of over 1,100 mother-child pairs, reported that mothers who experience unwanted births have lower happiness and higher depression scores than those who do not (Barber, Axinn, & Thornton, 1999).

Unwanted childbearing is thought to affect the child through its influence on the quality of mother-child relationships, both early in the child's life and from late adolescence through adulthood (Barber et al., 1999). There are no studies in the United States that examine the psychosocial consequences of being born unwanted. The most definitive study is the Prague study that followed 220 children born to women twice denied abortion and a similar number of pair-matched controls (David, Drytrch, & Matejcek, 2003). The psychosocial differences of the participants during childhood, adolescence, and adulthood were not great and varied over time, but the differences that did occur suggested that, despite similar intelligence and levels of health, the individuals born from an unwanted pregnancy consistently had more maladaptive behavior. This was characterized by indicators such as poorer school performance, more employment problems, more conflict with others, greater mental health problems, and fewer and less satisfying social relationships.

Effects of Unintended Births for Adolescent Mothers

Over 80% of pregnancies to women under age 18 in the United States are unintended (Henshaw, 1998). Therefore, most research that confronts the issues of teenage pregnancy and births fails to distinguish between consciously wanted and unwanted pregnancies, intended and unintended pregnancies. Pregnancy and birth rates are higher among African American and Hispanic/

Latina American teens than non-Hispanic/Latina White adolescents (Henshaw, 1997). Unintended pregnancy among adolescents has raised great concerns because of the presumed negative effects on the health, psychological well-being, and educational achievements of adolescent women and questions about their ability to adequately address the physical and emotional needs of the children that they bear. As Zabin and Cardona (2002) note, such effects *cannot* be presumed due to the pregnancy itself but rather are related to childbearing and parenting.

The effects of childbearing are believed greater for adolescent girls than adult women because the birth of a child can interfere with an adolescent's ability to complete developmental tasks, and it limits her social contacts with peers, thereby affecting psychological growth. Early parenthood can delay or limit women's educational achievement goals, resulting in lower socioeconomic status (Zabin & Cardona, 2002). Recent studies that have focused on adolescent mothers' environmental context suggest that family and community factors need to be considered in research on the consequences of adolescent childbearing and that perhaps the negative consequences of adolescent childbearing have been overstated (Hoffman, 1998). Nevertheless, concern about the negative outcomes of adolescent childbearing has led to a host of primary and secondary prevention programs emphasizing contraceptive use and/or sexual abstinence. Based on data suggesting possible causes of adolescent childbearing, programs have been developed that address peer and media pressure, teach life skills, promote sexual abstinence, and heighten future educational aspiration. Most of the primary prevention programs have not included rigorous evaluation. However, the most successful programs are multidimensional and programs need to be targeted toward specific communities (Zabin & Cardona, 2002).

Postpartum Mood Disturbance

Many women experience postpartum mood disturbances whether or not pregnancy is unintended or unwanted. Depressive symptoms experienced during the postpartum period range from mild "baby blues" to more serious disorders such as postpartum depression and postpartum psychosis. The "baby blues," which generally occur in the first 10 days after delivery, peaking about Day 4 and dissipating relatively rapidly, are extremely common, occurring in 30–75% of women (Nonacs & Cohen, 1998). This postpartum mood disturbance generally does not require treatment.

Although postpartum psychosis is extremely rare, postpartum depression occurs in 10–15% of women after birth (Nonacs & Cohen, 1998; Seyfried & Marcus, 2003). Because postpartum mood changes are common in women, postpartum depression often goes untreated, which can lead to declines in the health of both mother and infant and negatively influence child behavior and development (Nonacs & Cohen, 1998). Most recently, postnatal depression in women has been linked in longitudinal research with higher levels of preteen violent behavior in offspring (Hay, Pawlby, Angold, Harold, & Sharp, 2003). Effective treatments include both psychotropic drug and psychotherapeutic approaches (Seyfried & Marcus, 2003). Because many women breastfeed and the effects of antidepressant medication on infant development are not known, these medications often are not desired by lactating women (Nonacs & Cohen, 1998) and therefore may not be prescribed for them. A recent meta-analysis of predictors of postpartum depression found that unplanned/unwanted pregnancy was one of its several predictors (Beck, 2001). Prenatal depression, self-esteem, child-care stress, life stress, social support, and marital relationship were even stronger predictors. Other research suggests women at risk are those with previous episodes of major depression or other serious mood disorders. Also, lack of social support may lead to increased risk (Nonacs & Cohen, 1998).

Researchers do not agree about whether the "baby blues" are a mild form of postpartum depression or a qualitatively different phenomenon. Some suggest that mild negative affect and postpartum depression are opposite ends of a continuum of reactions involved in adjustment to motherhood (e.g., Lee, 1997). Parenthood, especially the birth of a first child, is a major life event that involves structural changes in life situation and major readjustments for most women. The recognition and meaning of their new status and the emotional and tangible support given to new mothers are dependent on culture. European American culture is characterized by individualism and geographic separation from family of origin; Hispanic/Latino culture is characterized by close family ties and intervention and help from other family members for the new mother; and African American culture emphasizes community interdependence and collective responsibility (Wile & Arechiga, 1999). In mainstream U.S. culture (i.e., European American culture), the cultural expectations of child care as the women's role and new parents as not wanting or needing much support, coupled with the reality that most women work outside the home and do not receive paid parenthood leave, may result in guilt, work overload, and depression in new mothers (Lee, 1997). Changes in gender roles (e.g., greater male involvement in child care, greater tangible social support from others) and employment practices (e.g., more flexible work schedules, feeding facilities in the workplace) could alleviate women's postpartum mood distress.

Abortion

Of all the issues involving women's reproductive health, abortion is the most controversial, volatile, and divisive, particularly in the United States. In the United States, close to half of unintended pregnancies terminate in an elective abortion, and it has been estimated that by age 45, 43% of all women will have had an abortion (Henshaw, 1998). Data on abortion attitudes and practices of different ethnic groups in the United States are limited. African American, Hispanic/Latina American, poor, and unmarried adolescent and adult women appear to have higher rates of abortion (Physicians for Reproductive Choice and Health [PRCH] and Alan Guttmacher Institute [AGI], 2003). Differences among ethnic groups in attitudes toward abortion and pregnancy termination behavior partially reflect differences in situational context, cultural and religious distinctions, and socioeconomic differentials. There also is considerable within-group variation in attitudes and opinions.

If abortion is so widely used, why does it provoke such great controversy? The most likely reason is that not only does abortion invoke moral values about the meaning and beginning of life but also abortion beliefs are closely linked with a constellation of deeply rooted values and beliefs about women's roles, sexuality, and parenthood. Luker's classic study (1984) found women who were pro-choice or pro-life activists had different life circumstances, goals, and worldviews, especially regarding gender roles, sexuality, and motherhood.

One important question involves the short- and long-term psychological consequences of abortion. The bulk of research evidence supports the conclusion that abortion has neutral or positive rather than negative psychological outcomes for most women (Bradshaw & Slade, 2003; Russo & Denious, 2000). Moreover, consequences appear fairly similar for adolescent and adult women (Adler, Smith, & Tschann, 1998). Women report significant levels of anxiety and other negative psychological states prior to the abortion; one review suggests that 40–45% experience high levels of anxiety and 20% experience high levels of depression (Bradshaw & Slade, 2003). Usually these negative emotional states are transitory, showing significant declines after abortion, although there is some controversy about how quickly this may occur (Bradshaw & Slade).

Most research on the outcomes of abortion is limited by relatively short-term follow-up, often a few months or less, and lack of comparison groups of women who continue their pregnancies. The few prospective studies of the longer term (up to 10 years) emotional sequelae of abortion that include compare groups have found minimal differences in the psychological outcomes of women who have abortions and women who give birth (Bradshaw & Slade, 2003). Adequate comparison studies require that baseline information on preexisting group differences in factors such as mental and emotional status, sociodemographic characteristics, and experiences of violence and abuse be taken into account. Analyses of longitudinal data sets (e.g., Russo & Dabul, 1997) generally confirm that abortion is not independently related to well-being once other variables are controlled. Rather, preexisting psychological well-being and contextual and childbearing factors are the key predictors of well-being among young women. Yet a few clinicians have postulated the existence of a "post abortion syndrome" (e.g., Rue & Speckard, 1992) somewhat similar to posttraumatic stress disorder (PTSD) and characterized by sadness, depression guilt, anger, and preoccupation with the aborted child. There is no methodologically sound empirical evidence to support such an assertion. Moreover, a handful of recent prospective analyses claiming to support abortion's negative effect on mental health have shown serious methodological flaws that make their conclusions questionable.

Despite the minimal negative long-term effects for most women who select to terminate pregnancies, a small minority of women experience negative psychological states of varying magnitudes after a legal abortion. These negative psychological outcomes appear related to pre-abortion characteristics of the women rather than to the abortion itself. Women who are more likely to experience psychological disorders postabortion are those who have preexisting psychological disorders or mental health problems, are ambivalent about the procedures, have strong religious values against abortion, lack social support, or experience conflict with their sexual partner or family about the decision.

In the United States, abortions primarily occur in freestanding clinics that are not integrated into other reproductive heath services. These freestanding clinics have often been sites of antiabortion picketing, harassment, and in some cases violence that may intimidate women, causing them distress (Cozzerelli & Major, 1998) and discouraging trained clinicians from providing abortion. Moreover, 84% of counties in the United States do not have an abortion provider. These conditions may make access difficult, particularly for women who are poor, young, or live in rural areas. In recent years, medical abortion, which involves administration of one or more drugs to induce evacuation of the uterus, has been publicized as a method to increase women's access to abortion. The most popular drug is mifepristone (marketed as RU-486 abroad and Mifeprex in the U.S.). This drug regimen is available in the United States from licensed physicians who sign a prescriber's agreement that specifies certain safeguards with the FDA.

Medical abortion expands the options available to women and is highly effective and safe for termination of early pregnancy. This abortion method may better fit the life circumstances of some women than surgical abortion. Women who elect to have or state they would prefer a medical abortion often mention fear of and desire to avoid surgery, taking a drug as a more natural and gentle process, and preference for a method that can be used early in pregnancy (Harvey, Sherman, Bird, & Warren, 2002). Although ready access to medical abortion is desirable for women, obstacles to its use exist. More widespread availability of this option for American women requires increasing the types of clinicians who legally can provide it, the number of physicians who provide the procedure, and the types of health settings in which abortions occur.

Contraception

The best way to reduce abortion and unintended pregnancy among sexually active women is through use of effective contraception (Deschner & Cohen, 2003), as evidenced by the decline in abortion rates in the United States, particularly since 1990. Women have a great variety of effective contraceptive options available to them today. A number of new methods, including the female condom, contraceptive ring, and contraceptive patch, are currently on the market (Severy & Newcomer, 2005). Other chemical and mechanical barrier methods, hormonal methods, immuno-contraceptives (e.g., a vaccine), and transcervical sterilization are on the horizon (Schwartz & Gabelnick, 2002). The development of methods that provide protection against both HIV/STDs and pregnancy is a particularly important need.

The large proportion of unintended pregnancies suggests that it is not enough for a contraceptive method to be efficacious; it also must be acceptable to its users, the woman and her sexual partner. No single method is acceptable to all users. Survey research suggests that women want and need methods that are congruent with their life circumstances (Schwartz & Gabelnick, 2002). Acceptability differs for the individual during different life phases and types of relationships. For instance, when a woman is in her 20s and has multiple partners she may need a different method than when she is in her 30s, married with children and in a monogamous relationship. A method must be used consistently and correctly over time to be effective. In addition, because unprotected sexual intercourse is now the single most common path of HIV transmission worldwide, and the most common route of male to female transmission, the use of dual methods or different products for different purposes also is important to consider. Past research highlights the importance of characteristics of the methods, sociocultural context, partner attitudes, and relationship factors on method acceptability (Severy & Newcomer, 2005).

Emergency Contraception

Emergency contraception pills (ECPs) are unique because they are used *after* rather than before or during intercourse. ECPs involve high doses of common oral hormonal contraceptives that are taken within 72 hours of unprotected intercourse. The method has been shown to be safe and effective (American College of Obstetrics & Gynecology [ACOG], 2003). Its use after an episode of unprotected intercourse reduces the risk of pregnancy by at least 75% (ACOG, 2003). ECPs act by one of three modes, depending on the timing of their use during the menstrual cycle. The most common actions appear to be to delay ovulation or prevent fertilization; prevention of implantation does not appear to be a primary mode (ACOG, 2003; Sherman, 2005). In fact, ECPs are not effective if used after implantation. ECPs frequently get confused with medical abortion in public discourse and the minds of women of childbearing age. Leading medical organizations and authorities state that a woman becomes pregnant only after a fertilized egg is implanted in her uterus. Thus, although most health providers believe ECPs are not a form of abortion, individuals who believe that life begins at the moment of fertilization consider ECPs to be abortion. Anti-abortion advocates who hold these beliefs have introduced bills to allow providers to refuse to prescribe ECPs and to require parental notification before minors can receive ECPs (Sherman, 2005).

A panel of experts for the U.S. Food and Drug Administration recently recommended that a progestin-only ECP (PlanB) be made available without prescription, an action supported by five major professional medical associations including the American Medical Association (Sherman, 2005). ECPs, especially if available without prescription at one's local drugstore, have the potential to reduce drastically the number of unintended pregnancies in the United States, some claim by as much as 50% (ACOG, 2003). Because of the potential negative psychological effects of unwanted pregnancies and births, use of ECPs can improve the psychological health of women. Moreover, they can be used to prevent pregnancy among victims of sexual assault. Surveys indicate that most health-care professionals are aware of ECPs and have positive attitudes toward their use; users also find them acceptable and report high levels of satisfaction (Sherman, 2005). Therefore, it is particularly important that this contraceptive method be made readily accessible to all women of childbearing age.

INFERTILITY

An estimated 11–15% of couples have infertility problems at some point during the woman's reproductive years (Burns & Covington, 1999; Centers for Disease Control [CDC], 2003). Although infertility rates have remained relatively stable for almost a century, the availability of various types of "high tech" infertility treatments has greatly increased during the last three decades (Burns & Covington, 1999). Most couples with infertility problems do not utilize these recent infertility treatments. However, these techniques exacerbate psychological stress, require couples to make complex decisions under conditions of uncertainty, and raise several ethical issues.

Assisted Reproductive Technology

Assisted reproductive technologies (ART) are methods of conception that manipulate eggs and sperm. The most common method of ART involves in vitro fertilization (IVF), used in over 70% of such procedures (Resolve of Minnesota, n.d.). In IVF, first drugs are used to stimulate egg production. Then eggs are surgically removed from a woman's ovaries, fertilized with sperm in the laboratory, and one or more of the resulting embryos are placed into woman's uterus (CDC, 2003). ARTs are expensive (averaging about $8,000–$10,000 per cycle [Resolve of Minnesota, n.d.]), time-consuming, involve multiple unpleasant physical procedures (e.g., drug injections), and are only modestly successful. About 23–25% of IVF treatment cycles are estimated to result in a live birth (CDC, 2003). IVF and other similar techniques often are not covered by insurance, although some insurers provide partial coverage and 13 states mandate some type of insurance coverage for infertility treatment (Resolve of Minnesota, n.d.). Still, access to ARTs may largely be limited to relatively affluent women, most of whom are non-Hispanic/Latina White women.

Culture affects couples' reactions to infertility and infertility treatment and can influence subsequent psychological well-being (Burns & Covington, 1999). Cultural groups differ in the stigma associated with childlessness, beliefs about the causes of childlessness and infertility, communication about medical and psychological problems, and attitudes toward technological medical interventions such as ARTs, as well as attitudes toward counseling. Also, they differ in their perceptions of male infertility and the significance of the male and/or female parent having a genetic link to the child.

The participation in ART treatment appears to have more profound effects on women's psychological health than the experience of infertility itself. The decisions necessary to attempt and then complete an ART cycle are complex and raise ethical considerations. These include how to deal with multiple fetuses and the selective reduction of multiple implanted embryos, what to tell a child who is the product of donor egg or sperm, and whether to disclose the identity or even the existence of egg or sperm donors to the resultant child or other family members. Both the number of unpleasant, sometimes painful procedures involved and the financial cost can heighten women's stress and anxiety levels (Abbey, 2000; Pasch & Christensen, 2000). Although research indicates that the vast majority of infertile women do not suffer from significant psychological maladjustment or trauma, treatment with ART adds many additional stressors that may decrease psychological well-being and increase psychological distress (Burns & Covington, 1999). Not surprisingly, some studies suggest that infertility is associated with negative psychological outcomes such as depression and lower self-esteem. It is generally accepted, however, that psychological problems related to infertility are consequences of the infertility rather than factors that play a role in its etiology (Burns & Covington, 1999). Methodologically rigorous research finds that the majority of infertile women do not suffer from negative reactions that are clinically significant—that is, psychological distress, relationship problems, or sexual difficulties that are severe (Stanton & Danoff-Burg, 1995). However, there is great diversity in the responses of infertile couples, and some do experience serious relationship difficulties. Psychological resources that may moderate the effects of stress associated with infertility and infertility treatment include perceived social support and perceived personal control and meaning (Abbey, 2000). Identification of these resources is important for healthcare professionals who counsel couples who use ARTs. Some authors provide detailed recommendations for professionals working with infertile couples (e.g., Pasch & Christensen, 2000).

Surrogacy

Surrogacy, also known as contractual parenting or third-party assisted reproduction, is a situation in which a woman agrees to carry a child to term for a couple. In the most common type of arrangement, traditional surrogacy, the surrogate mother (also known as the birth mother) is impregnated with the sperm of the intended father. In gestational carrier surrogacy, the fertilized egg (embryo) of the intended mother is implanted in the womb of the surrogate mother. In one case the surrogate is the genetic mother of the child she carries wherein the other case she is not.

Surrogate arrangements are often controversial and thus surrogacy arrangements remain relatively infrequent. Studies suggest that it is the least acceptable of all ARTs, particularly when money is paid to the birth mother (Ciccarelli & Beckman, 2005). Some people have been concerned about the potential for exploitation of poor women as surrogate mothers, yet the majority of surrogate mothers are White, married, have children of their own, and do not see money as a primary motivator. Their main motives are altruistic concerns and enjoyment of pregnancy. Despite the highly publicized court cases such as the Baby M case, most women are generally satisfied with their experiences as surrogates, although a minority report unmet expectations regarding the intended parents' relationship with them. Interestingly, the quality of the relationship with the intended parents appears the primary determinant of the surrogate's satisfaction with her experiences. Some surrogate mothers develop regrets over time about the experience as the child ages and their contact with the parents raising the child decreases. There are few studies of the intended parents who instigate a surrogacy arrangement, but the existing evidence shows they are of relatively high socioeconomic status and that the intended mother and the surrogate tend to bond while the intended father may experience awkwardness during contact with the surrogate (Ciccarelli & Beckman, 2005). Intended parents also have to cope with the ambiguity of their legal situation in some jurisdictions and the fear that something could jeopardize their relationship with the surrogate (Ciccarelli & Ciccarelli, 2005). Since a surrogacy arrangement is usually the last resort, these are couples who already have undergone the stress and uncertainty of other methods of infertility treatment.

Despite the obvious need for more data on the psychological health effects and issues involving surrogacy, the stigma surrounding this procedure and its limited acceptability within some cultures makes research difficult. Psychologists and other health professionals can make this anxiety-provoking relationship easier for all parties by providing accurate information to all about the processes involved, adequately screening both intended parents and surrogate mothers, and providing support to participants at all stages of the process (pre-pregnancy, pregnancy, postnatal and long term; Ciccarelli & Beckman, 2005). In addition, legislation that defines the rights and obligations of intended parents and gestational or traditional surrogates would help to improve the psychological well-being of women in both intended mothers and birth mothers (Ciccarelli & Ciccarelli, 2005).

CONCLUSIONS

Reproductive events offer a series of challenges for women's reproductive health. Women's options for limiting fertility, terminating unwanted pregnancies, and combating infertility are associated with choices or lack of choices that lead to short-term stress and anxiety for them, greatly improve their quality of life and psychological health, or in some cases have longer term negative psychological sequelae. This review has documented some of these outcomes, as well as their antecedent factors and confounding variables, while emphasizing the importance of the accessibility of acceptable reproductive options for *all* women.

REFERENCES

Abbey, A. (2000). Adjusting to infertility. In J. D. Harvey, & E. D. Miller (Eds.), *Loss and trauma: General and close relationship perspectives* (pp. 331–344). Ann Arbor, MI: Edwards Brothers.

Adler, N. E., Smith, L. B., & Tschann, J. M. (1998). Abortion among adolescents. In L. J. Beckman & S. M. Harvey (Eds.), *The new civil war: The psychology, culture and politics of abortion* (pp. 269–284). Washington, DC: American Psychological Association.

American College of Obstetrics and Gynecology. (2003, December 15). ACOG to testify before FDA in support of over-the-counter emergency contraception. Retrieved March 6, 2004, from http://www.acog.com/from_home/publications/press_releases/nr12-15-03.cfm

Barber, J. S., Axinn, W. G., & Thornton, A. (1999). Unwanted childbearing, health, and mother-child relationships. *Journal of Health and Social Behavior, 40,* 231–257.

Beck, C. T. (2001). Predictors of postpartum depression: An update. *Nursing Research, 50,* 275–285.

Bradshaw, Z., & Slade, P. (2003). The effects of induced abortion on emotional experiences and relationships: A critical review of the literature. *Clinical Psychology Review, 23,* 929–958.

Burns, L. M., & Covington, S. N. (1999). Psychology of infertility. In L. H. Burns & S. N. Covington (Eds.), *Infertility counseling* (pp. 3–25). Pearl River, NY: Parthenon.

Centers for Disease Control. (2003). 2000 Assisted Reproductive Technology success rates: Commonly asked questions about U.S. ART clinic reporting system. National Center for Chronic Disease and Prevention and Health Promotion. Retrieved May 20, 2003, from www.cdc.gov/nccdphp/drh/ART00/faq.htm

Ciccarelli, J., & Beckman, L. (2005). Navigating the rough waters: An overview of psychological aspects of surrogacy. *Journal of Social Issues, 61*, 21–43.

Ciccarelli, J., & Ciccarelli, J. (2005). The legal aspects of parental rights in assisted reproductive technology. *Journal of Social Issues, 61*, 127–137.

Cozzerelli, C., & Major, B. (1998). In L. J. Beckman & S. M. Harvey (Eds.), *The new civil war: The psychology, culture and politics of abortion* (pp. 25–60). Washington, DC: American Psychological Association.

David, H. P., Drytrch, Z., & Matejcek, Z. (2003). Born unwanted: Observation from the Prague study. *American Psychologist, 58*, 224–229.

Deschner, A., & Cohen, S. A. (2003). Contraceptive use is key to reducing abortion worldwide. *The Guttmacher Report on Public Policy, 6*(4), 2–7. Retrieved February 15, 2004, from www.futtmacher.org/pubs/journals/gr06047.html

Harvey, S. M., Sherman, S. A., Bird, S. T., & Warren, J. (2002). *Understanding medical abortion: Policy, politics and women's health* (Policy Matters Paper #3). Center for the Study of Women in Society, University of Oregon, Eugene.

Hay, D. F., Pawlby, S., Angold, A., Harold, G. T., & Sharp, D. (2003). Pathways to violence in the children of mothers who were depressed postpartum. *Developmental Psychology, 39*, 1083–1094.

Henshaw, S. K. (1997). Teenage abortion and pregnancy statistics by state, 1992. *Family Planning Perspectives, 29*, 115–122.

Henshaw, S. K. (1998). Unintended pregnancy in the United States. *Family Planning Perspectives, 30*, 24–29 & 46.

Hoffman, S. (1998). Teenage childbearing is not so bad after all . . . or is it?: A review of the literature. *Family Planning Perspectives, 30*, 236–239, 243.

Lee, C. (1997). Social context, depression and the transition to motherhood. *British Journal of Health Psychology, 2*, 93–108.

Luker, K. (1984). The war between the women. *Family Planning Perspectives, 16*, 105–110.

Murphy, E. M. (2003). Being born female is dangerous for your health. *American Psychologist, 58*, 205–210

Nonacs, R., & Cohen, L. S. (1998). Postpartum mood disorders: Diagnosis and treatment guidelines. *Journal of Clinical Psychiatry, 59*(Suppl. 2), 34–40.

Pasch, L. A., & Christensen, A. (2000). Couples facing fertility problems. In K. B. Schmaling & T. G. Sher (Eds.), *The psychology of couples and illness: Theory, research and practice* (pp. 241–267). Washington, DC: American Psychological Association.

Physicians for Reproductive Choice and Health & Alan Guttmacher Institute. (2003, January). An overview of abortion in the United States (PowerPoint presentation). Retrieved January 14, 2004, from http://www.agi-usa.org/sections/abortion.html

Resolve of Minnesota. (n.d.). Assisted reproductive technologies. Retrieved May 20, 2003, from www.resolvemn.org/art.htm

Rue, V., & Speckard, A. (1992). Post-abortion syndrome: An emerging public health concern. *Journal of Social Issues, 48*, 95–119.

Russo, N. F., & Dabul, A. J. (1997). The relationship of abortion to well-being: Do race and religion make a difference. *Professional Psychology: Research and Practice, 28*, 23–31.

Russo, N. F., & Denious, J. (2000). The socio-political context of abortion and its relationship to women's mental health. In J. Ussher (Ed.), *Women's health: Contemporary international perspectives* (pp. 431–439). London: British Psychological Society.

Schwartz, J. L., & Gabelnick, H. L. (2002). Current contraceptive research. *Perspectives on Sexual and Reproductive Health, 34*, 10–316.

Severy, L., & Newcomer, S. (2005). Critical issues in contraceptive and STI acceptability research: The impact of new technologies on intimate behavior. *Journal of Social Issues, 61*, 45–65.

Seyfried, L. S., & Marcus, S. M. (2003). Postpartum mood disorders. *International Review of Psychiatry, 15*, 231–241.

Sherman, C. (2005). Emergency contraception: The politics of post-coital contraception. *Journal of Social Issues, 61*, 139–157.

Stanton, A. L., & Danoff-Burg, S. (1995). Selected issues in women's reproductive health: Psychological perspectives. In A. L. Stanton & S. J. Gallant (Eds.), *The psychology of women's health* (pp. 87–108). Washington, DC: American Psychological Association.

Wile, J., & Arechiga, M. (1999). Sociocultural aspects of postpartum depression. In L. J. Miller (Ed.), *Postpartum mood disorders* (pp. 83–98). Washington, DC: American Psychiatry Press.

Zabin, L. S., & Cardona, K. M. (2002). Adolescent pregnancy. In G. Wingood & R. DiClemente (Eds.), *Handbook of women's sexual and reproductive health* (pp. 231–253). New York: Kluwer Academic/Plenum.

According to the 2000 U.S. Census, nearly one third of American women are raising children. However, each mother's experience is unique. More than two thirds of these women are in the labor force. Over one sixth of American women raising children head their households; over one third of these women live below the poverty level. Over 6 million of the women raising children are lesbians. Although motherhood is shared by many women, it is difficult to make accurate generalizations about their experiences. In addition, no woman resembles the romanticized notion of the ideal mother. This chapter offers a brief review of current research reflecting the themes of modern psychology's views of motherhood and the mixed messages to contemporary mothers.

THE SOCIAL CONSTRUCTION OF MOTHERHOOD

The construction of motherhood by modern psychological theories has provided an often unfair portrayal of mothers. Mothers have been simultaneously revered for their vital nurturance and blamed for their children's unsatisfactory well-being. The theories rarely address the psychological experience of motherhood (i.e., how it feels to be a mother) and have tended to focus on the needs of the child rather than on those of the mother. They have reinforced the motherhood mandate, arguing that women are fully developed only once they have borne children. Following brief overviews of developmental and psychoanalytic perspectives on motherhood, woman-centered perspectives are discussed as alternative frameworks. Then five issues regarding the myths surrounding motherhood are discussed, including the myth of choice; the role of fathers; mothers' experiences of guilt, ambivalence, and depression; stereotypes of "ideal" motherhood; and the purported qualities that make a "good" mother. Implications for clinicians are also included.

Developmental Perspectives

Historically, developmental psychologists have always focused on mothers; however, this focus

JOY K. RICE
and NICOLE ELSE-QUEST

The Mixed Messages of Motherhood

36

has typically been on the needs and welfare of the child. In the framework of classic developmental theory mothers are not endowed with unique identities and are seen principally as catalysts for child development. Attachment theory strongly influenced our ideas about the importance of early mothering for a child, proposing that infants must form an emotional attachment to their mother in order for subsequent emotional development to commence (Bowlby, 1969/1982). Early attachment theory held mothers solely responsible for their children's emotional development and assumed that mothers *know* how to foster their children's emotional development.

Contemporary to attachment theory was Harlow's (1974) nonhuman primate research, which revealed that physical contact between mother and infant was essential to rhesus monkey emotional development. Monkeys that were deprived of maternal contact were incapable of developing relationships with other monkeys. The research helped to reform child-care facilities and practices, and also bolstered the case that mothers per se were necessary and responsible for healthy emotional development. Harlow argued, "Nature has not only constructed women to produce babies, but has also prepared them from the outset to be mothers" (1974, p. 6). Arguments such as this have served primarily to reinforce traditional gender roles for both women and men.

In a similar vein, bonding theory emerged as an explanation for the roots of mothers' sensitivity to their children's needs. Klaus et al. (1972) proposed that hormonal processes present during childbirth prime the mother to bond with her newborn in early postpartum. If contact with the infant does not occur during this sensitive period, the mother is considered at risk for abusing or neglecting her child. Bonding theory implied that adequate maternal behavior is instinctive, not learned. Thus, biological mothers are presumed to be inherently ideal caregivers, particularly if they have contact with their newborns early in the postpartum.

Psychoanalytic Perspectives

The psychoanalytic tradition has discussed motherhood at great length, but the discussion has tended to reinforce sex roles and blame mothers. Freud (1949) viewed both maternal behavior and the meaning of the mother-child relationship as biologically based. He held the mother responsible for much of her child's later personality development. Psychoanalyst Helene Deutsch (1945) theorized that the feminine need for self-love is transferred to her child, and her willingness to endure pain and self-sacrifice exists now for the sake of her child. Deutsch placed a high value on motherhood as essential to women's psychological development. Such a view set the stage for psychological perspectives that assume adulthood for women is achieved only with motherhood.

Woman-Centered Perspectives

Chodorow's *The Reproduction of Mothering* (1978) maintains a psychoanalytic emphasis on the role of mothering and motherhood in psychological development. She contends that women mother (i.e., nurture and socialize children) because they are mothered by women, and that this cycle is fostered by a social structure that devalues women's labor. Daughters identify with their mothers and have a unique relationship with their mothers, and thus want to become mothers themselves. Sons, on the other hand, do not identify with their mothers and recognize that mothering, as women's labor, is devalued by their masculine society. They reject femininity and their ability to nurture never fully develops. Chodorow's theory influenced more woman-centered approaches to the study of motherhood.

Hrdy provides a perspective on motherhood that integrates feminist theory and sociobiology (1999). She argues that conceptualizations of the ideal mother as self-sacrificing, unconditionally loving, and devoting all energy to nurturing her children are inaccurate. Mothers have always needed to make choices that conflict with gender roles in order to ensure their own survival, sometimes at the cost of their children's welfare. In addition, mothers have always combined work and family, whether it entails foraging for food or commuting to the office, enlisting "alloparents" (i.e., friends, family, or other members of their community) for child-care help. This theoretical framework is unique in that it is woman-centered; moreover, mothers are neither blamed nor canonized.

Social cognitive theory is strikingly different from that of psychoanalytic or traditional developmental theories in that it emphasizes the interaction of environmental, cognitive, and behavioral factors, and allows for multiple processes to construct a woman's experience of motherhood (Bussey & Bandura, 1999). Among these is modeling, in which women learn the rules and patterns of maternal behavior. There are multiple sources available for modeling, including images in the mass media and one's own experiences and interactions. Unlike classic developmental or psychoanalytic theories, social cognitive theory contends that women *learn* to be mothers. The theory stipulates that mothers are not strictly confined by any particular experience or destined by their biology; there are individual differences in response. Our evolved biology makes it possible for us to become pregnant, birth, and lactate, but it does not govern our emotions or behavior.

Although traditional psychological theories on motherhood have focused primarily on the needs of the child, more recent theories have been woman-centered. Though the practice of mother-blaming is pervasive throughout traditional psychological theories, feminist theory has aimed to give credit to mothers' challenging work without idolizing them, recognizing that the existence of the ideal mother is a delusion. Nonetheless pervasive myths of mother persist. As clinicians and teachers, we can use woman-centered perspectives to help mothers examine, dispel, and even transform these myths into the experience of their own reality.

THE MYTH OF IDEALIZED MOTHERHOOD

The Myth of Choice

If you asked the average woman whether she had more choices about having children today than her mother or grandmother did, she would probably say yes. She might refer to the effects of improved contraceptive and fertility technology, the liberating force of the women's movement on attitudes about compulsory motherhood and reproductive rights, and the greater economic independence of women owing to workforce participation. More women today make choices to divorce, cohabit, parent alone, delay childbearing, have fewer children, or have no children. While census data do not distinguish between involuntary and voluntary childlessness, in two decades childless rates have almost doubled to 20% in 1995 (U.S. Bureau of the Census, 1997).

Yet in some ways these very "liberating" forces have paradoxically acted as further constraints for women deciding whether to become mothers. The media act to increase anxiety about "right" choices for timing, child care, parenting, fertility, and motivation. It tells women:

> Want to have a child? Well don't do it too early. Don't do it too late. Don't do it before you are settled. Don't have an abortion. Don't have an unwanted child. Don't be a single parent. Don't sponge off the State. Don't miss out on the joy of childbirth. Don't think you can do it alone. Don't let your children be reared by strangers. Don't be childless for selfish reasons. Don't have a child for selfish reasons. Don't end up in barren solitude. (Bennett, as cited in Letherby, 2002, p. 2791)

While more women are choosing to be childless, still others have no real choice, being infertile or involuntarily childless. These conditions garner more judgment than sympathy, are marginalized in the most literature, and are portrayed in terms of desperation and lack of choice (Letherby, 2002). Similarly with choices about timing and number of children, women today may feel no option but to delay motherhood if they want to have a career and job advancement. There is an increased trend toward later parenting, and births in the mother's thirties, and over-forties groups have more than doubled since 1970 in the United States. The opportunity costs of leaving the labor force to have a child and to parent also limit choice, as confirmed by the rapid increase in participation of women with young children and infants in the labor force. Three quarters of new mothers are back at work within a year of the birth (Barrow, 1999). Psychotherapists see more women, especially low-income women, complaining of a forced return to work, much earlier than they would choose. This trend is compounded by the welfare-to-work legislation of the last decade. Societal unwillingness to enact social policy for universal child care and flexible work arrangements also limits women's choices about combining motherhood with work. Motherhood is valued rhetorically (though in actuality possessing little social status nor economic reward), but nonmotherhood is still regarded as a lesser state. Pro-natalism is normative, and the voluntarily childless are still negatively stereotyped as selfish and less mature (Hird & Abshoff, 2000). Such norms also act to limit choice.

Finally one's "social location," in terms of cultural and ethnic cohort and social class, also significantly influences the way women experience mothering and their choices about mothering. The most obvious example is how cultural constraints and customs impact definitions of motherhood, and how poverty influences choice (or nonchoice) in birthing and mothering. Poverty is the context in which the great majority of instances of motherhood under 20 years of age occur. Low-income mothers from ethnic minority groups are less valued than are other mothers in Western societies, have less power, and are more subject to interventions by the state in family life and decisions (Seccombe, James, & Walters, 1998). Pro-life and pro-family legislation impacts the politics of choice in motherhood. Choice about motherhood for women, then, is relative, complex, multidetermined, and ongoing. Choice is also determined by ideology, economics, and social class, and is likely more related to these structural and societal factors than to individual factors (Hertz & Ferguson, 1996).

The Invisible Father

Pro-natalist attitudes and policies and recent cultural expectations all assume an increasing involvement of fathers in the traditional mothering, but myth abounds here as well. In reality, mothers continue to spend more time with children and do twice as much custodial care as fathers, even when mothers are in the paid labor force (Hofferth, 2003). Mothers also tend to perceive much less father involvement in *actual* parenting than fathers perceive, leading to more stress en-

gendered by discrepancies between ideal and actual levels of paternal involvement (Milkie, Bianchi, Mattingly, & Robinson, 2002). Fathers are more likely to be involved when the child is first born, male, a good student, and emotionally stable; when the relationship with the mother is good; and when the mother is more involved. Ethnic minority differences in parenting by fathers are not significant when controls are employed for family size, family structure, and employment (Hofferth, 2003).

In 2000, about 22% of children lived with single-parent mothers (America's Youth Census, 2002). Social policy and research repeatedly assert the importance of biological fathers and other male role models for children in both intact and single-mother families. Warmth and discipline from fathers is related to better academic achievement from children, and the provision of control by nonpaternal men is also related to reports of fewer school behavior problems and better behavior with peers (Coley, 1998). This research points to the potential positive outcomes of children's involvement with adult males in the family, nonpaternal as well as paternal. Ferrari (2002) finds that cultural factors and beliefs, as well as gender and ethnicity, are significantly related to the use of verbal and physical punishment by fathers. *Machismo* attitudes predict the use of physical punishment by fathers, but not by mothers. Thus father absence is not a negative solitary influence. The complex interaction of gender and cultural beliefs influence parental behavior and its results on children.

Guilt, Ambivalence, and Depression

With complex, contradictory messages about when, how, and whether to mother, and when, how, and whether to involve a father, it is not surprising that today's mothers often feel great ambivalence, guilt, and/or depression about their choices and behaviors. The mixed messages can lead to contradictory and conflicting expectations about behaviors. Opinion research consistently finds that continuously employed mothers are perceived as less committed to motherhood and more selfish than stay-at-home mothers (Gorman & Fritzsche, 2002). On the other hand, women with professional or graduate degrees who work part time or choose to stay home with children are criticized for wasting educational opportunities and not living up to their potential. Mothers are also continuously exposed to the contradictory messages of the child-care experts and developmental psychologists. They are told repeatedly that early attachment is critical, and the need for an intimate and continuous relationship with the *mother* is necessary for healthy development, but also reminded that a secure early childhood is not an insurance policy against later psychological damage. Another message, however, is that mothers need not fear, because children are extraordinarily resilient, and other people and experiences can significantly contribute to a child's security and long-term emotional health.

As clinicians and teachers we need to help women and mothers resolve and come to terms with contradictory cultural messages. The positive hallmarks of the motherhood experience, joy, pride, creativity, intense love, and satisfaction usually provide no problem for women. It is imperative, however, for clinicians to normalize the almost universal negative hallmarks that also accompany the motherhood experience: guilt and ambivalence and at the extreme, depression. There is also a need to help mothers in conflict to transcend the dualistic opposition of either children's or mother's needs. Traditionally, mothers have borne the responsibility for everything good and everything bad with children. Psychotherapists can help dispel these stereotyped perceptions by "expanding the context" for the client. This means helping clients understand how their guilt is not just caused by their individual behavior but is also influenced by the societal messages they have received about what it means to be a "good" mother. They can also note how creative thinking about parenting is characterized by the ambivalent melding of love and anger. This ambivalence is apparent in the common narrative themes of mothers of preadolescents and adolescents (Kurz, 2002; Seagram & Daniluk, 2002): sense of complete responsibility; sense of profound connection to their children; strong desire to positively impact on their children's development; fear of harm and strong desire to

protect and control freedom of movement; sense of depletion; and sense of guilt and inadequacy.

The uncertainty of children's long-term outcomes can intensify maternal ambivalence (Arendell, 2000). Thus the hallmark of ambivalence continues well into the mothering of adult children (Pillemer & Suitor, 2002). Problematic themes that mothers bring us that can be worked through in psychotherapy and counseling are: sense of conflict about adult children's independent lives and emotional distance; sense of failure about their adult children's nonconformance to maturational norms; conflict about how much to assist adult children; and simultaneous and continuous positive and negative feelings about adult children.

The Matrix of Tensions

A useful model of mothering for psychotherapy describes it as a "matrix of tensions" (Oberman & Josselson, 1996). In this model, mothers struggle to balance themselves between polar tensions that include several key developmental issues:

1. *Loss of self versus expansion of self.* This is the first and foremost developmental task stemming directly from the unique experience of another body growing *within one's own body.* From the recognition of that reality comes the gradual understanding that "you" who are "mine" are also different, new and outside of me. The act of mothering always represents both an expansion the self and the loss of self and is one of the most central dynamics of mothering.

2. *Experience of omnipotence versus liability.* Mother blaming and mother idealization are almost universal. Coming to terms with one's power over another vulnerable being, one's desire to execute power, and one's growing diminution of power and limited liability is a developmental challenge. Society's messages about being able to do it all, to be a "supermom," do not help, and many women are caught in internalized, unrealistic expectations of perfection about maintaining full-time careers as mothers and workers and

sometimes in addition, as caretakers of adult parents.

3. *Life creation and destruction.* Very few mothers will act out the anger and ambivalence they feel toward a child and, at the extreme, kill their child. Yet psychotherapists can help most mothers understand the polarities of intense love and murderous rage that a child's actions can engender, and can suggest cognitive behavioral strategies that invoke healthy separation, timeouts, limits, and consequences. About 50% of women will experience postpartum blues on a continuum of severity. In cases of postpartum nonpsychotic and psychotic depression, clinicians can be helpful in differential diagnosis, treatment, support, and referral for medication. It is also important to recognize the effects of culture on this diagnosis. Cultures with low levels of reported postpartum depression are characterized by strong social support, help, and special attention for new mothers (Miller, 2002).

4. *Cognitive versus intuitive parenting.* A tension between thinking and feeling, cognitive and emotional reacting to children, and balancing expert advice with one's gut feeling about a particular child is a sustaining theme of the mothering experience. Psychotherapists help mothers both to trust their intuitive responses and to be rational in their thoughts and behaviors regarding their children.

5. *Isolation versus community.* Most mothers and children do not function in isolation. Yet relationships with other mothers usually do not mitigate the loneliness that can exist in a day–to-day mother-child dyad. A theme of psychotherapy is coming to terms with this shifting equilibrium and expanding the maternal dyad to include other adults, children and experiences.

6. *Desexualization versus sexualization.* A woman's sexuality is expected to go underground during pregnancy, breast feeding, and early mothering, yet the early mother-child relationship is and should be erotic for the child and the mother, especially in breast feeding. Expressing and normalizing these feelings helps a woman recognize her sexuality and not split it from motherhood.

Shared and Shadow Mothering

Mothering is and has always been a shared experience in many cultures around the world and in some ethnic minority cultures in the United States (Hrdy, 1999). Of the nearly 21 million children under age 5 in 1995 in the United States, about 40% were cared for regularly by parents, 21% by other relatives, 31% in child-care centers, 14% in family day-care homes, and 4% by sitters in the child's home (Scarr, 1998). The last 30 years has seen a shift from home-based to center-based child care, but ethnic and cultural differences persist. African American women rely more on extended family for child care, White women more on neighbors and friends, and Hispanic women more on their partner or other children (Arendell, 2000).

The mandate of intensive mothering for dominant White middle-class culture in the United States flies in the face of women's need to work and to share mothering with child-care providers. How do women handle the stress of these conflicting mandates? How does one replace oneself when you have probably grown up believing that a mother is irreplaceable? Some mothers respond by becoming depressed. Across studies, depression levels are twice as high among employed women with young children who handle child care mostly alone and have difficulty in finding child care than among mothers who have sufficient resources (Arendell, 2000). Contemporary mothers also positively adjust to sharing the identity and the work of mothering in a variety of ways other than the more negative ones involving guilt, blame, and internalized depression. Often they compensate, deny, rationalize, and reframe their role and definition as "mother." Many compensate for absence from the children during work hours by increasing the amount of time they spend in intensive interaction with children during nonwork hours (Amato & Booth, 1997; Booth, Clarke-Stewart, Vandell, McCartney, & Owen, 2002). Women who try to be supermoms (having essentially two careers, one at home and one outside) maintain essentially the same views as at-home mothers in terms of their obligations for certain household tasks and child care. Employed mothers spend fewer hours doing household tasks, but perform the same amount and range of child-care tasks as at-home mothers. Instead of delegating these tasks or lowering expectations, they are more likely to reframe their attitudes to more positive interpretations of their situations (DeMeis & Perkins, 1996). By calling the day care a "learning environment," day care becomes an enrichment experience rather than a parenting substitute. Others "deskill" motherhood. These mothers break apart what was once a holistic pattern of practices into those that are presumed to be custodial and general (assigned to child-care personnel) and those that are individual and assumed to be indicative of quality care and more specifically unique to the role of the mother-child dyad. Deskilling motherhood has not been the crisis task for African American mothers, who historically have not questioned the legitimacy of necessary work outside the home or shared child care (Hertz & Ferguson, 1996).

Mothers also manufacture an image of shared mothering with paid child-care providers that helps to deny competitive roles, yet contradicts the actual day-to-day reality of the provision of affection and attachment by paid caregivers. The ideology of intensive mothering is maintained in the reality of shared parenting practice. Macdonald calls the work of such caregivers "shadow parenting." Their work is important, even critical, both in permitting maternal employment and in raising children, but they always must remain in the shadow of the mother's dominant role. This system also may involve social class and ethnic divisions as lower income and minority women provide the infrastructure of so-called menial mothering, maintaining majority women's investment in "spiritual" mothering (Macdonald, 1998). When mothers cannot ignore dominant and authoritative messages, they may employ some aspects, reject others, and even play a part in defining them (Letherby, 2002). They are not passive participants. They maintain a positive view of themselves as mothers by defining themselves as exceptional and others as less deserving or worse than themselves. Some young mothers on public assistance, for example, are able to include themselves in the "good mother" category by following conventional patterns in remaining at home with their young children and their parents, avoiding both shared child care and work outside the home.

Psychotherapists can help mothers with realistic appraisals and adjustments to shared mothering. It is important for women to realize that exclusive maternal care of infants and young children is a cultural myth of the idealized 1950s and that, until recently, child care for most North American children of working parents was shared, usually by other relatives. Other relevant information is the extensive research from several countries that shows that differences in child-care experience, both qualitative and quantitative, do not have persistent effects on children's development. Parents, through genetics and the environments they provide, are a far more powerful influence (Scarr, 1998). Nor do employed and at-home mothers differ in the quality of mother-infant interaction (Booth et al., 2002). Maternal education is a stronger predictor of maternal sensitivity than either child-care hours or quality (NICHD, 1999). Finally, developmental and clinical psychologists would also do well to consider the economic legitimacy of child care to serve the goal of maternal employment—in other words, child care for the good and need of the mother as well as for the welfare of the child. The job of the psychotherapist is (a) to help mothers understand the social-cultural context with its mixed messages that so strongly influence the internalized pressures and expectations they feel; (b) to differentiate those often confusing messages from their own expectations; and (c) to revise their internalized expectations to more rational and personally satisfying compromises.

CONCEPTIONS OF IDEAL MOTHERHOOD

While intensive mothering remains the dominant ideology, and married heterosexual employed mothers find and manufacture strategies to preserve the image of intensive mothering, other mothers are subjects of negative stereotypes of ideal motherhood. Single mothers, low-income minority mothers, divorced mothers, and lesbian mothers become the targets of criticism and censure. The first common denominator they share is the lack of a provider/partner/spouse; the second is often poverty.

Poverty and Single Motherhood

Minority and poorly educated women are over-represented among never-married mothers, contributing to popular stereotypes of single mothers of color dependent on public assistance. Single mothers' ability to parent consistently and firmly can be affected by the amount and kind of social support they receive from other adults (Coley, 1998). Concern for children's safety and efficacy in doing so is directly affected by the supports and safety of the neighborhood, and some African American mothers report that they cannot trust the police to help support them (Kurz, 2002). Poor mothers and mothers on public assistance are also less likely to obtain the support of high-quality child care. In the United States, there is a steadily evolving two-tier system of higher quality child care for more affluent parents and a lower quality one for middle and lower income parents (Scarr, 1998).

Financial stress emerges as a key variable in the parenting success of low-income African American mothers with serious mental illness. Oyserman and her associates (2002) found that mothers who were better off financially and had more education reported higher levels of mental health and more positive parenting attitudes and behaviors, leading them to conclude that poverty is the starting point for many of the difficulties these mothers face. Politicians, however, may point to the lack of marriage and, some psychologists, to a diagnosis of mental illness.

The Mother Hierarchy

Just as economics is a bottom-line variable in the emotional well-being of poor single mothers, economic self-sufficiency is the critical characterization of their opposite, the SMC, or single mothers by choice. SMCs are a small group of mothers who are, for the most part, middle to upper middle class, older, well-employed and educated, politically aware and dedicated to motherhood, having carefully made the decision to become a SMC (Mannis, 1999). Because of these characteristics, they argue for their place in the circle of mothers who earn praise. Thus we can see a fairly well developed "mother hierarchy" in

the United States closely related to the degree of deviancy from the mother ideal: married, heterosexual, White, employed, middle class. According to the presence of these factors, the social status lineup of mothers might look like this: (a) married mothers; (b) divorced employed mothers (a father is still presumed around); (c) single parent mothers by choice (educated, affluent); (d) single parent employed White mothers (not on welfare); (e) single ethnic minority mothers on public assistance; (f) lesbian mothers.

Where stepmothers fit into this hierarchy is unclear, but they, too, are faced with societal prejudice and stereotypes about their role as legitimate mothers. Note that the most prejudice and criticism of departure from the dominant motherhood ideology is reserved for lesbian mothers who openly challenge the religious and state-mandated policies of heterosexual marriage and family life. Research finds that children of lesbian parents fare as well or better on a variety of adjustment measures as children in intact heterosexual families. Lesbian parents and children have been found to be characterized by less sex role–stereotyped attitudes and behaviors (Flaks, Fisher, Masterpasqua, & Joseph, 1995). Yet the extreme bias against these families and lesbian mothers remains. Their greatest challenge is facing the enormous societal stigma and remaining grounded and confident in the face of prejudice and rejection (Rice, 2001).

The Deficit Comparison Model

While divorced mothers do not generally experience the kind of extreme stigma of the single poor mother, the teenage mother, or the lesbian mother, they still must navigate the continual messages of deficit parenting. Deficit parenting is characterized by negative comparative terms like "broken home" and "fatherless" children. At best, divorced motherhood is regarded as a transitory deviant state, ending when the mother remarries. This deficit comparison model is also applied to African American female–headed families and lone mothers (Rice, 1994). Part of why divorce is seen as so threatening to pro-marriage factions, political and religious, is that when women choose to leave a marriage, they choose a form of resistance to patriarchy, abuse, and dominance in marriage. Divorce becomes a form of resistance by women and mothers and is thus punished economically with women bearing the brunt of lesser incomes, lack of child support, and the often sole burden of providing for their children (Rice, 2003). On the average, economic well-being declines for mothers by 36% and improves for fathers 28% after divorce (Bianchi, Subaiya, & Kahn, 1999).

Not surprisingly, the child-rearing effectiveness of divorced mothers is related to mothers' education, financial stability, and social support. Adjustment among custodial mothers is also related to the difficulty in finding child care, to the number of children and if they have behavior problems, and to continuing discord with the former spouse. The introduction of a stable new partner, however, can have beneficial effects in other areas of postdivorce adjustment (Amato, 2000). While the divorce literature has been critical of mothers' emotional reliance on children, other data suggest that this can also lead to a sense of equality, closeness, and friend status in the relationships with their children, especially as they grow older (Arditti, 1999). Clinicians, then, need to balance the deficit/disaster model of divorce with the opportunity for enrichment and personal development in their women clients. A shift away from a framework of pathology and deficit comparison helps psychotherapists to support the unique strengths of these families, as well as to recognize their special challenges.

CONCLUSIONS

In this chapter we have discussed how discrepancies are prevalent between the ideologies of mothering and motherhood and the actual experiences of real women; how myths of choice are co-opted by scientific and medical experts, economic constraints, and pro-natalist policies; and how women themselves are redefining what it means to be a mother in today's modern world. What does it take to be a "good" mother? First, it is important to note that mothering carries multiple and often shifting meanings. A large body of research documents that mothering practices differ across historical eras and in ethnic, cul-

tural, and socioeconomic groups. For example, among African Americans, authoritarian and "no nonsense" parenting strategies are correlated with positive child outcomes (Hill & Bush, 2001). While there is no unitary standard or experience of good motherhood, few would disagree that the quality of emotional care offered to children in their early years has important consequences for later development. Mothers who have experienced neglect or abuse, who lack general knowledge, or who have unmanageable stress or psychological dysfunction, may be at higher risk of problematic parenting than other mothers in more fortunate circumstances (Mowbray, Oyserman, Bybee, & MacFarlane, 2002; Oyserman et al., 2002).

Contemporary mothering involves extensive, continuous emotional work. Feelings constantly change as children change, and a mother's emotions may vary not only within the course of a day but also over time and according to her given level of support and resources. A critical component is her ability to deal with ambivalence, changing feelings, and contradictory emotions. There are dialectic tensions inherent in an asymmetrical relationship in which one gives so much yet is never sure of the outcome or reward. As noted previously, there is an inevitable conflict in mothering between desiring both autonomy and dependence for the child. The essence of the paradox is that each person maintains early desires for a mother who is a need-satisfying other, but also desires to be in control of one's life. This tension surfaces very early in any mother-child dyad and is the overarching theme that extends to parenting adult children. Fortunately, it is becoming easier for women to discuss the "unacceptable" side of mothering, including the conflicting emotions of anger, sadness, and relief, to normalize ambivalence and sometimes negativity.

We do know that certain behaviors are constantly associated with the demands of the motherhood experience: managing/monitoring, caretaking, and nurturing. How well a particular woman is able to satisfy these demands, on herself and for her child, may depend also on maternal personality and the capacity for empathy. Maternal empathic capacity has been found to be negatively related to child neglect, whereas depressive symptoms have not. This implies that stable trait markers, rather than transient mood states, are more predictive of good or bad parenting. The capacity for empathy or emotional insight is a key component of what has been termed "emotional intelligence" (Shahar, 2001). The capacity for empathy implies an ability to tune in to another person, to read changing cues and feedback in a dyadic exchange. The mutual mother-infant and mother-child "dance" has been called by various terms as contingency, attunement, emotional availability, reciprocity, or mutuality (Barnard & Martell, 1995). The underlying composite personality trait here seems to be an *empathic capacity* that can transcend individual circumstances and situations.

It is easy to understand that empathic ability would affect success in fine-tuning solutions to the inherent tensions of mothering—for example, constant monitoring—but also assisting self-regulatory behavior and freedom. Empathy, after all, is a key capacity for human development in general. Since achieving better empathic skills in the client is a usual goal of most psychotherapy, psychotherapists can indirectly promote better mothering and the needs of the child. The thrust of this chapter, however, also strongly encourages psychotherapists to consider the needs of mothers. If women can understand the inevitable conflicts and myths of motherhood, they are better able to extend empathy to themselves as mothers. Such empathy can lead to a greater sense of acceptance and compassion for the dialectic tension and ambivalence in this most maligned and revered of all life's roles.

REFERENCES

Amato, P. R. (2000). The consequences of divorce for adults and children. *Journal of Marriage and Family, 62,* 1269–1287.

Amato, P. R., & Booth, A. (1997). *A generation at risk: Growing up in an era of family upheaval.* Cambridge, MA: Harvard University Press.

America's Youth Census. (2002, October). *Youth Today, 11,* 18.

Arditti, J. A. (1999). Rethinking relationships between divorced mothers and their children: Capitalizing on family strengths. *Family Relations, 48,* 109–119.

Arendell, T. (2000). Conceiving and investigating motherhood: The decade's scholarship. *Journal of Marriage and Family, 62,* 1192–1207.

Barnard, K. E., & Martell, L. K. (1995). Mothering. In M. H. Bornstein (Ed.), *Handbook of parenting, Vol. 3: Status and social conditions of parenting* (pp. 3–25). Hillsdale, NJ: Erlbaum.

Barrow, L. (1999). Child care costs and the return-to-work decisions of new mothers. *Economic Perspectives, 23,* 42–55.

Bianchi, S. M., Subaiya, L., & Kahn, J. R. (1999). The gender gap in the economic well-being of nonresident fathers and custodial mothers. *Demography, 36,* 195–203.

Booth, C. L., Clarke-Stewart, K. A., Vandell, D. L., McCartney, K., & Owen, M. T. (2002). Child-care usage and mother-infant "quality time." *Journal of Marriage and Family, 64,* 16–26.

Bowlby, J. (1969/1982). *Attachment.* New York: Basic Books.

Bussey, K., & Bandura, A. (1999). Social cognitive theory of gender development and differentiation. *Psychological Review, 106,* 676–713.

Chodorow, N. J. (1978). *The reproduction of mothering.* Berkeley: University of California Press.

Coley, R. L. (1998). Children's socialization experiences and functioning in single-mother households: The importance of fathers and other men. *Child Development, 69,* 219–230.

DeMeis, D. K., & Perkins, H. W. (1996). "Supermoms" of the nineties: Homemaker and employed mothers' performance and perceptions of the motherhood role. *Journal of Family Issues, 17,* 777–792.

Deutsch, H. (1945). *The psychology of women.* New York: Grune & Stratton.

Ferrari, A. M. (2002). The impact of culture upon child rearing practices and definitions of maltreatment. *Child Abuse & Neglect, 26,* 793–813.

Flaks, D. K., Fisher, I., Masterpasqua, F., & Joseph, G. (1995). Lesbians choosing motherhood: A comparative study of lesbian and heterosexual parents and their children. *Developmental Psychology, 31,* 105–114.

Freud, S. (1949). *An outline of psychoanalysis.* New York: Norton.

Gorman, K. A., & Fritzsche, B. A. (2002). The good mother stereotype: Stay at home (or wish that you did!). *Journal of Applied Social Psychology, 32,* 2190–2201.

Harlow, H. F. (1974). *Learning to love.* New York: Aronson.

Hertz, R., & Ferguson, F. I. T. (1996). Childcare choice and constraints in the United States: Social class, race and the influence of family views. *Journal of Comparative Family Studies, 27,* 249–280.

Hill, N. E., & Bush, K. R. (2001). Relationships between parenting environment and children's mental health among African American and European American mothers and children. *Journal of Marriage and Family, 63,* 954–966.

Hird, M. J., & Abshoff, K. (2000). Women without children: A contradiction in terms? *Journal of Comparative Family Studies, 31,* 347–366.

Hofferth, S. L. (2003). Race/ethnic differences in father involvement in two-parent families: Culture, context, or economy? *Journal of Family Issues, 24,* 185–216.

Hrdy, S. B. (1999). *Mother nature: Maternal instincts and how they shape the human species.* New York: Ballantine.

Klaus, M., Jerauld, R., Kreger, N. C., McAlpine, W., Steffa, M., & Kennell, J. H. (1972). Maternal attachment: Importance of the first postpartum days. *New England Journal of Medicine, 286,* 460–463.

Kurz, D. (2002). Caring for teenage children. *Journal of Family Issues, 23,* 748–767.

Letherby, G. (2002). Challenging dominant discourses: Identity and change and the experience of "infertility" and "voluntary childlessness." *Journal of Gender Studies, 11,* 278–288.

Macdonald, C. L. (1998). Manufacturing motherhood: The shadow work of nannies and au pairs. *Qualitative Sociology, 21,* 25–53.

Mannis, V. S. (1999). Single mothers by choice. *Family Relations, 48,* 121–128.

Milkie, M. A., Bianchi, S. M., Mattingly, M. J., & Robinson, J. P. (2002). Gendered division of childrearing: Ideals, realities and relationship to parental well-being. *Sex Roles, 47,* 21–38.

Miller, L. J. (2002). Postpartum depression. *Journal of the American Medical Association, 187,* 762–765.

Mowbray, C., Oyserman, D., Bybee, D., & MacFarlane, P. (2002). Parenting of mothers with a serious mental illness: Differential effects of diagnosis, clinical history, and other mental health variables. *Social Work Research, 26,* 225–240.

NICHD Early Child Care Research Network. (1999). Child care and mother-child interaction in the first 3 years of life. *Developmental Psychology, 35,* 1399–1413.

Oberman, Y., & Josselson, R. (1996). Matrix of tensions: A model of mothering. *Psychology of Women Quarterly, 20,* 341–359.

Oyserman, D., Bybee, D., Mowbray, C. T., & MacFarlane, P. (2002). Positive parenting among African American mothers with a serious mental illness. *Journal of Marriage and Family, 64,* 65–77.

Pillemer, K., & Suitor, J. J. (2002). Explaining mothers' ambivalence toward their adult children. *Journal of Marriage and Family, 64,* 602–613.

Rice, J. K. (1994). Reconsidering research on divorce, family life cycle, and the meaning of family. *Psychology of Women Quarterly, 18*(4), 559–584.

Rice, J. K. (2001). Family roles and patterns: Contemporary trends. In J. Worell (Ed.), *Encyclopedia of women and gender* (Vol. 1, pp. 411–424). San Diego, CA: Academic Press.

Rice, J. K. (2003). I can't go back: Divorce as resistance. In L. Silverstein and T. Goodrich (Eds.), *Feminist family therapy: Empowerment in social context.* Washington, DC: American Psychological Association, 2003.

Scarr, S. (1998). American child care today. *American Psychologist, 53,* 95–108.

Seagram, S., & Daniluk, J. C. (2002). "It goes with the territory": The meaning and experience of maternal guilt for mothers of preadolescent children. *Women & Therapy, 25,* 61–88.

Seccombe, K., James, D., & Walters, K. B. (1998). "They think you ain't much of nothing": The social construction of the welfare mother. *Journal of Marriage and Family, 60,* 849–865.

Shahar, G. (2001). Maternal personality and distress as predictors of child neglect. *Journal of Research in Personality, 35,* 537–545.

U.S. Bureau of the Census. (1997). *Statistical abstract of the United States: 1997.* Washington, DC: U.S. Government Printing Office.

FAYE J. CROSBY
and LAURA SABATTINI

Family and Work Balance

37

In years gone by, the problem of balancing work and family was thought to be a women's issue. We now know better. Men live in families, too. And the welfare of families is not simply a matter of concern for individuals. Balancing paid and domestic work is a social issue.

According to U.S. Census statistics, in 2001 approximately 57% of women (across ethnic groups) were working full time outside the home and about 23% worked part time (U.S. Bureau of Labor Statistics, 2002, 2003). The trend toward increased labor force participation is particularly dramatic among mothers. That same year, 78.7% of single and 69.6% of married mothers with children under 18 years of age were employed (U.S. Bureau of Labor Statistics, 2002). Among mothers of infants, Black women have the highest labor force participation rate (66% in 2000), followed by White and Asian American women (57%) and Hispanic women (Latinas) (42%; U.S. Census Bureau, 2000). Approximately 53% of all American mothers return to the labor force within six months following the birth of their first child (Haley, Perry-Jenkins, & Armenia, 2001).

Earnings of employed women have increased slowly. Census Bureau statistics report that median earning levels for women who work full time rose 3.5% from $28,227 in 2001 to $29,215 in 2002 (men's median income that year was $38,275; *Boston Globe*, 2003). College-educated women, who are ever more numerous, have been the primary beneficiaries of the increase. Meanwhile, men's real wages have declined in recent decades so that the gap between women's and men's earnings has narrowed (*Boston Globe*, 2003).

As a consequence of the increasing number of women working outside the home, the percentage of dual-earner families in the United States has grown considerably in recent decades. In 1992, the percentage of married couples where the husbands could be labeled as breadwinners (i.e., who earned at least 70% of the family income) made up only 42% of White and 33% of Black families (Steil, 2001). By 2001, and across ethnic groups, the number of married couples where both partners are employed full time was 53.7%, while families where only the husband is employed characterized 19.4% of married couples (U.S. Bureau of Labor Statistics, 2002). Also, between 1947 and 1997, married women's employment contributed to a 150% increase in the median income of dual-earner couples (U.S. Census Bureau, 1998).

In spite of increased workforce participation, women still contribute the lion's share of household and child-care labor (Hochschild & Machung, 1989; Mikula, 1998; Steil, 1997, 2000). Among married couples in the United States, 70% of wives are still in charge of most of the laundry, cooking, shopping, and child care, while the relative size of husbands' contribution is between 20 and 35%. While fathers and mothers tend to spend a similar amount of time playing with the children, women do 80% of the routine and time-consuming activities and 90% of the planning, supervising, and scheduling of child-care tasks (Coltrane, 1996; Steil, 2000).

Men tend to spend less time performing sporadic household tasks as well. Sociologist Scott Coltrane (1996) reports that married women do on average two thirds more of the routine, daily work than their male partners (an average of 32 vs. 10 hours per week), while married men do on average little less than twice as much the occasional household task (e.g., mowing the lawn, household repairs, and so on) than the average married woman (an average of 10 vs. 6 hours per week). Finally, women are more likely to be in charge of the emotional work and caregiving within the family, including taking care of children and elderly parents or relatives, adding up to an extra week on their monthly workload (Gerstel & McGonagle, 1999). Accordingly, married women report spending less time doing leisure activities than married employed men, especially when they have young children (Thrane, 2000). What women have experienced is role expansion rather than role redefinition (Crosby, 1991).

THE DIVISION OF FAMILY WORK

Given women's entry into the paid labor market, some social scientists have wondered how women feel about continuing asymmetries in domestic responsibilities. Most women appear rather content to carry a disproportionate burden of family responsibilities. Only about 30% of married women typically report that they consider the division of work within their fam-ily unfair, whether or not they work outside the home (Major, 1994; Mikula, 1998). The finding has led psychologist Janice Steil (2000) to wonder about "the paradox of the contented wife."

Ideologies

People tend to interpret their worlds through the lenses of ideology. And one reason for women's contentment concerns unspoken but prevalent ideologies. Often the disadvantaged subscribe to the status quo as fervently as do the privileged (Jost, Pelham, Sheldon, & Sullivan, 2003). When the prevalent ideology excuses gender imbalances in the home or sees them as natural, perhaps even as laudatory, it is hardly surprising that women accept as unproblematic the fact that they, in the words of Hochschild and Machung (1989), work "a second shift" while their husbands do not.

Data show that, in the United States, ideologies are changing. Attitudes about gender and family roles—considered in the abstract—appear to have become more egalitarian in the last couple of decades (Steil, 2000, 2001). In a 1996 national survey, for example, 85% of respondents said that it is desirable for both spouses to contribute to the family income, and 67% believed that dual-earner spouses should share the housework (Steil, 2000). Typically, women are more likely to endorse egalitarian beliefs than men; among women, surveys also indicate that Latinas tend to hold more traditional gender beliefs than White and Black women (Steil, 2001).

Other data speak to the persistence of traditional ideologies, usually held outside of conscious awareness. Examination of both public discourses and private conversations shows that, to a considerable extent, home is still seen as the natural province of women and work the natural province of men (Cabrera, Tamis-LeMonda, Bradley, Hofferth, & Lamb, 2000; Pasquera, 1993; Steil, 2000). While many Americans agree that women, including mothers, ought to contribute to the family's income, people tend to express more ambivalence in terms of the role that fathers should assume within the family (Coltrane & Adams, 2001). Society's ideological assumptions result in men being praised when they contribute to household work and in women's earnings being seen as supplementary to men's (Barnett, 1997). And both genders tend to take for granted that women should do the caregiving tasks (Gerstel & McGonagle, 1999).

Steil (2000) draws our attention to the circular nature of economic reality and social ideology. Women's limited access to good jobs may increase married women's financial dependence on their husbands, and thus decrease their sense of deservingness in terms of family work. Women's restricted sense of entitlement then hampers them from pushing for changes that could enlarge their financial and emotional independence. The gender gap in earnings makes it easy to justify a division of labor in the early years of family living when young couples struggle to pay for new expenses (Becker & Moen, 1999; Hochschild & Machung, 1989). Deutsch (2001) notes that "the key decisions parents made about employment when they first had children may have had long term effect on their earning potential and their place in the labor force" (p. 27). Men and women often claim that their work and family arrangements are inevitable, owing to the salary and time demand of each partner's job.

Social comparisons also help reality and ideology reinforce each other. Social justice theories maintain that people's sense of entitlement is largely defined through processes of social comparison and that we tend to compare with others who are assumed to be similar to us on the dimension under evaluation (Crosby, 1982; Major, 1994). Women tend to compare their own situations to the situations of other women (Zanna, Crosby, & Lowenstein, 1986), including their mothers (Silberstein, 1992). Thus, many women feel that they are, at least, better off than their mothers. Men, meanwhile, tend to see themselves as more involved in domestic life than their fathers (Silberstein, 1992).

Against All Odds

Hemmed in by unanalyzed ambient ideologies and by structural factors, individual couples face many obstacles to renegotiating traditional roles. Just how couples deal with those obstacles has been the focus of sociological and psychological inquiry. Several studies have looked closely at

what couples do when persistent gender imbalances clash with egalitarian desires.

One common strategy is to redefine behaviors to make them appear more egalitarian than they are. Both women and men often actively reinterpret their arrangements to make them appear fair and legitimate (Major, 1994; Zvonkovic, Greaves, Schmiege, & Hall, 1996). Hochschild and Machung (1989) documented how dual-earner couples ignored imbalances in the division of household labor when, for example, his "half" involved walking the dog and washing the car while her "half" included all other tasks. Couples also used personal preferences (e.g., "I like to cook") to justify imbalanced divisions of labor. Similarly, in interviews of White married couples, Dryden (1999) observed that most women could make the connection between gender inequality and the institution of marriage in general, but were reluctant to see the same link within the context of their own relationships.

Interested in how negotiation and other decision-making processes can help maintain conventional family roles, Becker and Moen (1999) conducted in-depth interviews with 117 middle-class men and women in dual-earner couples living in upstate New York. Becker and Moen found that families actively constructed their environment using a number of cognitive and behavioral strategies. For example, men and women would sometimes "place limits" by selecting a less demanding job over a more demanding one from the very beginning, or "scale-back" in their already established careers (in essence, one way or the other, choosing "the mommy track"). Some couples would consciously decide to "trade off," so that they would focus on one partner's career first and on the other's at a later time. Seventy-five percent of the couples interviewed used at least one of the strategies in the course of their relationship. Paradoxically, while participants often claimed that the strategies helped them maintain a sense of being in an egalitarian relationship, the ways in which the strategies were utilized often reproduced traditional gender dynamics.

Another strategy for bringing behavior and ideology into alignment is to press for changes in behavior that accord with contemporary equalitarian views. In a study of 128 dual-earner couples with young children conducted in the

Netherlands, Kluwer, Heesink, & Van de Vliert (2000) found that husbands and wives disagreed more frequently over the division of housework than over decisions regarding paid work or even child care. According to Kluwer and colleagues (2000), any conflict over household labor is asymmetrical because it involves a complainant, who wants to change the current situation, and a defendant, who wants to maintain the status quo. Most conflicts, furthermore, are gendered. To a large extent women find themselves in the role of the complainant while men assume the role of defendant (see also Thoits, 1987).

Research has found that, in the case of marital conflict over the division of labor, husbands typically hold more power than wives. Often wives attempt discussion, but husbands retain their privileged position by avoiding discussion (Kluwer et al., 2000; Pasquera, 1993; Sagrestano, Christensen, & Heavey, 1998). In her study about the division of family labor among Latino dual-earner couples, Pasquera (1993) describes how, in addition to "stalling" change by avoiding discussion, husbands would block change by agreeing to participate in domestic labor but then forgetting to get tasks done or doing them incorrectly. Given men's relative clout in negotiating change, it is not be surprising that Greenstein (1996) has found that husbands do relatively little domestic labor unless both they and their wives hold nontraditional beliefs about gender and marital roles.

In contrast to the difficulty in changing sex-role ideologies to produce consistent change, especially when it is the women whose ideologies have shifted, practical considerations have been shown to be quite important. At least two in-depth studies have illustrated how necessity is still the mother of invention. The studies have also shown that those with traditional sex-role ideologies and nontraditional behaviors are as adept as others in convincing themselves that their behaviors conform to their beliefs.

Zvonkovic and colleagues (1996) conducted a study of 61 married couples from a variety of socioeconomic backgrounds who had to make an important work or family decision in the previous six months. They found that couples' attitudes about gender and marriage influenced the ways in which decisions were made. Hence, decisions about the husbands' employment would gener-

ally take up more time and consideration by both marital partners than decisions about the wife's job. They also found that couples would reinterpret their decisions regarding work when they seemed to contradict their gender-role ideology. So, for example, a woman who held traditional gender roles explained her job as a teacher as an opportunity to learn about children and school and thus improve her parenting skills.

Even more depth of understanding is provided by Deutsch's (1999) study of White working- and middle-class couples. Deutsch compared the marital interactions of parents who reported child-care arrangements that varied from traditional to egalitarian. Only 26 of the 150 families interviewed by Deutsch were egalitarian at the time of the study, in that fathers actively participated in decisions and did at least half of the child care and housework, including highly maternal tasks such as feeding, bathing, and changing diapers. Deutsch found that, often, day-to-day practical decisions (e.g., the inability to pay for child care) fueled the behavior more than ideology.

In conclusion, research shows that men and women utilize a wide range of strategies to make decisions about and define their responsibilities within the family. These strategies can at times become a means to challenge unequal gender roles. According to Deutsch (1999), equal sharing increases intimacy because, by challenging society's expectations about the roles that they should perform, men and women create new identities for themselves and within their relationship. Egalitarian arrangements also positively influence the emotional quality of intimate relationships through the valuing of each partner's aspirations, abilities, needs and, consequently, through an equal investment in their relationship (Steil, 2000).

MULTIPLE ROLES AND WELL-BEING

Given the persistence of gender imbalances, many scholars have wondered how multiple roles influence women's physical and mental health. Do women, especially mothers, who combine paid labor with significant domestic responsibilities suffer negative consequences? Such questions preoccupied sociologists, psychologists, and public health experts from the mid-1960s (after Friedan [1963] ignited the women's movement with her *Feminine Mystique*) to the early 1990s. Early scholarship on work and family life was based on the assumption that engaging in multiple roles would unavoidably lead to role strain (Goode, 1960). As prevalent social norms expected women to be in charge of family responsibilities, adding paid work to family life was thought to be inherently stressful for the woman and potentially harmful for her children (Sieber, 1974).

Feminist scholars began to challenge the so-called scarcity hypothesis in the 1970s. Since then, a large number of empirical investigations have shown that employment can actually benefit women, including mothers, just as it can benefit men, including fathers (see Barnett & Hyde, 2001 for a review). Nor is it simply paid labor that fuels well-being. A growing body of evidence shows that people who engage in multiple roles report better physical and mental health than people with fewer roles (Ayers, Cusack, & Crosby, 1993; Barnett & Hyde, 2001).

Crosby (1991) has explained the salutary effects of multiple roles in terms of both practical and psychological benefits. In practical terms, having several roles provides important tools for both women and men to fulfill family obligations. Making an income, for example, may help families avoid the stresses associated with economic uncertainty.

Just as important, and perhaps more important than the material benefits of "juggling" multiple roles, are the emotional benefits (Barnett & Hyde, 2001). Crosby speculated that role combination promotes good mental health through at least three mechanisms. First, each role enriches the others by producing variety in life. Change is important because it creates balance among different experiences. All major theories of adult developments indicate that involvement in social roles is a crucial component of health and well-being (Vanderwater, Ostrove, & Stewart, 1997). Second, role combination allows people to amplify their positive experiences by increasing the chances of meeting different people—and different audiences—on a regular basis. Third, different roles can provide a "buffer" from negative events in any one role and thus diminish the likelihood of depression and anxiety. Having

more than one role provides alternative perspectives, as well as "time-outs" from difficult situations associated to other roles. A difficult situation at work can be put in a different perspective by changing a more pleasant scenario at home, such as a birthday party for one of the children, or in one's personal life, such as visiting with friends. On the other hand, going to work can become an opportunity to shift gears and temporarily divert the attention from, for example, a difficult family situation. Having different identities at work and at home also protects one's self-esteem by extending potential sources of positive experiences and support. Employed women often cite coworkers as an important source of social support in their lives (Repetti, Matthews, & Waldron, 1989).

Variations

Consistent with the enhancement hypothesis, multiple roles are found to be more beneficial in some circumstances than in others. As Holcomb (1998) observes, "work and family life are not static, but moving targets, and the cost and benefits of working change over time as circumstances change" (p. 109). When looking at how multiple roles influence individuals' well-being, it is thus important to consider not only the number of roles but also the quality of each role (Barnett & Hyde, 2001; Barnett & Rivers, 1996). The very reasons, both practical and emotional, why multiple roles enhance functioning mean that enactment of many roles can sometimes be more positive than other times.

Consider variations in the spouse role. Gender inequality within the family can actually have significant costs for both men and women. As Hochschild and Machung (1989) noted, keeping up the illusion of egalitarianism in the face of gender imbalances requires a lot of energy; unequal domestic arrangements lead to role overload and, thus, increase stress. In a review of numerous studies on the relationship between partners' involvement in housework labor and women's psychological well-being, for example, Steil (1997) consistently found the two variables to be positively correlated. Specifically, both equality in decision making and husbands' participation in domestic work were associated with higher relationship satisfaction, better communication, increased intimacy, and enhanced well-being. Spousal support—either of a practical or of an emotional nature—positively influences marital quality and decreases perceptions of work-family conflict among working women (Barnett & Rivers, 1996). As noted earlier, working together to reach equality within the family benefits women and men also by increasing intimacy between partners (Barnett & Rivers, 1996; Deutsch, 1999).

Similarly, some work is more rewarding and easier to combine with family responsibilities than is other work. Professional jobs, typically held by middle-class women and men, tend to provide greater rewards and flexibility of arrangements than working-class jobs (Roschelle, 1999). Sociologists have found that low-wage and low-quality jobs contribute to rendering low-income women particularly susceptible to role overload (Pasquera, 1993; Sidel, 1992). So does lack of social support. A working mother who is having difficulties finding affordable child care may feel particularly overwhelmed even if she is really happy with her job. The high levels of unemployment and underemployment among the poor makes flexible household arrangements particularly important, as housework and child care can become more of a burden in the context of ever-changing life and employment demands (Romero, 2001; Seccombe, 2000).

Finally, the qualities of role enactment are sometimes influenced by normative understandings. Women's attitudes toward their paid work influences their sense of well-being (Perry-Jenkins, Seery, & Crouter, 1992). Specifically, wives who view their paid work as equally important to their husbands' report less depression and less overload than wives who view their provider role as secondary to their spouse. In an qualitative investigation of Latina mothers, Segura (1994) interviewed Mexicanas (i.e., women who emigrated to the United States from Mexico) and Chicanas (women of Mexican heritage who were born and raised in the United States). Mexicanas, who were raised in a context in which family and employment are strictly interrelated, did not perceive conflict between employment and motherhood. Chicana participants, on the other hand, exposed to the ideology of separate spheres prevalent in the United States, reported that they felt ambivalence between their responsibilities as mothers and on the job.

CHILD CARE CHOICES AND FAMILY-FRIENDLY POLICIES

Although "workplace policies and practices still lag behind contemporary reality" (Moen & Han, 2001, p. 44), many companies have been responsive to the urgings of work-family researchers and to their own economic self-interest. Research showing that employee stress is not an inevitable consequence of multiple roles, but rather comes about because of identifiable factors, has led many to recognize the need for family-friendly policies (Lewis & Cooper, 1999). Sophisticated understandings of the multiplicity of factors that may affect individual well-being have increasingly contributed both to a focus on work and family synergy, rather than conflict (Galinsky, 2001) and to a willingness to identifying problems with an eye to finding solutions (Gerstel & McGonagle, 1999).

Workplaces that promote family-friendly policies claim to find such practices profitable. For example, Galinsky (2001) reports how companies that implement flextime, extended parental leaves, and manager training programs are able to significantly decrease employee turnover and thus save considerable resources. Employees who utilize family-friendly policies, furthermore, are often the ones with the highest performance evaluations. Interestingly, companies with a large proportion of women and/or people of color in executive positions are most likely to have family-friendly policies in place (Galinsky, 2001).

While the stress of caring for young children is substantial among all working parents (Haley et al., 2001), in the United States, the burden of work-family conflict is greater among women and the greatest among low-income women. Little has been done by either the private or public sector to help working-class and low-income families, who are increasingly the object of study among scholars (for extensive reviews see McLoyd, Cauce, Takeuchi, & Wilson, 2000; Seccombe, 2000). One consistent finding is that *lack* of affordable child care affects low-income women in particular.

Unfortunately, as noted earlier, innovative policies, including work arrangements that offer flexibility, autonomy, and control, are by and large available only to middle-class, professional women and men (Gerson & Jacobs, 2001).

Class inequalities appear to be connected with gender inequalities in important ways (Galinsky, 2001). Recent federal policies, for example, tend to pressure poor women to take low-wage jobs with few benefits (Deitch & Huffman, 2001). Paradoxically, families who can afford hired help to assist with household and child care generally employ low-paid immigrant women. Hence in order to protect their career opportunities, middle- and upper-class women may partly diminish other women's ability to manage their own work and family issues (Coltrane, 1996; Romero, 2001).

Progressive governmental policies in the United States may help prevent situations in which the needs of women from different social strata seem antagonistic. In her book *Saving Our Children From Poverty: What the United States Can Learn From France*, Barbara Bergman (1996) reminds us of positive effects that institutionalized family-friendly policies have on society at large, and on children in particular. In particular, Bergman contrasts the negative consequences of lack of family-responsive policies in the United States with the benefits of governmental policies providing medical care, housing assistance, and low-cost child care in France. In the United States, after taxes and cash benefits, nearly one in four children (21%) still live below the poverty line, compared to only 6 percent in France.

Bergman's observations stand as a reminder of a feminist truth. Whatever affects a woman affects her family. And whatever affects families is of concern for the nation. Even as we focus on how women balance paid labor and labor within the home, we must remember that the point is not simply for women to seek solutions to our problems; the point is to help move the nation toward a path of greater balance for all citizens.

REFERENCES

Ayers, L., Cusack, M., & Crosby, F. J. (1993). Combining work and home. In D. M. Headapohol (Ed.), *Occupational medicine* (pp. 821–831). Philadelphia: Hanley & Belfus.

Bergman, B. (1996). *Saving our children from poverty: What the United States can learn from France.* New York: Russell Sage Foundation.

Barnett, R. C. (1997). How paradigms shape the stories we tell: Paradigm shifts in gender and health. *Journal of Social Issues, 53*, 351–368.

Barnett, R. C., & Hyde, S. J. (2001). Women, men, work, and family: An expansionist theory. *American Psychologist, 56*, 781–796.

Barnett, R. C., & Rivers, C. (1996). *She works he works: How two income families are happier, healthier, and better off.* San Francisco: Harper Books.

Becker, P. E., & Moen, P. (1999). Scaling back: Dual earner couples' work-family strategies. *Journal of Marriage and the Family, 61*, 995–1007.

Boston Globe. (2003, March 25). Number of woman managers at a high, but salaries lag men's. Retrieved March 25, 2003, from http://www.boston.com/dailyglobe2/084/business/number_of_woman_managers

Cabrera, N. J., Tamis-LeMonda, C. S., Bradley, R. H., Hofferth, S., & Lamb, M. E. (2000). Fatherhood in the twenty-first century. *Child Development, 71*, 127–136.

Coltrane, S. (1996). *Family man: Fatherhood, housework, and gender equality.* New York: Oxford University Press.

Coltrane, S., & Adams, M. (2001). Men's family work: Child-centered fathering and the sharing of domestic labor. In R. Hertz & N. L. Marshall (Eds.), *Working families: The transformation of the American home* (pp. 72–99). Berkeley: University of California Press.

Crosby, F. J. (1982). *Relative deprivation and working women.* New York: Oxford University Press.

Crosby, F. J. (1991). *Juggling: The unexpected advantages of balancing career and home for women and their families.* New York: Free Press.

Deitch, C. H., & Huffman, M. L. (2001). Family responsive benefits and the two-tiered family benefits structure in the United States. In R. Hertz & N. L. Marshall (Eds.), *Working families: The transformation of the American home* (pp. 103–130). Berkeley: University of California Press.

Deutsch, F. M. (1999). *Having it all: How equally shared parenting works.* Cambridge, MA: Harvard University Press.

Deutsch, F. M. (2001). Equally shared parenting. *Current Directions in Psychological Science, 10*, 25–28.

Dryden, C. (1999). *Being married, doing gender: A critical analysis of gender relationships in marriage.* New York: Routledge.

Friedan, B. (1963). *The feminine mystique.* New York: Norton.

Galinsky, E. (2001). Toward a new view of work and family life. In R. Hertz & N. L. Marshall (Eds.), *Working families: The transformation of the American home* (pp. 168–186). Berkeley: University of California Press.

Gerson, K., & Jacobs, J. A. (2001). Changing the structure and culture of work: Work and family conflict, work flexibility, and gender equity in the modern workplace. In R. Hertz & N. L. Marshall (Eds.), *Working families: The transformation of the American home* (pp. 207–226). Berkeley: University of California Press.

Gerstel, N., & McGonagle, K. (1999). Job leaves and the limits of the Family and Medical Leave Act: The effects of gender, race, and family. *Work and Occupation, 26,* 510–534.

Goode, W. J. (1960). A theory of role strain. *American Sociological Review, 25,* 483–496.

Greenstein, T. N. (1996). Husbands' participation in domestic labor: Interactive effects of wives' and husbands' gender ideologies. *Journal of Marriage and the Family, 58,* 585–595.

Haley, H., Perry-Jenkins, M., & Armenia, A. (2001). Workplace policies and the psychological well-being of first-time parents: The case of working-class families. In R. Hertz & N. L. Marshall (Eds.), *Working families: The transformation of the American home* (pp. 227–250). Berkeley: University of California Press.

Hochschild, A. R., & Machung A. (1989). *The second shift.* New York: Avon Books.

Holcomb, B. (1998). *Not guilty! The good news about working mothers.* New York: Scribner's.

Jost, J. T., Pelham, B. W., Sheldon, O., & Sullivan, B. N. (2003). Social inequality and the reduction of ideological dissonance on behalf of the system: Evidence of enhanced system justification among the disadvantaged. *European Journal of Social Psychology, 33,* 13–36.

Kluwer, E. S., Heesink, J. A. M., & Van de Vliert, E. (2000). The division of household labor: An asymmetrical conflict issue. *Personal Relationships, 7,* 263–282.

Lewis, S., & Cooper, C. L. (1999). The work-family research agenda in changing contexts. *Journal of Occupational Health Psychology, 4,* 382–393.

Major, B. (1994). From social inequality to personal entitlement: The role of social comparisons, legitimacy appraisals, and group membership. In M. Zanna (Ed.), *Advances in experimental social psychology* (pp. 293–355). New York: Academic Press.

McLoyd, V., Cauce, A. M., Takeuchi, D., & Wilson, L. (2000). Marital processes and parental socialization in families of color: A decade review of research. *Journal of Marriage and the Family, 62,* 1070–1093.

Mikula, G. (1998). Justice in the family—multiple perspectives on the division of labor: Introduction. *Social Justice Research, 11,* 211–213.

Moen, P., & Han, S. K. (2001). Gendered careers: A life-course perspective. In R. Hertz & N. L. Marshall (Eds.), *Working families: The transformation of the American home* (pp. 42–57). Berkeley: University of California Press.

Pasquera, B. M. (1993). "In the beginning he wouldn't lift even a spoon": The division of household labor. In A. De La Torre & B. M. Pasquera (Eds.),

Building with our hands: New directions in Chicana studies (pp. 181–195). Berkeley: University of California Press.

Perry-Jenkins, M., Seery, B., & Crouter, A. C. (1992). Linkages between women's provider-role attitudes, psychological well being, and family relationships. *Psychology of Women Quarterly, 16,* 311–329.

Repetti, R. L., Matthews, K. A., & Waldron, I. (1989). Employment and women's health: Effects of paid employment on women's mental and physical health. *American Psychologist, 44,* 1394–1401.

Romero, M. (2001). Passing between the worlds of maid and mistress: The life of a Mexican maid's daughter. In R. Hertz & N. L. Marshall (Eds.), *Working families: The transformation of the American home* (pp. 323–339). Berkeley: University of California Press.

Roschelle, A. R. (1999). Gender, family structure, and social structure: Racial ethnic families in the United States. In M. M. Ferree, J. Lorber, & B. B. Hess (Eds.), *Revisioning gender* (pp. 311–340). Walnut Creek, CA: AltaMira Press.

Sagrestano, L. M., Christensen, A., & Heavey, C. L. (1998). Social influence techniques during marital conflict. *Personal Relationships, 5,* 75–89.

Seccombe, K. (2000). Families in poverty in the 1990s: Trends, causes, consequences, and lesson learned. *Journal of Marriage and the Family, 62,* 1094–1113.

Segura, D. A. (1994). Working at motherhood: Chicana and Mexican immigrant mothers and employment. In E. Nakano Glenn, G. Chang, & L. Rennie Forcey (Eds.), *Mothering: ideology, experience, and agency* (pp. 211–233). New York: Routledge.

Sidel, R. (1992). Toward a more caring society. In P. S. Rothenberg (Ed.), *Race, class and gender in the United States: An integrated study* (pp. 417–431). New York: St. Martin's.

Sieber, S. D. (1974). Toward a theory of role accumulation. *American Sociological Review, 39,* 567–578.

Silberstein, L. R. (1992). *Dual-career marriage: A system in transition.* Hillsdale, NJ: Erlbaum.

Steil, J. M. (1997). *Marital equality: Its relationship to the well being of husbands and wives.* Thousand Oaks, CA: Sage.

Steil, J. M. (2000). Contemporary marriage: Still an unequal partnership. In C. Hendrick & S. S. Hendrick (Eds.), *Close relationships: A sourcebook* (pp. 125–152). Thousand Oaks, CA: Sage.

Steil, J. M. (2001). Family forms and member well-being: A research agenda for the decade of behavior. *Psychology of Women Quarterly, 25,* 344–363.

Thoits, P. A. (1987). Negotiating roles. In F. J. Crosby (Ed.), *Spouse, parent, worker: On gender and multiple roles* (pp. 11–22). New Haven, CT: Yale University Press.

Thrane, C. (2000). Men, women, and leisure time: Scandinavian evidence of gender inequality. *Leisure Science, 22,* 109–122.

U.S. Bureau of Labor Statistics. (2002, March 29). *Employment characteristics of families in 2001.* Retrieved March 1, 2003, from http://www.bls.gov/news.release/famee.nro.htm

U.S. Bureau of Labor Statistics. (2003). *Table A-2. Employment status of the civilian population by race, sex, and age.* Retrieved September 17, 2003, 2003, from http://www.bls.gov/news.release/empsit. to2.htm

U.S. Census Bureau. (1998). *Married women joining work force spur 150% family income increase, Census Bureau finds in 50-year review* (Press Release). Retrieved March 1, 2003, from http://www.census.gov/Press-Release/cb98-181.html

U.S. Census Bureau. (2000, June). *Fertility of American women: Population characteristics* (P20-543RV). Washington, DC: Government Printing Office.

Vanderwater, E. A., Ostrove, J. M., & Stewart, A. J. (1997). Predicting women's well being in midlife: The importance of personality development and social role involvement. *Journal of Personality and Social Psychology, 72,* 1147–1160.

Zanna, M. P., Crosby, F., & Lowenstein, G. (1986). Male reference groups and discontent among female professionals. In B. A. Gutek & L. Larwood (Eds.), *Women's career development* (pp. 28–41). Newbury Park, CA: Sage.

Zvonkovic, A. M., Greaves, K. M., Schmiege, C. J., & Hall, L. D. (1996). The marital construction of gender through work and family decisions: A qualitative analysis. *Journal of Marriage and the Family, 58,* 91–100.

"Midlife" as a distinct period is a 20th-century construction made possible by the dramatic increase in the numbers of adults who enjoy healthy active lives well into older age. There is no firm consensus on when middle age begins, although it is popularly thought to begin around age 40 and end in the mid-60s (Etaugh & Bridges, 2004). No one biological or psychological event signals its beginning. Rather, individuals typically experience a number of life events and role changes during these years, including those related to physical changes, sexuality, marital status, parenting, caregiving for ill family members, grandparenting, and entry into or retirement from the workforce. Historically, women have been allocated the major responsibility for child care, kin relations, and care of impaired relatives in midlife, thereby restricting their participation in the labor force. Fundamental changes in social attitudes regarding gender roles over the past several decades have begun to broaden the opportunities available to women in midlife as well as in other life stages. Important to understanding the impact of role transitions in midlife is the timing or degree of predictability of these changes. For example, having the last child leave home and becoming a grandparent are frequently expected and welcome role transitions, whereas divorce, death of a spouse or partner, and providing care for ailing parents are often unplanned and stressful changes.

HEALTH

Although midlife is generally a time of good health, the first indications of physical aging become noticeable and signs of chronic health conditions may appear. There are enormous individual differences in rates of aging and emergence of chronic illness. Genetic makeup and lifestyle choices involving good nutrition, physical activity, and not smoking all contribute to health during the middle years (Goldman & Hatch, 2000).

In our youth-oriented society, the prospect of getting older generally is not relished by either sex. For women, however, the stigma of aging is greater than it is for men, a phenomenon labeled the "double standard of aging." The same gray hair and wrinkles that enhance the perceived

CLAIRE A. ETAUGH
and JUDITH S. BRIDGES

Midlife Transitions

38

status and attractiveness of an older man diminish the perceived attractiveness and desirability of an older woman. Some researchers account for this by noting that a woman's most socially valued qualities—her ability to provide sex and bear children—are associated with the physical beauty and fertility of youth. As she ages, she is seen as less attractive because her years of social usefulness as childbearer are behind her. Men, on the other hand, are seen as possessing qualities—competence, autonomy, and power—that are not associated with youth but rather increase with age. Given these societal views, it is not surprising that midlife women, compared with midlife men, are more dissatisfied with their appearance (McConatha, Hayta, Riley, & Leach, 2002) and use more age concealment techniques (Noonan & Adler, 2002).

The most distinct physiological change for most midlife women is menopause, the cessation of menses. In Western societies, menopause is often viewed in terms of loss of reproductive capability and decline in sexual functioning. Menopause continues to be defined in medical and psychological literature by a long list of negative symptoms and terms such as "estrogen deprivation" and "total ovarian failure." The popular press reinforces the notion of menopause as a condition of disease and deterioration that requires treatment by drugs (Derry, 2002).

Most middle-aged North American women minimize the significance of menopause, viewing it as only a temporary inconvenience, and feeling relief when their menstrual periods stop (Ayubi-Moak & Parry, 2002). Postmenopausal women have more positive attitudes toward menopause than younger midlife women, with young women holding the most negative views of all (Sommer et al., 1999). Women in other cultures often have menopausal experiences and attitudes very different from those reported by Western women, indicating that menopausal symptoms are at least in part socially constructed. For example, women of high social castes in India report very few negative symptoms, and hot flashes are virtually unknown among Mayan women. Similarly, Japanese women are much less likely than U.S. and Canadian women to report hot flashes (Etaugh & Bridges, 2004).

While most midlife adults enjoy good health, the frequency of chronic illness begins to increase during this time. Men have a higher prevalence of fatal diseases (e.g., heart disease, cancer, stroke) while women have a higher incidence of nonfatal ones (e.g., arthritis, gallstones, and urinary incontinence). This so-called gender paradox is summed up in the saying "Women are sicker; men die quicker" (Goldman & Hatch, 2000). Women spend 64 of their years in good health and free of disability, compared with only 59 years for men. But because women live longer than men, it is women who more often live many years with chronic, often disabling, illnesses (Etaugh & Bridges, 2004). Health risks and mortality rates for women vary by ethnic group and socioeconomic status. African American and Native American women, who have lower family income than do Asian American and White women, also have higher mortality rates (Torrez, 2001).

Many factors contribute to individual and gender differences in disease and injury, including biological predispositions and lifestyle. One biological explanation for women's greater longevity is that their second X chromosome protects them against certain potentially lethal diseases such as hemophilia and some forms of muscular dystrophy that are more apt to occur in individuals (men) who have only one X chromosome. Another biological reason for women's greater longevity may be their higher estrogen level, which, prior to menopause, may provide protection against heart disease (Gaylord, 2001).

One lifestyle factor accounting for the gender gap in mortality is that men are more likely than women to engage in potentially risky behaviors such as smoking, drinking, violence, and reckless driving. In addition, women make greater use of preventive health services and are more likely to seek medical treatment when they are ill (Addis & Mahalik, 2003). This may help explain why women live longer than men after the diagnosis of a potentially fatal disease. Women also are more likely than men to have extensive social support networks of family and friends, another factor related to living longer (Etaugh & Bridges, 2001).

On the other hand, midlife women are more likely than men to engage in certain deleterious health habits. More women are overweight and physically inactive. These factors contribute to a host of diseases and medical conditions including heart disease, many kinds of cancer, and stroke, the three leading causes of death for both women and men. Also, while the frequency of men's smoking has declined, that of women's has increased. The result is that smoking-related deaths from cancer, including lung cancer, have increased for women but decreased for men (Centers for Disease Control and Prevention, 2002).

SEXUALITY

Sexual activity and satisfaction vary among midlife women just as they do among young women. Sexual activity decreases only slightly and gradually for most middle-aged women, but some experience greater declines as a result of physical or psychological changes. Furthermore, while some women report a decline in sexual interest and the capacity for orgasm during these years, others report the opposite pattern, and some women report an increased desire for non-genital sexual expression such as cuddling, hugging, and kissing (Etaugh & Bridges, 2001).

Menopausal changes in sexual physiology and in hormone levels affect female sexuality in the middle years. Decline in the production of estrogen causes the vaginal walls to become less elastic, thinner, and more easily irritated, leading to painful intercourse. Although sexual arousal is slower, and the number and intensity of orgasmic contractions are reduced, few women either notice or complain about these changes. Furthermore, slower arousal time for both women and men may lengthen the time of pleasurable sexual activity (Etaugh & Bridges, 2004). The sexual lives of midlife women also are influenced by past sexual enjoyment and experience. Women who in their younger years found sexual expression to be fulfilling typically continue to enjoy sex in their middle years and beyond (Etaugh & Bridges, 2004).

Psychological factors also affect midlife women's sexual experiences. Sexual interest and pleasure may be heightened by freedom from worries about pregnancy or by the increase in marital satisfaction that often develops during the postparental years. On the other hand, dissatisfaction with one's partner and worries about family matters, finances, or work can negatively affect sexual experience (Rathus, Nevid, & Fichner-Rathus, 2002).

MIDLIFE: CRISIS OR PRIME OF LIFE?

Contrary to popular literature's depiction of middle age as a time of crisis, turmoil, and self-doubt, empirical evidence shows that midlife women consider this period to be one of vibrancy and opportunity for growth. Mitchell and Helson (1990) characterize the early postparental period as women's prime of life. Others describe midlife as a period of "postmenopausal zest," in which women have an increased determination, energy, and ability to fulfill their dreams and gain control over their lives. Freedom from reproductive concerns, a sense of accomplishment accompanying the successful launching of children, and an increase in available time enable women to focus more on their self-development and on their partner, job, and community.

MIDLIFE ROLE TRANSITIONS: AN OVERVIEW

Although few women experience a midlife crisis, many women go through a process of life review, an intensive self-evaluation of numerous aspects of their lives. One characteristic theme in the life reviews of current midlife women is the search for an independent identity. Helson (1992) notes that for many women, the need to rewrite the life story in middle age is related to the lessening of the dependence and restriction associated with marriage and motherhood as children grow up. Thus, many women attempt to affirm their own being, independent of their family, through graduate education, beginning a career, or switching careers.

For many midlife women, paid work is a significant predictor of psychological well-being. Middle-aged women who are involved in either beginning or building their career are both psychologically and physically healthier than women who are maintaining or reducing their career involvement (Etaugh & Bridges, 2001). Also, women who have attained the occupational goals they set for themselves in young adulthood have a greater sense of life purpose and are less depressed in midlife than those who fall short of their expectations (Carr, 1997). Furthermore, satisfaction with work predicts a general sense of well-being: the more satisfied women are with their jobs, the better they feel in general (McQuaide, 1998).

For other women, being a full-time homemaker or student can be associated with the same degree of psychological well-being as that experienced by women who are employed. Midlife homemakers whose life goal was this domestic role have a comparable sense of purpose in life as women who aspired toward and achieved an occupational role. Not surprisingly, however, women who are involuntarily out of the workforce, owing to forced early retirement or layoff, are not as satisfied with midlife as women with a chosen role (Etaugh & Bridges, 2001). Thus, there are multiple routes to well-being in midlife, and it appears that a key factor influencing midlife role evaluation is not a woman's *role* per se but fulfillment of her *preferred role*.

Although some midlife women are satisfied with traditional roles, others are disturbed about missed educational or occupational opportunities. Some middle-class women who, as young adults, devoted themselves solely to marriage and motherhood, voice regrets in midlife about their earlier traditional decisions. Stewart and Vandewater (1999) examined regrets experienced by women who graduated from college in the mid-1960s. The concerns reported by these women centered on disappointments about not pursuing a more prestigious career, marrying before establishing a career, and not returning to work after having children. The women who acknowledged their regrets and made modifications based on these regrets experienced greater psychological well-being at midlife than did those who had regrets but did not use those as a basis for altering their life direction.

SPOUSAL ROLE TRANSITIONS

Experiences with marriage, divorce, widowhood, and remarriage during the middle years vary for women and men. Men in the United States are more likely than women to be married during midlife, especially during the years from 55 to 64,

when 78% of men but only 67% of women are still married (U.S. Census Bureau, 2003). Marital disruption is more common among African American women, poor women, and women with disabilities than among White, more affluent, and able-bodied women.

Following divorce or widowhood, women are less likely than men to remarry, and they do so less quickly. Remarriage rates are much lower for women than men because of several factors. For one thing, older women outnumber older men. In the United States, for example, there are only two men for every three women by age 65, and this difference widens with age (U.S. Census Bureau, 2003). Second, Western cultural values sanction the marriage of men to much younger women but frown on the opposite pattern, thus expanding the pool of potential mates for an older man but shrinking it for an older woman. Finally, previously married women are less inclined to remarry than previously married men (Etaugh & Bridges, 2004).

Despite the increasing divorce rate, most marriages are terminated not by divorce but by the death of a spouse. Women are much more likely to become widowed than are men, since women not only have a longer life expectancy but also tend to marry men older than themselves. As of 2000, there were 11 million widows but only 2.6 million widowers in the United States, a ratio of more than four to one (Spraggins, 2003).

Common reactions to losing a spouse or partner include restlessness, sleep problems, feelings of depression, emptiness, anger, and guilt. While most individuals adjust to their spouse's or partner's death within two to four years, feelings of loneliness, yearning, and missing their partner remain for extended periods of time (Cutter, 1999). Loss of a lesbian's partner is especially stressful if the relationship was not publicly acknowledged, but even when the relationship was an open one, friends may not comprehend the severity and nature of the loss (Etaugh & Bridges, 2004). As many as 10–20% of widows experience long-term problems, including clinical depression, abuse of alcohol and prescription drugs, and increased susceptibility to physical illness. Such problems are more prevalent among younger women, those with a prior history of depression, those whose marriages were less satisfactory, those whose husbands' deaths followed the deaths of other close relatives and friends, those whose spouses died unexpectedly, those who depended on their husbands for most social contacts, and those women with limited financial and social resources. Support from families and children, especially daughters, does much to enhance the psychological well-being of widows. Women friends who are themselves widowed can be particularly supportive. Interestingly, research has found more loneliness among women who have lived with a spouse for many years than among women who live alone (Fields & Casper, 2001; Fingerman, 2001).

Keep in mind that our knowledge of widows has been obtained primarily from older women, most of whom had traditional marriages. When the young women of today become widows, they will be more likely than the current population of widows to have had a different set of life experiences, including a college education and a job or career that will better prepare them for a healthy adjustment to widowhood.

PARENTAL ROLE TRANSITIONS

Although midlife women who had children during their teen years have already launched their children into young adulthood, and other midlife women are still chasing toddlers around the house, a major event for many mothers during their middle years is the departure of their children from the home. Similar to common folklore characterizing midlife as a time of crisis, this postparental period is popularly but inaccurately viewed as an unhappy "empty nest" stage of life for most women. Women generally describe the postparental years in positive rather than negative terms. Because children can be a source of tension in any marriage, women report higher marital satisfaction once their children have left home (Bee, 2000). Also, the decreased complexity of family relationships at this time enables women to develop greater intimacy with their partners. Furthermore, the departure of the last child from the home is an opportunity to begin or expand the development of a personal identity independent of family roles. For many women, as we have seen, this event marks the beginning of a midlife review period when they evaluate their lives and consider other options such as pursuing new careers, furthering their education, or pro-

viding service to their communities. However, the significant redefinition of their parenting responsibilities and the end to their identity as a child caregiver can be somewhat problematic for women whose primary identity has been that of mother. Mothers who are employed during the child-rearing years and establish an identity additional to their mother role find it easier to relinquish their child-care responsibilities when their children leave home than do women who have identified primarily with their role as mother (Lippert, 1997).

Of course, mothers do not stop being parents when their children move out. Instead, they redefine parenting to a less-involved phase. A new type of interpersonal relationship is created and mothers remain involved in their children's lives, although in somewhat different ways. While their contacts are generally less frequent, they continue to offer advice and encouragement and sometimes provide goal-directed help, such as financial assistance (Etaugh & Bridges, 2001).

Although most mothers experience the departure of their children at some point during midlife, there are variations in children's age of departure, and a significant number return home for some period of time after leaving, for financial reasons or following divorce. Nearly half of middle-aged parents with children over the age of 18 have an adult child living with them. Parents' reaction to their children's return is related to the degree to which the return is characterized by a continued dependence on the parents. Parents experience greater parent-child strain the greater the children's financial dependency and the lower their educational attainment. Furthermore, parents' satisfaction with the living arrangement is positively related to their child's self-esteem, possibly because low self-esteem signals difficulty in assuming independent adult roles. These findings suggest that parents are most satisfied with the parent-child relationship and experience the highest degree of well-being when they perceive their children assuming the normative roles of adulthood (Etaugh & Bridges, 2001).

CAREGIVER ROLE TRANSITIONS

Midlife adults are often referred to as the "sandwich" or "squeeze" generation because of the responsibilities that they assume for their adolescent and young adult children, on the one hand, and their aging parents, on the other. At the same time that middle-aged parents are providing assistance and support for the young adult children who are staying at home or returning home, they also maintain ties with and provide care for their elderly parents (Yaffe et al., 2002). The extent of assistance provided may range from no help at all (either because none is needed or because it is provided by others) to around-the-clock care, including household maintenance, transportation, cooking, grocery shopping, and personal and medical care. Typically it is the middle-aged (or even elderly) daughter or daughter-in-law who provides such services (Katz, Kabeto, & Langa, 2000). These unpaid caregivers are the core of the long-term care system in the United States, providing three quarters of the help needed by the frail elderly. Demographic changes in recent years are increasing the parent-care responsibilities of midlife women. More parents are living well into old age, and their caregiving children themselves are becoming old. Furthermore, as the birthrate declines, there are fewer siblings to share the burden of the care. In addition, middle-aged women are increasingly likely to be employed, adding to their list of competing roles and responsibilities. For some individuals, caring for a parent and the sense of reciprocating the nurturance and care once provided by that parent can be very rewarding. For many, however, caregiving can adversely affect psychological and physical well-being. Older women caregivers with few economic resources and a limited support system are the most likely to develop psychological distress (Etaugh & Bridges, 2001).

GRANDPARENTAL ROLE TRANSITIONS

The stereotypical portrayal of a grandmother is often an elderly white-haired woman providing treats for her young grandchildren. However, grandmothers do not fit into any one pattern. While more than 75% of Americans over age 65 are grandparents, some people become grandparents as early as their late 20s and over half of women experience this event by age 47 (Sheehy, 2002). Nowadays, many middle-aged grandmothers are in the labor force and may also have responsibilities for caring for their elderly parents (Velkoff & Lawson, 1998). Thus, they may have less time to devote to grandparenting activities.

During their grandchild's infancy, grandmothers often provide the children's parents with considerable emotional support, information, help with infant care and household chores, and, to a lesser degree, financial support. Nearly one half of all grandmothers in the United States provide such help on a regular basis (Black et al., 2002). The grandmother's role in providing child care as well as economic, social, and emotional support for her grandchildren is more active in many ethnic minority groups than among Whites. African American, Latina, and Native American grandmothers are significant figures in the stability and continuity of the family (Etaugh & Bridges, 2004).

For some children, grandparents are part of the family household. The number of American children living in homes with a grandparent has risen from 2.2 million in 1970 to 4.5 million in 2000 (Pruchno & McKenney, 2000), including 12.3% of African American children, 6.5% of Latin American children, and 3.7% of White children. Some of the increase results from an uncertain economy and the growing number of single mothers, which has sent young adults and their children back to the parental nest. In other cases, elderly adults are moving in with their adult children's families when they can no longer live on their own. The arrangement benefits all parties. Grandparents and their grandchildren are able to interact on a daily basis, and grandparents may assume some parental responsibilities (Etaugh & Bridges, 2004).

Increasing numbers of grandparents now find themselves raising their grandchildren as their own. Of the 4.5 million children in the United States living in a household with a grandparent, over half are being raised by the grandparents without a parent present (Pruchno & McKenney, 2002). These "skip-generation parents" overwhelmingly are grandmothers. Reasons that grandparents become full-time caregivers for their grandchildren include parental child abuse or neglect, substance abuse, psychological or financial problems, and the growth of AIDS cases among heterosexuals (Kinsella & Velkoff, 2001).

The belief that caregiving grandmothers are primarily poor women of color is a myth. Parenting grandmothers can be found across racial and socioeconomic lines (Harm, 2001). About two thirds of U.S. grandparents raising grandchildren are White, over 25% are African American, and 10% are Latin American. African American women who are raising their grandchildren, compared to White women, report feeling less burdened and more satisfied in their caregiving role, even though they are generally in poorer health, dealing with more difficult situations, and dealing with them more often alone (Etaugh & Bridges, 2004).

Rearing a grandchild is full of both rewards and challenges. While parenting a grandchild is an emotionally fulfilling experience, there are also psychological, health, and economic costs (Harm, 2001). A grandmother raising the young child of her drug-addicted adult daughter may concurrently feel delight with her grandchild, shame for her daughter, anxiety about her own future, health, and finances, anger at the loss of retirement leisure, and guilt for feeling angry. Grandparents raising grandchildren often are stymied by existing laws that give them no legal status unless they gain custody of the grandchild or become the child's foster parents. Each of these procedures involves considerable time, effort, and expense. Yet without custody or foster parent rights, grandparents may encounter difficulties in obtaining the child's medical records, enrolling the child in school, or becoming eligible for certain forms of financial assistance (Cox, 2000). In most instances, grandchildren are ineligible for coverage under grandparents' medical insurance, even if the grandparents have custody.

LABOR FORCE TRANSITIONS

Labor force participation of middle-aged and older women has increased sharply over the past three decades. Two thirds of married women and 70% of unmarried women age 45 to 64 now are in the U.S. labor force. During the same 30-year period, by contrast, men have been retiring earlier. By 2002, only 84% of 45- to 64-year-old married men were in the workforce, compared to 91% in 1970. As a consequence of these changes, which hold across all ethnic groups, the proportion of paid workers 45 and over who are women is higher than ever before (U.S. Census Bureau, 2003).

Many midlife and older women have been employed throughout adulthood. For some working-class women, women of color, and single women, economic necessity has been the driving force. But for many women, a more typical pattern has been movement in and out of the labor force in response to changing family roles and responsibilities. Some women decide to reenter the labor force after their children are grown or following divorce or the death of their spouse (Etaugh & Bridges, 2004).

Older women work for most of the same reasons as younger women. Economic necessity is a key factor at all ages. In addition, feeling challenged and productive, and meeting new coworkers and friends, give women a sense of personal satisfaction and recognition outside the family (Choi, 2000). Active involvement in work and outside interests in women's middle and later years appear to promote physical and psychological well-being. Work-centered women broaden their interests as they grow older and become more satisfied with their lives. Employed older women have higher morale than women retirees, whereas women who have never been employed outside the home have the lowest (Etaugh & Bridges, 2001).

As women get older, they also confront age discrimination in the workplace. While women's complaints filed with the Equal Employment Opportunity Commission primarily concern hiring, promotion, wages, and fringe benefits, men more often file on the basis of job termination and involuntary retirement. Women also experience age discrimination at a younger age than men (Rife, 2001). This is another example of the double standard of aging, with women seen as becoming older at an earlier age than men. Western society's emphasis on youthful sexual attractiveness for women, and the stereotype of older women as powerless, weak, sick, helpless, and unproductive, create obstacles for older women who are seeking employment or who wish to remain employed.

As retirement age approaches, women and men may differ in their readiness to retire. Compared to men, women arrive at the threshold of retirement with a different work and family history, less planning for retirement, and fewer financial resources (Kim & Moen, 2001). A man who has put in several decades in the workforce may be eager to retire once he meets Social Security or pension eligibility requirements. A woman, on the other hand, may have entered the labor force later, after children entered school or were launched. In addition to still being enthusiastic about her job, she may want to continue working in order to build up her pension and Social Security benefits. A growing number of women continue to work after their husbands retire. Women who did not work when their children were young, compared to those who did, are more likely to continue working after their husbands retire. Widowed and divorced women are more apt than married women to plan for postponed retirement or no retirement at all (Choi, 2000). In addition, women who have strong work identities have more negative attitudes toward retiring than those with weaker work identities. Professional women and those who are self-employed, who presumably have strong work identities, are less likely than other women to retire early (Etaugh & Bridges, 2001).

While some women delay their retirement, others retire early. Poor health is one of the major determinants of early retirement. Because aging African American women and men tend to be in poorer health than aging Whites, they are likely to retire earlier (Etaugh & Bridges, 2001). Women's role as primary caregiver to elderly parents, spouses, or other relatives is another factor contributing to their early retirement. Elder care responsibilities often result in increased tardiness and absenteeism at work, as well as health problems for the caregiver. Most businesses do not offer work flexibility or support to workers who care for elder relatives. As a result, nearly one quarter of women caregivers reduce their hours or take time off without pay. Of those who continue to work, some are forced to retire earlier than planned. Women whose husbands are in poor health are more likely to retire than women whose husbands enjoy good health. Some women, of course, simply want to retire, whether to spend more time with a partner, family, or friends, to start one's own business, to pursue lifelong interests, or to develop new ones (Etaugh & Bridges, 2001).

Retirement has long been seen as an individual—primarily male—transition. But now, couples increasingly must deal with two retirements, according to Moen and her colleagues (Moen, Kim, & Hofmeister, 2001). They found that retirement was a happy time for retired couples. But the transition to retirement, defined as the first two

years after leaving a job, was a time of marital conflict for both women and men. Wives and husbands who retired at the same time were happier than couples in which the spouses retired at different times. Marital conflict was highest when husbands retired first, perhaps because of uneasiness with the role reversal of a working wife and a stay-at-home husband.

CONCLUSIONS

The midlife experiences discussed here must be placed in their historical and social context. Because there are greater options for young women today than there were in the 1960s and 1970s, when current midlife women were making life choices, it is possible that fewer young women today will find the need to make significant revisions in their paths during middle age.

A second cautionary note is that most of the research on women's midlife transitions has been done with White, highly educated, middle-class Western women. The midlife experiences of women of color, less educated women, poor women, and those in non-Western cultures have been almost completely unexplored.

NOTE

From Claire A. Etaugh and Judith S. Bridges, Midlife transitions. In J. Worell (Ed.), *Encyclopedia of women and gender* (Vol. 2, pp. 759–769). Copyright 2001 by Academic Press. Adapted by permission from Elsevier.

REFERENCES

Addis, M. E., and Mahalik, J. R. (2003). Men, masculinity, and the contexts of help seeking. *American Psychologist, 58*, 5–14.

Ayubi-Moak, I., and Parry, B. L. (2002). Psychiatric aspects of menopause: Depression. In S. G. Kornstein & A. H. Clayton (Eds.), *Women's mental health: A comprehensive textbook* (pp. 132–143). New York: Guilford Press.

Bee, H. L. (2000). *The journey of adulthood* (4th ed.). Upper Saddle River, NJ: Prentice-Hall.

Black, M. M., Papas, M. A., Hussey, J. M., Hunter, W., Dubowitz, H., Kotch, J. B., et al. (2002). Behavior and development of preschool children born to adolescent mothers: Risk and 3-generation households. *Pediatrics, 109*, 573–580.

Carr, D. (1997). The fulfillment of career dreams at midlife: Does it matter for women's mental health? *Journal of Health and Social Behavior, 38,* 331–344.

Centers for Disease Control and Prevention. (2002). Women and smoking: A report of the Surgeon General. *Morbidity and Mortality Weekly Report, 51* (No. RR-12).

Choi, N. G. (2000). Determinants of engagement in paid work following Social Security benefit receipt among older women. *Journal of Women & Aging, 12,* 133–154.

Cox, C. B. (Ed.). (2000). *To grandmother's house we go and stay: Perspectives on custodial grandparents.* New York: Springer.

Cutter, J. A. (1999, June 13). Coming to terms with grief after a longtime partner dies. *New York Times,* p. WH10.

Derry, P. S. (2002). What do we mean by "The biology of menopause?" *Sex Roles, 46,* 13–23.

Etaugh, C. A., and Bridges, J. S. (2001). Midlife transitions. In J. Worell (Ed.), *Encyclopedia of women and gender* (pp. 759–770). San Diego, CA: Academic Press.

Etaugh, C. A., and Bridges, J. S. (2004). *Psychology of women: A life span perspective* (2nd ed.). Boston: Allyn & Bacon.

Fields, J., and Casper, L. M. (2001). *America's families and living arrangements: March 2000.* Current Population Reports, P20-537. Washington, DC: U.S. Census Bureau.

Fingerman, K. L. (2001). *Aging mothers and their adult daughters: A study in mixed emotions.* New York: Springer.

Gaylord, S. (2001). Women and aging: A psychological perspective. In J. D. Garner & S. O. Mercer (Eds.), *Women as they age* (2nd ed., pp. 49–68). New York: Haworth.

Goldman, M. B., and Hatch, M. C. (Eds.). (2000). *Women and health.* New York: Academic Press.

Harm, N. J. (2001). Grandmothers raising grandchildren: Parenting the second time around. In J. D. Garner and S. O. Mercer (Eds.), *Women as they age* (2nd ed., pp. 131–146). New York: Haworth.

Helson, R. (1992). Women's difficult times and the rewriting of the life story. *Psychology of Women Quarterly, 16,* 331–347.

Katz, S. J., Kabeto, M., and Langa, K. M. (2000). Gender disparities in the receipt of homecare for elderly people with disability in the United States. *Journal of the American Medical Association, 284,* 3022–3027.

Kim, J. E., and Moen, P. (2001). Moving into retirement: Preparation and transitions in late midlife. In M. Lachman (Ed.), *Handbook of midlife development* (pp. 487–527). New York: John Wiley & Sons.

Kinsella, K., and Velkoff, V. A. (2001). *An aging world: 2001.* U.S. Census Bureau, Series P95/01-1. Washington, DC: U.S. Government Printing Office.

Lippert, L. (1997). Women at midlife: Implications for theories of women's adult development. *Journal of Counseling & Development, 76,* 16–22.

McConatha, J. T., Hayta, V., Riley, L., & Leach, E. (2002, June). *Attitudes toward aging.* Poster presented at the meeting of the American Psychological Society, New Orleans, LA.

McQuaide, S. (1998). Women at midlife. *Social Work, 43,* 21–31.

Mitchell, V., and Helson, R. (1990). Women's prime of life: Is it the 50s? *Psychology of Women Quarterly, 14,* 451–470.

Moen, P., Kim, J. E., and Hofmeister, H. (2001). Couples work/retirement transitions, gender, and mental quality. *Social Psychology Quarterly, 64,* 55–71.

Noonan, D., and Adler, J. (2002, May 13). The Botox boom. *Newsweek,* pp. 50–58.

Pruchno, R. A., and McKenney, D. (2002). Psychological well-being of Black and White grandmothers raising grandchildren: Examination of a two-factor model. *Journal of Gerontology: Psychological Sciences, 57B,* 444–452.

Rathus, S., Nevid, J., and Fichner-Rathus, L. (2002). *Human sexuality in a world of diversity* (5th ed.). Boston: Allyn & Bacon.

Rife, J. C. (2001). Middle-aged and older women in the workforce. In J. M. Coyle (Ed.), *Handbook on women and aging* (pp. 93–111). Westport, CT: Greenwood.

Sheehy, G. (2002, May 12). It's about pure love. *Parade Magazine,* pp. 6–8.

Sommer, B., Avis, N., Meyer, P., Ory, M., Madden, T., Kagawa-Senger, M., et al. (1999). Attitudes toward menopause and aging across ethnic/racial groups. *Psychosomatic Medicine, 61*(6), 868–875.

Spraggins, R. E. (2003). *Women and men in the United States: March 2002.* Current Population Reports, P20-544. Washington, DC: U.S. Census Bureau.

Stewart, A. J., and Vandewater, E. A. (1999). "If I had it to do over again": Midlife review, midcourse corrections, and women's well-being in midlife. *Journal of Personality and Social Psychology, 76,* 270–283.

Torrez, D. J. (2001). The health of older women: A diverse experience. In J. M. Coyle (Ed.), *Handbook on women on aging* (pp. 131–148). Westport, CT: Greenwood.

U.S. Census Bureau. (2003). *Statistical abstract of the United States: 2003* (123rd ed.). Washington, DC: U.S. Government Printing Office.

Velkoff, V. A., & Lawson, V. A. (1998). *Gender and aging: Caregiving* (1B/98-3). Washington, DC: U.S. Bureau of the Census.

Yaffe, K., Fox, P., Newcomer, R., Sands, L., Lindquist, K., Dane, K., et al. (2002). Patient and caregiving characteristics and nursing home placement in patients with dementia. *Journal of the American Medical Association, 287,* 2090–2097.

Older Adults: Winding Down and Summing Up

SUSAN KRAUSS WHITBOURNE
and KARYN M. SKULTETY

Aging and Identity: How Women Face Later Life Transitions

39

The study of women in later adulthood poses a number of theoretical and methodological challenges. By far, the preponderance of late-life research has failed to give specific attention to the psychosocial processes involved in women's adaptation to aging. Most research on aging and women either derives from a medical model, focusing on menopause and related health concerns, or fails to examine the roles that women play outside the home in the workplace and the community. In this chapter, we explore the implications of a model that examines identity in adulthood to better understand the psychology of women in later life. This exploration is based on cross-sectional data comparing women and men across the adult years. Following the examination of this model, we review the research on women in the roles of family member and retiree, interpreting the existing data and providing real-life examples in terms of the identity process model. Finally, we suggest potential areas for intervention to improve the experience of women as they age.

An important backdrop for understanding late life transitions for women is the by now well-known "double standard" of aging (Sontag, 1979). The double standard refers to the dual stereotypes faced by aging women of ageism (negative stereotypes of and attitudes toward older people) and sexism. Women in our culture gain value based on their appearance, and therefore as they age they move further away from what is most valued by society. The challenge is even greater for women of color, owing to the existence of "multiple jeopardy"—the combined impact of ageism, sexism, and racism. Against this backdrop, women must attempt to maintain a positive view of the self as they age while society communicates a largely negative message about their value.

IDENTITY PROCESS THEORY AND RESEARCH

The theory of identity processes is a merging of the theories of Piaget and Erikson. Identity process theory proposes that age-related changes in adulthood are negotiated through the processes of *identity assimilation, identity accommodation,* and *identity balance.* The propositions from this theory were derived from a semistructured interview study of middle-aged adults regarding their views on family, work, values, and aging (Whitbourne, 1986). Subsequent research based on identity process theory has involved the Identity and Experiences Scale (IES; Whitbourne, 1996) developed to measure the extent to which an individual uses each of the three identity processes. Studies using the IES have developed the theory into a framework for understanding transitions throughout adulthood and have expanded it to address age-related changes in physical and cognitive functioning (Whitbourne, 1998), self-esteem, and personality variables including defense mechanisms (Whitbourne, Sneed, & Skultety, 2002), depression (Jones, Skultety, & Whitbourne, 2003), and private versus public self-consciousness (Sneed & Whitbourne, 2003).

In identity process theory, identity is conceptualized as a broad biopsychosocial self-definition encompassing the individual's self-representation in the areas of physical functioning, cognition, personality, relationships, occupation, and social roles. Normal, healthy (i.e., nondepressed) adults attempt to maintain a positive view of themselves in these realms. This set of positive self-attributions is maintained primarily through the process of identity assimilation, which (as in Piaget's theory) is defined as the interpretation of new experiences through the existing identity. When experiences become sufficiently discrepant from identity, the individual may then begin to make shifts through identity accommodation. According to the theory, as in Piaget's, it is assumed that the ideal state is one of balance between identity assimilation and identity accommodation.

Investigations of identity processes in middle and later adulthood have established a consistent pattern of relationships among identity, self-esteem, age, and gender. For both sexes, identity balance is positively correlated with self-esteem; and identity accommodation is negatively correlated with self-esteem. Identity accommodation is also correlated with depression. Women are more likely to use identity accommodation throughout adulthood than are men. For women only, identity assimilation is positively related both to self-esteem and age. For both sexes, identity accommodation is negatively related to age. We have concluded that although identity bal-

ance is most strongly related to self-esteem, identity assimilation is an important mechanism for women to maintain positive self-esteem in middle and later adulthood (Skultety & Whitbourne, 2004).

There are important implications of these findings for understanding identity and aging women. When a woman uses identity assimilation, she minimizes or ignores an experience relevant to aging, allowing her to continue to view herself as both competent and worthy of regard. For example, an aging woman who is slighted or discriminated against by a younger coworker or supervisor may use identity assimilation to dismiss this experience by attributing it to lack of manners or an inadvertent oversight. Given the negative value attached to the aging woman's appearance and importance, it would seem that identity assimilation is the primary way for an older woman to survive constant threats to her identity and maintain positive self-esteem.

On the other hand, throughout their lives, women have learned to redefine themselves in ways consistent with their experiences, rather than to impose their own views of themselves onto the events that occur and the people who are around them. If the woman in the example was using identity accommodation, she would conclude that she is worthy of blame or criticism due to her age; she might believe that her job contributions and experience are not as valuable as the younger coworker's new ideas. Thus, women face a tension in later life between the tendency to use the more familiar mode of identity accommodation and the need to maintain a positive sense of self through the defensive shield provided by identity assimilation. Compared to men, they vacillate more sharply between avoiding threats to the self from the negative social context and the lifelong tendency to define themselves in terms of external criteria.

Older women also appear to engage in and benefit from identity assimilation in ways that are not true for men. However, identity assimilation may be simply a defense mechanism, a form of denial. The positive relationship between self-esteem and identity assimilation found for women may reflect the preference of aging women to avoid looking inward as a protection against anxiety. In work on identity and defense mechanisms women's, but not men's, identity balance scores were positively related to the use of denial and similar defense mechanisms that distort or minimize the truth. Some aging women are ashamed to admit to using identity assimilation, preferring to portray themselves as using identity balance. Not only must women contend with viewing themselves more negatively as they grow older in response to society's negative portrayal of aging women, but they also must appear to be flexible and open to this negative input. This adds another layer of complexity to an already complicated relationship for women between the aging self and late life experiences.

One might argue that as difficult as it may be for a woman to accommodate to age-related changes in later life, a life-long pattern of identity accommodation may benefit aging women. In addition, without use and familiarity with the costs of accommodation, assimilation may not be as important to self-esteem. The ability to adapt is associated with insight, a sense of meaning, and social relations in middle-aged women (Klohnen, Vandewater, & Young, 1996). Thus, identity accommodation may help women successfully interact with their changing bodies and social contexts by allowing them to be flexible and to adjust to age-related changes. However, given the consistent finding that identity accommodation relates negatively to self-esteem, there are obvious costs involved in the accommodative strategy. In fact, women's vulnerability to depression is related to low scores in instrumentality (the perceived ability to control the environment) and high scores in expressivity (Bromberger & Matthews, 1996). It is clear that identity accommodation lends itself to placing control outside of one's self and relying on the environment and the experiences it provides to define identity. Therefore, it may be that identity accommodation serves to increase the risk of experiencing depression for women; not by being an absolute predictor of women's self-esteem, but rather a risk factor for lower self-esteem and possible depression.

FAMILY TRANSITIONS

It is useful to consider the specific contexts within family relationships and work in which women's identities are challenged as they move from the middle to the later years of adulthood. In the area of family relationships, two major types of transitions are most likely to affect women's identities: the empty nest, or period when children leave the home, and widowhood. In addition, changes in living situations that accompany these role transitions as well as changes in health and physical functioning, present additional challenges to women's identities.

Empty Nest

Early research on the empty nest suggested that this period was often associated with a "syndrome" in which parents, particularly mothers, would experience grief, sadness, and depressive symptoms. In addition, many women reported an increase in anxiety, guilt, and stress related to their concern over their children's well-being during this time of transition. The women found most susceptible to this syndrome were those who experienced the change as losing their role as a mother and did not have other significant roles with which they could identify themselves (Raup & Myers, 1989).

However, contemporary researchers are finding there can be positive aspects of children moving away from the home and that most women do not experience the more negative responses described in the early literature. When reporting the transitions or turning points of their lives, midlife and older women rarely mentioned the empty nest as important. When it was discussed, role loss and sadness were not the main focus. Instead, women discussed pride in the child's independence as well as freedom to pursue their own interests (Leonard & Burns, 1999).

In a longitudinal study, children's leaving the home was found to lead to significant improvements in women's happiness and overall well-being and a reduction in number of daily "hassles." However, women who worried about their children leaving home beforehand did not experience the same benefits. These findings on the empty nest appear to generalize across cultures. A longitudinal study conducted in Hong Kong examined whether depressive symptoms were predicted by stressful life events common in midlife and later adulthood. For women, the experience of having children move out of the home was not accompanied by an increase in symptoms. On the contrary, a slight decrease in depressive symptoms occurred during the transition (Chou & Chi, 2000).

Findings on the empty nest transition are clouded somewhat by the fact that the transition is not always a clear cut change. The phenomenon of the 1990s, in which young adult children returned to live at home again in significant numbers alters the picture of what happens during the empty nest transition. As many as 25% of young adults return to live at home. The return of children to the home creates its own adjustment difficulties for the parents. Those parents who enjoyed a honeymoon of sorts after the children left home find that it is more awkward to maintain their sexual relationship because they are now sharing their home with their adult children (Dennerstein, Dudley, & Guthrie, 2002). The need to care for grandchildren also alters the empty nest. Increasingly, particularly in low-income and ethnic minority families, the grandparents are being called upon to become surrogate parents when their children work or are unable to fulfill the parenting role.

It seems empty nest women who define themselves predominantly in terms of their roles as mother face particular difficulty, unless they are able to use identity assimilation and minimize the impact on their sense of self. However, this strategy means that the woman may become unable to give up her role in her children's lives. She communicates to her children that they will hurt her if they establish separate lives. Therefore, the use of accommodation would allow the woman to recognize that her family role has changed. These processes become more complex when children move in and out of the home throughout this period. Nevertheless, by seeking alternative modes of self-definition, women can experience the empty nest as a positive and growth-enhancing transition.

For example, Carol is a successful architect in her early 60s. She enjoys her work and spends her free time with a large social network of friends. When Carol's children left the home, the event did not negatively impact her identity. She continued to define herself as a mother of grown children, but because she valued her identity as an architect and friend she was not negatively affected by the empty nest.

Widowhood

As women age, they are increasingly likely to face widowhood. About 800,000 older adults in the United States become widows each year (U.S. Department of Health and Human Services, 1999). Women at all ages and among all ethnic minority groups are more likely than men to become widows. Nearly half (46%) of all women over 65 years are widows, which is almost triple the rate for men (14%). The chances of becoming a widow increase substantially after the age of 65 years, particularly for African American women, of whom 83% are widows.

When a marriage ends in the death of a partner, the survivor is faced with enormous readjustments in every aspect of life. Adjustment to widowhood is a difficult and painful process even when there is time to prepare. For some women, bereavement may persist for years after the loss and may become diagnosable as depression (Lichtenstein, Gatz, Pedersen, Berg, & McClearn, 1996). It is important for providers and family members to be aware that long-lasting depressive symptoms are not part of the normal grieving process and should encourage these women to seek further mental health treatment. However, most women will take time to adjust to the change and may experience some depressive symptoms. Without remarriage, levels of well-being may not return to preexisting levels for as long as eight years after the loss (Lucas, Clark, Georgellis, & Diener, 2003). Negative effects on health can persist years after death of the spouse (Goldman, Koreman, & Weinstein, 1995). These effects are more pronounced for men than for women. Studies based on data from the National Survey of Families and Households found that widowhood is predictive of depressive symptoms in men but not women. In addition, men's depression appears to be directly associated with the loss of the spouse (Lee, DeMaris, Bavin, & Sullivan, 2001).

There is an adaptive value to the fact that women suffer fewer depressive symptoms than men following the loss of the spouse because women are less likely to remarry after becoming widows. Women who remarry report fewer concerns both in their day-to-day lives and in retrospectively recalling their concerns following their spouse's death. However, widows who choose not to remarry feel that they have more freedom and do not desire a new relationship (Davidson, 2001).

The loss of a spouse has the potential to alter many aspects of a woman's life. In terms of identity, widowhood also changes a woman's self-definition. No longer a wife, she may find family members, friends, and others in her community treat her differently. Identity accommodation is demanded by the changes brought about in her social status as well as by the changes in her daily routines and relationships with others. If she was emotionally close to her husband, feelings of loss of companionship and her valued life partner are added to the amount of readjustment required. Identity assimilation can serve a protective function in a situation that might otherwise become intolerable. Although the loss of the partner must be recognized, there can be benefit in maintaining a sense of the self as a woman who was in a close relationship for many years. Eventually, after the most difficult adjustment period has passed, identity accommodation can allow her to redefine the aspects of her identity that were related to her role as spouse.

Miriam was married for 52 years prior to her husband's sudden death from a stroke. Miriam's husband was a minister and they enjoyed a satisfying relationship, both with each other and in their involvement in the church. Identity assimilation was useful for Miriam in the time of her loss; she continued to define herself in terms of her important role as a minister's wife and remained involved in church activities. In addition, she continued to view her relationship with her husband as a model for other married couples. Over time, however, Miriam needed to use identity accommodation to redefine her identity as a widow to address living alone and finding new sources of social support. Throughout this process, she achieved a sense of balance between her past identity as a minister's wife and her new identity as a widow.

Identity plays a very different role in the ending of a relationship late in life as a result of divorce. Divorce rates are lower among adults aged 60 years and older than in the general population, but are remarkably high, with about 32% of first marriages ending in divorce (U.S. Bureau of the Census, 2000). Divorce has become more accepted in society, but there remains a sense of shame for many older adults. Older divorced women face a number of challenges to their identities. Identity assimilation is a far more adaptive strategy than ruminating on one's failures, at least until the shock and pain of the breakup subsides. As a woman develops alternative ways of defining herself outside of the role of wife, identity accommodation may allow her to achieve a more realistic view of the contribution each partner made to the relationship's dissolution.

Friendships are not a replacement for the deceased spouse or divorced partner, but they do offset the loss and help to maintain the older woman's sense of well-being. Women are more likely than men to be committed to and benefit from their roles as friends. Commitment to the role of friend and the self-identification as a friend predicts well-being, even more so than income or marital status (Siebert, Mutran, & Reitzes, 1999).

For both widowhood and divorce in older women, the risks to physical and psychological well-being are exacerbated by ethnic minority status. There is a much greater chance that they will live in poverty than women who are White and middle class, although they may find more support from extended family and social networks. The strain to meet their needs for adequate housing, food, and health care means that they may not have the luxury to rely on identity assimilation until they can adjust their identities to their new situations.

Relocation

Widowhood and changes in health status often lead to the older woman's decision to move out of her own home. Relocation is a common fact of life for older adult women, although relatively few studies examine how women are affected by changes in living arrangements. One longitudinal investigation followed 31 women over the course of one year throughout the moving process from their own homes to an assisted living facility. Those women who were healthy and moved for social reasons or concerns about future health had a higher quality of life and fewer depressive symptoms than those who moved for health reasons or those who felt uncertain about their reasons for the move (Rossen, 1999). In fact, older adults who move as a result of an active goal-directed process are likely to improve their well-being, in contrast to those who feel forced to move due to family influence or health reasons (Oswald, Schilling, Wahl, & Gaeng, 2002).

A number of factors may influence the well-being of women when they move into community facilities. In a longitudinal study, Smider, Essex, and Ryff (1996) examined psychological factors (environmental mastery, autonomy, and desire for personal growth) and contextual factors (pressure to move, difficulty of move, and unexpected gains experienced) that influence women's emotional reactions to the move. Women with greater psychological resources were more resilient when faced with negative circumstances related to relocation. However, there was a significant emotional "boost" for women with fewer psychological resources when they discovered unexpected positive gains in their new living situation.

Relocation is potentially stressful, but it can stimulate identity accommodation in a positive direction. Older women who cope successfully with the demands of a new environment and make independent decisions may experience positive identity change. In addition, women who value their independence will likely view the decision to move as a positive indication of their continued ability to care for themselves.

RETIREMENT

The majority of research on retirement has been conducted on men. The early research on women's retirement in the 1970s suggested that women had more positive attitudes toward retirement than did men. However, it is likely that the labor force experience of women who retired at that time was very different from the experience of current cohorts of women. The older cohorts of women had a less consistent work history than later cohorts of women; most were employed for financial necessity rather than strong work commitment. By the 1980s, researchers reported significantly lower retirement satisfaction for women than men, as well as more initial stress immediately following women's exit from the workforce (Seccombe & Lee, 1986). Problems are experienced both by women holding lower status jobs (Richardson & Kilty, 1991) and women in professional level occupations (Price, 2000).

A large-scale study of the retirement experience was the Cornell Retirement and Well-Being Study, conducted in the mid-1990s on a sample of more than 750 retired individuals between the ages of 50 and 72 years. The women in this study, whose work lives spanned the mid-1940s to the 1990s, had less continuous work histories than men. They spent fewer years in the labor force, took more breaks from employment, and did more part-time work than did men. Unlike the men in the sample, women who had spent more time in the labor force (fewer gaps and part-time employment) had higher satisfaction during their retirement years than women who had less continuous work histories. These differences remained even after other relevant factors were controlled, such as income, health, the nature of the job, and the reason for and timing of retirement. Unlike men, for whom the extent of advance planning predicted degree of satisfaction with retirement, women's retirement satisfaction was predicted by the timing of their work patterns (Quick & Moen, 1998).

There are other differences between men and women in the retirement experience. Women are more likely to spend time with relatives and become involved in organization work (Dorfman, 1995). The retirement of women is more likely to be affected by the poor health of their spouse or other family members. If wives are caring for their husbands, they are five times more likely to retire than if they do not have this responsibility (Dentinger & Clarkberg, 2002). Ethnic minority and marital status may influence the extent to which family obligations determine women's decision to retire. African American women are less likely to retire when they have ill family members. However, African American women with a child living in the household are more likely to retire than White women, who are less likely to retire when there is still a child living in the household (Szinovacz & Davey, 2001).

Similar to the transitions in relationship and family life, retirement has the potential to stimulate identity processes. The extent to which retirement affects a woman's identity depends heavily upon the salience of the work role to her sense of self. For example, retired professional women may face threats to their identities related to the loss of high social status, social contacts, and professional challenges, as well as threats related to the emergence of stereotypes and discrimination they did not experience while working (Price, 2000). For women at all occupational levels, the work role itself is a part of identity and helps to define sense of competence. The loss of this role may threaten some of the fundamental assumptions a woman makes about herself and her abilities.

The circumstances under which retirement occurs must also be considered. Women who view their retirement more favorably when they first retire are more likely to have positive morale and high levels of well-being throughout the retirement period (Kim & Moen, 2002). Perhaps the women with the more positive attitudes are using identity assimilation and prefer not to think about the negative side of retirement, or perhaps they truly view the experience in a positive light. Alternative sources of identity within the community, volunteer organizations, or family relationships may help these women retain favorable views of themselves over time. Women's involvement in these activities may allow them to view retirement as a way to gain time for developing new skills and interests, rather than as lost time for work. Conversely, using identity accommodation to the exclusion of identity assimilation carries other risks. A woman may experience loss and identity confusion if she no longer recognizes the important economic and societal contributions she made while working.

These psychological processes are confounded by the loss of financial resources available to women after they retire. As important as finding an alternative source of identity may be to women's postretirement self-esteem is, their primary set of needs is to maintain adequate nutrition, housing, and health care. Beyond these basic needs, women who can afford to travel, shop, exercise, maintain their household, and engage in social activities will find many more ways divert themselves in the hours formerly spent working and will reinforce their core sense of competence.

Laura is a successful lawyer who was forced to retire owing to her husband's development of dementia. In approaching this change, Laura could have used identity assimilation, by viewing herself as the loving and supportive wife she has always been. She could also have continued to view herself as a successful career woman whose retirement was due to her need to care for her husband. However, the tendencies toward identity assimilation were outweighed by the severe and sudden changes that relegated her to the role of caretaker, an identity that she did not value and that did not provide the same social supports and status she had as a lawyer. Laura was able to establish a state of balance in which she continued to feel proud of her outstanding law career. She began to enjoy the financial rewards from her work by pursuing new hobbies, while also coming to value herself in a new way, as a caretaker.

INTERVENTIONS

Late-life transitions pose challenges that threaten women's well-being and for some women may lead to the development of symptoms of depression or anxiety. Unfortunately, these symptoms are often viewed as part of the normal aging process and ignored by both the aging woman and those around her. Women are most likely to report these symptoms to their primary practice physicians (Arean, Alvidrez, Barrera, Robinson, & Hicks, 2002), and it is important for these providers and family members to assist older women in seeking further support and treatment.

Cognitive-behavioral and interpersonal individual psychotherapy are effective treatments for depression and anxiety in older adults (Scogin, Floyd, & Forde, 2000). Through individual psychotherapy, an older woman could explore her feelings regarding her retirement or changes in her family roles, as well as develop new behaviors to increase her sense of well-being. Effective group therapies developed for older adults provide both treatment for depression and opportunities for socialization with others (Thompson,

Coon, & Gallagher-Thompson, 2001). In addition to therapy groups, many support groups are available particularly for those women experiencing bereavement (Gottlieb, 2000). These groups help women to share their experiences with other newly widowed women and gain support during their time of loss. Older women may choose to utilize any of these services to help them through their difficult periods of transition and maintain their well-being through the aging process.

CONCLUSIONS

Older women face many challenges to the sense of self established earlier in life. Nevertheless, the majority of older women are able to define themselves in ways that foster a positive view of who they are and what they have accomplished, despite the possibility of discrimination from the multiple domains of ageism, sexism, and (for ethnic minority women), racism. Identity assimilation appears to be the primary method used by women to preserve their sense of self, although they also incorporate changes through identity accommodation. Both family and career transitions require older women take on new, or at least modified, self-definitions of their roles. Fortunately, the majority of women are remarkably successful in making these transitions and achieving a sense of balance as they move through their later years.

REFERENCES

Arean, P. A., Alvidrez, J., Barrera, A., Robinson, G. S., & Hicks, S. (2002). Would older medical patients use psychological services? *The Gerontologist, 42,* 392–398.

Bromberger, J. T., & Matthews, K. A. (1996). A "feminine" model of vulnerability to depressive symptoms: A longitudinal investigation of middle-aged women. *Journal of Personality and Social Psychology, 70,* 591–598.

Chou, K. L., & Chi, I. (2000). Stressful events and depressive symptoms among old women and men: A longitudinal study. *International Journal of Aging and Human Development, 51,* 275–293.

Davidson, K. (2001). Late life widowhood, selfishness, and new partnership choices: A gendered perspective. *Ageing and Society, 21,* 297–317.

Dennerstein, L., Dudley, E., & Guthrie, J. (2002). Empty nest or revolving door? A prospective study of women's quality of life in midlife during the phase of children leaving and re-entering the home. *Psychological Medicine, 32,* 545–550.

Dentinger, E., & Clarkberg, M. (2002). Informal caregiving and retirement timing among men and women: Gender and caregiving relationships in late midlife. *Journal of Family Issues, 23,* 857–879.

Dorfman, L. T. (1995). Health, financial status, and social participation of retired men and women: Implications for educational intervention. *Educational Gerontology, 21,* 653–669.

Goldman, N., Koreman, S., & Weinstein, R. (1995). Marital status and health among the elderly. *Social Science and Medicine, 40,* 1717–1730.

Gottlieb, B. H. (2000). Self-help, mutual aid and support groups among older adults. *Canadian Journal on Aging, 19,* 58–74.

Jones, K. M., Skultety, K. M., & Whitbourne, S. K. (2003, November). *Identity processes and concerns about aging in middle and later adulthood.* Paper presented at the 56th Annual Meeting of the Gerontological Society of America, San Diego, CA.

Kim, J. E., & Moen, P. (2002). Retirement transitions, gender, and psychological well-being: A life-course, ecological model. *Journals of Gerontology: Psychological Sciences, 57,* P212–P222.

Klohnen, E. C., Vandewater, E. A., & Young, A. (1996). Negotiating the middle years: Ego-resiliency and successful midlife adjustment in women. *Psychology and Aging, 11,* 431–442.

Lee, G. R., DeMaris, A., Bavin, S., & Sullivan, R. (2001). Gender differences in the depressive effect of widowhood in later life. *Journals of Gerontology: Social Sciences, 56,* S56–S61.

Leonard, R., & Burns, A. (1999). Turning points in the lives of midlife and older women. *Australian Psychologist, 34,* 87–93.

Lichtenstein, P., Gatz, M., Pedersen, N. L., Berg, S., & McClearn, G. E. (1996). A co-twin-control study of response to widowhood. *Journal of Gerontology: Psychological Sciences, 51,* 279–289.

Lucas, R. E., Clark, A. E., Georgellis, Y., & Diener, E. (2003). Reexamining adaptation and the set point model of happiness: Reactions to changes in marital status. *Journal of Personality and Social Psychology, 84,* 527–539.

Oswald, F., Schilling, O., Wahl, H., & Gaeng, K. (2002). Trouble in paradise? Reasons to relocate and objective environmental changes among well-off older adults. *Journal of Environmental Psychology, 22,* 273–288.

Price, C. A. (2000). Women and retirement: Relinquishing professional identity. *Journal of Aging Studies, 14,* 81–101.

Quick, H. E., & Moen, P. (1998). Gender, employment, and retirement quality: A life course approach to the differential experiences of men and women. *Journal of Occupational Health Physiology, 3,* 44–64.

Raup, J. L., & Myers, J. E. (1989). The empty nest syndrome: Myth or reality? *Journal of Counseling and Development, 68,* 180–183.

Richardson, V., & Kilty, K. (1991). Adjustment to retirement: Continuity versus discontinuity. *International Journal of Aging and Human Development, 32,* 151–169.

Rossen, E. K. (1999). Older women in relocation transition. *Dissertation Abstracts International: Section B: The Sciences and Engineering, 59.*

Scogin, F., Floyd, M., & Forde, J. (2000). Anxiety in older adults. In S. K. Whitbourne (Ed.), *Psychopathology in later life* (pp. 117–140). New York: John Wiley & Sons.

Seccombe, K., & Lee, G. R. (1986). Gender differences in retirement satisfaction and its antecedents. *Research on Aging, 8,* 426–440.

Siebert, D. C., Mutran, E. J., & Reitzes, D. C. (1999). Friendship and social support: The importance of role identity to aging adults. *Social Work, 44,* 522–533.

Skultety, K. M., & Whitbourne, S. K. (2004). Gender differences in identity processes and self-esteem in middle and later adulthood. *Journal of Women and Aging, 16,* 175–188.

Smider, N. A., Essex, M. J., & Ryff, C. D. (1996). Adaptation to community relocation: the interactive influence of psychological resources and contextual factors. *Psychology and Aging, 11,* 362–372.

Sneed, J. R., & Whitbourne, S. K. (2003). Identity processing and self-consciousness in middle and later adulthood. *Journals of Gerontology: Psychological Sciences, 58,* P313–P319.

Sontag, S. (1979). The double standard of aging. In J. Williams (Ed.), *Psychology of women* (pp. 462–478). San Diego, CA: Academic Press.

Szinovacz, M. E., & Davey, A. (2001). Retirement effects on parent-adult child contacts. *Gerontologist, 41,* 191–200.

Thompson, L. W., Coon, D. W., & Gallagher-Thompson, D. (2001). Comparison of desipramine and cognitive/behavioral therapy in the treatment of elderly outpatients with mild-to-moderate depression. *American Journal of Geriatric Psychiatry, 9,* 225–240.

U.S. Bureau of the Census. (2000). Detailed tables for Current Population Report, P20-537. Retrieved December 6, 2003, from http://www.census.gov/population/www/socdemo/hh-fam/p20-537_00.html

U.S. Department of Health and Human Services. (1999). *Mental health: A report of the Surgeon General.* Bethesda, MD: U.S. Public Health Service.

Whitbourne, S. K. (1986). *The me I know: A study of adult identity.* New York: Springer-Verlag.

Whitbourne, S. K. (1996). *The aging individual: Physical and psychological perspectives.* New York: Springer-Verlag.

Whitbourne, S. K. (1998). Physical changes in the aging individual: Clinical implications. In I. H. Nordhus & G. R. VandenBos (Eds.), *Clinical geropsychology* (pp. 79–108). Washington, DC: American Psychological Association.

Whitbourne, S. K., Sneed, J. R., & Skultety, K. M. (2002). Identity processes in adulthood: Theoretical and methodological challenges. *Identity, 2,* 29–45.

S. DEBORAH MAJEROVITZ

Physical Health and Illness in Older Women

40

Advances in health care over the last century have radically altered our experience of old age. First, average life expectancy has increased dramatically over the past century. Vaccines, antibiotics, and improved obstetric care have all but eradicated many common causes of death for children and young adults, so that the majority of people can expect to become old. Improved treatment for chronic illness has further increased life expectancy.

At every age and in every country that reports health statistics, women have lower rates of mortality than men (Idler, 2003). As a result, the majority of older adults are female and this gender gap widens with age. There are several theories attempting to explain this gender gap in health and longevity, including a biologically based health advantage for women resulting from sex hormones or genetic differences, better health behaviors and use of health care, less stressful and dangerous work environments, and lower risk-taking behavior (Gold, Malmberg, McClearn, Pedersen, & Berg, 2002). Older women report more symptoms of illness and live with more chronic health conditions than men, although life-threatening chronic conditions are more prevalent among older men, even within brother-sister twin pairs (Gold et al., 2002).

Longer life span adds a layer of complexity to the study of physical health in old age. First, old age is not the brief and fairly homogeneous time of life it once was. Age 65 is commonly considered the start of old age. With more and more people, particularly women, living into their late 80s and beyond, old age will last for 20 years or more. The health concerns of a 65-year-old are very different from those of an 85-year-old. As a result, gerontologists commonly speak of at least two distinct age groups: the young-old (65–75) and the old-old (late 70s and beyond). Some even add the oldest-old, referring to those over 85 (Smith, Borchelt, Maier, & Jopp, 2002). In the early decade of older adulthood, most people can expect to live a relatively healthy and active life. Among the old-old, the overwhelming majority live with at least one chronic health problem, and many must cope with two or more. Even more important, functional limitations resulting from these health problems become more common with advancing age, increasing the need for assistance with day-to-day needs. In addition to health declines related to chronic illness, older adults experience natural declines in physical and cognitive functioning as part of the normal aging process. While medical interventions and lifestyle changes can slow down or even reverse functional deficits associated with illness, older adults must learn to compensate for age-related changes in functioning.

Despite the prevalence of chronic illness among older adults, any consideration of physical health in older women must look beyond counting chronic illnesses and listing their symptoms. Physical health at all ages is inextricably linked to psychological well-being (Smith et al., 2002). There is ample evidence that illness and disability can be associated with depression and other indicators of psychological distress (Williamson & Schulz, 1992) while psychological stress can negatively affect physical health (Marsland, Bachen, Cohen, & Manuck, 2001). Research also suggests that it is functional limitation and disability, not the mere presence of chronic illness, that negatively affect psychological well-being among older women (Smith et al., 2002).

This chapter addresses functional disability in general, as well as a number of chronic illnesses common in old age. For each illness, the discussion includes its impact on functional status and psychological well-being with a particular focus on older women, as well as interventions shown to ameliorate some of these negative effects. Finally, this chapter explores factors that moderate the relationships among illness, disability, and psychological distress, allowing older women to lead satisfying lives and maintain independence.

FUNCTIONAL IMPAIRMENT AFFECTS QUALITY OF LIFE

Many of the natural age-related changes in sensorimotor systems can be associated with functional impairment in old age, particularly among the oldest old. Older adults may experience declines in neurological and muscular function, changes in proprioception leading to difficulty maintaining balance, decreased bone density and muscle mass, age-related declines in vision and hearing, and reduced reaction time (Ketcham

& Stelmach, 2001). These changes can compromise balance and motor control among older adults, leading to fear of falling and increased functional limitation. For older women who suffer from osteoporosis, fear of falling and suffering a fracture can further limit mobility and autonomy. Prospective research indicates that mobility impairment is associated with increased risk of mortality, particularly for individuals who engage in little physical activity (Hirvensalo, Rantanen, & Heikkinen, 2000).

In addition to changes associated with normal aging, a number of chronic illnesses prevalent in old age contribute to functional impairment. However, there is great variability in the impact of chronic illness on physical functioning. Health behaviors and personal resources such as social support and self-efficacy can help older women maintain functional independence despite chronic illness. For example, in a large longitudinal study of older adults with and without chronic illness (Seeman & Chen, 2002) regular exercise was associated with less functional decline over the course of the study for all participants, with or without chronic illness. Among participants with chronic illness, social support buffered its effects on functional ability, while negative social interactions were associated with greater disability.

Much of the research on functional impairment in old age measures disability as need for assistance with activities of daily living (ADL) and instrumental activities of daily living (IADL). ADL include basic self-care functions such as bathing, dressing, and mobility. IADL encompass more complex activities required for truly independent living, such as paying bills, using the telephone, or shopping. This reflects the central role that continued independence plays in quality of life for older adults (Gignac, Cott, & Badley, 2000).

In order to maintain independence in the face of diminished functional abilities, Baltes and Baltes (1990) have outlined a complex adaptational process called selective optimization with compensation. Older adults maintain their sense of well-being and functional independence by selectively concentrating on activities that are more highly valued and still within their capabilities. At the same time, they are able to compensate for the loss of other abilities through cognitive restructuring or behavioral substitutions. This may help explain the wide variability in response to chronic illness and age-related disability. In a study of older adults with osteoarthritis or osteoporosis, older adults used a variety of active strategies of activity selection, optimization of existing abilities, and compensation through assistive devices or changed routines in order to maintain maximum functional independence (Gignac et al., 2000). Traditional gender roles influence the activities and life domains that women value and feel most skilled in performing. As women age, they are likely to "select" these valued and familiar domains over others, possibly explaining gender differences in behavior and activity levels.

Each of the different chronic illnesses and disabilities prevalent in old age has differential impact on performance of individual ADL and IADL (Furner, Rudberg, & Cassel, 1995). Some conditions, such as hypertension, have little impact on daily functioning. Others, such as stroke and visual impairment, are associated with limitations across a wide range of activities. Older adults living with progressive conditions, such as arthritis, will show increasing disability over time.

COMMON CHRONIC ILLNESSES OF OLDER WOMEN

While it would be impossible to discuss every chronic health condition and its impact on health and well-being, a selection of major age-related chronic conditions will be considered independently to highlight these differential effects.

Arthritis

Arthritis is the most common chronic illness among older adults (U.S. Bureau of the Census, 1996). While arthritis is not life threatening, it is a major cause of pain and functional limitations. Younger adults are at elevated risk for psychological distress as a result of their arthritis symptoms, whereas older adults with arthritis tend to experience greater functional disability but better psychological adjustment (Burke, Zautra, Schultz, Reich, & Davis, 2002). However, older women with osteoarthritis or rheumatoid arthritis are at risk for depression when pain is elevated, while women with rheumatoid arthritis also may experience depressive symptoms in response to stress (Zautra & Smith, 2001).

Health-related quality of life for older adults with arthritis is linked to subjective evaluations of the illness context. When older people with arthritis place a high value on an activity, difficulty performing that activity is related to reduced satisfaction with physical functioning (Rejeski, Martin, Miller, Ettinger, & Rapp, 1998). Similarly, in a study of Latina women (of varying ages) with rheumatoid arthritis, inability to fulfill culturally valued family roles was related to greater emotional distress (Abraido-Lanza, 1997). For the current cohort of old-old women, pain and functional impairment associated with arthritis may impinge on traditionally valued roles and identities such as grandparent or homemaker. For young-old women, who are more likely to have entered the workforce or to have developed interests in sports or travel, arthritis would be perceived as stressful when it interfered with fulfillment of these valued roles and interests.

Although we cannot reverse age-related declines or cure chronic illness, research shows that lifestyle changes can dramatically improve quality of life for older women, slowing down physical decline and improving pain and functional ability. Longitudinal research with large representative samples provides strong evidence that even low levels of physical activity can improve physical functioning and slow down the progression of functional declines (Miller, Rejeski, Reboussin, Ten Have, & Ettinger, 2000). Unfortunately, many older women, particularly among the oldest cohorts, hold many unrealistic beliefs about risks associated with exercising at their age (O'Brien Cousins, 2000). Nonmedical barriers to exercise appear to be stronger for older women than for older men (Satariano, Haight, & Tager, 2000). Many older women grew up at a time when exercise was considered a man's domain and the health benefits of physical activity were not widely known. Interventions involving group walking programs for older women have shown promise in encouraging increased physical activity among older women across diverse ethnic backgrounds (Clark, 1999; Shin, 1999).

Vision and Hearing Impairment

Declines in sensory acuity and sensorimotor integration are inevitable as we age. However, research shows that for most people, significant sensory impairment occurs primarily in the oldest old (Fozard & Gordon-Salant, 2001). Sensory impairment, especially visual impairment, is a strong predictor of functional disability among older adults across studies (e.g., Reuben, Mui, Damesyn, Moore, & Greendale, 1999).

Older adults experience a range of changes in vision, including visual acuity, sensitivity to light and glare, color discrimination, decreased vision in low light, and presbyopia (Fozard & Gordon-Salant, 2001). Chronic illnesses associated with advancing age, such as glaucoma and cataracts, further impair vision for some older adults. Women are more likely than men to report disability related to vision loss (Raina, Wong, Dukeshire, Chambers, & Lindsay, 2000).

Hearing loss among older adults combines age-related changes with damage to the auditory system resulting from long-term exposure to noise and other environmental factors (Fozard & Gordon-Salant, 2001). Hearing loss tends to occur earlier and is more pronounced in men than in women (Fozard & Gordon-Salant, 2001; Raina et al., 2000). Studies suggest that women report greater acceptance of hearing loss than men yet they also experience more distress over the loss of social functioning and interpersonal communication than older men (Fozard & Gordon-Salant, 2001). They also report greater benefits from the use of hearing aids, possibly related to gender differences in the nature or severity of hearing loss.

Personal resources such as social support are crucial in helping older adults to adapt to sensory impairment. For example, in a study of older adults with visual impairment, social support from both family and friends were related to positive psychological well-being (McIlvane & Reinhardt, 2001). This was particularly true for women, who seemed to require support across a range of network members in order to accrue benefits.

Heart Disease

Heart disease, the leading cause of death in the industrialized world, can strike at any age. However, prevalence of heart disease and its risk factors, such as hypertension and elevated cholesterol, increases with age. Among younger adults, men have a much greater risk of serious heart disease than women, but this gender difference diminishes with age (Smith & Ruiz, 2002). Women who do experience myocardial infarction or undergo bypass surgery have less favorable outcomes than their male counterparts. They are at higher risk for depression and other negative changes in psychological adjustment (Brezinka & Kittel, 1996) and report more symptoms and physical limitations, particularly in household responsibilities (Sharpe, Clark, & Janz, 1991). Women may continue to engage in stressful role responsibilities such as housework and caregiving, or they may receive less aggressive or inappropriate treatment from health-care professionals. Comorbidity, particularly with diabetes or with depression, is associated with poorer prognosis (Clouse et al., 2003).

Lifestyle changes such as diet, exercise, and stress management are particularly important in controlling the impact of heart disease. As discussed above, older women, especially those in the current age cohort, may find it difficult to incorporate exercise into their daily routine (O'Brien Cousins, 2000; Satariano et al., 2000). Social support from family and friends and the ability to maintain social activities are particularly important in managing heart disease, buffering stress and encouraging positive health behaviors (Janz et al., 2001; Smith & Ruiz, 2002).

Diabetes

Diabetes is a disease of the endocrine system involving abnormal glucose metabolism. There are two types of diabetes. Type I diabetes typically begins early in life and involves malfunction of the pancreas so that the body does not produce enough insulin. Without insulin, the body cannot metabolize glucose leading to elevated blood glucose levels. Type II diabetes is the more common form among older adults, although it is currently seen more and more in younger individuals and even in children. In this condition, the body becomes resistant to insulin, damaging pancreatic cells. Obesity and overconsumption of simple carbohydrates are risk factors for developing type II diabetes (Gonder-Frederick, Cox, & Clarke, 2002). Native Americans, Hispanic Americans, and African Americans are at higher risk of developing type II diabetes while type I is more prevalent among Caucasians. Both forms of diabetes can have serious health consequences including blindness, kidney failure, vascular disease, and neuropathy. Type II diabetes also has been associated with cognitive impairment, especially among older adults (Coker & Shumaker, 2003). Unfortunately, cognitive impairment complicates compliance with dietary and treatment regimens for controlling diabetes.

Type I diabetes requires daily injections of insulin to reduce blood glucose levels. Type II diabetes is often controlled with changes in diet and exercise alone or in combination with medications. However, treatment regimens are complex and require close daily monitoring of blood glucose levels to prevent complications (Gonder-Frederick et al., 2002; Schoenberg & Drungle, 2001). Older women may find compliance with this treatment regimen difficult, especially if they also have visual impairment making it difficult to use testing equipment (Schoenberg & Drungle, 2001). Financial constraints also effect compliance, making it difficult to purchase testing materials, medications, and healthier food choices. Barriers to exercise also hinder diabetes management.

Although the prevalence of diabetes increases dramatically with age, the majority of research on disease management and prevention focuses on adolescents and younger adults. Research suggests that self-efficacy and realistic health beliefs predict better compliance with diabetes treatment regimens. Among older adults, perceptions of treatment benefits encourage compliance whereas young people are more concerned about the costs of their diabetes regimen (Gonder-Frederick et al., 2002).

Comorbidity is associated with more serious health consequences of diabetes, particularly the combination of diabetes and heart disease. Depression and anxiety disorders also are more prevalent among women with diabetes and these, in turn, are associated with poorer health outcomes and greater disability (Clouse et al., 2003; Gonder-Frederick et al., 2002). When diabetes complications such as visual impairment, loss of limbs, or kidney failure lead to functional disability, psychological distress is exacerbated.

Cancer

Cancer may be the most feared of all diseases, particularly to older cohorts who associate a cancer diagnosis with a death sentence. Recent strides in cancer treatment have made this view outdated. Still, it remains the second leading cause of death in the United States, and cancer treatment remains a long and difficult process accompanied by unpleasant side effects and fear of recurrence. Although we often think of cancer as a disease that strikes young people, the risk of developing cancer increases steadily with age, making it most prevalent among older adults. Among older women, breast and colorectal cancers are most common, followed by lung and gynecological cancers. However, lung cancer is the leading cause of cancer death among women, followed by breast and colorectal cancers (Andersen, Golden-Kreutz, & DiLillo, 2001).

Interventions with older women have focused primarily on cancer screening to promote early detection. In its early stages, cancer is less likely to have spread, enhancing survival rates and allowing patients to use less aggressive treatment. Cancer screening programs such as mammography have been associated with decreased mortality among older women (McCarthy et al., 2000). Knowledge about cancer screening and beliefs in personal control over one's health are two factors associated with greater use of screening tests (Bundek, Marks, & Richardson, 1993; Suarez, Roche, Nichols, & Simpson, 1997). Unfortunately, research suggests that older women are less knowledgeable about cancer screening than younger women, particularly those with less education or poor English skills (Suarez et al., 1997).

Cancer prevention also involves many of the same lifestyle changes recommended to prevent heart disease and diabetes. A diet high in fiber and low in fat, exercise and weight reduction, and good stress management all have been shown to enhance immunity and lower cancer risk (Andersen et al., 2001). For women already diagnosed with cancer, these lifestyle changes can improve response to treatment and prognosis. As discussed above, many older women experience barriers to lifestyle changes that can complicate living with cancer.

Cancer treatment itself is a highly stressful process involving uncomfortable and sometimes disabling side effects. Chemotherapy and radiation treatments are associated with severe fatigue, nausea, and loss of appetite in many people. Some patients leave treatment because they cannot tolerate these side effects. Interventions designed to prepare cancer patients for side effects and to ease the symptoms through stress management and cognitive and behavioral strategies have been successful for many people (Andersen et al., 2001). For older women already experiencing declines in daily functioning, cancer treatment can lead to more serious disability and loss of independence. Treatment effects that threaten positive body image, such as hair loss or mastectomy, may exacerbate existing concerns over age-related physical changes. Stereotypes of older women as unattractive and asexual can lead practitioners to overlook or devalue these concerns.

Cognitive Impairment and Dementia

Older adults experience some cognitive decline as part of the normal aging process, primarily in the area of "fluid intelligence" (Horn, 1982). This encompasses processing speed and the capacity to learn new information and solve novel problems. However, the majority of healthy older adults are able to compensate for these losses and maintain cognitive function.

Research on the relative contributions of normal age-related declines and the impact of disease on cognitive function has yielded inconsistent findings. Some studies suggest that physical health problems have little impact on cognitive function in old age (Anstey, Stankov, & Lord, 1993). Other studies suggest a link between health and cognitive function with positive health behaviors, such as exercise, related to better cognitive func-

tion (Laurin, Verreault, Lindsay, MacPherson, & Rockwood, 2001). While depression has been associated with cognitive changes among older adults, it does not appear to be a factor in the onset of dementia (Gallassi, Morreale, & Pagni, 2001).

Dementia is a chronic, progressive illness characterized by cognitive impairment, memory loss, behavior changes, and neurological deficits. Common causes of dementia are Alzheimer's disease and vascular dementia. It is a major cause of disability and loss of independence in old age, particularly among the oldest old (Suthers, Kim, & Crimmins, 2003). People with dementia can engage in dangerous behavior such as wandering or leaving the stove on and require assistance with activities of daily living, making them highly dependent on caregivers. Women are at higher risk of developing Alzheimer's disease than men, while there are no gender differences in incidence of vascular dementia (Andersen et al., 1999).

Very little research documents the experience of older women with severe cognitive impairment associated with dementia. Instead, research has focused almost exclusively on the stress that dementia caregivers experience (Cotrell & Schulz, 1993). The few existing studies of people with dementia reveal a high incidence of depression, exacerbating disability (Gallassi et al., 2001). Qualitative research examining the experience of dementia reveals a pervasive sense of loss and stressful interpersonal relationships (Ostwald, Duggleby, & Hepburn, 2002).

Successful Health Interventions With Older Women

While many older women experience barriers to health enhancing lifestyle changes, research suggests a number of possible avenues for successful intervention. As discussed above, regular exercise can be the key to a variety of positive health outcomes including lowered risk for chronic illness and enhanced physical and cognitive functioning. Group walking programs have been particularly successful in encouraging exercise among older women, and benefits are evident even when the increase in activity is modest (Clark, 1999; Shin, 1999). Given the association between knowledge about health screening and utilization of these vital services (Suarez et al., 1997), educational programs, especially those geared to specific ethnic or cultural groups, should become a focus of health care for older women. These programs should include family members whenever possible to facilitate social support and involve the social network in encouraging positive health behaviors.

MAINTAINING PSYCHOLOGICAL HEALTH IN THE FACE OF CHRONIC PHYSICAL ILLNESS

Despite the physical and cognitive declines associated with aging and the prevalence of chronic illness and loss of function, the majority of older women maintain a positive outlook and high levels of life satisfaction (Heidrich & Ryff, 1993). How is this possible? Researchers have suggested a number of mechanisms by which these women adapt to their situations and maintain mental health and quality of life. As discussed earlier, mobilization of social and personal resources such as social support and feelings of self-efficacy and mastery allow older women to maintain psychological well-being in the face of disability (Jang, Haley, Small, & Mortimer, 2002). Women who remain active into old age and are able to substitute new activities when disability interferes with previously enjoyed activities are able to maintain psychological well-being in the face of chronic illness (Duke, Leventhal, Brownlee, & Leventhal, 2002). Here, too, psychosocial resources such as social support and optimism facilitate this adaptive response.

In an interesting study of older women, Heidrich and Ryff (1993) explored the role of the psychological processes involved in maintaining well-being in the face of age-related declines. While physical disability was associated with psychological distress, this relationship was mediated by social integration and social comparisons. Women who felt integrated into a social network and were able to maintain meaningful social roles maintained positive mental health in the face of declining health. Similarly, women who were able to compare themselves favorably to others their own age maintained a sense of well-being.

Taken together, these findings highlight the adaptability and resilience of older women. They also highlight the reciprocal connection between physical health and psychological well-being, and the crucial role that social and personal resources play in adaptation to chronic illness and disability.

REFERENCES

Abraido-Lanza, A. F. (1997). Latinas with arthritis: Effects of illness, role identity, and competence on psychological well-being. *American Journal of Community Psychology, 25,* 601–627.

Andersen, B. L., Golden-Kreutz, D. M., & DiLillo, V. (2001). Cancer. In A. Baum, T. A. Revenson, & J. E. Singer (Eds.), *Handbook of health psychology* (pp. 709–726). Mahwah, NJ: Erlbaum.

Andersen, K., Launer, L. J., Dewey, M. E., Letenneur, L., Ott, A., Copeland, J. R. M., et al. (1999). Gender differences in the incidence of Alzheimer's disease and vascular dementia. *Neurology, 53,* 1992–1997.

Anstey, K., Stankov, L, & Lord, S. (1993). Primary aging, secondary aging, and intelligence. *Psychology and Aging, 8,* 562–570.

Baltes, P. B., & Baltes, M. M. (1990). Psychological perspectives on successful aging: The model of selective optimization with compensation. In P. B. Baltes & M. M. Baltes (Eds.), *Successful aging: Perspectives from the behavioral sciences.* Cambridge: Cambridge University Press.

Brezinka, V., & Kittel, F. (1996). Psychosocial factors of coronary heart disease in women: A review. *Social Science & Medicine, 42,* 1351–1365.

Bundek, N. I., Marks, G., & Richardson, J. L. (1993). Role of health locus of control beliefs in cancer screening of elderly Hispanic women. *Health Psychology, 12,* 193–199.

Burke, H. M., Zautra, A. J., Schultz, A. S., Reich, J. W., & Davis, M. C. (2002). Arthritis. In A. J. Christensen, & M. H. Antoni (Eds.), *Chronic physical disorders* (pp. 268–287). Malden, MA: Blackwell.

Clark, D. O. (1999). Identifying psychological, physiological, and environmental barriers and facilitators to exercise among older low income adults. *Journal of Clinical Geropsychology, 5,* 51–62.

Clouse, R. E., Lustman, P. J., Freedland, K. E., Griffith, L. S., McGill, J. B., & Carney, R. M. (2003). Depression and coronary heart disease in women with diabetes. *Psychosomatic Medicine, 65,* 376–383.

Coker, L. H., & Shumaker, S. A. (2003). Type 2 diabetes mellitus and cognition. An understudied issue in women's health. *Journal of Psychosomatic Research, 54,* 129–139.

Cotrell, V., & Schulz, R. (1993). The perspective of the patient with Alzheimer's disease: A neglected dimension of dementia research. *Gerontologist, 33,* 205–211.

Duke, J., Leventhal, H., Brownlee, S., & Leventhal, E. A. (2002). Giving up and replacing activities in response to illness. *Journal of Gerontology: Psychological Sciences, 57B,* P367–P376.

Fozard, J. L., & Gordon-Salant, S. (2001). Changes in vision and hearing with aging. In J. E. Birren & K. W. Schaie (Eds.), *Handbook of the psychology of aging* (5th ed., pp. 241–266). San Diego, CA: Academic Press.

Furner, S. E., Rudberg, M. A., & Cassel, C. K. (1995). Medical conditions differentially affect the development of IADL disability: Implications for medical care and research. *Gerontologist, 35,* 444–450.

Gallassi, R., Morreale, A., & Pagni, P. (2001). The relationship between depression and cognition. *Archives of Gerontology & Geriatrics, 33*(Suppl. 7), 163–171.

Gignac, M. A. M., Cott, C., & Badley, E. M. (2000). Adaptation to chronic illness and disability and its relationship to perceptions of independence and dependence. *Journal of Gerontology: Psychological Sciences, 55B,* P362–P372.

Gold, C. H., Malmberg, B., McClearn, G. E., Pedersen, N. L., & Berg, S. (2002). Gender and health: A study of older unlike-sex twins. *Journal of Gerontology: Social Sciences, 57B,* S168–S176.

Gonder-Frederick, L., Cox, D. J., & Clarke, W. L. (2002). Diabetes. In A. J. Christensen & M. H. Antoni (Eds.), *Chronic physical disorders* (pp. 137–164). Malden, MA: Blackwell.

Heidrich, S. M., & Ryff, C. D. (1993). Physical and mental health in later life. The self system as mediator. *Psychology & Aging, 8,* 327–338.

Hirvensalo, M., Rantanen, T., & Heikkinen, E. (2000). Mobility difficulties and physical activity as predictors of mortality and loss of independence in the community-living older population. *Journal of the American Geriatrics Society, 48,* 493–498.

Horn, J. L. (1982). The theory of fluid and crystallized intelligence in relations to concepts of cognitive psychology and aging in adulthood. In F. I. M. Craik & S. Trehub (Eds.), *Aging and cognitive processes* (pp. 201–238). New York: Plenum Press.

Idler, E. L. (2003). Discussion: Gender differences in self-rated health, in mortality, and in the relationship between the two. *Gerontologist, 43,* 372–375.

Jang, Y., Haley, W. E., Small, B. J., & Mortimer, J. A. (2002). The role of mastery and social resources in the associations between disability and depression in later life. *Gerontologist, 42,* 807–813.

Janz, N. K., Janevic, M. R., Dodge, J. A., Fingerlin, T. E., Schork, M. A., Mosca, L. J., et al. (2001). Factors influencing quality of life in older women with heart disease. *Medical Care, 39,* 588–598.

Ketcham, C. J., & Stelmach, G. E. (2001). Age-related declines in motor control. In J. E. Birren, & K. W. Schaie (Eds.), *Handbook of the psychology of aging* (5th ed., pp. 313–348). San Diego, CA: Academic Press.

Laurin, D., Verreault, R., Lindsay, J., MacPherson, K., & Rockwood, K. (2001). Physical activity and risk of cognitive impairment and dementia in elderly persons. *Archives of Neurology, 58,* 498–504.

Marsland, A. L., Bachen, E. A., Cohen, S., & Manuck, S. B. (2001). Stress, immunity, and susceptibility to infectious disease. In A. Baum, T. A. Revenson, & J. E. Singer (Eds.), *Handbook of health psychology* (pp. 683–695). Mahwah, NJ: Erlbaum.

McCarthy, E. P., Burns, R. B., Freund, K. M., Ash, A. S., Shwartz, M., Marwill, S. L., et al. (2000). Mammography use, breast cancer stage at diagnosis, and survival among older women. *Journal of the American Geriatrics Society, 48,* 1226–1233.

McIlvane, J. M., & Reinhardt, J. P. (2001). Interactive effect of support from family and friends in visually impaired elders. *Journal of Gerontology: Psychological Sciences, 56,* P374–P382.

Miller, M. E., Rejeski, W. J., Reboussin, B. A., Ten Have, T. R., & Ettinger, W. H. (2000). Physical activity, functional limitations, and disability in older adults. *Journal of the American Geriatrics Society, 48,* 1264–1272.

O'Brien Cousins, S. (2000). "My heart couldn't take it": Older women's beliefs about exercise benefits and risks. *Journals of Gerontology: Psychological Sciences & Social Sciences, 55B,* P283–P294.

Ostwald, S. K., Duggleby, W., & Hepburn, K. W. (2002). The stress of dementia: View from the inside. *American Journal of Alzheimer's Disease and Other Dementias, 17,* 303–312.

Raina, P., Wong, M., Dukeshire, S., Chambers, L. W., & Lindsay, J. (2000). Prevalence, risk factors and self-reported medical causes of seeing and hearing-related disabilities among older adults. *Canadian Journal on Aging, 19,* 260–278.

Rejeski, W. J., Martin, K. A., Miller, M. E., Ettinger, W. H., & Rapp, S. (1998). Perceived importance and satisfaction with physical function in patients with knee osteoarthritis. *Annals of Behavioral Medicine, 20,* 141–148.

Reuben, D. B., Mui, S., Damesyn, M., Moore, A. A., & Greendale, G. A. (1999). The prognostic value of sensory impairment in older persons. *Journal of the American Geriatrics Society, 47,* 930–935.

Satariano, W. A., Haight, T. J., & Tager, I. B. (2000). Reasons given by older people for limitation or avoidance of leisure time physical activity. *Journal of the American Geriatrics Society, 48,* 505–512.

Schoenberg, N. E., & Drungle, S. C. (2001). Barriers to non-insulin dependent diabetes mellitus self-care practices among older women. *Journal of Aging & Health, 12,* 443–466.

Seeman, T., & Chen, X. (2002). Risk and protective factors for physical functioning in older adults with and without chronic conditions: MacArthur studies of successful aging. *Journal of Gerontology: Social Sciences, 57B,* S135–S144.

Sharpe, P. A., Clark, N. M., & Janz, N. K. (1991). Differences in the impact and management of heart disease between older women and men. *Women & Health, 17,* 25–43.

Shin, Y. (1999). The effects of a walking exercise program on physical function and emotional state of elderly Korean women. *Public Health Nursing, 16*, 146–154.

Smith, J., Borchelt, M., Maier, H., & Jopp, D. (2002). Health and well-being in the young old and oldest old. *Journal of Social Issues, 58*, 715–732.

Smith, T. W., & Ruiz, J. M. (2002). Coronary heart disease. In A. J. Christensen, & M. H. Antoni (Eds.), *Chronic physical disorders* (pp. 83–111). Malden, MA: Blackwell.

Suarez, L., Roche, R. A., Nichols, D., & Simpson, D. M. (1997). Knowledge, behavior, and fears concerning breast and cervical cancer among older low-income Mexican-American women. *American Journal of Preventive Medicine, 13*, 137–142.

Suthers, K., Kim, J. K., & Crimmins, E. (2003). Life expectancy with cognitive impairment in the older population of the United States. *Journal of Gerontology: Social Sciences, 58B*, S179–S186.

U.S. Bureau of the Census. (1996). *Statistical abstract of the United States 1996*. Washington, DC: U.S. Government Printing Office.

Williamson, G. M., & Schulz, R. (1992). Pain, activity restriction, and symptoms of depression among community-residing elderly adults. *Journal of Gerontology: Psychological Sciences, 47*, P367–P372.

Zautra, A. J., & Smith, B. W. (2001). Depression and reactivity to stress in older women with rheumatoid arthritis and osteoarthritis. *Psychosomatic Medicine, 64*, 687–696.

Women need to feel secure, at whatever age. Minimally, physical requirements for survival must be met. To thrive, however, women need to develop confidence that the social and physical environment will adequately respond to them and can be adapted to meet their needs, at least to some degree. As girls grow into women, and as women mature, they develop increased mastery over their environment, decreased dependency, and greater self-sufficiency. These qualities also contribute to positive self-esteem. By the time a woman is in her seventh or eighth decade of life she is likely to have a stable sense of self that includes purpose, value, and control in the world, or using Susan Whitbourne's terms, "personal power, strength, and effectiveness" (1996, p. 9). Aging and its associated changes can challenge mastery, independence, and self-sufficiency. Under the best of circumstances there is opportunity for continued growth, creativity, and fulfillment.

Other chapters in this book speak to identity, risks, strengths, and coping styles throughout the life span, each of which affects security. This chapter focuses on the impact of a woman's life circumstances and her physical, social, and cultural environment on the experience of security in older age. It is not always possible for a woman to achieve and maintain security on her own. Social policy and government support may be necessary. Psychological interventions can be helpful.

BONNIE MARKHAM

Older Women and Security

DEFINITION OF SECURITY

A woman's security can be affected by the most ordinary aspects of life: where she lives and with whom, how she takes care of her physical needs, how she copes with her financial resources, how safe she feels in her environment. *Safety* refers to external factors—aspects of the environment that reduce danger, both physical and psychological. *Security* refers to an internal state of well-being. While safe conditions can promote a sense of security, it should not be assumed that the absence of external threat necessarily leads to feelings of security, or the reverse, that security can not occur even in relatively dangerous circumstances.

41

LIVING ARRANGEMENTS— WHERE AND WITH WHOM

Aging in place is the norm. Older people tend to remain in the same community as long as they are able to do so. For all older persons, and especially for a woman alone, the factors that support a sense of security are a familiar neighborhood, an established social network, and connections to area services. Most women over 65 live alone, a circumstance that is likely to become even more prevalent in the future (Administration on Aging, 2002).

Since the 1960s, when the first leisure-oriented retirement communities were built, many models for older adult living have been created. Age-segregated housing and communities, assisted living, and other residential arrangements, when they meet needs for social life, activities, and services, can have a positive impact on the experience of security. However, there is no "one size fits all." Developers ignored cultural differences when they imported Australian "Granny Flats" to the United States, and the project failed. American grandmothers did not want to live in small, temporary modular homes on someone else's land (Folts & Muir, 2002).

Living arrangements for older women are affected by level of disability and the availability of care assistance. An increase in frailty and ill health may precipitate a woman's need for nursing home care. Of the 4.5% of the population 65 and older who were in nursing homes in 2000, twice as many residents were women (Administration on Aging, 2002). Given the population trends, nursing home care will become even more of a woman's issue in the future. Leaving a familiar environment and losing control over one's own life seriously threatens security. According to an AARP study, older people with disabilities fear most the loss of independence. They want to be able to make choices regarding their living arrangements and other aspects of their lives (Nicholson, 2003). Even in a highly restricted environment, approaches such as the Eden Alternative for nursing homes offer opportunities for resident participation and control (C. Burt, personal communication, July 14, 2003).

There are many steps between full independence and nursing home living. Older women may rely on the assistance of spouses, children, other relatives, friends, religious congregation members, or community volunteers to continue functioning in the community and feel secure. Others move near or with family or friends, or bring a paid caretaker into the home. Living alone, however, is the most likely arrangement. Women baby boomers (born between 1946 and 1964) can expect to be alone for 15 to 20 years because this group usually marries older men, has a life expectancy that is increasing at a faster rate than that for men, and is not likely to remarry (Administration on Aging, 2002).

Cultural values affect a woman's comfort with accepting social support. Women from cultures that revere the oldest among them and favor living in multigenerational family groups can be expected to have an easier time relying on others than those from cultures that devalue older women and have a strong bias toward individuality and independence. Psychological factors make a difference as well. For those women who associate getting help with being loved, a certain amount of dependency may be gratifying and increase a sense of security. For those who value self-sufficiency above all else, the need for help may be threatening. Women whose identity includes being in charge of a household may find living under someone else's roof a blow to their self-esteem.

Older women continue to be expected to nurture their extended families. For example, an increasing number of older women are making a home for their young grandchildren, the fastest growing type of household in the United States (Hayslip & Patrick, 2003). In recognition of this trend, one that is more stressful for poor families, the Older Americans Act was amended in 2000 to include the National Family Caregiver Support Program. A recent study compared the role satisfaction of African American and White grandmothers rearing grandchildren on their own (Pruchno & McKenney, 2002). African American grandmothers were less affected by the nature of their relationship to the child's parents, perhaps owing to the more central and directive role grandmothers play in those families.

The financial and emotional cost experienced by some informal caregivers has a current and future negative impact on their security. A study conducted by MetLife Insurance for the National Center on Women and Aging (1999) identifies women as the primary providers of informal care; in doing so, they make a tremendous financial contribution to the community and the economy, for which they are not compensated. The amount of care provided does not correlate with a woman's experience of burden; however, mastery, control, emotional support, and the relationship between giver and receiver of care all reduce caregiver strain (Tennstedt, 1999). For those women in the study whose spouse was suffering from dementia, specific training increased the sense of efficacy and made it possible for the patient to remain in the home longer.

PHYSICAL CARE—NUTRITION, EXERCISE, AND ACCESS TO MEDICAL CARE

Adequate nutrition goes hand in hand with health and longevity. Habits, health status, and life circumstances may interact with aging to create a number of nutritional risk factors: an increase in health problems and medications that impairs ability to obtain nutrients from food, decreased mobility that affects shopping and food preparation, poor appetite, stress, lack of money to buy food or afford transportation, social isolation, little knowledge of nutrition, specific food preferences, and poor eating habits. Women, who are usually responsible for meal planning and preparation, may improve their own health and that of others in their household by reducing risk factors.

Nutritional adequacy is a complex problem for women in the United States and other developed countries where thinness is associated with physical attractiveness and social success. Weight gain, loss of bone density leading to decreased height, and other changes that occur with aging move older women away from the ideal of thin, firm, and wrinkle-free bodies. Though normative, these changes can threaten self-worth. Late-onset eating disorders, bizarre fad diets, and distorted body images are fairly common among older White women, less so for older African American women, and not so for older men who are more generally satisfied with their bodies (Fey-Yensan, McCormick, & English, 2002).

There are a number of programs to help those women who are frail or housebound for other reasons. For example, Meals on Wheels (MOW), started in 1972, has been shown to improve the nutritional status of participants. Assessment and socializing opportunities are an added benefit of the contact with volunteers who deliver the food. Not all elders choose to remain in the program. Research on MOW dropouts found that 28.2% of African American participants and 12.8% of White participants did not like the food (Choi, 1999). The inclusion of ethnically sensitive foods and more individual choice of menu items could improve the effectiveness of this program.

The health benefits of exercise throughout the life span are well documented, as they are for nutrition. Sandra O'Brien Cousins (2000) found that women who feel vulnerable, "My heart would hemorrhage" (p. 286), choose not to exercise. Social support can be crucial in counteracting the prevailing cultural stereotypes about older woman being too frail to work out. For example, 80% of older women in the United Kingdom who were participating in a doctor-prescribed exercise program learned of the program through their informal social network, not from their general practitioner (Hardcastle & Taylor, 2001). These women consistently reported that the encouragement of friends, classmates, and exercise instructors allowed them to get past their fear of health risks or the norms to "act their age."

Focus on one's own needs in the absence of role demands was linked to vigorous physical activity for a sample of Native American women (Henderson & Ainsworth, 2001). Exercise in their middle years was seen as integral to their roles: child rearing, housework, chopping wood, and gardening. Those women who did not become sedentary in later life, called "rejuvenators" by the authors, maintained or returned to an active lifestyle for self-fulfillment rather than role fulfillment.

Fitness programs can contribute to a woman's experience of agency. A tremendous increase in confidence, efficacy, and well-being for older women who exercise in a gym was reported by Poole (2001). Here, too, the comradeship with other women was an important part of the desirable effect. Primary care physicians are often very influential with their older female patients. Doctors knowledgeable about the psychological and physical benefits of exercise for the elderly could have a large positive impact. Legislation that reduces discrimination against girls in sports, such as Title IX, and changes in cultural attitudes, may result in women baby boomers feeling more empowered and competent to express their athletic ability or interest in exercise when they are young and when they reach 65 and beyond.

Government funding of exercise plans for older persons is cost effective (Matro, 2002). A wide variety of programs, including those targeted to address particular disabilities, can reduce the need for medical care and other expensive support services. Exercise programs can save lives. In her policy recommendation to New York City regarding fall prevention, Jennifer Matro identifies fear of falling as a major concern of elders, and falls as the leading cause of accident-related death in people over 65. Exercise to improve balance could change this statistic while saving health-care dollars. An important psychological benefit for women is the increase in security that comes from being more trusting of their bodies.

Discriminatory and culturally insensitive attitudes toward older women are a barrier to adequate health-care services and create a sense of distrust. Many older African American women report feeling disrespected by those White male physicians who address them by their first names (Christmas, 1994). Lesbian and gay older people have been found to avoid health-care institutions and practitioners, even when ill (Brotman, Ryan, & Cormier, 2003). Susan Feldman (1999) worked with 70–85-year-old women who participated in a writing program in Australia. The women wrote poignantly about the importance of good health, independence, and not being a burden. In all too many cases, ageism challenged their sense of security and limited their confidence in their medical practitioners.

Lack of insurance is another barrier to health-care access for women. Supplementary insurance, in addition to Medicare, has been found to be associated with increased survival rates and decreased transition from independence to disability (Porell & Miltiades, 2001). Insurance was not a factor for those already moderately disabled. Women, who are more likely to rely solely on Medicare, could benefit from programs to in-

crease knowledge and provide assistance with applications for available supplemental coverage. Affordable alternatives that augment reimbursement early in the disability process will ultimately reduce expenditures for more costly disabled care later on. The "medical necessity" model of many health-care insurance plans, including Medicare, has disincentives for women to engage in health-promoting behaviors such as good nutrition, smoking cessation, and exercise. Legislators and insurance carriers should remember that "an ounce of prevention is worth a pound of cure."

FINANCES

Older women are poorer than older men. Consequently, they are more likely to experience depression, poor health care, inadequate housing, isolation, and other risks to well-being. Widowhood and poverty go hand-in-hand for more than half of the women whose husbands died. The oldest Americans, over 75, are even more likely to be living in poverty than those a decade younger. Older Hispanic women living alone or with nonrelatives have the highest poverty rates (50.5%). African American and foreign-born elderly are also more likely to be poor (Administration on Aging, 2002).

Most of the poorest Americans live in central cities, rural areas, and the South. Yet the federal government poverty standard, often a trigger for benefits, does not consider regional and local differences in the real cost of living, nor does it factor in the availability of community services such as transportation, senior centers, and housing subsidies. Cost of living and availability of state and local entitlement programs varies widely from place to place and region to region. A uniform national poverty standard creates an opportunity for gross inequities in the distribution of support to poor women, and probably leads to an underestimate of the number of older women in dire straits.

At all ages, adult men are employed at higher rates than adult women, are more likely to work consistently and full time, and command higher positions and salaries. As a result, only half as many women as men receive pension benefits. Women are more likely to depend totally on Social Security for their income and to receive Supplemental Security Income (SSI). Three fourths of all people with sufficiently low incomes to receive SSI are women over the age of 65 (Administration on Aging, 2002). This picture may be changing. Women baby boomers will begin turning 65 in 2011. Many work full time and do not plan to retire. Some of those women want to continue to work as a personal choice, and a significant number will work out of economic necessity. A very high number expect that they will have some paid post-retirement employment. These women are aware of and express concern about age discrimination as a factor limiting both their advancement and their ability to be employed as long as they would want or need to work (National Center on Women and Aging, 2002). Nevertheless, the next cohort of women will have better economic health than their mothers and grandmothers.

Inadequate financial resources threaten all aspects of living for older women. The data quite consistently demonstrate a positive relationship between health and wealth and a negative relationship between economic inequity and well-being (Belle & Doucet, 2003). At all ages women feel less secure than men. For older women this disadvantage may be accounted for by their lower economic status, widowhood, poor health, and lesser everyday competence (Pinquart & Sorensen, 2001). A survey of older women conducted by the National Center on Women and Aging (2002) concluded that taking control of those aspects of life that can be controlled improves their chances for positive aging and security. Specifically, those surveyed offered two keys for fiscal control: saving money, no matter how tight one's budget, and living within one's means. A large proportion of women with health limitations do not save because they can't afford to put money aside, or fear that it would cause them to be ineligible for entitlement programs. Some do not save because they do not know how to make investments.

Many older women, not only those with some health limitations, find the steadily rising cost of health care prohibitive. Women with little disposable income spend a disproportionate amount on health care and spend even more if they have some physical disability. Today, even with Medicare, a person over the age of 65 in the United States pays approximately $3,500 a year

for medical expenses, including insurance premiums and prescribed medications (Administration on Aging, 2002). A new Medicare drug benefit will take effect in January 2006 for people who enroll. In the new plan, the poorest have no premiums or deductibles and will pay only a small amount for their prescriptions. Those not meeting the poverty criteria will have no coverage for expenses between $2,250 and $3,600 in any one year. This gap and other cost issues have been the focus of much debate. The need to pay out of pocket for prescription drugs is a common source of economic strain and anxiety. Some local communities have arranged discounts and subsidies to help their elderly obtain medicine. Questions about who is responsible to assure the best possible health outcomes for an increasing number of older women with disabilities need to be answered.

The next generation can expect to be better able to afford health care. It is predicted that by 2030 many more women will be able to pay for drugs and long-term care from their personal assets, and will have enough disposable income to cover new technologies for improving physical health not likely to be reimbursed by medical insurance (Knickman, Kleey, Snell, Alecxih, & Kennell, 2003). These authors caution that "tweeners"—those who are middle class but do not have many assets, will be hardest hit by rising medical costs and should begin purchasing insurance for long-term care and uncovered procedures at around age 40 or 50, when the premiums are lower. People often find it difficult to make choices that limit current disposable income for a need that has not yet arisen. Women who have goals and plan ahead will be contributing to their security in later life.

Women with significant financial assets face different issues. Widowed women new to managing finances may find themselves initially overwhelmed by learning about taxes, balancing a checkbook, understanding investments, dealing with property, or running a business. Paradoxically, these older women with assets may feel quite insecure and alone until they adjust. Those who learn how to identify a competent financial advisor and are prepared to develop other new skills will be able to move from anxiety to mastery.

Feelings of efficacy and competence can result from having enough money to be self-sufficient and to benefit others, in small or large ways. The distribution or anticipated distribution of wealth may occasion a great deal of interpersonal conflict. Donations to charities, often a source of well-being and connection, can test the limits of a woman's assertiveness through pressure from fund-raisers. Income and assets to be self-supporting indefinitely do not always ensure feelings of security. Fears, such as of outliving one's means, may appear reality oriented on the surface but could mask depression and isolation or unresolved mourning.

Older women, especially those in a life transition, are particularly vulnerable to scams. Telemarketing, home repair, and investment fraud are the most common. Americans lose billions of dollars each year in this way (National Center on Women and Aging, n.d.). Some scammers take advantage of group affiliations to gain trust. They contact the elderly through their houses of worship, community social clubs, or other group settings and solicit donations for nonexistent programs. Psychological loss and social isolation increase the chances that a woman may succumb to a scam and not make a formal complaint. Role specialization in marriage may have limited the wife's acquisition of some practical skills necessary to detect and deal with scammers. Interventions to improve awareness of deceptive business practices, and community-run group shopping trips to increase knowledge and reduce isolation may decrease susceptibility.

SAFETY

The dynamic interplay between needs for autonomy and needs for safety creates an ever-changing balance point for the individual's experience of well-being. It is estimated that somewhere between 25–39% of the elderly need some assistance in their home. A high percentage of these individuals could be fully functional with appropriate modifications such as tub grab bars, ramps, and accessible bathrooms. Those with unmet needs are more likely to be women, ethnic minorities, and have low income, much of which goes to housing costs (Newman, 2003).

Because women are most likely to be cooking, cleaning, and doing household chores, safety features in the home would significantly reduce their injuries. Such safety features, informed by human factors research and tested by the older people for whom they are designed, can increase the ability of elders to function effectively.

Maximum mobility and autonomy occur when women continue to drive their own cars. Older drivers can also pose a safety hazard for themselves and others. A review of current crash data for older drivers led to the projection that there will be a steady increase in fatal crashes involving a driver 65 and older, men having a somewhat higher rate than women (Bedard, Stones, Guyatt, & Hirdes, 2001). A more thorough understanding of risk factors can be used to direct the development of training for older drivers and safety initiatives. While some older drivers voluntarily surrender their licenses or just stop driving, many are reluctant to do so because of the limitations that would result. The elderly nondriver may have difficulty getting basic needs met, especially in those areas without public transportation, where stores and doctors are far apart.

Women's safety can be compromised by situations involving other people, both strangers and those with whom they are familiar. Poor women living in urban areas and women of color are most likely to be targets of criminals and to report being fearful. Women over 75 are usually attacked in or near their homes. In general, older women are the least likely targets of criminals, but they are ten times as likely to be victimized by an intimate (spouse, ex-spouse, dating partner, relative) than a stranger. African American women are even more at risk than White women and are twice as likely to be targets of violence (Administration on Aging, 2002).

According to the National Center on Women and Aging (n.d.), eight times more elder abuse occurs than is reported and this rate is rising. Women are the more likely victims and the abuse includes neglect, financial exploitation, physical, emotional, or sexual abuse. Most perpetrators are adult children but may also be a spouse, other relative, friend or neighbor, service provider, grandchild, or sibling. It is estimated that 10% of all Americans over 65 are subjected to abuse and that 4% of elders suffer moderate to severe abuse

(Smith, 1996). The abuse is usually recurring rather than a one time event, and those abused have at least one disability, either mental or physical. Women who believe they could not function without assistance may feel that reporting or resisting abuse could risk the loss of their needed caretaker, perhaps a more frightening possibility than the abuse itself. This is not just a problem experienced by women living in the community; it occurs in nursing homes as well. Public policy and legislation is needed to protect those institutionalized elders who cannot protect themselves.

POLICY IMPLICATIONS

The lesser status of women is compounded for older women by ageism and negative attitudes toward disability. Historical inequities in access to resources are perpetuated in the entitlement and benefit programs that women need as they age (Quadagno & Reid, 1999). If society agrees that women, poor and rich alike, have a right to safe, healthy, long lives, then policies regarding occupational pensions, public pensions such as Social Security, medical insurance, prescription drug coverage, safety modifications in the home, public transportation, and the like should reflect that value. A significant cost saving in human and financial resources will accrue from instituting programs that prevent predictable problems. Aging successfully is more likely when environmental conditions are favorable and affordable, need-specific services are available.

The anticipated rising numbers of elderly women will require housing, medical care, recreation, transportation, and other special services designed for their needs, especially those of older women who live alone. Communities that are responsive to aging women will find that these elders are also a potential market for local businesses and a source of loyal and hard-working employees. For women still in the workforce, flexible work schedules and family leave for child-rearing grandparents would improve well-being. Programs to train spouses of dementia patients, offer respite care, and provide support groups are also valuable and cost-effective. Public and private programs are known to be more effective when personal and cultural preferences are considered, and when the needs for mastery, independence, and self-sufficiency are supported.

PSYCHOLOGICAL IMPLICATIONS

In working with older women, time is of the essence. People who reach a ripe old age often have learned to be more selective, focus on the most essential, and pick and choose what is right for them from among their available options. Consequently, targeted interventions to address an immediate threat to security in a pragmatic, personal, and culturally sensitive way can have a surprisingly rapid positive impact. Life transitions provide an excellent stimulus for self-exploration and can create an opportunity to complete unfinished psychological business, such as unresolved mourning that has been reactivated by a recent event. It is never too late to feel better.

Mental and behavioral health professionals can be enormously helpful in very practical ways. A recent widow may need assistance in grieving and may also need advice about getting her refrigerator repaired. One woman might need encouragement and support to start exercising. Another might be helped by a call to her primary care physician to discuss drug interactions or the emotional concomitants of her medications. Psychological interventions are likely to be more effective when the practitioner works collaboratively with the woman's other care providers and her social system. Since those are the people to whom the woman turns for direction, their involvement can provide additional support for change. In fact, primary care physicians and nurses are typically the first professionals to see an older woman. Their screening for and alertness to security issues in the aging women they serve is an important part of assuring prompt and cost-effective help for these patients. Questions about living arrangements, finances, physical care, and safety need to focus not only on the facts but also on the woman's experience of her life in those areas.

Close relationships can be the greatest source of gratification or the greatest source of danger for elderly women. Challenges in their roles and their relationships may prompt them to seek help. Losses and conflicts in these areas are potentially devastating to self-esteem and sense of purpose, and thus to security. It can be anticipated that much of the therapeutic work with women of significant age will be around such issues. Women will feel empowered and more secure when the work focuses on things over which they have some control and supports a problem-solving orientation.

NOTE

My research assistant, Melissa Gartenberg, deserves much credit for being a sensitive, knowledgeable, and substantial support during all phases of the development of this chapter. Grateful appreciation for close readings of the drafts is extended to Myron Gessner, Thomas Matro, and Susan Newman. And particular thanks to Carol Goodheart for her encouragement and editing.

REFERENCES

Administration on Aging. (2002). *A profile of older Americans* [Electronic version]. Retrieved May 13, 2003, from http://www.aoa.gov/aoa/statistics/profile/2002/7.html

Bedard, M., Stones, M. J., Guyatt, G. H., & Hirdes, J. P. (2001). Traffic-related fatalities among older drivers and passengers: Past and future trends. *The Gerontologist, 41,* 751–756.

Belle, D., & Doucet, J. (2003). Poverty, inequality, and discrimination as sources of depression among U.S. women. *Psychology of Women Quarterly, 27,* 101–113.

Brotman, S., Ryan, B., & Cormier, R. (2003). The health and social service needs of gay and lesbian elders and their families in Canada. *The Gerontologist 43,* 192–202.

Choi, N. (1999). Determinants of frail elders' lengths of stay on meals on wheels. *The Gerontologist, 39,* 397–404.

Christmas, R. J. (1994). Dealing with doctors. *Essence, 25*(1), 30–32.

Feldman, S. (1999). Please don't call me "dear": Older women's narratives of health care. *Nursing Inquiry, 6,* 269–276.

Fey-Yensan, N., McCormick, L., & English, C. (2002, September/October). Body image and weight preoccupation in older women: A review. *Healthy Weight Journal,* 68–71.

Folts, W. E., & Muir, K. B. (2002). Housing for older adults: New lessons from the past. *Research on Aging, 24,* 10–28.

Hardcastle, S., & Taylor, A. H. (2001). From Looking for more than weight loss and fitness gain: Psychosocial dimensions among older women in a primary-care exercise-referral program. *Journal of Aging and Physical Activity, 9,* 313–328.

Hayslip, B., Jr., & Patrick, J. H. (Eds.). (2003). *Working with custodial grandparents.* New York: Springer.

Henderson, K. A., & Ainsworth, B. E. (2001). Physical activity and human development among older Native American women. *Journal of Aging and Physical Activity, 9,* 285–299.

Knickman, J. R., Kleey, A. H., Snell, E. K., Alecxih, L. M. B., & Kennell, D. L. (2003). Wealth patterns among elderly Americans: Implications for health care affordability. *Health Affairs, 22*(3), 168–174.

Matro, J. M. (2002). *Fall prevention for New York's elderly: An integrative approach.* Unpublished manuscript, Council of Senior Centers and Services of New York City, Inc.

National Center on Women and Aging, Brandeis University. (1999, December). *Americans pay a staggering price in lost wages and other costs* [Electronic version], from *To care for elderly relatives and friends according to MetLife study.* Retrieved May 13, 2003, from http://heller.brandeis.edu/national/metpress.htm

National Center on Women and Aging, Brandeis University. (2002, November). *2002 national poll: Women 50+* [Electronic version]. Retrieved May 13, 2003, from http://heller.brandeis.edu/national/poll_2002inst.pdf

National Center on Women and Aging, Brandeis University. (n.d.). *Facts on Midlife and Older Women and Crime* [Electronic version]. Retrieved May 13, 2003, from http://www.heller.brandeis.edu/national/Crime_Brief_M8.pdf

Newman, S. (2003). The living conditions of elderly Americans. *The Gerontologist, 43,* 99–109.

Nicholson, T. (2003, May). Good/bad news for the disabled: "Independent living" a growing option, but not for everybody. *AARP Bulletin,* pp. 8–9.

O'Brien Cousins, S. (2000). "My heart couldn't take it": Older women's beliefs about exercise benefits and risks. *Journal of Gerontology: Psychological Sciences, 55B,* P283–P294.

Pinquart, M., & Sorensen, S. (2001). Gender differences in self-concept and psychological well-being in old age: A meta-analysis. *Journal of Gerontology: Psychological Sciences, 56B,* P195–P213.

Poole, M. (2001). Fit for life: Older women's commitment to exercise. *Journal of Aging and Physical Activity, 9,* 300–312.

Porell, F. W., & Miltiades, H. B. (2001). Access to care and functional status change among aged Medicare beneficiaries. *Journal of Gerontology: Social Sciences, 56B,* S69–S83.

Pruchno, R. A., & McKenney, D. (2002). Psychological well-being of Black and White grandmothers raising grandchildren: Examination of a two-factor model. *Journal of Gerontology: Psychological Sciences, 57B,* P444–P452.

Quadagno, J., & Reid, J. (1999). The political economy perspective in aging. In V. L. Bengston & K. W. Schaie (Eds.), *Handbook of theories of aging* (pp. 344–358). New York: Springer.

Smith, G. P., II. (1996). *Legal and healthcare ethics for the elderly.* Washington, DC: Taylor & Francis.

Tennstedt, S. (1999, March). *Family caregiving in an aging society.* Paper presented at the U.S. Administration on Aging Symposium on Longevity in the New American Century, Baltimore [Electronic version]. Retrieved May 13, 2003, from http://www.aoa.gov/prof/research/famcare.pdf

Whitbourne, S. K. (1996). *The aging individual: Physical and psychological perspectives.* New York: Springer.

The death of a loved one is among the most stressful of all life events (Holmes & Rahe, 1967). The loss of one's husband or significant other, in particular, requires important psychological and behavioral adaptations. The survivor must cope with the loss of an enduring intimate relationship, establish a new identity as an "unmarried" woman, and learn to manage the daily routines and activities that were once shared by both partners (Utz, Reidy, Carr, Nesse, & Wortman, 2004). In general, bereavement in later life is less distressing than losses that occur earlier in the life course. Older women are believed to cope better with death than younger women because they have more experience with loss and because they may find support from their peers who also are experiencing their partner's illness and death (Moss, Moss, & Hansson, 2001). Older women also are better than young women at regulating their emotions, and thus may experience less intense emotions such as grief (Carstensen, Fung, & Charles, 2003).

Still, widowhood poses distinctive challenges for older women and these challenges may require different readjustments than those made by widowers. In this chapter, we describe the ways that gendered patterns of social roles, relationships, and economic inequality over the life course affect older women's adjustment to their partner's death, and suggest ways that late-life bereavement may change for future cohorts of women. The particular challenges and resources of two specific subgroups, African Americans and lesbians, also are highlighted. Finally, we suggest policies and practices that can potentially minimize the economic, social, and psychological strains associated with late-life bereavement.

DEBORAH CARR
and JUNG-HWA HA

Bereavement

42

GENDER AND BEREAVEMENT

In the United States today, late-life widowhood is primarily a women's issue. Among persons age 65 and older, 45% of women and just 15% are men are widowed (U.S. Bureau of the Census, 2001). This pattern reflects men's elevated mortality risk and their tendency to marry women younger than themselves. Women also are more likely to *remain widowed* at every stage in the life course; men are five times more likely than women to remarry after their spouses die, reflecting men's much larger pool of eligible partners (Mastekaasa, 1992). Among persons over age 65 in the United States, roughly 2% of widowed women ever remarry, while the figure is as high as 20% among widowed men (Smith, Zick, & Duncan, 1991). However, as men live longer and women start to marry men who are their own age or younger, then widowhood may become a more gender-egalitarian transition for future cohorts of older adults.

Who Adjusts Better to Loss, Men or Women?

Although widowhood is much more likely to befall women than men, both genders face distinctive challenges as they cope with their partner's death. An estimated 40–70% of widowed persons experience a period of two weeks or more marked by feelings of sadness immediately after the loss (e.g., Zisook & Shuchter, 1991). Gender differences in emotional distress following late-life widowhood have been researched extensively, yet results remain inconclusive. Several studies report that widows are more likely to become depressed than widowers (e.g., Thompson, Gallagher, Cover, Galewski, & Peterson, 1989), whereas most others find widowhood to have a more adverse effect on men than women (Lee, DeMaris, Bavin, & Sullivan, 2001; Umberson, Wortman, & Kessler, 1992). A third group finds no gender differences in the psychological consequences of widowhood (e.g., Zisook & Shuchter, 1991).

Methodological Issues in Studying Gender and Bereavement

The conflicting findings in past research reflect both methodological and substantive issues. First, men are more likely than women to remarry, and remarriage is likely to "select" those persons with the highest levels of emotional and physical well-being. As a result, the average well-being of persons remaining widowed is lower than for those who remarry; this pattern may artificially inflate the observed health problems of persons who remain widowed. Second, widowhood is believed to increase the risk of mortality for men more than for women (Kaprio, Koskenuvo, & Rita, 1987). Mortality risk is elevated among depressed persons. Thus, men who "survive" through the years after their wives' deaths will likely have greater psychological well-being than those men who have died.

Third, gender differences in psychological health *in general* need to be taken into consideration before one can conclude that widows or widowers fare worse. Women have higher rates of depression than men; most studies estimate that women's rates of depressive disorders are between 50–100% greater than men's (Rieker & Bird, 2000). In contrast, men have significantly higher rates of alcohol and drug dependence and antisocial behavior disorders than women (Rieker & Bird, 2000). In order to ascertain whether the event of widowhood affects women and men differently, researchers must examine the combined (i.e., interactive) effects of gender and widowhood. Studies that compare only widowed women and men may find that widows are more depressed, but cannot necessarily attribute this gender difference to the event of widowhood. Finally, gender differences in psychological reactions to the loss of one's partner may be understated (or overstated) in studies that do not control the mediator (or suppressor) variables that may account for the observed gender gap. Importantly, the key pathways that link bereavement to psychological adjustment reflect gendered patterns of social interaction over the life course, as well as characteristics of the late marriage or long-term relationship, and the context of the partner's death.

UNDERSTANDING GENDER DIFFERENCES IN BEREAVEMENT EXPERIENCE

"His" and "Her" Marriage

The ways that older women experience and adjust to the loss of their partners is inextricably linked to the social roles they have held both within and outside of marriage. Feminist writings, exemplified by Bernard (1972), have argued that traditional marriages—where men specialize in the "breadwinner" role and women are responsible for childbearing and child rearing—benefit women much less than men. Although marriage brings men health, power, and life satisfaction, the institution subjects women to stress, dissatisfaction, and the loss of self. According to this perspective, women are purported to suffer less upon the loss of their spouses because they have less to lose (Thompson & Walker, 1989). Recent empirical studies counter, however, that marriage benefits *both* men and women, yet in different ways (Simon, 2002). Women typically benefit economically, whereas men receive richer social and psychological rewards. These gendered patterns of advantage and disadvantage within marriage provide a framework for understanding older women's adjustments to the spousal loss.

Economic Issues

One of the most widely documented sources of women's distress upon widowhood is economic strain. Women are more likely than men to experience economic hardship, upon either divorce or widowhood (Zick & Smith, 1991). Although age-based income assistance programs such as Social Security provide economic support for older widowed persons (Hungerford, 2001), the bereaved remain significantly worse off than their married peers. Widowed persons are more likely to live below the poverty line than are their married counterparts, and they tend to cyclically reenter poverty after losing their partner (Rank & Hirschl, 1999). Direct costs associated with the funeral, long-term care, medical care, and estate-related legal proceedings can devastate the fixed income of older adults. For younger women, remarriage is an important pathway out of poverty yet demographic constraints make this option difficult for most older women. Women ages 65 and older outnumber men by roughly 1.5 to 1, and by age 85 women outnumber men by roughly 4 to 1 (U.S. Bureau of the Census, 2001).

Women's economic disadvantage upon loss reflects lifelong patterns of gendered inequality. In traditional marriages—particularly among current cohorts of older adults—wives tended to child rearing and family responsibilities while husbands were responsible for supporting the family financially. As a result, older women have had disrupted work lives (if they worked for pay,

at all) and fewer years of paid work experience than their male peers. Women's accumulated pension and Social Security benefits based on their own earnings are typically much lower than those based on their husband's lifetime earnings. Moreover, the pension benefits and Social Security income of their husband may not be available or may be reduced after his death. Third, older widows who try to reenter the labor force may lack the experience to secure a good job or may face age discrimination (Harrington, 1996).

These financial stressors, in turn, are an important source of psychological strain. Stressful life events, such as widowhood, may cast off a chain of secondary stressors that have either direct or combined effects on the survivor's well-being. Financial strain is a risk factor for depression (Vinokur, Price, & Caplan, 1996). Moreover, bereaved women who lack expertise or experience in paying bills, managing money, and making major financial or legal decisions may face considerable stress and anxiety when forced to assume sole responsibility for the financial management of the household (Umberson et al., 1992).

Social and Instrumental Support

In traditional marriages, women typically provide emotional, social, instrumental, and health-promoting support to their spouses and children. As a result, men often have difficulty in managing household tasks, maintaining their own health, and seeking alternative sources of emotional support after their wives have died. In contrast, women's richer sources of social support over the life course are an important resource as they adjust to the loss of their husbands. Women typically receive more instrumental and emotional support from their children following widowhood than do men, given mothers' closer relationships with their children at earlier stages in the life course (Connidis, 2001). Women also are more likely to have larger and more varied friendship networks than men, and these friendships provide an important source of support to women as they cope with their loss (Antonucci, 1990). These patterns reflect lifelong processes of gender-role socialization (particularly in current cohorts of older adults), where women are raised to develop close and intimate interpersonal relationships, and men are socialized to be self-reliant and independent, with few emotional confidantes other than their spouse.

Marital Quality

The extent to which bereaved elders mourn the loss of their partners also is linked to the emotional climate of the late marriage or long-term relationship. Early research, guided by the psychoanalytic tradition, suggested that persons with the most troubled marriages suffered heightened and delayed grief following their spouse's death (Freud, 1917/1957). This perspective held that persons who had conflicted or ambivalent marital relationships find it hard to let go of their spouses, yet feel angry at the deceased for abandoning them; as a result, they experience elevated grief. Recent research shows, conversely, that persons in conflicted marriages mourn less for their spouses while persons with the most loving marriages grieve most upon their loss (Carr et al., 2000).

The Nature of the Late Partner's Death

Late-life loss is distinct from earlier losses in that it typically occurs at the end of a long chronic illness, and intensive caregiving often is required during the ailing person's final weeks (Field & Cassel, 1997). The timing of and conditions surrounding a partner's death have implications for the psychological adjustment of the bereaved widow. On one hand, the knowledge that one's partner is going to die in the imminent future provides the couple with the time to address unresolved emotional, financial, and practical issues before the actual death. This preparation for death is believed to enable a smoother transition to widowhood. However, long-anticipated deaths due to chronic illness may be accompanied by potentially stressful experiences such as difficult caregiving duties, financial strains imposed by long-term care, emotional isolation from other family members and friends, and neglect of one's own health symptoms (Carr, House, Wortman, Nesse, & Kessler, 2001; Field & Cassel, 1997).

The conditions of a spouse's death can affect women and men in different ways (Carr et al., 2001). For women, sudden spousal deaths are associated with greater psychological distress, while men mourn most for their wives when they died after a prolonged illness. These relationships reflect gendered patterns of socialization and social interaction. Men typically have fewer sources of social support than do women (e.g., Antonucci, 1990) and may become even more emotionally bonded to their wives during their final weeks. Men also may have few same-sex peers who are caring for a dying spouse, and thus have few sources of peer support and advice. Women, in contrast, may rely on their female friends' direct experience with spousal illness to prepare them for the difficult dying process and thereafter (Lopata, 1996).

OTHER LOSSES: CHILDREN, SIBLINGS, AND FRIENDS

Older women anticipate the loss of their parents, and to a lesser degree, the loss of their spouse. However, the deaths of grown children may be particularly distressing because they are considered "off-time" (i.e., unnaturally early) and are typically unexpected; most parents anticipate that their children will outlive them (Leahy, 1992–1993). Most women experience depression upon the loss of a child, regardless of the child's age (Fish, 1986), yet the intensity of this distress is linked to women's social roles and identity. Those who grieve most report that the loss of their child is the loss of their "whole existence," while women adjust more smoothly to the loss when they viewed their child as just one part of themselves and maintained other important identities (Talbot, 1996–1997).

Surprisingly little research has explored adjustment to the deaths of friends and siblings in later life, although research on gender differences in personal relationships suggests that both losses are particularly distressing for older women. Friends are accorded fewer rights as mourners than members of the deceased person's family (Sklar, 1991–1992), and this may be particularly problematic for women as they mourn this loss. As noted earlier, women have richer friendship networks than men (Antonucci, 1990), and these friendships typically are based on sharing their personal experiences and feelings (Rubin, 1985). Consequently, the loss of a close confidante may involve a profound loss, yet one that goes unacknowledged. Sibling deaths may also be particularly difficult, given that sisters tend to maintain particularly close relationships over the life course (Matthews, 2002). Sibling deaths are most problematic for older women who have never married and who co-resided with their siblings; in this setting, sibling grief is just as powerful as spousal or partner grief (Pickard, 1994).

SUBGROUP VARIATIONS IN BEREAVEMENT EXPERIENCE FOR AFRICAN AMERICANS AND LESBIANS

Bereavement creates special challenges for African American women and lesbians, reflecting patterns of social interaction and inequalities that persist throughout the life course. However, both groups also have distinctive resources that may enable highly effective coping and readjustment to the death of their partners.

Ethnic Variation in Bereavement

Surprisingly little research has focused on the distinctive sources of risk and resilience among African American, Hispanic/Latino, Asian American, and Native American older widows in the United States. How people grieve varies widely across ethnic groups owing to cultural and religious differences in how death is understood, beliefs about the possibility for future reunion with the deceased, and beliefs and ways of communicating about death (Rosenblatt, 2001). Although small qualitative studies have documented the ways that specific ethnic and religious groups grieve (see Rosenblatt, 2001), little systematic comparative research has been conducted. This omission reflects the fact that few sample surveys include adequate numbers of older ethnic minorities, even African Americans, who currently constitute 8% of the older U.S. population. Older African Americans' underrepresentation in large-scale surveys reflects their elevated risk of pre-

mature death (Gibson, 1994). Studies of newly bereaved older African Americans are particularly difficult, given that Blacks are less likely than Whites to marry and remain married over the life course (Lugaila, 1998).

Research on ethnic and racial differences in stress and coping suggest that African Americans have several resources that may enable a more successful adjustment to loss. First, older African Americans women are more likely than White women to participate in formal religious activities (such as church attendance) and to rely on their religious beliefs as a strategy for coping with stressful life events (e.g., Levin, Chatters, & Taylor, 1995). The beneficial effects of religion—particularly for older women—have been widely documented (Koenig, 1998).

Second, African American married couples have been found to have lower levels of marital quality, higher levels of marital conflict, shorter marriages, and a more egalitarian division of household labor than do White married couples (Orbuch & Eyster, 1997). Because of their more strained emotional ties within marriage, and reduced dependence on their spouse for performing gender-typed household tasks, African American widows may experience less distress and anxiety upon the loss of spouse. Third, African American women are less likely than Whites to depend upon and interact with members of the nuclear family only, and instead maintain a more diffuse social network that may include friends, distant relatives, neighbors, and members of their church congregation (Ajrouch, Antonucci, & Janevic, 2001). Given that social support is one of the most important resources for coping with stressful life events, African American women's more varied interpersonal relationships and frequent contacts may provide an important source of instrumental and expressive support as they adjust to loss.

Further research on ethnic differences in bereavement will be critically important for future cohorts of older adults. Among persons age 65 and older today, roughly 4% are of Hispanic origin and 8% are African American; however, by the year 2050 the African American elderly population will quadruple while the number of Hispanic elderly will increase sevenfold (U.S. Bureau of the Census, 2001). Health-care providers, counselors, and social workers will need to develop an understanding of the distinctive challenges faced by ethnic minority widows.

Older Bereaved Lesbians

Researchers know very little about how older lesbians adjust to the loss of their long-term life partners. This lack of research reflects the fact that no official statistics are available for same-sex unions, given the lack of social and legal approval for these relationships. Moreover, current cohorts of older adults grew up during an historical era marked by lack of awareness and acceptance of homosexuality. Older lesbians may face both unique challenges and advantages as they cope with loss.

On one hand, bereavement may be particularly difficult. Bereaved lesbians may encounter conflict with their deceased partner's family, particularly with respect to the dispersion of personal possessions following death (DeSpelder & Strickland, 1992). Lack of institutionalized support compounds the difficulty faced by lesbian partners. Although there are serious shortcomings in Social Security benefit levels and eligibility criteria for surviving spouses who were married, no benefits are available for surviving partners in lesbian relationships. Other rights extended to heterosexual married couples are not typically available for same-sex couples, including the opportunity to make health-care and end-of-life decisions for ill partners. Bereaved lesbian partners may not receive sufficient emotional support upon loss because the end of homosexual relationships may not be recognized or acknowledged in the wider community. Some lesbians receive insufficient emotional support from their families of origin, if these relatives disapprove of their lifestyle or sexuality (Friend, 1990).

However, lesbians have some resources that may enable better coping with later life strains. They may create their own support networks of friends, significant others, and selected biological family members. Lesbians are more likely than heterosexual women to enact flexible gender roles throughout the life course; these roles, in turn, may foster greater adaptability to change and more positive self-identities, particularly

upon the loss of one's life partner (Kimmel, 1992). Richard Friend (1990) argued that older lesbians have had greater freedom than their heterosexual peers to learn skills that are nontraditional for their gender. Because they are not bound to traditional family roles, they may be better prepared for changes associated with aging, and for the daily challenges and responsibilities faced by the newly bereaved.

FORECASTING THE FUTURE: A "NEW" PARTNER BEREAVEMENT?

Changing Gender Roles, Changing Widowhood

The research discussed thus far describes widowhood as it is currently experienced, and not how it may be for *future cohorts* of bereaved elders. Many older adults today were raised to maintain traditional gender roles in the home and workplace. Women were largely dependent on their husbands' incomes for their economic well-being, and unhappily married persons seldom divorced, given the stigma of divorce. In contrast, current generations of young adult women have higher levels of education, more years of work experience, and more egalitarian divisions of labor in their families than do past cohorts. Thus, they may be less dependent on their husbands for income, home repair, and financial management tasks (Spain & Bianchi, 1996). Under this scenario, distress may be minimized among future cohorts of widows.

At the same time, adaptation to spousal loss may become more difficult for future cohorts of widows. Two important demographic trends—increasing divorce rates and declining fertility rates—may have important consequences for how the bereaved adjust to loss. Current cohorts of married couples are more likely than past generations to dissolve dissatisfying marriages. Consequently, women who remain married until late life may have higher levels of marital closeness and may suffer elevated grief following the loss of these close relationships. Declining fertility rates and increases in geographic mobility mean that older women will have fewer children upon whom they can rely for social support, and these children will be less likely than past generations to live close to their parents (Connidis, 2001). Future cohorts of older bereaved spouses may need to develop more expansive social networks that include friends and family members who are more proximate, to counterbalance the fact that their children are fewer and less proximate than in past generations.

Changing Sociolegal Context of Death and Dying

Changes in when, how, and under what conditions older persons die will have important ramifications for how older women adjust to loss. Wives typically outlive their husbands (U.S. Bureau of the Census, 2001), and women are more likely than men to provide care to dying friends, siblings, and parents (Cancian & Oliker, 2000); consequently the management of death and dying falls overwhelmingly upon older and midlife women. Most older adults today die of long-term chronic illness; heart disease, stroke, and cancer are now the leading causes of death and account for two thirds of all deaths to older adults (Brock & Foley, 1998). Although advanced medical technologies and treatments now enable chronically ill older adults to increase the length of their life, their quality of life during the final days is poor (Field & Cassel, 1997). Most dying elderly have limited mobility, cognitive functioning difficulty, pain, and difficulty recognizing family. In many cases, the dying have little control over the medical treatment they receive, and difficult decisions about stopping, starting, or continuing treatment fall upon distressed wives, daughters, and sisters (Brock & Foley, 1998).

However, recent policies and practices, including the establishment of the Patient Self-Determination Act (1990) and expanded use of palliative care (Pan, Morrison, & Meier, 2001), may give future cohorts of older women greater control over the conditions surrounding their loved ones' death. These changes may help to reduce the strains associated with widowhood and other family deaths. Deaths that are painful to the patient and where physicians provide unsatisfactory care are associated with poorer spousal adjustment (Carr, 2003). However, medical advancements that extend the length of life may create the need for more intensive caregiving, a task that typically falls to women. If the duration and intensity of late-life caregiving increases, and if women continue to bear the burden for personal care, then future cohorts of women may face a more difficult adjustment to spousal loss.

IMPLICATIONS OF RESEARCH FOR POLICY AND PRACTICE

The research reviewed thus far underscores an important message for policy makers and practitioners: women and men experience marriage differently and thus experience spousal loss in different ways. By identifying precisely what is lost upon spousal death, clinicians can provide individually tailored interventions that address at least one of the following areas for newly bereaved older women: psychological, social, instrumental, or economic support.

Recently widowed women may experience declines in their economic well-being and subsequent anxiety about their financial well-being. The development of support groups, where the bereaved gain mastery over those tasks for which they lack skills, training, or experience, may be particularly useful. For example, the Pathfinders program was designed to provide a supportive environment where widowed persons can discuss their frustrations with daily tasks, and learn practical skills related to household management (Caserta, Lund, & Rice, 1999).

Federal policy initiatives could help to reduce economic-related distress among bereaved women, especially African Americans and lesbians. Financial aid through more equitable and generous Social Security survivor benefits that recognize the economic value of women's unpaid caregiving labor may help to offset the declines in income often experienced upon widowhood. Moreover, recognition of the ways that women's contributions to the home (i.e., unpaid domestic labor, child care, and elder care) impede their pension earnings may be used to guide future policy decisions.

At the community or senior center level, the provision of social activities and social support also may be effective interventions for helping older adults to cope with the stress and loneliness that accompany widowhood. However, we caution against the development of informal community programs that are based on a simple "keep busy" philosophy. Rather than creating new recreational or social opportunities for the bereaved, intervention efforts should instead enable older adults' maintenance of their pre-loss social activities, interpersonal relationships, and hobbies—provided these activities are still enjoyable and meaningful to the newly bereaved.

Clinicians should recognize that while widowed persons may experience grief, widows may be particularly likely to also have depressive symptoms, given that women are much more likely than men to be depressed—even in the absence of loss (Rieker & Bird, 2000). Clinicians and medical professionals should identify soon-to-be or recent widows with past histories of major depression, even before the onset of grief or grief-related depressive symptoms. Both short and longer term treatment goals should take into account that depression may be a chronic and recurring condition for women, and that grief is an ongoing process that some bereaved persons may deal with for years (Zisook & Shuchter, 2001).

More generally, bereavement is a process that may begin far earlier than the actual moment of death. Interventions targeted toward older women who are providing care to their ailing partners, or witnessing their partner die of a long and painful illness, may be as important for alleviating bereavement-related distress as interventions offered *after* the loss. Improved medical care; affordable nursing home, long-term, or hospice care; and increased availability of pain management programs will not only benefit the dying person but also may enable a smoother transition for the bereaved survivor.

REFERENCES

Ajrouch, K., Antonucci, T. C., & Janevic, M. R. (2001). Social networks among Blacks and Whites: The interaction between race and age. *Journal of Gerontology: Social Sciences, 56B*, S112–S118.

Antonucci, T. C. (1990). Social support and social relationships. In R. H. Binstock & L. K. George (Eds.), *Handbook of aging and the social sciences* (3rd ed., pp. 205–226). San Diego, CA: Academic Press.

Bernard, J. (1972). *The future of marriage.* New York: Bantam.

Brock, D., & Foley, D. (1998). Demography and epidemiology of dying in the U.S., with emphasis on deaths of older persons. *The Hospice Journal, 13,* 49–60.

Cancian, F. M., & Oliker, S. J. (2000). *Caring and gender.* Walnut Creek, CA: AltaMira Press.

Carr, D. (2003). A "good death" for whom? Quality of spouse's death and psychological distress among older widowed persons. *Journal of Health and Social Behavior, 44,* 215–232.

Carr, D., House, J. S., Kessler, R. C., Nesse, R., Sonnega, J., & Wortman, C. B. (2000). Marital quality and psychological adjustment to widowhood among older adults: A longitudinal analysis. *Journal of Gerontology: Social Sciences, 55,* S197–S207.

Carr, D., House, J. S., Wortman, C. B., Nesse, R. M., & Kessler, R. C. (2001). Psychological adjustment to sudden and anticipated spousal death among the older widowed. *Journal of Gerontology: Social Sciences, 56,* S237–S248.

Carstensen, L. L., Fung, H., & Charles, S. (2003). Socioemotional selectivity theory and the regulation of emotion in the second half of life. *Motivation and Emotion, 27*(2), 103–124.

Caserta, M. S., Lund, D. A., & Rice, J. A. (1999). Pathfinders: A self-care and health education program for older widows and widowers. *The Gerontologist, 39,* 615–620.

Connidis, I. (2001). *Family ties and aging.* Thousand Oaks, CA: Sage.

DeSpelder, L., & Strickland, A. (1992). *The last dance: Encountering death and dying* (3rd ed.). Mountain View, CA: Mayfield.

Field, M. J., & Cassel, C. K. (1997). *Approaching death: Improving care at the end of life.* Washington, DC: Institute of Medicine.

Fish, W. C. (1986). Differences in grief intensity in bereaved parents. In T. A. Rando (Ed.), *Parental loss of a child* (pp. 415–428). Champaign, IL: Research Press.

Freud, S. (1917/1957). Mourning and melancholia. In J. Strachey (Trans. and Ed.), *Standard edition of complete psychological works of Sigmund Freud, Volume 14* (pp. 239–258). London: Hogarth Press and Institute of Psychoanalysis.

Friend, R. A. (1990). Older lesbian and gay people: A theory of successful aging. *Journal of Homosexuality, 23,* 99–118.

Gibson, R. (1994). The age-by-race gap in health and mortality in the older population: A social science research agenda. *The Gerontologist, 34,* 454–462.

Harrington, M. M. (1996). Making claims as workers or wives: The distribution of Social Security benefits. *American Sociological Review, 61,* 449–465.

Holmes, J. H., & Rahe, R. H. (1967). The social readjustment scale. *Journal of Psychosomatic Research, 11,* 213–228.

Hungerford, T. L. (2001). The economic consequences of widowhood on elderly women in the United States and Germany. *The Gerontologist, 41,* 103–110.

Kaprio, J., Koskenuvo, M., & Rita, H. (1987). Mortality after bereavement: A prospective study of 95,647 widowed persons. *American Journal of Public Health, 77,* 283–287.

Kimmel, D. (1992). The families of older gay men and lesbians. *Generations, 16,* 37–38.

Koenig, H. G. (1998). Religious beliefs and practices of hospitalized medically ill older adults. *International Journal of Geriatric Psychiatry, 13,* 213–224.

Leahy, J. M. (1992–1993). A comparison of depression in women bereaved of a spouse, child, or a parent. *Omega, 26,* 207–217.

Lee, G. R., DeMaris, A., Bavin, S., & Sullivan, R. (2001). Gender differences in the depressive effect of widowhood in later life. *Journal of Gerontology: Social Sciences, 56,* S56–S61.

Levin, J. S., Chatters, L. M., & Taylor, R. J. (1995). Religious effects on health status and life satisfaction among Black Americans. *Journal of Gerontology: Social Sciences, 50B,* S154–S163.

Lopata, H. (1996). *Current widowhood: Myths and realities.* Thousand Oaks, CA: Sage.

Lugaila, T. A. (1998). *Marital status and living arrangements: March 1998* (update). Washington, DC: U.S. Department of Commerce.

Mastekaasa, A. (1992). Marriage and psychological well-being: Some evidence on selection into marriage. *Journal of Marriage and the Family, 54,* 901–911.

Matthews, S. H. (2002). *Sisters and brothers/daughters and sons: Meeting the needs of old parents.* Bloomington, IN: Unlimited Publishing.

Moss, M., Moss, S., & Hansson, R. O. (2001). Bereavement and old age. In M. S. Stroebe, R. O. Hansson, W. Stroebe, & H. Schut (Eds.), *Handbook of bereavement research : Consequences, coping, and care.* Washington, DC: American Psychological Association.

Orbuch, T. L., & Eyster, S. L. (1997). Division of household labor among black couples and white couples. *Social Forces, 76,* 301–332.

Pan, C. X., Morrison, R. S., & Meier, D. E. (2001). How prevalent are hospital-based palliative care programs? Status report and future directions. *Journal of Palliative Medicine, 4,* 315–324.

Patient Self-Determination Act. (1990). 554206, 4751 of the Omnibus Reconciliation Act of 1990. Pub.L. No. 101–508.

Pickard, S. (1994). Life and death: The experience of bereavement in South Wales. *Ageing and Society, 14,* 191–217.

Rank, M. R., & Hirschl, T. A. (1999). Estimating proportion of Americans ever experiencing poverty during their elderly years. *Journal of Gerontology, 54B,* S184–S193.

Rieker, P., & Bird, C. E. (2000). Sociological explanations of gender differences in mental and physical health. In C. Bird, P. Conrad, & A. Fremont (Eds.), *Handbook of medical sociology* (5th ed., pp. 79–97). New York: Prentice-Hall.

Rosenblatt, P. C. (2001). A social constructionist perspective on cultural differences in grief. In M. S. Stroebe, R. O. Hansson, W. Stroebe, & H. Schut (Eds.), *Handbook of bereavement research: Consequences, coping, and care* (pp. 285–300). Washington, DC: American Psychological Association.

Rubin, L. (1985). *Just friends.* New York: Harper & Row.

Simon, R. (2002). Revisiting the relationship among gender, marital status, and mental health. *American Journal of Sociology, 107,* 1065–1096.

Sklar, F. (1991–1992). Grief as a family affair: Property rights, grief rights, and the exclusion of close friends as survivors. *Omega, 24,* 109–121.

Smith, K. R., Zick, C. D., & Duncan, G. J. (1991). Remarriage patterns among recent widows and widowers. *Demography, 28,* 361–374.

Spain, D., & Bianchi, S. M. (1996). *Balancing act: Motherhood, marriage and employment among American women.* New York: Russell Sage.

Talbot, K. (1996–1997). Mothers now childless: Survival after the death of an only child. *Omega, 34,* 177–189.

Thompson, L., & Walker, A. J. (1989). Gender in families: Women and men in marriage, work, and parenthood. *Journal of Marriage and Family, 51,* 845–871.

Thompson, L. W., Gallagher, D., Cover, H., Galewski, M., & Peterson, J. (1989). Effects of bereavement on symptoms on psychopathology in older men and women. In D. A. Lund (Ed.), *Older bereaved spouses: Research with practical applications* (pp. 17–24). New York: Hemisphere.

Umberson, D., Wortman, C. B., & Kessler, R. C. (1992). Widowhood and depression: Explaining long-term gender differences in vulnerability. *Journal of Health and Social Behavior, 33,* 10–24.

U.S. Bureau of the Census. (2001). *Statistical abstract of the United States: 2001* (112th ed.). Washington, DC: U.S. Government Printing Office.

Utz, R., Reidy, E. B., Carr, D., Nesse, R., & Wortman, C. B. (2004). The daily consequences of widowhood: The role of gender and intergenerational transfers on subsequent housework performance. *Journal of Family Issues, 25,* 683–712.

Vinokur, A. D., Price, R. H., & Caplan, R. D. (1996). Hard times and hurtful partners: How financial strain affects depression and relationship satisfaction of unemployed persons and their spouses. *Journal of Personality and Social Psychology, 7,* 166–179.

Zick, C. D., & Smith, K. R. (1991). Patterns of economic change surrounding the death of a spouse. *Journal of Gerontology, 46,* S310–S320.

Zisook, S., & Shuchter, S. R. (1991). Early psychological reaction to the stress of widowhood. *Psychiatry, 54,* 320–332.

Zisook, S., & Shuchter, S. R. (2001). Treatment of the depression of bereavement. *American Behavioral Scientist, 44,* 782–797.

Helping older individuals deal with end-of-life (EOL) issues is a topic of increasing significance to psychological and medical communities. In 1997, the Institute of Medicine issued its landmark report on improving care at the end of life (Field & Cassel, 1997). In 1998, the American Psychological Association (APA) established a working group on assisted suicide and EOL decisions that resulted in a report to the APA Board of Directors delineating historical changes in EOL care, including the relative invisibility of psychology in this arena and current and potential roles for psychologists interested in working with EOL issues (APA Ad Hoc Committee on End-of-Life Issues, 2000). In 2000, the APA established the Ad Hoc Committee on End-of-Life issues that helped to create an APA-sponsored Web site on this topic and also developed a fact sheet on EOL care based on behavioral and social science research findings. Most recently, in 2004, clinical practice guidelines for an interdisciplinary approach to palliative care were published, which represent a consensus of five major United States palliative-care organizations (National Consensus Project for Quality Palliative Care, 2004). Taken together, these publications provide a context for understanding this important domain of clinical practice.

DEMOGRAPHIC BACKGROUND INFORMATION

In the United States at present, a dramatic increase is occurring in the proportion of both the oldest old (those aged 85 and above) and elders of color, who represent a wide array of culturally, racially, and ethnically distinct groups. In the year 2000, individuals over the age of 65 were numbered at 35 million and individuals over the age of 85 were numbered at 4.2 million; together these groups accounted for about 13% of the population. Their proportion is expected to increase to approximately 30% by 2030 (U.S. Department of Health and Human Services, 2002). Within this large cohort, it is anticipated that African American, Asian and Pacific Islander, and Hispanic/Latino persons, who now account for about 25% of the 65+ age group in the United States, will increase significantly overall to account for about 35% by 2030. Because women

DOLORES GALLAGHER-THOMPSON,
JENNIFER DILLINGER,
HEATHER L. GRAY,
VERONICA CARDENAS,
LANI SINGER,
and SHANNON HSU

Women's Issues at the End of Life

live an average of seven years longer than men, they represent the majority of older adults. In fact, women who are approximately age 85 make up the most rapidly growing age group in the United States.

Aging women of all ethnicities face the problem of surviving other family members and being isolated at a time when they often need the most care. Of the 20.6 million women aged 65 and older in the United States, about 46% are widowed, 40% live alone, and 12% are below the poverty line. Older Hispanic women who live alone are in the most dangerous situation, with 50% in poverty (U.S. Department of Health and Human Services, 2002). Further, older women in generally are more likely to have limited Social Security and retirement benefits, reflecting a lifetime of disadvantages including discontinuous work histories and low pay while employed (Gatz, Harris, & Turk-Charles, 1995).

FRAMEWORKS FOR UNDERSTANDING DEATH AND DYING

Unlike individuals who die young or suddenly, the older population has time to contemplate death. In her popular book *On Death and Dying*, Kubler-Ross (1969, 1981) presents a five-stage model that has proved to be an influential theory to describe the process of dying. This five-stage model includes (a) denial, (b) anger, (c) bargaining, (d) depression, and eventually (e) acceptance. This model has helped to provide order and clarity to many people's understanding of dying. However, some clinicians and theorists have criticized Kubler-Ross's model for being too rigid and oversimplified (Copp, 1998). An excellent discussion of other theories about dying can be found in Copp's (1998) article.

The "Good Death"

Integral to understanding the meaning of death for most people is the desire to have a completed, full life. According to some authors (e.g., Brody, 1992), a full life is one that has run its "natural life span" (not necessarily the biological maximum) and that has brought a sense of completion to the person's psychological narrative. While there

can be no single definition of a "good death," Steinhauser et al. (2000), for example, found several components to be integral to this idea including (a) pain and symptom management, (b) EOL preparation (medical, emotional, and social), (c) development of a sense of completion (in terms of faith, relationships, resolutions, and saying good-bye), (d) the ability to contribute to other's well-being (generativity), and (e) empathetic treatment as a whole person. This and similar studies indicate the importance of psychological, physical, social, spiritual, and emotional support at the end of one's life, combined with sensitive and appropriate medical treatment.

PSYCHOLOGICAL HEALTH

There are a number of psychological health issues to consider with regard to EOL concerns, which can best be understood against the backdrop of humanity's attempt to find meaning in life even in the face of life-threatening illness and death. As Doka (1999) points out, "The central question becomes the human question: 'How can we live fully in the face of death' " (p. 247)? Some people are successful in finding meaning in death and so are more likely to experience a "good death," whereas others develop problems such as depression, anxiety, and other disorders. Three key interrelated constructs that seem to strongly influence one's ability to find meaning at the end of life are resilience, spirituality, and hope.

Resilience encompasses the confrontation of one's essential aloneness in life, along with the ability to construct meaning for one's life. According to major writers in the field such as Kastenbaum (1999), resilience provides a mechanism by which negatively viewed events such as life-threatening illness transform into opportunities for growth and satisfaction. Similarly, Neimeyer (2001) explains that human beings seek meaning in mourning and do so by constructing a coherent account of their losses. This account preserves a sense of continuity with who they have been while at the same time integrating the reality of who they must be now.

Existential concerns in general, such as "why" questions regarding purpose and spiritual reasons for death, are common among people at the end of their lives (Lander, Wilson, & Chochinov, 2000). For many older adults, religious beliefs and spirituality may provide a source of meaning and comfort when faced with these questions. Kaut (2002) emphasizes the value of a "bio-psychosocial-spiritual" approach to the dying patient, which recognizes the relationships among mind, body, and spirit. Religion and spirituality can also be powerful sources of hope for the person who is dying. In fact, researchers theorize that hope is one of the primary mediators in the common finding that religiosity is associated with increased psychological well-being among terminally ill individuals (Van Ness & Larson, 2002).

Hope is essential for the well-being of any person, especially one who is facing the end of life. Even when death is approaching, the absence of a medical cure in no way negates the possibility of hope (Rousseau, 2000). While women may initially seek hope in a cure or long-term survival, maintaining hope in impossible outcomes can lead to hopelessness and depression. Instead, close relationships, dignity, inner peace, and religious faith are described by many as alternative sources of hope (Sullivan, 2002).

As well, there are often a number of unmet psychological needs facing women at the end of life. Many authors have pointed out that as physical symptoms and disability increase, so do the incidence of pain, depression, and delirium (Breitbart, Chochinov, & Passik, 1998). Psychological factors such as depression, anxiety, and negative expectations for the future can also influence the experience of physical symptoms—for example, perceived pain (Turk & Feldman, 2000). Individuals with advanced disease frequently feel anxious about current pain and fear having more. It is estimated that 20–70% of dying patients experience inadequate pain relief, that over one third are clinically depressed, and that a similar proportion have unmet emotional needs, most of which go unaddressed by professionals (Bradley, Fried, Kasl, & Idler, 2000).

Death Anxiety and Fears Related to End of Life

Despite the lack of a uniform definition of this term, death anxiety is a conscious concern in Western societies. It encompasses fear of the unknown after death, fear of obliteration, and fear of the dying process itself. In older adults it appears to be linked to fewer remaining years to live and reduced likelihood of personal control over one's physical and mental health status (Cicirelli, 1999). According to the APA fact sheet on EOL care (APA, 2003), older adults fear that their pain, emotional suffering, and family concerns will be ignored. Many critically ill people who die in hospitals receive unwanted treatments, have prolonged pain, and have their advance directives disregarded. According to Peter Singer and colleagues (1999), older adults want more information about EOL issues and an opportunity to influence decisions about their care. Unfortunately, most Americans are referred too late to hospice or palliative care so they are unable to derive the maximum benefits possible from those services.

Elderly dying women may fear both being a burden to loved ones and being abandoned by them due to caregiving stress. For women who have been in caregiving roles for much of their lives, this reversal of roles may be particularly distressing (Brody, 2002). Several studies have shown that older women experience higher levels of death anxiety than men since they perceive themselves as having weaker instrumental control over external events, yet conversely, improvement in perceived self-efficacy is associated with reduced fear of dying, suggesting the important mediating role of self-beliefs (self-esteem, self-confidence, and self-efficacy) in coping with death anxiety (Fry, 2003).

Grief and Depression

Most women experience at least some sadness when faced with the imminent prospect of their own death. This sadness appears to be a natural part of preparatory grief, and fluctuates in intensity and salience over time (Hallenbeck, 2003). In itself, this is not a diagnosable condition, but rather a normal process of detaching oneself from loved ones and from one's roles in life. Preparatory grief has been described as a process of mourning both past and future abilities, experiences, people, objects, and hopes (Haley,

Kasl-Godley, Larson, Neimeyer, & Kweilosz, 2003). In addition to the emotional experience, physical symptoms of grief may include changes in appetite or weight, fatigue, low energy, sleep disturbances, and sexual dysfunction. These symptoms may also indicate the need for better control of physical symptoms; or, they may also be indicative of clinical depression, which does not seem to be a normal part of the dying process. Depression must be identified and treated in order for individuals to die as comfortably as possible. This is particularly relevant here since women are more likely than men to suffer from clinical depression at any given point in life, a finding consistently reported in epidemiological studies conducted in the United States and in other parts of the world (Alegria & Canino, 2000).

Distinguishing between grief and depression can pose a confusing task for clinicians, as many of their symptoms overlap. Nevertheless, these two states differ on both psychological and physical dimensions. While grief is highly variable, depression is relatively continuous and will often worsen unless treated. Patients with depression commonly feel an inability to experience pleasure, a lack of interest in nearly all activities, a sense of hopelessness, and a negative self-image, none of which are inherent to the grieving process. Physicians and family members may suspect depression in an elderly dying patient if she becomes continuously socially withdrawn or has requested an early death even when her symptoms and social issues have been adequately addressed (Lander et al., 2000). Wilson, Chochinov, de Faye, and Breitbart (2000) provide a review of measures to assess depression in terminally ill patients. They also discuss the importance of assessing for delirium (referring to temporary cognitive impairment, often resulting from medication interaction and/or other medical causes), and include a section on screening tools for that condition as well.

Despite the insidiousness of depressive disorders, there is cause for hope in individuals suffering from these symptoms. Numerous types of psychological therapies are available to aid a person's recovery from depression (see chapter 5, this volume); and Gatz and colleagues (1998) for review of psychotherapies for depressed older adults).

CULTURAL PERSPECTIVES ON END OF LIFE

Psychological health and well-being occur in a cultural context. While culture is a difficult term to define, Kleinman and Kleinman (1991) explain that, "Culture is now viewed not merely as a fixed top-down organization of experience by the symbolic apparatuses of language, aesthetic preference, and mythology; it is also 'realized' from the bottom-up in the everyday negotiation of the social world, including the rhythms and processes of interpersonal interactions" (cited in Koenig, 1997, p. 365). In their classic study on ethnicity and death, Kalish and Reynolds (1976) showed that ethnicity affects attitudes, feelings, beliefs, and expectations regarding the dying process and death itself. They also caution that there is substantial heterogeneity, not only *between* various racial and ethnic categorizations used in this country at this time (e.g., Asian and Pacific Islanders) but also *within* these groups. This implies that simply knowing an individual's racial or ethnic identification does not provide conclusive information about his or her views on death, typical coping strategies, role of family, religious practices, and so on. Keeping this in mind, we next present brief illustrations from two distinct cultural groups.

Latino culture includes rich traditions and religious beliefs surrounding death that may influence a Latino woman's (Latina's) views of death (Block, 1998). For example, it is common for Latinas with religious faith to believe that death is not the end of existence, but rather an opportunity to join God and ancestors in heaven. Emotional responses to death are often quite open and demonstrative, and the Latina client may even view death in a festive and celebratory fashion. For example, *Día de los Muertos* (Day of the Dead), a popular holiday celebrated in many Latin countries, includes remembering dead relatives by inviting their spirits to return and join in the festivities. Families may visit the graves of their close kin, sitting out to have a picnic and playing music that the relative once enjoyed (Applewhite, 1998). It is important, however, to stress that just because a Latina client understands, celebrates, and accepts death does not mean she does not find it distressing. Regardless of her fears, a Latina client may still feel that death is a very natural part of life.

Both Japanese and Japanese Americans' attitudes toward death are greatly influenced by the religious denomination of Buddhism. Buddhists believe that death is part of a natural cycle of birth, death, and rebirth (Braun & Nichols, 1997). The goal of each life is to achieve enlightenment and escape that cycle. A person who has followed Buddhist teachings will be reborn in a peaceful, better place. Although Japanese regard death as a positive experience, there still is a taboo against an open discussion of dying. Traditionally, Japanese do not explain to a dying individual the gravity of the situation as they believe that by concealing this information, the family is spared from discussing this difficult situation (Sharts-Hopko, 1998). Contrary to the nondiscussion of dying itself, Japanese honor their ancestors through a variety of ways, one of which is to celebrate them in an annual Obon festival that, similar to Latin cultures, reflects an old Japanese belief that the spirits of the dead ancestors come home to visit their families. Even after the passing of a loved one, filial piety remains, as the Obon festival serves as a means through which family members can continue their obligation of expressing gratitude for a "debt that can never be repaid" (Hashizume, 2000).

Family Roles and Culture

Families play an extremely important and integral role in the EOL issues that older women face. They not only serve as a source of strength but also often provide considerable direct care to dying individuals. In their national survey, Emanuel and his colleagues (2000) underscored both that family members provide high levels of care to dying relatives and are often considerably burdened by this process. In fact, depression has been found to be high in family caregivers of individuals with substantial care needs irrespective of the terminal illness. Therefore, an understanding of the psychological and physical needs of both the care recipient and her family is crucial for practitioners working with older adults.

For many cultures, providing care to ill elders is the community's duty and obligation, although the strength with which such cultural beliefs are endorsed varies according to generational

status—that is, the further removed a particular generation is from the original immigrant group, the less strongly endorsed these values are (Kagawa-Singer & Blackhall, 2001). Nevertheless, overall, Japanese families are very likely to provide substantial support to their dying members.

Similar values are found in the African American community. Because African American elders maintain substantial status in their families, churches, and communities (despite physical and/or cognitive impairments), family caregiving is highly socially valued and strongly encouraged. Lawton and his colleagues (1992) found that African Americans subscribe more strongly than Whites to traditional values of caring for a loved one with dementia. Values that were reported in their study included repaying the debt of being cared for as a child, continuing the family tradition of mutual concern, fulfilling personal values, and setting an example for one's children. An early survey of African American daughters caring for their mothers supported this view of the importance of filial responsibility. However, it was also associated with lower receptivity to using formal services such as hospice. Recent studies have confirmed these views, as the values of responsibility to family and to the extended family network, along with provision of in-home care for relatives for as long as possible, appear to be integral to the African American community (Phipps et al., 2003). Thus, the African American family generally serves as a strong support for its dying members.

Latino elders facing the end of their lives traditionally have a strong familial network for care and support. Although Latino culture comprises a variety of subcultures, the one consistent feature that they share is the strength of, and reliance on, *la familia*. Latino families commonly live within close proximity to each other and maintain strong emotional ties, creating a large extended family composed of both biological and nonblood relations (Tennstedt, Chang, & Delgado, 1998). Traditional values require that Latino family members have a duty (*deber*) to provide lifelong help and care for each other. Family members are thus expected to volunteer to help care for ailing kin without the need for solicitation on the part of the care recipient.

According to the construct of acculturation, however, attitudes, beliefs, and behaviors are modified as new immigrant groups attempt to accommodate to the dominant culture (Berry, 2003). As an illustration, apart from the Chinese living in Mainland China, Taiwan, Hong Kong, and other countries, subgroups exist within the United States Chinese community, depending on original language (Cantonese, Mandarin, or other regional dialect). Unavoidably, values and attitudes vary among different environments and generations. Filial piety is also no longer weighted as heavily as in previous generations, although it is still important. Studies are finding that not only are elderly Chinese Americans beginning to report a shift from traditional expectations of filial piety to more reliance on neighbors and friends for assistance with dying issues, but also they have increasing flexibility in combining Eastern and Western health-care modalities (Pang, Jordan-Marsh, Silverstein, & Cody, 2003).

PREFERENCES FOR TREATMENT IN END OF LIFE

Treatment preferences are strongly influenced by both family and cultural values, underscoring the importance of advance planning and discussion. Advance directives serve as tools that enable an individual to clearly communicate her EOL wishes regarding medical treatment. Unfortunately, although 86% of adults surveyed recognize the benefits of having advance directives, few actually execute them or have adequately communicated their existence or meaning to family members or health-care professionals (The SUPPORT Principal Investigators, 1995).

The role of the family in the EOL decision-making process is a complex topic. There is evidence that concerns about costs can influence a family member's perception of the value of life-extending measures (Covinsky et al., 1996). Other factors, such as religious and cultural preferences, complicate the picture. Clinicians need to be aware of the fact that there may be competing agendas at work; for example, some family members may wish to continue care as long as possible and others may be anxious to "pull the plug" (Farrenkopf & Bryan, 1999). Family counseling may hold promise as a way to enable distraught family members to communicate better with one another.

Even when family members agree over the desired treatment for their dying loved one, they may still tend to overestimate the care recipient's desire for aggressive rather than palliative care. As Haley and his colleagues (2002) point out, this may reflect family members' own sense of guilt in expressing a preference for nonaggressive care as well as their own emotional attachment to keeping their loved one alive.

The frequency of the use of advance directives various considerably among ethnic groups (Eleazer et al., 1996). One possible explanation for this finding is lack of knowledge about the value and role of advance directives. For example, one study found that African Americans appear to have limited knowledge or understanding of how to create an advance directive (Waters, 2000). Among Latinos, factors related to the low rates of completion of advanced directives include both education and level of acculturation (Murphy et al., 1996). In the Chinese American community, discussions of options for EOL care are often avoided because they connote disrespect for the privacy the elderly (Crain, 1997). Elderly Chinese also avoid preparing advance directives because they do not want to disturb emotional balance in the family by focusing on negative rather than positive thoughts (Bowman & Singer, 2001). This perspective may be partly explained by the fact that Confucian, Taoist, and Buddhist teachings all emphasize the importance of social harmony in maintaining both physical health and strong family ties.

In addition to these ethnic differences, people who do and do not complete advance directives vary on other dimensions as well. For example, one study found that among older HMO patients, those who completed advance directives reported greater faith in their clinicians to understand their desires for life-sustaining treatment. Completers also reported less desire for family members to choose appropriate treatments once they have become incapable of doing so (Beck, Brown, Boles, & Barrett, 2002). Preferences for EOL care, however, often change as a patient progresses toward death; therefore, these advance directives should be considered an ongoing process rather than a one-time, stable decision (Field & Cassel, 1997). Psychologists can play the important role of helping families to understand, communicate with each other, and communicate with the health-care system on these issues.

Hospice provides an alternative to placement in a hospital or institution, and the opportunity for many Americans to die at home among their families. The rapidly growing hospice movement in this country is flourishing because it provides comprehensive multidisciplinary care for dying individuals in a comfortable environment. Although little is currently known about the hospice decision-making process, a recent study by Hays, Gold, Flint, & Winer (1999) found that family members, not the patient themselves, made this decision in almost half of the cases studied. As for the patient's wishes, the 1996 Gallup poll found that nine out of ten Americans would prefer to die at home if they were terminally ill, and about seven out of ten would desire hospice care (National Hospice Organization, 1996). Nevertheless, this desire is unfortunately met in only a minority of cases: merely 11% of women who are 85 years and older die at home, and 42% of women in this same age group die in nursing homes (National Hospice and Palliative Care Organization, 2003).

With the growing availability of hospice services in the United States, however, the preference to die at home is becoming more of a reality. Even so, ethnic minority groups in the United States have a relatively low hospice-utilization rate compared to Whites (Hopp & Duffy, 2000). A number of barriers have been proposed in order to explain this low utilization rate, including lack of knowledge of how the hospice system works, cultural aversion to care by outsiders at the end of life, financial constraints (e.g., no health insurance), and unequal access to medical resources (Werth, Blevins, Toussaint, & Durham, 2002). This may change in the future as the hospice-care benefit becomes easier to obtain (through Medicare, for example) and as older adults and their families begin to understand the benefits of the extensive support that palliative care settings can provide.

RECOMMENDATIONS FOR CLINICIANS

Psychologists and other mental health providers face multiple professional challenges when at-tempting to work directly with their own dying process. First, it is essential to become well-versed in current trends of thought on common assessment and treatment issues (e.g., depression; decision-making capacity). The APA Web site contains a wealth of information about psychology's role in this process (APA, 2003), including specific recommendations for assessment and treatment. The Institute of Medicine report (Field & Cassel, 1997) presents specific information on domains to assess in order to determine and prioritize areas for intervention. These include evaluating the intensity of various physical and emotional symptoms; determining global quality of life and extent of family burden; estimating perceived survival time; and then following up for postdeath bereavement reactions.

Perhaps most pertinent to this chapter is the work by William Haley et al. (2003), which delineates several key roles that can be assumed by psychologists with appropriate training. These include assisting healthy individuals who wish to do advance planning for their own future care by helping them work through issues they may have about actually completing an advance directive; working directly with patients and families facing issues of death and dying, using a variety of therapeutic methods, appropriate to the situation; and providing supportive services to health-care providers experiencing burnout and strain. These authors suggest specific interventions that psychologists can provide, such as teaching cognitive and behavioral coping skills for management of pain, anxiety, and depressive symptoms (e.g., relaxation and breathing techniques), and teaching communication skills for improving ongoing communication among family members and with the larger health-care system. Family members can be taught these techniques (as well as the patient herself) and have been enlisted as coaches to provide additional support for implementation of treatment recommendations between formal sessions. Psychologists can also teach stress management and conflict resolution skills to multidisciplinary palliative-care team members so that the team itself will remain healthy in the face of ongoing patient care challenges.

Other approaches to counseling include, first, targeting specific health dimensions when addressing client preferences for life-sustaining treatments (Coppola & Trotman, 2002), such as prognosis for improvement and/or recovery, and the extent to which pain can be controlled through medication. While not disease-specific, these are common concerns on the minds of most individuals with terminal illnesses. A second approach utilizes family therapy to help resolve conflicts among family members about care at the end of life, including such issues as whether or not to continue life-sustaining treatments (Farrenkopf & Bryan, 1999), and a third suggests the value of existential psychotherapy to help women deal with EOL concerns (Brody, 1999).

One additional area that seems very appropriate for intervention by psychologists is that of providing psychoeducation to older adults and their families about what support and what outcomes they should reasonably be able to expect, given their particular medical situation and the overall bio/psycho/social/spiritual/cultural context of their lives. They should, for example, not be permitted to believe that pain is inevitable or that supportive care is incompatible with efforts to continue to diagnose and treat them. This seems particularly relevant as a promising intervention approach to use with diverse ethnic and cultural groups whose ability to obtain top quality EOL care has been compromised historically by a variety of factors including significant lack of knowledge about the overall process.

NOTE

Preparation of this chapter was substantially supported by grants # AG 18784-03 and AG 13289-07 from the National Institute on Aging, as well as grant # IIRG-01-3157 from the national office of the Alzheimer's Association.

REFERENCES

Alegria, M., & Canino, G. (2000). Women and depression. In L. Sherr & J. S. St. Lawrence (Eds.), *Women, health, and the mind* (pp. 185–210). Chichester, UK: John Wiley & Sons.

American Psychological Association. (2003). General fact sheet on end of life. *APA public interest: End-of-life issues and care.* Retrieved January 4, 2004, from http://www.apa.org/pi/eol

American Psychological Association Ad Hoc Committee on End-of-Life Issues. (2000). *Report to the Board of Directors of the American Psychological Association from the APA Working Group on Assisted Suicide and End-of-Life Decisions.* Retrieved March 10, 2004, from http://www.apa.org/pi/aseolf.html

Applewhite, S. L. (1998). Culturally competent practice with elderly Latinos. *Journal of Gerontological Social Work, 30*(1), 1–15.

Beck, A., Brown, J., Boles, M., & Barrett, P. (2002). Completion of advance directives by older health maintenance organization members: The role of attitudes and beliefs regarding life-sustaining treatment. *Journal of the American Geriatrics Society, 50*, 300–306.

Berry, J. W. (2003). Conceptual approaches to acculturation. In K. M. Chun, P. B. Organista, and G. Marin (Eds.), *Advances in theory, measurement, and applied research* (pp. 17–37). Washington, DC: American Psychological Association.

Block, J. (1998). In D. E. Hayes-Bautista & R. Chiprut (Eds.), *Healing Latinos: Realidad y fantasia* (pp. 111–121). Los Angeles: Cedars-Sinai Health System.

Bowman, K. W., & Singer, P. A. (2001). Chinese seniors' perspectives on end-of-life decisions. *Social Science & Medicine, 53*, 455–464.

Bradley, E. H., Fried, T. R., Kasl, S. V., & Idler, E. (2000). Quality-of-life trajectories of elders in the end of life. *Annual Review of Gerontology and Geriatrics, 20*, 64–96.

Braun, K. L., & Nichols, R. (1997). Death and dying in four Asian American cultures: A descriptive study. *Death Studies, 21*, 327–359.

Breitbart, W., Chochinov, H. M., & Passik, S. (1998). Psychiatric aspects of palliative care. In D. Doyle, G. W. C. Hanks, & N. MacDonald (Eds.), *Oxford textbook of palliative medicine* (pp. 933–954). Oxford: Oxford University Press.

Brody, C. M. (1999). Existential issues of hope and meaning in late life therapy. In M. Duffy (Ed.), *Handbook of counseling and psychotherapy with older adults* (pp. 91–106). New York: John Wiley & Sons.

Brody, C. M. (2002). An existential approach: End-of-life issues for women. In F. K. Trotman & C. M. Brody (Eds.), *Psychotherapy and counseling with older women: Cross-cultural, family, and end-of-life issues* (pp. 221–238). New York: Spring Publishing.

Brody, H. (1992). Assisted death—a compassionate response to a medical failure. *New England Journal of Medicine, 327*, 1384–1388.

Cicirelli, V. G. (1999). Personality and demographic factors in older adults' fear of death. *The Gerontologist, 39*, 569–579.

Copp, G. (1998). A review of current theories of death and dying. *Journal of Advanced Nursing, 28*, 382–390.

Coppola, K. M., & Trotman, F. K. (2002). Dying and death: Decision at the end of life. In F. K. Trotman

& C. M. Brody (Eds.), *Psychotherapy and counseling with older women: Cross-cultural, family, and end-of-life issues* (pp. 221–238). New York: Spring Publishing.

Covinsky, K. E., Landerfeld, C. S., Teno, J., Connors, A. A., Dawson, N., Youngner, S., et al. (1996). Is economic hardship on the families of the seriously ill associated with patient and surrogate care preferences? *Archives of Internal Medicine, 156,* 1737–1741.

Crain, M. K. (1997). *Medical decision-making among Chinese-born and Euro-American elderly: A comparative study of values.* New York: Garland.

Doka, K. J. (1999). The quest for meaning in illness, dying, death, and bereavement. In S. Strack (Ed.), *Death and the quest for meaning: Essays in honor of Herman Feifel* (pp. 241–255). Northvale, NJ: Jason Aronson.

Eleazer, G. P., Hornung, C. A., Egbert, C. B., Egbert, J. R., Eng, C., Hedgepeth, J., et al. (1996). The relationship between ethnicity and advance directives in a frail older population. *Journal of American Geriatric Society, 44,* 938–943.

Emanuel, E. J., Fairclough, D. L., Slutsman, J., & Emanuel, L. L. (2000). Understanding economic and other burdens of terminal illness: The experience of patients and their caregivers. *Annals of Internal Medicine, 132,* 451–459.

Farrenkopf, T., & Bryan, J. (1999). Psychological consultation under Oregon's 1994 Death With Dignity Act: Ethics and procedures. *Professional Psychology: Research and Practice, 30,* 245–249.

Field, M. J., & Cassel, C. K. (1997). *Approaching death: Improving care at the end of life.* Washington, DC: National Academy Press.

Fry, P. S. (2003). Perceived self-efficacy domains as predictors of fear of the unknown and fear of dying among older adults. *Psychology and Aging, 18,* 474–486.

Gatz, M., Fiske, A., Fax, L. S., Kaskie, B., Kasl-Godley, J. E., & McCullum, T. J. (1998). Empirically validated psychological treatments for older adults. *Journal of Mental Health and Aging, 4,* 9–46.

Gatz, M., Harris, J. R., & Turk-Charles, S. (1995). The meaning of health for older women. In A. L. Stanton & S. J. Gallant (Eds.), *The psychology of women's health* (pp. 491–529). Washington, DC: American Psychological Association.

Haley, W. E., Allen, R. S., Reynolds, S., Chen, H., Burton, A., & Gallagher-Thompson, D. (2002). Family issues in end-of-life decision making and end-of-life care. *American Behavioral Scientist, 46,* 284–298.

Haley, W. E., Kasl-Godley, J., Larson, D. G., Neimeyer, R. A., & Kweilosz, D. M. (2003). Roles for psychologists in end-of-life care: Emerging models of practice. *Professional Psychology: Research and Practice, 34,* 626–633.

Hallenbeck, J. L. (2003). *Palliative care perspectives.* New York: Oxford University Press.

Hashizume, Y. (2000). Gender issues and Japanese family-centered caregiving for frail elderly parents-in-law in modern Japan: From the sociocultural and historical perspectives. Retrieved August 4, 2003, from http://www.nurseCe.com

Hays, J. C., Gold, D. T., Flint, E. P., & Winer, E. P. (1999). Patient preferences for place of death: A qualitative approach. In B. de Vries (Ed.), *End-of-life issues: Interdisciplinary and multidisciplinary perspectives* (pp. 3–21). New York: Springer.

Hopp, F. P., & Duffy, S. A. (2000). Variations in end-of-life care. *Journal of the American Geriatrics Society, 48,* 658–663.

Kagawa-Singer, M., & Blackhall, L. J. (2001). Negotiating cross-cultural issues at the end of life: "You got to go where he lives." *Journal of the American Medical Association, 286,* 2993–3001.

Kalish, R. A., & Reynolds, D. K. (1976/1981). *Death and ethnicity: A psychocultural study.* New York: Baywood.

Kastenbaum, R. (1999). Dying and bereavement. In J. C. Cavanaugh & S. K. Whitbourne (Eds.), *Gerontology: An interdisciplinary perspective* (pp. 155–185). New York: Oxford University Press.

Kaut, K. P. (2002). Religion, spirituality, and existentialism near the end of life: Implications for assessment and application. *American Behavioral Scientist, 46,* 220–234.

Kleinman, A., & Kleinman, J. (1991). Suffering and its professional transformation: Toward an ethnography of interpersonal experience. *Culture, Medicine, and Psychiatry, 15,* 275–301.

Koenig, B. A. (1997). Cultural diversity in decision-making about care at the end of life. In M. J. Field, & C. K. Cassel (Eds.), *Approaching death: Improving care at the end of life* (pp. 363–382). Washington, DC: National Academy Press.

Kubler-Ross, E. (1969). *On death and dying.* New York: Macmillan.

Kubler-Ross, E. (1981). *Living with death and dying.* New York: Macmillan.

Lander, M. L., Wilson, K., & Chochinov, H. M. (2000). Death and dying: Depression and the dying older patient. *Clinics in Geriatric Medicine, 16,* 335–356.

Lawton, M., Rajagopal, D., Brody, E., & Kleban, M. (1992). The dynamics of caregiving for a demented elder among Black and White families. *Journal of Gerontology B: Social Sciences, 47,* S156–S164.

Murphy, S. T., Palmer, J. M., Azen, S., Frank, G., Michel, V., & Blackhall, L. J. (1996). Ethnicity and advanced directives. *Journal of Law, Medicine & Ethics, 24,* 108–117.

National Consensus Project for Quality Palliative Care. (2004). *Clinical practice guidelines for quality palliative care.* Retrieved May 15, 2004, from http://www.nationalconsensusproject.org

National Hospice Organization. (1996). New findings address escalating end-of-life debate. Press release. Arlington, VA.

National Hospice and Palliative Care Organization. (2003). 885,000 terminally ill Americans serviced by hospice in 2002. Press release. Alexandria, VA.

Neimeyer, R. A. (Ed.). (2001). *Meaning reconstruction and the experience of loss.* Washington, DC: American Psychological Association.

Pang, E. C., Jordan-Marsh, M., Silverstein, M., & Cody, M. (2003). Health-seeking behaviors of elderly Chinese Americans: Shifts in expectations. *The Gerontologist, 43,* 864–874.

Phipps, E., True, G., Harris, D., Chong, U., Tester W, Chavin, S. I., et al. (2003). Approaching the end of life: Attitudes, preferences, and behaviors of African-American and white patients and their family caregivers. *Journal of Clinical Oncology, 1,* 549–554.

Rousseau, P. (2000). Hope in the terminally ill. *Western Journal of Medicine, 173,* 117–118.

Sharts-Hopko, N. C. (1998). Japanese-Americans. In D. Purnell & B. Paulanka (Eds.), *Transcultural health care: A culturally competent approach* (pp. 1–56). Philadelphia: F. A. Davis.

Singer, P. A., Martin, D. K., & Kelner, M. (1999). Quality end-of-life care: Patients' perspectives. *Journal of the American Medical Association, 281,* 163–168.

Steinhauser, K. E., Clipp, E. C., McNeilly, M., Christakis, N. A., McIntyre, L. M., & Tulsky, J. A. (2000). In search of a good death: Observations of patients, families, and providers. *Annals of Internal Medicine, 132,* 825–832.

Sullivan, M. D. (2002). Hope and hopelessness at the end of life. *American Journal of Geriatric Psychiatry, 11,* 393–405.

The SUPPORT Principal Investigators. (1995). A controlled trial to improve care for seriously ill hospitalized patients: The study to understand prognoses and preferences for outcomes and risks of treatments. *Journal of the American Medical Association, 274,* 1591–1598.

Tennstedt, S. L., Chang, B., & Delgado, M. (1998). Patterns of long-term care: A comparison of Puerto Rican, African-American, and non-Latino White elders. *Journal of Gerontological Social Work, 30,* 179–199.

Turk, D. C., & Feldman, C. S. (2000). A cognitive-behavioral approach to symptom management in palliative care. In H. M. Chochinov & W. Breitbart (Eds.), *Handbook of psychiatry in palliative medicine* (pp. 223–240). New York: Oxford University Press.

U.S. Department of Health and Human Services. (2002). *A profile of older Americans: 2002.* Retrieved October 25, 2003, from http://www.aoa.gov/prof/Statistics/profile/2002profile.pdf

Van Ness, P. H., & Larson, D. B. (2002). Religion, senescence, and mental health. *American Journal of Geriatric Psychiatry, 10,* 386–397.

Waters, C. M. (2000). End-of-life directives among African-Americans: Lessons learned—a need for community centered discussion and education. *Journal of Community Health Nursing, 17,* 25–37.

Werth, J. L., Blevins, D., Toussaint, K. L., & Durham, M. R. (2002). The influence of cultural diversity on end-of-life care and decisions. *American Behavioral Scientist, 46,* 204–219.

Wilson, K. G., Chochinov, H. M., de Faye, B. J., & Breitbart, W. (2000). Diagnosis and management of depression in palliative care. In H. M. Chochinov and W. Breitbart (Eds.), *Handbook of psychiatry in palliative medicine* (pp. 25–50). Oxford: Oxford University Press.

MARY M. GERGEN
and KENNETH J. GERGEN

Positive Aging: Reconstructing the Life Course

Across the life span, the stereotype of the aging woman is the most negative of all age and gender groups. She is often portrayed as a marginalized figure—ugly, undesirable, and weak—in the late stages of physical and mental decline. The reputation of being old is so negative that most older people refuse to define themselves as such (Friedan, 1993). Also contributing to this negative view of aging is the traditional value of productivity. With deep roots in the Protestant ethic and the spirit of capitalism, this view of aging shows a strong tendency to equate personal worth with productive achievement. As feminist critics point out, because women's "production" is so frequently allied with their capacity to bear children, older women, who no longer reproduce, are doubly vulnerable to being found wanting (Martin, 1997). The onset of menopause signals for them a loss of worth. This "retirement" is seen as no small matter; as Matlin (2000) reported, since 1990, biological "retirement" was the topic of psychological research in 21,000 published articles, while only 116 were about retirement from paid employment.

Loss of productivity is also associated with loss of intellectual and bodily strength. Older women are presumed to become less able to think rationally, act decisively, or have the physical stamina to manage simple everyday tasks. Most of the literature on aging reflects this negative view. For example, in 2002, one issue of the *Journal of Gerontology* featured articles on Alzheimer's disease, diabetes, dementia, balance impairment, heart disease, and depression. Only a single article focused on the positive possibilities of aging. In certain respects this emphasis on decline serves the needs of those professions—scientific, medical, social service, and charitable—that depend on aging-as-a-problem to remain viable. While acknowledging the importance of these groups, we also ask, How might gerontologically focused professions reform their agendas so that they are able to acknowledge and enhance the resilience, strength, wisdom, and creativity of their target populations?[1]

For the past several years many psychologists have been seeking to redress this negative view of aging. We have been among those deeply engaged in developing a perspective called "positive aging" and providing resources that may facilitate this refocus.[2] In this chapter, we examine women's lives within this positive framework. In particular, we explore a pattern of research that has profound implications for living well across the life span. Our focus then shifts to social policies that could expand the potentials of positive aging for women.[3]

THE SOCIAL CONSTRUCTION OF AGE

Our work on positive aging is importantly guided by a longstanding commitment to social constructionist theory. From a constructionist standpoint, descriptions and explanations of the world are not demanded by the nature of the world itself. Rather, it is through the active negotiation and collaboration of people that such understandings are constructed (K. Gergen, 1999; M. Gergen, 2001). With regard to the concept of aging, constructionist theses are particularly catalytic. They unsettle the widespread tendency within the social and biological sciences to search for the naturalized life course—that is, to chart the innate development and decline of human capacities over the life span. From a constructionist perspective, to find someone biologically or cognitively impaired constitutes a collaborative accomplishment, which is produced when various parties concur that something is the case—for example, medical authorities, gerontologists, advertisers, and social scientists, among others (Gubrium, Holstein, & Buckholdt, 1994). There is nothing about changes in the human body that requires a concept of aging or of decline, although it would be difficult to argue that there is no change in bodies over the life course. Too much of our commonsense wisdom rejects this possibility. There are serious consequences of this narrative of inevitable and lengthy decline over the life span. In accord with Foucault (1979), we propose that cultural constraints imposed upon older women, such that they accept themselves as undesirable, create the condition of self-denigration, sustain power relations that are unhealthy for women, and limit their options in living. When we avoid tendencies toward naturalizing, we can begin to appreciate possibilities of a cultural transformation of aging. With this constructionist orientation in place, let us consider the grounds for viewing aging as a generative period of life.

INDIVIDUAL WELL-BEING: THE LIFE SPAN DIAMOND

While much research has been done on the many ways in which the brain and body deteriorate over the years, caution about conclusions is essential. At the outset such research is highly selective. That is, of the many complex dimensions related to living over an extended period of time, researchers regularly select only those that demonstrate decline. Why, one ponders, is not more attention paid to forms of growth and generativity? This negative pattern is further intensified by the fact that scientific journals tend to exclude research reports in which no significant results emerge. If older people are not significantly less able than younger people on some dimension, the findings are generally not published. One might say that the aging population has been the "victim of mismeasurement" (Allaire & Marsiske, 2002). Additionally whether a pattern manifests decline and how significant this decline is are matters of interpretation. With a large sample size, statistically significant differences in reaction time, for example, do not necessarily mean that there are substantial differences in reaction time; the differences could be very slight, with a high degree of overlap between the two groups. Lastly, issues of sample selection, variable naming, context familiarity, and researcher conduct with the participants all play a role in producing results that affirm forms of decline with aging. And, as with the research on minority-group achievement under "stereotype threat," if people are perceived as "old folks" they may behave in stereotypical ways (Steele, 1997).

In the shift toward positive aging we attempt to readjust the balance. We review the literature on research that demonstrates the many ways in which aging people retain their capacities or increase them. We also look at those facets of life that enhance the art of living. For example, research by Diener, Suh, Lucas, and Smith (1999) indicates that as people age they become more comfortable with themselves, more contented, and less concerned with striving to meet the expectations of others. As women age they regard themselves as better able to cope with their environments and in relationships with others. Many older women see themselves as on an upward trajectory psychologically, having internalized the idea of progress in their life narratives (Greene, 2003). Such research suggests that aging allows people the opportunity for life enhancing strategies (Baltes & Baltes, 1990; Rowe & Kahn, 1998).

In this chapter, we highlight research findings from a variety of areas that lend support to this view of aging. These results suggest an overall pattern of substantial significance. We term this pattern "the life span diamond," not only because it speaks to well-being throughout the life course but also because its four points of departure invite us to think in terms of continuing life enrichment. The four points serving both as an origin and as an outcome in this design are:

1. *Relational Resources:* Supportive family and friends, conversational partners, and mediated connections, such as with chat room members and imaginal others—that is, those with whom we imagine interactions such as celebrities, fictional characters, or people who have died or who are no longer a part of our lives (M. Gergen, 2001; Watkins, 1986).

2. *Physical Well-Being:* Optimal functioning of brain and body as determined by medical tests, as well as through self-reports of health.
3. *Positive Mental States:* Well-being, happiness, optimism, and satisfaction with life.
4. *Engaging Activity:* Active participation in mental and physical activity.

As we find, there is a steadily expanding body of research in gerontology in which investigators trace relationships that exist between one of these points and another. Such research strongly suggests the possibility of bidirectional influences. For example, positive mental states may bring about physical well-being, and physical well-being can simultaneously contribute to positive mental states. The model of positive functioning suggested by these patterns is that of the diamond featured in figure 44.1.

We shall not review here all the many findings and arguments that contribute to this engaging pattern. However, its significance can be appreciated more fully by scanning the supportive reasoning and representative research.

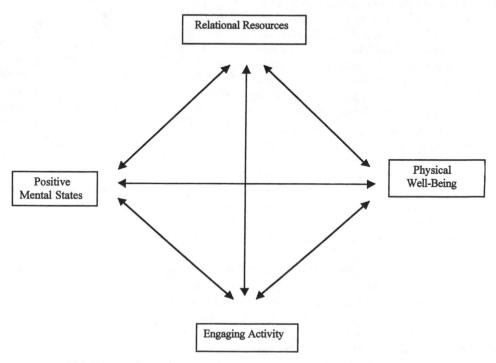

FIGURE 44.1 The life span diamond.

Relational Resources ↔ Physical Well-Being

Family, friends, and our mediated "others" influence our physical well-being in a multitude of ways; they may exercise or play games with us, influence us to go on a diet, and express their opinions about our appearance and health. They provide information that invites one to deliberate, to act, and, at times, to seek professional advice. Husbands often rely upon their wives to determine when they should go to the doctor; women tend to rely upon one another for such advice. Thus close relationships help people to be healthier. At the same time, when the body is functioning well and people feel healthy, they are more likely to seek others' company and be more deeply involved in relationships. Numerous studies provide support for this vision of a two-way link between relational resources and physical well-being. For example, we find that the availability of social support for widowed people is associated with better health (Stroebe and Stroebe, 1996), and as well with the speed with which one recovers from injury (Kempen, Scaf-Klomp, Ranchor, Sanderman, & Ormel, 2001). People who have strong emotional attachments to others recover from loss (e.g., the death of a spouse) more rapidly (Abbey & Andrews, 1985). Finally, people who are married enjoy far more years of life than those who never married or are separated or divorced (Coombs, 1991).

Relational Resources ↔ Positive Mental States

Having a satisfying network of others with whom to relate is correlated with having positive mental states. Positive relations with others bolsters one's self confidence, provides a sense of personal worth, lifts one's spirits, helps one generate meaningful goals, and provides many pleasures, as well as comfort and solace in times of trouble. At the same time, when people are feeling good about themselves and life, they will often approach others in a positive way, evidencing more empathy, love, nurturance, and forgiveness. Their positive states of mind enhance their relationships. Again, there is much research to support this connection. For example, studies in-

dicate that people high in social contact are more likely to feel supported and cared for; they are also less likely to become depressed (Pierce, Frone, Russell, Cooper, & Mudar, 2000). One of the strongest predictors of happiness is a good marriage (Myers, 1993). People who live alone, never marry, or are widowed, divorced, or separated are less likely to feel happy (Argyle, 1999).

Positive Mental States ↔ Engaging Activity

Positive mental states are related to engaging activity. Again, we find good reason for bidirectional influence. Positive mental states provide a sense of purpose, confidence, and optimism, all of which favor engaging in various mental and physical activities. At the same time, engaging activity can often yield good memories, a sense of accomplishment, and a feeling of zestfulness and joy. Engaging activity can also increase one's sense of internal control. Relevant research indicates that life satisfaction is positively related to engaging in the planning of future activities (Prenda & Lachman, 2001). Couples engaging in arousing activities together have more positive feelings toward each other and are happier (Aron, Aron, Norman, McKenna, & Heyman, 2000). Participating in leisure activities with friends, doing volunteer work, dancing, and engaging in sports, sexual activity, and outside events are all positively related to feelings of happiness (Argyle, 1999). Greater involvement in religion is also positively related to life satisfaction. Within the African American community, especially for older women, the church is an extremely important source of satisfaction. As Larson, Sherrill, and Lyons (1999) found, among African Americans, religious involvement is associated with physical health and psychological well-being. In addition, being religious is more important to health status for these women than financial well-being, despite the fact that many of them have low incomes.

Positive Mental States ↔ Physical Well-Being

One of the most theoretically interesting connections is that between positive mental states and physical well-being. On the one hand, it is not surprising that feeling good is related to physical well-being. After all, if one is in good bodily condition, feeling good about life is favored. And, too, feeling good about oneself should favor taking good care of one's body. With depression, one may even seek ways of damaging the body; older people, especially men, are at a higher risk for suicide than any other age group, perhaps because they are depressed and alone (Canetto, 1992). The intrigue with this connection lies in another realm; specifically, investigators increasingly believe that positive mental states may lead to better states of physical health. Many research findings are congenial with the notion that there is a relationship between mental health and the immune system. Additionally, people who exhibit greater positive affect are at a reduced risk of stroke (Oster, Markides, Peek, & Goodwin, 2001). People who are disposed to positive feelings during their youths live longer than those who are negative and pessimistic (Harker & Keltner, 2001). In a longitudinal study of late-life Catholic nuns, researchers found a strong relationship between emotions as expressed in teenage diaries and mortality. Of those nuns who had expressed few positive emotions in their diaries, 54% had died by the age of 80. Of those who used a high number of expressions of positive emotions, only 24% had died by age 80 (Danner, Snowdon, & Friesen, 2001). Further, having a positive sense of purpose is positively related to physical health. Research by Krause and Shaw (2000) found that maintaining a sense of control over an important social role increases a woman's longevity. Finally, as survey research in 1998 by the Drexel University Center for Employment Futures in Philadelphia indicated, approximately 90% of the people over 65 feel satisfied with their lives, feel they have contributed positively to society, and also claim to be in good health.

Physical Well-Being ↔ Engaging Activity

It comes as little surprise that physical health enhances one's capability to engage in a wider range of activities. Conversely, engaging in activity keeps one physically healthy. Numerous research findings support the link. For example, engaging in low-impact aerobic dance classes three times a week for 12 weeks improved the flexibility, muscle strength, body agility, and balance in women aged 57–77 (Hopkins, Murrah, Hoeger, & Rhodes, 1990). Other activities also are important for maintaining health. Being a volunteer is positively related to physical health (Van Willigen, 2000). The same is true of engaging in religious activities, such as attending church and participating in church activities (Larson et al., 1999). Engaging in a wide range of activities, from reading, to playing cards, to devoting time to community services, is positively related to rapid recovery from losses of various kinds (Bar-Tur, Levy-Shiff, & Burns, 2000).

Relational Resources ↔ Engaging Activity

Relationships with others invite engagement, both mental and physical. Often one is invited into new realms of activity, thus broadening one's spectrum of interests, curiosity, and potential for action. And, of course, engaging activity often functions to enhance social relationships (e.g., playing bridge, bowling, and dancing). It can also enhance one's ability to relate to others (providing topics of conversation, information to relate, amusing stories). Activity can also yield social rewards (appreciation and love from neighbors, family members, and friends through giving help to them). While this relationship between social relationships and activity has been researched less than the others in our model, there is evidence to support this mutuality. For example, widows who engage in activities with friends following loss are more comforted than if they are involved only with their family members. In addition, despite their loss, most widows, especially those who keep engaged in outside interests, cope very well over time (O'Bryant & Morgan, 1990). Through their activities, widows seem to make a shift from their established marital patterns to a new, positive, and very active phase of adult life (Feldman, Byles, & Beamont, 2000).

THE CRITICAL FULCRUM: RELATIONAL RESOURCES

As our diamond model suggests, positive aging among women has at least four important points of entry. Time spent in developing and sustaining family and friendship networks, maintaining good health practices, engaging in mental and physical activity, and maintaining positive attitudes about life are all important in themselves. However, an interlocking system of reverberating effects has multiple positive outcomes. To engage in physical activity is not simply enjoyable in itself; it constitutes a potential lift to one's health, personal relationships, and sense of well-being. And with each of these effects, there may be further reverberations, which ultimately yield increased interest in one's activities. Once set in motion, the interrelated parts of the system are self-sustaining. Further, it is never too late to enter the system—to develop a friendship, take on an activity, or improve one's diet. The system will change over a lifetime, depending on one's choices and the level of one's vigor and vitality, as well as one's opportunities for activity and one's relational resources.

However, one might ask if the diamond model is valid: Would not declines in physical activity, for example, affect all other aspects of life? Would not relationships be subverted and a sense of well-being decline? Do not bodily ills and failings eventually overtake us all regardless of the condition of our relationships? These are all possible outcomes. Yet consider again the constructionist orientation introduced above. From this perspective what we might term the objective state of affairs is so by virtue of one's interpretations. These interpretations, in turn, are dependent on relations with others. Our relational ties are essentially the source of all meaning-making. In this light, with the support of others, people are able to adjust their level of aspiration to their level of expectation and find satisfaction, regardless of the "objective" state of affairs. If, for example, people all share a view that restricted movement is normal, it is no longer an "impairment." Additionally, older women also feel good if they can compare themselves favorably with others of their own age (Kwan, Love, Ryff, & Essex, 2003). Cultural differences in perception are also important, as studies on pain have shown (Melzack & Wall, 1982). We are only now beginning to understand the enormous impact of socially embedded interpretation for one's sense of life satisfactions and physical well-being.

POSITIVE AGING IN ACTION AND POLICY MAKING

We finally turn from research to social practices involving positive aging. There is much to be said here about initiatives that encourage and facilitate adult education, artistic creativity, career changes, economic security, medical care, political involvement, travel, and volunteerism. There is also much to be said, as well, concerning the need to undermine cultural attitudes that foster multiple forms of prejudices against older women, who tend to be among the most maligned of social groups. All such initiatives enrich the possibilities of aging positively. One major avenue for advancing this goal is to follow the inspiration of the positive psychology movement and focus on the positive possibilities available at all stages of life, as opposed to the problems. One form of practice that has caught the attention of many practitioners is Appreciative Inquiry.[4] Professionals working with older people have begun to adopt an appreciative orientation to this time of life, with good effects. For example, while developmentalists previously spoke of the period when children leave the home as "the empty nest problem," now most accept that the vast majority of women describe this period in their lives as rejuvenating (Logothetis, 1993). As Dennerstein, Dudley, and Guthrie (2002) recently noted, in the first year without children in the home, women's moods and sense of well-being improved and the number of daily hassles dropped.

Of special concern to older women is the topic of menopause, which is customarily labeled as a "medical problem" in the United States. This view predominates despite cross-cultural research that demonstrates how women's views of menopause are dependent on the cultural milieu in which they live (Gullette, 1997). The medical community needs to recognize the impact of the deficit model on the well-being of patients and work toward a framework for helping women that is less pathologizing. Often women who no longer menstruate feel very liberated from the "curse." Based on interviews with 65 American post-childbearing women, Martin (1997) found that the vast majority of women saw menopause in a positive light, as an end to discomforts and worries associated with menstruation and to fears of pregnancy, as well as a time for achieving greater happiness and for feeling a renewal of physical energy and strength.

Gerontologists also are implicated in the search for a more positive approach to their work. Presently many gerontologists are finding evidence that older women enjoy a great deal of autonomy and pleasure in their senior years. This may be a well-guarded secret, but one of the earliest claims was made by feminist scholar Bernice Neugarten, in 1968. She found that older women rated their quality of life as high, in part because they relished the freedom offered to them as they escaped the constraints of the traditional female sex role. Similarly, Carol Ryff (1985) found that older women valued achievement or success in the eyes of others less as they age and valued having a sense of freedom and being happy more (regardless of what the neighbors think). Research on personality traits over the life span found that women became less and less "neurotic," according to the "Big Five" personality indicator terminology (Costa & McCrae, 1992), and more emotionally stable as they age (Srivastava, John, Gosling, & Potter, 2003). Adding support is the work of Stewart and Ostrove (1998), whose sample of U.S. college graduates aged 26–80 rated their early 50s as the most satisfying of their lives.

To enhance the lives of older women, especially, the most important changes include supporting public policies that enhance economic well-being, provide adequate health care, reduce sexual and age inequality, and end prejudice and discrimination. Specifically, raising the minimum wage, supporting Living Wage laws, advocating total medical care coverage with drug benefits, and encouraging unions and grassroots community organizing can all be helpful to older women. Proposals to increase economic security for older women are especially relevant to African American women, who are the poorest of elderly adults, and to those who have never married. Through political activism with the support of educational and religious organizations, efforts to promote positive aging can be expanded (Belle & Doucet, 2003).

Health-care professionals and family therapists are also working to produce more positive perspective on issues of aging. The challenge is to help people find opportunities for significant de-

velopment, creativity, invigoration, and inspiration. People who are working directly with aging populations, including nursing home administrators and other care takers, are becoming involved in the positive aging practices. Theresa M. Bertram (personal communication, November 12, 2002), CEO of the Cathedral Foundation, a large, multifaceted gerontological organization, in Jacksonville, Florida, reports the following about the changes made in her organization as a result of this shift to a more positive approach to aging:

> For its first thirty-five years, the Cathedral Foundation was a national leader in providing the "answers" for . . . thousands of seniors day in and day out. For the last five years, using an appreciative approach, we have begun to understand elders . . . from a position of strength, not of weakness. . . . They are robust, often reaching across generations to build a better society—and they are spiritual and take the time to explore fully this dimension of their lives. They are so different from the sick, frail, sexless, weak, disabled, powerless, passive, and unhappy persons portrayed in many segments of our society. Today, we are exploring ways to undergird seniors in their daily lives rather than fostering dependency by doing everything for them and making decisions on their behalf.

In our view, the potentials of approaching the aging process in a positive way are enormous, and older women, who are the majority of those who survive to very old ages, are the primary beneficiaries of this new perspective. There are significant overtures being played out by many professionals, informal groups, and individuals in the field; we look forward to the full symphony.

NOTES

1. The present effort is resonant with what is called the "Positive Psychology Movement." The major message of this movement is that psychology has been overly focused on the deficits of people—for example, on categorizing mental illness—and not enough time and resources on the ways in which people thrive, are resilient, or otherwise overcome deficits. See the *Amer-*

ican Psychologist, January, 2000, Volume 55, No. 1, which is a special issue emphasizing positive psychology, and has articles on happiness, excellence, and optimal human functioning.

2. Many of our efforts are expressed in an electronic newsletter, *Positive Aging*, sponsored by the Taos Institute and the Novartis Foundation on Aging. Past issues of the newsletter and additional materials are archived at: http://www.positiveaging.net

3. While we do not wish to neglect those who are variously afflicted, so extensive has been the attention to the problems of aging that no other possibility is entertained. We believe that these negative images of aging have colored all aspects of this time of life and have suppressed appreciation for its potentials.

4. Appreciative Inquiry is a new, dynamic organization behavior approach (Cooperrider, Whitney, & Stavros, 2003; Watkins & Mohr, 2001; Whitney, Trosten-Bloom, & Cooperrider, 2003. Also see www.Taos Institute.net.

REFERENCES

Abbey, A., & Andrews, F. M. (1985). Modeling the psychological determinants of life quality. *Social Indicators Research, 16,* 1–34.

Allaire, J. C., & Marsiske, M. (2002). Well- and ill-defined measures of everyday cognition: Relationship to older adults' intellectual ability and functional status. *Psychology and Aging, 17,* 101–115.

Argyle, M. (1999). Causes and correlates of happiness. In D. Kahneman, E. Diener, & N. Schwarz (Eds.), *Well-being: The foundations of hedonic psychology* (pp. 353–374). New York: Russell Sage.

Aron, A., Aron, E. N., Norman, C., McKenna, C., & Heyman, R. (2000). Good relationships through arousing activities: A research report. *Journal of Personality and Social Psychology, 78,* 272–284.

Baltes, P. B., & Baltes, M. M. (Eds.). (1990). *Successful aging.* New York: Cambridge University Press.

Bar-Tur, L., Levy-Shiff, R., & Burns, A. (2000). The importance of mental and emotional engagement in off-setting the effects of loss. *Journal of Aging Studies, 12,* 1–17.

Belle, D., & Doucet, J. (2003). Poverty, inequality, and discrimination as sources of depression among U.S. women. *Psychology of Women Quarterly, 27,* 101–113.

Canetto, S. S. (1992). Gender and suicide in the elderly. *Suicide and Life-Threatening Behavior, 22,* 80–97.

Coombs, R. H. (1991). Marital status and personal well-being. A literature review. *Family Relations, 40,* 97–102.

Cooperrider, D. R., Whitney, D., & Stavros, J. M. (2003). *Appreciative inquiry handbook.* Bedford Heights, OH: Lakeshore Communications.

Costa, P. T., & McCrae, R. R. (1992). Revised NEO Personality Inventory (NEOPI-R) and Five Factor Inventory (NEO-FFI) professional manual. Odessa, FL: Psychological Assessment Resources.

Danner, D. D., Snowdon, D. A., & Friesen, W. V. (2001). Positive emotions in early life and longevity: Findings from the nun study. *Journal of Personality and Social Psychology, 80,* 804–813.

Dennerstein, L., Dudley, E., & Guthrie, J. (2002). Empty nest or revolving door? A prospective study of women's quality of life in midlife during the phase of children leaving and reentering the home. *Psychological Medicine, 32,* 545–550.

Diener, E., Suh, E. M., Lucas, R. E., & Smith, H. L. (1999). Subjective well-being: Three decades of progress. *Psychological Bulletin, 125,* 276–302.

Drexel University Center for Employment Futures. (1998, April 22). Survey of aging suggests a bright future. *Philadelphia Inquirer,* p. D-1.

Feldman, S., Byles, J. E., & Beamont, R. (2000). "Is anybody listening?" The experiences of widowhood for older Australian women. *Journal of Women and Aging, 12,* 155–176.

Foucault, M. (1979). *Discipline and punish: The birth of the prison.* New York: Random House.

Friedan, B. (1993). *The fountain of age.* New York: Simon & Schuster.

Gergen, K. J. (1999). *An invitation to social construction.* Thousand Oaks, CA: Sage.

Gergen, M. (2001). *Feminist reconstructions in psychology: Narrative, gender & performance.* Thousand Oaks, CA: Sage.

Greene, S. (2003). *The psychological development of girls and women: Rethinking change in time.* New York: Routledge.

Gubrium, J. F., Holstein, J. A., & Buckholdt, D. R. (1994). *Constructing the life course.* Dix Hills, NY: General Hall.

Gullette, M. M. (1997). Menopause as magic marker: Discursive consolidation in the United States, and strategies for cultural combat. In P. Komesaroff, P. Rothfield, & J. Daly (Eds.), *Reinterpreting menopause: Cultural and philosophical issues* (pp. 176–199). New York: Routledge.

Harker, L., & Keltner, D. (2001). Expressions of positive emotion in women's college yearbook pictures and their relationship to personality and life outcomes across adulthood. *Journal of Personality and Social Psychology, 80,* 112–124.

Hopkins, D. R., Murrah, B., Hoeger, W. W. K., & Rhodes, R. C. (1990). Effect of low-impact aerobic dance on the functional fitness of elderly women. *Gerontologist, 30,* 189–192.

Kempen, G., Scaf-Klomp, W., Ranchor, A. V., Sanderman, R., & Ormel, J. (2001). Social predictors of recovery in late middle-aged and older persons after injury to the extremities: A prospective study. *Journal of Gerontology, 56B*(4), S229–S236.

Krause, N., & Shaw, B. A. (2000). Role-specific feelings of control and mortality. *Psychology and Aging, 15,* 617–626.

Kwan, C. M. L. K., Love, G. D., Ryff, C. D., & Essex, M. J. (2003). The role of self-enhancing evaluations in a successful life transition. *Psychology and Aging, 18,* 3–12.

Larson, D. B., Sherrill, K. A., & Lyons, S. S. (1999). What do we really know about religion and health among the aging populations? In J. S. Levin (Ed.), *Religion in aging and health* (pp. 183–199). Thousand Oaks, CA: Sage.

Logothetis, M. L. (1993). Disease or development: Women's perceptions of menopause and the need for hormone replacement therapy. In J. C. Callahan (Ed.), *Menopause: A midlife passage* (pp. 123–135). Bloomington: University of Indiana Press.

Martin, E. (1997). The woman in the menopausal body. In P. Komesaroff, P. Rothfield, & J. Daly (Eds.), *Reinterpreting menopause: Cultural and philosophical issues* (pp. 239–254). New York: Routledge.

Matlin, M. (2000). *The psychology of women* (4th ed.). Fort Worth, TX: Harcourt Brace.

Melzack, R., & Wall, P. D. (1982). *The challenge of pain.* Harmondsworth, UK: Penguin Books.

Myers, D. G. (1993). *The pursuit of happiness.* New York: Avon.

Neugarten, B. (1968). Adult personality: Toward a psychology of the life course. In B. Neugarten (Ed.), *Middle age and aging* (pp. 3–37). Chicago: University of Chicago Press.

O'Bryant, S. L., & Morgan, L. A. (1990). Recent widows' kin support and orientations to self-sufficiency. *Gerontologist, 30,* 391–398.

Oster, G., Markides, K. S., Peek, K., & Goodwin, J. S. (2001). The association between emotional well-being and the incidence of stroke in older adults. *Psychosomatic Medicine, 63,* 210–215.

Pierce, R. S., Frone, M. R., Russell, M., Cooper, M. L., & Mudar, P. (2000). Social contact, depression and alcohol. *Health Psychology, 19,* 28–38.

Prenda, J. M., & Lachman, M. E. (2001). Planning for the future: A life management strategy for increasing control and life satisfaction in adulthood. *Psychology and Aging, 16,* 206–216.

Rowe, J. W., & Kahn, R. L. (1998). *Successful aging.* New York: Pantheon.

Ryff, C. D. (1985). The subjective experience of life span transitions. In A. Rossi (Ed.), *Gender and the life course* (pp. 143–167). New York: Aldine.

Srivastava, S., John, O. P., Gosling, S. D., & Potter, J. (2003). Development of personality in early and middle adulthood: Set like plaster or persistent change? *Journal of Personality and Social Psychology, 84,* 1041–1053.

Steele, C. M. (1997). A threat in the air: How stereotypes shape intellectual identity and performance. *American Psychologist, 52,* 613–629.

Stewart, A. J., & Ostrove, J. M. (1998). Women's personality in middle age: Gender, history and midcourse corrections. *American Psychologist, 53,* 1185–1194.

Stroebe, W., & Stroebe, M. (1996). The social psychology of social support. In E. T. Higgins & A. W. Kruglanski (Eds.), *Social psychology: Handbook of basic principles* (pp. 597–621). New York: Guilford.

Van Willigen, M. (2000). Differential benefits of volunteering across the life course. *Journal of Gerontology, 55,* S308–S318.

Watkins, J. M., & Mohr, B. J. (2001). *Appreciative inquiry.* San Francisco: Jossey-Bass.

Watkins, M. (1986). *Invisible guests: The development of imaginal dialogues.* Hillsdale, NJ: Analytic Press.

Whitney, D., Trosten-Bloom, A., & Cooperrider, D. (2003). *The power of appreciative inquiry: A practical guide to positive change.* San Francisco: Barrett Kohler.

Special Problems and Resources

IV

LENORE E. A. WALKER

Legal Issues Influencing Girls' and Women's Psychological Health

A discussion of the many legal issues that can impact on girls' and women's mental health in this book is an important acknowledgment of the high degree of emotional stress that interacting with the legal system places on most people. In the United States, especially, it seems that it is a rare person who goes through life without at least some contact with the legal system. Women in the 1970s used the legal system to continue the civil rights accorded in the previous decade, create new social change specific to women, and attain many of the current legal rights that exist today, such as access to credit in our own names, stronger laws against sexual and physical assault, and the right of reproductive choice (Kaye, 1990). However, the gender bias that was studied in the 1990s (Schafran, 1990; Singleton, 1990; Wikler, 1990) still exists today, placing even more emotional stress on those who believe they can exercise their civil and legal rights only to be disappointed that the system still does not work very well for women, especially those women who are not of the majority culture. As Singleton states, "myths about the woman's economic and social place can cause a decision to be based on something other than the realities of life" (p. 39).

Gender bias can cause disparities in the criminal justice system with inappropriate prosecution and sentencing for girls and women, especially those of African American descent (Chesney-Lind, 2001; New Freedom Commission on Mental Health, 2004), family law with custody, access to and support of children and women based on misogynist and racist beliefs, violation of the civil rights of women of color, minimal attention given to prosecution of domestic violence and rape cases, harassment and denial of the legal rights of lesbians, and the devaluing of women's work in the home when awarding damages for personal injuries. The links between child sexual abuse and later prostitution need to be carefully explained to juvenile court judges so that girls who are arrested for running away are not punished twice, once in their abusive homes and once again in the courts (see the recommendations of the New Freedom Commission on Mental Health report released in 2004, as well as other Office of Juvenile Justice and Delinquency Prevention [OJJDP] documents on their Web site). Other areas where litigation can impact on women and girls can be found in table 45.1.

TABLE 45.1 Frequent Legal Issues for Women and Girls

Area	Issues	Area	Issues
Marriage and the family	Marriage as a legal contract Reproductive rights Using new technologies to get pregnant Adoption Abortion and family planning issues Divorce Protection of assets Child custody, visitation, and access Widowhood Protection of assets	Juvenile delinquency	Status crimes for girls Juveniles in need of supervision Girls who run away from home Other frequent arrests Prostitution Drug crimes Shoplifting Truancy Relationship crimes Crimes of violence committed by girls Statistics on increase Waiver to adult court
Criminal law	Sexual assault Domestic and family violence Special domestic violence courts Restraining orders Ex parte financial arrangements Girls and women as victims Women as perpetrators Women who kill in self-defense Child abuse Caretakers and abuse Substance abuse Drug-exposed fetuses Crimes to support addictions Women and crime Women and sentencing guidelines Women in prison Right to treatment Right to refuse treatment including medication Right to treatment including proper medication		Typical crimes Domestic violence School violence Group murders
		Contracts	Access to money Mortgages Credit cards Access to health care and enforcement of insurance contracts Duress in signing contract
		Personal injury	Civil torts Car accidents and other injuries Product liability cases Dalkon Shield cases Bad blood cases Sexual harassment and discrimination cases Federal court State court Domestic violence and sexual abuse claims Malpractice against health-care providers

This chapter will deal with some of the more common issues that are faced by women and girls when thrust into the legal arena, understanding that the scenarios described here are repeated day after day in courtroom after courtroom in the United States and other countries. (See Schafran, 1990, for descriptions of the findings of the many Gender Bias Task Force studies that were done by most states and the federal government, and the National GAINS Center Web site for information on co-occurring disorders in women and their children involved in the justice system.)

ORIGINS OF THE PRESENT U.S. LEGAL SYSTEM

The U.S. legal system is based on what is called *common law* that has been adapted from British common law. Many countries in the world use a form of this legal system while others may use models adapted from Napoleonic or Roman law. However, despite whatever legal system is used, the laws were mostly written for and by men, and the struggle for women's legal rights has had to be vigorously pursued. This struggle has been especially evident during the last three decades, with the help of the United Nations worldwide programs designed to enhance women's and children's lives. Unfortunately, in most countries including the United States, girls still have very few legal rights, even fewer than boys in some areas. For example, in the United States, the new laws passed within the last two decades have forced sexually active girls to obtain parental consent if they become pregnant and seek to terminate the pregnancy. The transparent political nature of these laws is obvious, as these girls do not need parental permission to obtain obstetric care for themselves and pediatric care for any babies they choose to carry to term.

If their parents obtain a divorce, girls can be court-ordered into the custody of one or both parents without a voice or legal representation of their rights even if they state that they have been physically, sexually, and psychologically abused by a parent. The closest they can come to being heard in the court is having a legal guardian (called a *guardian ad litem,* or GAL) represent their best interests but not necessarily to represent their wishes, as would be possible if they could have their own lawyer and own legal standing. In many cases, the GAL never even meets the girl before making recommendations. Rarely is psychological research used to support an argument when attempting to meet the legal standard that is the "best interests of the child" in most countries around the world. Rather, as is described below, the law is based on untested presumptions or beliefs about what is right and wrong for children.

FAMILY LAW

Perhaps family law, the area of the law with which most women will have experience, has been the most resistant to changing norms for women and children. A family is legally defined as a man and a woman with their children. Lesbian couples and their children are not considered a family under the law in most places. Mixed racial couples may not be treated fairly even though the older laws that forbade such relationships are no longer present. There are many assumptions, called legal *presumptions,* that must be overcome if someone wants to de-

viate from the expected socialized standards and norms set in the marriage contract. Marriage and family are constructs that benefit the state; here the presumption is that people in the family will take care of each other (and the state doesn't have to do so). Obviously, the high rate of child abuse and domestic violence demonstrate that this presumption is not based on reality (see Walker, 1994, for further discussion of how these areas impact on women). Nonetheless, the state will not intervene in the family unless something occurs that is a sufficiently high enough trigger. Unfortunately the trigger seems to be lower in families from nondominant cultures where practices are different from the rest of the community. Although each state has its own definition of the standard used, in general a criminal conviction requires *beyond a reasonable doubt,* often thought to be around 99%. Civil cases require *clear and convincing evidence,* which is around 75%, or *preponderance of the evidence,* which is just over 50% or more likely than not that something occurred.

For example, the state may intervene to protect an abused child and place him or her in a foster home at the lower standard of proof (preponderance), but may not choose to terminate parental rights and permit the child to be adopted unless a higher standard of proof (clear and convincing) is met. In a highly publicized case, a 12-year-old who wished to be adopted by the foster parent was ruled to have no legal standing by the court, despite the fact that the parents had such severe substance-abuse problems that they could not overcome them to raise the child. In another example, if a 15-year-old girl who has her own money wishes to attend a school that is not chosen by her parents, she may not be legally allowed to do so unless she is emancipated. Emancipation is often not a good decision as a 15-year-old may not be ready to completely support herself, even though she may be perfectly competent to choose a school or profession and has money in her own name or trust to pay for it. There have been other highly publicized cases of children who have tried to "divorce" their parents, usually those whose parents are unable to care for them (see Walker & Shapiro, 2004, for a full discussion of the movement for children's legal rights).

No-Fault Divorce

In the 1970s there was strong social pressure to permit dissolution of marriage upon the testimony of at least one party that the marriage was irretrievably broken. These new laws were often called "no-fault divorce." Prior to the change, people had to prove that the other spouse was generally unfit as a partner or parent. The courts also changed the standard practice of awarding women alimony from their usually more affluent husbands, instead granting "maintenance" for a time-limited period. Although hailed as a positive reform by women who were often trapped in unhappy marriages, in fact, it has proved to be a disaster for many, especially older women who worked as homemakers and have no ability to earn the type of salary that will permit them to continue their predivorce lifestyle. They rarely have good medical or health care or sufficient income to support themselves after their children leave home even if they were lucky enough to collect the full amount of child support the courts awarded them. According to the data, their former husbands rapidly replaced the money and property they were required to share in the divorce and often began a new family that lived in the style in which the former wife and children no longer could afford to live (Schafran, 1990).

Singleton (1990) found that few divorced women ever receive alimony, and those who do find it substantially below their needs. She cites a University of Michigan study that found divorced men had incomes at least 17% above their needs while divorced women had incomes at least 7% below their needs. Divorced women tended to contribute more money to supporting their children than divorced men even though women are employed in lower paying jobs. In *community property* states, where property is divided equally when purchased with marital assets, lawyers and judges reported less gender bias than when distribution attempts to be done "*equitably*" or in states where property is shared according to how much nonmarital money each partner contributed. For many years, women tended to receive the family home while the men received investment property. However, this appears to have changed in more recent years. Singleton believes that the biggest problem for divorcing women is the long delay in the court so that women have less access to resources with which to properly investigate and litigate the distribution of these financial assets before the economically dominant spouse disposes of them.

Child Custody and Support

Although there have been many important reforms in the collection of child support today, in reality, the advent of joint custody has become a popular way for the higher wage-earner (still the man in most families) to pay only an equal share of the support that is required by the courts. The problem is worsened if the woman must try to collect a child support award from a partner who has been abusive toward her or the children. In many states, child support is allocated by amount of time spent with a child in addition to or instead of ability to pay, creating a financial interest in shared legal and residential custody. So, for example, in Pennsylvania a man who is awarded 51% of the time with his children may pay significantly less in child support than if he was awarded 49% of the access time despite his earning ability. In these cases, it is usually the woman and children who were previously living in an affluent home who suffer the most. Men who do not pay child support may be subject to heavy penalties including *garnished wages* or even jail time. However, the woman still must have sufficient money to obtain an attorney to go to court to collect the money owed. The system works better if the woman is receiving welfare assistance as then the state has an interest in collecting the back-owed child support. Either way the woman or children still get little or nothing.

Battered Women and Family Court

Women who are battered by their husbands are rarely able to afford the necessary health care during or after a divorce (Singleton, 1990). Although there has been reform in the way criminal courts handle domestic violence cases, in fact, the family court may unwittingly serve to keep a woman in an abusive relationship just to meet the necessities of life by not awarding sufficient resources to live independent from the batterer's control. In most states, if the woman has young children, the courts will demand that she not move out of state or even out of the neighborhood or she will lose custody and access to her children. These clauses are so standard in most dissolution decrees today that the mother must file what is now called a *removal* petition to ask the court for permission to leave even if it is for a new job or a new marital obligation. In many cases, the actual physical injuries from the abuse will not be evident until these women get older. A type of adult *shaken-baby syndrome* is most common when women have been shaken and had their heads banged on soft objects such as sofas, bed mattresses, or carpets. In some cases, the women function marginally until another injury such as an automobile accident occurs. Then, they cannot recover and appear to continue on a downward spiral. These are many of the cases seen in disability courts daily (Walker, 2000).

CIVIL TORT LAWS

Separate civil *tort* actions are possible to obtain sufficient money from an abusive partner if they are filed within a timely period, usually one to two years after the last injury. However, it is often difficult to get an attorney to take a case on a contingency fee, as most women do not have sufficient money to fund this often costly litigation, nor do they have the psychological strength to know they have been damaged within the statutory limitations. In some tort actions against nonfamily members, such as in the priest-abuse cases, women may be more likely to find attorneys who will assist in trying *to toll the statute* or get the time limits extended to when the woman first knew that the trauma caused an injury. Definitions of what *know* means vary from place to place, but most have some kind of psychological understanding that they have been harmed, not just objectively knowing what happened to them and that it was bad or wrong.

It is interesting that the laws in the civil courts are far more favorable to women who have been abused and harmed than in family court. For example, definitions of sexual discrimination and harassment in Title VII of the Civil Rights Act of 1964 and 1992 have been informed by the psychological research that delineates the harm that may be caused by various forms of discrimination, prejudice, and stereotyping behaviors. Therefore, it is not necessary for a woman to prove she suffered specific damages in federal court, but rather, only that a pattern of unwanted sexual acts, a pattern of discrimination based on being female, or a pattern of *quid pro quo* or expectation to trade sex for other favors has occurred. However, if the case is filed in those state courts that permit personal injury cases because of sex discrimination or harassment, it is necessary to prove not only that the acts of discrimination or abuse occurred but also that the person has physical or mental health problems and that the acts specified caused the person's current problems.

In state civil court these issues can come in front of a jury that will make the decision, while in family court it is usually a judge who decides how to divide the family's assets. In domestic-violence cases that result in personal injury and require financial compensation, the family court judge might be called upon to decide if a battered woman signed a prenuptial agreement under duress, fearing that she would be physically harmed if she didn't obey her soon-to-be husband's orders. In fact, each state's family law code describes a whole body of case law that specifies how many days prior to the wedding a valid prenuptial agreement must be signed, whether there was a total disclosure of the assets, and if the agreement is fair, honest, and free from coercion. For many battered women who signed away their rights to obtain adequate financial compensation for injuries caused by a husband who can file for dissolution of marriage without cause, these laws may make the difference between good nutrition and medical care as well as safety as they grow older.

Personal Injury Lawsuits

In cases of abuse, battered women, rape victims, and others who have been assaulted or exploited may choose to file a personal injury lawsuit against the perpetrator in state civil rather than family court. These laws provide for financial compensation both for the actual costs of their injuries (e.g., medical expenses, time lost from work, etc.) and punitive damages that supposedly teach perpetrators a lesson not to do it again! Unfortunately, these cases can get messy as the abusers and their attorneys know what might really upset the woman, such as calling her aging parents for a deposition or demanding all her prior therapy records. In many individual cases, however, women do obtain sufficient money to rebuild their lives after these injuries, although attorneys also take a good percentage of the financial award for their own work. In other cases where family laws are not favorable in protecting contractual rights, the civil courts may also be used. In most cases where a civil lawsuit is filed together with a dissolution for marriage petition, the parties reach a fair settlement of the marital assets prior to litigating the tort action. Lesbians, who frequently are unable to use the family law system to gain a share of property if the relationship breaks up, may be legally able to sue an abusive partner in civil court for financial compensation under tort law.

Some believe that filing tort cases against individual abusers will have more of an impact on stopping men who abuse women than do criminal charges, since those with sufficient assets to mount a good defense rarely go to jail or prison but do fear losing those assets to the woman. In the 1990s, women who claimed to have been sexually abused as children by adults began filing similar lawsuits. The issue of statute of limitations was raised here, as was described earlier. Women who began to remember more incidents of child abuse while in therapy filed these lawsuits against their abusers, who then used as a defense to them allegations that the therapists were implanting false memories of abuse. Although there were a few such inadequately trained or unethical therapists who confused their clients, in fact there were far more women who actually were harmed by their abusers than the cases against therapists that went to court would suggest. Nonetheless, the charges and counter-charges proved to be a deterrent to filing more of these cases as the courts were not sympathetic to these women or to therapists, in general (see, for example, the publications and Web site of

the Leadership Council for Mental Health, Justice, and the Media, n.d., and Dallam et al., 1998).

More often than not, even the good personal injury cases settle for a sum less than sufficient for women to benefit from the stress of several years in litigation. Once a woman makes a claim for damages, all of her personal history may be exposed in the legal setting, especially any other physical or mental health issues not related to the current injury. Although the *plaintiff*, the person who brings the lawsuit, must prove only that the last injury was caused by the *defendant*, who then is liable for all the damages the person currently suffers, in fact many cases settle by parsing out those injuries from earlier events. All of these factors must be taken into account before a woman leaps into a personal injury lawsuit.

Class Action Lawsuits

Some of the major lawsuits designed to obtain financial compensation for women who were harmed by one or more large corporations have been part of a *class action*, which is defined by Rule 23 of the Federal Rules of Procedure as having "common questions of law or fact, that the claims are so numerous that the joinder of all members is impractical, that the claims of the names representative(s) are typical of the class, and that the representative(s) will fairly and adequately protect the interests of the class" (Rheingold, 1990, p. 60). Some of these lawsuits settle out of court for a minimum amount of money and actually the attorneys get more money from the settlement for expenses and fees. Relatively little money goes to the women themselves. This situation occurred with the Dalkon Shield cases filed against large corporation, A. H. Robbins, who manufactured intrauterine devices (IUDs) that caused infections and serious damage to women's reproductive health (Rheingold, 1990; see also *In re A. H. Robbins Co., Inc.*, 1989, and *In re Northern District of California "Dalkon Shield,"* 1981). The company eventually filed for bankruptcy as it claimed it could not pay all the claims, which by then had grown to over 200,000. Eventually they settled the case for a limited amount of money and the manufacturer no longer makes the

IUDs, but it did little to bring back or compensate individuals for the loss of their reproductive health and ability to bear children in some cases.

On the other hand, some class action lawsuits have been beneficial such as those against the tobacco growers and cigarette manufacturers who knew that there was a clear relationship between their product and cancer in people who became addicted to cigarettes. A recent class action certification was issued by a federal court in a lawsuit filed against Wal-Mart stores by women employees who claimed discrimination because of disparate salaries and promotions in Wal-Mart stores across the United States (reported by National Public Radio in June 2004). If their lawsuit is successful, all women who work for Wal-Mart stores and were similarly discriminated against (who are then in the class) would be eligible for whatever settlement is awarded.

Class action lawsuits such as *Hodgson v. State of Minnesota* and *Casey v. Planned Parenthood* reaffirmed *Roe v. Wade* and won the right of all women in their states to terminate a pregnancy without the interference of the state unless it was to protect the woman's health. In *Casey,* the disparate requirement for a married woman to obtain consent from her husband as opposed to no such burden for a single woman to obtain consent from her co-conceiver was overturned. In *Hodgson,* the U.S.S.C. created a bypass procedure for teens who declared that they could not obtain permission from both parents in order to have an abortion. These are special kinds of civil lawsuits, often handled in federal, not state, court by experienced attorneys, and women should be cautious when entering into such agreements.

Other Contracts

Although it may be difficult to believe today, women's ability to sign a contract in her own name (without having a father or husband as a co-signer) has been an important gain in women's legal rights, especially to make sure that they have access to adequate money with which to live. Until about 30 years ago, women could not obtain credit in their own name to make big or small purchases. The U.S. health-care system is based on financing through employment, so women who choose to be homemakers or work fewer than the typical 35 or 40 hour work week often must give up health and other benefits when making these choices.

The new reproductive technologies have brought a whole area of legal issues. This is especially true for a child conceived after a man has died. For example, there have been cases where zygotes fertilized by a man's previously frozen sperm after his death were implanted in the mother's uterus and the children from the man's previous marriage challenged that child's rights as a true heir. The law stated that the child's birthright was secure and the court upheld it in this case. However, in other cases where the ownership of frozen zygotes was challenged by divorcing partners, the case law determined that the person who would be most harmed by the destruction of the zygote got ownership. In the cases where the man claimed harm from having to support a resulting child and the woman was unable to conceive another child, she got to keep the zygotes. If the man was the one who could no longer produce sperm or father a child, he got them. Parents who have children conceived with a surrogate also may have legal difficulties, with some states permitting contracts between biological and adoptive parents and other states not permitting it. As is evident, the new reproductive technologies have brought with them a whole new set of laws covering these legal issues.

JUVENILE CASES

Although the history of a separate justice system for children began in Chicago over 100 years ago, we are still not much closer to obtaining juvenile justice today. Children develop at different rates and are not biologically, cognitively, or emotionally the same as adults. Children, especially adolescents, are still in their formative years; the brain is not yet totally formed and personality can be more easily changed and shaped than once they become adults. Thus, the nature of their misconduct should not be considered demonstration that they will become hardened or career criminals as adults to be eligible for delinquency court. In fact, today we have data that suggest that less than 20% of those arrested as youth will go on to become "career criminals" (Wettstein, 1998). Nonetheless, there is still a large disparity between the crimes that boys and girls are arrested for today.

Like adult males, boys are more likely to commit crimes of violence according to the Bureau of Justice statistics, while girls are more likely to be arrested for status crimes (OJJDP, 2003). Here is a major area of gender discrimination. *Status* crimes are those where there would be no violation of the law if the person were an adult, but by virtue of their age, they have committed an offense. The most common offense for girls is running away from home followed by truancy and incorrigibility or being uncontrollable by a parent. As might be expected, many criminal acts such as perpetrating sexual offenses are much higher for boys than girls. However, Schafran (1990) contends that the goal of the state in prosecuting status crimes against girls is to control their sexuality. Surely the facts are that girls are arrested while the men who abuse them or in cases of prostitution, men who are their clients, often go free. These statistics are supported by both intuitive understanding and research on gender and juvenile crime (Walker & Shapiro, 2004, Wettstein, 1998). Perhaps most egregious is the lack of services to these youth despite the accepted knowledge that abuse, neglect, culture, racism, poverty, and other factors have damaged many of them who could be healed through better access to health and mental health care. Health care in the juvenile detention centers is bare minimum, which is dangerous especially because the chance of exposure to many different infections, including ones with serious consequences such as hepatitis C, HIV, and tuberculosis, is high.

The gender disparity between crimes of violence, especially murder committed, needs further study. Offenses against other persons by teens occur as much in a gendered role as they do in adults. In 1992, four out of every five violent offenses against other persons were committed by males. In 1992, 6% of violent offenses were reportedly committed by girls, but newer data from the Office of Juvenile Justice suggests that there is an increase in use of violence by girls at an even younger age (Wettstein, 1998). Girls are more likely to engage in relational violence or aggressive behavior toward friends and family members, while boys are more likely to engage in gang violence, homicides, and sexual offenses. Girls are less likely to be arrested for antisocial behavior and crimes of violence than are boys.

School Violence

The known school shooters, such as Eric Harris and Dylan Klebold, from the 1999 Columbine High School murders, are all boys from different cultures and ethnic minorities. Most of the reported violent incidents in schools are committed by boys against other boys, although girls seem to be getting "meaner," as the recent movie *Mean Girls* portrays. Most educators and juvenile detention center service providers believe that the types of violent behaviors committed by teenage girls today are more serious than ever before. In my own research, I have hypothesized that girls exposed to domestic violence or child abuse, and forced to spend unsupervised time with a father who abused their mother, may well use more physical aggression in their adolescent years. For some girls, as the dating violence literature suggests, they are both victims and aggressors when they are in the teen years, but more likely to be victims as adults (Walker, 2000).

Abuse and Aggressive Behavior

On the other hand, girls who experience psychological effects from being abused as children are more likely to develop symptoms similar to post-traumatic stress disorder (PTSD) and use alcohol and other drugs to self-medicate the symptoms. The illicit use of these substances may be a factor for many of the young girls who are later arrested for selling their bodies in order to obtain drugs. If we provided adequate mental health care for these abuse victims, they may not turn to illegal substances. Many turn to prostitution as a way to survive out of their abusive homes even though it often leads to further criminal behavior such as shoplifting and other forms of stealing. As described below, the child abuse–drugs–aggressive behavior–run away–prostitution–shame–pregnancy–welfare (and sometimes other nonviolent crimes) cycle is often more difficult to break in women than if caught and intervened earlier when they are still girls.

Some girls, like boys, are misdiagnosed as having attention deficit disorders and placed on prescription stimulants rather than given therapy to overcome their abusive experiences. The increasing and inappropriate use of medication for children's anxiety, depression, and other behavioral symptoms is finally getting the attention it needs in the psychological community. At this time, we do not know either the efficacy of using such powerful psychotropic drugs or their potential long-term effects on the health of those for whom they are prescribed. However, psychologists do know the efficacy of specialized trauma treatment, which should be an option for all youth who are adjudicated as delinquents.

WOMEN AND CRIME

Women, like girls reported above, also are known to commit fewer violent crimes than men, according to the Bureau of Justice Statistics (OJJDP, 2003). Again, women's crimes are more relational especially if they kill someone. Usually those victims are abusive intimate partners or very young children. Most women who kill their babies suffer from undiagnosed postpartum depression while others have different but equally severe mental illnesses that are rarely recognized or treated until a tragedy occurs. The numbers of women who are incarcerated in jails and prisons around the world has increased in the past 20 years, and large numbers of them have a mental illness for which they require treatment. Unfortunately, the typical attempt at treatment in prison or jail is administration of psychotropic medication—usually insufficient, inappropriate, and dangerous to their well-being.

Battered Women Who Kill in Self-Defense

Over 25 years ago, the first known battered woman self-defense case, as these cases came to be known, appeared in the appellate case law. In *U.S. v. Ibn-Tamas* (1979), the court decided

that the introduction of psychological testimony about Beverly Ibn-Tamas's state of mind at the time she killed her husband, summarized in the description of battered woman syndrome, could assist the trier of fact in understanding the often counter-intuitive behavior of the battered woman, such as not leaving the relationship or other such myths (see Walker, 1989, for further details). Since then all U.S. states and some other countries have permitted testimony about the battered woman syndrome, considered a subcategory of posttraumatic stress disorder by many clinicians. The expert witness testimony focuses on how battered woman syndrome impacted upon a woman's state of mind, causing her to hold a reasonable belief that she was in imminent danger at the time she committed homicide or other criminal acts. Although some feminist advocates for battered women do not accept the psychological constructs of PTSD, or even battered woman syndrome to describe the effects on abused women, claiming that it is unfair to further pathologize women who are only acting to protect themselves against the injustice of male dominance and abuse, the legal system requires psychological data as a entry point to attempt to obtain justice for battered women and their children. Further, the diagnosis makes it possible for women to obtain the right type of psychotherapy as an intervention, without having inappropriate labels put on them by therapists untrained in abuse issues.

At the time the admissibility of this testimony was being debated, there were fears that women would use this as a license to kill men with whom they were angry rather than utilize more lawful means of terminating a relationship. This has not happened and in fact, fewer women resort to killing the abuser than before, according to the latest Bureau of Justice statistics (OJJDP, 2003). In 2002 approximately 500 women killed an abusive partner, while in 1988, the numbers were closer to 1,200. However, this has not stopped women from being battered by intimate partners, and they still are more likely to be seriously injured or killed at the point of separation through two years postdivorce, indicating that termination of the relationship will not always stop the man's violent behavior.

Rape Victims and Prosecution

Women and girls who are raped by men who know them rather than by strangers are still more likely to be treated in a hostile manner, with their credibility and integrity attacked. Although women who are raped by strangers are treated much better today than in the past, meaning they are less likely to be required to take lie detector tests or cross-examined about why they were out of their homes late at night or why they were wearing provocative sexy clothing, those who experience date or acquaintance rape are still treated as if they were the guilty parties. We only have to look at the case against Kobe Bryant to see how the whore-madonna construct about women's sexuality still plays out in the courts. Bryant's lawyers made much of the fact that the woman who accused him of rape may have had other sexual partners, as if that would negate his responsibility if he had indeed sexually assaulted her.

The debate has centered on how far a man can go before he is not required to stop his sexual behavior. Instead, the focus should be on how much aggression indicates that consensual sex has stopped and violence has begun. This case demonstrated the widening gulf between a woman's belief that if she says "stop" at any time, the man must do so, and a man's belief that her consent at the beginning of a sexual encounter is all that is needed, no matter how rough it gets. It remains to be seen if the publicity this case has generated will have a chilling effect on other women reporting sex crimes.

THERAPEUTIC JUSTICE AND MENTAL HEALTH COURT

The rise in the numbers of women in the criminal justice system may also be due to the lack of care for the seriously and persistently mentally ill in the community. Many blame the closing of the state hospitals for the lack of resources for women with schizophrenic spectrum and affective disorders. However, the advent of antipsychotic, antidepressant, and mood stabilizing medications, especially the second generation of atypical antipsychotics, has made it possible for many people with serious mental illnesses to be main-

tained in the community with good case management and therapy to stabilize rather than cure them of their illnesses. Unfortunately, many of these people, especially women, are poor, abused by family members and/or the community, without adequate treatment, and homeless. Many also came from homes where their families lacked resources and were already disenfranchised from the majority culture. Without adequate treatment they prefer to self-medicate with alcohol and other drugs. These women (and men) often end up being arrested for petty misdemeanor crimes such as trespassing, having an open bottle of beer in public, stealing food, or aggressive acts against those mistreating them.

Mental health courts are a part of the new wave of therapeutic or restorative justice in the criminal justice system (Peters & Osher, 2004). Many jurisdictions have specialty courts such as drug courts, where those who are addicted to drugs but not selling them may be deferred for treatment. Domestic violence courts may provide withheld adjudication with court-ordered treatment for first-time batterers instead of jail or prison terms. While these offender-specific treatment programs may be useful in stopping some of the abusers' physical violence, there are some reports that they become better psychological abusers afterwards. Batterers who are also sex offenders or have other mental illnesses need more psychological treatment than these programs can provide in the 6 to 12 or even 26 weeks that they are mandated to attend. Even when they violate again, few men experience any further consequences by a court system that is truly inadequate to protect women and girls.

Women in prison for more serious crimes are also advocating for more treatment programs while they are incarcerated, especially programs that deal with the effects of trauma and substance abuse. Health care in the women's prisons barely meets minimum standards especially since infections such as impetigo, streptococcus, HIV, hepatitis C, and new strains of tuberculosis are rampant there. Women can wait months after finding a lump on their breasts to be eligible to even get a physical examination by a doctor. In a recent case where I evaluated a woman in a local jail, she suffered permanent scaring because infections in gunshot wounds were not promptly treated. Pain medication is often nonexistent or inadequate and women are kept on major psychotropic medications without proper evaluation (see New Freedom Commission on Mental Health's subcommittee report on criminal justice, 2004, for recommendations to upgrade mental health care in the prison system).

Although it is true that most women with nonmajority-culture status are more likely to remain in prison longer than their Caucasian counterparts, just like men who languish in prison, there are hierarchies in prisons where women of different cultural and racial groups fight among themselves for power. For example, in prisons that house mostly Hispanic prisoners, those from the various Latin American countries may treat each other differently. It is difficult for African American, Haitian, and Hispanic women to relate to each other in therapy or psychoeducational groups, so the psychologists providing services there need to be sensitive to these cultural issues.

EXERCISING CIVIL AND LEGAL RIGHTS

Finding the Right Lawyer

Perhaps the most important way for women and girls to obtain justice and avoid the health problems that may result from legal difficulties, as described in this chapter, is to find the right lawyer to assist them. The legal field is filled with requirements that only trained lawyers can figure out. Women's credibility is often devalued in the legal system simply because of being a woman rather than the substance of the claims. As Schafran (1990) points out, "Women in the courts, particularly women lawyers, are sometimes subjected to demeaning forms of address, comments on their physical appearance and clothing, sexist remarks and 'jokes,' unwanted touching, and verbal and physical sexual harassment" (p. 32).

Emotional Toll of Litigation

It is also important to understand that being involved in the legal system is an exhausting and often demeaning experience for most people. The U.S. legal system is based on an advocacy model, with both parties permitted to present their best version of the truth. Often, only one side can win, although in equity courts such as family court, there is an attempt to settle so that each side wins some and loses some of whatever they are fighting for. Women often do not like how ugly the fight by an advocate can get, so they settle too soon and lose more than they should. It may be prudent to have an impartial support system such as a therapist, legal advocate, or other group support while pursuing justice. This is especially true for women with physical challenges that require them to obtain assistance from the government to support themselves.

Women in highly contested litigation often constrain their attorneys from fairly representing them because they do not want to be seen as mean or unfair. Sometimes they get pushed into a settlement without much time to think about the ramifications and remain unhappy afterwards. It is wise to get advice about various possible legal strategies prior to starting out so that there are no major surprises along the way. Sometimes sufficient information about what to expect in a legal case can reduce the emotional impact when difficulties arise which, is almost always the case.

CONCLUSIONS

This chapter has attempted to describe some of the most common legal situations where women and girls have contact with the courts today. It is proposed that despite over two decades of attention paid to gender bias and the addition of large numbers of women lawyers and judges, the laws still do not usually work on behalf of women even when they have substantive claims. This is especially true for women who are from nonmajority cultures and racial groups as they are most often disenfranchised by their status.

REFERENCES

Casey v. Planned Parenthood, No. 93-1503, 1504, U.S. Court of Appeals for Third Circuit, 14 F.3d 848 (1993).

Chesney-Lind, M. (2001). Women and the criminal system: Gender matters. *Topics in Community Corrections*, 5, 7–10.

Dallam, S. J., Gleaves, D. H., Cepeda-Benito, A., Silberg, J. L., Kraemer, H. C., & Spiegel, D. (1998). The effects of child sexual abuse. *Psychological Bulletin, 127,* 715–733.

Hodgson v. State of Minnesota, 497 U.S. 417 (1990).

In re A. H. Robbins Co., Inc., 880 F.2d 694, 4th Cir. (1989).

In re Northern District of California "Dalkon Shield" IUB Prod. Liab. Litig., 521 F. Supp. 1188 and 566 F. Supp. 887, N.D. Cal. (1981).

Kaye, J. S. (1990). Women and the law. Creating profound social change. *Trial,* 52–56.

The Leadership Council for Mental Health, Justice, and the Media. (n.d.). Web site on issues impacting the mental health, justice, and the media response to abuse of children. Available at www.theleadershipcouncil.com

National GAINS Center for People with Co-Occurring Disorders in the Justice System. (2001). The Prevalence of Co-Occurring Mental Illness and Substance Use Disorders in Jails. Fact sheet series. Delmar, NY: National GAINS Center. See also Web site at www.gainsctr.com (issues with justice-involved women with mental health and substance abuse disorders and their children; this center also houses the TAPA Center, which provides technical assistance to government funded programs for women with co-occurring disorders).

New Freedom Commission on Mental Health. (2004). Subcommittee on criminal justice: Background paper. DHHS Pub. No. SMA-04-3880. Rockville, MD. See also Web site at www.newfreedomcommissiononmentalhealth (Report of the Presidential Commission on Mental Health and its subcommittee reports).

Office of Juvenile Justice and Delinquency Prevention. (2003). *Statistical Briefing Book.* Washington, DC: National Center for Juvenile Justice. See also Web site at www.ojjdp.gov (Office of Juvenile Justice and Delinquency Prevention documents, including statistical briefing book).

Peters, R. H., & Osher, F. C. (2004). *Co-occurring disorders and specialty courts* (2nd ed.). Delmar, NY: National GAINS Center.

Rheingold, P. D. (1990). Tort class actions: What they can and cannot achieve. *Trial,* 59–63.

Schafran, L. H. (1990). Overwhelming evidence: Reports on gender bias in the courts. *Trial,* 28–35.

Singleton, S. M. (1990). Gender bias skews justice for women. *Trial,* 39–43.

U.S. v. Ibn-Tamas. (1979).

Walker, L. E. A. (1989). *Terrifying love: Why battered women kill and how society responds.* New York: Harper/Collins.

Walker, L. E. A. (1994). *Abused women and survivor therapy: A practical guide for the psychotherapist.* Washington, DC: American Psychological Association.

Walker, L. E. A. (2000). *Battered woman syndrome* (2nd ed.). New York: Springer.

Walker, L. E. A., & Shapiro, D. L. (2004). *Introduction to forensic psychology: Clinical and social psychology perspectives.* New York: Kluwer/Plenum.

Wettstein, R. M. (Ed). (1998). *Treatment of offenders with mental disorders.* New York: Guilford Press.

Wikler, N. J. (1990). Gender and justice: Navigating the curves on the road to equality. *Trial,* 36–37.

Immigrant and refugee girls' and women's psychological health and well-being in the United States may best be understood by incorporating their realities prior to immigration, their reasons for immigration, and their adaptation to living in the United States. For many, their collectivistic ethnic origins and heritages, as well as the sociopolitical and economic realities in their countries of origin, give them little preparation to deal with the postmigration individualistic context of living in the United States. What might generally be normative challenges and tasks across the life span may be monumental for these populations because of conflicting traditional and American cultural expectations and values of what is considered developmentally desirable, optimal, and acceptable. Moreover, migration-related losses, traumas, adjustment issues, prolonged hardships, and oppression often mire normal developmental processes. Yet girls, women, and their families demonstrate a variety of strengths and resilience in the face of these challenges (de las Fuentes & Vasquez, 1999; Fong, 2004). Clinical as well as societal strategies to promote optimism and hope among immigrant girls and women, and their families, are essential elements in a socially responsible profession and society.

This chapter provides an overview of female immigrant and refugee experiences, and discusses pertinent issues including documentation status, migration, reasons for immigration, and adjustment challenges. It uses the "Guidelines on Multicultural Education, Research, Practice, and Organizational Change for Psychologists," a policy endorsed by the American Psychological Association (APA, 2003) for its members, as a framework for discussing the role of the therapist and elements of culturally competent practice with immigrant and refugee girls and women.

MELBA J. T. VASQUEZ,
AY LING HAN,
and CYNTHIA DE LAS FUENTES

Adaptation of Immigrant Girls and Women

46

DEFINITIONS

The term immigrant is typically applied to foreign-born persons who have left their nation of birth to dwell in another country (Fong, 2004). Migration is a global issue; according to the United Nations (1995), 70 to 100 million immigrants and refugees have migrated to other countries as a result of war, political instability, expulsion, economic, social, and environmental pressures, population expansion, and poverty.

Legal or documented immigrants are those who have received the official papers that allow them to enter a country. A permanent resident is an immigrant, not a citizen of the United States, who is living in the United States under legally recognized and lawfully recorded permanent residence status. Other terms used synonymously include permanent resident alien, lawful permanent resident, resident alien permit holder, and green card holder (U.S. Citizenship and Immigration Services [USCIS], 2003). Legal immigrants may work if employment can be found, although some foreign-born residents, such as students, may be restricted in their freedom to accept work (Fong, 2004).

Refugees and asylum seekers may have temporary protective status granted by the Immigration and Naturalization Service (INS) while petitions for permanent residence are considered. These petitions are based on the threat of persecution should they return to their native country.

Undocumented immigrants are those who enter the country without official sanction. They have no legal status in the United States (Fong, 2004). The Immigration and Nationality Act (INA) broadly defines an immigrant as any alien in the United States except one legally admitted under specific nonimmigrant categories (INA Section 101[A][15]). An illegal alien who entered the United States without inspection, for example, would be strictly defined as an immigrant under the INA but is not a permanent resident (USCIS, 2003). We recommend using the term undocumented resident to refer to this category of immigrant.

CURRENT IMMIGRATION TRENDS

Approximately 10% of the U.S. population is foreign-born (Fong, 2004). In addition, 20% of all youths in the United States are from immigrant families (Suarez-Orozco & Suarez-Orozco, 2001). A breakdown of foreign-born populations by country of birth as a percentage of the total foreign-born population is available from the Global Data Center (2003). The top ten sending countries in 2001 included: Mexico, 19.4%; India, 6.6%; mainland China, 5.3%; the Philippines,

5.0%; Vietnam, 3.3%; El Salvador, 2.9%; Cuba, 2.6%; Haiti, 2.5%; Bosnia and Herzegovina, 2.2%; and Canada, 2.1%; with all other countries combined representing 48%. The top five languages among the English language learner population (ELL) are Spanish, Vietnamese, Hmong, Haitian Creole, and Korean (National Clearinghouse for English Language Acquisition, 2002). Seventy-seven percent of the ELL population is composed of Spanish speakers. Interestingly, for 2000, the most recent year for which data are available, more females (55.5%) than males were considered immigrants (Global Data Center, 2003).

American attitudes toward immigrants have always been ambivalent and frequently negative. Throughout the history of this nation, such attitudes have influenced regulations concerning who may immigrate to the United States and what rights and legal protections they may have once here. While undocumented residents are a vital part of the economic fabric of the United States, the nation's dependence on immigrant labor is seldom acknowledged and is not reflected in immigration policy. An estimated 8–10 million undocumented immigrants, including women, are currently living, working, and paying taxes in the United States (Martinez-Wenzl, 2003). Women in particular tend to work as domestics caring for children and older adults, in restaurant and clothing industries, and in farm fields. Undocumented immigrants live with the chronic stress of trying to avoid identification and deportation, the threat of discrimination and victimization through hate crimes, economic exploitation by employers, and sweatshop labor conditions.

Immigrants are often active in their attempts to influence legislation and public perception. In October 2003, for example, the Immigrant Workers Freedom Riders, representing a wide range of nationalities, traveled across the country to Washington, DC, to mobilize national support for changes in immigration policies. The Freedom Riders asked Congress to support four main principles: legalization and a path to citizenship for immigrant workers, family unification, workplace protections, and civil rights and civil liberties. Modeled after the Freedom Rides of the 1960s, the Immigrant Workers Freedom Ride highlighted the challenges immigrants face today with a nationwide plea for justice. In early 2004,

President Bush proposed a plan that would provide temporary legal status for millions of undocumented workers in the United States. The plan would provide legal status for three years, renewable for a yet-to-be-determined number of times, and the guest workers could freely leave and re-enter the country and bring dependents as long as they could show an ability to support them (Castillo, 2004). The plan is welcomed in part by immigrant advocates, but it is also criticized for not including a plan for earning citizenship; and anti-immigration groups are concerned it will drive down wages. Regardless of the outcome of this particular plan, public policy significantly affects the well-being of immigrant girls and women.

Martinez-Wenzl (2003) suggests that the national movement for immigrant rights took a blow after the horror of the terrorist acts of September 11, 2001. Suddenly, immigrants were viewed with renewed wariness and suspicion. For example, much of the progress toward developing a legalization program, made only days earlier in talks between U.S. President George W. Bush and Mexican President Vicente Fox, came to a halt. The changed climate in the wake of September 11 has made it more difficult for immigrant families in this country.

REASONS FOR IMMIGRATION

Both premigration and postmigration factors are important in assessing the challenges of acculturation and psychosocial adjustment (Bemak, 2000). Reasons that lead to decisions to immigrate to the United States point to significantly different experiences prior, during, and after migration as experienced by immigrants and refugees.

Push-pull theory is the classic explanation for the international migration of immigrants and refugees (Lee, in Potocky-Tribody, 2002). The theory posits that people migrate in response to "push" factors in the country of origin and "pull" factors in the country of destination (Potocky-Tribody, 2002, p. 13). Refugees and asylum seekers are pushed out of their home countries by harrowing experiences, including killings of family and community members, torture, rape, and other atrocities. Their pre-immigration experi-

ences often result from war, ethnic cleansing or genocide, political or religious persecution, and severe sociopoliticoeconomic destabilization. Because of their fear of persecution, these refugees and asylum seekers are unable or unwilling to return (USCIS, 2003).

In contrast, documented immigrants tend to be pulled into their country of destination by prospects of a better future. Refugees' departures are involuntary, sudden, tumultuous, and often involve life-threatening risks, whereas immigrants come voluntarily, with a planned and relatively smooth transition and without risks to their lives. Refugees tend to leave in groups of family and nonfamily members, while immigrants typically leave as individuals or with members of their families.

Women and girl refugees are among the world's most vulnerable populations. They are subject to gender-based violence, not only before migration but also in refugee settings, where violence is sometimes perpetrated by the very people charged with protecting them: the peacekeepers and relief workers from international and nongovernmental organizations. Reports of such gender-based violence over the past two decades include intimidation, physical harm, sexual abuse, rape, and unequal access to humanitarian assistance. The U.S. General Accounting Office (GAO) reported that "sexual abuse of refugee women and girls is pervasive and present in almost all refugee settings" (U.S. GAO, 2003, p. 1.). For refugee girls and women, posttraumatic stress disorder is a likely consequence when there is a history of sexual trauma and other violations to their basic human rights.

CHALLENGES FOR GIRLS AND WOMEN IN IMMIGRANT AND REFUGEE FAMILIES: POSTMIGRATION ADJUSTMENT

Both immigrant and refugee families face postmigration culture shock, typically accompanied by feelings of helplessness and confusion. In addition, survivor's guilt is a potential barrier to successful adjustment for those haunted by feelings of guilt from having escaped dangerous or dire political and economic conditions in their home countries while leaving behind family and friends.

Psychosocial adjustment to a different culture can be very stressful and difficult. What was formerly normative behavior may be unacceptable in the host country. For example, some practices such as corporal punishment in child rearing or spousal domination and abuse are illegal in this country. Additionally, traditional healing practices may be perceived as negative (Bemak, 2000).

Most refugees and immigrants come from male-dominated societies where husbands or fathers are the sole breadwinners, decision-makers, and arbiters of power. Women and men are accorded clear and separate gender roles. Yet, once in the United States, women must often enter the paid workforce to support their families; and they tend to find work faster than men (Potocky-Tribody, 2002). This crossing of the gender-role lines may result in a decrease of immigrant men's traditional power, status, and respect. In addition, as female immigrants are exposed to nontraditional values through school, work, their children, and mainstream Americans they may become more independent and may make changes to traditional family dynamics at home (Bemak, 2000). For example, a girl or woman may learn to value assertive communication, something that may be considered disrespectful and unacceptable by those whose heritages value patriarchal and generational hierarchy. In addition, because immigrant children more quickly acquire English fluency, the older generations must often rely on them as translators and cultural brokers, roles found to be the norm rather than the exception (Ying, 1999). While some families are able to adapt to marked changes in traditional gender and generational hierarchies, others may not. Unexpected conflicts, owing to the impact of acculturation on the rearrangement of these hierarchies, understandably result in disagreements that may escalate to violent abuse of women and girls (Potocky-Tribody, 2002). Notwithstanding the challenges, there are many girls and women who are resilient and who thrive in their new cultures. For example, in an inspiring story of how a daughter of immigrants can learn to be true to herself, Eng (1999) described her process of integrating American and Asian cultures in order to survive successfully in both worlds.

Adult or middle-aged immigrant women are often caught in multiple binds and conflicts with spouses, children, and older parents and parents-in-law. Moreover, a woman's normative developmental tasks may be complicated by language barriers, racism, ethnocentrism, sexism, and classism. Later, the elderly immigrant or refugee woman faces the special challenge of coming to terms with and finding integrity in the meaning of her life (Potocky-Tribody, 2002). Such a challenge is likely to include the profound losses of her homeland, significant others, and all those familiar signifiers that contributed to her identity, resulting in a "discontinuity in her sense of self or identity" (Feinberg, 1996, p. 42). It is also likely to include the losses of her traditional hopes and expectations about her place in the life of the family, the role of elders in the community, and the loss of connections to her descendants owing to language and cultural barriers. These elderly immigrant women must cope with isolation caused by a lack of traditional support networks. Thus, for an older immigrant woman, a re-evaluation of her identity and a search for integrity in the meaning of her life may at times seem insurmountable within the context of her migration and resettlement experiences and in the face of likely ongoing familial strain (Potocky-Tribody, 2002).

THE ROLE OF THE THERAPIST

In general, the clinician should view immigrant women and girls presenting for psychotherapy and other psychological services in the context of the family, even when they come alone. Since most immigrants come from collectivistic cultures, their presenting problems in psychotherapy typically reflect conflicts and concerns about one or more members of the family. Marital conflict, parent-child conflict, and academic problems in children are common presenting problems. The clinician's role, therefore, includes determining the degree of acculturation of the family, including discrepancies in acculturation among family members, in order to facilitate an understanding of the presenting problem (de las Fuentes, 2003). For many immigrant women and girls, family concerns are complicated by issues of loss, grief, and isolation.

Knowledge of the immigrant client's dominant language and its use in psychotherapy with bilingual speakers are essential because it is through language that customs, values, and social and cultural beliefs are expressed. According to Altarriba and Santiago-Rivera (1994), the therapist's responsibility in developing cultural sensitivity includes understanding the client's language. If psychotherapists are unable to communicate in the dominant language of their clients, the quality of services delivered to them is compromised (Bamford, 1991; Padilla et al., 1991) because language differences create barriers to cultural understanding and, perhaps more troubling, can cause a great deal of misinterpretation by the therapist (Altarriba & Santiago-Rivera, 1994).

Asking the question, "Where is your family from?" and listening to the girl's or woman's immigration story provides the therapist with an invaluable opportunity to learn about the country and people she left behind, her culture, and the reasons for leaving (McGoldrick, Giordano, & Pearce, 1996). The therapist then can explore issues about pre-immigration experiences, immigration decision making, and changes to family processes as a result of living in the United States (de las Fuentes, 2003). Together with the discussion of acculturative stressors and concerns, it is important for a therapist to explore what the family has learned as a result of the immigration process and what strengths and resources they have discovered within themselves and their networks. With such a balanced exploration, therapists can be more equipped to provide multiculturally resonant services and may facilitate clients to incorporate their relevant strengths, resources, and resilience to deal with their acculturative challenges. Additionally, therapists can play a crucial part in facilitating immigrants' reflections on cultural similarities and differences, and on what they value and appreciate from each culture as well as what they do not. Such reflection may significantly assist them in negotiating the acculturative process (Garcia-Preto, 1994).

ELEMENTS OF CULTURALLY COMPETENT PRACTICE WITH IMMIGRANT GIRLS AND WOMEN

Most experts agree that an understanding of cultural contexts is essential in planning, developing, and offering mental health services for immigrant girls and women and their families (Bemak, 2000; Fong, 2004). The APA (2003) endorsed the "Guidelines on Multicultural Education, Training, Research, Practice, and Organizational Change for Psychologists" as policy for the APA and its members. These guidelines address psychologists' work and interactions with individuals from other nations, including international students, immigrants, and temporary workers. They reflect knowledge and skills needed for the profession in a time of historic, sociopolitical, and demographic changes across the nation. Although the "Guidelines" are not intended to be mandatory or exhaustive, and may not be applicable to every professional and clinical situation, they are informative for psychologists who work with immigrant and ethnic minority populations in the United States.

The first two guidelines inform the remaining four guidelines and will be described here. They apply to all psychologists from two primary perspectives: (a) knowledge of self with a cultural heritage and varying social identities, and (b) knowledge of other cultures. The remaining guidelines address the application of multiculturalism in education and training, research, practice, and organizational change.

Guideline 1 focuses on knowledge of self with a cultural heritage and states: "Psychologists are encouraged to recognize that, as cultural beings, they may hold attitudes and beliefs that can detrimentally influence their perceptions of and interactions with individuals who are ethnically and racially different from themselves" (APA, 2003, p. 382). In other words, our worldviews, the way we perceive our lives, our experiences and those of others, are all shaped in large measure by our cultural experiences. Every individual holds a set of cultural experiences and backgrounds. We encourage psychologists and other health care professionals to learn how cultures differ in basic premises that shape worldview. Culturally competent health-care professionals recognize differing cultural contexts, assess for cultural differences, look for variations, and most important, validate multiple cultural perspectives rather than attaching labels or stereotypes. Psychologists should also be aware of how their own culture contributes to attitudes and biases.

A defining value of mainstream American culture is a preference for individuals who are independent and focused on achievement and success. Americans prefer self-determination and value rational decision making (Fiske, Kitayama, Markus, & Nisbett, 1998; Oyserman, Coon, & Kemmelmeier, 2002). Western psychological practice is grounded in a medical model that focuses on mental health problems while emphasizing optimum individual functioning and self-development (Bemak, 2000). Yet the cultural context of many immigrants is a collectivistic sensibility in which family and social networks define identity and self, and underscore collective harmony rather than individual assertiveness, tactful indirectness rather than directness, interdependence rather than independence. Beliefs about resilience, strength, and healing may involve the support of extended family, a sense of community and social networks, the importance of ancestral guidance, and a spirituality that includes the interdependence of living and nonliving forces (Bemak, 2000). These cultural standards tend to differ from mainstream American belief systems and may even be misinterpreted or pathologized by U.S. health-care providers.

The categorization of immigrant groups is particularly complex and can lead to a dangerous we/they dichotomy. It is normal and even helpful for people to rely on categories in the process of making sense of their world. The most commonly used theoretical framework for understanding this practice is social categorization theory, which was originally conceptualized by Allport (1954). In this framework, people understand their social context by creating categories of the individuals around them, which includes separating the categories into ingroups and outgroups (Fiske et al., 1998). Categorization becomes problematic when one group holds much more power than another, when resources are not distributed equitably among groups, or when ingroups judge outgroups negatively, as is the case in the United States (and much of the world) today.

Many people distance themselves from others who are different or foreign, sometimes unconsciously. Health-care professionals who provide services to immigrant and ethnically diverse client populations must be aware of and be prepared to manage their own negative reactions. One of the most constructive therapeutic strategies for dealing with the potential pitfalls of clinician-client cultural differences in psychotherapy is to become attuned to the immigrant girl or woman, hear her narratives, and connect with her as a human being. In essence, Guideline 1 calls upon therapists to be aware of their own cultural assumptions, values, and biases; explore, acknowledge, and respect differences; and suspend negative judgments and reactions, even if doing so causes discomfort. At the same time, therapists must find culturally appropriate ways to give feedback about genuinely problematic behaviors and attitudes.

Guideline 2 encourages knowledge of other cultures, and states: "Psychologists are encouraged to recognize the importance of multicultural sensitivity/responsiveness, knowledge, and understanding about ethnically and racially different individuals" (APA, 2003, p. 385). It is incumbent upon psychologists, and all health professionals, to be sensitized to the Western cultural biases that underlie general psychological theories and to increase our knowledge of the multiple cultural foundations that inform the lives of immigrant clients.

Compared to the general U.S. population, immigrants, especially refugees, have a higher incidence of loneliness and alienation, guilt, negative self-esteem, somatization, depression, anxiety, and posttraumatic stress disorders (Kinzie, 1993; Potocky-Tribodi, 2002). A review of major findings suggests that predictors of psychological distress for migrants include older age, loss of a spouse, divorced or single marital status, low socioeconomic status, unemployment, limited education, and discrimination (Bemak, 2000). Adolescent girls face particular challenges because they have lost peers and a familiar culture that would have served in the development of identity (de las Fuentes & Vasquez, 1999). Moreover, parental loss of power and capability to function as effectively in the new society may leave adolescents feeling unsafe and unable to rely on their parents for protection (Espin, 1997).

In working with immigrant girls and women, it is important to assess psychological problems and experiences from each period of the immigrant experience, including premigration situations, transition, and postmigration adjustment.

Bemak (2000) outlined three phases of immigration adjustment that serve to establish emotional safety and security: (a) initial skill development, (b) integration of previously learned skills from the country of origin with new skills in the resettlement country, and (c) creation of skills and values that foster a realistic acquisition of future goals. These are crucial stages for immigrant girls' and women's acculturation and creation of a new life for themselves. Problems may emerge at different intervals, typically ranging over a period of six months to several years after immigration, but psychological intervention can be an important tool in fostering successful adjustment in those phases (Bemak, 2000).

Focusing on and validating the girls' and women's strengths, capabilities, and resources is an important intervention. A systemic view of resilience should take into account the strengths and support of the family as well as the environment, which contributes to the "hardiness" for weathering changes and uncertainties. For many immigrant families, the family itself often serves as an important protective factor, especially those families able to convey warmth, affection, and emotional support for one another. Fostering a close connection to one's cultural roots also seems to be a positive mediating factor (de las Fuentes & Vasquez, 1999).

In summary, psychologists—including clinicians, researchers, and educators—must develop skills and practices that are attuned to the unique worldviews and cultural contexts of immigrant girls and women. Psychologists must incorporate a nuanced understanding of these girls' and women's ethnic, linguistic, and cultural backgrounds into their professional practice. In psychotherapy with immigrant girls and women, psychologists must continuously examine traditional interventions for cultural appropriateness, and expand their own clinical interventions to incorporate multicultural awareness and culturally resonant strategies.

Among such strategies, psychologists must be prepared to conduct psychotherapy sessions in the immigrant girl's or woman's preferred language—while respecting her boundaries by using interpreters who are neither family members nor authorities in the community, or who lack skill in the area of mental health practice.

This includes making sure that all documents, including informed consent for assessment or procedures, are accurately translated. In addition, psychologists must assess each client's culturally preferred approaches to communicate to both peers and authority figures in her traditional as well as mainstream American contexts. For example, she may communicate her wishes, agreement, disagreements, or feelings in tactful indirect ways in the former context but in assertive ways in the latter. However, she may communicate indirectly in all contexts, which is especially relevant for psychologists to be able to decipher so that bidirectional misinterpretations in therapy can be clarified and minimized, thereby providing a therapeutic opportunity to develop a multiculturally relevant and inclusive working alliance. Last but not least, psychologists must assess immigrant girls' and women's problem-solving skills, strengths, and resiliencies. According to an empowerment theory and strengths perspective, immigrant families have the traditional means to cope with the stressors in their lives (Fong, 2004). It is the psychologist's job to recognize and encourage those skills, strengths, and resiliencies as part of psychotherapy, using them to facilitate cross-cultural adjustment and integration.

REFERENCES

Allport, G. W. (1954). *The nature of prejudice*. Cambridge, MA: Addison-Wesley.

Altarriba, J., & Santiago-Rivera, A. L. (1994). Current perspectives on using linguistic and cultural factors in counseling the Hispanic client. *Professional Psychology: Research & Practice, 25*, 388–397.

American Psychological Association. (2003). Guidelines on multicultural education, training, research, practice, and organizational change for psychologists. *American Psychologist, 58*, 377–402.

Bamford, K. W. (1991). Bilingual issues in mental health assessment and treatment. *Hispanic Journal of Behavioral Sciences, 13*, 377–390.

Bemak, F. P. (2000). Migrants. In A. E. Kazdin (Ed.), *Encyclopedia of psychology* (pp. 244–247). Washington, DC: American Psychological Association; New York: Oxford University Press.

Castillo, J. (2004, January 8). Migrants could get 3-year legal status. *Austin American-Statesman*, pp. A1, A10.

de las Fuentes, C. (2003). Latino mental health: At least you should know this. In J. S. Mio & G. Y.

Iwamasa (Eds.), *Culturally diverse mental health: The challenges of research and resistance* (pp. 159–172). New York: Brunner-Routledge.

de las Fuentes, C., & Vasquez, M. J. T. (1999). Immigrant adolescent girls of color; Facing American challenges. In N. G. Johnson, M. C. Roberts, & J. Worell (Eds.), *Beyond appearance: A new look at adolescent girls* (pp. 131–150). Washington, DC: American Psychological Association.

Eng, P. (1999). *Warrior lessons: An Asian American woman's journey into power.* New York: Pocket Books.

Espin, O. M. (1997). Crossing borders and boundaries: The life narratives of immigrant lesbians. In B. Greene (Ed.), *Ethnic and cultural diversity among lesbians and gay men* (pp. 191–125). Thousand Oaks, CA: Sage.

Feinberg, R. I. (1996). Use of reminiscence groups to facilitate the telling of life stories by elderly Russian Jewish immigrants. *Smith College Studies in Social Work, 67,* 39–51.

Fiske, A. P., Kitayama, S., Markus, H. R., & Nisbett, R. E. (1998). The cultural matrix of social psychology. In D. T. Gilbert & S. T. Fiske (Eds.), *The handbook of social psychology, Vol. 2* (4th ed., pp. 915–981). New York: McGraw-Hill.

Fong, R. (Ed.). (2004). *Culturally competent practice with immigrant and refugee children and families.* New York: Guilford Press.

Garcia-Preto, N. (1994). On the bridge. *Family Therapy Networker, 18,* 35–37.

Global Data Center. (2003). Migration information source: Fresh thought, authoritative data, global reach. Retrieved from www.migrationinforma tion.org/GlobalData

Kinzie, D. (1993). Posttraumatic effects and their treatment among Southeast Asian refugees. In J. Wilson & B. Raphael (Eds.), *International handbook of traumatic stress syndromes* (pp. 311–329). New York: Plenum Press.

Martinez-Wenzl, M. (2003, November 2). Guest viewpoint: Immigration freedom rides a catalyst. *The Register-Guard* (Eugene, OR). Retrieved from http://www.registerguard.com/news/2003/11/06/a11.ed.col.martinez.1106.html

McGoldrick, M., Giordano, J., & Pearce, J. K. (Eds.). (1996). *Ethnicity and family therapy* (2nd ed.). New York: Guilford Press.

National Clearinghouse for English Language Acquisition and Language Instruction Educational Programs. (2002). *United States most commonly spoken languages.* Retrieved from http://www.ncbe.gwu.edu/askncela/05toplangs.html

Oyserman, D., Coon, H. M., & Kemmelmeier, M. (2002). Rethinking individualism and collectivism: Evaluation of theoretical assumptions and meta-analyses. *Psychological Bulletin, 128,* 3–72.

Padilla, A. M., Lindholm, K. J., Chen, A., Duran, R., Hakuta, K., Lambert, W., et al. (1991). The English-only movement. *American Psychologist, 46,* 120–130.

Potocky-Tribody, M. (2002). *Best practices for social work with refugees and immigrants.* New York: Columbia University Press.

Suarez-Orozco, C., & Suarez-Orozco, M. (2001). *Children of immigration.* Cambridge, MA: Harvard University Press.

United Nations. (1995). *Notes for speakers: Social development.* New York: Department of Public Information.

U.S. Citizenship and Immigration Services. (2003). Information retrieved from http://uscis.gov

U.S. General Accounting Office. (2003). *Humanitarian assistance: Protecting refugee women and girls remains a significant challenge.* GAO-03-663, released May 23, 2003. Information retrieved from http://www.gao.gov/

Ying, Y. (1999). Strengthening intergenerational/intercultural ties in migrant families: A new intervention for parents. *Journal of Community Psychology, 27,* 89–96.

There are times when pharmacotherapy may contribute to a woman's optimal health, and there are many differences in the assessment and treatment of women and men. Women are bigger consumers of health care than men; they make more visits to health-care professionals, undergo more surgical procedures, occupy more hospital beds, have more chronic diseases, spend more for health care, and are given more prescriptions for medications (Burt & Hendrick, 2001). There are significant psychodiagnostic, sociocultural, and psychological differences, as well as physiological differences, between women and men that have implications for pharmacotherapy. For some drugs the pharmacokinetics (the body's processing of the drug) and pharmacodynamics (the body's response to the drug) are different for women and men. Levels of a psychotropic medication may vary across the menstrual cycle, and when used with exogenous hormones—for example, oral contraceptives (OC) and estrogen or combined hormone replacement therapy (ERT/HRT; Anthony and Berg, 2002a,b; Food and Drug Administration [FDA], 1993). Knowledge of such differences and a mindfulness of them are required when engaging in psychodiagnostic assessment and treatment. This chapter provides an overview of gender-specific elements of the evaluation and psychopharmacologic treatment of adult women during childbearing and perimenopausal years. (See Phelps, Brown, & Power, 2002; and Sadavoy, Lazarus, Jarvik, & Grossberg, 1996, respectively, regarding children and the elderly.)

DEBRA LINA DUNIVIN

Psychopharmacotherapy and Women: Issues for Consideration

DEFINITIONS, DISTINCTIONS, AND CONCEPTS

Gender sensitive pharmacotherapy is a term used to describe a practice that "incorporates knowledge of sex and gender related variables into clinical decision-making, research and education in pharmacotherapy" (Jensvold, Halbreich, & Hamilton, 1996, p. 3). This approach incorporates a range of biopsychosocial factors that influence drug therapies. Often when talking about sex differences, terms are used interchangeably that should be distinguished. Some important distinctions include sex (a biological category, female or male), gender (a more complex, socially and culturally constructed dimension of human functioning), sexuality (i.e., sexual functioning), and sexual reproduction (behavioral and hormonal functioning related to reproductive system). Sexual side effects of medications fall into two different, overlapping sets of adverse drug reactions that affect sexual functioning and reproductive system functioning. The endocrine system creates the biochemical environment into which we add psychotropic medications. This hormonal milieu provides the background for women's conditions and is particularly influential during childbearing years. The functioning of some endocrine glands is similar for females and males (e.g., pineal, pancreas, kidney) and some quite different (e.g., thyroid); some glands are specific to the sex (e.g., ovaries and testes). Adding to the complexity of the hormonal milieu for women are fluctuations of endocrine levels across the menstrual cycle, which may be quite variable throughout a woman's childbearing years and become disrupted during the perimenopausal years. For many teens and women, significant behavioral and emotional fluctuations accompany the hormonal and physiological changes across the menstrual cycle. (See Burt & Hendrick, 2001; and Toot, Surrey, & Lu, 1992, respectively, for concise and detailed discussions of female hormonal functioning.)

AN INTEGRATED TREATMENT APPROACH

When drug therapy is indicated, the optimal approach fully integrates psychological therapies with pharmacotherapy. Emphasis on psychosocial versus pharmacologic components of treatment may be expected to vary with the condition being treated. For example, pharmacotherapy might be contraindicated in some conditions (e.g., adjustment disorders) while psychotherapy might be counterproductive in others (e.g., acute mania). For some conditions pharmacotherapy is generally considered essential (e.g., schizophrenia) and for some (e.g., obsessive-compulsive disorder) drug therapy and psychotherapy may have an additive or synergistic benefit. Use of combined therapies is supported by clinical, anecdotal, and research data for many conditions and for some disorders has been found superior to either single mode of treatment (Arana & Rosenbaum, 2000; Sammons & Schmidt, 2001).

Fundamental to any treatment is the relationship between the doctor and patient. For both psychotherapy and pharmacotherapy, adherence to a treatment regimen is enhanced by a positive therapeutic alliance. Transference and countertransference phenomena impact pharmacologic management of symptoms just as they do psychological treatments. For many consumers of mental and behavioral health care, treatment is not provided by a single provider. Instead, one health-care provider administers the psychological treatment while another provides the pharmacologic treatment. The participation of multiple providers complicates provision of integrated services and challenges health-care professionals to coordinate care and work as a team. Ideally, communication between collaborating providers should include keeping all clinicians informed regarding assessment and treatment, as well as the role of each provider in the care of the patient. Providers of psychological therapies often see patients much more frequently than prescribers and are therefore in a better position to monitor target symptoms and adverse drug reactions. This makes knowledge of psychopharmacology in general and the specific plan for pharmacotherapy of individual patients essential.

GENDER-SPECIFIC ASPECTS OF A PSYCHODIAGNOSTIC EVALUATION

Areas worthy of particular focus in the comprehensive assessment of female patients include: elements of history specifically relevant to women (relationship of symptoms to menstrual cycle, plans regarding pregnancy, seasonality of mood symptoms, menopausal status, especially if there are sleep disturbances in middle-aged women); family history of premenstrual dysphoric disorder (PMDD) and depression (since reproduction-related mood symptoms often run in families); particular issues related to sexually transmitted diseases (including gynecological conditions that affect sexual functioning or fertility); effects of surgery (influence of breast surgery or hysterectomy on sense of femininity and relationship with partner); alcohol and drug abuse (although once less prevalent than in men, now about equal in younger adults). A history of psychiatric symptoms in relation to one reproductive life event (e.g., when using oral contraceptives, or during premenstrual, postpartum or perimenopausal phases) indicates a risk of psychiatric symptoms at the time of subsequent reproductive life events. During the assessment, the psychologist must be aware of social roles and pressures that may influence a woman's coping capacity, vulnerability to psychopathology, and access to health care. Sexual orientation is also an important consideration; patterns of mental health morbidity and treatment use are shown to differ between lesbians and heterosexual women (Bernhard, 2001; Cochran, Sullivan, & Mays, 2003). There are special considerations in the laboratory assessment of women, just as there are in the psychosocial assessment. Although most psychologists do not have the training necessary to order and interpret laboratory studies, it is helpful for appropriate referral and follow-up to know something about which tests should be included and which symptoms or conditions should be worked up in a comprehensive psychodiagnostic assessment. (See Burt & Hendrick, 2001.)

SPECIAL CONSIDERATIONS IN THE PSYCHOPHARMACOTHERAPY OF WOMEN

Some psychiatric disorders are exclusive to women—for example, depressions associated with pregnancy, perimenopause, and menopause; PMDD; and postpartum psychosis. For many other psychological disorders, women and men differ in terms of factors such as lifetime prevalence, expression and course of the disorder, and comorbid conditions and response to treatment (Kessler et al., 1994).

The Hormonal Milieu: Impact on Pharmacokinetics and Pharmacodynamics

The backdrop to any discussion of psychiatric disorders occurring across the life span of a woman is the significant role of hormonal fluctuations—the cyclic fluctuations across the menstrual cycle during childbearing years, the extreme variations during pregnancy and puerperium, and the erratic fluctuations during the perimenopausal phase. For decades pharmacotherapy was based on the assumption that metabolism and response to drugs were the same for women and men, an assumption that remained unchallenged by research data based solely on men. It has been only about a decade since the FDA (1993) revised the guidelines excluding women with childbearing potential from clinical trials that established therapeutic doses of medications, and that aspects of illness and treatment specific to women have been the focus of study. Creation of the Women's Health Initiative and the National Institutes of Health Office of Research on Women's Health reflects recognition of the need to study these previously neglected aspects of women's health care (Matthews et al., 1997; Schwartz, 2001).

Sex differences in pharmacokinetics (the phases of absorption, distribution, metabolism, and elimination or clearance of the pharmacologic agent from the body) and pharmacodynamics (the biochemical and physiological effects of the agent) have been demonstrated for some drugs. It is known that some drugs affect women differently from men and that women process some drugs differently than do men. For example, it has been reported that women have an increased incidence of adverse effects to medications and also that these adverse reactions are associated with greater health risks in women (M. A. Miller, 2001). Reviews of sex differences in psychopharmacologic agents (Anthony & Berg, 2002a,b; Jensvold et al., 1996) highlight the importance of establishing menstrual phase in research studies investigating gender differences in pharmacokinetics and pharmacodynamics. They likewise highlight the importance of establishing menstrual phase in the clinical setting when adverse drug reactions or fluctuations in efficacy occur. "The prudent clinician will remember that every time a therapy is initiated for an individual patient, especially a female patient, it is a clinical trial and the outcome is uncertain" (Schwartz, 2001, p. 17). Ethnicity is also an important factor to consider since pharmacogenetic differences have been found for many pharmacological agents (Gaw, 2001). Although a full discussion of various pharmacologic agents is beyond the scope of this chapter, the clinical relevance of these sex differences is apparent in the following summation:

> Examination of specific psychotropic agents indicates that (1) the effects of benzodiazepines are influenced by gender, menstrual cycle phase and concurrent use of OCs; (2) antipsychotic agents may be more effective in women, although women are more likely to experience adverse drug reactions; and (3) women may respond better to different classes of antidepressant agents than men, specifically the SSRIs and the MAOIs. (Brawman-Mintzer & Yonkers, 2001, p. 413)

Pregnancy

The possibility of pregnancy must always be kept in mind whenever the pharmacologic treatment of a woman is considered. Many psychiatric disorders cluster during childbearing years and often women experience onset of these conditions during pregnancy (L. J. Miller, 2001). A full discussion with every female patient of her fertility status, plans for pregnancy, and contraception is warranted (Cohen & Rosenbaum, 1998) and may inform choice of treatment for women maintained on psychotropics who plan to become pregnant. Estimates of unplanned pregnancy are as high as 49% (Henshaw, 1998); thus it is not uncommon that a woman may unintentionally become pregnant while taking psychotropic medications. Careful consideration of the relative risks and benefits of pharmacotherapy for the mother and fetus, as well as the risks and benefits of not treating the psychiatric disorder with a medication, is required.

The absolute risks associated with fetal drug exposure are very difficult to quantify, as are the risks of untreated psychiatric disorders in pregnant women. Controlled randomized trials are understandably lacking in this population, and most data must be compiled from various sources including series of anecdotal and case reports, as well as drug registry information. Risks to the fetus

of prenatal exposure to drugs include teratogenic effects, direct neonatal toxicity, and the potential for long-term neurobehavioral sequelae (Cohen & Rosenbaum, 1998). Discontinuation of a psychotropic medication upon learning of pregnancy may not be the best solution despite the potential risks of continuing the drug and may be associated with high rates of relapse and the associated risks to mother and fetus of the untreated disorder (including higher rates of obstetrical complications; Cohen, 2003; L. J. Miller, 2001). No psychotropic drug is currently approved the FDA for administration during pregnancy, and a multidisciplinary task force has been established to develop new guidelines (Stewart & Robinson, 2001). It is expected that the FDA's Use in Pregnancy labeling system will be revised and that in the future package labeling will include the number of exposures reported from various sources along with outcomes (Cohen, 2003).

Clearly no decision regarding use of a psychotropic drug during pregnancy is risk-free; all psychotropics diffuse across the placenta and enter fetal circulation (Altshuler et al., 1996; Stewart & Robinson, 2001). During the first two weeks of gestation, the embryo is usually not susceptible to teratogens (Moore & Persaud, 1999). During these preembryonic stages a teratogen may damage all or most of the cells, often resulting in death, or may damage only a few cells, allowing the embryo to develop without birth defects. The next 10 weeks is a time when exposure to teratogens may result in major congenital anomalies, while after the 12th week functional defects and minor congenital anomalies may occur. Biological interventions (medication or ECT) during pregnancy may be indicated when the potential risk to the fetus from exposure to the mother's untreated psychiatric disorder is outweighed by risk of exposure to the intervention (Cohen, 2003; L. J. Miller, 2001). The clinician's role is to provide the best available information and assist the patient in making a risk-benefit analysis, knowing that women with similar histories often make different decisions regarding pharmacotherapy during pregnancy. Whenever possible the patient's partner and her obstetrician/gynecologist should be involved in the treatment-planning process.

Thoughtful discussions of the complex process of consulting about use of psychotropics with a pregnant woman who is experiencing psychiatric symptoms may be found in Altshuler et al. (1996), Cohen and Rosenbaum (1998), and L. J. Miller (2001). Factors to consider include: prior course and severity of the illness, the woman's capacity to tolerate symptoms, her potential for decompensation, and the reproductive safety of the medications. Currently available data indicate increased relative risk of congenital malformations with first-trimester exposure to some phenothiazine antipsychotics, mood stabilizers (lithium, carbamazepine, and valproic acid) and benzodiazepines, as well as the relative safety of tricyclic antidepressants, fluoxetine, citalopram, and two antipsychotics, haloperidol and trifluoperazine (previously cited reviews). The goal of pharmacotherapy during pregnancy is to maintain psychological stability with the lowest effective dose and minimize fetal drug exposure—that is, symptom-reduction rather than cure while maximizing use of psychosocial interventions.

Lactation/Breast-Feeding

The postpartum period presents the special challenge of newborn drug exposure through breast milk. Recognition of the significant benefits of breast-feeding for both mother and child has resulted in worldwide interest and the decision by increasingly more mothers to nurse their infants (Hale & Ilett, 2002). Psychopharmacotherapy may be indicated during the postpartum period given the increased vulnerability to psychiatric illness during the puerperium (Nonacs, 2002) and the fact that many women will have been taking psychotropic medications prior to delivery. Thus there is an increased need for information to facilitate the risk-benefit analysis by mothers and health-care providers. The American Academy of Pediatrics (AAP) has placed emphasis on increasing breast-feeding in the United States and has commented on the transfer of drugs and chemical into human milk since 1983. The AAP maintains that "most drugs likely to be prescribed to the nursing mother should have no effect on milk supply or on infant well-being" (2001, p. 776) and that advice to cease breast-feeding

when taking medication is often unwarranted. Nevertheless there are many drugs (including nicotine, alcohol, and prescribed and over-the-counter medications, food, and environmental agents) that have known adverse effects on nursing infants and many others for which the effect is unknown of concern.

Reviews of agents transferred into human milk and their possible effect on the nursing infant (AAP, 2001; Hale, 2002; Stewart & Robinson, 2001) inform discussions with a patient about the effective pharmacologic management of a breast-feeding mother and impact on infant well-being. Lactation risk categories have been established for many pharmacologic agents based on available safety data (Hale, 2002); these are different from FDA Use in Pregnancy ratings and may assist in determining appropriate pharmacotherapy when indicated. Some general guidelines for the pharmacotherapy of a lactating woman include: avoidance of medication when possible, selecting drugs for which breast-feeding data exists, taking fetal physiology into account and recognizing that some enzyme systems are immature in newborns and inhibit biotransformation of some agents, measuring blood concentrations in the infant when exposure may cause risk, exercising more caution with preterm or low-birth-weight infants, and timing infant feeding and maternal dosing to minimize drug exposure to the nursing infant (AAP, 2001; Auerback, 1999; Hale & Ilett, 2002; Nonacs, 2002). The consultative process with the lactating woman is similar to that regarding pregnancy; the clinician's role is to provide best available information and assist the patient in a careful risk-benefit analysis, maximize use of psychological interventions, and involve the pediatrician in treatment planning and decision making whenever possible.

The Menopausal Transition

The period of time, often five to seven years, between regular ovulatory menstrual cycles and complete cessation of ovarian function is referred to as perimenopause. It marks the transition between a woman's reproductive years and reproductive quiescence and is characterized by extreme fluctuations in sex hormones. Susan Love

(1998) describes the life stages of perimopause and puberty as mirror images of the same mechanism. They have in common dramatic hormonal changes; however, during puberty the ovarian mechanism is gearing up to an estrogen-dominant hormonal balance while during perimenopause the system is shifting into a new hormonal balance. Menopause is defined as cessation of menses for 12 months; it is marked by prolonged exposure to relatively low levels of estrogen. Baby boomers entering the menopausal transition have called attention to the medicalization of menopause and facilitated its recharacterization from a disease that should be medicated away to that of a normal developmental phase for which only some women will require medical intervention (Doress-Worters, 1998; Love, 1998).

A natural menopause usually occurs between 45 and 55 with an average age of about 51; with an expected life span of almost 81 years, women can expect to live about one third of their lives in the postmenopausal phase (Sherwin, 2001). Some women experience a premature menopause in their early 30s. Menopause may also be induced: surgically through bilateral oophorectomy (removal of both ovaries, with or without a hysterectomy) or medically through chemotherapy for treatment of various kinds of cancer or radiation therapy for colon cancer. Severity of symptoms seems to vary with the form of menopause, with less severe symptoms associated with a naturally occurring menopause and most severe symptoms occurring with a surgically induced menopause (Love, 1998). Regardless of the form of menopause, it is accompanied not only by changes in hormonal balance but also changes in physiology, mood, sexuality, and increased comorbid medical conditions including osteoporosis, cardiovascular disease, obesity, diabetes, thyroid dysfunction, and hypertension. Comorbid conditions and polypharmacy complicate treatment of psychological disorders during this phase of life.

Data regarding increased incidence of psychological disorders during the menopausal transition are equivocal; however, women who experience severe vasomotor symptoms (hot flashes, cold sweats) do appear at greater risk for developing depressive symptoms and as physical symptoms resolve, mood often returns to baseline (Altshuler et al., 2001; Burt & Hendrick, 2001). Evaluation of a middle-aged woman with affective or other psychological symptoms should include assessment of menstrual patterns, vasomotor symptoms, sexual function, and hormonal levels. Working closely with a woman's gynecologist or primary care physician is optimal for the comprehensive evaluation and treatment of these symptoms. Mild to moderate symptoms may remit with HRT; however, HRT is usually insufficient to treat a major depressive episode and standard psychological and/or pharmacological interventions may be required. The decision regarding use of ERT/HRT is complicated; it must be made individually and on the basis of inadequate data, much as are the decisions regarding pharmacotherapy during the reproductive years. (See Love, 1998; Sherwin, 2001.) Assisting a woman in a risk-benefit analysis and offering alternative and adjunctive treatments (such as diaphragmatic breathing for vasomotor symptoms) is a very valuable role for health professionals.

CONCLUSIONS

This chapter provides an overview of issues involved in gender-specific psychopharmacology in hopes of facilitating practitioners' comprehensive assessment and treatment of women and their development of a useful conceptual framework for incorporating new data as it emerges.

NOTE

Opinions expressed in this chapter are the private views of the author and should not be construed as official views of the Departments of the Army or Defense.

REFERENCES

Altshuler, L. L., Cohen, L. S., Moline, M. L., Kahn, D. A., Carpenter, D., & Docherty, J. P. (2001, March). The Expert Consensus Guideline Series: Treatment of depression in women, 2001. *Postgraduate Medicine: A Special Report*, 5–28.

Altshuler, L. L., Cohen, L., Szuba, M. P., Burt, V. K., Gitlin, M., & Mintz, J. (1996). Pharmacologic management of psychiatric illness during pregnancy: Dilemmas and guidelines. *American Journal of Psychiatry, 153*(5), 592–606.

American Academy of Pediatrics, Committee on Drugs. (2001). The transfer of drugs and others chemicals into human milk. *Pediatrics, 108*(3), 776–789.

Anthony, M., & Berg, M. J. (2002a). Biologic and molecular mechanisms for sex differences in pharmacokinetics, pharmacodynamics, and pharmacogenetics: Part I. *Journal of Women's Health and Gender-Based Medicine, 11*(7), 601–615.

Anthony, M., & Berg, M. J. (2002b). Biologic and molecular mechanisms for sex differences in pharmacokinetics, pharmacodynamics, and pharmacogenetics: Part II. *Journal of Women's Health and Gender-Based Medicine, 11*(7), 617–629.

Arana, G. W., & Rosenbaum, J. F. (2000). *Handbook of psychiatric drug therapy* (4th ed.). Philadelphia: Lippincott, Williams & Wilkins.

Auerback, K. G. (1999). Breastfeeding and maternal medication use. *Journal of Obstetric, Gynecologic, and Neonatal Nursing, 28*(5), 554–563.

Bernhard, L. A. (2001). Lesbian health and health care. *Annual Review of Nursing Research, 19*, 145–177.

Brawman-Mintzer, O., & Yonkers, K. A. (2001). Psychopharmacology in women. In N. L. Stotland & D. E. Stewart (Eds.), *Psychological aspects of women's health care: The interface between psychiatry and obstetrics and gynecology* (2nd ed., pp. 401–420). Washington, DC: American Psychiatric Press.

Burt, V. K., & Hendrick, V. C. (2001). *Concise guide to women's mental health*. Washington, DC: American Psychiatric Press.

Cochran, S. D., Sullivan, J. G., & Mays, V. M. (2003). Prevalence of mental disorders, psychological distress, and mental health services use among lesbian, gay, and bisexual adults in the United States. *Journal of Consulting and Clinical Psychology, 71*(1), 53–61.

Cohen, L. S. (2003, October). *Course and treatment of mood disorders during pregnancy: From clinical lore to reproductive neuroscience.* Paper presented at the Psychopharmacology Conference, Boston.

Cohen, L. S., & Rosenbaum, J. F. (1998). Psychotropic drug use during pregnancy: Weighing the risks. *Journal of Clinical Psychiatry, 59*(Suppl. 2), 337–347.

Doress-Worters, P., with Ditzion, J. (1998). Women growing older. In the Boston Women's Health Book Collective, *Our bodies, ourselves for the new century* (pp. 547–589). New York: Simon & Schuster.

Food and Drug Administration. (1993). Guidelines for the study and evaluation of gender differences in the clinical evaluation of drugs. *Federal Register, 58*(139), 39406–39416.

Gaw, A. C. (2001). *Concise guide to cross-cultural psychiatry.* Washington, DC: American Psychiatric Press.

Hale, T. W. (2002). *Medications and mother's milk* (10th ed.). Amarillo, TX: Pharmasoft.

Hale, T. W., & Ilett, K. F. (2002). *Drug therapy and breastfeeding: From theory to clinical practice.* Washington, DC: Parthenon.

Henshaw, S. K. (1998). Unintended pregnancy in the United States. *Family Planning Perspectives, 30*(1), 24–46.

Jensvold, M. F., Halbreich, U., & Hamilton, J. A. (1996). *Psychopharmacology & women: Sex, gender, & hormones.* Washington, DC: American Psychiatric Press.

Kessler, R. C., McGonagle, K. A., Zhao, S., Nelson, C. B., Hughes, M., Eshleman, S., et al. (1994). Lifetime and 12-month prevalence of *DSM-III-R* psychiatric disorders in the United States: Results from the National Comorbidity Survey. *Archives of General Psychiatry, 51*(1), 8–19.

Love, S. M., with Lindsey, K. (1998). *Dr. Susan Love's hormone book: Making informed choices about menopause.* New York: Times Books.

Matthews, K. A., Shumaker, S. A., Bowen, D. J., Langer, R. D., Hunt, J. R., Kaplan, R. M., et al. (1997). Women's Health Initiative: Why now? What is it? What's new? *American Psychologist, 52*(2), 101–116.

Miller, L. J. (2001). Psychiatric disorders during pregnancy. In N. L. Stotland & D. E. Stewart (Eds.), *Psychological aspects of women's health care: The interface between psychiatry and obstetrics and gynecology* (2nd ed., pp. 51–66). Washington, DC: American Psychiatric Press.

Miller, M. A. (2001). Gender-based differences in the toxicity of pharmaceuticals—the Food and Drug Administration's perspective. *International Journal of Toxicology, 20*, 149–152.

Moore, K. L., & Persaud, T. V. N. (1999). *The developing human: Clinically oriented embryology* (6th ed.). Philadelphia: W. B. Saunders.

Nonacs, R. (2002). Postpartum mood disorders: Diagnosis and treatment considerations. In K. H. Pearson, S. B. Sonawalla, & J. F. Rosenbaum (Eds.), *Women's health and psychiatry* (pp. 127–136). Philadelphia: Lippincott, Williams & Wilkins.

Phelps, L., Brown, R. T., & Power, T. J. (2002). *Pediatric psychopharmacology: Combining medical and psychosocial interventions.* Washington, DC: American Psychological Association.

Sadavoy, J., Lazarus, L. W., Jarvik, L. F., & Grossberg, G. T. (1996). *Comprehensive review of geriatric psychiatry-II* (2nd ed.). Washington, DC: American Psychiatric Press.

Sammons, M. T., & Schmidt, N. B. (2001). *Combined treatments for mental disorders: A guide to psychological and pharmacological interventions.* Washington, DC: American Psychological Association.

Schwartz, J. B. (2001). The evaluation of pharmacologic therapy in humans: A brief summary of the drug evaluation process and guidelines for clinical trials as they relate to women. *Journal of Gender-Specific Medicine, 4*(4), 13–17.

Sherwin, B. B. (2001). Menopause: Myths and realities. In N. L. Stotland & D. E. Stewart (Eds.), *Psychological aspects of women's health care: The interface between psychiatry and obstetrics and gynecology* (2nd ed., pp. 241–260). Washington, DC: American Psychiatric Press.

Stewart, D. E., & Robinson, G. E. (2001). Psychotropic drugs and electroconvulsive therapy during pregnancy and lactation. In N. L. Stotland & D. E. Stewart (Eds.), *Psychological aspects of women's health care: The interface between psychiatry and obstetrics and gynecology* (2nd ed., pp. 67–94). Washington, DC: American Psychiatric Press.

Toot, P. J., Surrey, E. S., & Lu, J. K. H. (1992). The menstrual cycle, ovulation, fertilization, implantation, and the placenta. In N. F. Jacker & J. G. Moore (Eds.), *Essential of obstetrics and gynecology* (pp. 36–51). Philadelphia: W. B. Saunders.

VERONICA M. HERRERA,
MARY P. KOSS,
JENNIFER BAILEY,
NICOLE P. YUAN,
and ERIKA L. LICHTER

Survivors of Male Violence: Research and Training Initiatives to Facilitate Recovery From Depression and Posttraumatic Stress Disorder

48

Violence against women encompasses physical and sexual abuse perpetrated against a woman or female child by persons known or unknown to her, such as spouses, partners, boyfriends, fathers, brothers, acquaintances, or strangers (Saltzman, Fanslow, McMahon, & Shelley, 1999). At least one woman in three globally is beaten, coerced into sex, or otherwise abused in her lifetime (Heise, Ellsberg, & Gottemuller, 1999). Because women represent 85% of the victims of the 1 million incidents of nonfatal intimate assaults that occur each year in the United States (Greenfield et al., 1998), violence is a women's health concern, a human rights issue, and a major public health problem. The present review focuses on two predominant psychological responses among survivors of male violence: depression and posttraumatic stress symptoms. This review summarizes state-of-the-art empirical data documenting the extensiveness of victimization, prevalence of diagnosable depression and posttraumatic stress disorder (PTSD) among survivors, their course and co-occurrence, and mediators and moderators of the traumatic response. The chapter concludes with recommendations to improve mental health care for survivors of male violence.

THE SCOPE OF VIOLENCE AGAINST WOMEN AND ITS IMPACT ON MENTAL HEALTH

Defining Terms

According to the Centers for Disease Control and Prevention (Saltzman et al., 1999), intimate partner violence consists of four categories: physical violence, sexual violence, threat of physical or sexual violence, and psychological/emotional abuse. *Physical violence* involves "punching, shoving, throwing, grabbing, biting, choking, shaking, poking, hair pulling, slapping, hitting, burning, use of a weapon, restraints, or body size and strength against another person." *Sexual violence* involves "physical force to compel a person to engage in a sexual act against his or her will, whether or not the act is completed," attempted or attempted acts with persons unable to decline participation, and abusive sexual contact (Saltzman et al., 1999). *Child sexual abuse* includes noncontact abuse such as modeling of inappropriate sexual behavior, forced involvement in child pornography, or exhibitionism and contact abuse that ranges from fondling to rape.

Adult Survivors of Childhood Sexual Abuse

Prevalence

Because 54% of women reporting rape on the National Violence Against Women Survey (NVAWS) were victimized before the age of 18, the authors conclude that "rape is primarily a crime against youth" (Tjaden & Thoennes, 1998). The national prevalence of childhood sexual abuse, based on retrospective reports, is from about 9% (Saunders, Kilpatrick, Hanson, Resnick, & Walker, 1999) to up to 75% in highly traumatized populations such as women prisoners (Browne, Miller, & Maguin, 1999). Prevalence rates depend on the sample, specific definitions of sexual abuse, and age limit for childhood sexual abuse. However, most estimates converge around 20–30%. Existing data suggest that childhood sexual abuse cuts across social boundaries such as socioeconomic status and race/ethnicity, occurring with nearly equal frequency among various social groups (Finkelhor, 1994).

Studies using detailed, behaviorally specific questions and face-to-face interviewing tend to report higher rates of childhood sexual abuse, as do studies that address high-risk groups of incarcerated or homeless women (Goodman, 1991). Drawing conclusions about the national prevalence of childhood sexual abuse based on questions about rape occurring at any age is problematic because childhood sexual abuse includes many acts that are not rape, such as exhibitionism, fondling, coerced or forced manual stimulation of the perpetrator, or taking pictures of children nude or simulating sex acts. Restricting the definition of child sexual abuse to rape has the impact of reducing its apparent magnitude. It is incorrect to assume that noncontact abuse is less serious or less likely to produce negative effects. Pretrauma characteristics, such as personality variables, influence perceptions and cognitive appraisals of sexual victimization. Thus, the severity of abuse depends in part on to whom it happened to, as well as what happened (Barker-Collo, Melnyk, & McDonald-Miszczak, 2000).

Impact

Childhood sexual abuse has been linked to depression and PTSD, with both retrospective and prospective investigations. Among a sample of sexual abuse victims identified by Child Protective Services, Widom (1999) found that 37.5% met *Diagnostic and Statistical Manual for Mental Disorders* (3rd. rev. ed.; *DSM-III-R*) criteria for lifetime PTSD by young adulthood. A 17-year longitudinal study showed that victims of childhood sexual abuse were significantly more likely to meet criteria for both major depression and PTSD at age 21, with 44% meeting criteria for two or more disorders (Silverman, Reinherz, & Giaconia, 1996). Among women who were raped in childhood, the lifetime rate of PTSD was 32% versus 10% among nonvictimized women. The rate of lifetime depression among survivors was 52% compared to 27% among nonvictimized women (Saunders et al., 1999). The female survivors also experienced elevated risk of current depression and PTSD compared to the nonvictimized women. Similar risks have been reported among samples of medical patients. Women who were severely sexually abused in childhood were 5.3 times as likely to have a lifetime diagnosis of major depression, 3.3 times as likely to experience dysthymia, and 2.8 times as likely to have current depression (Dickinson, de Gruy, Dickinson, & Candib, 1999).

An association between suicidality and child sexual abuse also has been documented. In one study, 22% of sexually abused women reported suicidal ideation in the previous 12-month period compared to 7% of nonabused women. Twenty-six percent of abused women reported at least one suicide attempt by age 21 years compared to 2.4% of nonvictims. These findings must be interpreted with caution because retrospective studies may overestimate the size of relationships between sexual abuse and its outcomes, particularly in clinical or help-seeking samples (Statham et al., 1998). Community samples and student populations, however, identify relatively few severe cases and, therefore, may not adequately capture the most devastating effects of abuse as often encountered among women who are homeless, living in prisons, and/or chronically mentally ill.

Course

Equally disturbing is the evidence that victimization in childhood elevates the risk for repeat victimization. The few longitudinal studies on the course of depression and PTSD suggest that childhood sexual abuse contributes to chronicity (Brown & Moran, 1994), and to increased susceptibility to dissociation among victims with PTSD following sexual revictimization in adulthood (Dancu, Riggs, Hearst-Ikeda, & Shoyer, 1996). There are also reports that the impact of multiple victimization experiences is cumulative, though it has not yet been determined if they are additive or multiplicative (Dickinson et al., 1999).

Mediators and Moderators

Investigators have begun to develop and test hypotheses about the mediators and moderators that translate abuse into psychological distress and other health outcomes. A moderator is a variable that affects the relationship between two variables, changing the direction or magnitude of the effects. Studies have shown that moderators of sexual abuse include characteristics of the abuse experience(s), such as penetration, duration of exposure to abuse, the use of force, and the relatedness of the perpetrator (e.g., Rodriguez, Ryan, Rowan, & Foy, 1996), all of which serve to make abuse experiences more damaging to victims. A mediator, or intervening variable, is a link in a causal chain and transmits the effect from independent to dependent variable. Mediating effects of event-related cognitions and appraisals, such as characterological and behavioral self-blame, have been confirmed (e.g., Andrews, Brewin, Rose, & Kirk, 2000). For example, sexual abuse leads to negative appraisals of the self, which are then associated with emotional distress and social dysfunction. Lastly, giving testimony or being involved in civil litigation is associated with increased PTSD (e.g., Mackey et al., 1992).

Sexual Violence in Adulthood

Incidence and Prevalence

To date, there are many different approaches to obtaining incidence and prevalence rates of sexual violence. Most national data focus on rape, the most severe form of sexual violence. The incidence of rape is the number of new cases occurring in any given year. Several federal sources provide incidence data. For example, the FBI Uniform Crime Report (UCR) provides data representing those rapes that were reported to U.S. law enforcement. In 2001, approximately 90,491 forcible rapes of females were reported (Federal Bureau of Investigation, 2002). These data only hint at the actual occurrence of rape, since just 16% (National Violence Against Women's Survey estimate) to 43% (National Crime Victimization Survey estimate) of all sexual assaults are ever reported. The National Crime Victimization Survey (NCVS), conducted by the Bureau of Justice Statistics, measures incidence of both reported and unreported crime (including rape and sexual assault defined more broadly) from a national sample of households. Critics have asserted that these data underdetect rape because of inherent features of the methodology used to collect them. For example, in 2001 the NCVS projected 83,620 rapes (Bureau of Justice Statistics, 2003), yet this number is lower than the actual number of rapes reported to law enforcement.

A number of national surveys have been designed to improve the detection of sexual assault, including the NVAWS (Tjaden & Thoennes, 1998), the National Women's Study (NWS; Kilpatrick, Edmunds, & Seymour, 1992), and the National Survey of Adolescents (NSA; Kilpatrick & Saunders, 1996). In addition to incidence, these surveys also measured prevalence, which is the percentage of the population affected during a defined period. For example, the NVAWS estimated that 14.8% of adult women in the United States had been raped sometime during their lives and that another 2.8% had been victims of an attempted rape. The NSA estimated that 13% of female adolescents had been victims of sexual assault in their lifetime.

Two understudied areas are the prevalence of women raped within marital or cohabiting relationships (estimated at between 10–14%) and rape rates by ethnicity, socioeconomic status, and other important demographic variables that would permit the delineation of high-risk groups. The sparse data that exist on rape rates by ethnicity suggest that Asian/Pacific Islander women have the lowest reported rates and Native American/Alaskan Native women the highest (Tjaden & Thoennes, 2000). These data and similar studies are difficult to interpret because culture may not only influence the frequency of sexual assault, but also the likelihood of disclosure to an interviewer. Low prevalence rates do not necessarily indicate that violence is less frequent. They may reflect the effects of cultural variables (e.g., norms relating to gender relations and divulgence of sensitive information, acculturation, and language facility) on disclosure. In addition, there is danger in presenting ethnic comparisons that lump all American Indian, Asian, or Hispanic groups together because such comparisons may mask important intragroup differences. Finally, any analysis that fails to control for income may present findings that reflect the influence of poverty rather than culture.

Some authors have argued that the sexual victimization of girls and women is a continuous phenomenon (McCloskey, 1997). In other words, the risks for and effects of sexual victimization may be quite similar across the life span. Many studies examining the impact of victimization have measured both childhood and adulthood sexual victimization and presented data that cannot be disaggregated. Thus, some of the studies presented below could equally have been presented in the preceding section describing the impact of child sexual victimization.

Impact

Rape is considered to be one of the most severe among all types of traumas, and its psychological impact has been extensively researched. Both acute and chronic depressive symptoms have been identified among women who were raped. Frank and Stewart (1984) documented depressive symptoms in 56% of rape survivors one month following the rape, with 43% of the women meeting criteria for major depression. Data from the Los Angeles Epidemiologic Catchment Area Study

suggested that, for women and men combined, sexual assault in either childhood or adulthood resulted in a 2.4 times greater likelihood of major depression compared to matched, nonassaulted controls (Burnam et al., 1988). Female medical patients who had been raped were three times more likely to meet criteria for lifetime major depression, almost twice as likely to qualify for dysthymia, and 2.5 times more likely to report recent depression compared to nonraped women. Age of first victimization appeared to be important because the rate of depression in women sexually assaulted in childhood was 25% compared to 12% among women raped the first time as adults and 6% among women who were never raped (Dickinson et al., 1999).

Lifetime prevalence rates of PTSD range from approximately 24% for women exposed to any trauma (Breslau, Davis, Andreski, & Peterson, 1991) to 65% for women who have experienced a completed rape (Rothbaum, Foa, Riggs, Murdock, & Walsh, 1992). In one study, 31% of all rape survivors developed PTSD at some point during their lifetimes, and they were 6.2 times more likely to suffer from PTSD than women who had never been victims (Kilpatrick et al., 1992). In family practice patients, anxiety disorders, including PTSD, are the class of disorder most strongly associated with victimization. Fifty-six percent of sexually abused and assaulted patients suffered from PTSD compared to 30% of nonvictimized women (Dickinson et al., 1999).

Course

Prospective studies have demonstrated that within two weeks of assault, 90% of rape victims meet symptom criteria for PTSD while 50% continue to meet the criteria three months later (Rothbaum et al., 1992). In a review of the literature, Neville and Heppner (1999) found that the majority of rape survivors suffer an intense psychological reaction immediately following the assault, such as fear, anxiety, self-esteem issues, and sexual dysfunction. Many of these early reactions to rape lessen in approximately two to three months, improving in most rape survivors although not necessarily returning to normal. Approximately one fourth of women who are several years beyond rape continue to experience negative effects (Hanson, 1990).

Mediators and Moderators

Characteristics of the rape attack, such as the use of escalated physical force or weapons, high perceived fear of death, and physical injuries, have all been named as significant moderators that exacerbate psychological distress and disorder (Acierno, Resnick, Kilpatrick, Saunders, & Best, 1999). Previous victimization history, including various forms of attack in childhood and/or adulthood, is also associated with increased depression and longer recovery. In addition, negative social reactions absorb and magnify the effects of rape on PTSD (Ullman & Filipas, 2001). Researchers and clinicians have recently turned attention to the processes that transform rape into deleterious outcomes and contribute to the persistence of chronic symptoms. When combined in a structural model framework, the most powerful class of mediators in accounting for the physical, social, and psychological consequences of rape were social cognitions including self-blame and core beliefs about self and others such as esteem, trust, power, and vulnerability. Past exposure to violence and the behavioral impact of these experiences also contributed to shaping distress (Koss, Figueredo, & Prince, 2002).

Physical Violence in Adulthood

Incidence and Prevalence

Each year about 10–15% of U.S. women, approximately 2 million persons, are abused by their intimate partners and 4% sustain assaults serious enough that they could or did produce injury (Tjaden & Thoennes, 1998). (It is important to note that neither the UCR nor the NCVS provides separate reporting for intimate assault; instead it is folded into the numbers for simple and aggravated assault.) The yearly incidence among women patients seen in primary care is 16–26% compared to a national average of 12% (reviewed in Hamby & Koss, 2004). And, lifetime prevalence of intimate assault among women seeking medical care is 6–30%. The Conflict Tactics Scale (CTS; Straus, 1979) is the most commonly used assessment tool to measure partner violence among women. This scale has several limitations, including lack of attention to context and temporal sequence of violence, insensitivity to high frequencies of ongoing abuse, equation of serious physical with minimal verbal forms of aggression, and absence of a scoring procedure that addresses women's general tendency to endorse a higher number of items than men on psychological assessments. As a result, the CTS creates an artifactual, but robust finding that women are just as violent as men.

Research in the area suggests that both poverty and ethnicity may play a role in intimate violence. For example, Russo, Denious, Keita, and Koss (1997) found that partner violence increases as income levels decrease. Findings from the NVAWS documented different rates of partner assault by ethnicity: 21.3% among Whites, 26.3% among African Americans, 27% among persons of "mixed race," 12.8% among Asian Pacific Islanders, and 30.7% among American Indian/Alaska Natives (Tjaden & Thoennes, 2000). As mentioned earlier, these statistics must be interpreted with caution since poverty and race are often confounded. Some cultures may have mores that preclude disclosure of partner violence.

Impact

Depression is prevalent among women who experience partner violence. It is one of the strongest factors that distinguish abused women from nonabused women (Orava, McLeod, & Sharpe, 1996). A meta-analysis of 18 studies on depression and intimate violence calculated that the mean prevalence rate of depression among battered women was 48% (Golding, 1999), with studies showing a range from 39% to 83%. Prevalence rates vary across studies depending on assessment tools and sample characteristics (e.g., living situation). Women who access services specifically for domestic violence report moderate to severe levels of depressive symptoms and experience higher levels of distress compared to women who are maritally distressed (Cascardi & O'Leary, 1992).

The mental health consequences of physical abuse appear to go beyond depression. Several studies have found that battered women suffer from a range of symptoms, such as hyperarousal, nightmares, anxiety, fear, and sleep and eating disorders (Saunders, 1994). They often experience intrusive memories of the abuse and they tend to avoid reminders of the violence. As a result, PTSD has become the main psychiatric diagnosis associated with partner violence. Rates of PTSD in battered women range from 31% to 84%; a meta-analysis of 11 studies of PTSD in battered women found a mean prevalence of 64% (Golding, 1999). Measurement, however, is also a primary concern when diagnosing PTSD among battered women. Self-report measures tend to document higher rates of PTSD than structured interviews, but structured interviews are more accurate and consistent in diagnosing PTSD (Houskamp & Foy, 1991).

Whereas most studies on battered women's mental health assess *either* PTSD symptoms *or* depression, only a few studies have considered both diagnoses. Among existing studies, only two examined the co-occurrence of PTSD and depression (Cascardi, O'Leary, & Schlee, 1999). The findings indicate that PTSD and depression are correlated, but not necessarily co-occurring among physically abused women. Cascardi and colleagues (1999) found that 30% of their sample met the criteria for PTSD, 32% met the criteria for depression, and 17% met the criteria for both. Their results indicate different predictors for experiencing PTSD and depression. Both PTSD and depressive symptoms were related to intensity of husband to wife physical aggression. PTSD symptoms alone were associated with spouse's dominance/isolation tactics, while depressive symptoms were related to marital discord. Women with comorbid depression and PTSD and women with PTSD alone reported higher levels of spousal fear and physical aggression compared to women with depression or neither disorder. Although the authors suggest a distinct difference between PTSD and depression diagnoses, the question remains equivocal (Golding, 1999).

The behavioral impacts of partner abuse are similar to rape, made more salient by the significant overlap of these forms of victimization, including an increased risk for suicide (Thompson, Kaslow, & Kingree, 2002). Among women who are in violent relationships, depression, drug abuse, hopelessness, and history of childhood abuse or neglect all increase the likelihood of suicide attempts (Thompson et al., 2002). The risk of suicide attempts for women with two, three, and four, or five of these risk factors, compared to women with no risk factors, was elevated 10, 25, and 107 times, respectively.

Course

A dose-response relationship exists between battering and mental health symptoms. As the severity and frequency of violence increase, the severity of depression and PTSD also increases (Cascardi et al., 1999). Ongoing abuse is particularly potent in maintaining depressive symptom severity. Once a battered woman is away from the abusive environment, her symptoms often decrease. We are unaware of any longitudinal studies of PTSD in battered women.

Mediators and Moderators

Whether or not a battered woman develops depression or PTSD may depend on several variables, one of which is the severity of the abuse. In addition, psychological and sexual abuse within a physically violent relationship increases depressive symptoms above and beyond the effects of physical abuse (Orava et al., 1996). Women who are exposed to violence for a long duration are more likely to develop symptoms of PTSD than women who experience shorter exposure (Houskamp & Foy, 1991). A woman's experiences with childhood abuse also place her at elevated risk for mental health problems if she is battered. In addition, battered women who have low levels of social support are more likely to develop major depressive disorder or PTSD (Campbell, Kub, Belknap, & Templin, 1997). The provision of social support has been shown to reduce PTSD among battered women (Sullivan & Bybee, 1999). Specifically, battered women who had advocates to help them access services, such as financial assistance or employment counseling, scored significantly lower in PTSD at follow-up compared to a control group who received standard shelter services.

RESPONSES TO THE MENTAL HEALTH NEEDS OF VIOLENCE SURVIVORS: CURRENT CLINICAL PRACTICE

Female survivors of violence are everywhere—in our families and religious institutions, the criminal justice system, the welfare system, prisons, psychiatric hospitals, medical populations, and the military. Many of these women have recovered from their victimization using their own support systems and personal resources. But as the foregoing review establishes, the mental health toll of violence on female victims is high. It was recognized over a decade ago that radical changes in traditional medical care would be necessary to meet the needs of victimized women. In 1991, Surgeon General Koop challenged health providers to address the issues of violence (cited in Stark, 2001). In the early 1990s, our major health organizations, including the American Medical Association, Joint Commission on Accreditation of Healthcare Organizations, American College of Obstetrics and Gynecology, and the American Academy of Pediatries, all recommended polices and procedures for identifying, treating, and referring victims of abuse (Stark, 2001). Common features of these recommendations was the development of emergency room protocols that outline steps to be taken to provide appropriate care for violence victims and standard screening procedures of all female patients who enter the health-care system through its major portals including emergency services, obstetric, pediatric, mental health, and primary-care services.

Despite significant organizational encouragement, change has been disappointing. Formal policies and procedures remain slow to appear in primary-care settings (for a review, see Koss, Ingram, & Pepper, 1997). For example, 80% of hospitals in a Massachusetts survey had no written protocol and 585 of the hospitals reported that they identified fewer than 5 domestic violence patients per month (Stark, 2001). And, even when a protocol is in place, the results are not encouraging. One study found that the establishment of a protocol to identify victims of partner violence in an emergency department increased the rates of identification of domestic violence cases five to six times compared to standard practice informal record keeping. However, when the same emergency department was studied 10 years later to determine whether screening continued, identification had fallen to pre-training levels (McLeer & Anwar, 1989). Even when on-site referral services were available, researchers found that 79% of providers did not increase their screening practices (McKibben, Hauf, Must, & Roberts, 2000).

Barriers to Routine Screening and Ways to Improve Compliance

Barriers to screening include provider characteristics, especially lack of education about violence against women, fear of offending the patient, and the erroneous belief that there are no effective interventions. There are also barriers attributed to infrastructure factors, including lack of time, and patient factors, such as the decision not to disclose to the provider even if asked directly (Waalan, Goodwin, Spitz, Petersen, & Saltzman, 2000). The most successful approach to increasing screening rates is a system intervention (Salber & McCaw, 2000) that involves training with a simple protocol for screening and responding, an on-site resource for identified cases, medical records audit with quarterly feedback at the department level on their rates of screening, and prompts such as posters and cards, some asking "Did you screen?" As an integrated approach, this method has been shown to double the rates of screening, especially due to the use of posters and on-site specialized responders. An excellent measurement tool of provider attitudes, beliefs, and behaviors is available (Maiuro et al., 2000). Comparisons of providers who were exposed to workshops, journal articles, and other experiences to a control group of providers showed positive changes in overcoming barriers following intervention. However, other investigations have found increases in screening rates following systematic training that while clinically significant, lacked practical significance (i.e., documentation in charts rose from 3.5% to 21%; Thompson et al., 2000). Thus, the authors recommended abandoning attempts to modify the behavior of providers and moving toward written screening.

Patient Preferences in Screening and Reporting

Although health-care providers may be hesitant to ask about abuse, research has indicated that the majority of women favor routine inquiry about physical and sexual assault and believe that health-care professionals can be helpful. When asked their opinions about screening, 86% of women patients agreed that screening would make it easier to get help and 96% said they would be glad if someone showed interest. However, African American women were twice as likely as other women to feel that women who were not being abused would be insulted and feared it might put abused women at risk. Nevertheless, African American women agreed that screening would make it easier to get help. In recent years, 14 states have passed legislation requiring mandatory reporting to criminal justice when domestic abuse is disclosed (Gielen et al., 2000). Surveys of attitudes toward mandatory reporting reveal that more than half (54%) of abused women preferred to make the choice themselves whether or not to report to law enforcement; two thirds thought requiring physicians to report abuse would make women less likely to disclose, and half thought it put them in danger from the abuser. Clearly, these policies demand careful evaluation for unintended negative effects.

Accessibility of Services

Are survivors accessing appropriate mental health services? Patients with depression were found less likely to be screened for violence (16%) than patients with chronic pelvic pain (21%; Thompson et al., 2000). And, the care received by victims of violence is strongly biomedically focused. For example, abused, depressed women were much *less* likely to receive outpatient mental health care than to be treated with biomedically oriented approaches targeting physical problems (Scholle, Rost, & Golding, 1998). And, outpatient mental health care was the one service that victimized women indicated was most difficult to access.

The most visible and accessible source of help for physical and sexual assault in most communities are centers against sexual assault, family agencies, and domestic violence shelters. These agencies offer a comprehensive menu of services including advocacy, prevention education, group and individual counseling (Renzetti, Edleson, & Bergen, 2001). In addition to counseling provided by these centers, the routine duties of advocates for survivors involve finding resources and facilitating referrals to the formal mental health system. However, lack of funding for these services severely limits their options. On their own, survivors of male violence are unlikely to contact mental health assistance. Even when mental health care was offered as a covered benefit and provided on the work site, only 9% of physical and sexual assault survivors utilized it (Koss, Woodruff, & Koss, 1991). Another obstacle to reaching out for help is that survivors of male violence fear their credibility will be questioned or they will be partly blamed for what happened to them. For example, most rape survivors who had contacted legal or medical services experienced two or more responses that left them feeling revictimized (Campbell et al., 1999). In contrast, the majority of rape survivors in another sample who utilized the mental health system, rape crisis centers, and their clergy perceived their services as healing and beneficial (Campbell, Wasco, Ahrens, Sefl, & Barnes, 2001).

A number of manual-based, empirically validated therapies for treating rape are also available (e.g., Foa, Keane, & Friedman, 2000). Solomon and Johnson (2002) recently published a practice-friendly review of outcome research for psychosocial treatment of PTSD. However, a recent analysis of the National Comorbidity Survey (1990–1992) found service-seeking behaviors by sexual assault victims was lower among those with less education who were members of ethnic minority groups, lower social support, and poor or no access to medical insurance coverage. In addition, survivors in need of mental health care must contend with double stigmas—the stigma of being an intimate violence victim and the stigma of experiencing emotional problems. Finding ways to make services more accessible and reducing stigma would help, but these efforts will fall short unless survivors can identify mental health symptoms and are aware of their treatment options. For example, the highly disseminated Depression Screening Day initiative could make more explicit links between depression and living with current or past experiences of violence. Despite the foregoing comments, it is important to recognize that diverse groups living in the United States do not equally value seeking formal psychotherapy (Bletzer & Koss, 2004). For example, rape victims in some American Indian tribes prefer to speak to horizontal kin including sisters and cousins. Likewise, relatively unacculturated Mexican American rape victims confide in their mothers. Only Anglos spontaneously spoke with people outside their family about sexual victimization.

Recommendations to Improve Response to Victimized Women

Numerous policy recommendations have been made to improve response to victimized women (e.g., Heise et al., 1999; Kilpatrick, Resnick, & Acierno, 1997; Koss et al., 1994; Koss et al., 1997). We believe that the weight of findings reviewed earlier support the following implications for service delivery and mental health policy.

1. *Reference victimization in campaigns that attempt to de-stigmatize mental illness.* Any plan to reduce the stigma of mental illness should address the subject of victimization, one of the major etiologies of psychological distress among women.
2. *Design prevention strategies that aim to limit the damage of victimization.* Primary prevention aims to prevent victimization for FROM occurring in the first place. Although prevention education programs can provide women and girls with skills that might reduce risks, stopping sexual abuse, rape, and battering depends on reaching potential perpetrators. Women and girls may be helped by secondary prevention that aims to reduce the impact of victimization that has already occurred. A fruitful avenue may be media campaigns that model supportive response to those disclosing sexual and physical abuse and encourage seeking help among whose victimization has not been disclosed to any system of care in the community. Such interventions might eliminate some of the nega-

tive social support victims receive, such as people who feel rape victims should just snap back, or think that victims who were drinking deserved what happened to them. It is well known that negative support is much more powerful in predicting distress than positive support. For example, a recent ad campaign in Arizona targeted sexual assault and focused on influencing the public to "believe her." The public service television ads resulted in a one-third increase in calls to sexual assault services (Machelor, 2002).

3. *Incorporate links with violence into the Depression Screening Day initiative.* Such linkage would help women tie their feelings to environmental causes and establish mental health services as an avenue to heal the consequences of victimization.
4. *Forge links between the formal mental health system and community-based services.* Many survivors are served by specialized sexual assault and battered women community agencies that are available to individuals who are unable to pay. We call upon the mental health system to forge links with these agencies and develop models for providing consultation and training in these settings. Also, we need to continue work to develop services that are culturally competent, recognizing the intersections of culturally based knowledge, coping strategies, and resources for the woman living with violence.
5. *Use system approaches to develop screening and treatment protocols, increase training of psychological service providers, and monitor adherence to recommended practices with violence survivors.* Routine screening should be conducted in a wide range of settings including mental health and substance-abuse treatment centers and health-care delivery sites (Kilpatrick et al., 1997). Using a short self-administered survey of experiences with violence rather than depending on provider-administered questions might result in higher compliance rates. Training initiatives embedded in a coordinated system intervention could establish violence as a potential etiology of depression. Such a strategy might increase the likelihood that women will have the opportunity to discuss this vital subject

within the medical arena. Many primary care providers are experienced in addressing issues of grief and loss and they receive special training in the identification of depression. Involving health-care providers provides a means of identifying and educating patients who could benefit from mental health care for their victimization related aftereffects. Because of the interrelationships of mental and physical symptoms, many people seek medical care before they consider the potential that mental health care could help them.

6. *Increase the accessibility of the formal mental health system.* This recommendation emphasizes the need to make mental health care accessible and affordable. Lack of insurance coverage is an identified barrier for victimized women and initiatives to achieve universal coverage with parity for mental and physical health care are needed to remove them.

7. *Initiate research studies to evaluate victimization-specific interventions for seriously mentally ill populations.* Given the prevalence and impact of trauma among individuals with severe mental illness, exposure to violence is a serious public mental health concern for this population. Future directions should include controlled clinical trials under conditions of routine care and widespread implementation of evidence-based interventions (Rosenberg et al., 2001).

CONCLUSIONS

Although we have achieved a greater understanding of the prevalence and consequences of violence against women, many issues in this area have not been adequately addressed. As women continue to be victims of physical and sexual abuse in our society, we must challenge ourselves, as researchers, health-care professionals, policy makers, and community members, to avoid further revictimization of survivors, highlight the responsibilities of perpetrators, and develop collaborative services that address the diverse needs of female survivors in the United States. This chapter has outlined several avenues for such future endeavors.

REFERENCES

Acierno, R., Resnick, H., Kilpatrick, D. G., Saunders, B., & Best, C. L. (1999). Risk factors for rape, physical assault, and posttraumatic stress disorder in women: Examination of differential multivariate relationships. *Journal of Anxiety Disorders, 13,* 541–563.

Andrews, B., Brewin, C. R., Rose, S., & Kirk, M. (2000). Predicting PTSD symptoms in victims of violent crime: The role of shame, anger, and childhood abuse. *Journal of Abnormal Psychology, 109,* 69–73.

Barker-Collo, S. L., Melnyk, W. T., & McDonald-Miszczak, L. (2000). A cognitive-behavioral model of post-traumatic stress for sexually abused females. *Journal of Interpersonal Violence, 15,* 375–392.

Bletzer, K. V., & Koss, M. P. (2004). Narrative constructions of sexual violence as told by female rape survivors in three populations of the southwestern United States: Scripts of coercion, scripts of consent. *Medical Anthropology, 23,* 113–157.

Breslau, N., Davis, G., Andreski, P., & Peterson, E. (1991). Traumatic events and posttraumatic stress disorder in an urban population of young adults. *Archives of General Psychiatry, 48,* 216–222.

Brown, G. W., & Moran, P. (1994). Clinical and psychosocial origins of chronic depressive episodes: I. A community survey. *British Journal of Psychiatry, 165,* 447–456.

Browne, A., Miller, B., & Maguin, E. (1999). Prevalence and severity of lifetime physical and sexual victimization among incarcerated women. *International Journal of Law and Psychiatry, 22,* 301–322.

Bureau of Justice Statistics. (2003). *Criminal Victimization in the United States, 2001 Statistical Tables* (NCJ-197064). Washington, DC: U.S. Department of Justice.

Burnam, M. A., Stein, J. A., Golding, J. M., Siegel, J. M., Sorenson, S. B., Forsythe, A. B., et al. (1988). Sexual assault and mental disorders in a community population. *Journal of Consulting & Clinical Psychology, 56,* 843–850.

Campbell, J. C., Kub, J., Belknap, R. A., & Templin, T. N. (1997). Predictors of depression in battered women. *Violence Against Women, 3,* 271–293.

Campbell, R., Sefl, T., Barnes, H. E., Ahrens, C. E., Wasco, S. M., & Zaragoza-Diesfeld, Y. (1999). Community services for rape survivors: Enhancing psychological well-being or increasing trauma? *Journal of Consulting and Clinical Psychology, 67,* 847–858.

Campbell, R., Wasco, S. M., Ahrens, C. E., Sefl, T., & Barnes, H. E. (2001). Preventing the "second rape": Rape survivors' experiences with community service providers. *Journal of Interpersonal Violence, 16,* 1239–1259.

Cascardi, M., & O'Leary, K. D. (1992). Depressive symptomatology, self-esteem, and self-blame in battered women. *Journal of Family Violence, 7,* 249–259.

Cascardi, M., O'Leary, K. D., & Schlee, K. A. (1999). Co-occurrence and correlates of posttraumatic stress disorder and major depression in physically abused women. *Journal of Family Violence, 14,* 227–249.

Dancu, C. V., Riggs, D. S., Hearst-Ikeda, D., & Shoyer, B. G. (1996). Dissociative experiences and post-traumatic stress disorder among female victims of criminal assault and rape. *Journal of Traumatic Stress, 9,* 253–267.

Dickinson, L. M., de Gruy, F. V., III, Dickinson, W. P., & Candib, L. M. (1999). Health-related quality of life and symptom profiles of female survivors of sexual abuse in primary care. *Archives of Family Medicine, 8,* 35–43.

Federal Bureau of Investigation. (2002). *Crime in the United States 2001 Uniform Crime Reports.* Washington, DC: U.S. Department of Justice.

Finkelhor, D. (1994). Current information on the scope and nature of sexual abuse. *The Future of Children, 4,* 31–53.

Foa, E. B., Keane, T. M., & Friedman, M. J. (Eds.). (2000). *Effective treatment in PTSD: Practice guidelines from the International Society for Traumatic Stress Studies.* New York: Guilford Press.

Frank, E., & Stewart, B. D. (1984). Depressive symptoms in rape victims: A revisit. *Journal of Affective Disorders, 7,* 77–82.

Gielen, A. C., O'Campo, P. J., Campbell, J. C., Schollenberger, J., Woods, A. B., Jones, A. S., et al. (2000). Women's opinions about domestic violence screening and mandatory reporting. *American Journal of Preventive Medicine, 19,* 279–285.

Golding, J. M. (1999). Intimate partner violence as a risk factor for mental disorders: A meta-analysis. *Journal of Family Violence, 14,* 99–132.

Goodman, L. A. (1991). The prevalence of abuse among homeless and housed poor mothers: A comparison study. *American Journal of Orthopsychiatry, 61,* 163–169.

Greenfield, L. A., Rand, M. R., Craven, D., Klaus, P. A., Perkins, C. A., Ringel, C., et al. (1998). *Violence by intimates: Analysis of data on crimes by current or former spouses, boyfriends, and girlfriends* (NCJ-167237). Washington, DC: U.S. Department of Justice.

Hamby, S. L., & Koss, M. P. (2004). The epidemiological debate: Prevalence, risk factors, and consequences of violence against women. In J. M. Liebschutz, S. M. Frayne, & G. Saxe (Eds.), *Violence against women: A physician's guide to identification and management* (pp. 3–38). Philadelphia: ACP-ASIM Press.

Hanson, R. K. (1990). The psychological impact of sexual assault on women and children: A review. *Annals of Sex Research, 3,* 187–232.

Heise, L., Ellsberg, M., & Gottemuller, M. (1999). Ending violence against women (*Population Reports,* Series L, No. 11, 1–43). Baltimore: Johns Hopkins University School of Public Health, Population Information Program.

Houskamp, B. M., & Foy, D. W. (1991). The assessment of posttraumatic stress disorder in battered women. *Journal of Interpersonal Violence, 6,* 367–375.

Kilpatrick, D. G., Edmunds, C., & Seymour, A. (1992). *Rape in America: A report to the nation.* Charleston: National Victims Center & the Crime Victims Research and Treatment Center, Medical University of South Carolina.

Kilpatrick, D. G., Resnick, H. S., & Acierno, R. (1997). Health impact of interpersonal violence: III. Implications for clinical practice and public policy. *Behavioral Medicine, 23*(2), 79–85.

Kilpatrick, D. G., & Saunders, B. E. (1996). *Prevalence and consequences of child victimization: Results from the National Survey of Adolescents.* Washington, DC: U.S. Department of Justice, Office of Justice Programs.

Koss, M. P., Figueredo, A. J., & Prince, R. J. (2002). A cognitive mediational model of rape's mental, physical, and social health impact: Preliminary specification and evaluation in cross-sectional data. *Journal of Consulting and Clinical Psychology, 70,* 926–941.

Koss, M. P., Goodman, L. A., Browne, A., Fitzgerald, L. F., Keita, G. P., & Russo, N. F. (1994). *No safe haven: Male violence against women at home, at work, and in the community.* Washington, DC: American Psychological Association.

Koss, M. P., Ingram, M., & Pepper, S. (1997). Psychotherapists' role in the medical response to male-partner violence. *Psychotherapy, 34,* 386–396.

Koss, M. P., Woodruff, W. J., & Koss, P. G. (1991). Criminal victimization among primary care medical patients: Prevalence, incidence, and physician usage. *Behavioral Sciences & the Law, 9,* 85–96.

Machelor, P. (2002, April 14). Sex assault crisis center facing crunch [electronic version]. *Arizona Daily Star,* p. B1.

Mackey, T., Sereika, S. M., Weissfeld, L. A., Hacker, S. S., Zender, J. F., & Heard, S. L. (1992). Factors associated with long-term depressive symptoms of sexual assault victims. *Archives of Psychiatric Nursing, 6,* 10–25.

Maiuro, R. D., Vitaliano, P. P., Sugg, N. K., Thompson, D. C., Rivara, F. P., & Thompson, R. S. (2000). Development of a health care provider survey for domestic violence: Psychometric properties. *American Journal of Preventive Medicine, 19,* 245–252.

McCloskey, L. A. (1997). The continuum of harm: Girls and women at risk for sexual abuse across the lifespan. In D. Cicchetti & S. Toth (Eds.), *Rochester symposium on developmental psychopathology, vol. 8: Developmental perspectives on trauma: Theory, research, and intervention* (pp. 553–578). Rochester, NY: University of Rochester Press.

McKibben, V., Hauf, A. C., Must, A., & Roberts, E. L. (2000). Role of victims' screening services on improving violence screening by trained maternal and child health-care providers, Boston, Massachusetts, 1994–1995. *MMWR Morbidity and Mortality Weekly Report, 49,* 114–117.

McLeer, S. V., & Anwar, R. (1989). A study of battered women presenting in an emergency department. *American Journal of Public Health, 79,* 65–66.

Neville, H. A., & Heppner, M. J. (1999). Contextualizing rape: Reviewing sequelae and proposing a culturally inclusive ecological model of sexual assault recovery. *Applied & Preventative Psychology, 8,* 41–62.

Orava, T. A., McLeod, P. J., & Sharpe, D. (1996). Perceptions of control, depressive symptomatology, and self-esteem of women in transition from abusive relationships. *Journal of Family Violence, 11,* 167–186.

Renzetti, C., Edleson, J., & Bergen, R. (2001). *Sourcebook on violence against women.* Thousand Oaks, CA: Sage.

Rodriguez, N., Ryan, S. W., Rowan, A. B., & Foy, D. W. (1996). Posttraumatic stress disorder in a clinical sample of adult survivors of childhood sexual abuse. *Child Abuse & Neglect, 20,* 943–952.

Rosenberg, S. D., Mueser, K. T., Friedman, M. J., Gorman, P. G., Drake, R. E., Vidaver, R. M., et al. (2001). Developing effective treatments for posttraumatic disorders among people with severe mental illness. *Psychiatric Services, 52,* 1453–1461.

Rothbaum, B. O., Foa, E. B., Riggs, D. S., Murdock, T., & Walsh, W. (1992). A prospective examination of posttraumatic stress disorder in rape victims. *Journal of Traumatic Stress, 5,* 455–475.

Russo, N. F., Denious, J. E., Keita, G. P., & Koss, M. P. (1997). Intimate violence and Black women's health. *Women's Health: Research on Gender, Behavior, and Policy, 3,* 315–348.

Salber, P. R., & McCaw, B. (2000). Barriers to screening for intimate partner violence: Time to reframe the question. *American Journal of Preventive Medicine, 19,* 276–278.

Saltzman, L. E., Fanslow, J. L., McMahon, P. M., & Shelley, G. A. (1999). *Intimate partner violence surveillance uniform definitions and recommended data elements. Version 1.0.* Atlanta, GA: Centers for Disease Control and Prevention, National Center for Injury Prevention and Control.

Saunders, B. E., Kilpatrick, D. G., Hanson, R. F., Resnick, H. S., & Walker, M. E. (1999). Prevalence, case characteristics, and long-term psychological correlates of child rape among women: A national survey. *Child Maltreatment, 4,* 187–200.

Saunders, D. G. (1994). Posttraumatic stress symptom profiles of battered women: A comparison of survivors in two settings. *Violence & Victims, 9,* 31–44.

Scholle, S. H., Rost, K. M., & Golding, J. M. (1998). Physical abuse among depressed women. *Journal of General Internal Medicine, 13,* 607–613.

Silverman, A. B., Reinherz, H. Z., & Giaconia, R. M. (1996). The long-term sequelae of child and adolescent abuse: A longitudinal community study. *Child Abuse & Neglect, 20,* 709–723.

Solomon, S. D., & Johnson, D. M. (2002). Psychosocial treatment of posttraumatic stress disorder: A practice-friendly review of outcome research. *Journal of Clinical Psychology, 58,* 947–959.

Stark, E. (2001). Health intervention with battered women: From crisis intervention to complex social prevention. In C. M. Renzetti, J. L. Edleson, & R. K. Bergen (Eds.), *Sourcebook on violence against women* (pp. 345–370). Thousand Oaks, CA: Sage.

Statham, D. J., Heath, A. C., Madden, P. A. F., Bucholz, K. K., Beirut, L., Dinwiddie, S. H., et al. (1998). Suicidal behaviour: An epidemiological and genetic study. *Psychological Medicine, 28,* 839–855.

Straus, M. A. (1979). Measuring intrafamily conflict and violence: The conflict tactics scales. *Journal of Marriage & the Family, 41,* 75–88.

Sullivan, C. M., & Bybee, D. I. (1999). Reducing violence using community-based advocacy for women with abusive partners. *Journal of Consulting and Clinical Psychology, 67,* 43–53.

Thompson, M. P., Kaslow, N. J., & Kingree, J. B. (2002). Risk factors for suicide attempts among African American women experiencing recent intimate partner violence. *Violence & Victims, 17,* 283–295.

Thompson, R. S., Rivara, F. P., Thompson, D. C., Barlow, W. E., Sugg, N. K., Maiuro, R. D., et al. (2000). Identification and management of domestic violence: A randomized trial. *American Journal of Preventive Medicine, 19,* 253–263.

Tjaden, P., & Thoennes, N. (1998). Prevalence, incidence, and consequences of violence against women: Findings from the National Violence Against Women Survey. *Research in Brief.* Washington, DC: National Institute of Justice, U.S. Department of Justice.

Tjaden, P., & Thoennes, N. (2000). *Extent, nature, and consequences of intimate partner violence. Findings from the National Violence Against Women Survey* (NCJ-18167). Washington, DC: U.S. Government Printing Office.

Ullman, S. E., & Filipas, H. H. (2001). Predictors of PTSD symptom severity and social reactions in sexual assault victims. *Journal of Traumatic Stress, 14,* 369–389.

Waalan, J., Goodwin, M. M., Spitz, A. M., Petersen, R., & Saltzman, L. E. (2000). Screening for intimate partner violence by health care providers: Barriers and interventions. *American Journal of Preventive Medicine, 19,* 230–237.

Widom, C. S. (1999). Posttraumatic stress disorder in abused and neglected children grown up. *American Journal of Psychiatry, 156,* 1223–1229.

Although the connection between social policy and individual psychological health is rarely transparent, a woman's psychological development is likely to be shaped not only by intrinsic factors (biological and biographical) but also by various aspects of the social and cultural context, including social institutions such as the government (Zigler and Finn-Stevenson, 1996). In modern societies, including the United States, government actions—whether through raising revenues, spending public funds, or regulating private behavior—influence almost every aspect of life. The design of public policy, both what it includes and what it does not include, is likely to have important consequences for the development and maintenance of well-being in girls and women.

In practice, the connections between public policy and women's psychological health are rarely simple. In this chapter, we provide an overview of public policy and its limitations, describe the problems of policy design in two general areas, and illustrate the design dilemmas in more detail in situations of particular importance to girls' and women's psychological health.

SHERRY GLIED
and SHARON KOFMAN

An Overview of Policies That Impact the Psychological Well-Being of Girls and Women

49

PUBLIC POLICY: ITS FUNCTIONS AND LIMITATIONS

Public policy is a general term that describes all government actions, whether federal, state, or local. Public policy includes distributive, regulatory, and redistributive policies (Lowi, 1972). The latter two forms will be our focus. Distributive policies are those that provide goods available to all, such as parks or national defense. Regulatory policies are government-established limits on private actions. Redistributive policies are those that use the government's taxation and spending authority to change the distribution of resources among people.

The process of translating policy problems—including problems of importance to women's psychological health—into policy proposals of any of these types is inevitably complicated. Public policy occurs through politics. Politicians make decisions based on public opinion, interest group pressure, and arguments colored by values rather than facts. Policy makers almost always balance competing imperatives as they design and implement policy. The provision of goods or services through distribution or redistribution rarely occurs without affecting the behavior of recipients, often in ways that are less than desirable. Regulatory policy imposes costs on the private sector. Optimally designed policy can correct underlying problems without generating new costs, but in practice, policy is rarely so precisely calibrated.

Further obstacles arise in designing policy that responds to the specific needs of girls and women. Public policies are usually intended to be gender-neutral. Yet women and men may experience different consequences of the same policy because their social and economic circumstances differ. These differences are continually changing, reflecting the evolution of gender and parenting roles, the changing nature of work, and changing sociopolitical attitudes. Policy that seeks to address the needs of girls and women may, wittingly or unwittingly, create incentives that promote or restrain traditional gender roles.

REGULATORY POLICY—UNINTENDED CONSEQUENCES

Regulatory policy encompasses a broad range of interventions. Criminal justice policies, for example, safeguard people from deliberate actions that might impede their ability to conduct their lives and to profit from their own endeavors. A considerable literature emphasizes gender-specific aspects of criminal law, particularly law concerning sexual and domestic violence (see, e.g., Buzawa & Buzawa, 2003). Much of criminal law, however, is relatively gender-neutral in both intent and effect. The existence of a reasonable criminal law (and the police power and legal system that enforce it) gives women more security in conducting their lives and, thus, may contribute directly or indirectly to their psychological health.

Other government regulations affect the safety of the air we breathe, the water we drink, the products we purchase, the jobs at which we work, the food we eat, the cars we drive, the highways we drive on, and so on. In general, these policies intend to protect the population as a whole. They may, however, have differential effects on women and men because of physiological or circumstan-

tial differences between the genders. There is controversy, for example, about whether standards for occupational safety should make particular allowances for women of reproductive age because of concerns that hazards have teratogenic effects (Bertin, 1998). In a very different context, there are concerns that automobile airbag standards, which were designed based on the height and weight of the average man, are inappropriate for women who are typically shorter and lighter (Insurance Institute for Highway Safety, 1998).

The impacts of regulatory policies on well-being may be both intended and unintended. Policies such as these intend to improve physical health and safety, which may be correlated with psychological health. But protective regulatory policies may also have indirect negative effects on psychological health. Harsh criminal laws may ultimately limit rather than enhance freedom. Safety regulations typically increase the costs of production and may price women out of the market for some goods and services they desire. Protections that have disparate impacts on women may also narrow the range of economic opportunities available to them. The effects of regulatory policies also often depend on how they are combined with distributive and redistributive policies. For example, rights to reproductive health services are not very meaningful unless women have the means to obtain such services.

We next examine how the unintended consequences and the links between redistributive and regulatory policy play out in two areas of regulatory focus that affect women's psychological health: parental leave and child care.

Family and Medical Leave— The Cost of Opportunity

By the early 1990s, every industrialized country except the United States had a provision for maternity leave, often paid. Such policies respond to a clear need related to women's and children's psychological health. Epidemiological research has documented the vulnerability of women to distress and psychiatric disorder during the postpartum period (Glied and Kofman, 1995). Breakthroughs in developmental science and brain research confirm the important role of parenting, and the importance of time for women to bond with their babies in the early postnatal period (Coates, 2003; Hofer, 2003). A burgeoning research underscores the important role of the early caregiving relationship and of maternal psychological well-being on child health (Aber, Jones, & Cohen, 2000; Kamerman, 2000; Shonkoff & Phillips, 2000).

President Clinton's first legislative action, signing the Family and Medical Leave Act (FMLA) of 1993, extended some leave benefits to American workers. The law requires private employers with 50 or more workers and public employers to offer a job-protected family or medical leave of up to 12 weeks to qualifying employees (those who have worked at least 1,250 hours in the previous 12 months). The benefits are available to employees (women or men) who are absent from work for birth, adoption, or foster care placement of a child; care for the employee's own parent, child, or spouse with a serious health condition; or the employee's own serious health condition. In practice, women make more use of the FMLA than do men, but only about 20% of new mothers work and meet all the eligibility conditions for FMLA benefits (Ruhm, 1997).

The FMLA makes it more viable for women to forgo working immediately after birth, and empirical evidence suggests that it has, as hoped, led to some increase in postpartum leaves (Waldfogel, 1999). Yet the FMLA is quite limited (particularly in comparison to laws in most European countries). FMLA leaves are relatively short, they are unpaid, and many women do not qualify for them. Women who choose to take advantage of FMLA leaves must sacrifice income for time with their infants.

A longer, paid benefit with broader scope would certainly benefit more new mothers. Yet there would also be costs associated with such an expansion. Women's wages or employment have not fallen as a consequence of the FMLA (Waldfogel, 1999), but research examining the more generous European legislation has often found that working women pay for part of the cost of leave policy through lower wages (Ruhm, 1997). Research on a similar law that mandated the inclusion of maternity benefit in all health insurance policies in the United States found that the costs of this policy were borne by women of childbearing age—its intended beneficiaries (Gruber, 1994). This type of unintended result is often a consequence of policies that seek to achieve socially desirable redistributive outcomes through regulation alone.

Child Care—The Cost of Quality

Many American families rely on paid child care, even in the first year of life (Hungerford, Brownell, & Campbell, 2000). In 1997, 45% of 3- and 4-year-olds, and 22% of children younger than 3 received some form of paid child care (U.S. Bureau of the Census, 1997). The high rates of use of child care have spawned an interest in the regulation of the quality of child-care programs and facilities.

The quality of child care has been linked with diverse dimensions of children's health, including their cognitive, linguistic, emotional, and interpersonal functioning (Hungerford et al., 2000; Kagan & Neuman, 2000). Research evidence suggests that children in centers subject to more rigorous facility licensing requirements have enhanced developmental outcomes (Kagan & Neuman, 2000).

Current child-care arrangements vary widely in quality. Concerns have been raised with regard to the safety and adequacy of responsive supervision and stimulation within some of these settings, as well as the stability of providers. Many children in early child-care programs nationwide are unprotected by state regulation (Adams, 1990).

Scientific research suggests that improving the quality of child-care arrangements would improve children's psychological health. Yet raising the quality of formal child-care settings might actually reduce the quality of child care received by many children, particularly those most vulnerable to the effects of poor-quality child care. More stringent regulations tend to reduce the supply of regulated centers and to drive up prices in those centers that remain, reducing demand for these centers (Hofferth & Chaplin, 1998). Faced with high costs for formal centers, families, particularly low-income families, may turn to informal, unregulated arrangements that offer worse quality. While regulation of child-care arrangements has the clear potential to improve psychological health, designing policies that effectively do this may be quite complicated, especially if regulations are not coupled with complementary redistributive policies.

REDISTRIBUTIVE POLICY—
BALANCING ACTS

Tax-financed redistributive policy is the most directly measurable component of public policy and, as noted above, may be an important adjunct to regulatory policy. Redistributive policies may be non-means-tested (providing benefits regardless of income) or means-tested (with benefits targeted by income group), and they may distribute cash or in-kind benefits. Specific provisions of these programs are constantly changing. For reference, table 49.1 provides a summary of the features of the main redistributive programs in the United States with links to sources that provide up-to-date information about their provisions.

The best-known non-means-tested programs are the social insurance programs, Social Security and Medicare, which provide income and health insurance benefits to retired and disabled people with work experience. Workers' compensation insurance and Unemployment Insurance are also non-means-tested programs, with cash benefits available to workers who have been injured or have lost their jobs.

Means-tested cash assistance programs include Temporary Assistance for Needy Families (TANF), the Earned Income Tax Credit (EITC), and the Supplemental Security Income (SSI) program; the latter provides assistance to low-income disabled people. Means-tested in-kind assistance programs include food stamps, housing vouchers, child-care credits, Medicaid, school lunch programs, WIC, and a variety of other smaller programs that target needy families.

Many government programs, particularly those that operate through provisions of the tax system, confer benefits primarily on higher income tax filers (these are not summarized in the table). For example, the deductibility of mortgage interest provided $70 billion in benefits to taxpayers in 2003, nearly three times as much as the government spends on TANF, with most of the benefits going to higher income taxpayers who own their own homes. Similarly, the exclusion of employer payments for health insurance from income and payroll taxation conferred $80 billion of benefit—about three fourths as much as the cost of Medicaid—on taxpayers who obtain employer-sponsored insurance (U.S. Congress, Joint Committee on Taxation, 2002).

Tax-financed programs direct resources to people and alter the distribution of income and goods. Collectively, these programs provide a social safety net that protects people who are unable or fail to provide for themselves. The U.S. social safety net is relatively lean compared to that of most other developed countries. Relatively fewer people are eligible for government benefits in the United States than elsewhere and the generosity of benefits received is, in many cases, lower here than in other countries.

The relatively limited scope of U.S. tax-financed programs is, in part, a consequence of concerns that the size and design of tax-financed programs can also have negative effects. For example, the existence of income-support programs for retired people may discourage them from working longer, even if they are able to do so. Similarly, higher tax rates may make it less desirable for spouses of high-income earners to enter paid employment. Distortions induced by redistribution and taxes may have untoward effects by putting financial penalties on behaviors (such as entering the labor force) that might otherwise improve people's well-being and psychological health.

We focus on two areas of redistributive policy that are of particular significance to women's psychological health: income support policies and health insurance policies.

Income Support Policies—Balancing Redistribution and Incentives

Rates of psychological distress are higher among people in poverty than among higher income people (Aber et al., 2000; Belle, 1990; Belle and Doucet, 2003). Multiple mediating factors, at the individual, familial, community, and societal level, operate to translate poverty into mental health problems (Aber et al., 2000; Cummings, Davies, & Campbell, 2000). Poverty also appears to interfere with the healthy development of young children, through diverse causal pathways

TABLE 49.1 Characteristics of Selected Major Redistribution Programs

Title	Benefits	Eligibility	Administration	Participants (millions); Spending (billions)
Temporary Assistance for Needy Families (TANF)[a]	3-person, single-parent family, maximum monthly cash benefit in 2001 was between $164 (AL) and $923 (AK)	Very low-income families with children. Income eligibility varies by state (in 2000, monthly income cutoff was $205 in AL to $1425 in HI). Eligibility is time limited. Work requirements exist.	Federal block grant to states	5.4 monthly; $25.5 (2001)
Earned Income Tax Credit (EITC)[b]	Up to $4,140 annually (2002). Size of credit is based on earnings and number of children.	2002 annual income below: $11,060 (no children); $29,201 (one child); $33,178 (more than one child)	Federal Internal Revenue Service (IRS)	19.6 tax returns; $33.4 (2001)
Old Age Survivors and Disability Program—Social Security (OAISD)[c]	Maximum individual monthly benefit if retiring at 65 in 2002, $1,661; additional 50% for spouse. Amount of benefits depends on earnings.	Must have worked for 10 years. Age for maximum benefits rising by 2 months per year beginning in 2003. Spouses, widow(ers), and surviving minor children also receive benefits.	Federal Social Security Administration (SSA)	39; $372 (2001)
Social Security Disability Insurance (SSDI)[c]	Earnings based. Average monthly benefit for those entitled in 2001 was $1,056 for men and $774 for women.	Disabled workers unable to engage in substantial gainful activity who worked ½ of the calendar quarters between age 21 and becoming disabled.	Federal SSA	6.2, about 53% men; $60 (2001)
Supplemental Security Income (SSI)[c]	(1/03) Federal monthly payment for individuals is $552 and $829 for couples. Many states supplement.	Age 65 or older, disabled, and blind. (1/02) With countable monthly income must be less than $545 and countable resources below $2,000 (more at state option).	States and federal SSA	6.7 monthly; $35 (2002)
Federal-State Unemployment Insurance Program[d]	Varies by state, but earnings based. Average weekly benefit in 2002 was $232. Typically, benefits last 26 weeks.	Involuntary unemployment in covered industries only. State requirements on wages and duration of employment.	States under guidelines set by federal law	Estimated 8.5; $2.2 (2002)
Workers Compensation Program[e]	Periodic cash payments based on worker's earnings	Limited to injuries or diseases traceable to industrial exposure or accident	States and Office of Workers' Compensation (OWCP)	2.1; $11.5 (2001)
Medicare[f]	Part A: most inpatient hospital expenses. Part B: outpatient health care expenses, including doctor fees. Rx not covered.	Over 65, disabled, and end-stage renal disease, not means tested. Eligible if self or spouse worked and paid Medicare taxes for 10 years. Others can buy in.	Centers for Medicare and Medicare Services (CMS)	Enrolled in either or both part A and B—40; $217.7 (2001)
Medicaid[g]	Hospital, MD, Rx, medical equipment, nursing facility, home health care, family planning, lab and X-ray services, health screening, diagnosis, and treatment (EPSDT)	Recipients of TANF, SSI, state supplementary payments. Pregnant women and children based on family income thresholds (at least 133% of federal poverty level).	States and CMS	36; $128 (2002)
State Children's Health Insurance (SCHIP)[h]	Health insurance for low-income children. Benefits similar to private insurance.	Varies by state: generally under age 19, not eligible for Medicaid, income below 200% federal poverty level (FPL).	States and CMS	5.3 children (2002); $217 (2001)

(continued)

TABLE 49.1 Characteristics of Selected Major Redistribution Programs (*Continued*)

Title	Benefits	Eligibility	Administration	Participants (millions); Spending (billions)
Child Care and Development Fund (CCDF)[j]	Assists for child care programs and subsidies to families	TANF families	Block grant to states	Up to 500,000 families; $4.5 (2001)
Child and Dependent Care Credit[i]	Non-refundable credit for 20–30% of dependent care expenses. Family maximum is $720 for one dependent and $1,440 for two or more dependents.	Available to working taxpayers who incur expenses in caring for their dependents while they are working or looking for work	IRS	3.6 returns; $1.6 (2000)
The Head Start Program[k]	Meals, care, education, health-care services	Children <5 in families <100% FPL, TANF or SSI, or foster care	Department of Health and Human Services (DHHS), Head Start Bureau	0.91 children; $6.5 (2002)
Food Stamp Program[l]	Coupons or electronic cards for purchase of food. In 2002, average monthly benefit about $80 and $186 per household.	TANF, SSI, and very low-income (<130% FPL) households	U.S. Department of Agriculture—Food, Nutrition, and Consumer Services (FNS), states	17.2 (2000); $20.1 (2001)
Women, Infants and Children (WIC)[m]	Food, formula, nutrition education and counseling	Low-income pregnant, postpartum, or breastfeeding women, infants, and children with family income <85% FPL, TANF, or SSI and at nutrition risk	FNS and WIC state agencies	7.25 monthly; $4.3 (2002)
National School Lunch Program[n]	Nutritionally balanced, low-cost or free lunches	Low-income children with family income <130% (free) or <185% (subsidized)	FNS and state education agencies	25.4 children; $6.4 (2001)

See the Web sites given in the notes below for additional information.

[a] www.spdp.org/tanf.htm, http://www.acf.dhhs.gov/programs/ofa/
[b] www.irs.gov/eitc
[c] www.ssa.gov
[d] http://workforcesecurity.doleta.gov/unemploy/aboutui.asp; http://www.workforcesecurity.doleta.gov/unemploy/ocia.asp
[e] Money and income 2001: http://ferret.bls.census.gov/macro/032002/perinc/new09_000.htm
[f] http://cms.hhs.gov/
[g] http://cms.hhs.gov/medicaid/mover.asp
[h] http://cms.hhs.gov/schip/
[i] www.acf.hhs.gov/programs/ccb/geninfo/index.htm
[j] www.irs.gov; individual tax statistics
[k] www.acf.dhhs.gov/programs/hsb/about/generalinformation/index.htm
[l] www.fns.usda.gov/fsp/faqs.htm#1
[m] www.fns.usda.gov/wic
[n] www.fns.usda.gov/cnd/Lunch/default.htm

and cumulative risks (Aber et al., 2000). Redistribution of income and in-kind benefits may alleviate poverty and thus, reduce the incidence of poverty-related distress.

Americans qualify for government assistance in consequence of meeting the criteria associated with one of a series of eligibility categories. Major categories of eligibility are defined around the presence of children, disability, and old age. In a minority of states, people may receive state or locally funded general assistance payments if they have very low incomes, even if they do not meet these categorical criteria. People with very low incomes may also qualify for in-kind food and housing benefits. There is, however, no national, comprehensive system of income support based solely on need.

Two programs—TANF and the EITC—are the mainstays of income support for families with children.[1] Women make up the overwhelming majority of adult recipients of TANF and three fourths of adult recipients of the EITC (http://www.now.org/issues/legislat/03-07-96.html). Both these programs underwent significant changes in the 1990s.

In 1996, the federal government replaced the 61-year-old Aid to Families with Dependent Children (AFDC) entitlement program with TANF. As had been the case for AFDC, income eligibility for TANF is generally limited to families with incomes well below the poverty line. Cash benefits offered are likewise limited. In the median state, a single-parent three-person family receiving TANF benefits alone would have an annual cash income of just over $5,000 in 2002, leaving them below 40% of the federal poverty level (calculations based on U.S. Congress, House Ways and Means Committee, 2000). Prior research on AFDC showed that many recipients supplemented their benefits with income from family members and undocumented work (Edin & Lein, 1997).

Under TANF, states receive federal block grants that can be used only to provide time-limited support to recipients. Federal law limits most adult recipients to five years of federally funded TANF benefits over their lifetimes and most recipients must work as a condition of receiving TANF benefits. TANF benefits to a family do not increase with the birth of an additional child born while receiving benefits. Legal immigrants are not eligible for federally funded TANF benefits for five years after arrival in the United States. Beyond these requirements, TANF offers states considerable flexibility in designing their programs, so that there is substantial cross-state variation in requirements and benefits.

There has been extensive research on the effects of TANF on low-income families and children (see Grogger, Karoly, & Klerman, 2002; Blank, 2002, for reviews). TANF was initially implemented during a period of economic expansion in the late 1990s, which makes it difficult to identify the effects of the program itself. Nonetheless, there is substantial consensus that the program achieved several of its goals. Program participation fell 56.5% between 1994 and 2000; employment rates among single mothers with children increased by 10 percentage points; and poverty levels fell to historically low levels (Blank, 2002). TANF sanctions do not appear to have affected birth rates and effects on child welfare are mixed (Grogger et al., 2002). The greatest economic benefits of TANF reform appear to have occurred among those who were dissuaded from entering the program at all (Grogger, Haider, & Klerman, 2003). By contrast, some recipients who lost TANF benefits because of program time limits and sanctions have fallen into deeper poverty (Blank, 2002).

The EITC was introduced in 1975. Benefit levels increased substantially under President Clinton.[2] The EITC program provides refundable credits to beneficiaries, meaning that it pays refunds that exceed the amount of income taxes owed. In 1999, the EITC provided a family with two children and income of $9,540, a 40% earnings supplement (U.S. Congress, House Ways and Means Committee, 2000).

These substantial payments mean that the EITC has been quite successful in raising incomes, lifting over 4 million people above poverty in 1998 (Meyer, 2000). Economic research suggests that it has been an important contributor to the growth in labor force participation among single mothers (Meyer & Rosenbaum, 2001). Because EITC payments fall as work increases, the EITC also appears to have had led to a reduction in work hours among low-income married women (Ellwood, 2000).

The combination of TANF and the expanded EITC have created a new structure of income support for families with children that has a very different set of incentives and distributional effects associated with it than did the system characterized by AFDC and the more limited EITC. These differences reflect a difference in the balance between redistribution and incentives in the two systems. The older system focused on ensuring that women and children in families without a wage earner would have a source of subsistence income. Providing this income, however, gave recipients and potential recipients disincentives for work and positive incentives for out-of-wedlock birth. TANF was designed to offer temporary incentives while limiting these undesirable incentives. The EITC further strengthened these incentives by "making work pay" for low-income women.

The policy evaluation literature suggests that, on the whole, the combination of TANF welfare changes and expansions of the EITC in the late 1990s has improved the well-being of lower income women and children. These benefits accrue most to those women who responded to the strong work incentives in the new programs and entered the labor market. The economic benefits achieved by these women may well have translated into improved psychological health. By contrast, those women who did not respond to these incentives and remained dependent on public assistance have suffered as a consequence of these changes. This population includes a disproportionate number of women with significant mental health problems (U.S. General Accounting Office, 2002). Overall, income support reform focused on incentives has shifted the direction of public assistance payments away from the very lowest income families toward slightly higher income working families.

Income Security—Balancing Redistribution and Gender Neutrality

In contrast to the income support system for families with children, almost all Americans of retirement age receive benefits through the Social Security system. Social Security provides benefits to retired workers who contributed to the system for 10 years or more, and to the spouses and survivors of these workers (Dobelstein, 2002). Women constitute a majority of Social Security recipients, primarily because they live longer than do men.

Social Security has been extremely effective in lifting older Americans out of poverty. While poverty among the elderly has historically been quite high, in 2001, people over 65 were about equally likely to be in poverty as were working-age adults and they were only 60% as likely to be in poverty as were children (Proctor & Dalaker, 2002). Among elderly people, however, nonmarried women and minorities have the highest rates of poverty (Hungerford, Rassette, Iams, & Koenig, 2002).

The Social Security system began in 1935, and in many respects, its benefit structure continues to reflect the social circumstances of its origins (Favreault, Sammartino, & Steurle, 2002). Social Security payments are based on contributions, so higher income workers receive greater payments than do lower income workers. Benefits are also based on the number of years of earnings.

This structure leads female retirees to receive, on average, lower benefits than male retirees. Female retirees' Social Security benefits reflect the historically lower wages they have earned. They also reflect the fact that many women did not participate in the labor market continuously. The income of female retirees is also depressed because women retirees are much more likely than men to rely exclusively on Social Security as a source of retirement income. Women workers are much less likely to enter retirement with private pension benefits from their jobs than are men (Hungerford et al., 2002).

Many currently retired women did not work in the paid labor market when they were younger. They rely on the Social Security benefits of their spouses. Nonworking spouses of retired workers receive benefits equal to 50% of the worker's benefit. Upon the workers' death, however, the surviving spouse receives just 75% of the worker's basic benefit.

Low payments to surviving spouses contribute to the higher poverty rates among nonmarried women. Spousal payments reflect traditional family patterns and represent compensation for the value of a spouse's contributions outside the workplace. On the other hand, this spousal payment implicitly acts as a tax on two-earner couples. Two-earner couples receive only the benefits to which each spouse is entitled, implicitly assigning no value to any contributions outside the workplace by either spouse (Favreault et al., 2002).

Patterns of labor market participation and earnings have changed across cohorts of women. The existing system of payments in Social Security cements into place a particular configuration of gender roles. A challenge for policy makers as the system moves on will be to ensure adequate income to surviving spouses who did not work in the paid labor market, while adequately rewarding the contributions of spouses who do.

Health Insurance—Balancing Cost Containment and Access

Unlike the situation in all other wealthy industrialized countries, health insurance in the United States is not universal. Most people who have coverage obtain it in the private insurance market. Governments participate in the system primarily by providing coverage to about 22% of Americans through Medicare, Medicaid, State Child Health Insurance Programs (SCHIP), and smaller programs that serve the military and veterans.

Medicare provides health insurance to Americans 65 and over and long-term disabled people who qualify for Social Security Disability income. Medicare coverage includes the cost of hospital inpatient and outpatient care, care in physicians' offices, laboratory tests, and some rehabilitation and home-care services, but until 2004, did not include prescription drugs.

Medicaid provides coverage for certain low-income beneficiaries.[3] Medicaid covers a very extensive set of benefits (although these may vary by state), including prescription drugs and mental health services. Medicaid, however, tends to pay very low rates to providers, reducing access to services. SCHIP provides insurance coverage to low-income children. In addition to financing these public insurance programs, governments subsidize private insurance by exempting from income and Social Security taxes employer contributions to employee health insurance and health insurance purchased by the self-employed.

Despite these programs, many Americans continue to lack health insurance coverage. In 2002, an estimated 41 million Americans were uninsured, and 47% of this group were women (Mills, 2002).

Health insurance is an important contributor to general health (Institute of Medicine, 2003). Having health insurance is particularly important for people with mental health problems. A broad array of effective treatments is available for the treatment of such problems, and health insurance provides people with enhanced access to these treatments (U.S. Department of Health and Human Services, 1999). Better insurance is associated with higher levels of mental health service use (Greenley & Mullen, 1990; Keeler, Wells, & Manning, 1986).

Health care, however, is very expensive, and the price of health insurance, in both the private and public sectors, reflects these high costs. These high costs lead both public and private programs to consider strategies that aim to control service utilization. Ideally, efforts to control utilization would reduce the use of unnecessary services without limiting valuable care.

The problem of controlling utilization under insurance is particularly acute with respect to mental health services. Results of a randomized social experiment indicate that a person who can obtain outpatient mental health services at no cost uses about four times as many services as would an identical person who had to pay full cost for these services. By contrast, a person who can obtain general health services at no cost uses only about two times as many services as would an identical person who had to pay full cost (Keeler et al., 1986; Newhouse, 1999). This high response to insurance coverage has led to the use of strategies for controlling use and costs.

Historically, utilization control in mental health has been achieved through the use of higher copayment and deductible levels in mental health coverage (Sharfstein, Stoline, & Goldman, 1993). The Mental Health Parity Act, passed by Congress in 1996 and implemented in 1998, prohibits the use of lifetime and annual limits on coverage that are different for physical and mental health in firms with 50 or more employees but continues to permit higher cost-sharing rates (U.S. Department of Health and

Human Services, 1999). High cost-sharing rates reduce access to services and lead some people who could benefit from service use to go without.

More recently, health plans in the public and private sector have turned to managed care to control costs. Managed care converts the form of cost containment in health insurance from reliance on patient financial incentives to provider incentives and more direct utilization control. These changes have been very effective in reining in the costs of mental health treatment, and they have been coincident with increases in the percentage of people who use such services, but their effects on the quality of care are more ambiguous.

Certain aspects of managed care may make it difficult for people with mental health symptoms to receive services. In some traditional managed care plans, patients require a referral from a primary care practitioner before they can see a specialist, which may limit use of mental health specialty care if primary care physicians fail to diagnose illness. Managed care plans may place more stringent utilization review restrictions on mental health services than on general health services (Burnham & Escarce, 1999). Plans that separate mental health services from general health services may limit the coordination of care between primary care doctors and specialists (Glied, 2002). Behavioral managed care plans also face strong incentives to shift patients from psychotherapy treatment (where they are responsible for costs) to medication treatment (where costs are often covered by a different plan).

Rising health care costs make it difficult for legislatures to expand benefits to the many Americans who lack insurance altogether or whose benefits are limited. Furthermore, increasing costs lead some of those who are currently insured to lose their coverage. Yet available cost containment techniques are crude and often discourage both more and less valuable care.

CONCLUSIONS

We have reviewed policies that are aimed at significant policy problems with clear linkages to mental health: child care, poverty, and health insurance. Our analysis illustrates the complexity of designing policies that address such problems.

The range of public policies is vast and the effects of a given policy are almost inevitably complex, necessitating the balancing of conflicting imperatives and entailing both desired and unintended consequences. The effects of such a policy on individual psychological health are, likewise, multifaceted and often obscure. The mechanisms that lead from environment to outcomes are poorly understood and may change over time.

The challenge of addressing problems that pose risks to psychological health through policy is huge. It is also essential. Poorly designed public policies—even if well-intentioned—can exacerbate problems, rather than solving them. The enormous potential of public policy to improve—or diminish—our lives suggests that an understanding of public policy is an important contributor to an understanding of the determinants of psychological health. The implementation of wisely designed policy is a critical component of women's psychological health.

NOTES

1. Low-income workers without children may also be eligible for a more limited earned income credit.

2. The Child Tax Credit program, introduced in 1998 and since expanded, increases program benefits for families with children.

3. Three groups of beneficiaries are eligible for Medicaid: those categorically eligible for coverage because they are eligible for TANF, SSI, or would have been eligible for Aid to Dependent Children (ADC) if the program were continued; pregnant women and children under 6 with incomes below 133% of the federal poverty level (FPL) and children under 19 with incomes below 100% of the FPL; low-income Medicare beneficiaries and additional groups of "optional" beneficiaries who qualify under federal rules and whom the state has chosen to cover, such as certain institutionalized persons and certain designated "medically needy" individuals (U.S. Congress, House Ways and Means Committee, 2000).

REFERENCES

Aber, L., Jones, S., & Cohen, J. (2000). The impact of poverty on the mental health and the development of very young children. In C. H. Zeanah (Ed.), *Handbook of infant mental health* (pp. 113–128). New York: Guilford Press.

Adams, G. (1990). *Who knows how safe? The status of state efforts to ensure quality child care.* Washington, DC: Children's Defense Fund.

Belle, D. (1990). Poverty and women's mental health. *American Psychologist, 445*(3), 385–389.

Belle, D., & Doucet, J. (2003). Poverty, inequality, and discrimination as sources of depression among women. *Psychology of Women Quarterly, 27,* 101–113.

Bertin, J. (1998). Health, safety, and equity in the workplace. In J. M. Stellman (Ed.), *Encyclopedia of occupational health and safety* (4th ed., pp. 24.5–24.9). Geneva: International Labor Organization.

Blank, R. M. (2002). *Evaluating welfare reform in the United States.* National Bureau of Economic Research, Working Paper 8983.

Burnham, M. A., & Escarce, J. J. (1999). Equity in managed care for mental disorders. *Health Affairs, 18*(5), 22–31.

Buzawa, E. S., & Buzawa, C. G. (2003). *Domestic violence: The criminal justice response* (3rd ed.). Thousand Oaks, CA: Sage.

Coates, S. W. (2003). Chapter 1: Introduction. In S. Coates, J. L. Rosenthal, & D. Schechter, *Trauma and human bonds* (pp. 1–14). Hillsdale, NJ: Analytic Press.

Cummings, E. M., Davies, P. T., & Campbell, S. B. (2000). *Developmental psychopathology and family process.* New York: Guilford Press.

Dobelstein, A. W. (2002). *Social welfare policy and analysis* (3rd ed.). Pacific Grove, CA: Thomson Brooks/Cole.

Edin, K., & Lein, L. (1997). *Making ends meet: How single mothers survive welfare and low-wage work.* New York: Russell Sage Foundation.

Ellwood, D. T. (2000, December). The impact of the Earned Income Tax Credit and social policy reforms on work, marriage, and living arrangements. *National Tax Journal, 53*(4:2), 1063–1103.

Favreault, M. M., Sammartino, F. J., & Steurle, C. E. (2002). Social Security benefits for spouses and survivors: Options for change. In M. M. Favreault, F. J. Sammartino, & C. E. Steurle (Eds.), *Social Security and the family* (pp. 177–227). Washington, DC: Urban Institute Press.

Glied, S. (2002). Mental health carve-outs and the fragmentation of physical and mental health. In S. Feldman (Ed.), *Managed behavioral health services: Perspectives and practice* (2nd ed., pp. 125–145). Springfield, IL: Charles C. Thomas.

Glied, S., & Kofman, S. (1995, March). *Women and mental health: Issues for health reform* (background paper). New York: Commonwealth Fund, Commission on Women's Health.

Greenley, J. R., & Mullen, J. (1990). Help-seeking and the use of mental health services. In J. R. Greenley (Ed.), *Research in community and mental health* (Vol. 6, pp. 325–351). Greenwich, CT: JAI Press.

Grogger, J., Haider, S. J., & Klerman, J. (2003, May). Why did the welfare rolls fall during the 1990's?

The importance of entry. *The American Economic Review, 93*(2), 288–292.

Grogger, J., Karoly, L. A., & Klerman, J. A. (2002). *Consequences of welfare reform: A research synthesis.* DRU-2676-DHHS. Santa Monica, CA: RAND Corporation.

Gruber, J. (1994, June). The incidence of mandated maternity benefits. *The American Economic Review, 84*(3), 622–641.

Hofer, M. A. (2003). The emerging neurobiology of attachment and separation. In S. W. Coates, J. L. Rosenthal, & D. Schechter (Eds.), *Trauma and human bonds* (pp. 191–209). Hillsdale, NJ: Analytic Press.

Hofferth, S. L., & Chaplin, D. D. (1998). State regulations and child care choice. *Population Research and Policy Review, 17,* 111–140.

Hungerford, A., Brownell, C. A., & Campbell, S. B. (2000). *Childcare in infancy: A transactional perspective.* In C. H. Zeanah (Ed.), *Handbook of infant mental health* (pp. 519–532). New York: Guilford Press.

Hungerford, T., Rassette, M., Iams, H., & Koenig, M. (2002). Trends in the economic status of the elderly, 1976–2000. *Social Security Bulletin, 64*(3), 12–22.

Institute of Medicine. (2003). *Hidden costs, value lost: Uninsurance in America.* Washington, DC: National Academies Press.

Insurance Institute for Highway Safety. (1998, October 10). *Status Report, 33*(9), 1–3.

Kagan, S. L., & Neuman, J. L. (2000). Early childcare and education: Current issues and future strategies. In J. P. Shonkoff, & S. J. Meisels (Eds.), *Handbook of early childhood intervention* (2nd ed., pp. 339–360). Cambridge: Cambridge University Press.

Kamerman, S. (2000). Early childhood intervention and policies: An international perspective. In J. P. Shonkoff, & S. J. Meisels (Eds.), *Handbook of early childhood intervention* (2nd ed., pp. 613–629). Cambridge: Cambridge University Press.

Keeler, E. B., Wells, K. B., & Manning, W. G. (1986). *The demand for episodes of mental health services.* R-3432-NIMH. Santa Monica, CA: The RAND Corporation.

Lowi, T. (1972). Four systems of policy, politics, and choice. *Public Administration Review, 32,* 298–310.

Meyer, B. D. (2000, December). Introduction to special issue. *National Tax Journal, 53*(4:2), v–viii.

Meyer, B. D., & Rosenbaum, D. T. (2001, August). Welfare, the Earned Income Tax Credit, and the labor supply of single mothers. *Quarterly Journal of Economics, 116*(3), 1063–1114.

Mills, R. J. (2002). U.S. Census Bureau, Current Population Reports, P60–220, *Health Insurance Coverage: 2001.* Washington, DC: U.S. Census Bureau.

Newhouse, J. P. (1999). *Free for all? Lessons from the RAND health insurance experiment.* Cambridge, MA: Harvard University Press.

Proctor, B. D., & Dalaker, J. (2002). U.S. Census Bureau, Current Population Reports, P60 219, *Poverty in the United States: 2001*. Washington, DC: U.S. Government Printing Office.

Ruhm, C. (1997, Summer). Policy watch: The Family and Medical Leave Act. *Journal of Economic Perspectives, 11*(3), 175–186.

Sharfstein, S. S., Stoline, A. M., & Goldman, H. H. (1993). Psychiatric care and health insurance reform. *American Journal of Psychiatry, 150*(1), 7–18.

Shonkoff, J. P., & Phillips, D. A. (Eds.). (2000). *From neurons to neighborhoods: The science of early child development*. Washington, DC: National Research Council and Institute of Medicine/National Academy of Science.

U.S. Bureau of the Census. (1997, November). *Who's minding our preschoolers? Fall 1994 (Update)*. P70-62 and PPL-81. Washington, DC: U.S. Department of Commerce.

U.S. Congress, House Ways and Means Committee. (2000). *Green book on program participation*. Washington, DC: U.S. Government Printing Office.

U.S. Congress, Joint Committee on Taxation. (2002, December 19). *JCS-5-02 Estimates of federal tax expenditures for fiscal years 2003–2007*. Washington, DC: U.S. Government Printing Office.

U.S. Department of Health and Human Services. (1999). *Mental health: A report of the Surgeon General*. Rockville, MD: U.S. Department of Health and Human Services, Substance Abuse and Mental Health Services Administration, Center for Mental Health Services, National Institutes of Health, National Institute of Mental Health.

U.S. General Accounting Office. (2002, December). *Former TANF recipients with impairments less likely to be employed and more likely to receive federal supports*. GAO-03-210. Washington, DC: U.S. Government Printing Office.

U.S. Social Security Administration. (2002, September). *Annual statistical report on the Social Security Disability Insurance Program, 2001*. Retrieved January 15, 2005, from http://www.ssa.gov/policy/docs/statcomps/di_asr/2001/

Waldfogel, J. (1999). The impact of the Family and Medical Leave Act. *Journal of Policy Analysis and Management, 18*(2), 281–302.

Zigler, E., & Finn-Stevenson, M. (1996). National policies for children, adolescents, and families. In M. Lewis (Ed.), *Child and Adolescent Psychiatry: A Comprehensive Textbook* (2nd ed., pp. 1186–1195). Baltimore: Williams & Wilkins.

Conclusion

V

CAROL D. GOODHEART
and JUDITH WORELL

Afterword

50

The contributors to the *Handbook* have presented a kaleidoscopic view of psychological health. These viewpoints converge into a biopsychosocial perspective on girls and women. The multifaceted approach takes into account their risks, needs, and strengths, as well as the social, economic, and cultural realities of their lives. The four major sections of the book allow the reader to assimilate an overview, consider factors across the life span, examine topics specific to particular phases of life, and assess special problems and resources. Now we look forward and extrapolate from the lessons learned. What is needed in the future?

The world is growing smaller and it will be important to consider the status of women globally; national boundaries are likely to become increasingly fluid and health risks can readily cross borders. For example, at the 1994 International Conference on Population and Development (ICPD) in Cairo, members of the United Nations established goals for the year 2015: improve women's reproductive health, education, and rights; reduce infant mortality; and curb population growth. An interim report released in September 2004 by the United Nations Population Fund (which may be accessed at http://www. unfpa.org/index.htm) shows significant progress in conditions related to reproduction and education for women in 23 countries. However, there was little progress in 17 other countries, and some lost ground. Across much of the world, the HIV epidemic is growing rapidly among women and children, deaths in pregnancy and childbirth remain high, and prevention efforts for adolescent girls is lacking. There is more work to do.

It will be important to build on the gains and to address the persistent problems through expanded efforts in research, education, practice, and social policy. The most promising avenues for health intervention are likely to be those approaches based on solid psychological, physiological, and epidemiological research with girls and women; those approaches directed toward parity, strengths, function, prevention, and cultural applicability; and those approaches grounded in social justice. The best approaches will integrate all three facets.

We hope the *Handbook* proves to be a rich resource for professionals who seek stimulating questions for research, effective bases for practice, and heuristic frameworks for improved social policy. However, the *Handbook* remains a work in progress. Other dimensions may be worth illuminating to enhance an understanding of the complexities of psychological health. We welcome readers' suggestions for new and emerging topics for discussion in future editions.

Index

biological explanations, 52
body dissatisfaction, 69
cultural messages, 246
dating relationships, 55–56
diathesis-stress models, 52
early puberty, 254
emotional self-care of women, 185
end-of-life issues and older women, 408–409
entitlement and, 179
family relationships, 54–55
females vs. males, 51–52
gender, 19
gender role, 52–54
healthy environments, 225
marital relations, 20, 56–57
motherhood, 342–343
physical violence in adulthood, 459–460
postpartum, 332
poverty, 51, 124
problematic relationships, 54–57
psychological and social factors, 52
psychological health, 8–9
research on psychology of women and gender, 234
sexual violence in adulthood, 457–459
suicide and women, 131
supportive friends and less, 32
survivors of male violence, 455
treatment, 57, 109
widowhood, 373–374
women with disabilities, 98
Depression Screening Day initiative, 463
DESNOS (disorders of extreme stress not otherwise specified), 104
development. *See* gender development
diabetes, 184, 256–258, 382–383
Diagnostic and Statistical Manual of Mental Disorders, Fourth Edition (*DSM–IV*)
anxiety disorders in girls and women, 62–63
classification system, 11
gender and mental disorders, 79–80
posttraumatic stress disorder (PTSD), 104
sexual dysfunctions, 195
women and body dissatisfaction, 70
dialectical behavior therapy (DBT), 134, 146
diathesis-stress models, depression, 52
dieting, girls, 253
disabilities
abuse, 99
comparison of nondisabled and disabled persons, 96, 97
demographics and disadvantage, 95–96
depression, 98
gender and, 94
health and wellness, 99–100
identity and coming of age with, 96–98
intervention, 100–101
living arrangements of older women with, 389
participation in workforce, 99
risk factors, 98–99
self-esteem, 98
stress, 98
women and stereotype, 94–95
discrimination, disrupted body practices for women, 303–304

disorders of extreme stress not otherwise specified (DESNOS), 104
divorce
deficit comparison model, 346–347
environment, 223
girls' physical functioning, 255
loss of romantic relationship, 327
no-fault, 430
nondisabled and disabled persons, 97
psychological health, 9–10
rates and effect on bereavement, 402–403
spousal role transitions, 362–363
women with disabilities, 99
divorced mother household, 264, 347
domestic captivity, term, 105
domestic violence, 107, 429
double standard, aging, 370
driving, older women, 393
drop-outs from high school, gender, 286
drug treatments, gender bias, 42
drug use. *See* substance use
dual-earner families. *See also* work and family
demographics, 350–351
gendered asymmetries, 175
home and career, 27, 235–236
dyslexia, 44, 47

Earned Income Tax Credit (EITC), 471, 473–474
eating disorders
adolescent girls, 256, 258, 302–303
body image, 70, 235, 302–303
cognitive-behavior therapy, 235
cultural messages, 246
exercise, 255
gender bias, 44
self-esteem, 18–19
suicide and women, 131
eclectic orientation, psychotherapists, 230
ecological models, strength and well-being, 29–30
ecology models, healthy environments, 219–221
economic issues, 122–123, 399
education. *See also* gender and schooling; school achievement
barriers to career choices, 315–316
gendered asymmetries, 175
poor women, 126–127
postsecondary, for women, 307
promoting well-being, 26–27
pursing higher, and balance, 205
pursuing higher, for attaining balance, 204–205
self-esteem, 19
suicide intervention, 132–133
women with and without disabilities, 96, 97
elder abuse, 91, 393–394
elderly persons. *See* older women
Elementary and Secondary Education Act, 26–27, 284–285
emergency contraception pills, 335
emotion, expression and suppression of, 269–270
emotional closeness, psychological health, 269
emotional health, sexual health and, 194–195
emotional intelligence, term, 186
emotional investment, 19–20